Frommer's®
Las Vegas

My Las Vegas
by Mary Herczog

SOME PEOPLE SAY, "I'M NOT GOING TO LAS VEGAS. IT'S JUST NOT my kind of place." And I think, "What does that have to do with anything?"

The Grand Canyon is a wonder of the natural world, but Vegas is a wonder of the artificial world. It is, at once, everyone's kind of town and no one's kind of town. It has a little bit of a lot of places, recreated in meticulous, scale detail and then covered in neon and lights. As a visitor, I feel both at home and out of this world. It's loud and gaudy, it's heartbreaking and ridiculous, and it exists for one reason only: to take your money. And to make sure you have a ball doing it.

I don't like to gamble—except when I win, in which case I like it a lot—but I remain fascinated. Vegas is glamorous; remember, a "glamour" is a type of hypnotic, magic spell. Something is always new in a town that periodically tears everything down to start again. So, I will always come back. Because my brother can eat a steak at 3am, my sister can gamble on the penny slots, my niece can dance all night at a club, my parents can marvel at Mystère, and my husband and I can giggle and enjoy the spectacle.

You have to go. At least once. Okay, maybe twice. In a few years, the town will be all new, yet again. You can't say that about the Grand Canyon.

© Siegfried & Roy's Secret Garden at The Mirage

They may not strut their stuff on the Strip any more, but you can still coo at **SIEGFRIED & ROY'S WHITE TIGERS (left)** at the Secret Garden, a mini-zoo behind the Mirage hotel—a visit with them and the playful mammals of the adjacent Dolphin Habitat are about the most un-Vegas thing to do in Vegas.

This **MGM GRAND (above)** kitty isn't real (unlike his tiger pals over at the Mirage). But the hotel is—real big, that is, with the most rooms in Vegas (over 5,000) and the largest casino in town. Translation: this cat has a big appetite for your money...

OOH, LA, LA! A perfect two-thirds scale replica of the Eiffel Tower stands at the front of the **PARIS HOTEL (left)**. Inside, the casino is set amid a Parisian street scene—just the right mix of class and gimmick. Move over to Egypt and behold the wonders of **LUXOR'S (below)** glass pyramid and a spiffed-up Sphinx. Locals will tell you that the beam of light that emanates from the pyramid's top can be seen from outer space. Personal experience in a 747 puts that claim in serious doubt.

The best free show on the Strip is the **WATER FOUNTAINS OUTSIDE THE BELLAGIO (above, right)** that dance, dip, and sway in time to tunes ranging from Sinatra to opera. Sound cheesy? It's actually delightful. And also complex; set on a 22-million-gallon lake, the show involves 5,000 lights and a sound system cranking up 56,000 watts.

In other cities, hotels are built near the attractions. In Las Vegas, hotels are the attractions. Here, the skyline of New York City is replicated—not to mention seriously compacted—to create **THE NEW YORK–NEW YORK HOTEL (below, right)**.

Taste. Subtlety. Neither word applies to the late, great Liberace, which is why we love him so much. See this understated garment, and so much more, at the **LIBERACE MUSEUM (left).**

We all need constants in an ever-changing world. In Vegas, that means the over-the-top production shows, complete with topless feathered showgirls like the ones here, at *JUBILEE!* **(above).** Good taste and class are all well and good, but sometimes, one just wants to look at a bunch of pretty girls. Preferably in Bob Mackie–designed headdresses.

Slot machines, like the ones pictured here at **NEW YORK–NEW YORK (left)**, will be happy to take your money. And maybe, just maybe, they might give some of it back.

The otherworldly landscape of **VALLEY OF FIRE (above)** is the perfect natural-world accompaniment to the artificial weirdness of Vegas. Clear your head for a day and take a tour of this gorgeous state park.

Oh! It's **O, THE DAZZLING CIRQUE DU SOLEIL SHOW (left)** that takes place over, on and in water, one of the finest productions on the Strip. Despite the town's storied reputation for entertainment, most Vegas productions would be laughed right off Broadway. Cirque is the exception.

THE FORUM SHOPS (below) at Caesar's Palace aren't like the shops in Rome, but they are like the shops in Vegas, which has its own unique pleasures. After all, in the real Rome, can you walk across the street to go shop in Venice? Well, you can in Vegas!

The Neon Museum has rescued many fabulous old signs from the junk heap, like this fellow here, **VEGAS VIC (above, right)** himself, who reminds us that Vegas is still a smoker's paradise.

CIRQUE DU SOLEIL'S *MYSTÈRE* (below, right) presents the kind of arresting, erotic and magical human circus that might have been styled by Dali. It was the first Cirque show in town, and it's still a dream.

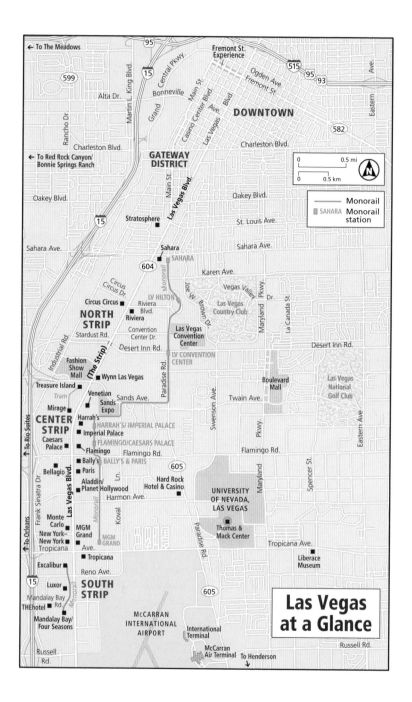

Las Vegas
at a Glance

Blackjack

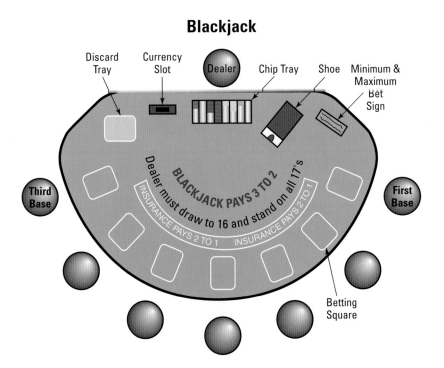

Basic Strategy										
The Dealer Is Showing:	**2**	**3**	**4**	**5**	**6**	**7**	**8**	**9**	**10**	**Ace**
Your Total Is: 4–11	H	H	H	H	H	H	H	H	H	H
12	H	H	S	S	S	H	H	H	H	H
13	S	S	S	S	S	H	H	H	H	H
14	S	S	S	S	S	H	H	H	H	H
15	S	S	S	S	S	H	H	H	H	H
16	S	S	S	S	S	H	H	H	H	H
	S = Stand					**H = Hit**				

Poker Hands

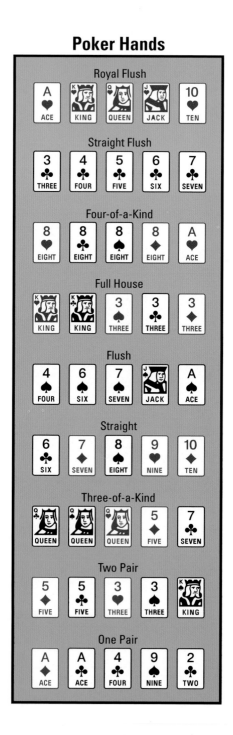

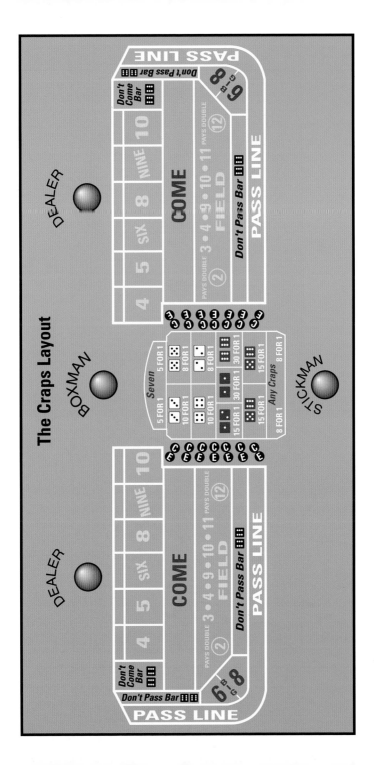

The Craps Layout

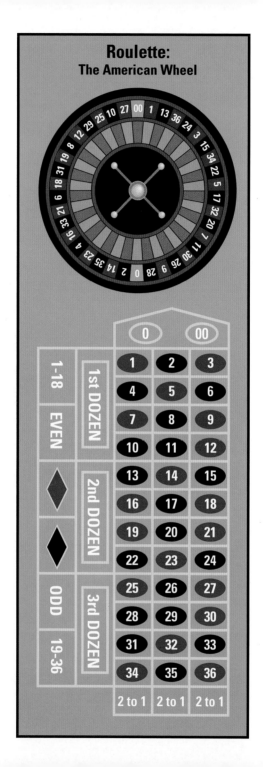

Frommer's®

Las Vegas

2009

by Mary Herczog

Here's what the critics say about Frommer's:

"Amazingly easy to use. Very portable, very complete."

—*Booklist*

"Detailed, accurate, and easy-to-read information for all price ranges."
—*Glamour Magazine*

"Hotel information is close to encyclopedic."

—*Des Moines Sunday Register*

"Frommer's Guides have a way of giving you a real feel for a place."
—*Knight Ridder Newspapers*

WILEY

Wiley Publishing, Inc.

About the Author

Mary Herczog lives in Los Angeles and works in the film industry while also attending graduate school. She is the author of *Frommer's New Orleans, California For Dummies, Frommer's Portable Las Vegas for Non-Gamblers, Las Vegas Day by Day,* and *Las Vegas For Dummies,* and she has contributed to *Frommer's Los Angeles.* Craps make her nervous, so she sticks to blackjack—even though she is never sure when to hit on thirteen.

Published by:

Wiley Publishing, Inc.

111 River St.
Hoboken, NJ 07030-5774

ISBN 978-0-470-38431-2

Editor: Billy Fox with Cate Latting
Production Editor: Katie Robinson
Cartographer: Elizabeth Puhl
Photo Editor: Richard Fox
Production by Wiley Indianapolis Composition Services

Front cover photo: Casino sign, night, low angle view
Back cover photo: Mountain biking on the Cottonwood Valley Trail System, Red Rock Canyon Conservation Area

For information on our other products and services or to obtain technical support, please contact our Customer Care Department within the U.S. at 800/762-2974, outside the U.S. at 317/572-3993 or fax 317/572-4002.

Wiley also publishes its books in a variety of electronic formats. Some content that appears in print may not be available in electronic formats.

Manufactured in the United States of America

5 4 3 2 1

Contents

(5) Where to Dine   115

(6) What to See & Do in Las Vegas   171

(7) About Casino Gambling   199

(8) Shopping   227

List of Maps

An Invitation to the Reader

In researching this book, we discovered many wonderful places—hotels, restaurants, shops, and more. We're sure you'll find others. Please tell us about them, so we can share the information with your fellow travelers in upcoming editions. If you were disappointed with a recommendation, we'd love to know that, too. Please write to:

Frommer's Las Vegas 2009
Wiley Publishing, Inc. • 111 River St. • Hoboken, NJ 07030-5774

An Additional Note

Please be advised that travel information is subject to change at any time—and this is especially true of prices. We therefore suggest that you write or call ahead for confirmation when making your travel plans. The authors, editors, and publisher cannot be held responsible for the experiences of readers while traveling. Your safety is important to us, however, so we encourage you to stay alert and be aware of your surroundings. Keep a close eye on cameras, purses, and wallets, all favorite targets of thieves and pickpockets.

Acknowledgments

As always, thank you to Frommer's for a job that's really cool even when the desert temps are high, and for their patience with me during difficult times. Billy Fox knows what to query and what to leave alone, and, for an author, that's even better than knowing when to hit and when to hold. Lisa Derrick got my facts in order, and I am grateful. Rick Garman is even better than winning a lot of money on a slot machine; he knows firsthand about that sort of thing, whereas I do not. My biggest win is Steve Hochman, and for that I am most grateful of all.

—Mary Herczog

Other Great Guides for Your Trip:

Frommer's Portable Las Vegas

Frommer's Portable Las Vegas for Non-Gamblers

Las Vegas For Dummies

The Unofficial Guide to Las Vegas

Frommer's USA

Frommer's American Southwest

Frommer's Star Ratings, Icons & Abbreviations

Every hotel, restaurant, and attraction listing in this guide has been ranked for quality, value, service, amenities, and special features using a **star-rating system**. In country, state, and regional guides, we also rate towns and regions to help you narrow down your choices and budget your time accordingly. Hotels and restaurants are rated on a scale of zero (recommended) to three stars (exceptional). Attractions, shopping, nightlife, towns, and regions are rated according to the following scale: zero stars (recommended), one star (highly recommended), two stars (very highly recommended), and three stars (must-see).

In addition to the star-rating system, we also use **seven feature icons** that point you to the great deals, in-the-know advice, and unique experiences that separate travelers from tourists. Throughout the book, look for:

Finds	Special finds—those places only insiders know about
Fun Fact	Fun facts—details that make travelers more informed and their trips more fun
Kids	Best bets for kids and advice for the whole family
Moments	Special moments—those experiences that memories are made of
Overrated	Places or experiences not worth your time or money
Tips	Insider tips—great ways to save time and money
Value	Great values—where to get the best deals

The following **abbreviations** are used for credit cards:

AE	American Express	DISC	Discover	V	Visa
DC	Diners Club	MC	MasterCard		

Frommers.com

Now that you have this guidebook to help you plan a great trip, visit our website at **www.frommers.com** for additional travel information on more than 4,000 destinations. We update features regularly to give you instant access to the most current trip-planning information available. At Frommers.com, you'll find scoops on the best airfares, lodging rates, and car rental bargains. You can even book your travel online through our reliable travel booking partners. Other popular features include:

- Online updates of our most popular guidebooks
- Vacation sweepstakes and contest giveaways
- Newsletters highlighting the hottest travel trends
- Podcasts, interactive maps, and up-to-the-minute events listings
- Opinionated blog entries by Arthur Frommer himself
- Online travel message boards with featured travel discussions

2010, it will have more than 5,300 rooms in four distinct properties—Echelon Resort (a mega-casino-style place) and three boutique hotels with high-cache names: Mondrian, Delano, and Shangri-La (a high-end Asian hotelier)—plus the typical casino, meeting, shopping, restaurant, entertainment, and other facilities one would expect in a place that will cost this much money.

On the drawing boards is yet another massive project; Station Casinos is dreaming of Viva, to be built at the former corner of Flamingo and Dean Martin, on the former Wild West site. Their modest proposal would be the largest hotel complex in Vegas, with 10,000 rooms and at least three casinos.

As usual, rumors fly about the fate of other venerable properties. At press time, the Sahara's new owner intends to give the place a top-to-bottom redo. Still up for sale, the fate of the venerable and rather shabby Rivera continues to hang in the balance. The Tropicana has been the subject of all sorts of plans for rebuilds, implosions, makeovers, and more, all of which have failed to materialize for various reasons, while the property itself sits in fading limbo. And who knows what Harrah's has in mind for that swath of property that runs from Harrah's to Paris? Surely envy over CityCenter is going to produce something equally grand. For the time being, figure that the Imperial Palace's budget Strip rooms are in peril, as are those in the former Barbary Coast (currently carrying the moniker Bill's).

For complete details on the lodging scene in Las Vegas, see chapter 4.

DINING The celebrity chefs continue to come to Vegas, making it one of the most exciting places to eat in the country. And those who are already here just open up additional places. The Palazzo has brought along all sorts of celebrity chefs, starting with another Emeril entry, **Table 10,** as well as a second Mario Batali eatery, steakhouse **Carnevino,** quite possibly the most expensive steakhouse in town. The latter gets to compete with The Palazzo neighbor, **Cut,** Wolfgang Puck's own much lauded house of beef. And Charlie Trotter has opened a haute cuisine seafood venture, **Restaurant Charlie.** And it's not just name chefs; Los Angeles's favorite paparazzi stalking spot, **Sushi Roku,** has opened up a branch in the newer part of Caesars Forum shops.

For more dining options in Las Vegas, see chapter 5.

ABOUT CASINO GAMBLING Perhaps the oddest experience these days in Vegas is the quietest one. The volume in casinos has dimmed some—notably, if you've been to Vegas before—thanks to a gradual change in all slot and other gaming machines. Every casino has changed its machines over to a cashless system, wherein the payouts come in the form of printed slips you exchange at the cages. No more can you thrill to that distinct sound of coins dropping—*clinkclinkclinkclinkclink*—as you cash out on your slot (or poker) machine. These days, that sound is just a programmed audio track. And slots and other machines won't even take coins; gone are the days when one could dump that pocketful of loose change in a slot as one passed by. Meanwhile, many casinos, especially the ones belonging to "resort hotels," are easing up on the noise factor; there is considerably less *bingbingdingding dingdingding* going on in the casinos, which is fine in terms of noise pollution, but still . . . gambling will never be the same again.

And more revolutions are on the way. Casinos in The Venetian and The Palazzo are field-testing portable devices that will allow you take the gambling experience out of the casino and in to any other public area of the building like the pool, some restaurants, bars, lounges, and more. Boy, as if the city didn't already enable gambling problems. The exact details on how these things will work are still a bit of a mystery, but the state has approved the technology, which may well be widely available by the end of 2008.

Another big change hitting casino floors in the near future is the concept of server-based gaming. Currently, each slot machine has its own computer, but in the future they will be "shells" run by one server computer (hidden, we like to imagine, in a bunker somewhere in each casino guarded by dogs and guys with sub-machine guns). Fantasy aside, the end result for you will be the ability to "download" any video-based slot or video poker to any console, eliminating the need to hunt for your "favorite" machine. This is already being tested in certain markets around the country, so expect to see it in Vegas at some point.

Vegas not fast-paced enough for you? Certain newer slot machines are now equipped so that if you are too impatient to wait for the reels to go through their entire spinning cycle, you can punch the "spin" button a second time, and it will go instantly to its final lineup. Doing this does not affect the outcome—it was going to get to that position regardless. If you find yourself pressed for time and don't want to wait for results, try this option.

For tips on maximizing your wins and choosing a casino, see chapter 7.

SHOPPING   With the evolution of the former Aladdin into Planet Hollywood now more or less complete, the owners of the attached shopping center have transformed it, in stages, from the Middle Eastern–themed Dessert Passage into the Times Square/Glamorous Big City–themed **Miracle Mile.** Can't this city leave anything alone? Wait, don't answer that. Anyway, $90 million or so later, it looks an awful lot like a generic fancy shopping mall, albeit one with all kinds

of whiz-bang electronics and lights. It's keenly disappointing. We are getting tired of big and bland, but the list of shops is enough to keep us spending our hard-earned jackpots there.

Another high-end shopping experience is available for you now that **The Palazzo** has opened. The star of the retail show is a branch of Barney's New York, the boutique department store where pretty much every up-to-the-minute brand is represented, but there is plenty else to drool over thanks to the likes of Christian Louboutin, Bottega Veneta, and more. The coming of Encore will bring even more shops right out of the pages of Vogue.

For more on the shopping scene, see chapter 8.

LAS VEGAS AFTER DARK   Broadway continues to stumble when making the transition to the Strip. Tony-winners **The Producers** and **Spamalot** both closed, as did the long-running **Mamma Mia!,** though the Vegas-ized version of **Phantom** continues to bring in its phans. Still, the resort hotels aren't quite giving up on the thea-tah; The Palazzo is hoping for the kind of appeal that classic pop hits can bring (and that Frankie Valli and the Four Seasons have the same kind of support as Abba) as they present the award winning **Jersey Boys.**

Meanwhile, other hotels continue to bank on the ubiquitous Cirque de Soliel. Gothic magician Criss Angel, star of his own Broadway show *Mindfreak,* is pairing up with the po-mo circus troop, which is actually fairly inspired given both acts' use of surreal visuals. *Criss Angel: Believe* will combine Cirque's non-linear, daydream spectacle with his own original illusions, ideally breathing new life into a nearly dead Vegas genre—that of the awe-inspiring magician. Look also for Cirque to follow up its Beatles-salute **LOVE** with an Elvis-themed show due to arrive at CityCenter in 2009.

What's New in Las Vegas

Gee, what *isn't* new in Las Vegas? That they want to take your money and will do so by any means necessary. Cynical? Hardly. That is, after all, why this town was built, and don't, for a minute, think anything else.

Otherwise, everything is constantly new in Las Vegas. This town is afflicted with terminal restlessness and must keep finding new ways of attracting visitors who can then be relieved of their money. Heck, by the time we've finished writing this, everything we've written, everything in the entire town, will be outdated, changed, or somehow different.

Perhaps we exaggerate. But really, only a little. Hotels are routinely renovating, upgrading, redecorating their rooms, and changing their themes (because everyone knows that a Spanish theme will bring in more tourist dollars than a Mardi Gras theme—that is, until they decide it's been long enough with the Spanish theme and then switch to an Asian one), and that's only if they aren't blowing up the hotel and starting over from scratch. New restaurants with celebrity chefs and big prices open, and longtime stalwarts with comfort food for the ages close. Shows that have been touted with enormous billboards and bigger budgets close in the blink of an eye. Please remember this and think kindly of us if anything in this book is inaccurate. Because that's why.

So, as we write this, what's new? Or even, what's going to be new?

PLANNING YOUR TRIP The iconic sign outside of the city reading WELCOME TO LAS VEGAS is a favorite photo op for many. And no wonder—it fits in the frame a lot better than those gargantuan hotels. Unfortunately, snapping a shot has meant risking life and limb as the sign is right on the highway. To help prevent unfortunate starts (or conclusions) to a nice vacation, a parking lot is being constructed in the median just south of the sign. At press time, bids were still being taken, but the hopes are that construction will be finished by late 2008.

Long the last best hope for smokers, Vegas is considerably less smoky these days. A recent ban forbids smoking in any place that serves food, such as a restaurant, supermarket, or bar with a pub menu. Stand-alone bars and casinos are exempt, which, in theory, means you can't smoke in a hotel lobby, but you can a few feet away in a casino. It's an interesting evolution for a town so dedicated to hedonistic pursuits.

ACCOMMODATIONS This being Vegas, "top this" is the mantra. All sorts of significant new properties are due to open in either late 2008 or 2009, with still more coming in the two years after that, giving the city a massive wave of novelty unlike anything since the Strip started its process of reinvention in the late 1980s/early 1990s. It's going to be interesting to see how these properties do given the current economic issues.

There are already newcomers to the Strip scene. The latest entry is **The Palazzo,** 3325 Las Vegas Blvd. S. (© **877/ 883-6423** or 702/607-7777; www.palazzo lasvegas.com). Operating along the lines of Mandalay Bay's THEhotel, it is at once a separate entity from, but tied into, the original Venetian. It contains another 3,000 rooms and is approximately 53 stories tall. In some ways, it may be even grander than The Venetian, though in other ways it's even blander. Along with it come new dining and entertainment options, plus still more shopping. Right next door, Wynn will be opening **Encore,** another billion-dollar-plus addition with 2,000 more suites, more casino, more restaurants, more everything—except it's two whole stories shorter than The Palazzo. Due to open in late 2008, it will include not only entertainer Danny Gans (poached from Wynn's former property, The Mirage), but also a 40,000-square-foot nightclub—in other words, about as big as the hotel's own casino. Bigger is, of course, better, and taller is better still—so Donald Trump has decided he can't possibly be outdone in such matters, and therefore *his* **Trump International,** two towers of hotel rooms and condos, is 60-something stories. The town giggles delightedly over all this display of architectural macho.

For that matter, right in front of Trump's property, the New Frontier is making way for a project courtesy of the Elad Group. The new hotel will be called the **Plaza,** thus liberally borrowing the goodwill generated by fond memories of New York's much-loved Plaza Hotel (also owned by Elad). Whether the Vegas version will resemble its Manhattan sibling in any way remains to be seen. Elad intends to spend $5 billion to produce 3,000 rooms, plus 300 super-high-end luxury residences, a casino, theaters, and the rest. It should be opening in 2011.

Going for sprawl rather than tall—though there is that, too—the hefty MGM MIRAGE (which controls most of the properties on the Strip—Harrah's controls nearly all the rest) is at the helm of the town's most ambitious project yet—the massive **CityCenter.** Get this: It will contain (if it all comes to fruition) not just a 4,000-room megaresort and casino and all that goes with it (shops, restaurants, clubs), but also two 400-room boutique hotels (one being a part of the ultraluxe Mandarin Oriental chain), plus a couple thousand condo units and even more shopping, clubs, and restaurants separate from those belonging to the hotel complex. There will be 7,000 rooms total, plus its own people-mover, which is just as well since CityCenter covers more than 60 acres. With a well over $8 billion price tag, it's the largest privately funded construction project in U.S. history. Its opening in 2009 will make The Palazzo and Encore look like mere penny ante additions.

As if that wasn't enough for that stretch of real estate, hot on CityCenter's heels is its neighbor, the nearly $2-billion **Cosmopolitan,** which will include a Hyatt-run hotel and a big casino when it is complete in 2009. Assuming everything goes according to schedule, 2009 will bring yet another new tower to the ever-expanding **Caesars Palace,** at the cost of a cool billion. Also opening should be **Fontainebleau,** a $3-billion version of the famous Miami resort of the same name. Containing 4,000 rooms, theaters, restaurants, and the rest, it is being built on the site of the newer of the two El Ranchos (Vegas history—it's complicated) right across from Circus Circus.

Not quite CityCenter but right up there in sheer size and scope will be **Echelon Place,** the $4-billion-plus development that is replacing the Stardust on the north end of the Strip. When it opens in

List of Maps

An Invitation to the Reader

In researching this book, we discovered many wonderful places—hotels, restaurants, shops, and more. We're sure you'll find others. Please tell us about them, so we can share the information with your fellow travelers in upcoming editions. If you were disappointed with a recommendation, we'd love to know that, too. Please write to:

Frommer's Las Vegas 2009
Wiley Publishing, Inc. • 111 River St. • Hoboken, NJ 07030-5774

An Additional Note

Please be advised that travel information is subject to change at any time—and this is especially true of prices. We therefore suggest that you write or call ahead for confirmation when making your travel plans. The authors, editors, and publisher cannot be held responsible for the experiences of readers while traveling. Your safety is important to us, however, so we encourage you to stay alert and be aware of your surroundings. Keep a close eye on cameras, purses, and wallets, all favorite targets of thieves and pickpockets.

Acknowledgments

As always, thank you to Frommer's for a job that's really cool even when the desert temps are high, and for their patience with me during difficult times. Billy Fox knows what to query and what to leave alone, and, for an author, that's even better than knowing when to hit and when to hold. Lisa Derrick got my facts in order, and I am grateful. Rick Garman is even better than winning a lot of money on a slot machine; he knows firsthand about that sort of thing, whereas I do not. My biggest win is Steve Hochman, and for that I am most grateful of all.

—Mary Herczog

Other Great Guides for Your Trip:

Frommer's Portable Las Vegas
Frommer's Portable Las Vegas for Non-Gamblers
Las Vegas For Dummies
The Unofficial Guide to Las Vegas
Frommer's USA
Frommer's American Southwest

Frommer's Star Ratings, Icons & Abbreviations

Every hotel, restaurant, and attraction listing in this guide has been ranked for quality, value, service, amenities, and special features using a **star-rating system.** In country, state, and regional guides, we also rate towns and regions to help you narrow down your choices and budget your time accordingly. Hotels and restaurants are rated on a scale of zero (recommended) to three stars (exceptional). Attractions, shopping, nightlife, towns, and regions are rated according to the following scale: zero stars (recommended), one star (highly recommended), two stars (very highly recommended), and three stars (must-see).

In addition to the star-rating system, we also use **seven feature icons** that point you to the great deals, in-the-know advice, and unique experiences that separate travelers from tourists. Throughout the book, look for:

Finds	Special finds—those places only insiders know about
Fun Fact	Fun facts—details that make travelers more informed and their trips more fun
Kids	Best bets for kids and advice for the whole family
Moments	Special moments—those experiences that memories are made of
Overrated	Places or experiences not worth your time or money
Tips	Insider tips—great ways to save time and money
Value	Great values—where to get the best deals

The following **abbreviations** are used for credit cards:

AE	American Express	DISC	Discover	V	Visa
DC	Diners Club	MC	MasterCard		

Frommers.com

Now that you have this guidebook to help you plan a great trip, visit our website at **www.frommers.com** for additional travel information on more than 4,000 destinations. We update features regularly to give you instant access to the most current trip-planning information available. At Frommers.com, you'll find scoops on the best airfares, lodging rates, and car rental bargains. You can even book your travel online through our reliable travel booking partners. Other popular features include:

- Online updates of our most popular guidebooks
- Vacation sweepstakes and contest giveaways
- Newsletters highlighting the hottest travel trends
- Podcasts, interactive maps, and up-to-the-minute events listings
- Opinionated blog entries by Arthur Frommer himself
- Online travel message boards with featured travel discussions

One good diva deserves another, or even two, and so the indomitable **Bette Midler** and **Cher** have replaced Céline Dion at Caesars Palace with their own annual lengthy residencies. Both are pure entertainers, through and through, and if the Divine One's vocals outshine those of Cher's, the latter makes up for it with Bob Mackie gowns that are stars in their own right. Both are producing the kind of shows Vegas used to be known for, quality music and dancing acts, though the prices are anything but retro. Speaking of retro, **Toni Braxton** is ending her run at The Flamingo to be replaced by—wait for it—Donny and Marie. Huh. And here we thought all the family fun was gone from Vegas.

See chapter 9 for more details on Vegas's nightlife.

RUMORS   Vegas just loves gossiping about big plans and changes. None of the following is confirmable—we can't even get most hotels to confirm their rates—and much of it may have changed by the time you read this. But, this gives you an idea of the dreams this city dreams.

At press time, it was announced that the Star Trek Experience exhibit at the Hilton would be closing by September, 2008. This has lead to a most delicious rumor. Vegas watchers have noted two things: the Star Trek ten-year contract runs out in 2008 and has not been renewed. And Michael Jackson's ranch Neverland was saved from a foreclosure-induced bidding auction by a last minute loan from . . . the company that owns the Hilton. Dots have been connected and—well, who knows? Whether anything manifests, it seems reasonable to assume that something very, very interesting was discussed. By the time you read this, it could all be a foregone conclusion—but still . . . isn't it interesting?

1

The Best of Las Vegas

The point about [Las Vegas], which both its critics and its admirers
overlook, is that it's wonderful and awful simultaneously. So one
loves it and detests it at the same time.

—*David Spanier, Welcome to the Pleasuredome: Inside Las Vegas*

As often as you might have seen it on TV or in a movie, nothing can prepare you for your first sight of Las Vegas. The skyline is hyper-reality, a mélange of the Statue of Liberty, a giant lion, a pyramid, and a sphinx, and preternaturally glittering buildings. At night, it's so bright, you can actually get disoriented—and suffer from a sensory overload that can reduce you to hapless tears or fits of giggles. And that's without setting foot inside a casino, where the shouts from the craps tables, computer-generated noise from the slots, and the general roar combine into either the greatest adrenaline rush of your life or the ninth pit of hell.

Las Vegas is a true original; there is nothing else like it in the world. In other cities, hotels are built near the major attractions. Here, the hotels *are* the major attractions. What other city has a skyline made up of buildings from other cities' skylines?

Once you get to Vegas, you'll want to come back again, if only to make sure you didn't dream it all. It's not just the casinos with their nonstop action and sound, the almost-blinding lights, or the buildings that seek to replicate some other reality (Paris, Venice, New York, ancient Egypt). It's not the mountains of shrimp at the buffets, the wedding chapels that will gladly unite two total strangers in holy wedlock, or the promise of free money. It's the whole package. It's Frank and Dino and Sammy. It's Elvis—the Fat Years. It's Britney and Paris behaving scandalously at nightclubs. It's volcanoes and magic shows and cocktail waitresses dressed in short-short Roman togas. It's cheesy, sleazy, and artificial and wholly, completely unique. It's wonderful. It's awful. It's wonderfully awful and awfully wonderful.

Las Vegas can be whatever a visitor wants, and for a few days, a visitor can be whatever he or she wants. Just be prepared to leave all touchstones with reality behind. Here, you will rise at noon and gorge on endless amounts of rich food at 3am. You will watch your money grow or (more likely) shrink. You will watch fountains dance and pirates fight sexy showgirls. This is not a cultural vacation, okay? Save the thoughts of museums and historical sights for the real New York, Egypt, Paris, and Venice. Vegas is about fun. Go have some. Go have too much. It won't be hard.

The Vegas of the Rat Pack years does not exist anymore. Even as ancient civilizations are replicated, "old" in Vegas terms is anything over a decade. Indeed, thanks to teardowns and renovations, there is virtually nothing original left on the Strip. In a way, that is both admirable and ghastly, and it's also part of what makes Vegas so *Vegas*.

Las Vegas & Environs

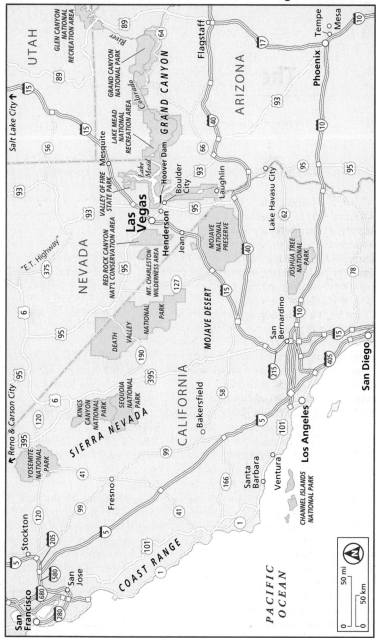

What other city can completely shed its skin in such a short amount of time? But as much as one might mourn the loss of such landmarks as the Sands, one has to admit that time marches on, and Vegas has to keep pace. Nostalgia for the vanished does not mean you can't enjoy what turns up in its place. Even as you might sneer at the gaudy tastelessness of it all, you have to admit that what's out there is remarkable.

And when it's all lit up at night...well, even those who have lived here for years agree there is nothing like the sight of the Strip in all its evening glory. Everything is in lights in Vegas: hotels, casinos, 7-Elevens, the airport's parking garage. Stand still long enough, and they'll probably cover *you* in neon.

Oh, the gambling? Yep, there's plenty of that. Let's not kid ourselves: Gambling is the main attraction of Vegas. The rest—the celebrity-chef restaurants, the shows, the cartoonish buildings—is so much window dressing to lure you and your money to the city. But even a non-gambler can have a perfectly fine time in Vegas, though the lure of countless slot machines has tempted even the most puritanical of souls in their day.

Unfortunately, the days of an inexpensive Las Vegas vacation are gone. The cheap buffets and meal deals still exist, as do some cut-rate rooms, but both are likely to prove the old adage about getting what you pay for. Be prepared to pay if you want glamour and fine dining.

However, free drinks are still handed to anyone lurking near a slot, and even if show tickets aren't in your budget, you won't lack for entertainment. Free lounges, some with singers or go-go dancers, abound, and the people-watching opportunities never disappoint. From the Armani-clad high rollers in the baccarat rooms to the polyester-sporting couples at the nickel slots, Vegas attracts a cross section of humanity.

Yes, it's noisy and chaotic. Yes, it's really just Disneyland for adults. Yes, it's a shrine to greed and the love of filthy lucre. Yes, there is little ambience and even less "culture." Yes, someone lacking self-discipline can come to great grief. But in its own way, Vegas is every bit as amazing as the nearby Grand Canyon, and every bit as much a must-see. It's one of the Seven Wonders of the Artificial World. And everyone should experience it at least once.

1 Frommer's Favorite Las Vegas Experiences

- **Strolling on the Strip after Dark:** You haven't really seen Las Vegas until you've seen it at night. This neon wonderland is the world's greatest sound-and-light show. Begin at Luxor and work your way past the incredible hotels and their attractions. You'll pass the gotta-see-it-to-believe-it New York–New York on your way, and if your strength holds out, you will end at Circus Circus, where live acrobat acts take place overhead while you gamble. Make plenty of stops en route to take in the *Sirens* show at Treasure Island, see The Mirage volcano erupt, take a photo of the full moon over the Eiffel Tower, and marvel at the choreographed water-fountain ballet at Bellagio.

- **Casino-Hopping on the Strip:** The interior of each lavish hotel-casino is more outrageous and giggle-inducing than the last. Just when you think they can't possibly top themselves, they do. From Venice to Paris, from a rainforest to a bit of Paris, from New York City to the ultraluxurious Wynn Las Vegas, it is all, completely and uniquely, Las Vegas.

- **Spending an Evening in Glitter Gulch:** Set aside an evening to tour the Downtown hotels and take in the overhead light show of the **Fremont Street Experience** (p. 174). Unlike the lengthy and exhausting Strip, here you can hit a dozen casinos in about 5 minutes.

- **Binging at Buffets:** Many are no longer the very best of bargains, but there is something about the endless mounds of food that just scream "Vegas" to us. Our choices for the best in town are listed in the dining section, later in this chapter.

- **Taking a Creative Adventures Tour:** Char Cruze of **Creative Adventures** (© **702/893-2051;** www.creativead-venturesltd.net) provides personalized tours unlike anything offered by a commercial tour company, full of riveting stories and incredible facts about both natural and artificial local wonders. See p. 193.

- **Marveling at the Liberace Museum:** It's not the Smithsonian, but then again, the Smithsonian doesn't have rhinestones like these. Only in Vegas. See p. 177.

- **Visiting the Dolphins at The Mirage:** This is a most un-Vegas experience. Watch these gorgeous mammals frolic in their cool blue pool. If you're really lucky, they'll play ball with you. See p. 181.

- **Playing Penny Slots:** Even the most budget-conscious traveler can gamble for hours. Penny slots used to be as rare as a non-silicone-enhanced showgirl, but now they're in all the major casinos. See chapter 7.

- **Shopping the Big Three Casino Arcades:** Take what Napoleon called "the greatest drawing room in Europe," replicate it, add shops, and you've got the **Grand Canal Shoppes at The Venetian** (p. 233)—it's St. Mark's Square, complete with canals and working gondolas. It's now connected to its sister property, **The Palazzo,** where it is not themed, but is still quite impressive, with envy-inducing designer stores. Then there are the **Forum Shops at Caesars Palace** (p. 230), which replicate an ancient Roman streetscape, with classical piazzas and opulent fountains. Don't miss the scary audio-animatronic statues as they come to glorious, cheesy life. And while **Miracle Mile at Planet Hollywood** (p. 232) is no longer the Middle Eastern–themed souk of our dreams—it's now sort of a glitzy generic mall—the variety of shops makes it one of the better hotel shopping experiences.

- **Being Amazed by Cirque du Soleil's *O, KÀ,* and *Mystère:*** You haven't really seen Cirque du Soleil until you've seen it performed in a showroom equipped with state-of-the-art sound and lighting systems and a seemingly infinite budget for sets, costumes, and high-tech special effects. It's an enchantment. See p. 245, 243, and 245.

- **Seeing Your Favorite Headliners:** As soon as you arrive in town, pick up a show guide and see who's playing during your stay. For the top showrooms, see chapter 9.

- **Finding the Worst Lounge Shows:** Some feel this is the ultimate Vegas experience. Be sure to watch out for **Mr. Cook E. Jarr.** See chapter 9 for some ideas.

- **Red Rock Canyon and Valley of the Fire State Park:** No money-grubbing businessperson caused these awe-inspiring desert rock formations to be built, and they will be standing long after Vegas.

A Funeral Director's Look Back at Vegas: No Tomorrow

Las Vegas is convention central. Orthodontists go there, as do architects, computer geeks, gynecologists, TV preachers, township clerks, postal workers, and pathologists. There's an abundance of good hotel rooms, cheap eats, and agreeable weather. Coming and going is reasonably painless. There are golf and gambling and ogling of girls—showgirls of unspeakable beauty—and, of course, the mountains, the desert, and the sky.

The National Funeral Directors Association advertised its 116th Annual Convention and International Exposition there in the trade press as "A Sure Bet." Debbie Reynolds was talking at the Spouse's Luncheon. Neil Sedaka was singing at the Annual Banquet. There was a golf outing, a new website, the installation of officers. I called the brother and the brother-in-law and said, "Let's get our funeral homes covered and go out to Vegas for the convention." Pat and Mike agreed. All of us are funeral directors. All of us were due for a break. Here's another coincidence: All of our wives are named Mary. The Marys all agreed to come along. They'd heard about the showgirls and high-stakes tables and figured Pat and Mike and I would need looking after. They'd heard about the great malls and the moving statues and the magic shows.

My publisher paid for my airfare and our room at the Hilton. "A Sure Bet" is what they reckoned, too. My book, *The Undertaking: Life Studies from the Dismal Trade,* was being featured in the Marketplace Booth at the exhibit hall. The association would be selling and I'd be signing as many copies as we could for a couple of days. So there I sat, behind a stack of books, glad-handing and autographing, surrounded by caskets and hearses, cremation urns and new computer software, flower stands and funeral flags and embalming supplies. Some things about this enterprise never change— the basic bias toward the horizontal, the general preference for black and blue, the arcane lexicons of loss and wonder. And some are changing every day. Like booksellers and pharmacists and oncologists, many of the small firms are being overtaken by the large consolidators and conglomerates. Custom gives way to convenience. The old becomes old, then new again.

Five thousand undertakers made it to Vegas—the biggest turnout since the last time here, in '74—and 2,300 sales reps and suppliers. It was bigger than Orlando or Kansas City or Chicago, or the next year in Boston.

Las Vegas seems perfect for the mortuary crowd—a metaphor for the vexed, late-century American soul that seems these days to run between

2 Best Hotel Bets

- **Best for Conventioneers/Business Travelers:** The **Las Vegas Hilton,** 3000 Paradise Rd. (© **888/732-7117;** www.lvhilton.com), adjacent to the Las Vegas Convention Center and the setting for many conventions, offers extensive facilities that include a full business center. And now it's a stop on the monorail, making access to the Strip easier than ever. See p. 103.

extremes of fantasy and desolation. Vegas seems just such an oasis: a neon garden of earthly delights amid a moonscape of privations, abundance amid the cacti, indulgence surrounded by thirst and hunger.

Or maybe it's that we undertakers understand these games of chance—the way life is ever asking us to ante up, the way the wager's made before the deal is dealt or dice are tossed, before we pull the lever. Some people play for nickels and dimes, some for dollars, some for keeps. But whatever we play for, we win or lose according to these stakes. We cannot, once winning is certain or losing is sure, change our bet. We cannot play for dollars, then lose in dimes or win in cash when we wager matchsticks. It's much the same with love and grief. They share the same arithmetic and currency. We ante up our hearts in love, we pay our losses off in grief. Baptisms, marriages, funerals—this life's casinos—the games we play for keeps.

Oh, we can play the odds, hedge our bets, count the cards, get a system. I think of Blaise Pascal, the 17th-century French mathematician who bet on heaven thus: "Better to believe in a God who isn't than not to believe in a God who is." Figure the math of that, the odds. Pascal's Wager is what they called it. All of us play a version of this game.

I came downstairs in the middle of the night and lost 200 bucks before it occurred to me that this is how they built this city—on folks like me, on what we'd be willing to lose. The next night, my Mary won $800 on one pull of the lever on the slots. They paid her off in crisp C-notes. We laughed and smiled. She tipped the woman who sold her the tokens. She went shopping the next day for a pair of extravagant shoes and came home, as they say, with money in her pockets.

We undertakers understand winners and losers. Our daily lives are lessons in the way love hurts, grief heals, and life—always a game of chance—goes on. In Vegas we get to play the game as if there's no tomorrow. And after a long night of winning or losing, it's good to have a desert close at hand into which we wander, like holy ones of old, to raise our songs of thanks or curse our luck to whatever God there is, or isn't.

—*Thomas Lynch*

Thomas Lynch is a poet and essayist and a funeral director in Milford, Michigan. *The Undertaking: Life Studies from the Dismal Trade* won the Heartland Prize and the American Book Award, and was a finalist for the National Book Award. His latest work is *Booking Passage: We Irish and Americans.*

- **Best Luxury Resorts:** The **Ritz-Carlton, Lake Las Vegas,** 1610 Lake Las Vegas Pkwy., Henderson (© **800/ 241-3333;** www.ritzcarlton.com), perched on the edge (and over part) of Lake Las Vegas in Henderson, wins the prize for its combination of setting (gorgeous, peaceful) and experience (such service!). See p. 111. But you might want something that's actually in town, and for that, you must go to the **Four Seasons,** 3960 Las Vegas Blvd. S. (© **877/632-5000;** www. fourseasons.com), because experience running luxury resorts around the world makes them the only true claimant to the throne within Vegas. See p. 62.

- **Best Resort for the Indecisive:** So you want a proper resort getaway, but you don't want to be too far from Vegas action. **Red Rock Resort,** 10973 W. Charleston Rd. (© **866/ 767-7773;** www.redrocklasvegas. com), is a smashing newer facility that has it all: luxe rooms, an excellent pool area, good and relatively inexpensive food, fab decor, and a breathtaking view of the red rocks of the canyon. Many a well-heeled celeb has already kept a low profile by the pool. See p. 113.

- **Best Archetypically Las Vegas Hotel:** To be honest, these days there aren't any. Las Vegas hotels are one and all doing such massive face-lifts that the archetype is mostly a memory. Still, despite some major changes, **Caesars Palace,** 3570 Las Vegas Blvd. S. (© **877/427-7243;** www.caesars.com), will probably continue to embody the excess, the romance (oh, yes) and, well, downright silliness that used to characterize Vegas—and to a certain extent still does. See p. 78.

- **Best Non-Vegas Vegas Hotel:** Mandalay Bay's **THEhotel,** 3950 Las Vegas Blvd. S. (© **877/632-7800;** www.thehotelatmandalaybay.com), is as elegant and sophisticated as any lodging in Manhattan. All accommodations are true suites, complete with flatscreen TVs and deep soaking tubs. Since it's a separate tower, you are far away from the clash and clang of Vegas—at least in spirit. In reality, it's just a medium walk down a long hallway. Quite possibly our favorite hotel in the city. See p. 71.

- **Best Swimming Pools:** Hands down, the acres of water park fun at **Mandalay Bay,** 3950 Las Vegas Blvd. S. (© **877/ 632-7000;** www.mandalaybay.com)— wave pool, lazy river, beach, regular swimming pools, even its own open-air casino . . . no wonder they check IDs carefully to make sure only official guests enter. Everyone wants to swim and splash here. See p. 66. If you can't, you won't be disappointed by the amorphously shaped pools with water fountains and slides, plus a rather festive atmosphere, at **The Mirage,** 3400 Las Vegas Blvd. S. (© **800/627-6667;** www.mirage. com). See p. 87. But if you've ever longed to swim at Hearst Castle, **Bellagio,** 3600 Las Vegas Blvd. S. (© **888/987-6667;** www.bellagio. com), with six swimming pools in a neoclassical Italian garden setting (and a more hushed, chic ambience), is for you. See p. 77. Then again, the pool at **Green Valley Ranch Resort,** 2300 Paseo Verde Pkwy. (at I-215), Henderson (© **866/782-9487;** www. greenvalleyranchresort.com), with its foliage, beach, and everything else, may have them both beat. But its distant location (in Henderson) takes it out of the running. But only just. See p. 112.

- **Best Spas/Health Clubs:** We only wish our own gym were as handsomely equipped as the one at the Canyon Ranch Spa in **The Venetian,** 3355 Las Vegas Blvd. S. (© **888/ 283-6423;** www.venetian.com), which also has a number of other high-priced amenities on which you can blow your blackjack winnings. See p. 82. We are also partial to the full complement of machines at the health club at **Bellagio,** 3600 Las Vegas Blvd. S. (© **888/987-6667;** www.bellagio.com), probably the best-equipped club of all. Attentive attendants, a well-stocked locker room, and comfortable lounges in which to rest up after your workout are other pluses. For a straight spa experience, the **Qua** at Caesars Palace, 3570 Las Vegas Blvd. S. (© **702/731-7110**), is a paean to quiet pleasure, a peaceful and aesthetically pleasing haven with all sorts of included-in-admission indulgences, such as an ice exfoliation room. See p. 80.

- **Best Hotel Dining:** Foodies can't miss the chance to eat French food from the hands of a true master, at **Joël Robuchon** and **L'Atelier de Joël Robuchon** (the latter is a more casual and somewhat cheaper experience, but just as lauded; © **702/891-7925**), in the MGM Grand. If, of course, you don't mind taking out a small bank loan to fund that gastronomic venture. Otherwise, you can work up a good case of gout trying all the haute-cuisine options at Bellagio, which has restaurants by Todd English (**Olives;** © **702/693-7223**) and Julian Serrano (**Picasso;** © **702/693-7223**). The hotel has seven James Beard Award–winning chefs on staff. Wynn Las Vegas has brought in a number of name-brand chefs, including Alex Strada (**Alex;** © **888/320-7110**) and Paul Bartolotta (**Bartolotta Ristorante di Mare;** © **888/320-7110**). The Venetian isn't too far behind, with restaurants from Emeril Lagasse (**Delmonico Steakhouse;** © **702/414-3737**), and Joachim Splichal (**Pinot Brasserie;** © **702/414-8888**), Mario Batali (**B&B Ristorante;** © **702/266-9977**) plus a version of Thomas Keller's bistro **Bouchon** (© **702/414-6200**). See chapter 5.
- **Best for 20-Somethings to Baby Boomers:** Palms Casino Resort, 4321 W. Flamingo Rd. (© **866/942-7777;** www.palms.com), is the single most happening hotel for the hip and hip-hop sets. See p. 89. The **Hard Rock Hotel & Casino,** 4455 Paradise Rd. (© **800/473-7625;** www.hardrockhotel.com), bills itself as the world's "first rock 'n' roll hotel and casino" and "Vegas for a new generation." See p. 98.
- **Best Interiors:** For totally different reasons, it's a tie between **New York–New York Hotel & Casino,** 3790 Las Vegas Blvd. S. (© **800/693-6763;** www.nynyhotelcasino.com), and **The Mirage,** 3400 Las Vegas Blvd. S. (© **800/627-6667;** www.mirage.com). The Mirage's (p. 87) tropical rainforest and massive coral-reef aquarium behind the registration desk may not provide as much relaxation as a Club Med vacation, but they're a welcome change from the hubbub that is usual for Vegas. Speaking of hubbub, New York–New York (p. 69) has cornered the market on it, but its jaw-dropping interior, with its extraordinary attention to detail (re-creating virtually every significant characteristic of New York City), makes this a tough act to beat.
- **Best for Families:** The classic choice is **Circus Circus Hotel & Casino,** 2880 Las Vegas Blvd. S. (© **877/434-9175;** www.circuscircus.com), with ongoing circus acts, a vast video-game arcade, a carnival midway, and a full amusement park. See p. 97. Less aged, and less hectic, **Mandalay Bay,** 3950 Las Vegas Blvd. S. (© **877/632-7000;** www.mandalaybay.com), is a more modern choice, right for families because you can gain access to both the guest rooms and the pool area (itself fun for kids, with a beach, a wave pool, and a lazy river) without trotting through the casino. See p. 66. Those of you with bigger budgets might want to try the **Ritz-Carlton, Lake Las Vegas,** 1610 Lake Las Vegas Pkwy., Henderson

(𝄢 **800/241-3333;** www.ritzcarlton.com), because not only is it well out of range of Sin City's temptations, but it also offers a variety of healthy and fun activities (from hikes to fly-fishing to stargazing). See p. 111.

- **Best Rooms off the Strip:** Again, we love the **Ritz-Carlton, Lake Las Vegas,** 1610 Lake Las Vegas Pkwy., Henderson (𝄢 **800/241-3333;** www. ritzcarlton.com), with its perfect decor, spacious interior, and gorgeous bathrooms, but you'll probably want something closer to town. Still not in the thick of things, but not quite as far away is **Red Rock Resort,** 10973 W. Charleston Rd. (𝄢 **866/767-7773;** www.redrockstation.com), where the smashing rooms include lush bathrooms and beds that are like sleeping in a bowl of whipped cream—both offering places to relax while watching big flatscreen TVs. See p. 113.

- **Best Rooms on the Strip:** We need to break this down. If one is talking actual suites, then **THEhotel,** 3950 Las Vegas Blvd. S. (𝄢 **877/632-7800;** www.thehotelatmandalaybay. com), wins the day, with its one-bedroom could-be-a-great-apartment-in-Manhattan sophisticated wonders. See p. 71. Best "suites" (because no matter how the hotel bills them, these accommodations are really just one big room) are clearly the 700-square-foot extravaganzas at **The Venetian,** 3355 Las Vegas Blvd. S. (𝄢 **888/283-6423;** www.venetian.com) and **The Palazzo,** 3325 Las Vegas Blvd S. (𝄢 **866/263-3001;** www.palazzo lasvegas.com) with separate sitting and bedroom areas, full of all sorts of special details. See p. 81. Best "room" goes to the **Wynn Las Vegas,** 3131 Las Vegas Blvd. S. (𝄢 **888/320-9966;** www.wynnlasvegas.com), where the rooms are quite big, the bathrooms not far behind, the beds are

plush, the TVs (plural!) are flatscreen, and the tubs are deep. See p. 93. The newly upgraded rooms at **The Flamingo,** 3555 Las Vegas Blvd S. (𝄢 **800/732-2111;** www.flamingo lasvegas.com) pay homage to its venerable past with vintage photos and hot pink accents—plus various luxuries and other style touches that make them ring-a-ding! See p. 85.

- **Best Rooms Downtown:** The rooms at the **Golden Nugget,** 129 E. Fremont St. (𝄢 **800/846-5336;** www.goldennugget.com), are getting some much-needed love that should return them to the top of the heap (p. 107), but don't forget about the lovely **Main Street Station,** 200 N. Main St. (𝄢 **800/465-0711;** www. mainstreetcasino.com), with lots to offer both in the rooms and beyond. It has done a terrific job of renovating an older space, boasting solidly good restaurants and surprisingly nice rooms for an inexpensive price (p. 110).

- **Best Bathrooms:** This honor goes to **THEhotel,** 3950 Las Vegas Blvd. S. (𝄢 **877/632-7800;** www.thehotelat mandalaybay.com), where each good-size marble bathroom features a large glass shower, a separate water closet, a flatscreen TV, and a soaking tub so deep that the water comes up to your chin. It's a wonder anyone ever leaves to go to the casino. See p. 71. Not far behind is **Wynn Las Vegas,** 3131 Las Vegas Blvd. S. (𝄢 **888/320-9966;** www.wynnlasvegas.com), which offers a similar layout, including a plasma TV and deep, long tub, plus lemon-grass-scented amenities and silky robes to cradle you afterward. See p. 93.

- **Best Non-Casino Hotel: Four Seasons,** 3960 Las Vegas Blvd. S. (𝄢 **877/632-5000;** www.fourseasons.com; p. 62), used to win this category, but now it's a tie with **THEhotel,** 3950 Las Vegas Blvd. S. (𝄢 **877/632-7800;**

www.thehotelatmandalaybay.com; p. 71). It can't be a coincidence that both are found around Mandalay Bay. Once you've experienced the Four Seasons's quiet good taste, superior service and pampering, and the serenity of their non-casino property, or the sophistication and elegance of THEhotel, it's hard to go back to traditional Vegas hotels. But best of all, should you want the best of both worlds, you need only pass through one door to have access to Mandalay Bay and all its traditional Vegas hotel accouterments, including that missing casino. Coming in a close second is the **Venezia,** 3355 Las Vegas Blvd. S. (☏ **888/283-6423;** www.venetian. com; p. 84) at The Venetian; same idea as THEhotel (a separate yet equal entity, the non-casino part of the casino hotel), though we prefer the decor and gestalt of THEhotel.

- **Best Casinos:** Our favorite places to gamble are anywhere we might win. But we also like the casinos in **The Mirage** (lively, beautiful, and not overwhelming; p. 87), **New York–New York** (because of the aforementioned attention to detail—it almost makes losing fun; p. 69), and **Main Street Station** (p. 110), because it's about the most smoke-free casino in town and because it's pretty.

- **Best Views:** From the high-floor rooms at the **Stratosphere Las Vegas Hotel & Casino,** 2000 Las Vegas Blvd. S. (☏ **800/998-6937;** www. stratospherehotel.com), you can see clear to the next county (p. 96), while the top floors in the **Wynn Las Vegas,** 3131 Las Vegas Blvd. S. (☏ **888/320-9966;** www.wynnlas vegas.com) and **The Palazzo,** 3325 Las Vegas Blvd. S. (☏ **866/263-3001;** www.palazzolasvegas.com), sit in the tallest buildings on the main part of the Strip. See p. 81. If you are lucky, your room at **Red Rock Resort,** 10973 W. Charleston Rd. (☏ **866/767-7773;** www.redrock lasvegas.com), will overlook those very same red rocks, though at some distance.

3 Best Dining Bets

A number of celebrity chefs are cooking in Vegas, awakening us to the opinion that Vegas's rep for lackluster restaurants is no longer deserved. Reviews for all of the restaurants listed below can be found in chapter 5.

- **Best Restaurant to Blow Your Money On:** You could lighten your wallet at the craps table—and why not?—or you could spend that same amount, and take a lot longer doing so, exalting in the culinary work being done at **Joël Robuchon** (☏ **702/891-7925;** p. 123), in the MGM Grand, where you will have a once-in-a-lifetime meal. Somewhat less in the stratosphere, but still plenty costly, are **Alex Strada's** (☏ **702/248-3463;** p. 143) and **Paul Bartolotta's** (☏ **702/248-3463;** p. 144) eponymous places in Wynn Las Vegas, and Hubert Keller's **Fleur de Lys** (☏ **702/632-7200;** p. 122) at Mandalay Place, not to mention **L'Atelier de Joël Robuchon,** the master chef's less formal venue that won the James Beard Award for Best New Restaurant 2007. Meals come dear at all five places, but each is turning out works of edible art, from four different inspired sources of creation. To us, this is what Vegas indulgence is all about, and the memories make us much happier than our losses at the table.

- **Best All Around:** Given our druthers, we are hard-pressed to choose between **Alizé** (© 702/951-7000; p. 130), at the top of the Palms, where nearly flawless dishes often compete with the sparkling view for sheer delight, and **Rosemary's Restaurant,** 8125 W. Sahara Ave. (© 702/869-2251; p. 156), a 20-minute drive off the Strip and worth twice as much effort, for some Southern-influenced cooking. Each of these may well put the work of those many high-profile chefs, so prominently featured all over town, to shame. Speaking of high-profile chefs, we have just sworn allegiance to Thomas Keller's **Bouchon** (© 702/414-6200; p. 137), in Venezia at The Venetian. Keller may be the best chef in America, and while this is simply his take on classic bistro food, you should never underestimate the joys of simple food precisely prepared. We also never ever turn down a chance to eat what Julian Serrano is making over at **Picasso** (© 702/693-7223; p. 135), at Bellagio.

- **Best Inexpensive Meal: Capriotti's,** 324 W. Sahara Ave. (© 702/474-0229; p. 147), serves beautiful, fresh, monster submarine sandwiches. They roast their own beef and turkey on the premises and assemble it (or cold cuts, or even vegetables) into delicious well-stuffed submarine sandwiches, ranging in size from 9 to 20 inches, and most of them under $10. We never leave town without one . . . or two.

- **Best Buffet:** On the Strip, it's **Le Village Buffet** (in Paris Las Vegas, © 888/266-5687; p. 166), where the stations break from standard form by adhering to regional French food specialties (from places such as Provence, Alsace, and Burgundy) and the results are much better than average. Though not cheap, this is a reasonable substitute for an even more costly fancy meal. If you want a little

more traditional buffet—as in, one not devoted to one particular cuisine—**Wynn Las Vegas** (in Wynn Las Vegas, © 702/770-3340) is terrific all the way, even through the usual buffet weakness, dessert. See p. 168. Downtown, the **Main Street Station Garden Court** (in Main Street Station, © 702/387-1896), has an incredible buffet: all live-action stations (where the food is made in front of you, sometimes to order); wood-fired brick-oven pizzas; fresh, lovely salsas and guacamole in the Mexican section; and better-than-average desserts. See p. 170.

- **Best Sunday Champagne Brunch:** Head for Bally's, at Mid-Strip, where the lavish **Sterling Sunday Brunch** (© 702/967-7999) features tables dressed with linen and silver. The buffet itself has everything from caviar and lobster to sushi and sashimi, plus fancy entrees that include the likes of roast duckling with black currant and blueberry sauce. See p. 165.

- **Best Group Budget Meal Deal: Capriotti's,** 324 W. Sahara Ave. (© 702/474-0229; p. 147), again—a large sandwich can feed two with leftovers, for about $5 each.

- **Best Bistro:** We ate nearly the entire menu at Thomas Keller's **Bouchon,** in The Venetian (© 702/414-6200; p. 137), and didn't find a misstep, just what you might expect from one of the most critically lauded chefs in the country. But don't overlook **Mon Ami Gabi** (© 702/944-4224), in Paris Las Vegas. Offering lovely, reasonably priced bistro fare (steak and *pommes frites,* onion soup), it's also a charming spot. See p. 141.

- **Best Restaurant/Nightclub Interiors:** The designers ran amok in the restaurants of **Mandalay Bay.** At **Aureole** (© 877/632-1766), a four-story wine tower requires that a pretty young thing be hauled up in a harness to fetch your chosen vintage. See p. 120. The post-Communist party decor at **Red Square** (② 702/632-7407; p. 124) is topped only by the fire-and-water walls at neighboring **rumjungle** (② 702/632-7408; p. 267). And then there is the futuristic fantasy of **Mix** (② 702/632-9500), on top of THEhotel, where stunning views of the Strip compete with a giant beaded curtain made of hand-blown glass balls, to say nothing of silver pods in lieu of booths. See p. 124.

- **Best Spot for a Romantic Dinner:** **Alizé** (② 702/951-7000), at the top of the Palms, has windows on three sides of the dining room, with no other buildings around for many blocks. You get an unobstructed view of all of Vegas, the desert, and the mountains from every part of the restaurant. Aren't you in the mood already? See p. 130.

- **Best Spot for a Celebration:** Let's face it, no one parties like the Red Party, so head to **Red Square** (② 702/632-7407) in Mandalay Bay, where you can have caviar and vodka in the ultimate capitalist revenge. See p. 124.

- **Best Free Show at Dinner:** At Wynn Las Vegas, **Daniel Boulud Brasserie** (② 702/770-9966), provides front-and-center seating for the strange yet compelling Lake of Dreams show. And then there is the vista offered by the restaurants in Bellagio—**Picasso** (② 702/693-7223), **Le Cirque** (② 877/234-6358), **Olives** (② 702/693-7223), and **Circo** (② 702/693-8150)—which are grouped to take advantage of the view of the dancing water fountains. See chapter 5 for reviews of all the Bellagio restaurants.

- **Best Wine List:** It's a competitive market in Vegas for such a title, and

with sommeliers switching around, it's hard to guarantee that any wine list will retain its quality. Still, you can't go wrong at Mandalay Bay's **Aureole** (② 877/632-1766), which has the largest collection of Austrian wines outside of that country, among other surprises. See p. 120.

- **Best Beer List: Rosemary's Restaurant,** 8125 W. Sahara Ave. (② 702/869-2251), offers "beer pairings" suggestions with most of its menu options, and includes some curious and fun brands, including fruity Belgian numbers. See p. 156.

- **Best Views: Mix** (② 877/632-1766; p. 124), on top of THEhotel, and **Alizé** (② 702/951-7000; p. 130), at the top of the Palms, win with their floor-to-ceiling window views, but there is something to be said for seeing all of Vegas from the revolving **Top of the World** (② 702/380-7711), 106 stories off the ground in the Stratosphere Casino Hotel & Tower. See p. 136.

- **Best Italian:** You won't find anything more authentic outside of Italy than at **Bartolotta Ristorante di Mare** (② 888/320-7110), at Wynn Las Vegas. Given that the chef has his fish flown in daily from the Mediterranean, this also wins "best seafood." See p. 143. For personal takes on very traditional Italian—and in doing so, demonstrating how wide "traditional Italian" goes—head to **Corsa Cucina,** also in Wynn Las Vegas (② 702/352-3463), where the chef-owner is often right there in the open kitchen, ready to guide you to something interesting.

- **Best Deli:** Wars are fought over less, so all you New Yorkers can square off on behalf of **Carnegie Deli** in The Mirage (② 702/791-7310). Los Angeles residents will fight for the branch of their beloved **Canter's Deli**

(© **702/894-7111**), in TI–Treasure Island. The rest of us will find our mouths too packed with pastrami to weigh in. See p. 143.

- **Best New Orleans Cuisine:** Emeril's **Delmonico Steakhouse** (© **702/414-3737**), in The Venetian, brings the celebrity chef's "Bam!" cuisine to the other side of the Mississippi, and we are glad. See p. 132.

- **Best Red Meat: Lawry's The Prime Rib,** 4043 Howard Hughes Pkwy.

(© **702/893-2223;** p. 148), has such good prime rib, it's hard to imagine ever having any better. If you want cuts other than prime rib, **Charlie Palmer** (© **702/632-5120;** p. 121), in the Four Seasons, has some of the best steaks in town, though the more budget-conscious might want to either split the enormous cuts or try the justly popular **Austins Steakhouse** in Texas Station, 2101 Texas Star Lane (© **702/631-1033;** p. 154).

4 Best of Vegas After Dark

- **Best Production Show:** It's a total deadlock tie between **Cirque du Soleil's** *KÀ* and *O* (© **866/774-7117** for *KÀ,* and © **888/488-7111** for *O;* p. 243 and 245). The latter is more "traditional"—if you can call a human circus that uses a giant tank of water as a stage "traditional"—in that it has only a loose semblance of narrative, whereas *KÀ* actually has a plot. Both are dazzling and, given the extremely high production values, seem worth the extremely high ticket prices.

- **Best Old-Time Vegas Production:** You know: big, huge stage sets, pointless production numbers, showgirls, nipples on parade, Bob Mackie headdresses. Ah, *Jubilee!,* this world would be dreary without you (© **800/237-7469**). See p. 249.

- **Best Smart Show:** This town isn't good enough for either **Blue Man Group** (© **866/641-7469;** p. 243) or **Penn & Teller** (© **888/746-7784;** p. 251).

- **Best Local Hang:** Hard-core types (including punks, off-duty strippers, off-duty waitstaff, and, on certain nights, Blue Men sans makeup, doing weird percussion things) gather way after hours at the **Double Down Saloon,** 4640 Paradise Rd. (© **702/791-5775**). See p. 258.

- **Best Night Club:** If by "best" you mean "most popular," and by "most popular" you mean "people are willing to start standing in line hours before they open and pay $30 a pop, and that's before alcohol, just to get a foot in the door," then **Pure** in Caesars Palace, 3570 Las Vegas Blvd. S. (© **702/731-7110**), beats out the competition by a long shot.

- **Best Ultralounge:** That's just Vegas-speak for "fancy-pants hotel bar," but most of them are pretty nice, if trying too hard to be all that. Still, we like the vibe at **Tabú,** at MGM Grand (© **702/891-7183**). See p. 268.

- **Best Reason to Wait in Line:** We never think there is a good enough reason, but **ghostbar,** in the Palms (© **702/938-2666;** p. 259), is a fantastic hotel bar, especially because of its outstanding view, perched high above the Strip. Meanwhile, there's a good reason **Rain Nightclub,** 4321 W. Flamingo Rd. (© **702/940-7246;** p. 267), keeps packing them in—it's *plus ne ultra* for dance clubs. But the style of **Body English** (© **702/693-5000;** p. 265), in the Hard Rock Hotel, is terribly appealing to us as well. And then there is the egalitarian attitude at **Privé** (in **Planet Hollywood,** 3667 Las Vegas Blvd. S.,

(C) **702/492-3960**) where there is no VIP section, and everyone is encouraged to move about the club freely, and even dance on the furniture.

- **Best Burlesque:** Tough call, given the competition, but **Ivan Kane's Forty Deuce** ((C) **702/632-7000**), in Mandalay Bay, was the first establishment (back in Los Angeles) to cash in on the return of the high-class hoochie girl, and still does it the best here. See p. 259.

- **Best Strip Club:** You know you want to know. We give the honors to **Treasures,** 2801 Westwood Dr. ((C) **702/257-3030**), because we think all strip joints should insist on production numbers with stage effects and look like old-fashioned English brothels. See p. 272.

2

Planning Your Trip to Las Vegas

Before any trip, you need to do a bit of planning. In the pages that follow, you'll find everything you need to know to handle the practical details of planning your trip in advance: area airports, a calendar of events, a list of major conventions you may want to avoid, resources for those with special needs, and more.

For international visitors, the pervasiveness of American culture around the world may make you feel that you know the United States pretty well, but leaving your own country still requires an additional degree of planning. This chapter will help prepare you for the most common issues you may encounter in Las Vegas.

We also suggest that you check out chapter 9, "Las Vegas After Dark," before you leave home. If you want to see the most popular shows, it's a good idea to call ahead and order tickets well in advance to avoid disappointment. Ditto if you want to dine in one of the city's top restaurants: Head to chapter 5, "Where to Dine," for reviews and contact information.

For additional help in planning your trip and for more on-the-ground resources in Las Vegas, please turn to the "Fast Facts, Toll-Free Numbers & Websites" appendix on p. 292.

1 Visitor Information

For advance information, call or write the **Las Vegas Convention and Visitors Authority,** 3150 Paradise Rd., Las Vegas, NV 89109 (© **877/VISIT-LV** or 702/892-0711; www.visitlasvegas.com). They can send you a comprehensive packet containing brochures, a map, a show guide, an events calendar, and an attractions list; help you find a hotel that meets your specifications (and even make reservations); and tell you whether a major convention is scheduled during the time you would like to visit Las Vegas. Or stop by when you're in town. They're open daily from 9am to 5pm.

Another excellent information source is the **Las Vegas Chamber of Commerce,** 3720 Howard Hughes Pkwy., #100, Las Vegas, NV 89109 (© 702/735-1616; www.lvchamber.com). Ask them to send you their *Visitor Guide,* which contains extensive information about accommodations, attractions, excursions, children's activities, and more. They can answer all your Vegas questions. They're open Monday through Friday from 8am to 5pm.

For information on all of Nevada, including Las Vegas, contact the **Nevada Commission on Tourism** (© **800/638-2328;** www.travelnevada.com). They'll send you a comprehensive information packet on Nevada.

There's also lots of great info on the Web. We highly recommend the informative and comprehensive **www.vegas4visitors.com** as well as **www.vegas.com**. Both feature plenty of reviews, listings, hotel bookings and more. Blogs about Las Vegas include **www.everythinglv.com**, **www.ratevegas.com/blog**, and **www.stevefriess.com/podcast**.

Las Vegas Advisor

Professional gambler and longtime Las Vegas resident Anthony Curtis, author of *Bargain City: Booking, Betting, and Beating the New Las Vegas,* knows all the angles for stretching your hotel, restaurant, and, most importantly, gaming dollar. His 12-page monthly newsletter, the *Las Vegas Advisor,* is chock-full of insider tips on how to maximize your odds on every game, which slot tournaments to enter, casino promotions that represent money-making opportunities for the bettor, where to obtain the best *Fun Books* (coupon books full of freebies and discounts), which hotel offers a 12-ounce margarita for 99¢ or a steak dinner for $3, what the best buffet and show values in town are, and much, much more.

Subscribers get more than $3,400 worth of coupons for discounts on rooms, meals, show tickets, and car rentals, along with free slot plays, two-for-one bets, and other perks. A subscription is $50 a year, a single issue $5. To subscribe, call ✆ **800/244-2224** or send a check to *Las Vegas Advisor,* 3687 S. Procyon St., Las Vegas, NV 89103. You can also go to **www.lasvegasadvisor. com** and get the full membership or a special online membership that features everything except the mailed newsletters and reference guide for $37 per year.

2 Entry Requirements & Customs

ENTRY REQUIREMENTS
PASSPORTS

New regulations issued by the Department of Homeland Security now require virtually every air traveler entering the U.S. to show a passport. As of January 23, 2007, all persons, including U.S. citizens, traveling by air between the United States and Canada, Mexico, Central and South America, the Caribbean, and Bermuda are required to present a valid passport. As of January 31, 2008, U.S. and Canadian citizens entering the U.S. at land and sea ports of entry from within the western hemisphere will need to present government-issued proof of citizenship, such as a birth certificate, along with a government-issued photo ID, such as a driver's license. A passport is not required for U.S. or Canadian citizens entering by land or sea, but it is highly encouraged to carry one.

For information on how to obtain a passport, go to "**Passports**" in the "**Fast Facts**" appendix (p. 296).

VISAS

The U.S. State Department has a **Visa Waiver Program (VWP)** allowing citizens of the following countries to enter the United States without a visa for stays of up to 90 days: Andorra, Australia, Austria, Belgium, Brunei, Denmark, Finland, France, Germany, Iceland, Ireland, Italy, Japan, Liechtenstein, Luxembourg, Monaco, the Netherlands, New Zealand, Norway, Portugal, San Marino, Singapore, Slovenia, Spain, Sweden, Switzerland, and the United Kingdom. (*Note:* This list was accurate at press time; for the most up-to-date list of countries in the VWP, consult **www.travel.state.gov/ visa**.) Canadian citizens may enter the United States without visas; they will need to show passports (if traveling by

---

Tips   Prepare to Be Fingerprinted

Many international visitors traveling on visas to the United States are photographed and fingerprinted at Customs in a new program created by the Department of Homeland Security called **US-VISIT**. Non-U.S. citizens arriving at airports and on cruise ships must undergo an instant background check as part of the government's efforts to deter terrorism by verifying the identity of incoming and outgoing visitors. Exempt from the extra scrutiny are visitors entering by land or those (mostly from Europe; see p. 21) who don't require a visa for short-term visits. For more information, go to the Homeland Security website at **www.dhs.gov/dhspublic**.

---

air) and proof of residence, however. *Note:* Any passport issued on or after October 26, 2006, by a VWP country must be an **e-Passport** for VWP travelers to be eligible to enter the U.S. without a visa. Citizens of these nations also need to present a round-trip air or cruise ticket upon arrival. E-Passports contain computer chips capable of storing biometric information, such as the required digital photograph of the holder. (You can identify an e-Passport by the symbol on the bottom center cover of your passport.) If your passport doesn't have this feature, you can still travel without a visa if it is a valid passport issued before October 26, 2005, and includes a machine-readable zone, or between October 26, 2005, and October 25, 2006, and includes a digital photograph. For more information, go to **www.travel.state.gov/visa**.

Citizens of all other countries must have (1) a valid passport that expires at least 6 months later than the scheduled end of their visit to the U.S., and (2) a tourist visa, which may be obtained without charge from any U.S. consulate.

As of January 2004, many international visitors traveling on visas to the United States will be photographed and fingerprinted on arrival at Customs in airports and on cruise ships in a program created by the Department of Homeland Security called **US-VISIT**. Exempt from the extra scrutiny are visitors entering by land or those (mostly in Europe; see p. 21) that don't require a visa for short-term visits. For more information, go to the Homeland Security website at **www.dhs.gov/dhspublic**.

For specifics on how to get a visa, go to "**Visas**" in the "**Fast Facts**" appendix (p. 298).

For specifics on how to get a visa, go to "**Visas**" in the "**Fast Facts**" appendix.

MEDICAL REQUIREMENTS

Unless you're arriving from an area known to be suffering from an epidemic (particularly cholera or yellow fever), inoculations or vaccinations are not required for entry into the United States.

CUSTOMS
WHAT YOU CAN BRING INTO THE U.S.

Every visitor more than 21 years of age may bring in, free of duty, the following: (1) 1 liter of wine or hard liquor; (2) 200 cigarettes, 100 cigars (but not from Cuba), or 3 pounds of smoking tobacco; and (3) $100 worth of gifts. These exemptions are offered to travelers who spend at least 72 hours in the United States and who have not claimed them within the preceding 6 months. It is forbidden to bring into the country almost any meat products (including canned, fresh, and dried meat products such as bullion, soup mixes, and so on). Generally, condiments including vinegars, oils,

Cut to the Front of the Airport Security Line as a Registered Traveler

In 2003, the **Transportation Security Administration (TSA;** www.tsa.gov) approved a pilot program to help ease the time spent in line for airport security screenings. In exchange for information and a fee, persons can be pre-screened as registered travelers, granting them a front-of-the-line position when they fly. The program is run through private firms—the largest and most well-known is Steven Brill's **Clear** (www.flyclear.com), and it works like this: Travelers complete an online application providing specific points of personal information including name, addresses for the previous five years, birth date, social security number, driver's license number, and a valid credit card (you're not charged the **$99 fee** until your application is approved). Print out the completed form and take it, along with proper ID, to an "enrollment station" (this can be found in over 20 participating airports and in a growing number of American Express offices around the country, for example). It's at this point where it gets seemingly sci-fi. At the enrollment station, a Clear representative will record your biometrics necessary for clearance; in this case, your fingerprints and your irises will be digitally recorded.

Once your application has been screened against no-fly lists, outstanding warrants, and other security measures, you'll be issued a clear plastic card that holds a chip containing your information. Each time you fly through participating airports (and the numbers are steadily growing), go to the Clear Pass station located next to the standard TSA screening line. Here you'll insert your card into a slot and place your finger on a scanner to read your print—when the information matches up, you're cleared to cut to the front of the security line. You'll still have to follow all the procedures of the day like removing your shoes and walking through the X-ray machine, but Clear promises to cut 30 minutes off your wait time at the airport.

—*David A. Lytle*

spices, coffee, tea, and some cheeses and baked goods are permitted. Avoid rice products, as rice can often harbor insects. Bringing fruits and vegetables is not advised, though not prohibited. Customs will allow produce depending on where you got it and where you're going after you arrive in the U.S. Foreign tourists may carry in or out up to $10,000 in U.S. or foreign currency with no formalities; larger sums must be declared to U.S. Customs on entering or leaving, which includes filing form CM 4790. For details regarding U.S. Customs and Border Protection, consult your nearest U.S. embassy or consulate, or **U.S. Customs** (www.customs.ustreas.gov).

WHAT YOU CAN TAKE HOME FROM THE U.S.

Canadian Citizens: For a clear summary of Canadian rules, write for the booklet *I Declare,* issued by the **Canada Border Services Agency** (✆ 800/461-9999 in Canada, or 204/983-3500; www.cbsa-asfc.gc.ca).

Irish Citizens: The Irish government has organized their customs regulations at www.citizensinformation.ie. For more information, call the **Citizens' Information Board** at © 353/1-605-9000.

U.K. Citizens: For information, contact **HM Customs & Excise** at © **0845/010-9000** (from outside the U.K., 020/8929-0152), or consult their website at www.hmce.gov.uk.

Australian Citizens: A helpful brochure available from Australian consulates or Customs offices is *Know Before You Go.* For more information, call

the **Australian Customs Service** at © **1300/363-263,** or log on to **www.customs.gov.au**.

New Zealand Citizens: Most questions are answered in a free pamphlet available at New Zealand consulates and Customs offices: *New Zealand Customs Guide for Travellers, Notice no. 4.* For more information, contact **New Zealand Customs,** The Customhouse, 17–21 Whitmore St., Box 2218, Wellington (© **04/473-6099** or 0800/428-786; **www.customs.govt.nz**).

3 When to Go

Most of a Las Vegas vacation is usually spent indoors, so you can have a good time here year-round. The most pleasant seasons in this area are spring and fall, especially if you want to experience the great outdoors.

Weekdays are slightly less crowded than weekends. Holidays are always a mob scene and come accompanied by high hotel prices. Hotel prices also skyrocket when big conventions and special events are taking place. The slowest times of year are June and July, the week before Christmas, and the week after New Year's.

If a major convention is to be held during your trip, you might want to change your date. Check the box on p. 26 for convention dates, and contact the **Las Vegas Convention and Visitors Authority** (© **877/VISIT-LV** or 702/892-7575;

www.visitlasvegas.com), as convention schedules often change.

THE WEATHER

First of all, Vegas isn't always hot, but when it is, it's *really* hot. One thing you'll hear again and again is that even though Las Vegas gets very hot, the dry desert heat is not unbearable. We know this is true because we spent a couple of days there in 104°F (39°C) weather and lived to say, "It wasn't all that bad, not really." The humidity averages a low 22%, and even on very hot days, there's apt to be a breeze. Also, except on the hottest summer days, there's relief at night, when temperatures often drop by as much as 20°F.

But this is the desert, and it's not hot year-round. It can get quite cold, especially in the winter, when at night it can

Las Vegas's Average Temperatures (°F/°C) & Precipitation

		Jan	Feb	Mar	Apr	May	June	July	Aug	Sept	Oct	Nov	Dec
Average Temp.	(°F)	47	52	58	66	75	86	91	89	81	69	55	47
	(°C)	8	11	14	19	24	30	33	32	27	21	13	8
Avg. High Temp.	(°F)	57	63	69	78	88	99	104	102	94	81	66	57
	(°C)	14	17	21	26	31	37	40	39	34	27	19	14
Avg. Low Temp.	(°F)	37	41	47	54	63	72	78	77	69	57	44	37
	(°C)	3	5	8	12	17	22	26	25	21	14	7	3
Avg. Precip.	(in.)	0.59	0.69	0.59	0.15	0.24	0.08	0.44	0.45	0.31	0.24	0.31	0.40
	(cm)	1.5	1.8	1.5	0.4	0.6	0.2	1.1	1.1	0.8	0.6	0.8	1.0

drop to 30°F (−1°C) and lower. Although rare, it does snow occasionally in Las Vegas. The winter of 1998–99 dropped nearly 2 inches of snow on the Strip; a light dusting landed in January 2005. There's nothing quite like the sight of Luxor's Sphinx covered in snow. The breeze can also become a cold, biting wind of up to 40 mph and more. And so there are entire portions of the year when you won't be using that hotel pool at all (even if you want to because most of the hotels close huge chunks of those pool areas for "the season," which can be as long as the period from Labor Day to Memorial Day). If you aren't traveling in the height of summer, bring a jacket. Also, remember sunscreen and a hat—even if it's not all that hot, you can burn very easily and very fast.

LAS VEGAS CALENDAR OF EVENTS

You may be surprised that Las Vegas does not offer as many annual events as most other tourist cities. The reason is Las Vegas's very raison d'être: the gaming industry. This town wants its visitors spending their money in the casinos, not at Renaissance fairs and parades.

When in town, check the local paper and contact the **Las Vegas Convention and Visitors Authority** (© 877/VISIT-LV or 702/892-7575; www.visitlasvegas.com) or the **Chamber of Commerce** (© 702/735-1616; www.lvchamber.com) to find out about other events scheduled during your visit.

For an exhaustive list of events beyond those listed here, check http://events.frommers.com, where you'll find a searchable, up-to-the-minute roster of what's happening in cities all over the world.

March

NASCAR/Winston Cup. The **Las Vegas Motor Speedway,** 7000 Las Vegas Blvd. N. (© 800/644-4444; www.lvms.com), has become one of the premier facilities in the country, attracting races and racers of all stripes and colors. The biggest of the year are the Sam's Town 300 and the UAW–DaimlerChrysler 400 held in early March.

June

CineVegas Film Festival. This annual event, usually held in early June, is growing in popularity and prestige, with film debuts from both independent and major studios, plus lots of celebrities hanging around for the big parties. Call © **702/992-7979,** or visit **www.cinevegas.com**.

World Series of Poker. When Harrah's Entertainment bought the legendary Binion's Horseshoe in Downtown Vegas out of bankruptcy, it quickly turned around and sold the hotel but kept the hosting rights to this famed event and moved its location and place on the calendar. Now held at the **Rio All-Suite Hotel and Casino** (3700 W. Flamingo Rd.; © **800/PLAY-RIO**) in June, July, and August, the event features high-stakes gamblers and showbiz personalities competing for six-figure purses. There are daily events with entry stakes ranging from $125 to $5,000. To enter the World Championship Event (purse: $1 million), players must pony up $10,000. It costs nothing to crowd around the tables and watch the action, but if you want to avoid the throngs, you can catch a lot of it on TV. For more information, visit **www.worldseriesofpoker.com**.

October

Oktoberfest. This boisterous autumn holiday is celebrated from the first of October through the end of the month at the **Mount Charleston Resort** (© **800/955-1314** or 702/872-5408; www.mtcharlestonlodge.com), about a 35-minute drive northwest of Las Vegas, with music, folk dancers, singalongs around a fire, special decorations, and Bavarian cookouts.

Major Convention Dates for 2009

Listed below are Las Vegas's major annual conventions, with projected attendance figures for 2009; believe us, unless you're coming for one of them, you probably want to avoid the biggies. Since convention schedules frequently change, contact the **Las Vegas Convention and Visitors Authority** (© **877/VISIT-LV** or 702/892-7575; www.visitlasvegas.com) to double-check the latest info before you commit to your travel dates.

Event	Dates	Expected Attendance
Consumer Electronics Show	Jan 18–21	148,000
International Builders Show	Jan 21–23	60,000
Sports Licensing& Entertainment Marketplace	Jan 21–23	15,000
World of Concrete	Feb 3–6	85,000
American Academy of Orthopedic Surgeons	Feb 25–27	30,000
Ace Hardware	Mar 3–6	18,000
International Hospitality Week	Mar 3–4	31,000
Nightclub/Bar Convention	Mar 3–6	38,000
Associated Surplus Dealers	Mar 15–18	64,000
Global Shop	Mar 18–20	30,000
Wireless Communications Expo	Mar 18–20	15,000
National Association of Broadcasters (NAB)	Apr 20–23	115,000
National Hardware Show	May 5–7	50,000
Global Real Estate Convention	May 15–18	50,000
Licensing International Expo	June 2–4	25,000
Great West Truck Show	June 25–27	19,000
Association of Woodworking Suppliers	July 22–25	45,000
World Shoe Association (Fall)	July 27–29	37,000
Associated Surplus Dealers	Aug 12–16	60,000
Pack Expo	Oct 5–7	30,000
National Association of Convenience Stores	Oct 21–23	27,000
G2E	Nov 17–19	33,000
National Association of Amusement Parks	Nov 17–20	30,000
Clinical Meeting	Dec 6–10	23,000
Power Gen International	Dec 8–10	20,000

Frys.com Open. This televised 4-day PGA Tour event is played at TPC Summerlin and TPC at The Canyons. For details, call © **702/242-3000.**

November

The Comedy Festival. This festival, launched in 2005, was such a hit that they have turned it into an annual event and expanded it to 5 days. Some of the world's top comics and comedy troupes perform, and the event also includes workshops, film festivals, and more. It's held in mid-November, and the primary host hotel is Caesars Palace. For details, call ℂ **800/634-6661,** or go to **www.thecomedyfestival.com**.

December

National Finals Rodeo. This is the Super Bowl of rodeos, attended by about 200,000 people each year and offering nearly $5 million in prize money. Male rodeo stars compete in calf roping, steer wrestling, bull riding, team roping, saddle bronco riding, and bareback riding. And women compete in barrel racing. An all-around "Cowboy of the Year" is chosen. In connection with this event, hotels book country stars into their showrooms, and a cowboy shopping spree—the **NFR Cowboy Christmas Gift Show,** a trade show for Western gear—is held at Cashman Field. The NFR runs for 10 days during the first 2 weeks of December at the 17,000-seat Thomas & Mack Center of the University of Nevada, Las Vegas (UNLV). Order tickets as far in advance as possible (ℂ **702/895-3900**). For more information, see **www.nfrexperience.com**.

Las Vegas Bowl Week. A championship football event in mid-December pits the winners of the Mid-American Conference against the winners of the Big West Conference. The action takes place at the 32,000-seat Sam Boyd Stadium. Call ℂ **702/895-3900,** or visit **www.lvbowl.com** for ticket information.

New Year's Eve. This is a biggie (reserve your hotel room early). Downtown, on the Fremont Street Experience, there's a big block party with two dramatic countdowns to midnight (the first is at 9pm, midnight on the East Coast). The Strip is usually closed to street traffic, and hundreds of thousands of people pack the area for the festivities. Of course, there are fireworks.

4 Getting There

BY PLANE

Given the shambles the airline industry is in, writing this section makes us wince. Just be aware that the future of many airlines was in varying degrees of doubt as we went to press.

With the federalization of airport security, security procedures at U.S. airports are more stable and consistent than ever before. Bring a **current, government-issued photo ID** such as a driver's license or passport, and if you've got an e-ticket, print out the **official confirmation page;** you'll need to show your confirmation at the security checkpoint and your ID at the ticket counter or the gate. Children under 18 do not need photo IDs for domestic flights, but the adults checking in with them do.

Security lines are getting shorter than they were a couple of years ago, but some doozies remain. We've heard reports of security checks and gridlocks causing delays of up to 4 and 5 hours, with plenty of missed flights as a result. If it's a busy convention or holiday weekend, you might want to plan accordingly. Better a long wait at the airport than a missed flight. If you have trouble standing for long periods of time, tell an airline employee; the airline will provide a wheelchair. Speed up security by **not wearing metal objects** such as big belt buckles or clanky earrings. If you've got metallic body parts, a note from your doctor can prevent a long chat with the security screeners. Keep in mind that only **ticketed passengers** are allowed past

Moments   New Year's Eve in Las Vegas

Over the past couple of years, more and more people have been choosing Las Vegas as their party destination for New Year's Eve. Although not quite a rival, in terms of sheer numbers, for New York City's Times Square, Nevada still offers a viable alternative site for ringing in the New Year.

From experience, we can tell you that a lot of people come here on December 31. We mean a *lot* of people. Traffic is a nightmare, parking (at least legally) is next to impossible, and there is not 1 square inch of the place that isn't occupied by a human being. Las Vegas doesn't really need a reason to throw a party, but when an event like this comes along, they do it up right. It doesn't make a bit of difference to the many gamblers who remain perched at tables and in front of machines, barely looking up long enough to mumble "Happynewyear" at the key moment.

A major portion of the Strip is closed down, sending the masses and their substantial quantities of alcohol into the street. Each year's celebration is a little different but usually includes a streetside performance by a major celebrity, confetti, the obligatory countdown, and fireworks.

For New Year's 2001, the city launched a massive fireworks extravaganza called "America's Party." It involved blasting pyrotechnics from the roofs of 10 different hotels in succession up the Strip, with a grand finale at midnight that rivaled the worldwide millennium celebrations the year before. The event was considered such a success that the city has made it an annual event.

security, except for folks escorting passengers with disabilities or unaccompanied children.

Federalization has stabilized **what you can carry on** and **what you can't.** The general rule is that sharp things are out, nail clippers are okay, and food and beverages must be passed through the X-ray machine—but security screeners can't make you drink from your coffee cup. Bring food in your carry-on rather than checking it, as explosive-detection machines used on checked luggage have been known to mistake food (especially chocolate, for some reason) for bombs. Travelers in the U.S. are allowed one carry-on bag, plus a "personal item" such as a purse, briefcase, or laptop bag. Carry-on hoarders can stuff all sorts of things into a laptop bag; as long as it has a laptop in it, it's still considered a personal item. The **Transportation Security Administration (TSA)** has issued a list of restricted items; check its website (www.tsa.gov/travelers) for details.

The TSA has phased out **gate check-in** at all U.S. airports. Passengers with e-tickets and without checked bags can still beat the ticket-counter lines by using **electronic kiosks** or even **online check-in from home.** Ask your airline which alternatives are available, and if you're using a kiosk, bring the credit card you used to book the ticket. If you're checking bags, you will still be able to use most airlines' kiosks; again, call your airline for up-to-date information. **Curbside check-in** is also a good way to avoid lines, although a few airlines still ban curbside check-in entirely; call before you go.

At press time, the TSA is also recommending that you **not lock your**

checked luggage so screeners can search it by hand, if necessary. The agency says to use plastic "zip ties" instead, which can be bought at hardware stores and can be easily cut off.

ARRIVING AT THE AIRPORT

Las Vegas is served by **McCarran International Airport,** 5757 Wayne Newton Blvd. (© **702/261-5211,** TTY 702/261-3111; www.mccarran.com), just a few minutes' drive from the southern end of the Strip, where the bulk of casinos and hotels are concentrated. This big, modern airport—even bigger thanks to a $500-million expansion—is rather exceptional in that it includes several casino areas with more than 1,000 slot machines. Although these are reputed to offer lower paybacks than hotel casinos (the airport has a captive audience and doesn't need to lure repeat customers), it's hard to resist throwing in a few quarters while waiting for the luggage to arrive. We actually know someone who hit a $1,000 jackpot there on his way out of town, thereby recouping most of his gambling losses at the last possible moment, and putting a lie to our insistence that such wagers are sucker bets.

IMMIGRATION & CUSTOMS CLEARANCE International visitors arriving by air, no matter what the port of entry, should cultivate patience and resignation before setting foot on U.S. soil. U.S. airports have considerably beefed up security clearances in the years since the terrorist attacks of September 11, and clearing Customs and Immigration can take as long as 2 hours.

Getting into Town from the Airport

Getting to your hotel from the airport is a cinch. **Bell Trans** (© **800/274-7433** or 702/739-7990; www.bell-trans.com) runs 20-passenger minibuses daily between the airport and all major Las Vegas hotels and motels (7:45am–midnight). Several other companies run similar ventures—just stand outside on the curb, and one will be flagged down for you. Buses from the airport leave about every 10 minutes. When you want to check out of your hotel and head back to the airport, call at least 2 hours in advance to be safe (though often you can just flag down one of the buses outside any major hotel). The cost is $5 per person each way to Strip- and Convention Center–area hotels, $6.50 to Downtown or other Off-Strip properties (anyplace north of the Sahara Hotel and west of I-15). Other similarly priced shuttles run 24 hours and can be found in the same place.

Even less expensive are **Citizens Area Transit (CAT)** buses (© **702/CAT-RIDE;** www.rtcsnv.com/transit). The no. 108 bus departs from the airport and takes you to the Stratosphere, where you can transfer to the no. 301, which stops close to most Strip- and Convention Center–area hotels. The no. 109 bus goes from the airport to the Downtown Transportation Center (at Casino Center Blvd. and Stewart Ave.). The fares for buses on Strip routes are $2 for adults, 60¢ for seniors and children 6 to 17, and free for children under 6. *Note:* You might have a long walk from the bus stop to the hotel entrance, even if the bus stop is right in front of your hotel. Vans are able to get

---

Tips   Don't Stow It—Ship It

Though pricey, it's sometimes worthwhile to travel luggage-free, particularly if you're toting sports equipment, meetings materials, or baby equipment. Specialists in door-to-door luggage delivery include **Virtual Bellhop** (www.virtualbellhop.com) and **SkyCap International** (www.skycapinternational.com).

Long-Haul Flights: How to Stay Comfortable

- Your choice of airline and airplane will definitely affect your legroom. Find more details about U.S. airlines at **www.seatguru.com**. For international airlines, the research firm Skytrax has posted a list of average seat pitches at **www.airlinequality.com**.
- Emergency exit seats and bulkhead seats typically have the most legroom. Emergency exit seats are usually left unassigned until the day of a flight (to ensure that someone able-bodied fills the seats); it's worth checking in online at home (if the airline offers that option) or getting to the ticket counter early to snag one of these spots for a long flight. Many passengers find that bulkhead seating offers more legroom, but keep in mind that bulkhead seats have no storage space on the floor in front of you.
- To have two seats for yourself in a three-seat row, try for an aisle seat in a center section toward the back of coach. If you're traveling with a companion, book an aisle and a window seat. Middle seats are usually booked last, so chances are good you'll end up with three seats to yourselves. And in the event that a third passenger is assigned the middle seat, he or she will probably be more than happy to trade for a window or an aisle.
- To sleep, avoid the last row of any section or the row in front of an emergency exit, as these seats are the least likely to recline. Avoid seats near highly trafficked toilet areas. Avoid seats in the back of many jets—these can be narrower than those in the rest of coach. Or reserve a window seat so you can rest your head and avoid being bumped in the aisle.
- Get up, walk around, and stretch every 60 to 90 minutes to keep your blood flowing. This helps avoid **deep vein thrombosis,** or "economy-class syndrome."
- Drink water before, during, and after your flight to combat the lack of humidity in airplane cabins. Avoid caffeine and alcohol, which will dehydrate you.

right up to the entrance, so choose a van if you're lugging lots of baggage.

If you have a large group with you, you might also try one of the limos that wait curbside at the airport, and charge $45 to $65 for a trip to the Strip. However, the price may go up with additional passengers, so ask about the fee very carefully.

BY CAR

For listings of the major car rental agencies in Las Vegas please see the "Fast Facts, Toll-Free Numbers & Websites" appendix (p. 292).

The main highway connecting Las Vegas with the rest of the country is I-15; it links Montana, Idaho, and Utah with Southern California. The drive from Los Angeles is quite popular and, thanks to the narrow two-lane highway, can get very crowded on Friday and Sunday afternoons with hopeful weekend gamblers making their way to and from Las Vegas. An expansion project has widened most of that stretch of road to three lanes in each direction, which is helping the situation a lot. (By the way, as soon as you cross the state line, there are three casinos ready to handle your immediate gambling needs, with two more about 12 min. up the road, 30 miles before you get to Las Vegas.)

From the east, take I-70 or I-80 west to Kingman, Arizona, and then U.S. 93 north to downtown Las Vegas (Fremont St.). From the south, take I-10 west to Phoenix and then U.S. 93 north to Las Vegas. From San Francisco, take I-80 east to Reno and then U.S. 95 south to Las Vegas.

If you're driving to Las Vegas, be sure to read the driving precautions below.

Vegas is 286 miles from Phoenix, 759 miles from Denver, 421 miles from Salt Lake City, 269 miles from Los Angeles, and 586 miles from San Francisco.

DRIVING SAFETY

Because driving on the outskirts of Las Vegas—for example, coming from California—involves desert driving, you must take certain precautions. It's a good idea to check your tires, water, and oil before leaving. Take at least 5 gallons of water in a clean container that can be used for either drinking or the radiator. Pay attention to road signs that suggest when to turn off your car's air conditioner. And don't push your luck with gas—it may be 35 miles or more between stations. If your car overheats, do not remove the radiator cap until the engine has cooled, and then remove it very slowly. Add water to within an inch of the top of the radiator.

BY BUS

Bus travel is often the most economical form of public transit for short hops between U.S. cities, but it's certainly not an option for everyone. **Greyhound** (© **800/231-2222;** www.greyhound.com) is the sole nationwide bus line. International visitors can obtain information about the **Greyhound North American Discovery Pass.** The pass can be obtained from foreign travel agents or through their website (www.discoverypass.com) for unlimited travel and stopovers in the U.S. and Canada.

BY TRAIN

Amtrak (© **800/872-7245;** www.amtrak. com) does not currently offer direct rail service, although plans have been in the works to restore the rails between Los Angeles and Las Vegas for years. We've been hearing these reports for so long now, they just make us roll our eyes.

In the meantime, you can take the train to Los Angeles or Barstow, and Amtrak will get you to Las Vegas by bus.

5 Money & Costs

It's always advisable to bring money in a variety of forms on a vacation: a mix of cash, credit cards, and traveler's checks. You should also exchange enough petty cash to cover airport incidentals, tipping, and transportation to your hotel before you leave home, or withdraw money upon arrival at an airport ATM.

Because Las Vegas is a town built on the concept of separating you from your money, it should come as no surprise that gaining access to money is very easy—sometimes too easy. There are ATMs conveniently located about every 4 feet (okay, an exaggeration, but not by a lot), and check-cashing, credit-card-advance systems, and traveler's-check services are omnipresent. So getting to your money isn't a problem. Keeping it may be.

Las Vegas has grown progressively expensive in the recent past, with the concept of a cheap Sin City vacation a distant memory. Average room rates are over $200 a night, those formerly cheap buffets have been replaced by $30-a-person lavish spreads, and top-show tickets easily surpass $100 a head.

What Things Cost in Las Vegas	Average Cost ($)
Taxi from the airport to the Strip	10.00–15.00
Taxi from the airport to Downtown	15.00–20.00
One-way Las Vegas Monorail ticket	5.00
All-day "Deuce" bus pass	5.00
Standard room at Bellagio, Fri–Sat	300.00–400.00
Standard room at MGM Grand, Fri–Sat	200.00–300.00
Standard room at Bally's, Fri–Sat	100.00–200.00
Dinner for two at Picasso, prix fixe	220.00
Dinner for two at Austins Steakhouse	75.00
Wynn Las Vegas buffet, weekend Champagne brunch	35.00
Main Street Station Garden Court buffet Champagne brunch	10.00
Ticket to Cirque du Soleil's O	99.00–150.00
Ticket to Mac King's Comedy Magic Show	25.00
Domestic beer at Body English	7.00
Domestic beer at the Double Down Saloon	3.00

And then, of course, there are the casinos, a money-losing proposition for the traveler if there ever was one.

But there are Las Vegas vacations available for just about any budget, so pay (no pun intended) close attention to chapter 4, "Where to Stay," and chapter 5, "Where to Dine," which break down your choices by cost.

The most common bills are the $1 (a "buck"), $5, $10, and $20 denominations. There are also $2 bills (seldom encountered), $50 bills, and $100 bills. (The last two are usually not welcome as payment for small purchases.)

Coins come in seven denominations: 1¢ (1 cent, or a penny); 5¢ (5 cents, or a nickel); 10¢ (10 cents, or a dime); 25¢ (25 cents, or a quarter); 50¢ (50 cents, or a half dollar); the gold-colored Sacagawea coin, worth $1; and the rare silver dollar.

Vegas visitors used to require a great deal of change in order to play the slots and other gaming machines, but few, if any, accept coins any longer. Gone are the once-prevalent change carts. All machines now take bills in most denominations, and you get "change" in the form of a credit slip that appears when you cash out. You then take this slip to the nearest cashier's cage to exchange for actual money.

ATMs

The easiest and best way to get cash away from home is from an ATM, sometimes referred to as a "cash machine," or "cashpoint." The **Cirrus** (© 800/424-7787; www.mastercard.com) and **PLUS** (© 800/843-7587; www.visa.com) networks span the country; you can find them even in remote regions. Be sure you know your daily withdrawal limit before you depart.

Note: Many banks impose a fee every time you use a card at another bank's ATM, and that fee is often higher for international transactions (up to $5 or more) than for domestic ones (where they're rarely more than $2). In addition, the bank from which you withdraw cash may charge its own fee. To compare banks' ATM fees within the U.S., use

Fun Fact **Beating the Odds**

In 1995, Don Harrington entered a satellite event at the World Series of Poker for just $220, won his way into the $10,000 buy for the Championship Event, and went on to win the $1-million prize.

www.bankrate.com. Visitors from outside the U.S. should also find out whether their bank assesses a 1% to 3% fee on charges incurred abroad.

CREDIT CARDS & DEBIT CARDS

Credit cards are the most widely used form of payment in the United States: **Visa** (Barclaycard in Britain), **Master-Card** (EuroCard in Europe, Access in Britain, Chargex in Canada), **American Express, Diners Club,** and **Discover.** They also provide a convenient record of all your expenses, and offer relatively good exchange rates. You can withdraw cash advances from your credit cards at banks or ATMs, but high fees make credit card cash advances a pricey way to get cash.

It's highly recommended that you travel with at least one major credit card. You must have a credit card to rent a car, and hotels and airlines usually require a credit card imprint as a deposit against expenses.

ATM cards with major credit card backing, known as **debit cards,** are now a commonly acceptable form of payment in most stores and restaurants. Debit cards draw money directly from your checking account. Some stores enable you to receive cash back on your debit card purchases as well. The same is true at most U.S. post offices.

TRAVELER'S CHECKS

Though credit cards and debit cards are more often used, traveler's checks are still widely accepted in the U.S. Foreign visitors should make sure that traveler's checks are denominated in U.S. dollars; foreign-currency checks are often difficult to exchange.

You can buy traveler's checks at most banks. Most are offered in denominations of $20, $50, $100, $500, and sometimes $1,000. Generally, you'll pay a service charge ranging from 1% to 4%.

Be sure to keep a copy of the traveler's checks serial numbers separate from your checks in the event that they are stolen or lost. You'll get a refund faster if you know the numbers.

6 Health

STAYING HEALTHY

By and large, Las Vegas is like most other major American cities in that the water is relatively clean, the air is relatively clear, and illness-bearing insects and animals are rare. However, in a city with this many people coming and going from all over the world, there are a couple of specific concerns worth noting.

Over the past few years, there have been a few outbreaks of **norovirus** at Las Vegas hotels. This virus, most commonly associated with cruise ships, is rarely serious but can turn your vacation into a very unpleasant experience of intestinal illness. Because it is spread by contact, you can protect yourself by washing your hands often, especially after touching all of those slot machines.

Food preparation guidelines in Las Vegas are among the strictest in the world, but when you're dealing with the sheer volume that this city is, you're bound to run into trouble every now and then. All restaurants are required by law to display a health certificate and letter grade (A, B, or C) that indicates how well they did on their last inspection. An A grade doesn't mean you will never get **food poisoning,** but it does mean they do a better-than-average job in the kitchen.

GENERAL AVAILABILITY OF HEALTH CARE

Contact the **International Association for Medical Assistance to Travelers (IAMAT)** (© **716/754-4883** or, in Canada, 416/652-0137; www.iamat.org) for tips on travel and health concerns, and for lists of local doctors. The United States **Centers for Disease Control and Prevention** (© **800/311-3435;** www.cdc.gov) provides up-to-date information on health hazards by region or country and offers tips on food safety. The website **www.trip prep.com,** sponsored by a consortium of travel medicine practitioners, **Travel Health Online,** may also offer helpful advice.

COMMON AILMENTS

SUN/WEATHER EXPOSURE Las Vegas is the desert and the **sun exposure** is high. On sunny days, you can fry within minutes, and even on cloudy days burns are possible. During the summer, slather up with sunscreen before heading to the pool or even if you may be walking more than a few minutes outside. Don't believe us? Look at that lobster-red person moving uneasily at the craps table next to you. If you intend to do any kind of walking, even on the Strip, during the hot days, drink lots of water. This is especially important if you go out to Red Rock or Valley of the Fire.

WHAT TO DO IF YOU GET SICK AWAY FROM HOME

If you suffer from a chronic illness, consult your doctor before your departure. Pack **prescription medications** in your carry-on luggage, and carry them in their original containers, with pharmacy labels—otherwise they won't make it through airport security. Visitors from outside the U.S. should carry generic names of prescription drugs. For U.S. travelers, most reliable health-care plans provide coverage if you get sick away from home. Foreign visitors may have to pay all medical costs up front and be reimbursed later.

We list **emergency numbers and hospital information** in the "Fast Facts, Toll-Free Numbers & Websites" appendix, p. 292.

7 Safety

CSI, one of the nation's top-rated TV shows, may turn up new corpses each week, but the crime rate in real-life Vegas isn't higher than in any other major metropolis of its size.

With all that cash floating around town, pickpockets and thieves are predictably active. At gaming tables and slot machines, men should keep wallets well concealed and out of the reach of pickpockets, and women should keep handbags in plain sight (on laps). If you win a big jackpot, ask the pit boss or slot attendant to cut you a check rather than give you cash—the cash may look nice, but flashing it can attract the wrong kind of attention. Outside casinos, popular spots for pickpockets and thieves are restaurants and outdoor shows, such as the volcano at The Mirage or the fountains at Bellagio. Stay alert. Unless your hotel room has an in-room safe, check your valuables in a safe-deposit box at the front desk.

8 Specialized Travel Resources

TRAVELERS WITH DISABILITIES

Most disabilities shouldn't stop anyone from traveling in the U.S. Thanks to provisions in the Americans with Disabilities Act, most public places are required to comply with disability-friendly regulations. Almost all public establishments (including hotels, restaurants, museums, and so on, but not including certain National Historic Landmarks), and at least some modes of public transportation provide accessible entrances and other facilities for those with disabilities.

On the one hand, Las Vegas is fairly well equipped for travelers with disabilities, with virtually every hotel having accessible rooms, ramps, and other requirements. On the other hand, the distance between hotels (particularly on the Strip) makes a vehicle of some sort virtually mandatory for most people with disabilities, and it may be extremely strenuous and time-consuming to get from place to place (even within a single hotel, because of the crowds). Even if you don't intend to gamble, you still may have to go through the casino, and casinos can be quite difficult to maneuver in, particularly for a guest in a wheelchair. Casinos are usually crowded, and the machines and tables are often laid out close together, with chairs, people, and such blocking easy access. You should also consider that it is often a long trek through larger hotels between the entrance and the room elevators (or, for that matter, anywhere in the hotel), and then add a crowded casino to the equation.

The **America the Beautiful—National Park and Federal Recreational Lands Pass—Access Pass** (formerly the **Golden Access Passport**) gives visually impaired or permanently disabled persons (regardless of age) free lifetime entrance to federal recreation sites administered by the National Park Service, including the Fish and Wildlife Service, the Forest Service, the Bureau of Land Management, and the Bureau of Reclamation. This may include national parks, monuments, historic sites, recreation areas, and national wildlife refuges.

The America the Beautiful Access Pass can only be obtained in person at any NPS facility that charges an entrance fee. You need to show proof of a medically determined disability. Besides free entry, the pass also offers a 50% discount on some federal-use fees charged for such facilities as camping, swimming, parking, boat launching, and tours. For more information, go to www.nps.gov/fees_passes.htm or call the United States Geological Survey (USGS), who issues the passes, at ✆ **888/275-8747.**

For more on organizations that offer resources to travelers with limited mobility, go to www.frommers.com.

GAY & LESBIAN TRAVELERS

For such a licentious, permissive town, Las Vegas has its conservative side and is not the most gay-friendly city. This will not manifest itself in any signs of outrage toward open displays of gay affection, but it does mean that the local gay community is largely confined to the bar scene. This may be changing, with local gay pride parades and other activities gathering steam each year. See listings for gay bars in chapter 9.

For more gay and lesbian travel resources visit frommers.com.

SENIOR TRAVEL

One of the benefits of age is that travel often costs less. Mention the fact that you're a senior when you make travel reservations. Although the major U.S. airlines have canceled their senior discount and coupon book programs, many hotels still offer discounts for seniors. In most cities, people over the age of 60 qualify for reduced admission to theaters, museums, and other attractions, as well as discounted fares on public transportation.

Members of **AARP,** 601 E St. NW, Washington, DC 20049 (© **888/ 687-2277;** www.aarp.org), get discounts on hotels, airfares, and car rentals. AARP offers members a wide range of benefits, including *AARP The Magazine* and a monthly newsletter. Anyone over 50 can join.

The U.S. National Park Service offers an **America the Beautiful—National Park and Federal Recreational Lands Pass— Senior Pass** (formerly the **Golden Age Passport**), which gives seniors 62 years or older lifetime entrance to all properties administered by the National Park Service—national parks, monuments, historic sites, recreation areas, and national wildlife refuges—for a one-time processing fee of $10. The pass must be purchased in person at any NPS facility that charges an entrance fee. Besides free entry, the American the Beautiful Senior Pass also offers a 50% discount on some federal-use fees charged for such facilities as camping, swimming, parking, boat launching, and tours. For more information, go to www.nps.gov/ fees_passes.htm or call the United States Geological Survey (USGS), who issues the passes, at © **888/275-8747.**

Frommer's website (http://frommers. com) offers more information and resources on travel for seniors.

FAMILY TRAVEL

Family travel can be immensely rewarding, giving you new ways of seeing the world through smaller pairs of eyes. That said, Vegas is hardly an ideal place to bring the kids. For one thing, they're not allowed in casinos at all. Because most hotels are laid out so that you frequently have to walk through their casinos, you can see how this becomes a headache. Some casino hotels will not allow the children of nonguests on the premises after 6pm—and this policy is seriously enforced.

Note also that the Las Vegas Strip is often peppered with people distributing fliers and other information about decidedly adult entertainment options in the city. Sex is everywhere. Just walking down the Strip might give your kids an eyeful of items that you might prefer they avoid. (They don't call it Sin City for nothing!)

On top of everything else, there is a curfew law in Vegas: Kids younger than 18 are not permitted on the Strip without a parent after 9pm on weekends and holidays. In the rest of the county, minors can't be out without parents after 10pm on school nights and midnight on the weekends.

Although still an option at most smaller chain hotels and motels, the major casino-hotels on the Strip offer no discount for children staying in your room, so you may have to pay an additional fee (anywhere from $10–$40 per person per night) to have them bunk with you. You'll definitely want to book a place with a pool. Some hotels also have enormous video arcades and other diversions.

If you choose to travel here with the children, see the "Especially for Kids" section in chapter 6, and the "Family-Friendly" boxes in chapters 4, 5, and 9 for suggested hotels, restaurants, and shows. Also look for the "Kids" icon throughout this guide. For more great tips and suggestions for your Vegas family vacation, we strongly suggest that you pick up a copy of *Frommer's Las Vegas with Kids.*

Recommended family travel websites include **www.familytravelforum.com**, a comprehensive site that offers customized trip planning; **www.familytravelnetwork. com**, an online magazine providing travel tips; and **www.travelwithyourkids.com**, a comprehensive site written by parents

Frommers.com: The Complete Travel Resource

Planning a trip or just returned? Head to **Frommers.com,** voted Best Travel Site by *PC Magazine.* We think you'll find our site indispensable before, during, and after your travels—with expert advice and tips; independent reviews of hotels, restaurants, attractions, and preferred shopping and nightlife venues; vacation giveaways; and an online booking tool. We publish the complete contents of over 135 travel guides in our **Destinations** section, covering over 4,000 places worldwide. Each weekday, we publish original articles that report on **Deals and News** via our free **Frommers.com Newsletters.** What's more, **Arthur Frommer** himself blogs five days a week, with cutting opinions about the state of travel in the modern world. We're betting you'll find our **Events** listing an invaluable resource; it's an up-to-the-minute roster of what's happening in cities everywhere—including concerts, festivals, lectures, and more. We've also added weekly **podcasts, interactive maps,** and hundreds of new images across the site. Finally, don't forget to visit our **Message Boards,** where you can join in conversations with thousands of fellow Frommer's travelers and post your trip report once you return.

for parents offering sound advice for long-distance and international travel with children.

WOMEN TRAVELERS

Las Vegas, thanks to the crowds, is as safe as any other big city for a woman traveling alone. A woman on her own should, of course, take the usual precautions and should be wary of hustlers and drunken businessmen who may mistake her for a "working girl." (Alas, million-dollar proposals a la Robert Redford are a rarity.) Many of the big hotels (all MGM MIRAGE hotels, for example) have security guards stationed at the elevators at night to prevent anyone other than guests from going up to the room floors. Ask when you make your reservation. If you're anxious, ask a security guard to escort you to your room. *Always* double-lock your door *and* deadbolt it to prevent intruders from entering.

For general travel resources for women, go to http://frommers.com.

TRAVELING WITH PETS

Las Vegas is not a very pet-friendly town, at least not for visitors. **The Four Seasons** (p. 62) is the only hotel on the Strip that allows pets, and because it's one of the most expensive hotels in town, you may find it more economical to leave Fluffy or Fido with a sitter.

With the exceptions of helper-animals for persons with disabilities and Chihuahuas owned by Paris Hilton (which can apparently go anywhere they darned well please), pets are also not allowed in most public places, such as casinos and restaurants.

But if you can't bear the thought of leaving Snookums at home, the **Las Vegas Convention and Visitors Authority** (© **877/VISIT-LV** or 702/892-0711; www.visitlasvegas.com) can provide you with a list of pet-friendly lodgings away from the Strip, or you can check out the following websites: **www.petswelcome. com**, **www.pettravel.com**, and **www. travelpets.com.**

9 Packages for the Independent Traveler

Package tours are simply a way to buy the airfare, accommodations, and other elements of your trip (such as car rentals, airport transfers, and sometimes even activities) at the same time and often at discounted prices.

One good source of package deals is the airlines themselves. Most major airlines offer air/land packages, including **American Airlines Vacations** (© 800/321-2121; www.aavacations.com), **Delta Vacations** (© 800/654-6559; www.deltavacations.com), **Continental Airlines Vacations** (© 800/301-3800; www.covacations.com), and **United Vacations** (© 888/854-3899; www.unitedvacations.com). Several big **online travel agencies**—Expedia, Travelocity, Orbitz, Site59, and Lastminute.com—also do a brisk business in packages.

Travel packages are also listed in the travel section of your local Sunday newspaper. Or check ads in the national travel magazines such as *Budget Travel Magazine, Travel + Leisure, National Geographic Traveler,* and *Condé Nast Traveler.*

Before you invest in a package deal, always ask about the **cancellation policy** and **accommodations choices,** and look for **hidden expenses,** such as taxes.

For more information on Package Tours and for tips on booking your trip, see http://frommers.com.

10 Staying Connected

TELEPHONES

Generally, hotel surcharges on long-distance and local calls are astronomical; rates can start at $1 for a local call, but that sometimes is for up to only the first thirty minutes, whereupon the rates increase exorbitantly. You're better off using your **cellphone** or a **public pay telephone.** You are often charged even for making a toll-free or phone card call. Some hotels are now adding on an additional "resort fee" to the cost of the room, which is supposed to cover local calls (as well as using the pool and other elements that ought to be givens). The fee can range from $1 (Motel Six) to $15 per day. Many convenience groceries and packaging services sell **prepaid calling cards** in denominations up to $50; for international visitors, these can be the least expensive way to call home. Many public pay phones at airports now accept American Express, MasterCard, and Visa credit cards. **Local calls** made from pay phones cost from 25¢ to 50¢ (no pennies, please).

Most long-distance and international calls can be dialed directly from any phone. **For calls within the United States and to Canada,** dial 1 followed by the area code and the seven-digit number. **For other international calls,** dial 011 followed by the country code, city code, and the number you are calling.

Calls to area codes **800, 888, 877,** and **866** are toll-free. However, calls to area codes **700** and **900** (chat lines, bulletin boards, "dating" services, and so on) can be very expensive—usually a charge of 95¢ to $3 or more per minute, and they sometimes have minimum charges that can run as high as $15 or more.

For **reversed-charge or collect calls,** and for person-to-person calls, dial the number 0 and then the area code and number; an operator will come on the line, and you should specify whether you are calling collect, person-to-person, or both. If your operator-assisted call is international, ask for the overseas operator.

For **local directory assistance** ("information"), dial 411; for long-distance information, dial 1 and then the appropriate area code and 555-1212.

CELLPHONES

Just because your cellphone works at home doesn't mean it'll work everywhere in the U.S. (thanks to our nation's fragmented cellphone system). It's a good bet that your phone will work in major cities, but take a look at your wireless company's coverage map on its website before heading out; T-Mobile, Sprint, and Nextel are particularly weak in rural areas. If you need to stay in touch at a destination where you know your phone won't work, **rent** a phone that does from **InTouch USA** (© **800/872-7626;** www.intouch global.com) or a rental-car location, but beware that you'll pay $1 a minute or more for airtime.

If you're not from the U.S., you'll be appalled at the poor reach of the **GSM (Global System for Mobile Communications) wireless network,** which is used by much of the rest of the world. Your phone will probably work in most major U.S. cities; it definitely won't work in many rural areas. To see where GSM phones work in the U.S., check out www.t-mobile.com/coverage. And you may or may not be able to send SMS (text messaging) home.

VOICE-OVER INTERNET PROTOCOL (VOIP)

If you have Web access while traveling, consider a broadband-based telephone service (in technical terms, **Voice over Internet protocol,** or **VoIP**) such as Skype (www.skype.com) or Vonage (www.vonage. com), which allow you to make free international calls from your laptop or in a cybercafe. Neither service requires the people you're calling to also have that service (though there are fees if they do not). Check the websites for details.

INTERNET & E-MAIL
WITH YOUR OWN COMPUTER

Most resort hotels in Vegas offer wireless access, but for a hefty daily fee (usually around $17). Some chain hotels offer free Wi-Fi in public areas, while others still offer high-speed access. In Las Vegas, you can find free Wi-Fi at most stand-alone McDonald's, Starbucks, and in the Fashion Show Mall. To find additional public Wi-Fi hotspots, go to **www.jiwire.com**; its Hotspot Finder holds the world's largest directory of public wireless hotspots.

For dial-up access, most business-class hotels in the U.S. offer dataports for laptop modems.

Wherever you go, bring a **connection kit** of the right power and phone adapters, a spare phone cord, and a spare Ethernet network cable—or find out whether your hotel supplies them to guests.

For information on electrical currency conversions, see "Electricity," in the "Fast Facts" section in the appendix (p. 292).

WITHOUT YOUR OWN COMPUTER

Some Vegas hotels still offer Internet service through the television with a wireless keyboard (provided). Figure, on average, that you'll pay about $15 a day for the privilege.

There are usually no easily accessible cybercafes in Vegas, and even these tend to close without warning. To check for possibilities, try **www.cybercaptive.com** and **www.cybercafe.com**.

Most major airports have **Internet kiosks** that provide basic Web access for a per-minute fee that's usually higher than cybercafe prices. Check out copy shops such as **FedEx Kinkos,** which offers computer stations with fully loaded software (as well as Wi-Fi). A list of convenient locations is in the "Fast Facts" section of the appendix on p. 292.

3

Getting to Know Las Vegas

There has rarely been a time in Vegas's post-Bugsy history when the city wasn't booming, but lately it's redefining "booming". A new megaresort seems to go up every other week, and each brings something new to the party, sometimes things hitherto never invited: great works of art, five-star world-renowned chefs, rock clubs and arenas that attract significant and still-current acts—you get the idea. In other words, everything old is new again, and Vegas glamour is back.

1 A Look at the Past

THE EIGHTH WONDER OF THE WORLD

For many years after its creation, Las Vegas was a mere whistle-stop town. That all changed in 1928 when Congress authorized the building of nearby Boulder Dam (later renamed Hoover Dam), bringing thousands of workers to the area. In 1931, gambling once again became legal in Nevada, and Fremont Street's gaming emporiums and speak-easies attracted dam workers. Upon the dam's completion, the Las Vegas Chamber of Commerce worked hard to lure the hordes of tourists who came to see the engineering marvel (it was called "the Eighth Wonder of the World") to its casinos. But it wasn't until the early years of World War II that visionary entrepreneurs began to plan for the city's glittering future.

LAS VEGAS GOES SOUTH

Contrary to popular lore, developer Bugsy Siegel didn't actually stake a claim in the middle of nowhere—he just built a few blocks south of already-existing properties.

And in 1941, El Rancho Vegas, ultraluxurious for its time, was built on the same remote stretch of highway (across the street from where the Sahara now stands). Scores of Hollywood stars were invited to the grand opening, and El Rancho Vegas soon became the hotel of choice for visiting film stars.

Beginning a trend that continues today, each new property tried to outdo existing hotels in luxurious amenities and thematic splendor. Las Vegas was on its way to becoming the entertainment capital of the world.

Las Vegas promoted itself in the 1940s as a town that combined Wild West frontier friendliness with glamour and excitement. As Chamber of Commerce president Maxwell Kelch put it in a 1947 speech, "Las Vegas has the impact of a Wild West show, the friendliness of a country store, and the sophistication of Monte Carlo." Throughout the decade, the city was Hollywood's celebrity playground. The Hollywood connection gave the town glamour in the public's mind. So did the mob connection (something Las Vegas has spent decades trying to live down), which became clear when notorious underworld gangster Bugsy Siegel built the fabulous Flamingo, a tropical paradise and "a real class joint."

A steady stream of name entertainers came to Las Vegas. In 1947, Jimmy Durante opened the showroom at The Flamingo. Other headliners of the 1940s included Dean Martin and Jerry Lewis, tap-dancing legend Bill "Bojangles" Robinson, the Mills Brothers, skater Sonja Henie, and Frankie Laine. Future Las Vegas legend Sammy Davis, Jr., debuted at El Rancho Vegas in 1945.

While the Strip was expanding, Downtown kept pace with new hotels such as the El Cortez and the Golden Nugget. By the end of the decade, Fremont Street was known as "Glitter Gulch," its profusion of neon signs proclaiming round-the-clock gaming and entertainment.

THE 1950s: BUILDING BOOMS & A-BOMBS

Las Vegas entered the new decade as a city (no longer a frontier town) with a population of about 50,000. Hotel growth was phenomenal. The Desert Inn, which opened in 1950 with headliners Edgar Bergen and Charlie McCarthy, brought country-club elegance (including an 18-hole golf course and tennis courts) to the Strip.

In 1951 the Eldorado Club Downtown became Benny Binion's Horseshoe Club, which would gain fame as the home of the annual World Series of Poker. In 1954 the Showboat sailed into a new area east of Downtown. The Showboat not only introduced buffet meals, but it also offered round-the-clock bingo and a bowling alley (106 lanes to date).

In 1955 the Côte d'Azur–themed Riviera became the ninth big hotel to open on the Strip. Breaking the ranch-style mode, it was, at nine stories, the Strip's first high-rise. Liberace, one of the hottest names in show business, was paid the unprecedented sum of $50,000 a week to dazzle audiences in the Riviera's posh Clover Room.

Elvis appeared at the New Frontier in 1956 but wasn't a huge success; his fans were too young to fit the Las Vegas tourist mold. In 1958 the $10 million, 1,065-room Stardust upped the spectacular stakes by importing the famed *Lido de Paris* spectacle from the French capital. It became one of the longest-running shows ever to play Las Vegas.

Throughout the 1950s, most of the Vegas hotels competed for performers whose followers spent freely in the casinos. The advent of big-name Strip entertainment tolled a death knell for glamorous nightclubs in America; owners simply could not compete with the astronomical salaries paid to Las Vegas headliners. Two performers whose names have been linked to Las Vegas ever since—Frank Sinatra and Wayne Newton—made their debuts there. Mae West not only performed in Las Vegas, but also cleverly bought up ½-mile of desolate Strip frontage between the Dunes and the Tropicana.

Competition for the tourist dollar also brought nationally televised sporting events such as the PGA's Tournament of Champions. In the 1950s the wedding industry helped make Las Vegas one of the nation's most popular venues for "goin' to the chapel." Celebrity weddings of the 1950s that sparked the trend included singer Dick Haymes and Rita Hayworth, Joan Crawford and Pepsi chairman Alfred Steele, Carol Channing and TV exec Charles Lowe, and Paul Newman and Joanne Woodward.

On a grimmer note, the '50s also heralded the atomic age in Nevada, with nuclear testing taking place just 65 miles northwest of Las Vegas. A chilling 1951 photograph shows a mushroom-shaped cloud from an atomic bomb test visible over the Fremont Street horizon. Throughout the decade, about one bomb a month was detonated in the nearby desert (an event, interestingly enough, that often attracted loads of tourists).

THE 1960s: THE RAT PACK & A PACK RAT

The very first month of the new decade made entertainment history when the Sands hosted a 3-week "Summit Meeting" in the Copa Room that was presided over by "Chairman of the Board" Frank Sinatra with Rat Pack cronies Dean Martin, Sammy Davis, Jr., Peter Lawford, and Joey Bishop (all of whom happened to be in town filming *Ocean's Eleven*).

The building boom of the '50s took a brief respite. Most of the Strip's first property, the El Rancho Vegas, burned down in 1960. And the first new hotel of the decade, the first to be built in 9 years, was the exotic Aladdin in 1966.

During the '60s, negative attention focused on mob influence in Las Vegas. Of the 11 major casino hotels that had opened in the previous decade, 10 were believed to have been financed with mob money. Then, like a knight in shining armor, Howard Hughes rode into town and embarked on a $300 million hotel- and property-buying spree, which included the Desert Inn itself (in 1967). Hughes was as "bugsy" as Benjamin Siegel any day, but his pristine reputation helped bring respectability to the desert city and lessen its gangland stigma.

Las Vegas became a family destination in 1968, when Circus Circus burst onto the scene with the world's largest permanent circus and a "junior casino" featuring dozens of carnival midway games on its mezzanine level. In 1969, Elvis made a triumphant return to Las Vegas at the International's showroom and went on to become one of the city's all-time legendary performers. His fans had come of age.

Hoping to establish Las Vegas as "the Broadway of the West," the Thunderbird Hotel presented Rodgers and Hammerstein's *Flower Drum Song*. It was a smash hit. Soon the Riviera picked up *Bye, Bye, Birdie,* and, as the decade progressed, *Mame* and *The Odd Couple* played at Caesars Palace. While Broadway played the Strip, production shows such as the Dunes's *Casino de Paris* became ever more lavish, expensive, and technically innovative.

THE 1970s: MERV & MAGIC

In 1971 the 500-room Union Plaza opened at the head of Fremont Street on the site of the old Union Pacific Station. It had what was, at the time, the world's largest casino, and its showroom specialized in Broadway productions. The same year, talk-show host Merv Griffin began taping at Caesars Palace, taking advantage of a ready supply of local headliner guests. He helped popularize Las Vegas even more by bringing it into America's living rooms every afternoon.

The year 1973 was eventful: Over at the Tropicana, illusionists extraordinaire Siegfried & Roy began turning women into tigers and themselves into legends in the *Folies Bergère*.

Two major disasters hit Las Vegas in the 1970s. First, a flash flood devastated the Strip, causing more than $1 million in damage. Second, gambling was legalized in Atlantic City. Las Vegas's hotel business slumped as fickle tourists decided to check out the new East Coast gambling mecca.

As the decade drew to a close, an international arrivals building opened at McCarran International Airport, and dollar slot machines caused a sensation in the casinos.

THE 1980s: THE CITY ERUPTS

As the '80s began, Las Vegas was booming once again. McCarran Airport began a 20-year, $785-million expansion program.

Siegfried & Roy were no longer just the star segment of various stage spectaculars. Their own show, *Beyond Belief,* ran for 6 years at the Frontier, playing a record-breaking

3,538 performances to sellout audiences every night. It became the most successful attraction in the city's history.

In 1989, Steve Wynn made Las Vegas sit up and take notice. His gleaming white-and-gold Mirage was fronted by five-story waterfalls, lagoons, and lush tropical foliage—not to mention a 50-foot volcano that dramatically erupted regularly! Wynn gave world-renowned illusionists Siegfried & Roy carte blanche (and more than $30 million) to create the most spellbinding show Las Vegas had ever seen.

THE 1990s THROUGH TODAY: KING ARTHUR MEETS KING TUT

The 1990s began with a blare of trumpets heralding the rise of a turreted medieval castle fronted by a moated drawbridge and staffed by jousting knights and fair damsels. Excalibur reflected the '90s marketing trend to promote Las Vegas as a family-vacation destination.

More sensational megahotels followed on the Strip, including the *new* MGM Grand hotel, backed by a full theme park (it ended Excalibur's brief reign as the world's largest resort), Luxor Las Vegas, and Steve Wynn's Treasure Island.

In 1993 a unique pink-domed 5-acre indoor amusement park, Grand Slam Canyon, became part of the Circus Circus hotel. In 1995 the Fremont Street Experience was completed, revitalizing downtown Las Vegas. Closer to the Strip, rock restaurant magnate Peter Morton opened the Hard Rock Hotel, billed as "the world's first rock 'n' roll hotel and casino." The year 1996 saw the advent of the French Riviera–themed Monte Carlo and the Stratosphere Casino Hotel & Tower, its 1,149-foot tower the highest building west of the Mississippi. The unbelievable New York–New York arrived in 1997.

But it all paled compared with 1998–99. As Vegas hastily repositioned itself from "family destination" to "luxury resort," several new hotels, once again eclipsing anything that had come before, opened. Bellagio was the latest from Vegas visionary Steve Wynn, an attempt to bring grand European style to the desert, while at the far southern end of the Strip, Mandalay Bay charmed. As if this weren't enough, The Venetian's ambitious detailed re-creation of everyone's favorite Italian city came along in May 1999, and was followed in short order by the opening of Paris Las Vegas in the fall of 1999.

THE LUXURY RESORT YEARS

The 21st century opened up with a bang as the Aladdin blew itself up and gave itself a from-the-ground-up makeover (which in turn only lasted for a handful of years before Planet Hollywood took it over and changed it entirely), while Steve Wynn blew up the Desert Inn, and built a new showstopper named for himself. Along the way, everyone expanded, and then expanded some more, ultimately adding thousands of new rooms. Caesars produced two new towers, plus a multi-story addition to its Forum Shops. Bellagio and The Venetian followed suit with their own additional towers. Mandalay Bay upped the ante by making their new tower an entirely separate establishment, THEhotel, which sent the signal that the priorities in this latest incarnation of Vegas had shifted. There is no casino in THEhotel (though guests have adequate access to the one in Mandalay Bay), while rooms are all one-bedroom suites, permanently breaking with the convention that no one comes to Vegas to spend time in their room. Other hotels followed with similar plush digs. The watchword became luxury, with a secondary emphasis on adult. Little by little, wacky, eye-catching themes were phased out (as much as one can when one's hotel looks like a castle) and generic sophistication took its place. Gaming is still number one, but the newer hotels are trying to top each other in terms of other recreations—celebrity chef-backed restaurants, decadent nightclubs, fancy spas, and superstar shows.

More is more seems to be the motto, and so The Venetian's new annex The Palazzo is taller than Encore, the new extension of the Wynn. Even bigger hotels are currently under construction or well into the planning stages. Eclipsing all of it—for the moment, anyway—is the massive CityCenter, perhaps the most ambitious project in the city yet. Comprised of a 4000-room megaresort, two 400-room boutique hotels, condos, shopping, dining, clubs, and more, it covers 60 acres and as such is a city-within-the-city. Clearly, no one can rest on their laurels in Vegas, for this is not only a town that never sleeps, but also one in which progress never stops moving, even for a heartbeat.

For the latest shake-ups on the Strip, see "What's New in Las Vegas," at the beginning of this guide.

2 Books & Movies

Brinkley, Christina, *Winner Takes All: Steve Wynn, Kirk Kerkorian, Gary Loveman, and the Race to Own Las Vegas* (Hyperion, 2008). The explosion that is today's Las Vegas didn't just happen; it was largely the work of these three competing tycoons, who come together in a crush of money, ambition, and vision.

Cooper, Marc, *The Last Honest Place in America* (Nation Books, 2004). Long fascinated by Sin City, the reporter-author investigates its evolution into its current corporation-driven status.

Denton, Sally, *The Money and the Power: The Making of Las Vegas and Its Hold on America* (Vintage, 2002). An exhaustive, often behind-the-scenes investigative history of Vegas.

Fischer, Steve, *When the Mob Ran Vegas: Stories of Murder, Mayhem and Money* (Berkline Press, 2005). Ah, the good old days.

Hess, Alan, *Viva Las Vegas: After Hours Architecture* (Chronicle Books, 1993). Vegas doesn't have architecture as much as set design, and here you can learn all about how its bizarre skyline is really an icon of model American urban culture.

Martinez, Andrez, *24/7 Living It Up and Doubling Down in the New Las Vegas* (Villard, 1999). The author chronicles his efforts to spend his $50,000 book advance in a wild Vegas spree.

McCracken, Robert, *Las Vegas: The Great American Playground* (University of Nevada Press, 1997). A comprehensive history of Vegas up to the last decade.

McManus, James, *Positively Fifth Street* (Picador, 2004). The author came to write about the 2000 World Series of Poker and stayed to play, with surprising results that only demonstrate the seductive and strange lure of the city.

Mezrich, Ben, *Bringing Down the House: The Inside Story of Six MIT Students Who Took Vegas for Millions* (Free Press, 2002). The title says it all. Recently the basis for the movie *21*.

O'Brien, John, *Leaving Las Vegas* (Grove, 1995). The basis for the critically acclaimed movie, this novel demonstrates that not everything that happens in Vegas is fun and games, as the protagonist comes to town certain it's the perfect place wherein to drink himself to death.

Puzo, Mario, *Inside Las Vegas* (Grossett & Dunlap, 1972). Though out of print, it's not that hard to find, and well worth reading to get the take of the man who invented the Corleones on the city invented by the mob.

Anthony Zuiker's Top 7 Las Vegas Movies

A graduate of the University of Nevada at Las Vegas who's lived in Vegas for 35 years, Anthony Zuiker worked for The Mirage as a graveyard-shift tram driver, bellboy, and ad writer before he was inspired to create *CSI,* currently the number-one-rated TV show in the country. Here are Zuiker's seven favorite Las Vegas flicks and what he thinks about them.

- *Ocean's Eleven* **(the remake)**   It's our modern-day Rat Pack actors. Who can deny George Clooney and Brad Pitt?
- *Fear and Loathing in Las Vegas*   It epitomizes the surreal journey of coming to Las Vegas, and it captures the hyper-reality very well.
- *Indecent Proposal*   I remember seeing Demi Moore shooting the film at the Hilton, and Bruce Willis was playing blackjack at the tables while the filming was going on. She would run over to him and kiss him, and then go back and shoot the scene. That was my first taste of Hollywood glory long before I was in the business.
- *Ocean's Eleven* **(the original)**   It's timeless actors and classic Vegas, platinum swagger that can never be replicated. I watch it, remembering that Sinatra would do just one take and that was it. Being in the business now, I marvel at that. He was always dressed so amazingly in those sweaters, he always had a cocktail, and he was just so cool.
- *Viva Las Vegas*   To me, this was the first movie to put Las Vegas on the map, with the King of rock 'n' roll, no less, exemplifying what Vegas was all about, in its true glory days. Back then, times were good, it was all about the gambler, and it was amazing.
- *Casino*   I actually grew up in town during this era, so I remember these characters very well. It was one of the first movies that took us inside the world of the casino, not just on the floor, but also behind the scenes. It was the look of the mob era in Vegas, how it really was; and since I knew of those men, I could see both how accurate it was and where creative license was taken.
- *Leaving Las Vegas*   It's one of my top-five films of all time. The concept of an alcoholic going to Vegas because they never close the bars was a genius dramatic idea. And the way that director Mike Figgis shot Nick Cage, with Luxor in the background, with the red lights of Bally's blinking, the seedy hotel, it all just felt like the dark, surreal side of Vegas that we are used to as locals on a much more gut and emotional level. A wonderful movie.

Spanier, David, *Welcome to the Pleasure Dome: Inside Las Vegas* (University of Nevada Press, 1992). First-person history and analysis of the Las Vegas phenomenon.

Thompson, Hunter S., *Fear and Loathing in Las Vegas* (Random House, 1971). The gonzo journalist and his Samoan lawyer head to Sin City for the all-time binge. An instant classic, made into a movie starring Johnny Depp.

Tronnes, Mike, ed., *Literary Las Vegas* (Henry Holt, 1995). A terrific collection of different essays and excerpts from books about Vegas.

3 Orientation

Located in the southernmost precincts of a wide, pancake-flat valley, Las Vegas is the biggest city in the state of Nevada. Treeless mountains form a scenic backdrop to hotels awash in neon glitter. Although it is one of the fastest-growing cities in America, for tourism purposes, the city is quite compact.

VISITOR INFORMATION

All major Las Vegas hotels provide comprehensive tourist information at their reception and/or sightseeing and show desks.

Other good information sources are the **Las Vegas Convention and Visitors Authority,** 3150 Paradise Rd., Las Vegas, NV 89109 (© **877/VISIT-LV** or 702/892-7575; www.visitlasvegas.com), open daily from 9am to 5pm; the **Las Vegas Chamber of Commerce,** 3720 Howard Hughes Pkwy., #100, Las Vegas, NV 89109 (© **702/735-1616;** www.lvchamber.com), open Monday through Friday from 8am to 5pm; and, for information on all of Nevada, including Las Vegas, the **Nevada Commission on Tourism** (© **800/638-2328;** www.travelnevada.com), open 24 hours.

CITY LAYOUT

There are two main areas of Las Vegas: the **Strip** and **Downtown.** For many people, that's all there is to Las Vegas. But there is actually more to the town than that: Although maybe not as glitzy and glamorous as the Strip and Downtown—okay, definitely not—Paradise Road and east Las Vegas are home to quite a bit of casino action, Maryland Parkway boasts mainstream and some alternative-culture shopping, and there are different restaurant options all over the city. Many of the "locals hotels" (pretty much anything with "Station" in the name, for starters), most of which are off the regular tourist track, offer cheaper gambling limits plus budget food and entertainment options. Confining yourself to the Strip and Downtown is fine for the first-time visitor, but repeat customers (and you will be) should get out there and explore. Las Vegas Boulevard South (the Strip) is the starting point for addresses; any street that crosses it starts with 1 East and 1 West at its intersection with the Strip (and goes up from there).

THE STRIP

The Strip is probably the most famous 4-mile stretch of highway in the nation. Officially called Las Vegas Boulevard South, it contains most of the top hotels in town and offers almost all the major showroom entertainment. First-time visitors will, and

---

⌐*Tips* Help for Troubled Travelers

The **Travelers Aid Society** is a social-service organization geared to helping travelers in difficult straits. Its services include reuniting families separated while traveling, feeding people stranded without cash, and even providing emotional counseling. If you're in trouble, seek them out. In Las Vegas there is a Travelers Aid office at McCarran International Airport (© **702/798-1742**) that is open daily from 8am to 5pm. Similar services are provided by **Help of Southern Nevada,** 953–35B E. Sahara Ave., Suite 208, at Maryland Parkway in the Commercial Center (© **702/369-4357;** www.helpsonv.org). Hours are Monday through Friday from 8am to 4pm.

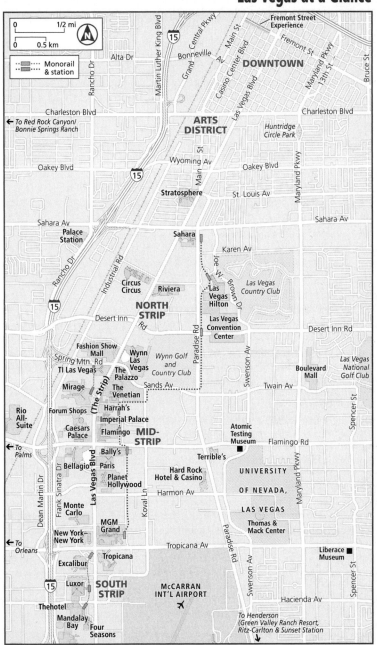

Las Vegas at a Glance

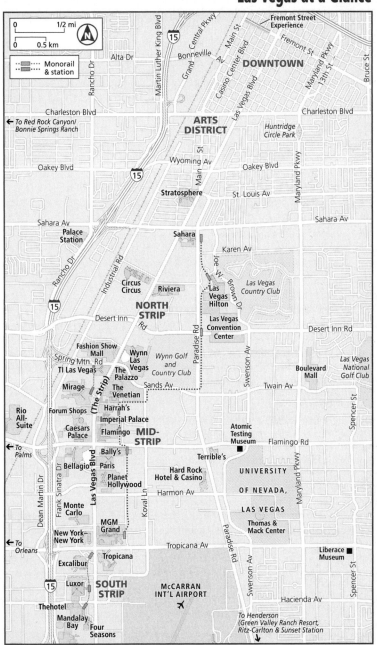

Downtown

Fremont Street Experience
Fremont St
Main St
Maryland Pkwy
13th St
Bruce St

0   1/2 mi
0   0.5 km

Monorail & station

Alta Dr
Bonneville Av
Grand Central Pkwy
Martin Luther King Blvd
Rancho Dr
Casino Center Blvd
Las Vegas Blvd

Charleston Blvd
← To Red Rock Canyon/
Bonnie Springs Ranch

ARTS DISTRICT

Charleston Blvd
Huntridge Circle Park

Wyoming Av
Main St
Maryland Pkwy

Oakey Blvd
Oakey Blvd

Stratosphere
St. Louis Av

Sahara Av
Sahara Av

Palace Station
Sahara
Karen Av

Rancho Dr
Industrial Rd
Joe W. Brown Dr
Las Vegas Country Club

Circus Circus
Riviera
Las Vegas Hilton

NORTH STRIP
Las Vegas Convention Center

Desert Inn Rd
Paradise Rd
Desert Inn Rd

Fashion Show Mall
Spring Mtn. Rd
TI Las Vegas
Wynn Las Vegas
Wynn Golf and Country Club
Swenson Av
Las Vegas National Golf Club
Boulevard Mall

The Palazzo
Mirage
(The Strip)
The Venetian
Sands Av
Twain Av
Spencer St

Forum Shops
Harrah's

Rio All-Suite
Imperial Palace

Caesars Palace
Flamingo
MID-STRIP
Atomic Testing Museum
Flamingo Rd

← To Palms
Bally's
Terrible's

Bellagio
Paris
UNIVERSITY
Maryland Pkwy

Frank Sinatra Dr
Las Vegas Blvd
Planet Hollywood
Hard Rock Hotel & Casino
OF NEVADA,

Dean Martin Dr
Monte Carlo
Harmon Av
Koval Ln
LAS VEGAS

New York–New York
MGM Grand
Thomas & Mack Center

← To Orleans
Tropicana Av
Paradise Rd
Liberace Museum

Excalibur
Tropicana
Swenson Av
Spencer St

Luxor
SOUTH STRIP
McCARRAN INT'L AIRPORT
Hacienda Av

Thehotel
Mandalay Bay
Four Seasons
To Henderson
(Green Valley Ranch Resort,
Ritz-Carlton & Sunset Station)
↓

47

probably should, spend the bulk of their time on the Strip. If mobility is a problem, we suggest basing yourself in a South or Mid-Strip location.

For the purposes of organizing this book, we've divided the Strip into three sections. The **South Strip** can be roughly defined as the portion of the Strip south of Harmon Avenue, including the MGM Grand, Mandalay Bay, the Monte Carlo, New York–New York, Luxor, and many more hotels and casinos.

Mid-Strip is a long stretch of the street between Harmon Avenue and Spring Mountain Road, including Bellagio, Caesars, The Mirage, and TI–Treasure Island, Bally's, Paris Las Vegas, The Flamingo Las Vegas, and Harrah's, among other hotels and casinos.

The **North Strip** stretches north from Spring Mountain Road all the way to the Stratosphere Casino Hotel & Tower and includes Wynn Las Vegas, Sahara, the Riviera, and Circus Circus, to name a few of the accommodations and attractions.

EAST OF THE STRIP/CONVENTION CENTER

This area has grown up around the Las Vegas Convention Center. Las Vegas is one of the nation's top convention cities, attracting around 3 million conventioneers each year. The major hotel in this section is the Las Vegas Hilton, but Marriott has a big presence here and the Hard Rock Hotel is a major draw. You'll find many smaller chain/name brand hotels and motels southward, along Paradise Road. All these hotels offer proximity to the Strip.

BETWEEN THE STRIP & DOWNTOWN

The area between the Strip and Downtown is a seedy stretch dotted with tacky wedding chapels, bail-bond operations, pawnshops, and cheap motels. However, the area known as the **Gateway District** (roughly north and south of Charleston Blvd. to the west of Las Vegas Blvd. S.) keeps trying to make a name for itself as an artists' colony. Studios, small cafes, and other signs of life continue to spring up.

DOWNTOWN

Also known as **"Glitter Gulch"** (narrower streets make the neon seem brighter), Downtown Las Vegas, which is centered on Fremont Street between Main and 9th streets, was the first section of the city to develop hotels and casinos. With the exception of the Golden Nugget, which looks like it belongs in Monte Carlo, this area has traditionally been more casual than the Strip. But between the **Fremont Street Experience** (p. 174) and other ongoing plans, more and more Downtown is offering a viable alternative to the Strip. Plans are in the works for new pleasant public areas and attractions, plus a narrowing of Fremont Street at 8th Street to allow for sidewalk expansion and new bars, so crowds can spill out and mingle convivially. With prices on the Strip running amok, there is more reason than ever to focus your tourist attention and dollars down here. The area is clean, the crowds are low-key and friendly, there is a collection of great bars just east of the Experience, and the light show itself is as ostentatious as anything on the Strip. Sure, by comparison with the overblown Strip, it feels more like a small town than even old time "Vegas," but don't let that allow you to overlook this area. Las Vegas Boulevard runs all the way into Fremont Street Downtown.

4 Getting Around

It shouldn't be too hard to navigate your way around. But remember, between huge hotel acreage, increased and very slow traffic, and lots and lots of people—like you—

trying to explore, getting around takes a lot longer than you might think. Heck, it can take 15 to 20 minutes to get from your room to another part of your hotel! Always allow for plenty of time to get from point A to point B.

BY CAR

Unless you plan to spend the bulk of your vacation in a city where walking is the best way to get around (read: New York City or New Orleans), the most cost-effective way to travel is by car.

If you plan to confine yourself to one part of the Strip (or one cruise down to it) or to Downtown, your feet will suffice. Otherwise, we highly recommend that visitors rent a car. The Strip is too spread out for walking (and Las Vegas is often too hot or too cold to make strolls pleasant), Downtown is too far away for a cheap cab ride, and public transportation is often ineffective in getting you where you want to go. Plus, return visits call for exploration in more remote parts of the city, and a car brings freedom, especially if you want to do any side trips at your own pace.

You should note that places with addresses some 60 blocks east or west of the Strip are actually less than a 10-minute drive—provided there is no traffic.

Having advocated renting a car, we should warn you that traffic is getting worse, and it's harder and harder to get around town with any certain swiftness. A general rule of thumb is to avoid driving on the Strip whenever you can, and avoid driving at all during peak hours (8–9:30am and 4:30–6pm), especially if you have to make a show curtain.

Parking is usually a pleasure because all casino hotels offer free valet service. That means that for a mere $1 to $2 tip, you can park right at the door, though the valet usually fills up on busy nights. In those cases, you can use the gigantic self-parking lots (free on the Strip, nominal fees Downtown) that all hotels have.

RENTING A CAR

National companies with outlets in Las Vegas include **Alamo** (✆ 877/227-8367; www.alamo.com), **Avis** (✆ 800/230-4898; www.avis.com), **Budget** (✆ 800/ 527-0700; www.budget.com), **Dollar** (✆ 800/800-3665; www.dollar.com), **Enterprise** (✆ 800/261-7331; www.enterprise.com), **Hertz** (✆ 800/654-3131; www.hertz.com), **National** (✆ 800/227-7368; www.nationalcar.com), **Payless** (✆ 800/729-5377; www.paylesscarrental.com), and **Thrifty** (✆ 800/847-4389; www.thrifty.com).

Car rental rates vary even more than airline fares. The price you pay depends on the size of the car, where and when you pick it up and drop it off, the length of the rental period, where and how far you drive it, whether you purchase insurance, and a host of other factors. A few key questions could save you hundreds of dollars.

- Are weekend rates lower than weekday rates? Ask if the rate is the same for pickup Friday morning, for instance, as it is for Thursday night.
- Is a weekly rate cheaper than the daily rate? Even if you need the car for only 4 days, it may be cheaper to keep it for 5.
- Does the agency assess a drop-off charge if you don't return the car to the same location where you picked it up? Is it cheaper to pick up the car at the airport than at a Downtown location?
- Are special promotional rates available? If you see an advertised price in your local newspaper, be sure to ask for that specific rate; otherwise, you may be charged the standard cost. Terms change constantly, and reservations agents are notorious for not mentioning available discounts unless you ask.

- Are discounts available for members of AARP, AAA, frequent-flier programs, or trade unions? If you belong to any of these organizations, you may be entitled to discounts of up to 30%.
- How much tax will be added to the rental bill? Local tax? State use tax?
- What is the cost of adding an additional driver's name to the contract?
- How many free miles are included in the price? Free mileage is often negotiable, depending on the length of the rental.
- How much does the rental company charge to refill your gas tank if you return with the tank less than full? Though most rental companies claim these prices are "competitive," fuel is almost always cheaper in town. Try to allow enough time to refuel the car yourself before returning it.

Some companies offer "refueling packages," in which you pay for an entire tank of gas up front. The price is usually fairly competitive with local gas prices, but you don't get credit for any gas remaining in the tank.

Many available packages include airfare, accommodations, and a rental car with unlimited mileage. Compare these prices with the cost of booking airline tickets and renting a car separately to see if such offers are good deals. Internet resources can make comparison-shopping easier. *Note:* Foreign driver's licenses are usually recognized in the U.S., but you should get an international one if your home license is not in English.

Surfing for Rental Cars

For booking rental cars online, the best deals are usually found at rental-car company websites, although all the major online travel agencies also offer rental-car reservations services. **Priceline** (www.priceline.com) and **Hotwire** (www.hotwire.com) work well for rental cars; the only "mystery" is which major rental company you get, and for most travelers, the difference between Hertz, Avis, and Budget is negligible. Also check out **Breezenet.com**, which offers domestic car-rental discounts with some of the most competitive rates around.

Demystifying Renter's Insurance

Before you drive off in a rental car, be sure you're insured. Hasty assumptions about your personal auto insurance or a rental agency's additional coverage could end up costing you tens of thousands of dollars—even if you are involved in an accident that was clearly the fault of another driver.

If you already hold a **private auto insurance** policy in the United States, you are most likely covered for loss of or damage to a rental car and liability in case of injury to any other party involved in an accident. Be sure to find out whether you are covered in the area you are visiting, whether your policy extends to all persons who will be driving the rental car, how much liability is covered in case an outside party is injured in an accident, and whether the type of vehicle you are renting is included under your contract. (Rental trucks, sport utility vehicles, and luxury vehicles may not be covered.)

Most **major credit cards** provide some degree of coverage as well—provided they were used to pay for the rental. Terms vary widely, however, so be sure to call your credit card company directly before you rent. If you don't have a private auto insurance policy, the credit card you use to rent a car may provide primary coverage if you decline the rental agency's insurance. This means that the credit card company will cover damage or theft of a rental car for the full cost of the vehicle. If you do have a private auto insurance policy, your credit card may provide secondary coverage—

which basically covers your deductible. *Credit cards do not cover liability* or the cost of injury to an outside party and/or damage to an outside party's vehicle. If you do not hold an insurance policy, you may want to seriously consider purchasing additional liability insurance from your rental company. Be sure to check the terms, however: Some rental agencies cover liability only if the renter is not at fault; even then, the rental company's obligation varies from state to state. Bear in mind that each credit card company has its own peculiarities; call your own credit card company for details before relying on a card for coverage.

The basic insurance coverage offered by most car rental companies, known as the **Loss/Damage Waiver (LDW)** or **Collision Damage Waiver (CDW),** can cost as much as $20 per day. The former should cover everything, including the loss of income to the rental agency, should you get in an accident (normally not covered by your own insurance policy). It usually covers the full value of the vehicle, with no deductible, if an outside party causes an accident or other damage to the rental car. You will probably be covered in case of theft as well. Liability coverage varies, but the minimum is usually at least $15,000. If you are at fault in an accident, you will be covered for the full replacement value of the car—but not for liability. In Nevada, you can buy additional liability coverage for such cases. Most rental companies require a police report in order to process any claims you file, but your private insurer will not be notified of the accident. Check your own policies and credit cards before you shell out money on this extra insurance because you may already be covered.

BY TAXI

Since cabs line up in front of all major hotels, an easy way to get around town is by taxi. Cabs charge $3.20 at the meter drop and 25¢ for each additional ⅛ mile, plus an additional $1.20 fee for being picked up at the airport and time-based penalties if you get stuck in a traffic-jam. A taxi from the airport to the Strip will run you $12 to $20, from the airport to Downtown $15 to $20, and between the Strip and Downtown about $10 to $15. You can often save money by sharing a cab with someone going to the same destination (up to five people can ride for the same fare). All this implies that you have gotten a driver who is honest; many cabbies take you the long way around, which sometimes means the shortest physical distance between two points—right down the Strip—but longest time on the clock and, thus, meter. Either way, you could end up paying a fare that...let's just say a new pair of shoes would have been a much more fun way to spend that jackpot. Your only recourse is to write down the cab number and call the company and complain. They may not respond, but you can try.

If you just can't find a taxi to hail and want to call one, try the following companies: **Desert Cab Company** (*©* **702/386-9102**), **Whittlesea Blue Cab** (*©* **702/ 384-6111**), or **Yellow/Checker Cab/Star Company** (*©* **702/873-2000**).

BY MONORAIL

The first leg of a high-tech monorail opened in 2004, offering riders their first and best shot of getting from one end of the Strip to the other with a minimum of frustration and expense. The 4-mile route runs from the MGM Grand at the southern end of the Strip to the Sahara at the northern end, with stops at Paris/Bally's, The Flamingo, Harrah's, the Las Vegas Convention Center, and the Las Vegas Hilton along the way. Note that some of the actual physical stops are not as geographically close to their namesakes, so there can be an unexpected—and sometimes time-consuming—

Tips Chopper Tom's Traffic Tips

"Chopper" Tom Hawley has watched Las Vegas grow since he was a little kid catching lizards in the desert back in the '60s. A self-described "traffic geek," Tom reports from the helicopter and from the studio most mornings and afternoons in Las Vegas on KVBC-TV/Channel 3. For further information on the following projects, tips, and much more, stop by Channel 3's website, at **www.kvbc.com**, and click "Traffic."

- **Monorail Mania:** After decades of abandoned plans and false starts, a commuter monorail serving the Strip is finally a reality! This 4-mile system is a larger, faster, and more modern version of the Disney hand-me-down that used to run between the MGM and Bally's. The Las Vegas Monorail now has seven stations sprinkled from the MGM to the Sahara, with a one-way fare running $5 per person. (Discounts are available for multiple trips.) You may have heard about some less-than-glorious months for the system, but we're happy to report that as of this writing, things seem to be in fine working order. The bad news is that the monorail has probably scuttled planned extensions to Downtown and the airport at least for now.

- **People Movers Galore:** Las Vegas has a greater variety of independent people-mover systems than any other city in the world, and they're a great way to get around without having to get into your car. In addition to the people movers at McCarran Airport, a variety of trains will take you from hotel to hotel. The Mandalay Bay Train whisks you from the Tropicana walkways to the Excalibur, Luxor, and Mandalay Bay hotels. Smaller shuttles operate between The Mirage and TI-Treasure Island and between the Circus Circus Big Top and East Tower. A new train is set to connect the Monte Carlo and Bellagio with CityCenter, set to open in late 2009.

- **Spaghetti Bowl:** The "Spaghetti Bowl" is what locals call the mess where I-15 intersects U.S. 95. The entire thing was reconstructed in 2000, but some studies indicate that it's carrying more traffic than it was designed for, so don't expect a congestion-free ride.

- **U.S. 95 Widening:** A seven-year project to widen the west leg of U.S. 95 (connecting to the busy northwest valley) is now complete. Though still busy in weekday rush hours, this freeway hasn't moved better in 20 years.

- **Keep Your Feet off the Streets:** Local engineers have been trying to improve traffic on the Strip by separating the cars from the pedestrians. The first overhead pedestrian walkways opened at Tropicana Avenue in 1995; similar bridges were completed at Flamingo Avenue in 2000 and Spring Mountain in 2003. Future pedestrian bridges will be installed at Sahara and Harmon.

- **Do D.I. Direct:** Most visitors seem to get a lot of mileage out of the Strip and I-15. But if you're checking out the local scene, you can bypass both of those, using Desert Inn Road, which is now one of the longest streets running from one side of the valley to the other. Plus, the 2-mile "Super-arterial" section between Valley View and Paradise zips you nonstop over the interstate and under the Strip.
- **Grin and Bear It:** Yes, there are ways to avoid traffic jams on the Strip. But at least these traffic jams are entertaining! If you have the time and patience, go ahead and take a ride along the Strip from Hacienda to Sahara. The 4-mile drive might take an hour, but while you're grinding along, you'll see a Sphinx, an active volcano, a water ballet, and some uniquely Vegas architecture.
- **Rat Pack Back Doors:** Frank Sinatra Drive is a bypass road that runs parallel to the Strip from Russell Road north to Industrial. It's a great way to avoid the traffic jams and sneak in the back of hotels such as Mandalay Bay, Luxor, Monte Carlo, and Bellagio. On the other side of I-15, a bunch of high-end condo developers talked the city into rechristening a big portion of Industrial Road as Dean Martin Drive. It's still called Industrial from near Downtown to Twain, and it lets you in the back entrances to Circus Circus, TI-Treasure Island, and others. It's a terrific bypass to the Strip and I-15 congestion.
- **Beltway Bypass:** The 53-mile 215 Beltway was completed in 2003, wrapping three quarters of the way around the valley, allowing easy access to the outskirts while bypassing the Resort Corridor. While the initial beltway is done, some portions still need to be built out from half-beltway and frontage road systems to a full freeway—a process that will take until 2013.
- **That Dam Bridge:** In 2002, work began on a magnificent bridge over the Colorado River to handle traffic between Arizona and Nevada. It was supposed to be done in 2008, but a construction mishap has pushed that back to 2010. If you want to visit Hoover Dam, watch out for delays of an hour or more approaching the construction zone. The best advice is to start your trip by 8am, and especially to avoid midday on Saturdays and Sundays.
- **Catch the CAT:** Some locals complain about Citizens Area Transit (CAT) bus service in certain neighborhoods. But the Strip routes are frequent and well serviced, running around the clock from the South Strip Transfer Terminal to the Downtown Transportation Center in the north. The 301 runs every 10 minutes during busy hours, and there's also a limited-stop express bus (no. 302) every 15 minutes. Other routes go for $1.25, but the 301 and 302 are the CAT's gravy trains and cost $2. Exact change, please.

additional walk from the monorail stop to wherever you intended to go. Factor in this time accordingly.

These trains can accommodate more than 200 passengers (standing and sitting) and make the end-to-end run in about 15 minutes. They operate Monday through Thursday from 7am until 2am and Friday through Sunday from 7am until 3am. Fares are $5 (!!!) for a one-way ride (whether you ride from one end to the other or just to the next station); discounts are available for round-trips and multiride/multiday passes.

Feelings are mixed about the monorail, which isn't generating the ridership as expected. A variety of behind-the-scenes issues, mostly having to do with money, may change the way it's run, extend the route, or even shut it down altogether, although that seems highly unlikely. None of this will happen before 2009, and even if it does change, it may not be in such a way that you will notice.

BY PUBLIC TRANSPORTATION

The no. 301 bus operated by **CAT** (② **702/CAT-RIDE;** www.rtcsouthernnevada. com/cat) plies a route between the Downtown Transportation Center (at Casino Center Blvd. and Stewart Ave.) and a few miles beyond the southern end of the Strip. The fare is $2 for adults, 60¢ for seniors 62 and older and children 6 to 17, and free for those under 6. A low $5 buys an all-day pass. CAT buses run 24 hours a day and are wheelchair-accessible. Exact change is required.

The Regional Transportation Commission (RTC) recently launched a service called **The Deuce** (② **702/CAT-RIDE;** www.rtcsouthernnevada.com/deuce), a fleet of modern double-decker buses that run the length of the Strip into downtown and near the airport. A one-way ride is $2 for adults, $1 for seniors 62 and older and children 6 to 17, and free for those under 6. For a remarkably low $5, you get an all-day pass that lets you get on and off as many times as you like and also lets you ride all the other RTC buses all day. They even provide recorded color commentary as you sit in the mind-numbing traffic-jams that plug up the Strip most of the time. Exact change is required.

At this writing, it was unclear if the Vegas.com Arrow, classic streetcar replicas, will still be in operation. Let's hope so—the old fashioned, dark green vehicles are nice on the eyes and better still, air-conditioned. Like the buses, they run northward from Hacienda Avenue, stopping at all major hotels en route to the Sahara (not to the Stratosphere or Downtown) and then go back from the Las Vegas Hilton. Trolleys run about every 15 minutes daily between 9:30am and 1:30am. The fare is $2.50 for a single one-way ticket or $6.50 for an all-day pass (free for children under age 5). Exact change is required.

There are also a number of free transportation services, courtesy of the casinos. A free monorail connects Mandalay Bay with Luxor and Excalibur, and a free tram shuttles between The Mirage and TI–Treasure Island. Given how far apart even neighboring hotels can be, thanks to their size, and how they seem even farther apart on really hot (and cold and windy) days, these are blessed additions.

4

Where to Stay

If there's one thing Vegas has, it's hotels. Big hotels. And lots of them. You'll find 9 of the 10 largest hotels in the United States—8 of the top 10 in the world—right here. And you'll find a whole lot of rooms: 140,000 rooms, give or take, as of this writing. Every 5 minutes, or so it seems, someone is putting up a new giant hotel or adding another 1,000 rooms to an existing one. So finding a place to stay in Vegas should be the least of your worries.

Or should it?

When a convention, a fight, or some other big event is happening—and these things are always happening—darn near all of those 140,000 rooms are going to be sold out. Over the course of a regular year, the occupancy rate for hotel rooms in Las Vegas runs at about 90%. A last-minute Vegas vacation can turn into a housing nightmare. If possible, plan in advance so that you can have your choice: Ancient Egypt (kinda) or Ancient Rome (kinda)? New York or New Orleans? Strip or Downtown? Luxury or economy? Vegas has all that and way too much more.

The bottom line is that with a few, mostly subtle differences, a hotel room is a hotel room is a hotel room. After you factor in location and price, there isn't that much difference between rooms, except for perhaps size and the quality of their surprisingly similar furnishings.

Hotel prices in Vegas are anything but fixed, so you will notice wild price ranges. The same room can routinely go for anywhere from $60 to $250, depending on demand. So use our price categories with a grain of salt, and don't rule out a hotel just because it's listed as "Very Expensive"—on any given day, you might get a great deal on a room in a pricey hotel. On the negative side, some hotels start with their most typical lowest rate, adding "and up." Don't be surprised if "up" turns out to be way up. Just look online or call and ask.

Yes, if you pay more, you'll probably (but not certainly) get a "nicer" establishment and clientele to match (perhaps not so many loud drunks in the elevators). On the other hand, if a convention is in town, the drunks will be there no matter how upscale the hotel—they'll just be wearing business suits and/or funny hats. And frankly, the big hotels, no matter how fine, have mass-produced rooms; at 3,000 rooms or more, they are the equivalent of '60s tract housing. Consequently, even in the nicest hotels, you can (and probably will) encounter plumbing noises, notice scratch marks on the walls or furniture, overhear conversations from other rooms, or be woken by the maids as they knock on the doors next to yours that don't have the DO NOT DISTURB sign up.

1 Coming Attractions

Part of the reason that we patiently tell people they haven't really been to Vegas, even if they have, is because if they haven't been by in the last, oh, week—okay, let's say 2 or 3 years—they might find several surprises awaiting them on the Strip. And if it's been more than a decade, well, forget it. All the classic old hotels are either gone (Sands, Hacienda; indeed, 2007 saw the end of the 1942 Frontier) or renovated virtually beyond recognition (Caesars, The Flamingo). In their place rise bigger and better and trendier resort hotels, changing the landscape and altering the welcome that Vegas visitors receive.

The new era of Vegas hotels was ushered in by The Mirage, and since then, everyone has been trying to up the ante. The year 1997 began with the opening of New York–New York, which set yet another level of stupendous excess that remained unmatched for at least 18 months.

The fall of 1998 saw the official beginning of the new era of Vegas luxury resorts (many with themes), with the opening of the opulent Bellagio, followed by Mandalay Bay and Four Seasons. And then these took a backseat (sort of) to The Venetian, which combines the jaw-dropping detail and extravagance of New York–New York (complete with canals and gondolas) with the luxury of Bellagio. Could anything top it? Possibly—hot on its heels was Paris, themed as you can imagine, and just a few months later, the new and improved Aladdin, with its desert-fantasy decor.

The first half of this decade was less about new stuff and more about old stuff getting bigger and/or better. Sure, Caesars opened its Roman Coliseum replica, built just to house Céline Dion's new show, but other than that, no grand new hotels or major expansions arrived, unless you count (and we sure do) the arrival of a true luxury resort, the Ritz-Carlton, Lake Las Vegas, over in nearby Henderson. One old hotel, The Maxim, was reborn as a business-swank Westin, complete with its trademark "Heavenly Beds." The rest of the action was all about expansions: The Venetian added 1,000 rooms, a new pool, a fancy restaurant, and more in the new Venezia Tower; Mandalay Bay added more than 1,000 rooms and other goodies in a facility they call THEhotel; Bellagio joined the fray with more than 900 new rooms and a swank new spa in a new tower; and Caesars Palace added a new 700-room tower to its empire.

The year 2005 kicked off what is an unprecedented wave of development, with the arrival of Wynn Las Vegas, the latest hotel concept from Steve Wynn, the man behind Mirage Corp., at a mere cost of $2.7 billion. (As you will see, that formerly record-breaking total is peanuts compared with what's coming up.) In 2006, we saw the addition of Red Rock Resort, designed to lure tourists away from the busy Strip, and two top-to-bottom overhauls, with the creaky old San Remo going pneumatic as the Hooters Casino Hotel (no, really) and the relatively new Aladdin getting an extreme makeover to become Planet Hollywood Resort & Casino (no, really, again).

But that won't be the end of it, not hardly. 2007 saw the debut of yet another expansion to The Venetian, a 3,000-room resort and casino called **The Palazzo,** seeking to continue the parent hotel's Italian aesthetic. 2008 brings an inaugural foray for The Donald in Vegas with **Trump International,** the first of two 1,200-unit condo/hotel towers going up behind what used to be the Frontier. Things really ratchet up with the late-2008 birth of Wynn's second baby, **Encore,** a more than $1.7-billion, 2,000-room hotel and casino, complete with its own indoor pool with a retractable roof. Condos seems to be the property development trend right now, so if you haven't been to Vegas in a while, and you wonder what that, and that over there, and also that really big tall tower is, it's more than likely a condo building.

But the biggest of the big new developments will come at the end of this decade, with the 2009 arrival of **CityCenter,** an $8-billion (yes, you read that right) complex of hotels, condos, casinos, shopping, and entertainment spread across 66 acres just north of Monte Carlo. Also due in 2009 is **Fontainebleau,** based on the famous Miami hotel and belonging to a company run by former Mandalay Resorts executives. It's a 4,000-room complex going up on the old El Rancho site across from Circus Circus.

2010 should see the opening of **Echelon Place,** a 63-acre, $4.4 billion multihotel development that is replacing the Stardust. Other plans are in various stages of development: the Elad Group, best known for their current transformation of New York's venerable Plaza Hotel into condos, bought the nearly as venerable, and notably aging, New Frontier for $1.2 billion. Of course, the plan is to promptly tear it down and spend another $3.8 billion to build a **Plaza Las Vegas.** The latter will have 3,500 hotel rooms plus residences, shopping, and all the rest. It's unclear whether the name Plaza will carry over into replicating the New York landmark's style and form, but that seems unlikely.

Meanwhile, Harrah's, which controls a significant portion of Strip properties, was bought in the biggest buyout of a public corporation in history, to the tune of about $27 billion. The new owners have plans to do something with their center strip casinos that could involve completely renovating or tearing down the Imperial Palace, Bill's (former Barbary Coast), and Bally's as well as major changes to Harrah's, Flamingo, Paris, and Caesars. And MGM Mirage bought all the land from Circus Circus to Sahara Boulevard, a property even bigger than the one occupied by their City-Center. Look for something huger than huge that will include a major renovation of Circus Circus. Stay tuned.

2 Three Questions to Ask before You Book a Room
WHERE SHOULD I STAY?

Your two main choices for location are the Strip and Downtown. The Strip, home to many of the most dazzling hotels and casinos in Vegas, is undeniably the winner—especially for first-timers—if only because of the sheer, overwhelming force of its "Vegas-ness." On the other hand, it is expensive, crowded, confining, and strangely claustrophobic. We say "strangely claustrophobic" because the hotels only *look* close together: In reality, they are situated on large properties, and it's a long (and often very hot or very cold) walk from one place to the next.

Contrast that with Downtown, which is nowhere near as striking but is more easily navigated on foot. Within 5 minutes, you can reach more than a dozen different casinos. The Fremont Street upgrade has turned a declining area into a very pleasant place to be, and the crowds reflect that: They seem nicer and more relaxed, and a calmer atmosphere pervades. Hotels certainly aren't state-of-the-art down there, but the rooms at many are not just clean and acceptable but rather pleasant. The establishments' smaller sizes often mean friendlier, faster service than at the big 'uns uptown, and you often can't beat the rates. There are also several other development plans afoot that might add even more aesthetic and entertainment appeal to the area. Since it's only a 5-minute ride by car between Downtown and Strip hotels (the Convention Center is more or less in between), there's no such thing as a bad location if you have access to a car. Main Street Station even provides a free shuttle to the Strip.

For those of you without a car and who don't want to spend the $10 to $15 on a cab ride between Downtown and the Strip: Although the bus ride between Downtown and the Strip is short in distance, it can be long in time if you get stuck in traffic. You should also be aware that the buses become quite crowded once they reach the

Reservations Service

The **Las Vegas Convention and Visitors Authority** runs a room-reservations hotline (© **877/VISIT-LV** or 702/892-0711; www.visitlasvegas.com) that can be helpful. They can apprise you of room availability, quote rates, contact a hotel for you, and tell you when major conventions will be in town.

A couple words of warning: Make sure they don't try to book you into a hotel you've never heard of. Try to stick with the hotels listed in this book. Always get your information in writing and then make some phone calls just to confirm that you really have the reservations that they say they've made for you.

Strip and may bypass a bus stop if no one signals to get out and the driver does not want to take on more passengers. Without a car, your ease of movement between different areas of town is limited.

Frankly, for first-timers, there probably isn't any point to staying anywhere but the Strip—you're going to spend most (if not all) of your time there anyway. For future visits, however, we'd strongly advise you to consider Downtown.

But the Strip vs. Downtown location isn't the end of the debate; there is also the issue of where to stay on the Strip. Staying on the **South Strip** end means an easy trip (sometimes in the air-conditioned comfort of covered walkways or monorail) to Mandalay Bay, MGM Grand, New York–New York, Tropicana, Luxor, and Excalibur—all virtually on one corner. **Mid-Strip** has CityCenter, Caesars, The Mirage, Bellagio, TI–Treasure Island, Paris, The Venetian, The Palazzo, Bally's, The Flamingo, Harrah's, and so forth. The **North Strip** gets you Wynn Las Vegas, Encore, the Riviera, Sahara, and Circus Circus, though with a bit more of a walk between them. For this reason, if mobility is a problem and you want to see more than just your own hotel casino, the South and Mid-Strip locations are probably the best bets.

WHAT AM I LOOKING FOR IN A HOTEL?

If gambling is not your priority, what are you doing in Vegas? Just kidding. But not 100% kidding. Vegas's current identity as a luxury, and very adult, resort destination means there are several hotels that promise to offer you all sorts of alternatives to gambling—lush pool areas, fabulous spas, incredible restaurants, lavish shopping. But if you look closely, much of this is Vegas bait and switch; the pools are often chilly (and often partially closed during non-summer months), and it will be years before there is more foliage than concrete in these newly landscaped environments. The spas cost extra (sometimes a whole lot extra), the best restaurants can require a small bank loan, and the stores are often the kinds of places where average mortals can't even afford the oxygen. So what does that leave you with? Why, that's right—gambling.

The other problem with these self-proclaimed luxury hotels is their size. True luxury hotels do not have 3,000 rooms—they have a couple of hundred, at best, because you simply can't provide first-class service and Egyptian-cotton sheets in mass quantity. But while Wynn, Bellagio, The Venetian, The Palazzo and, to a lesser extent, Mandalay Bay have done their best to offer sterling service and to make their rooms more attractive and luxurious than those at other Vegas hotels, there's only so much that any place that big can do. Don't get us wrong—these places are absolutely several steps up in quality from other large hotels, and compared to them, even the better older hotels really look shabby. But they are still sprawling, frequently noisy complexes.

Having said that, there is an additional trend in Vegas; many of the big hotels have put up new towers or additions that function as virtually separate hotels. This began with the Four Seasons, which occupies the top floors of Mandalay Bay and has its own separate entrance. Mandalay Bay has the sterling THEhotel, while The Venetian and Bellagio have separate towers. And The Venetian added The Palazzo, which is more or less The Venetian without the overt Venice elements. Each has its own check-in area and functions like a separate hotel entity. You gain some quiet (with the exception of The Palazzo, there are no casinos in these venues); in the case of THEhotel, considerable style; and, overall, at least the illusion of better service (and probably some reality of it, too, since there are fewer rooms under the special monikers). Classier grown-ups, or well-heeled families, should make these new additions first on their list.

Sadly, it's relatively easy for both you and us to make a mistake about a hotel; either of us may experience a particular room or two in a 1,000-plus-room hotel and from there conclude that a place is nicer than it is or more of a dump than it is. Maintenance, even in the best of hotels, can sometimes be running a bit behind, so if there is something wrong with your room, don't hesitate to ask for another. Of course, if it's one of those busy weekends, there may not be another room to be had, but at least this way you've registered a complaint, perhaps letting a busy hotel know that a certain room needs attention. And who knows? If you are gracious and persistent enough, you may be rewarded with a deal for some future stay.

If you want a true luxury-resort hotel, there are only two options: On the Strip it's the Four Seasons, and off, way off, in nearby Henderson, it's the Ritz-Carlton. In addition to that same service and level of comfort only found at a smaller hotel, both offer those extra goodies that pile on the hidden charges at other hotels—health club, poolside cabanas, and so on—as part of the total package, meaning that their slightly higher prices may be more of a bargain than you'd think. Actually, there is a third option: The Red Rock Resort is attracting well-heeled and high-profile tabloid types, who, presumably, know luxury. However, Red Rock charges for all the extras you get as a regular part of your stay at the Four Seasons and the Ritz.

(*Tips* **Who Kept the Kids Out?**

Some hotels—notably Bellagio, which started the practice, and Wynn Las Vegas—ban children who are not staying on-site from stepping foot on the hotel premises and ban strollers even if you are staying there. Child-free adults love the bans, but families who travel to Vegas (can we say yet again that this is not a family destination?) may be seriously inconvenienced by it. The policy doesn't appear to be uniformly enforced (hotels don't want to offend parents who have plenty of dough to gamble, after all), but we've seen families and teenagers get turned away from a hotel because they couldn't produce a room key. If you're traveling with your kids, or want to be free of someone else's, your best bet is to call your chosen hotel and ask what its policy is.

Surfing for Hotels

In addition to the online travel booking sites **Travelocity, Expedia, Orbitz, Price-line,** and **Hotwire,** you can book hotels through **Hotels.com; Quikbook** (www.quikbook.com); and **Travelaxe** (www.travelaxe.net). **HotelChatter.com** is a daily webzine offering smart coverage and critiques of hotels worldwide. Go to **TripAdvisor.com** or **HotelShark.com** for helpful independent consumer reviews of hotels and resort properties.

It's a good idea to **get a confirmation number** and **make a printout** of any online booking transaction.

Still, if you want peace and quiet and don't land in the tax bracket that Four Seasons/Ritz caters to, there are other, less high-profile hotels without casinos. Make certain the hotel has a pool, however, especially if you need some recreation. There is nothing as boring as a non-casino, non-pool Vegas hotel—particularly if you have kids.

Casino hotels, by the way, are not always a nice place for children. It used to be that the casino was a separate section in the hotel, and children were not allowed inside. (We have fond memories of standing just outside the casino line, watching Dad put quarters in a slot machine "for us.") But in almost all the new hotels, you have to walk through the casino to get anywhere—the lobby, the restaurants, the outside world. This makes sense from the hotel's point of view; it gives you many opportunities to stop and drop $1 or $10 into a slot. But this often long, crowded trek gets wearying for adults—and it's far worse for kids. The rule is that kids can walk through the casinos, but they can't stop, even to gawk for a second at someone hitting a jackpot nearby. The casino officials who will immediately hustle the child away are just doing their job, but, boy, it's annoying.

So, take this (and what a hotel offers that kids might like) into consideration when booking a room. Again, please note that those gorgeous hotel pools are often cold (and again, sometimes closed altogether) and not very deep. They look like places you would want to linger, but often (from a kid's point of view) they are not. Plus, the pools close early. Hotels want you inside gambling, not outside swimming.

Finally, the thing that bothers us the most about this latest Vegas phase; it used to be that we could differentiate between rooms, but that's becoming harder and harder. Nearly every major hotel has changed to more or less the same effect; gone is any thematic detailing and in its place is a series of disappointingly similar (if handsome and appealing) looks. Expect clean-lined wood furniture, plump white beds, and monochromes everywhere you go. All that may distinguish one from another would be size of the room or quality of furnishings.

Ultimately, though, if it's a busy time, you'll have to nab any room you can, especially if you get a price you like. How much time are you going to spend in the room anyway?

WHAT WILL I HAVE TO PAY?

The rack rate is the maximum rate that a hotel charges for a room. It's the rate you'd get if you walked in off the street and asked for a room for the night. Hardly anybody pays these prices, however, especially in Vegas, where prices fluctuate wildly with demand and there are many ways around rack rates. Here are some tips for landing a low rate.

- **Don't be afraid to bargain.** Get in the habit of asking for a lower price than the first one quoted. Always ask politely whether a less-expensive room is available than the first one mentioned or whether any special rates apply to you. If you belong to the players' clubs at the hotel casino, you may be able to secure a better deal on a hotel room there. Of course, you will also be expected to spend a certain amount of time, and money, gambling there. See below for more details on players' clubs.

- **Rely on a qualified professional.** Certain hotels give travel agents discounts in exchange for steering business their way, so if you're shy about bargaining, an agent may be better equipped to negotiate discounts for you.
- **Dial direct.** When booking a room in a chain hotel (Courtyard by Marriott, for example), call the hotel's local line, as well as the toll-free number, and see where you get the best deal. A hotel makes nothing on a room that stays empty. The clerk who runs the place is more likely to know about vacancies and will often grant deep discounts in order to fill up.
- **Remember the law of supply and demand.** Las Vegas hotels are most crowded and therefore most expensive on weekends. So the best deals are offered midweek, when prices can drop dramatically. If possible, go then. You can also call the **Las Vegas Convention and Visitors Authority** (© 877/VISIT-LV) to find out whether an important convention is scheduled at the time of your planned visit; if so, you might want to change your date. Some of the most popular conventions are listed under "When to Go," in chapter 2. Remember also that planning your vacation just a week before or after official peak season can mean big savings.
- **Look into group or long-stay discounts.** If you come as part of a large group, you should be able to negotiate a bargain, since the hotel can then guarantee occupancy in a number of rooms. Likewise, when you're planning a long stay in town (usually from 5 days to a week), you'll usually qualify for a discount.
- **Avoid excess phone charges.** We can't stress this enough. Virtually every hotel in Vegas charges like crazy for phone calls. At best, it will be $1 for a local call, and sky-high prices for long distance (a 7-min. call to California set us back $35). At worst, it's all that plus an additional charge—as much as 30¢ a minute—for all local calls lasting more than 30 minutes. This is particularly onerous if you are using a laptop with a dial-up Internet connection and stay online for any length of time.
- **Beware of hidden extras.** Almost all the major hotels (Four Seasons is one notable exception) charge extra for things that are always free in other destinations, such as health-club privileges. Expect to pay anywhere from $15 to $35 to use almost any hotel spa/health club. Wi-Fi also doesn't come free; usually there is a $12 to $15 charge per 24-hour period. (We've noted these charges in the listings that follow so that you won't be taken by surprise.) Some hotels even audaciously charge an additional mandatory "resort fee" that covers amenities that are commonly free elsewhere, such as pool use.
- **Watch for coupons and advertised discounts.** Scan ads in your local Sunday travel section, an excellent source for up-to-the-minute hotel deals. *The Fun Book,* available from the Las Vegas Convention and Visitors Authority (see above), offers some discounts on lodging.
- **Consider a suite.** If you are traveling with your family or another couple, you can pack more people into a suite (which usually comes with a sofa bed) and thereby reduce your per-person rate. Remember that some places charge for extra guests and some don't.
- **Investigate reservations services.** These outfits usually work as consolidators, buying up or reserving rooms in bulk and then dealing them out to customers at a profit. Most of them offer online reservations services as well.

As far as prices go, keep in mind that our price categories are rough guidelines, at best. If you see a hotel that appeals to you, even if it seems out of your price range, give them a call anyway. They might be having a special, a slow week, or some kind of promotion, or they may just like the sound of your voice (we have no other explanation for it). You could end up with a hotel in the "expensive" category offering you a room for $60 a night. It's a toll-free call, so it's worth a try.

Consider also, even if you think from the outset that this is your one and only trip to Vegas, joining a hotel's players' club—or possibly every hotel's players' club. This costs you nothing, and players/members often get nifty offers in the mail for heavily discounted, and occasionally even free, rooms (plus meals, shows, and so on). Players' clubs reward you with freebies and discounts when you play in their casinos, regardless of whether you win. Recently, ridiculous bargains were showing up in e-mail boxes—like the Bellagio for $59 a night. How much you have to play to get these deals varies, but if you are going to gamble anyway, why not make it work more to your advantage? You can sign up online, which will get you e-mail only offers. You can do this on almost every hotel's website, and it's worth it, though it does mean scheduling your Vegas vacation to take advantage of the times the offers are valid.

We've classified all our hotel recommendations based on the average rack rate that you can expect to be quoted for a double room on an average night (not when the Consumer Electronics Show is in town, and not on New Year's Eve). Expect to pay a little less than this if you stay only Sunday to Thursday, and a little more than this if you stay Friday and Saturday. And on any given night when business is slow, you might be able to stay at a "very expensive" hotel for a "moderate" price. For that matter, if the economy continues to slow, prices are very likely to fall considerably.

Note: All the casinos for the major hotels on the Strip and Downtown (and a few other ones) are reviewed in chapter 7.

3 South Strip

VERY EXPENSIVE

Four Seasons Hotel Las Vegas ✿✿✿ *Kids* Various mammoth Vegas hotels attempt to position themselves as luxury resorts, insisting that service and fine cotton sheets can be done on a mass scale. But there is only one true luxury resort—in some people's eyes, *the* luxury resort—in town (see later in this chapter for two more luxury options in Henderson), located on the top five floors of Mandalay Bay, though in many ways, the Four Seasons is light-years away from the vibe of Mandalay. A separate driveway and portico entrance, plus an entire registration area, set you up immediately. This is one fancy hotel in town where you are not greeted, even at a distance, with the clash and clang of slots and the general hubbub that is the soundtrack to Vegas.

Inside the hotel, all is calm and quiet. But it's really the best of both worlds—all you have to do is walk through a door, and instantly you are in Mandalay Bay, with access to a casino, nightlife, and, yes, general hubbub. The difference is quite shocking, and frankly, once you've experienced Vegas this way, it's kind of hard to go back to the constant sensory overload. So let's scurry quickly back to the womblike comfort of Four Seasons.

The rooms don't look like much at first—slightly bland but in good taste—but when you sink down into the furniture, you appreciate the fine quality. Here at last is a Vegas hotel where they really don't care if you ever leave your room, so the beds have

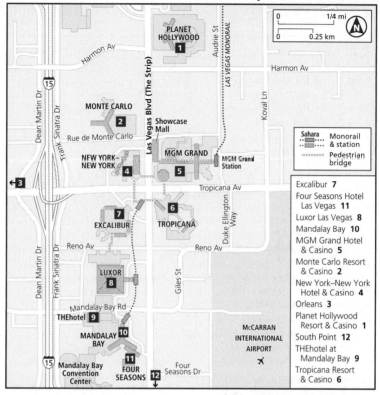

feather pillows and down comforters, robes are plush, and amenities (such as pricey L'Occitane products in the lush bathrooms) are really, really nice. Since Four Seasons has the southernmost location on the Strip, its Strip-view rooms (the most expensive units) give you the whole incredible panorama.

Service is superb (if they say 20 min. for room service, you can expect your food in 19½ min.). Your needs are anticipated so quickly that you're tempted to sink to the floor in the lobby because you know someone will have a chair under your rear before you land. Children are encouraged and spoiled with welcome gifts of toys and goodies, rooms are childproofed in advance, and the list of comforts available for the asking is a yard long. Once you factor in all the freebies (gym/spa access and various other amenities), not to mention the service and the blessed peace, the difference in price between Four Seasons and Bellagio (with all its hidden charges) is nothing.

3960 Las Vegas Blvd. S., Las Vegas, NV 89119. ☎ **877/632-5000** or 702/632-5000. Fax 702/632-5195. www.four seasons.com. 424 units. $450 and up double; $630 and up suite. Extra person $30. Children 17 and under stay free in parent's room. AE, DC, DISC, MC, V. Valet parking $18, no self-parking. Pets under 25 lb. accepted. **Amenities:** 2 restaurants; heated outdoor pool; elegant health club (free to guests); spa; concierge; car-rental desk; courtesy car; business center w/faxing, delivery, and secretarial service daily during business hours; 24-hr. room service; in-room massage; overnight laundry service; overnight dry cleaning; executive-level rooms. *In room:* A/C, TV/DVD w/pay movies, Wi-Fi (for a fee), minibar, fridge on request, coffeemaker, hair dryer, iron/ironing board, safe.

Locals' Hotels

No, not hotels where locals stay—they have that already, after all—but so-called because it's here that locals themselves often come to eat and gamble. Why? Because these places are cheap. The way Vegas used to be. See, an increasing frustration for the Vegas visitor, still under the impression that Vegas is a vacation bargain, is hotel prices, particularly those on the Strip, most of which have long left "bargain" behind. The solution is simple: Give up that Strip location, and suddenly, you have a host of budget-minded options, completely satisfying casino-hotels that may not have the luxury appointments of the big Strip palaces but also don't come with the luxury price tags.

Topping the list of these so-called locals' hotels are those managed by the Station Casinos chain. All the following hotels are admittedly located away from the main tourist areas, but if you have a car at your disposal, you can save yourself a great deal of money by being flexible with your location. None of them is more than 20 minutes from the Strip, and several offer free shuttles to other sister properties. Most of these properties offer a variety of family-friendly entertainment—bowling alleys, multiscreen movie theaters, and more.

On the southeast side of town there are three Station Casinos properties. **Sunset Station** 🎫🎫, 1301 W. Sunset Rd., Henderson (🕐 **888/786-7389;** www.sunsetstation.com), is probably the nicest. Rooms are simple but have all of the amenities you are likely to need, such as irons and ironing boards, high-speed Internet access (for a fee), pay-per-view movies, room service, and so on. Sure, the bathrooms may not be bigger than those in an apartment, and the beds may not be as plush, but if all you need is a nice room for a moderate amount of money, this is a fine option. On-site you'll find more than a dozen restaurants, including a Hooters, a bowling alley, movie theaters, bars, lounges, a nightclub, an outdoor amphitheater with regular concerts by retro (read: has-been) performers, a microbrew pub, and a huge casino with much lower gaming limits than the Strip ($5 blackjack tables abound!). It's really more of an entertainment complex than a hotel, and it even has a mall across the street, so it isn't totally isolated. Prices at Sunset Station are usually well below $100 a night during the week (we've seen them as low as $60), and usually not too much above $100 on the weekends.

Just down the street a bit is the Mexican pueblo–themed **Fiesta Henderson** 🎫, 777 W. Lake Mead Dr., Henderson (🕐 **800/388-8334** or 702/558-7000; www.fiestacasino.com), where they are slowly stripping away the Mexican jungle theme to go Santa Fe (it underwent a massive expansion in 2006). It has equally basic yet comfortable lodgings, plus plenty of gaming options, a decent and dirt-cheap buffet, other restaurants, bars, movie theaters, and more. Things are even cheaper here, with rooms going for as low as $30 a night during the week. You'll also find **Boulder Station** 🎫, 4111 Boulder Hwy. (🕐 **800/683-7777** or 702/432-7777; www.boulderstation.com), a little closer to the Strip, with more than 300 guest rooms, a 75,000-square-foot casino, movie theaters, a day-care facility, a big video-game arcade, restaurants and bars, and a concert venue called The Railhead. Rates at Boulder Station usually run from $75 to $125 a night, but rooms can be had for as little as $49 per night.

A couple of other properties in this area are worth knowing about, even though they aren't managed by the Station Casinos chain. **Sam's Town Hotel & Gambling Hall** (p. 104) is listed separately in this chapter, and nearby is **Arizona Charlie's Boulder** ✖, 4575 Boulder Hwy. (© **800/632-4040** or 702/951-5900; www.arizonacharlies.com), a sister hotel to the Stratosphere, with 300 minisuites, a 37,000-square-foot casino, an on-site laundry facility, several restaurants, and a casino lounge. It's only a step or two above budget accommodations but still very well maintained. It has very low limits in the casino, a cheap and reliable coffee shop, and a buffet priced like buffets used to be. This place is also very inexpensive, with weekday rooms as low as $30 and weekends often as low as $50.

On the north and west sides of town are three more Station properties. **Texas Station** ✖, 2101 Texas Star Lane (© **800/654-8888** or 702/631-1000; www.texasstation.com), has a 91,000-square-foot casino, 200 rooms, movie theaters, a bowling alley, concert venues, bars, and a number of very fine restaurants, including the recommended and justly popular Austins Steakhouse (p. 154). You can often get rooms for as low as $40 a night here. Right across the street is **Fiesta Rancho** ✖, 2400 N. Rancho Rd. (© **888/899-7770** or 702/631-7000; www.fiestacasino.com), another Station hotel similar in concept and execution to its sister property mentioned above, only with more adobe and less jungle. In addition to the 100 rooms, they have a big casino and a regulation-size ice-skating rink, complete with equipment rentals and lessons. Prices go as low as $40 a night. Continue north on Rancho Road, and you'll run into **Santa Fe Station** ✖✖, 4949 N. Rancho Rd. (© **866/767-7771**; www.santafestationlasvegas.com), a place that used to be a really dingy affair until Station Casinos got hold of it. They redid the place from top to bottom, including an unexpectedly spiffy casino, upgraded rooms with stylish furnishings and all the amenities you could reasonably want or need, lots of restaurants and bars, a revamped bowling alley, movie theaters and an addition that includes movie theaters, a showroom, a video-game arcade, a kids' day-care center, and more. They've recently added some new restaurants, including a highly recommended buffet. All this for rates as low as $35 a night and rarely over $100, even during the busiest times.

Also on the north side of town is **The Cannery** ✖, 2121 E. Craig Rd. (© **866/999-4899**; www.cannerycasinos.com), a '40s patriotic World War II–themed hotel and casino with a couple hundred fine and very inexpensive rooms (usually well under $100 a night), a fun casino, a terrific buffet and a few other restaurants, a really cool indoor/outdoor events center that hosts regular concerts and festivals, movie theaters, and more.

EXPENSIVE

Mandalay Bay *Kids*   Mandalay Bay is one of our favorite hotels. Why? Well, we love that the lobby (impossibly high ceilings, calm, gleaming with marble, and housing a large aquarium), and the other public areas really do make this seem more like an actual resort hotel than just a Vegas version of one. You don't have to walk through the casino to get to any of these public areas or the guest-room elevators, the pool area is spiffy, and the entire complex is marginally less confusing and certainly less overwhelming than some of the neighboring behemoths.

We wouldn't say it really evokes colonial Southeast Asia—oh, maybe around the edges, if you squint, thanks to the odd bit of foliage or Balinese carving. This may well keep out the gawkers, who are looking for bigger visual thrills, but we find a place whose theme doesn't bop you over the head refreshing.

The freshly redone spacious rooms are among the most desirable on the Strip. There is no tropical influence; they've gone with geometrics like everyone else, though theirs are very handsome indeed. The bathrooms are the crowning glory: downright large with impressive, slightly sunken tubs, glassed-in showers, double sinks, and separate water closets, plus lots of fab amenities. Rooms on higher floors have some of the best Strip views in town, but usually cost an additional fee.

Service overall is pretty good, and those pool-area employees are the tops in Vegas, though there were no security guards at the guest elevators. A monorail system connects the hotel with Luxor and Excalibur, which are located in the heart of the Strip action, and this should more than help you get over any feelings of isolation.

The restaurants in Mandalay Bay feature some of the most innovative interiors in Vegas, each one more whimsical and imaginative than the next. Even if you don't eat at the hotel, drop in and poke around the restaurants: **Aureole,** a highly rated branch of Charlie Palmer's renowned New York City restaurant; **Border Grill; Red Square;** and the **Bayside Buffet** are reviewed in chapter 5. And then there's **rumjungle,** which features a dramatically skewered all-you-can-eat multicourse Brazilian feast, which you'll enjoy while listening to world-beat drums, surrounded by walls of fire and water and other striking visual features. More casual food can be found at **House of Blues,** whose Southern delicacies are often quite palate-pleasing; HOB is probably the best place in town to see rock bands. Mandalay Bay has a showroom where *Mamma Mia!,* just finished a years-long run, and a separate arena that was inaugurated by none other than the late Luciano Pavarotti. See chapter 9 for details on the hotel's major nightlife offerings. There's also a big, comfortable casino, airier and less claustrophobic than most, plus three bars, often featuring live music at night.

There are no fewer than four pools (entering this area is like going to a water park, thanks to upgraded security—*all* guests, regardless of age, must show a room key), including the touted wave pool, which is, unfortunately, a classic example of Vegas bait-and-switch. It can't handle waves of any serious size, but bobbing in the mini-waves is delightful, as is floating happily in the lazy river (tubes are available for rental—we say save some bucks and share a tube with friends, taking turns using it). Though it was already the finest pool area in town, recent overhauls have given it even more style, adding in a poolside casino, restaurant, and bar. All in all, this area alone makes this resort a top choice for families (except, perhaps, in the topless swimming area).

The health club is sufficiently stocked to give you a good workout (it should be, as they charge guests $27 per day to use it—$20 for the gym only at THEhotel's facility).

The spa area proper—featuring hot and warm pools, plus a cold plunge pool—is exotically designed, as close to those found in the Turkish spas in Eastern Europe as we've come across, though without the weathered decay of decades or centuries, which can be a good thing. Load up on that rich moisturizer when dressing—it costs $17 a bottle in the store outside the door.

See the separate listing on p. 71 for Mandalay Bay's THEhotel addition.

3950 Las Vegas Blvd. S. (at Hacienda Ave.), Las Vegas, NV 89119. © 877/632-7000 or 702/632-7000. Fax 702/632-7228. www.mandalaybay.com. 3,309 units (excluding THEhotel). $99 and up double; $149 and up suite; $149 and up House of Blues Signature Rooms. Extra person $30. Children 14 and under free in parent's room. AE, DC, DISC, MC, V. Free self- and valet parking. **Amenities:** 22 restaurants; casino; 12,000-seat events center; 1,700-seat performing-arts theater; aquarium; wedding chapels; 4 outdoor pools w/lazy river and wave pool; health club; spa; Jacuzzi; sauna; watersports equipment/rentals; concierge; tour desk; business center; 24-hr. room service; in-room massage; laundry service; dry cleaning; executive-level rooms. *In room:* A/C, TV w/pay movies, dataport, Wi-Fi (for a fee), hair dryer, iron/ironing board, safe.

MGM Grand Hotel & Casino 🌟🌟 *Kids*   Vegas goes back and forth on its position on whether size does matter, and the MGM Grand is a perfect example of that. The hotel management now downplays the once-touted "hugeness," trying to pretend that the really big casino is actually several medium-big casinos. Whatever. Despite plenty of signage, it is still a lengthy, confusing schlep from anywhere to anywhere. The 80 or so 42-inch TV monitors (apprising registering guests of hotel happenings) in the vast white-marble lobby only add to the chaotic confusion a guest might feel—all the worse if you are toting kids. At least the lobby is now immediately accessible from the outside world.

Having said all of that, we've grown very fond of this hotel, and we have to admit that they've gone to some efforts to make the ridiculous size work to its—and, thus, your—advantage. Although the original standard rooms in the main tower with their 1930s-era Hollywood glam styling have been replaced by somewhat more blandly upscale decor (there are still black-and-white movie star photos and some deco-inspired curves to some of the furniture), there's nothing wrong, really, with blandly upscale. They are generously proportioned and equipped with pretty much everything you might need, and while they may not be as large or as opulent as some of the super-luxe hotels in town, they are also not as expensive (usually). A second section of the tower is called the West Wing, and it is here that you'll find the memorable accommodations. With a kicky contemporary style, these rooms are smaller (a rather tiny 350 sq. ft.) but full of the trendy touches we are complete suckers for. There is no counter space in the open bathroom plan, but frosted green glass doors preserve privacy. Rooms include DVD and CD players, TVs in the bathroom mirrors, and fluffy bedding, plus there's liberal use of electronic "gee whiz" moments such as lamps that turn on and off if you touch them, while all lights in the rooms are controlled by the insertion of your room key. Each has a king-size bed and shower-only bathroom. Overall, guests report that the staff couldn't be more friendly and helpful.

MGM houses a prestigious assemblage of dining rooms, among them **Joël Robuchon's** two new sterling entries, **Wolfgang Puck Bar & Grill,** and **Emeril's New Orleans Fish House.** These, along with buffet offerings and the **Rainforest Cafe,** are reviewed in chapter 5.

As befits a behemoth of this size, there's an appropriately gigantic casino. The show is *KÀ,* a dazzling offering from Cirque du Soleil. Plus, there's **MGM Grand's *Crazy Horse Paris,*** a very adult topless show; a hot lounge, **Tabú;** nightclub **Studio 54;** a headliner showroom; and a larger events arena that hosts sporting events and bigger concerts. See chapter 9 for details on all the nightlife options. The **Lion Habitat** is reviewed on p. 180.

The MGM Grand's **Grand Spa** 𝄞𝄞 is a Zen-Asian minimalist wonder, all natural stone and aged wood. The services offered are quite marvelous, with everything from standard massages to 2-hour "rituals" in a private room for over $300. The state-of-the-art health club is larger than most, with some serious machines, including ones equipped with fancy computer video monitors. It'll cost you $25 to work up a sweat here most of the day, but you can use the gym facilities only, without the whirlpools and other amenities of the spa, for $15 after 6pm.

The swimming pool area is a rousing success. The 6½ acres of landscaped grounds feature five pools, including the longest lazy river in town (though we wish portions of it weren't closed off for non-summer months). They've recently added a "pool club"—sort of like a nightclub but during the day—called Wet Republic, which only further pushes kids out of the picture.

Note that the MGM Grand has its own separate, non-casino, all-suite addition called **The Signature.** Prices are a bit high for what you get, but if money is not an issue, and a more grown-up atmosphere is, you might want to inquire.

3799 Las Vegas Blvd. S. (at Tropicana Ave.), Las Vegas, NV 89109. ℂ **800/929-1111** or 702/891-7777. Fax 702/891-1030. www.mgmgrand.com. 5,034 units. $99 and up standard double; $159 and up suite. Extra person $30. Children 12 and under stay free in parent's room. AE, DC, DISC, MC, V. Free self- and valet parking. **Amenities:** 15 restaurants; nightclub; casino; events arena; showroom; Lion Habitat, cabaret theater; 2 wedding chapels; 5 outdoor pools w/lazy river; large health club; spa; Jacuzzi; video-game arcade; concierge; tour desk; car-rental desk; business center; shopping arcade; salon; 24-hr. room service; in-room massage; laundry service; dry cleaning; executive-level rooms. *In room:* A/C, TV w/pay movies, dataport, high-speed Internet access (for a fee), hair dryer, iron/ironing board, safe.

Monte Carlo Resort & Casino 𝄞 A dramatic fire in 2008 charred the top of part of the Monte Carlo, but the hotel has not only fully recovered, it's using the incident as an excuse for long-overdue room makeovers. By the time that's done, in mid-2009, this should once again be a viable Strip location. When it was built, the massive Monte Carlo was the world's seventh-largest hotel. It's now considerably overshadowed by its high-profile, all the more luxe-intensive brethren. Entering it is still nice, as it comes off as a European casino hotel alternative, replete with Corinthian colonnades, triumphal arches, and big and busy statuary, with an entranceway opening onto a bustling casino. A separate entrance in the rear of the hotel leads to a splendid marble-floored, crystal-chandeliered lobby evocative of a European grand hotel. We love that the guest rooms are accessible without going through the casino, but we don't really love the rooms themselves, since they are smaller than what we've grown accustomed to, especially in terms of bathroom square-footage. Still, the revamp should help. The pool area, once the very last word in local pool fun, is now put to shame by better versions (including superior lazy rivers) at Mandalay Bay and the MGM Grand. It does have a number of child-/family-/budget-friendly restaurants. Note that it's right in the path of the massive CityCenter construction and so the noise from that could be a factor during your stay.

The **Monte Carlo Pub & Brewery, Dragon Noodle Co.,** and **buffet** are described in chapter 5. In addition, there is a highly recommended branch of the classic Downtown French restaurant **Andre's** (p. 160). There's also a large and overly ornate casino, plus a lavish showroom that currently hosts the recommended show by magician **Lance Burton** (p. 249).

Monte Carlo's health club and spa are nothing special and at $23 a day, not cheap.

3770 Las Vegas Blvd. S. (btw. Flamingo Rd. and Tropicana Ave.), Las Vegas, NV 89109. © **800/311-8999** or 702/730-7777. Fax 702/730-7250. www.montecarlo.com. 3,002 units. $99 and up double; $145 and up suite. Extra person $25. No discount for children. AE, DC, DISC, MC, V. Free self- and valet parking. **Amenities:** 7 restaurants; food court; casino; showroom; wedding chapel; outdoor pool w/wave pool and lazy river; health club; spa; Jacuzzi; watersports equipment/rentals; video-game arcade; concierge; tour desk; business center; shopping arcade; salon; 24-hr. room service; laundry service; dry cleaning; executive-level rooms. *In room:* A/C, TV w/pay movies, dataport, high-speed Internet access (for a fee), hair dryer, iron/ironing board.

New York–New York Hotel & Casino 🐨🐨 *Kids*   Isn't this exactly the kind of hotel you think about—or dream about or fear—when you think "Las Vegas"? There it is, a jumbled pile mock-up of the venerable Manhattan skyline—the Empire State Building, the Chrysler Building, the Public Library—all crammed together, along with the 150-foot Statue of Liberty and Ellis Island, all built to approximately one-third scale. And as if that weren't enough, they threw in a roller coaster running around the outside and into the hotel and casino itself.

And inside, it all gets better. There are details everywhere—so many, in fact, that the typical expression on the face of casino-goers is slack-jawed wonder. If you enter the casino via the Brooklyn Bridge (the walkway from the Strip), you'll find yourself in a replica of Greenwich Village, down to the cobblestones, the manhole covers, the tenement-style buildings, and the graffiti. (Yes, they even re-created that. You should see the subway station.) The reception area and lobby are done in an Art Deco, golden-age-of-Manhattan style; you'll feel like breaking into a 1930s musical number while standing there. It's a *wow!* all right. The word "subtle" was obviously not in the lexicon of the designers. We will leave it to you to decide, based on your own aesthetic values, if all this is a good or bad thing. Let's just say that to us, it's very, very good indeed. This is exactly what we come to Vegas for—unbridled, unrepentant, theme-gone-wild.

Upstairs—oh, yes, there's much more—is the arcade, which is Coney Island–themed (naturally), and just as crowded as the real thing. Kids play boardwalk games in the hopes of winning tickets redeemable for cheap prizes. (You're never too young to start learning about gambling.) The line for the roller coaster starts here. There are many restaurants, all housed in buildings that fit the theme of whatever New York neighborhood is represented in that particular part of the hotel.

Rooms are housed in different towers, each with a New York–inspired name. The place is so massive and mazelike that finding your way to your room can take a while. There are 64 different layouts for the rooms, which are currently undergoing their third makeover, probably moving them ever farther from the original Deco-inspired decor to something bland. Still, they should be comfortable, and though the bathrooms are small, they are done in a pleasing gray marble. There can be a looooonnnggg walk from the elevators, so if you have ambulatory issues, you had best mention this while booking. Rooms in the single digits seem to be in the Empire Tower, if that helps give you a clue to location. Light sleepers should request a room away from the roller coaster. The health club and spa just got an expensive new makeover and are much larger. The mediocre pool is right next to the parking structure.

In addition to a particularly nice food court and a number of more-than-decent restaurants, including reliable Italian chain Il Fornaio, there are several festive and beautifully decorated bars throughout the property. **Coyote Ugly** is a party-hearty bar where dancing on furniture is encouraged and the female bartenders are hired just to be sassy. At **The Bar at Times Square,** dueling pianos set the mood for a lively neighborhood bar conviviality. This is home to the topless and adults-only Cirque du Soleil production *Zumanity,* which we think is overrated. Chapter 9 offers more on the hotel's nightlife.

The main casino area is done as Central Park, complete with trees, babbling brooks, streetlamps, and footbridges. The change carts are little yellow cabs.

3790 Las Vegas Blvd. S. (at Tropicana Ave.), Las Vegas, NV 89109. © **800/693-6763** or 702/740-6969. Fax 702/740-6920. www.nynyhotelcasino.com. 2,023 units. $79 and up double. Extra person $30. No discount for children. AE, DC, DISC, MC, V. Free self- and valet parking. **Amenities:** 7 restaurants; food court; casino; showrooms; outdoor pool; health club; spa; Jacuzzi; video-game arcade w/midway games; tour desk; business center; salon; 24-hr. room service; laundry service; dry cleaning; executive-level rooms. *In room:* A/C, TV w/pay movies, dataport, high-speed Internet access (for a fee), hair dryer, iron/ironing board, safe.

Planet Hollywood Resort & Casino 🏝🏝

We were sad when the once fairy-tale fantastic Aladdin was purchased by Planet Hollywood—it was the end of yet another era. Sure, today's Aladdin wasn't the same building where Elvis married 'Scilla, but even so. But thanks to that same Planet Hollywood and its memorabilia gimmick, the rooms are currently the most distinctive in town. *Note:* At press time, the rooms were still undergoing makeovers, so you should be careful to request a remodeled unit.

The reconstructed Strip entrance, heavy on the LED screens (it's supposed to evoke the visual mania of Times Square), certainly makes the interior easier to access than the last incarnation of Aladdin. Inside, those looking for the pop kitsch sensibility of the Planet Hollywood restaurants will be disappointed; it's actually kind of classy and design intensive. But you are going to come here for the rooms. Each has a movie or entertainment theme, such as *Pulp Fiction,* which might have John Travolta's suit in a glass case and a glass coffee table filled with more original memorabilia from the film. Although more than one room may share the same movie theme, no two rooms will have the same objects. The vibe of the room can vary radically depending on if the theme is Judy Garland in some charming musical or Wesley Snipes in *Blade,* so ask when booking. As gimmicks go, it's a catchy one, and a good use for all that junk the company's accumulated over the years. Beds have purple-velour padded headboards and the beds themselves are the Sheraton Four Comforts pillow-top thing, and mighty darn comfortable at that. Bathrooms are larger than standard but neither the largest on the Strip nor special enough to match the sleeping areas.

Note: The parking lot is all the way on the other side of the Miracle Mile shopping area, thus requiring guests to drag their suitcases all the way through the mall and a good chunk of the hotel before getting to registration. It's a very, very long and unpleasant schlep. Do not self-park here if you have mobility issues of any kind. Instead, follow the signs for casino (as opposed to mall) valet parking, which is right outside the front desk.

Restaurants include their massively popular 24-hour coffee shop Planet Daily, a Trader Vic's (just in time for the original to close forever), P.F. Chang's, Striphouse (a New York steakhouse with a bordello theme), and the Earl of Sandwich, from the very same noble family that lent its name to the food, which in fact is what the cafe is serving.

And then there is the **Miracle Mile** shopping area (p. 232), winding its way in a giant horseshoe shape around the property, another one to rival the capitalist ventures over at Caesars and The Venetian. This also has a new owner (separate from Planet Hollywood), and while we resent its makeover from the aesthetically delightful Casbah theme to a much more generic upscale mall, as a shopping and dining option, it's still tops. The hotel also has its own arena, the **Center for the Performing Arts,** which is attracting big names back to Vegas. Finally, there is the **Mandera spa** ✸✸✸, maybe aesthetically our hands-down local favorite. The designers went to Morocco for ideas, and it shows in this Medina-flavored facility; just looking at it is pampering, and that's before one of their attentive staff puts you in a wrap and "dry float" (a womblike water bed–style cradle).

3667 Las Vegas Blvd. S., Las Vegas, NV 89109. ✆ 877/333-9474 or 702/785-5555. Fax 702/785-5558. www.planet hollywoodresort.com. 2,600 units. $99 and up double. Extra person $30. No discount for children. AE, DC, DISC, MC, V. Free self- and valet parking. **Amenities:** 19 restaurants; 7 bars/lounges; casino; performing-arts center; showroom; wedding chapel; 2 outdoor pools; health club; spa; 2 Jacuzzis; concierge; tour desk; car-rental desk; business center; extensive shopping arcade; 24-hr. room service; in-room massage; laundry service; dry cleaning; executive-level rooms. *In room:* A/C, TV w/pay movies, dataport, Wi-Fi (for a fee), hair dryer, iron/ironing board, safe.

THEhotel at Mandalay Bay ✸✸✸　The rather silly nomenclature of this utterly fabulous Vegas accommodation reminds us of our previous consideration regarding the Four Seasons' relationship with Mandalay Bay (located on the top floors but operated as a separate entity)—it's part *of* the hotel but not precisely *the* hotel. In this case, this really is *THE*hotel, in all senses, not the least of which is that even though we were quite fond of Mandalay Bay prior to the opening of this conjoined twin of a property, we now think of it as the frowzy sister from the sticks who looks tawdry and rumpled next to its sleek *Vogue*-magazine-editor sibling. (Actually, we still like Mandalay Bay a great deal.) Yes, if Prada were a hotel, it would look something like THEhotel. Certainly, if there are Prada wearers in town, we bet they are going to be staying here.

The new trend in Vegas hotels seems to be hotels that allow you, if you so choose, to forget you are in Vegas. Never mind that psychology. What that translates to here is an entirely separate entrance and an entirely different atmosphere. This is not a casino hotel—though it is connected to one by a long hallway—but a world of sleek towering walls of lighting, ambiguous modern art, and both guests and employees in head-to-toe black. Like any good Vegas hotel, it wows you from the start, but not in the usual Vegas marble-gilt-and-chandelier screaming over the top "look-how-you-can-live-if-only-you-hit-that-jackpot-over-there" way, but in a way that coolly says, "You probably already live like this, don't you?" while handing you a nicely chilled Cosmopolitan. In other words, this isn't Donald Trump's version of the best, but rather that of Mr. Big from *Sex and the City.* Don't get us wrong, everything here is still out-of-proportion large, but it's sophisticated and chic, all blacks, tans, woods, and mid-century modern sharp lines. We fell for it instantly, and that's before we went to our room.

Ah, the rooms: Every one is a genuine suite (not just separated living room and bedroom, but even a wet bar and second water closet), done in more black, tans, and gleaming woods, like your professionally decorated Manhattan dream apartment. There are plasma-screen TVs in every room, including the enormous marble bathroom, where the tub is so deep, the water comes up to your chin when you sit down. Bathroom amenities are posh, the comforters are down, and the sheets—well, remember our complaints about how you just can't get good sheets in big hotels? Feel the soft heft of these. *That's* what we want. Two complaints might be the excess of mirrors (the wall-length double closet and TV cabinet are covered in them, as is another wall) and the overall lack of good lighting. But seriously, you won't care. For once, a hotel room in Vegas designed to make you want to stay put. Not that you have to; as stated, all the amenities of Mandalay Bay (their incredible pool area, a number of terrific restaurants) are just down a long hall, though the instant you step from this grown-up world

(Kids Family-Friendly Hotels

We've said it before, and we'll say it again: Vegas is simply not a good place to bring your kids. Most of the major hotels have backed away from being perceived as places for families, no longer offering babysitting, much less exciting children's activities. Further, fewer hotels offer discounts for children staying in parents' rooms, and many of the others have lowered the age for children staying free.

In addition to the suggestions below, you might consider choosing a non-casino hotel, particularly a reliable chain, and a place with kitchenettes.

- **Circus Circus Hotel & Casino** (p. 97)   Centrally located on the Strip, this is our first choice if you're traveling with the kids. The hotel's mezzanine level offers ongoing circus acts daily from 11am to midnight, dozens of carnival games, and an arcade. And behind the hotel is a full amusement park.
- **Excalibur** (p. 72)   Though the sword-and-sorcery theme has been considerably toned down, Excalibur features an entire floor of midway games, a large video-game arcade, and more. It also has some child-oriented eateries and shows. It also now has a heavily promoted male-stripper show, though, so it's not perfect.
- **Four Seasons** (p. 62)   For free goodies, service, and general child pampering, the costly Four Seasons is probably worth the dough. Your kids will be spoiled!
- **Mandalay Bay** (p. 66)   Mandalay Bay certainly looks grown-up, but it has a number of factors that make it family friendly: good-size rooms, to start, which you do not have to cross a casino to access; a variety of restaurants; a family-appropriate show; a big ol' shark attraction; and,

into the world of, well, noisy grown-up pursuits, which isn't the same thing at all, you might well want to turn right back around.

Having raved about it all, we do have some complaints. The staff are hardly cuddly, and service reflects that. Costs at the sleek cafes are higher than even the usual elevated hotel restaurant prices. Then again, you can use just the workout facilities at the **Bathhouse Spa** ★★, the rather unfortunately named but gorgeous health club and spa, for only $20 (cheap compared to other comparable hotels, though it's $30 if you also want to use the saunas and the like). This is the place we would splash out on (and certainly would leap on any specials offered), but with the understanding that it's still, despite appearances, a Vegas hotel, though very likely the best there is.

3950 Las Vegas Blvd. S., Las Vegas, NV 89119. ℭ **877/632-7800** or 702/632-7777. Fax 702/632-9215. www.thehotel atmandalaybay.com. 1,120 units. $160 and up suite. Extra person $30. Children 13 and under stay free in parent's room. AE, DC, DISC, MC, V. Free self- and valet parking. **Amenities:** 2 restaurants; bar; access to Mandalay Bay restaurants/pool/casino; health club; spa; tour desk; car-rental desk; business center; 24-hr. room service; laundry service; dry-cleaning service. *In room:* A/C, 3 flatscreen TVs, CD/DVD player, Wi-Fi (for a fee), wet bar, hair dryer, iron/ironing board.

MODERATE
Excalibur ★ (Kids   One of the largest resort hotels in the world, Excalibur (also known as the Realm) is a gleaming white, turreted castle complete with moat, drawbridge,

best of all, the swimming area—wave pool, sandy beach, lazy river, lots of other pools—fun in the Vegas sun!

- **MGM Grand** (p. 67)   While decidedly no longer targeted toward families—their high-profile nudie show *Crazy Horse Paris!* should be your tip-off—MGM Grand is still frequented by families, thanks to an excellent swimming pool area, a decent arcade, and other goodies.
- **New York–New York** (p. 69)   Overstimulating and hectic, for sure, but between the roller coaster and the Coney Island–style midway, not to mention just looking around, this has options for children (though going almost anywhere requires walking through the casino).
- **Orleans** (p. 76)   With some kid-friendly possibilities (a bowling alley and movie theaters), a not particularly lascivious environment, and at a distance from the decidedly lascivious Strip, the Orleans is a viable family-appropriate hotel, with something for each age range—including a casino for those of age and desire.
- **Ritz-Carlton, Lake Las Vegas** (p. 111)   Like the Four Seasons, it's costly, but with so many recreational activities and the Lake Las Vegas setting (well out of the way of the path of Sin City), it offers a lot over the regular Vegas resorts.
- **Stratosphere Las Vegas Hotel & Casino** (p. 96)   For families looking for reasonably priced, if not particularly exciting, digs, this is a good choice. Plus, it's not in the middle of the Strip action, so you and your kids can avoid that. Thus far it's not moving in the "adult entertainment" direction, and it has thrill rides at the top.

battlements, and lofty towers. And it's huger than huge. To heck with quiet good taste; kitsch is cool. And it's becoming harder and harder to find in a town that once wore tacky proudly. If your soul is secretly thrilled by overblown fantasy locations—or if you just want a pretty good budget option on the Strip—the Excalibur is still here for you. And yet, we just know that any minute now, the Lords of Taste will bring an end to its sword and sorcery imagery. Actually, the decorating fairies have already made some quiet changes (the deep reds in the public areas have been switched to creams) but nothing that really sullies the silliness. There are some ominous rumblings in keeping with the rest of Vegas's careening away from the "family-friendly" image—gone is the animatronic dragon and wizard show out front, and inside there is a male-stripper act, *Thunder from Down Under*. It's really too bad because, without the excess, this is just another hotel—a mighty big and chaotic hotel, thanks to a sprawling casino full of families and small-time gamblers, which is located smack dab in the middle of everything, including, naturally, the path between you and the elevators to your room.

Newly redone rooms only slightly reflect the Olde English theme and feature the brown suede headboards that are all the rage, flatscreen TVs, spiffed-up bathrooms with new marble fixtures, and nice wallpaper. Guests who have stayed in Tower 2 have complained about the noise from the roller coaster across the street at New York–New York (it runs till 11pm, so early birds should probably ask to be put in a different part of the hotel). Frankly, we prefer stopping in for a visit rather than actually settling here, but we know single-minded others (read: Vegas is for gambling, and so is the majority of the vacation budget) who wouldn't consider staying anywhere else.

The second floor holds the Medieval Village, where Excalibur's restaurants and shops are peppered along winding streets and alleyways, a sort of permanent Renaissance Faire, which could be reason enough to stay away (or to come). Up here you can access the enclosed, air-conditioned, moving sidewalk that connects with the Luxor. The pool area is getting a face-lift to add in better landscaping, fancy cabanas, and the like. There are plenty of restaurants, including **The Roundtable Buffet** (p. 164), and a pretty good prime rib joint. **Dick's Last Resort** and the buffet are reviewed in chapter 5. Excalibur won our hearts forever by installing a branch of Krispy Kreme Doughnuts on the second level, on the way to the Luxor walkway. The *Tournament of Kings* (p. 254) is a medieval-style dinner show, and there's a very loud, claustrophobic casino.

3850 Las Vegas Blvd. S. (at Tropicana Ave.), Las Vegas, NV 89109. (© **800/937-7777** or 702/597-7700. Fax 702/597-7163. www.excalibur.com. 4,008 units. $59 and up double. Extra person $20. Children 12 and under stay free in parent's room. AE, DC, DISC, MC, V. Free self- and valet parking. **Amenities:** 5 restaurants; food court; casino; showrooms; wedding chapel; outdoor pools; video-game arcade; concierge; tour desk; car-rental desk; shopping arcade; 24-hr. room service; laundry service; dry cleaning. *In room:* A/C, TV w/pay movies, dataport, high-speed Internet access (for a fee), hair dryer, iron/ironing board.

Luxor Las Vegas ✷✷   Kitsch-worshippers were dealt a blow when the people behind this hotel came to the inexplicable decision to eliminate anything Egypt from it, casting aside identity in favor of generic luxury. Obviously, they can't get rid of certain elements—the main hotel is, after all, a 30-story onyx-hued pyramid, complete with a really tall 315,000-watt light beam at the top. (Luxor says that's because the Egyptians believed their souls would travel up to heaven in a beam of light. We think it's really because it gives them something to brag about: "The most powerful beam on Earth!") Replicas of Cleopatra's Needle and the Sphinx still dominate the exterior. But other than that, by some point in 2009, every other trace of the land of the Pharaohs will be gone. And some magic will be gone from Vegas. Now guests will be attracted only by the generally good prices, not by the giddy fun the theme produced. That is, unless said price rises in accordance with the place's lofty ambitions.

But they can't take away fundamentals and so staying in the pyramid part means you get to ride the 39-degree high-speed *inclinators*—that's what an elevator is when it works inside a pyramid. Really, they are part conveyance, part thrill ride—check out that jolt when they come to a halt. Rooms are scheduled for an overhaul throughout 2009, at which point all the Egypt details will be gone. You might want to grab one of the older ones while you can, unless you prefer the comfort the new rooms will doubtless provide. Rooms in the pyramid open onto the vast center that contains the casino—indeed, ground-level rooms open more or less right into the action (though many of these have been turned into offices), so if you want only a short drunken stumble back to your room, these are for you. Otherwise, ask for a room higher up. Marvelous views are offered through the slanted windows (the higher up, the better, of course), but the bathrooms are shower-only, no tubs. Bathrooms are better in the Tower rooms, including deep tubs. Decor renovations will produce more cookie-cutter blandness, though doubtless there will be welcome upgrades to the furnishings.

MORE, The Buffet at Luxor (p. 165), offers a cool archaeological-dig atmosphere. **Criss Angel: Believe** pairs the popular exotic magician with the spectacle of Cirque du Soleil (p. 247). Comedian Carrot Top is also in residency. Enormous nightclub LAX is state of the art, and attracting a fashionable crowd. Two notable attractions here are **Titanic: The Exhibition** (p. 183) and **Bodies: The Exhibition** (p. 174).

3900 Las Vegas Blvd. S. (btw. Reno and Hacienda aves.), Las Vegas, NV 81119. (C) **888/777-0188** or 702/262-4000. Fax 702/262-4478. www.luxor.com. 4,400 units. $69 and up double; $150 and up whirlpool suite; $249–$800 other suites. Extra person $30. Children 11 and under stay free in parent's room. AE, DC, DISC, MC, V. Free self- and valet parking. **Amenities:** 7 restaurants; food court; nightclub; casino; showrooms; 5 outdoor pools; health club; spa; 18,000-sq.-ft. video-game arcade; concierge; tour desk; car-rental desk; business center; shopping arcade; 24-hr. room service; dry cleaning; executive-level rooms. *In room:* A/C, TV w/pay movies, dataport, Wi-Fi (for a fee), hair dryer, iron/ironing board.

South Point ★★ *(Value)* Including the South Point in the South Strip category stretches the definition almost to the breaking point. Located about 6 miles south of Mandalay Bay, it is still on Las Vegas Boulevard but certainly not within walking distance to anything else of interest except for maybe a convenience store. Still, this hotel is a worthwhile addition both to the city and to this category, offering an "expensive" level of accommodations at a "moderate" price.

South Point follows the same formula established by its ancestors: nice rooms at reasonable costs; plenty of low-priced food outlets; tons of entertainment options, including movie theaters, a bowling alley, and more; and a massive casino with lower-than-average limits on everything from slots to craps tables. There's also a giant Equestrian Center out back, large enough for just about any rodeo, complete with air-conditioned horse stalls and a pen for thousands of head of cattle. A unique offering to be sure, but we'd recommend you choose a nonevent time to stay here, if possible, because no matter how much odor-absorbing wood chips you throw at them, 2,000 head of cattle emit a less-than-pleasant odor that may make an afternoon by the pool rather unenjoyable.

The overall scheme is Southern California modern, with plenty of sunny paint schemes and airy architectural details. Think Santa Barbara instead of Hollywood, and you're probably in the ballpark. Rooms are large and aesthetically pleasing, each over 500 square feet and crammed full of expensive and luxurious furnishings, 42-inch plasma televisions, and all the other pampering amenities one would expect in a room three times the price. Seriously, a weekend rate check had rooms here at $125 per night, while Bellagio and Wynn were well over $400. Although we wouldn't put these rooms on quite the same level as the ones at those two ultraluxe establishments, we have a hard time coming up with a $275 amount of difference. Venerable local restaurant Michael's recently relocated here, along with a number of other new restaurants, and a tower expansion should be completed by the end of 2008.

9777 Las Vegas Blvd. S., Las Vegas, NV 89183. (C) **866/796-7111** or 702/796-7111. Fax 702/365-7505. www.southpoint casino.com. 1,350 units. $79 and up double. Extra person $20. Children 5 and under stay free in parent's room. AE, DC, DISC, MC, V. Free self- and valet parking. **Amenities:** 6 restaurants; casino; 16-screen movie theater; 70-lane bowling center; 4,400-seat equestrian and events center; outdoor pool; spa; concierge; free shuttle service to Mandalay Bay; 24-hr. room service; dry cleaning. *In room:* A/C, TV w/pay movies, dataport, Wi-Fi (for a fee), hair dryer, iron/ironing board.

Tropicana Resort & Casino Thanks to a combination of factors, the Trop's future has been in flux for years, with the result that little has been done to this hotel for much too long. Staying here is advisable only if location and price are more important to you than upkeep. But as a result, we can't say precisely what you are going to get when you come here, and it should be understood that any Trop attractions referenced in the rest of this book could be gone by the time you read this. In the meantime, rooms are basically clean '70s motel rooms, but a little bit nicer. You are better off staying in the Trop's Paradise Tower, where the rooms are slightly bigger and much easier on the eyes—mock provincial, to be sure (check out the plaster molding and ceiling cornices—a curious and welcome little touch). Bathrooms are also bigger here, but dull, except for the ones with Jacuzzis. The pool area is one of the best around and is the place's biggest draw. Note, however, that their touted swim-up blackjack is seasonal (read: summer only). The showroom currently hosts the **Folies Bergere** revue (p. 248).

3801 Las Vegas Blvd. S. (at Tropicana Ave.), Las Vegas, NV 89109. ✆ **888/826-8767** or 702/739-2222. Fax 702/739-2469. www.tropicanalv.com. 1,878 units. $79 and up double. Extra person $25. Children 11 and under stay free in parent's room. AE, DC, DISC, MC, V. Free self- and valet parking. **Amenities:** 6 restaurants; 3 outdoor pools; casino; showrooms; wedding chapel; small health club; spa; video-game arcade; tour desk; car-rental desk; business center; salon; barber shop; laundry service; dry cleaning; executive-level rooms. *In room:* A/C, TV w/pay movies, dataport, Wi-Fi (for a fee), fridge (in some), hair dryer, iron/ironing board, safe.

INEXPENSIVE

Orleans 🎿 *Value* *Kids*   The Orleans is a little out of the way, and there is virtually nothing around it, but with an 18-screen movie complex, complete with a food court and day-care center, a bowling alley (that keeps ridiculously late hours; we know more than one recent guest who found a 3am game just the right way to wind down after a hectic clubbing night), and a 9,000-seat arena for a minor-league hockey team (but also available for concerts and the like), this is a reasonable alternative to staying on the hectic Strip. Plus, there is a shuttle that runs continuously to the Gold Coast, Sam's Town, and Suncoast. The facade is aggressively fake New Orleans, more reminiscent of Disneyland than the actual Big Easy. Inside, it's much the same.

As long as prices hold true (as always, they can vary), this hotel is one of the best bargains in town, despite the location, though the staff can be rotten, which can seriously sour a bargain experience (on the other hand, room service seems fine). The rooms are nice enough and have a definite New Orleans–French feel. Each is L-shaped, with a seating alcove by the windows, and comes complete with an old-fashioned, overstuffed chair and sofa. The beds have brass headboards, the lamps (including some funky iron floor lamps) look antique, and lace curtains flutter at the windows. The one drawback is that all these furnishings, and the busy floral decorating theme, make the rooms seem crowded (particularly down by the seating area in front of the bathrooms). Still, it's meant to evoke a cozy, warm Victorian parlor, which traditionally is very overcrowded, so maybe it's successful after all. The hotel has your basic Vegas-type places to eat. Worth noting are **Big Al's Oyster Bar,** a not-unauthentic Creole/Cajun–themed restaurant, and **Don Miguel's,** a basic but satisfying Mexican restaurant that makes its own tortillas while you watch. There are several bars, including one with live music at night. The **Orleans Showroom** is an 827-seat theater featuring live entertainment, the **Orleans Arena** is a large facility for concerts and sporting events, and, of course, there's a casino.

4500 W. Tropicana Ave. (west of the Strip and I-15), Las Vegas, NV 89103. ✆ **800/675-3267** or 702/365-7111. Fax 702/365-7505. www.orleanscasino.com. 1,886 units. $59 and up double; $185 and up suites. AE, DC, DISC, MC, V. Free self- and valet parking. **Amenities:** 12 restaurants; casino; showroom; 9,000-seat arena; 18-screen movie theater; 70-lane bowling center; 2 outdoor pools; health club; spa; children's center offering amusements and day care for kids 3–12; video-game arcade; concierge; tour desk; car-rental desk; 24-hr. room service; laundry service; dry cleaning; executive-level rooms. *In room:* A/C, TV w/pay movies, dataport, Wi-Fi (for a fee), hair dryer, iron/ironing board.

4 Mid-Strip

VERY EXPENSIVE

Bellagio ★★   This is the luxury resort that ushered in the new post-Vegas-is-for-families elegance epoch, and it was so successful that many of its attributes can now be found, in varying forms, up the street at the Wynn resort. It's hard not to compare the two, and which you prefer will depend on your aesthetics. We give the edge to Bellagio because even though it is not as theme-intensive as it could be, it still has some elements drawn from its charming Lake Como village namesake, and we do prefer even our resorts to have some of old school Vegas silliness, however slight. In this case, it's an 8-acre Lake Como stand-in out front, complete with a dazzling choreographed water-ballet extravaganza, plus a representation of an Italian lakeside village, while the pool area is sort of Hearst Castle Romanesque. However, don't think this is much like a getaway to a peaceful, romantic Italian village because it's not. But it is exactly like going to a big, grand, state-of-the-art Vegas hotel. To expect more probably isn't fair, but then again, they tried to set the tone with dreamy, soft-focus TV ads aired when the hotel debuted. Nothing with a casino stuck in the middle of it can be that serene and restful.

But does it work as a luxury hotel? Sort of. It certainly is much closer to a European casino hotel than a Vegas one. Fabulous touches abound, including a lobby that's unlike any other in Vegas. It's not just grand, with marble and an eye-popping Dale Chihuly blown-glass flower sculpture on the ceiling (the largest of its kind in the world), but it's also brave with plants, natural lighting, and actual seating. There's also a downright lovely conservatory, complete with a 100-year-old fountain stuffed full of gorgeous, brightly colored flowers and plants, preposterously (and delightfully) changed every few weeks to go with the season (yellows and whites for Easter, for example, though we could have done without the ginormous animatronic bald eagle chicks as part of the extremely gaudy July 4th decor)—it's one of the sweetest spots in all of Vegas.

On the downside, you still can't avoid a walk through the casino to get just about anywhere (with the inevitable ruckus shattering your blissful state every time you exit the elevators from your room). At least the casino is laid out in an easy-to-navigate grid with wide aisles. (*Tip:* Black floral carpets indicate the main casino paths.) Another downside is that there are hidden charges galore, such as a pricey fee for the spa, another one for poolside cabanas. The rooms are quite nice, better than ever thanks to a recent redo that changed the colors from the usual resort-sand to a more cosmopolitan look with handsome sage greens and dark woods, but given the relatively puny size, it may still not be enough for the price. Having said that, you can find deals on Bellagio's website, depending on day of week and time of year. Furnishings are plush (good, cushy beds with quality linens, comfy chairs), the roomy bathrooms even more so (marble and glass plus good-smelling soap and hair dryers—it works every time), but it's all just a busier and slightly more luxurious variation on what's found over at TI–Treasure Island. Strip-side rooms, while featuring a much-desired view of the hotel's dancing water fountains (see below), don't quite muffle the booms the fountains make as they explode (although we didn't find it annoying). Rooms in the newer Spa Tower are more desirable if you want a shorter walk to the pool and the gym and spa areas (guests in the original building will have a long jog around the casino perimeter instead), but only a "partial" (read: a bit set back with a parking lot in the foreground) view of the fountains. Note that a channel on the TV will play the songs as the fountains dance because you can't quite hear the music from your room. Still, service is top-notch, despite the size of the place; the staff is eager to please and nonpatronizing.

Meanwhile, many of the better restaurants are found in Bellagio. Full reviews of **Picasso, Le Cirque, Circo, Michael Mina, Fix, Sensi, Jean-Philippe Patisserie,** and **Olives** are found in chapter 5, as is a review of the **Bellagio Buffet.** And the man who brought us a free pirate show and a volcano explosion now brings us a **water ballet** ✫✫✫, courtesy of a dancing fountain with jets timed to a rotating list of songs (everything from pop to Sinatra to Broadway to opera). This sounds cheesy, but it absolutely is not. It's really quite delightful and even witty (no, really) and is the best free show in Vegas (p. 178).

Bellagio also features an upscale casino and ***O*** (p. 245), one of the most incredible shows yet from Cirque du Soleil. Bellagio is also home to **Petrossian Bar** (see chapter 9), and **The Bank,** a high-end nightclub.

The hotel's pool area has skidded to the top of our favorites list; it boasts six swimming pools (two heated year-round and two with fountains) geometrically set in a neoclassical Roman garden, with flowered, trellised archways and Italian opera piped in over the sound system. The Grand Patio could have come right off a movie set (pillars, domes, you get the idea). A more sophisticated environment than the tropical party over at The Mirage (our other favorite), it is surely the sort of place where thonged model types hang out with moneyed Eurotrash—it comes off as *that* chic.

The **health club** is marvelous, large, and well stocked with top-of-the-line machines, with natural light coming in through windows to the outside world, but at $25 a pop, it's pretty pricey if all you want is a simple session on a treadmill (though with your fee, you are allowed to return throughout the day for additional soakings/steamings/workouts). Attendants ply you with iced towels and drinks. The **spa** ✫✫ is not quite as pretty as some others around town, but it does offer a full range of pricey treatments and has a serene soaking area, with plunge pools ranging in temperature from icy to boiling. In addition to drinks and snacks, smoothies are sometimes offered—take one.

The shopping area, called **Via Bellagio,** features all the stores that advertise in color in glossy magazines: Tiffany, Armani, Gucci, Prada, Hermès, and the like. There's also an **art gallery** (p. 173) that boasts enough highly regarded works to draw some million visitors a year.

What does all this add up to? As good as a casino-hotel can provide and perform the duties of a luxury resort experience, certainly. If it doesn't quite work, that's probably more the fault of the initial concept than the hotel itself.

3600 Las Vegas Blvd. S. (at the corner of Flamingo Rd.), Las Vegas, NV 89109. ℂ **888/987-6667** or 702/693-7111. Fax 702/693-8546. www.bellagio.com. 3,933 units. $169 and up double, $450 and up suites. Extra person $35. No discount for children. AE, DC, DISC, MC, V. Free self- and valet parking. **Amenities:** 14 restaurants; nightclub; casino; showrooms; wedding chapel; 6 outdoor pools; large health club; spa; concierge; tour desk; car-rental desk; business center; elegant shopping arcade; salon; 24-hr. room service; in-room massage; laundry service; dry cleaning; executive-level rooms. *In room:* A/C, TV w/pay movies, dataport, high-speed Internet access (for a fee), hair dryer, iron/ironing board, safe.

Caesars Palace ✫✫   Since 1966, Caesars has stood simultaneously as the ultimate in Vegas luxury and the nadir (or pinnacle, depending on your values) of Las Vegas cheese. It's the most Vegas-style hotel you'll find, covering all the bases from the tacky fabulous schmaltz of the recent past to the current trend in high-end luxury.

Mid-Strip Accommodations

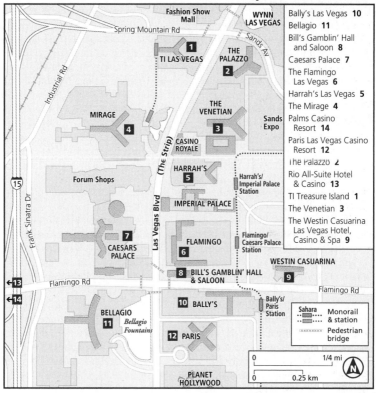

Bally's Las Vegas **10**

Bellagio **11**

Bill's Gamblin' Hall and Saloon **8**

Caesars Palace **7**

The Flamingo Las Vegas **6**

Harrah's Las Vegas **5**

The Mirage **4**

Palms Casino Resort **14**

Paris Las Vegas Casino Resort **12**

The Palazzo **2**

Rio All-Suite Hotel & Casino **13**

TI Treasure Island **1**

The Venetian **3**

The Westin Casuarina Las Vegas Hotel, Casino & Spa **9**

When Caesars was originally built to reflect Roman decadence, its designers probably had no idea how guffaw-inducing this would be some years later. It's the level of kitsch all should aspire to: Roman colonnades, Roman pillars, gigantic faux-marble Roman statues, staff attired in gladiator outfits—it's splendidly ridiculous. It's what Vegas ought to be.

But all things change, and Caesars was outshined over the years by more modern glamour. And frankly, that facade was looking dated 2 decades ago. Never one to rest on any kind of laurels, Roman or otherwise, Caesars gave itself a massive face-lift and keeps on building and expanding. Never fear, the Roman statues still remain, as do the toga-clad cocktail waitresses, and so does the Caesars giggle factor (it's still pretty campy). Past or future, Caesars remains spectacular. From the Roman temples, heroic arches, golden charioteers, and 50-foot Italian cypresses at its entrance, to the impressive interiors, it's the spectacle a good Vegas hotel should be. It still retains its core of Vegas romance, even if that core is getting harder to find. The haphazard layout has become ever more confusing and hard to negotiate, and it takes forever to get anywhere—especially out to the Strip. Sometimes you feel like just surrendering and staying in, which isn't necessarily a bad thing, especially since Caesars is also known for its service.

Accommodations occupy five towers (six by the time you read this), and there are too many decorating schemes to describe here. Until the latest tower opens, Augustus is the newest and somewhat biggest, while the Palace is the most recently upgraded. Standard rooms in the new tower are done in the sleek, unfussy neutrals that are all the rage, plus whirlpool tubs, marble and wood sinks, and little flatscreen TVs in the bathrooms. If you like elbow room, it's worth it. If you are looking for old-time Caesars romance, ask for rooms with a Greco-Roman theme (some have classical sculptures in niches); furnishings tend to neoclassic styles; Roman columns, pilasters, and pediments are common. Some may still have four-poster beds with mirrored ceilings. Some newer rooms have floor-to-ceiling windows that offer a hypnotizing panoramic view and, better still, older ones have lavish tubs in the middle of the room (which can be uncomfortable if you wish to shower and don't want your shower to turn into a spectator sport).

Caesars has a well-deserved reputation for superior in-house restaurants. There are quite a few in the hotel, plus dining facilities in the Forum shopping area. All are highly recommended. The hotel's sushi restaurant, **Hyakumi,** its Southwestern-themed **Mesa Grill,** and a replica of New York's famous **Rao's** are described in chapter 5, as are the hotel's food court and buffets. Restaurants in the Forum Shops arcade include **Spago** and the **Palm**—both are discussed in chapter 5. In the newer Atlantis section is a Cheesecake Factory. For a review of the nightclubs **Pure** and **Cleopatra's Barge,** see p. 267 and 265, respectively.

Having spent over $100 million renovating its **Garden of the Gods,** Caesars has created a tasteful, undeniably "Caesaresque" masterpiece. With three pools measuring a total of 22,000 square feet, there is plenty of space for frolicking in the hot sun. Inspired by the healing Baths of Caracalla in Rome, each of the pools is adorned with griffins or sea horses and inlaid with classic granite-and-marble mosaics. To feel even more regal, snatch one of the shaded cabanas that offer phones, TV, and air-conditioning, starting at $150 a day (reserve them early). Several amenities are also available by the pool area, including massage, two whirlpools, the Neptune Bar, and, of course, a Snackus Maximus.

The **Qua spa** is a knockout. Stone-and-water themed Roman baths with infinity pools, an ice room with shaved ice exfoliation, rain showers and best of all, heated tile curved lounge chairs. Add in a tea lounge with drinks and you've got the perfect place for post-party detox. If you have the energy, the fitness room is large, with plush padded equipment and plenty of windows. Go work off some of that Caesars indulgence and then get a little pampered.

The **Forum Shops** ✦✦✦ (p. 230) are in the grandest mall you can imagine (think of the *La Dolce Vita* walk on the Via Veneto), with stores ranging from the pedestrian (Gap) to the exclusive (Dolce & Gabbana). Not content to stop paying contractors, Caesars also added the 4,000-seat Coliseum, a replica of the original building in Rome. This was built for one purpose only—to give diva **Céline Dion** a place to play. No kidding. Céline moved on after some years of residency, but **Bette Midler** and **Cher** have taken her place. When they aren't in town, the venue is taken over by various über-names, such as Elton John and his *The Red Piano* production.

3570 Las Vegas Blvd. S. (just north of Flamingo Rd.), Las Vegas, NV 89109. ℂ 877/427-7243 or 702/731-7110. Fax 702/697-5706. www.caesarspalace.com. 3,348 units. $129 and up double; $549 and up suite. Extra person $30. No discount for children. AE, DC, DISC, MC, V. Free self- and valet parking. **Amenities:** 25 restaurants; nightclub; casino; 4 wedding chapels; 4 outdoor pools; health club; spa; concierge; tour desk; car-rental desk; business center; extensive shopping arcade; salon; 24-hr. room service; laundry service; dry cleaning; executive-level rooms. *In room:* A/C, TV w/pay movies, dataport, Wi-Fi (for fee), hair dryer, iron/ironing board, safe, robe/slippers.

The Palazzo ⭑⭑   An expansion of the impressive Venetian but one that functions as a separate hotel, with its own massive grand lobby, own restaurants, and own rates. It's even more expensive for roughly the same experience, so choosing this one over the other isn't a must-do. Though if we had to say it, the rooms are a wee bit nicer. Which is saying a lot since The Venetian has some of the nicest rooms in town. Like its sister property, The Palazzo's rooms are "suites"—a bedroom plus a sunken living room, with a sectional couch perfect for crashing and channel surfing. Three flatscreen TVs (two quite big, one smaller one badly positioned in the bathroom), a particularly squishy white bed with superior linens and pillows, remote control curtain and shades, and a deep bathtub in a generously sized, gleaming bathroom add up to the kind of accommodations that are hard to leave. Stay here only if what you mostly wanted to see in the city is your fabulous hotel room. On the other hand, they face the same problem as any behemoth Vegas hotel; it's luxury but for a luxury price, and it's luxury on a large scale, which doesn't permit the kind of personal pampering that price ought to bring.

Should you leave, there are 14 restaurants including **Table 10,** the new eaterie by Emeril, and **Carnevino,** a steakhouse from Mario Batali, while **Grand Lux Café** is a moderately priced alternative to the mostly higher end offerings. Hip hop star Jay Z is behind sports bar/club **40/40,** while the high-end shopping area (covered in the shopping chapter) is anchored by Barney's New York. And there is still more of all of that accessible in the adjoining Venetian. The pool area is unmemorable and the excellent Canyon Ranch spa and health club will set you back an additional $35 a day.

3325 Las Vegas Blvd. S., Las Vegas, NV 89109. ✆ **877/883-6423** or 702/607-7777. Fax 702/414-4805. www.palazzo lasvegas.com. 4,027 units. $199 and up double; $229 and up suite. Extra person $35. Children 12 and under stay free in parent's room. AE, DC, DISC, MC, V. Free self- and valet parking. **Amenities:** 15 restaurants; casino; showroom; 7 outdoor pools shared w/Venetian; health club and spa shared w/Venetian; concierge; tour desk; car-rental desk; business center; extensive shopping arcade; 24-hr. room service; laundry service; dry cleaning; executive-level rooms. *In room:* A/C, TV w/pay movies, fax, Wi-Fi (for a fee), fridge on request, hair dryer, iron/ironing board, safe.

Paris Las Vegas Casino Resort ⭑   *Sacre bleu!* The City of Light comes to Sin City in this, one of the few theme-run-amok hotels left to its giddy devices. Stay here if you came to Vegas for the silly fantasy. The outside reproduces various Parisian landmarks (amusing anyone familiar with Paris, as the Hotel de Ville is crammed on top of the Louvre), complete with a half-scale perfect replica of the Eiffel Tower. The interior puts you in the middle of a dollhouse version of the city. You can stroll down a mini Rue de la Paix, ride an elevator to the top of the Eiffel Tower, stop at an overpriced bakery for a baguette, and have your photo taken near several very nice fountains.

You'll find signage employing the kind of dubious use of the French language that makes genuine Frenchmen really cross ("le car rental" and so forth), while all the employees are forced to dust off their high school French ("Bonjour, Madame! Merci beaucoup!") when dealing with the public. Don't worry, it's not quite enough to make you sick to "le stomach."

Quel dommage, this attention to detail does not extend to the rooms, which are nice enough but disappointingly uninteresting, with furniture that only hints at mock French Regency. Bathrooms are small but pretty, with deep tubs. Try to get a Strip-facing room so that you can see Bellagio's fountains across the street; note also that north-facing rooms give you nice peeping-tom views right into neighboring Bally's.

Tips Staying off the Strip

First-time visitors, and even second-timers, will prefer, as they should, to stay on the Strip or Downtown, hang the cost (most of the time anyway). But if you can't get a room price to your liking, or if you are a habitual visitor, you might want to consider some alternatives. The following are out of the way, relatively speaking, but each hotel makes up for it with rack rates you just aren't going to get—well, not that often—on the Strip. We're talking as low as $49 a night. Maybe even lower. The rooms aren't anything to write home about, which is why we didn't bother writing much about them, but they are clean, comfortable, and sufficiently (in some cases) easy on the eyes. And several of the hotels, particularly those that are part of the Station chain, have so many extras to offer that they really could compete with some of the big boys on the Strip. However, you trade away location; for the most part; once you leave the hotel property, you enter a vast nothingness. So what? Get in that rental car—or take the shuttle that many of the hotels provide—and drive 15 minutes to the big boys' free parking lots, and use the money you saved to see *O* (p. 245), or to eat at a fancy restaurant, or to gamble. But, hey, even gambling is cheaper out here in the vast nothingness!

In northwest Las Vegas, the **JW Marriott** ⭐, 221 N. Rampart, Las Vegas, NV 89128 (🕿 **877/869-8777** or 702/869-8777; www.jwlasvegasresort.com), was the Resort at Summerlin but was bought out by the Marriott chain. With a handsome Spanish Mission–style building, fabulously landscaped grounds, and tricked-out rooms, this is much more of a true resort property than any Strip destination. But then again, what you gain there you lose in

The monorail has a stop out back, which adds to the convenience factor. Overall, not a bad place to stay but a great place to visit—*quel hoot!*

The hotel has eight more-or-less French-themed restaurants, including the highly lauded **Le Village Buffet,** the **Eiffel Tower restaurant** (located guess where), and bistro **Mon Ami Gabi,** all of which are covered in chapter 5. The bread for all these restaurants is made fresh on-site at the bakery. You can buy delicious, if pricey, loaves of it at the bakery, and we have to admit, that's kinda fun. There are also five lounges. The **Eiffel Tower** attraction is covered on p. 174.

3655 Las Vegas Blvd. S., Las Vegas, NV 89109. 🕿 **888/BONJOUR** (266-5687) or 702/946-7000. www.parislv.com. 2,916 units. $119 and up double; $350 and up suites. Extra person $30. No discount for children. AE, DC, DISC, MC. V. Free self- and valet parking. **Amenities:** 12 restaurants; casino; showrooms; 2 wedding chapels; outdoor pool; health club; spa; concierge; tour desk; business center; shopping arcade; 24-hr. room service; laundry service; dry cleaning; executive-level rooms. *In room:* A/C, TV w/pay movies, dataport, Wi-Fi (for fee), hair dryer, iron/ironing board, safe.

The Venetian ⭐⭐   One of the most elaborate hotel spectacles in town, The Venetian falls squarely between an outright adult Disneyland experience and the luxury resort experience currently dominating the Vegas landscape. The big draw here is the rooms, all suites, and all successful examples of that same luxury resort mindset, though the commitment to theme in the Grand Canal Shoppes is certainly appealing.

location—with traffic, it could take 40 minutes to get to the Strip. The **Fiesta Rancho** ⍟, 2400 N. Rancho Dr., Las Vegas, NV 89130 (℃ **800/731-7333** or 702/631-7000; www.fiestacasino.com), has a friendly local touch that used to be found in Downtown but is rarely seen there these days, plus a performance venue that frequently has some decent names, and a Mexican restaurant with more than 300 different kinds of margaritas.

Just west of the Strip can be found one of the best options, the **Palace Station.** Don't be put off by the old-fashioned—dark, crowded, noisy— casino and lobby area. This is a swell deal in a town rapidly losing such lures. It's plain, but comfortable and unexpectedly nice. Newly refurnished rooms—a lighter palate in a sleek spare modern design that is anything but old fashioned—offer pillow-top mattresses, a huge flatscreen TV (Tower rooms only), free Wi-Fi, a coffee machine (rare in Vegas these days, forcing guests to spend large amounts just for their morning cup of Joe), and large showers in spiffed up bathrooms. Tubs are available only in some rooms. Prices are often quite cheap (under $100 a night) but a mere additional $40 gets you a junior suite with even more space. The pool area has been redone, the entirely gutted and remodeled buffet is a steal at $8 for dinner. The locals love this place, and you might well too, given rising Strip prices. 2411 W. Sahara Ave., Las Vegas, NV. ℃ **800/634-3101** or 702/367-2411; www. palacestation.com.

For other great off-the-Strip hotel choices, see "Locals' Hotels" on p. 64.

The hotel's exterior, which re-creates most of the top landmarks of Venice (the Campanile, a portion of St. Mark's Square, part of the Doge's Palace, a canal or two), ranks right up there with New York–New York as a must-see, and since you can wander freely through the "sights," it even has a slight edge over New York–New York. This may be the only hotel in Vegas where it seems inviting to wander around outside in the front. As stern as we get about re-creations *not* being a substitute for the real thing, we have to admit that the attention to detail here is impressive indeed. Stone is aged for that weathered look, statues and tiles are exact copies of their Italian counterparts, security guards wear Venetian police uniforms—all that's missing is the smell from the canals, but we are happy to let that one slide.

Inside, it's more of the same, particularly in the lobby area and the entrance to the extraordinary shops, as ceilings are covered with hand-painted re-creations of Venetian art. With plenty of marble, soaring ceilings, and impressive pillars and archways, it's less kitschy than Caesars but more theme park than Bellagio. The lobby says classy hotel, if "classy hotel on steroids." The lobby, casino, and shops can all be accessed from outside through individual entrances, which helps avoid that irritating circuitous maneuvering required by most other locations. This is all the more appreciated because the casino seems to have a most confusing layout, with poor signage; perhaps it's just our problem with spatial navigation, but we consistently got lost on the way to the guest elevators.

A room makeover has pared down the previously over-the-top fussy decor, which is a good thing, but then again, apart from the size it's not as dreamily romantic on the eye. Now the suites have the same sleek new look as The Palazzo, though the beds lack The Palazzo's fluffy comforters. The towels are nicer here. You still can't see the bathroom TV from the tub. The marbled bathrooms rocketed virtually to the top of our list of favorites, in a tie for second place with those at Bellagio. (Mandalay Bay's THEhotel are the best.) Devices for the hearing-impaired (ranging from door-knock lights to vibrating alarm clocks and telecaption decoders) are available upon request.

Despite the niceties, there is a certain amount of price gouging at this hotel that unpleasantly reminds one of the real Venice. There is a charge for that in-room faxing and printing, and the minibar is automated so that if you so much as rearrange items inside, you are charged for it.

And all this is even before the **Venezia Tower,** with over 1,000 more rooms, with the same large and lush footprint and style as the originals. The tower has its own check-in and gestalt—somehow, it comes off even more lush than the original hotel, which is pretty frilly to start. It's like a Four Seasons on human growth hormones, with over-the-top opulence. The gas lamp–lit lobby hallway slays us, as do the flatscreen TVs in the bathrooms. Rooms here cost about $35 more a night (in theory—in practice, anything goes with hotel pricing in Vegas) and we would spend it. The trend toward casino hotels adding additions that are away from a casino—"Nope, no slot machines here. We are just a luxury hotel. Really!"—is a disingenuous stance that is actually entirely genius. There are many who prefer their Vegas at arm's length, whose finest compliment for a hotel is, "It doesn't seem like it's in Vegas." These people are willing to spend extra to stay in a grown-up atmosphere, and certainly are more inclined to want a comfortable room—and nothing says "comfortable room" like "plasma TV in the bathroom."

Many celebrity chefs and high-profile restaurants are in residence at The Venetian. Reviews of **Bouchon** (by Thomas Keller, perhaps America's top chef), **Delmonico Steakhouse, Canaletto, Valentino, Mario Batali's B&B Ristorante** and **Pinot Brasserie** can be found in chapter 5. Nightlife options include the **Blue Man Group** and a special production of the long-running **Phantom of the Opera** (both reviewed in the nightlife chapter). And, of course, there is an elegant but confusingly laid-out casino.

The Venetian has five pools and whirlpools, but its pool area is disappointingly sterile and bland. Pools are neoclassical (think rectangles with the corners lopped off), and the fourth-floor location probably means that more dense foliage is not going to be forthcoming. The Venezia Tower has a courtyard pool area that is amusing, but the water space is tiny.

The **Canyon Ranch SpaClub** ✦✦✦ is run by a branch of arguably the finest getaway spa in America. This is an unbelievably lavish facility, certainly the finest hotel spa in town. From the Bed Head and Bumble & Bumble products on sale in the shop to the nutritionists, physical therapists, and acupuncturists on the staff to the vibrating massage chairs that you rest in during pedicures—geez, what more could you want? Well, we want our own home gym to be as nice as the one here, with ample equipment, racks of big TVs, and a staff eager to help you with advice and bring you bottled water. The $35-a-day fee is high, but it does include a full day's worth of classes, ranging from regular aerobics to yoga, Pilates, and dance. Did we mention the rock-climbing wall, which, because this is Vegas, costs extra?

The **Grand Canal Shoppes** ⟪★★⟫ (p. 233) rank with the Caesars Palace shops as an absolute must-see. Like Caesars, the area is a mock Italian village with a blue, cloud-studded, painted sky overhead. But down the middle runs a canal, complete with singing gondoliers. (The 10-min. ride costs about $15, which seems steep, but trust us, it's a *lot* more in the real Venice.) The entire thing finishes up at a small re-creation of St. Mark's Square, which features glass blowers, traveling musicians, flower sellers, and the like. Expect to run into famous Venetians such as a flirty Casanova and a travel-weary Marco Polo. It's ambitious and a big step up from animatronic figures. Oh, and the stores are also probably worth a look—a decent mixture of high-end fashion and more affordable shops.

3355 Las Vegas Blvd. S., Las Vegas, NV 89109. ⟪C⟫ **888/283-6423** or 702/414-1000. Fax 702/414-4805. www.venetian. com. 4,027 units. $169 and up double. Extra person $35, $50 in executive level. Children 12 and under stay free in parent's room. AE, DC, DISC, MC, V. Free self- and valet parking. **Amenities:** 18 restaurants; casino; showroom; wedding chapels; 6 outdoor pools; health club; spa; concierge; tour desk; car-rental desk; business center; extensive shopping arcade; 24-hr. room service; laundry service; dry cleaning; executive-level rooms. *In room:* A/C, TV w/pay movies, fax, Wi-Fi (for a fee), fridge on request, hair dryer, iron/ironing board, safe.

EXPENSIVE

The Flamingo Las Vegas ⟪★⟫   The Flamingo is the Strip's senior citizen, boasting a colorful history. It's changed a great deal since Bugsy Siegel opened his 105-room oasis "in the middle of nowhere" in 1946. It was so luxurious for its time that even the janitors wore tuxedos. (Hey, new Vegas? That's class.) Jimmy Durante was the opening headliner, and the wealthy and famous flocked to the tropical paradise of swaying palms, lagoons, and waterfalls. Renovations and expansions over the years aren't going to make Siegel's a "real class joint" cause you to forget about, say, the rooms at The Palazzo, but they have freshened the joint up—including making it somewhat easier to reach the outside world, which in the past was often difficult. A recent addition is a branch of singer Jimmy Buffett's Margaritaville nightclub, a theme locale that makes us wince when it's in, say, New Orleans, but this one, here in Vegas? Not bad!

By Vegas standards, the old girl is Paleozoic, but not only is it hanging in there, some of the changes have made us reconsider it entirely. Gradually, all their dated rooms are getting upgraded. The first set off the conveyor belt are flatly terrific. Rushing headlong into the Dean Martin/Rat Pack retro vibe, they are kicky candy modern, with hot pink (the signature Flamingo color!) accent walls, hot pink lights in the bathroom where you can also find TV screens embedded in the mirror, candy-striped wallpaper, black-and-white photos of The Flamingo from its early days, squishy white beds with chocolate accents and vinyl padded headboards, huge flatscreens with HDTV, iPod docking stations, and more. Two-bedroom suites scream classic playboy bachelor pad. It's ring-a-ding fun and Dino would surely have approved, well worth the extra $50 currently charged for the upgraded rooms. It's uncertain whether further room renovations will follow this design, but thus far, the hotel has inspired confidence.

The Flamingo Paradise Garden Buffet (p. 167) is a decent choice. There are also several bars, plus a huge casino and the improv production show *The Second City* (p. 252). And the monorail has a stop out back.

For those planning some leisure time outside the casino, The Flamingo's exceptional pool area, spa, and tennis courts are big draws. Five gorgeous swimming pools, two whirlpools, and water slides are located in a 15-acre Caribbean landscape amid lagoons, meandering streams, fountains, waterfalls, a rose garden, and islands of live flamingos. Ponds have ducks, swans, and koi, and a grove of 2,000 palms graces an expanse of lawn. Although the water can be a little chilly, kids should be able to spend hours in the pool area.

A health club ($10 per day for machines only; $20 for spa and health club) offers a variety of weight machines, treadmills, stair machines, free weights, sauna, steam, a TV lounge, and hot and cold whirlpools. Spa services include massage, facials, salt glow, and body wraps.

3555 Las Vegas Blvd. S. (btw. Sands Ave. and Flamingo Rd.), Las Vegas, NV 89109. 📞 **800/732-2111** or 702/733-3111. Fax 702/733-3353. www.flamingolv.com. 3,517 units. $85 and up double; $350 and up suite. Extra person $30. Timeshare suites available. AE, DC, DISC, MC, V. Free self- and valet parking. **Amenities:** 8 restaurants; casino; show-rooms; wedding chapels; 5 outdoor pools; 3 night-lit tennis courts; health club; spa; small video-game arcade; car-rental desk; UPS store; shopping arcade; 24-hr. room service; laundry service; dry cleaning; executive-level rooms. *In room:* A/C, TV w/pay movies, dataport, Wi-Fi (for a fee), hair dryer, iron/ironing board, safe.

Harrah's Las Vegas 🐸 Here's another property that is doing its best to keep up with the pace in Vegas, to mixed success. Though parts of Harrah's benefited from a reworking of the place a few years ago, the rest of it evokes Old Las Vegas in the way the Riviera does—as in, dark, dated, and claustrophobic. Still, there is much to like here, and occasional quite good rates might make the so-so bits worth overlooking. Certainly, they want to be the fun and convivial place we wish more of Vegas were (instead of pretty much catering to high rollers and simply tolerating the rest of us with normal budgets). The monorail stop is a draw, too, because it is now easier to get to and from here.

The rooms have undergone some cosmetic fluffing to the tune of good new mattresses and those white bed covers now more or less standard in most local hotels. Dark masculine decor is an odd choice for such a festive place. The rooms aren't flashy, but they are reliable for what is ultimately a gamblers' hotel.

The Range (p. 135) steakhouse is one of the few hotel restaurants that overlooks the Strip. Other restaurant options include a Toby Keith–themed joint featuring down-home cooking and nightly entertainment, a buffet, and a food court for quick bites to eat. The casino has a fun, festive atmosphere. There's a showroom (that used to be home to Sammy Davis, Jr., back in the day), a comedy club, **Mac King's** wonderful comedy/magic act (p. 250), and other amusing entertainment diversions.

Carnaval Court (p. 231) is a festive, palm-fringed shopping plaza where strolling entertainers perform. It's notable because it's right on the Strip but entirely outdoors; similar ventures at other hotels are inside artificial environments. Note that lounge singer legend **Cook E. Jarr** often plays here late on varying nights (p. 239).

Harrah's has an Olympic-size swimming pool and sun-deck area with a waterfall and trellised garden areas, and a whirlpool. It's a pretty underwhelming pool by Vegas standards.

The hotel's health club is one of the better facilities on the Strip, with a full-range spa and a gym with Lifecycles, treadmills, stair machines, rowing machines, lots of Universal equipment, free weights, and TVs and a VCR for which aerobic exercise tapes are available. Its $20-a-day access charge is more reasonable than the fees in other hotels.

3475 Las Vegas Blvd. S. (btw. Flamingo and Spring Mountain roads), Las Vegas, NV 89109. 📞 **800/427-7247** or 702/369-5000. Fax 702/369-5283. www.harrahs.com. 2,526 units. $79 and up double; $199 and up suite. Extra person $30. No discount for children. AE, DC, DISC, MC, V. Free self- and valet parking. **Amenities:** 9 restaurants; casino; showrooms; outdoor pool; health club; spa; concierge; tour desk; car-rental desk; business center; shopping arcade; salon; 24-hr. room service; laundry service; dry cleaning; executive-level rooms. *In room:* A/C, TV w/pay movies, dataport, hair dryer, iron/ironing board.

⟨Tips⟩ So Your Trip Goes Swimmingly . . .

Part of the delight of the Vegas resort complexes is the gorgeous pools—what could be better for beating the summer heat? But there are pools and there are *pools,* so you'll need to keep several things in mind when searching for the right one for you.

During the winter, it's often too cold or windy to do much lounging, and even if the weather is amenable, the hotels often close part of their pool areas during winter and early spring. The pools also are not heated for the most part, but in fairness, they largely don't need to be.

Most hotel pools are shallow, chest-high at best, only about 3 feet deep in many spots (the hotels want you gambling, not swimming). Diving is impossible—not that a single pool allows it anyway.

And finally, during those hot days, be warned that sitting by pools next to heavily windowed buildings such as The Mirage and TI–Treasure Island allows you to experience the same thing a bug does under a magnifying glass with a sun ray directed on it. Regardless of time of year, be sure to slather on the sunscreen; there's a reason you see so many unhappy lobster-red people roaming the streets. Many pool areas don't offer much in the way of shade. On the other hand, if your tan line is important to you, head for Caesars, Mandalay Bay, Wynn Las Vegas, or Stratosphere (to name a few), all of which have topless sunbathing areas where you can toast even more flesh than at the other hotels.

At any of the pools, you can rent cabanas (which often include TVs, special lounge chairs, and even better poolside service), but these should be reserved as far in advance as possible, and with the exception of the Four Seasons' complimentary shaded lounging area, most cost a hefty fee. If you are staying at a chain hotel, you will most likely find an average pool, but if you want to spend some time at a better one, be aware that most of the casino-hotel pool attendants will ask to see your room key. If they are busy, you might be able to sneak in, or at least blend in with a group ahead of you.

The Mirage 𝄄𝄄 Imagine the levels of frustration of the Las Vegas hotel-casino. There you are, once the hottest thing on the Strip, and then everyone copies you and takes it to the next level of luxury, or theme, or lunacy, depending on what this year's trend is; and there you are, the former front runner, now years behind the ever-evolving curve. Desperate fashion crazes call for desperate measures, and so if you are The Mirage, you dump nearly all your tropical theme in favor of that sleek, sophisticated, dark wood look that is currently all the rage. It was a good choice. The Asian elegance produces unexpected sharp design touches—just peer in at the bar of Stack Steakhouse, full of sensuous wood curves. The place is looking sharp, stylish, and grown up, instead of tired. Even though it has become somewhat eclipsed by the very hotels whose presence it made possible, we still really like this place. From the moment you walk in and breathe the tropically perfumed air and enter the lush rainforest, it's just a different experience from most Vegas hotels.

The Mirage was Steve Wynn's first project built from the ground up. It seems funny now, but back in 1989, this was considered a complete gamble that was sure to be a failure. That was before the hotel opened, mind you. On opening day, the crowds nearly tore the place down getting inside, and The Mirage soon made its money back. Now it is the model upon which all recent hotels have been based.

Occupying 102 acres, The Mirage is fronted by more than a city block of cascading waterfalls and tropical foliage centering on a "volcano," which, after dark, erupts every 15 minutes, spewing fire 100 feet above the lagoons below. A total overhaul of the exhibit should produce a more impressive effect, because truth be told, it was always a little anticlimactic. (In passing, that volcano cost $30 million, which is equal to the entire original construction cost for Caesars next door.) The lobby is dominated by a 53-foot, 20,000-gallon simulated coral-reef aquarium stocked with more than 1,000 colorful tropical fish. This gives you something to look at while waiting (never for long) for check-in.

Impressions

Supercalifragilisticexpialidocious!
—Governor Bob Miller's reaction upon first visiting The Mirage

Next, you'll walk through the rainforest, which occupies a 90-foot domed atrium—a path meanders through palms, banana trees, waterfalls, and serene pools. If we must find a complaint with The Mirage, it's with the next bit because you have to negotiate 8 miles (or so it seems) of casino mayhem to get to your room, the pool, food, or the outside world. It gets old, fast. On the other hand, the sundries shop is located right next to the guest-room elevators, so if you forgot toothpaste, you don't have to travel miles to get more.

Fresh room renovations are turning the lodgings into that white bed/bold solid colors/70s-inspired look that everyone is sporting a variation of these days. Admittedly it does fit the current mod look of the hotel. Plus, pillow-top mattress and 42-inch LCD TVs do wonders for overcoming any decor concerns. The bathrooms remain small—though they have been given a solid makeover as well—which won't bother you unless you have space issues and/or have seen the bigger ones elsewhere on the Strip. **The Mirage Cravings Buffet** is detailed in chapter 5. The Cirque production *Love* is reviewed in chapter 9, while a show starring Terry Fator, winner of *America's Got Talent,* will be going on during 2009. The Mirage has one of our favorite casinos and some excellent nightclubs and bars. We miss the so-Vegas-it's-bad lounge but have to admit that the **Zen Japonais Lounge** is more appealing in every way, with its fluttering spalike curtains and proximity to the rainforest. It's an odd bit of serenity right off the casino bustle.

Out back is the pool, one of the nicest in Vegas, with a quarter-mile shoreline, a tropical paradise of waterfalls and trees, water slides, and so forth. It looks inviting, but truth be told, it's sometimes on the chilly side and isn't very deep. But it's so pretty you'll hardly care. There is also Bare, a "European-style pool" offering a more adult aquatic experience. Free swimming lessons and water-aerobics classes take place daily at the pool. Behind the pool are the **Dolphin Habitat** and Siegfried & Roy's **Secret Garden** (p. 181). **The Mirage Day Spa** ✦ teems with friendly staff anxious to pamper you, bringing you iced towels to cool you during your workout and refreshing juices and smoothies afterward. The gym is one of the largest and best stocked on the Strip.

3400 Las Vegas Blvd. S. (btw. Flamingo and Spring Mountain roads), Las Vegas, NV 89109. ℂ **800/627-6667** or 702/791-7111. Fax 702/791-7446. www.mirage.com. 3,044 units. $109 and up double; $275 and up suite. Extra person $30. No discount for children. AE, DC, DISC, MC, V. Free self- and valet parking. **Amenities:** 11 restaurants;

casino; showrooms; beautiful outdoor pool; health club; spa; concierge; tour desk; car-rental desk; business center; shopping arcade; salon; 24-hr. room service; laundry service; dry cleaning; executive-level rooms. *In room:* A/C, TV w/pay movies, dataport, Wi-Fi (for a fee), hair dryer, iron/ironing board, safe.

Palms Casino Resort 🍸🍸   Britney's base for her (first) wedding debacle and still the retreat of choice for tabloid staples. In keeping with the tropical-foliage name, it's more or less Miami-themed (but without the pastels), with a strange aversion to straight lines (really, check out all those curves). Inside a bland building is a pretty nice complex with some downright family-friendly touches—which we say only because it's a puzzle that the place is such a hot spot. That's mostly due to the nightlife options—**ghostbar, Playboy Club,** and the nightclubs **Rain** and **Moon** have lines of people every night the facilities are open, offering to sell their firstborn sons for a chance to go inside. Why did those two places catch on so? Quite possibly MTV's *The Real World: Las Vegas,* which featured seven strangers picked to live in the Palms and have their lives taped...oh, never mind...what you need to know is that the entrances to the clubs stand right by the elevators to your hotel room, which means on a busy weekend night, there can be upwards of 4,000 gorgeous and antsy (if not angry) people standing between you and access to your hotel room. If you are a Hilton sister, or wish to see whether one will date you, this could be heaven, but if encountering the beautifully dressed and coifed, with 0% body fat and sullen expressions of entitlement, and the 19-year-olds who seek to become all that (and usually affect a thuggish demeanor) makes you, like us, itch, this might not be the most comfortable place to stay. And yet there is an excellent child-care facility, **Kid's Quest,** plus movie theaters, and a family-ready food court (with a McDonald's, Panda Express, pizza, and subs). So it's both totally wrong for kids and rather right at the same time.

The Palms has perhaps some of the most comfortable beds in Vegas, thanks to fluffy pillows and duvets that make one reluctant to rise, plus big TVs and huge bathrooms. The workout room is decent size, but the spa is underwhelming, especially for a $25 daily admission fee, though it does offer yoga and Pilates classes. The pool areas got party-spot makeovers, turning what were kind of bland "stand and pose" watering holes into the kind of trendy must-visit beach areas this kind of crowd loves. Also on the property is **Alizé** (p. 130), in competition for the title Best Restaurant in Town (and owner of the title Most Gorgeous and Romantic Restaurant).

4321 W. Flamingo Rd. (just west of I-15), Las Vegas, NV 89103. 📞 **866/942-7777** or 702/942-7777. Fax 702/942-6859. www.palms.com. 703 units. $99 and up double. Extra person $30. No discount for children. AE, DC, DISC, MC, V. Free self- and valet parking. **Amenities:** 7 restaurants; food court; casino; movie theater; nightclub/showroom; outdoor pool; health club; spa; concierge; business center; salon; 24-hr. room service; laundry service; dry cleaning; executive-level rooms. *In room:* A/C, TV w/pay movies, dataport, Wi-Fi (for a fee), coffeemaker, hair dryer, iron/ironing board, safe, robe/slippers.

Rio All-Suite Hotel & Casino 🍸   Rio bills itself as a "carnival" atmosphere hotel, which in this case means hectic, crowded, and noisy, and an apparent edict requiring the Most Scantily Clad Waitresses in Town to burst into song and dance in between delivering beers. The Masquerade Village is actually pretty pleasant, with a very high ceiling, but the older section's low ceilings seem to accentuate only how crowded the area is in both the number of people and the amount of stuff (slot machines, gaming tables, and so on). This party atmosphere, by the way, is strictly for adults; the hotel actively discourages guests from bringing children.

The hotel touts its room size. Every one is a "suite," which does not mean two separate rooms, but rather one large room with a sectional, corner sofa, and coffee table at one end. The dressing areas are certainly larger than average and feature a number of extra amenities, such as fridges (unusual for a Vegas hotel room) and small snacks. Windows, running the entire length of the room, are floor to ceiling, with a pretty impressive view of the Strip, Vegas, or the mountains (depending on which way you're facing). The furniture doesn't feel like hotel-room standard, but otherwise the decor is fairly bland.

The hotel's first-rate **Carnival World Buffet** and barbeque restaurant **RUB** are described in chapter 5. You might consider checking out the **Wine Cellar Tasting Room,** which bills itself as "the world's largest and most extensive collection of fine wines," and hyperbole aside, it's certainly impressive and a must-do for any wine aficionado.

Penn & Teller, the smartest show in town, is reviewed in chapter 9, as is the **Voodoo Lounge** and other clubs. The casino, alas, is dark and claustrophobic. The party/carnival theme gets a distinct R rating with the newly reconceived **Masquerade Village in the Sky,** the Rio's free show. Sort of an homage to Rio Carnival, courtesy of floats that move on grids set in the ceiling above the casino, it now includes sets such as spas and 17-foot-long beds, with "performers of seduction" gyrating to the Pussycat Dolls. Performed Thursday through Sunday in the evening.

Out back is a pool with a sandy beach, and two others in imaginative fish and shell shapes that seem inviting until you get up close and see how small they are. It could be especially disappointing after you have braved the long, cluttered walk (particularly from the newer tower rooms) to get there. Three whirlpool spas nestle amid rocks and foliage, there are two sand-volleyball courts, and blue-and-white-striped cabanas (equipped with rafts and misting coolers) can be rented for $250 to $500 per day. The 18-hole championship **Rio Secco golf course,** located on the south side of town (transportation included), was designed by Rees Jones.

3700 W. Flamingo Rd. (just west of I-15), Las Vegas, NV 89103. © **888/752-9746** or 702/777-7777. Fax 702/777-7611. www.riolasvegas.com. 2,582 units. $99 and up double-occupancy suite. Extra person $30. No discount for children. AE, DC, MC, V. Free self- and valet parking. **Amenities:** 12 restaurants; sports book dining; casino; showrooms; 4 outdoor pools; golf course; health club; spa; concierge; car-rental desk; business center; shopping arcade; salon; 24-hr. room service; in-room massage; laundry service; dry cleaning; executive-level rooms. *In room:* A/C, TV w/pay movies, Wi-Fi (for a fee), fridge, coffeemaker, hair dryer, iron/ironing board, safe.

TI–Treasure Island 🏨🏨   Huh? What happened to Treasure Island? What happened to the pirates? Why, Vegas grew up, that's what. Or, rather, it wants the kids it once actively tried to court to grow up, or at least, not come around until they are able to drink and gamble properly.

Originally the most modern family-friendly hotel, the Treasure Island was a blown-up version of Disneyland's *Pirates of the Caribbean.* But that's all behind them now, and the slight name change is there to make sure you understand that this is a grown-up, sophisticated resort. There might still be the odd pirate element here and there, but only because someone absentmindedly missed it in a ruthless purging of the last remnants. One victim is the pirate stunt show out front; it's been revamped so that the pirates (and you have no idea how much we wish we were making this up) now "battle" scantily clad strippers . . . er, "sirens."

To be fair, none of this matters a whit, unless, like us, you got a kick out of the skulls and crossbones, and treasure chests bursting with jewels and gold, that originally decorated the place. What remains, after they stripped the pirate gilt, is such a nice place to stay that in some ways, it even outranks its older sister, The Mirage. The good-size rooms are getting redone and while they aren't breaking from the mold of geometric neutrals, they are more striking than some. Good bathrooms feature large soaking tubs—a bather's delight. Best of all, Strip-side rooms have a view of the pirate battle—views are best from the sixth floor on up. You know, so you can see right down the sirens' dresses.

The hotel offers half a dozen restaurants, including **Isla** (p. 141), **The Buffet at TI** (p. 167), and a branch of Los Angeles's **Canter's** deli (p. 143). Treasure Island is home to Cirque du Soleil's *Mystère* (p. 245), one of the best shows in town.

A free tram travels between TI and The Mirage almost around the clock. For a good photo op, sit in the front of the first car: As you leave the loading dock, note how The Mirage, palm trees, and a bit of the New York–New York skyline are framed in an attractive, and surreal, manner.

There's a full-service spa and health club with a complement of machines, plus sauna, steam, whirlpool, massage, on-site trainers, TVs and stereos with headsets, and anything else you might need (including a full line of Sebastian grooming products in the women's locker room). There's a $22-per-day fee to use the facilities.

The pool is not that memorable, with none of the massive foliage and other details that make the one at The Mirage stand out. So blah is it that the staff didn't even bother to check room keys when last we swam here. It's a large, free-form swimming pool with a 230-foot loop slide and a nicely landscaped sun-deck area. It's often crawling with kids, so if that's a turn-off, go elsewhere.

3300 Las Vegas Blvd. S. (at Spring Mountain Rd.), Las Vegas, NV 89109. (C) 800/944-7444 or 702/894-7111. Fax 702/894-7446. www.treasureisland.com. 2,885 units. $89 and up double; $140 and up suite. Extra person $30. No discount for children. Inquire about packages. AE, DC, DISC, MC, V. Free self- and valet parking. **Amenities:** 6 restaurants; casino; showrooms; wedding chapels; outdoor pool; health club; spa; concierge; tour desk; car-rental desk; business center; shopping arcade; salon; 24-hr. room service; laundry service; dry cleaning; executive-level rooms. *In room:* A/C, TV w/pay movies, fax, dataport, Wi-Fi (for a fee), hair dryer, iron/ironing board, safe.

The Westin Casuarina Las Vegas Hotel, Casino & Spa

When the ever-more-seedy Maxim was more or less stripped to its bones and turned into a Westin, we were thrilled. What Vegas needs, we kept saying, was a true kicky boutique hotel, one that puts real service and real style ahead of slot machines. This Westin won't fill that bill—coming a lot closer would be THEhotel at Mandalay Bay—but business travelers who want a little style, and don't mind if said style is just a tad generic and sterile, will be pleased with this hotel.

There is nothing wrong with the rooms—they are in excellent taste, done in eye-pleasing sages and wheats, complete with The Westin's self-congratulatory trade-marked "Heavenly Bed," which caused one occupant to dream she was sleeping on clouds (and the other to note it has a whole lot of polyester in its make-up). The bathrooms are gleaming, if small—but they pale compared to some of the (admittedly occasionally lurid) fantasies around town. For the price, especially if you were looking for something Vegas-riffic, you might be disappointed. It doesn't help that the cool exec-style lobby/check-in area melds into a casino area that seems to have been missed in the renovations; it's weirdly dated. It also doesn't help that the staff says, "No, that's not something we do or offer" more often than, "Yes, we can do that," though they say it nicely enough. There is an adequate (and free!) gym, reached by walking right by all the business meeting areas, and a decent pool. And this is the only hotel in Las Vegas that bans smoking in all rooms and public areas (except for the casino, where folks can still puff away). Ultimately, it's too good a property not to give a relatively high rating to, but you need to understand that, by Vegas standards—which means different things to different people—it's boring.

160 E. Flamingo Rd., Las Vegas, NV 89109. ⓒ 866/837-4215 or 702/836-9775. Fax 702/836-9776. www. starwood.com. 825 units. $139 and up double. Extra person $30. Children 17 and under stay free in parent's room. AE, DC, DISC, MC, V. Free self- and valet parking. Pets accepted, $35 fee and a deposit. **Amenities:** Restaurant; bar; coffee shop; casino; pool; health club; concierge; tour desk; business center; meeting rooms; 24-hr. room service; laundry service; dry cleaning. *In room:* A/C, TV, dataport, Wi-Fi (for a fee), minibar, hair dryer, iron/ironing board, safe.

MODERATE

Bally's Las Vegas ⚜   With all the fancy-pants new hotels in town, it's hard to keep up with the Joneses, or the Wynns, as the case may be. And here's poor Bally's, with a perfect location, and it's got no big fountain or Eiffel Tower or anything to make a passerby think "Gotta go gamble there," much less a tourist booking long distance to think "Gotta stay there." And we aren't really going to make you change your mind, though we might give you a reason to consider it. After all, you can get a room for a ridiculously low rate these days (not reflected in the official rack rates below, but give them a try), and those rooms, which are larger than average, have been redone to an admirable degree, with some swell touches, including modern curvy couches, big TVs, and marble this and that. The public areas still feel a little dated, but the hotel is connected to its sister property, Paris Las Vegas, which is swanky and modern enough. Also, it's a stop on the monorail system, so you'll be able to go just about everywhere by foot or by swift train, and, thanks to those nice rooms, you've got someplace pleasant to return to.

Bally's has the usual range of dining choices and is justly renowned for its **Sterling Sunday Brunch** (p. 165). The casino is large, well lit, and colorful, and there's also a headliner showroom and the splashy *Jubilee!* revue (p. 249).

3645 Las Vegas Blvd. S. (at Flamingo Rd.), Las Vegas, NV 89109. ⓒ 800/634-3434 or 702/739-4111. Fax 702/967-3890. www.ballyslv.com. 2,814 units. $99 and up double; $300 and up suite. Extra person $30. No discount for children. AE, DC, MC, V. Free self- and valet parking. **Amenities:** 13 restaurants; casino; showrooms; outdoor pool; 8 night-lit tennis courts; golf desk; health club; spa; video-game arcade; concierge; tour desk; car-rental desk; business center; shopping arcade; salon; room service; laundry service; dry cleaning. *In room:* A/C, TV w/pay movies, coffeemaker, high-speed Internet access (for a fee), hair dryer, iron/ironing board.

Bill's Gamblin' Hall and Saloon   You can't fault the location of this hotel. It's right on the busiest corner of the Strip, smack in the middle of the action. With all the hotel business (the itty-bitty reception desk and tiny sundries/gift-shop counter) set on the fringes of the small, dark, cluttered casino, this is very old Vegas, which is sort of a good thing; but unfortunately, it's becoming harder to wrap one's mind around it in these days of megacasino complexes. Further, as part of the massive Harrah's holdings, its future is somewhat in doubt. Too bad; a nice Strip boutique hotel would be just the ticket and this would provide good bones for one.

The rooms were completely redone to lighten up the formerly dark Victorian affairs they used to be. Regardless of the look, each has an extra corner of space for a couple of chairs or a couch alongside the very cramped bathroom. *Beware:* The very loud intersection outside can make rooms noisy.

3595 Las Vegas Blvd. S. (at Flamingo Rd.), Las Vegas, NV 89109. ⓒ 866/245-5745 or 702/737-2100. Fax 702/894-9954. www.billslasvegas.com. 200 units. $60 and up double. Extra person $19. No discount for children. AE, DC, DISC, MC, V. Free self- and valet parking. **Amenities:** 2 restaurants; casino; tour desk; car-rental desk; 24-hr. room service; dry cleaning. *In room:* A/C, TV w/pay movies, dataport, Wi-Fi (for a fee), hair dryer, iron/ironing board.

5 North Strip

VERY EXPENSIVE

Wynn Las Vegas ★★ Because Steve Wynn is a modern-day Vegas legend, because this town almost entirely owes its present-day look and outlook to him, because this hotel (built on the site of the old Desert Inn and opened on the same day, Apr 28, that grand old dame was originally opened) came with a $2.7-billion price tag, and because there was a great deal of hype that used words and phrases such as "like nothing you've ever seen before," there was a corresponding amount of anticipation and expectation surrounding the opening of this, Vegas's newest and perhaps most trumpeted resort. The result? Something that is at once pretty "wow" and a whole lot "It looks like Bellagio." In short, it was something many of us had, in fact, seen before, just down the street. And that is both fair and not; sure, the hotel does not live up to its *sui generis* claims, but that's obvious only if you have previous knowledge of other Vegas hotels. If you are new to town, this will look plenty spectacular. A better question might be "What's the visitor getting for that price tag?" This is especially relevant since the room rate can be upward of $400 a night (though even as soon as a month after it opened, certain e-mail–only offers went as low as $139). Just about everything here can generate sticker shock in all but those used to costly resorts, but note that costly resorts usually have one-tenth the number of rooms here.

The hotel feels a little bit cramped when you first enter—we are used to swooping Vegas lobby displays—and the reception area is impractically proportioned, resulting in some check-in wait issues. The suspicion is that all this makes the place seem less behemoth and more resort-size. The hotel has no discernible theme (apart from that tendency to prompt constant comparisons to Bellagio), which may be disappointing for those looking for, say, a New York–New York style of theme-aganza. The interior has some superior moments, including considerable use of natural light (via various skylights and atriums), unusual in this town and most welcome, and a floral motif reflected in eye-catching brightly hued floor mosaics, artistic fresh flower arrangements throughout, and, best of all, the atrium that runs down the center and, like its predecessor at Bellagio, features frequently changed displays. There are also some of the most garish lighting fixtures in a town not known for its subtlety in chandeliers. The layout is devoted to old-school Vegas floor planning, which forces guests to maneuver around and through the casino to get anywhere.

As with all other Wynn hotels, there is an installation in front of the building, a 150-foot tall man-made mountain covered in trees (many mature trees taken from the old Desert Inn golf course) and waterfalls, and like the others, this comes with a "free show." The quotation marks are because said show is not viewable from the street—neither, in fact, is the mountain itself. The latter can be glimpsed only in bits and pieces, though there is a decent shot at a portion of it as you enter from the Strip across from the pedestrian walkway; the former can be viewed only when either dining at the SW or Daniel Boulud Brasserie, or having a drink at a couple of bars, where you will be required to purchase two drinks per person, starting at $12 a glass. There is one truly free viewing platform, but it is tiny.

These complaints notwithstanding, there's nothing really wrong with the place; we just nitpick because the prehype invited it. In fact, there is much to like here. The rooms are the hands-down best on the Strip (at least, that aren't suites, such as at The Venetian or THEhotel). They're particularly large (and have kind of ruined us for even the more spacious of other rooms), with much-appreciated floor-to-ceiling views (west side shows off the mountain and waterfalls, east side the golf course; both are choice), deeply comfortable beds with high-thread-count sheets and feather beds atop good-quality mattresses plus down comforters, flatscreen TVs, and excellent up-to-the-minute bathrooms complete with quite long and deep tubs, their own flatscreen TVs, and lemony amenities. Take note of the silky-satiny robes (the best we've ever had in a hotel) and plush velour slippers. All the rooms are done in shades that happily break the recent trend toward bland parchment tones, but at least one of the palettes is a strange hybrid of salmon and terra cotta, so while we appreciate the effort, the result can be disconcerting. Love the Warhol flower prints, though. There is alleged turn-down service at night, but that can be spotty.

The gym is excellent, stuffed with up-to-the-minute equipment, most with individual TV screens, though we could do without the windows looking onto an interior hallway that make our workout visible to all passersby. The spa area is serene and particularly pretty, with an atrium emitting natural light into the bathing areas. The pool area has four oval-shaped numbers connected by some stretches long enough for laps, plus a "European sun-bathing" (read: topless) area that includes outdoor blackjack tables.

Dining options are superb (though generally exceptionally pricey), including **Alex, Bartolotta, Daniel Boulud Brasserie, Red 8,** and the **Wynn Las Vegas Buffet,** all reviewed in chapter 5. A shopping street features high-end choices—Chanel, Cartier, Manolo Blahnik, Gaultier—but still seems a bit more lower-economic (that's relative, mind you) than a similar one at Bellagio. Make special note of the apothecary-style shop next to the sundries shop; it stocks all sorts of fine lotions and potions, including, remarkably, the centuries-old, coveted (and still difficult-to-find) monk-produced line from the Santa Maria Novella Pharmacy in Florence. Monk-made products in Vegas? Well, why not? There's also a Ferrari dealership—no, really, and what's more, it's so popular that they actually charged admission to gawk for a while.

In the end, this is a very adult hotel, in the best sense—classy and mature. But still, so was the old Desert Inn, which hit all the right resort notes even in its last days, only to be replaced by the bigger-is-better ethos.

3131 Las Vegas Blvd. S. (corner of Spring Mountain Rd.), Las Vegas, NV 89109. ℂ **888/320-9966** or 702/770-7000. Fax 702/770-1571. www.wynnlasvegas.com. 2,716 units. $199 and up double. Extra person $50. No discount for children. AE, DC, DISC, MC, V. Free self- and valet parking. **Amenities:** 22 restaurants; casino; showrooms; 3 wedding chapels; 4 outdoor pools; health club; spa; concierge; tour desk; car-rental desk; business center; salon; 24-hr. room service; in-room massage for suites; laundry service; dry cleaning; executive-level rooms. *In room:* A/C, flatscreen TVs w/pay movies, CD/DVD player, dataport, Wi-Fi (for a fee), fax and printer, hair dryer, iron/ironing board, safe, robe/slippers.

EXPENSIVE

The Riviera Hotel & Casino *(Overrated*   At press time, the Riviera was for sale, and thus could land in the hands of people who will either want to tear it down or fix it up—so any, or all, of this could change at a moment's notice.

Its best days long past, this former Strip star is looking awfully dumpy these days. Between that and its promotion as an "alternative for grown-ups" and an "adult-oriented hotel," you should probably stay here only if you can get a deal and simply must be on the Strip. You certainly shouldn't bring the kids, who are actively discouraged as guests.

Opened in 1955 (Liberace cut the ribbon, and Joan Crawford was the official hostess of opening ceremonies), the Riviera was the first "high-rise" on the Strip, at nine stories. Today it tries to evoke the Vegas of the good old days—"come drink, gamble,

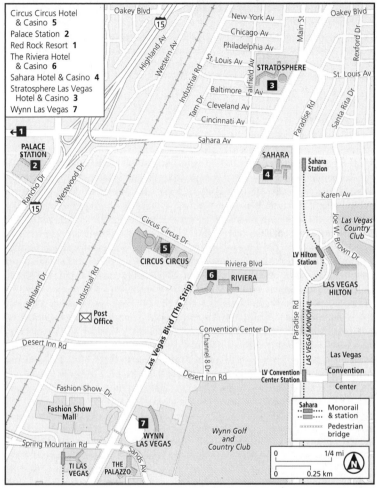

Circus Circus Hotel
& Casino **5**
Palace Station **2**
Red Rock Resort **1**
The Riviera Hotel
& Casino **6**
Sahara Hotel & Casino **4**
Stratosphere Las Vegas
Hotel & Casino **3**
Wynn Las Vegas **7**

and see a show"—and while it is appropriately dark and glitzy, it's also very crowded and has a confusing layout. Don't miss your chance to take your photo with the bronze memorial to the Crazy Girls (their premier, largely nekkid, show), and their butts, outside on the Strip. There is a pool here, but it's very dull.

Rooms are getting gradual makeovers, bringing in modern furnishings, the ubiquitous white comforters, flatscreen TVs, and the like. Be sure to ask for one of these. There is the predictable assortment of dining options—though an excellent choice for families, ironically, is the **Mardi Gras Food Court,** which, unlike most of its genre, is extremely attractive. White-canvas umbrella tables and Toulouse-Lautrec–style murals create a comfortable, French cafe ambience. Food choices are wide ranging, including burgers, pizza, gyros, falafel, and Chinese fare. The Riviera's enormous casino is one of the world's largest; see chapter 9 for reviews of its production shows, *An Evening at*

La Cage (female impersonators), *Crazy Girls* (sexy Las Vegas–style revue), and skating variety show *ICE.*

2901 Las Vegas Blvd. S. (at Riviera Blvd.), Las Vegas, NV 89109. ⓒ 800/634-6753 or 702/734-5110. Fax 702/794-9451. www.rivierahotel.com. 2,074 units. $79 and up double; $155 and up suite. Extra person $20. No discount for children. AE, DC, MC, V. Free self- and valet parking. **Amenities:** 5 restaurants; food court; casino; showrooms; wedding chapel; outdoor pool; health club; spa; video-game arcade; concierge; tour desk; car-rental desk; business center; shopping arcade; salon; 24-hr. room service; laundry service; dry cleaning; executive-level rooms. *In room:* A/C, TV w/pay movies, safe, Wi-Fi (for fee).

MODERATE

Sahara Hotel & Casino *Value*   One of the few venerable old casino hotels still standing in Vegas (it's come a long way since it opened in 1952 on the site of the old Club Bingo), how you now view the Sahara may simply depend on which direction the sun is shining. It's been a few years since a spiffy renovation really pulled in some solid Moroccan details (an arched neon dome with Moroccan detailing, plenty of marble and chandeliers, plus small tiles and other Arabian Nights decorations) and caused the loss of the landmark sign, once the tallest in Vegas. Then they added a roller coaster around the outside (quite a good ride, enthusiasts assure us), you know, just because. Meanwhile, the hotel was recently purchased, with plans for a top-to-bottom overhaul with an eye toward making it more like the Palms. This project, which probably won't start until sometime in 2008 or 2009, will be a good thing. The old place deserves another shot at Vegas significance.

Rooms are currently a bit too motel-room bland (though the windows open, which is unusual for Vegas). Again, this may simply be in comparison to the gleaming new kids in town, a comparison suffered by most of the older hotels. If you are looking for four walls and a mattress, this isn't a bad choice at all. It should be noted that the Sahara feels that it is not as well equipped as other hotels for children and discourages you from bringing yours—and yet, it added a roller coaster. Go figure.

The hotel includes the Sahara Buffet. The casino is a pretty pleasant one to gamble in, and there's a showroom as well. There is one pool.

2535 Las Vegas Blvd. S. (at E. Sahara Ave.), Las Vegas, NV 89109. ⓒ 888/696-2121 or 702/737-2111. Fax 702/791-2027. www.saharavegas.com. 1,720 units. $45 and up double. Extra person $20. No discount for children. AE, DC, DISC, MC, V. Free self- and valet parking. **Amenities:** 5 restaurants; casino; showroom and lounge w/free entertainment; outdoor pool; spa; salon; tour desk; car-rental desk; business center; shopping arcade; limited room service; executive-level rooms. *In room:* A/C, TV w/pay movies, high-speed Internet access (for a fee), fridge on request (free but limited availability), hair dryer, iron/ironing board.

Stratosphere Las Vegas Hotel & Casino *Kids*   A really neat idea, in that Vegas way, in a really bad location. At 1,149 feet, it's the tallest building west of the Mississippi. In theory, this should have provided yet another attraction for visitors: Climb (okay, elevator) to the top and gaze at the stunning view. But despite being on the Strip, it's a healthy walk from anywhere—the nearest casino is the Sahara, which is 5 very long blocks away. This, and possibly the hefty price charged for the privilege of going up to the top of the tower, may have conspired to keep the crowds away.

And although the crowds might have been justified before, they—and by "they," we mean "you"—might reconsider, especially if you are looking for a friendly place to hang your hat, but nothing more. The smaller-size rooms here are basically motel rooms—really nice motel rooms, but with that level of comfort and style. Then again, you can often get such a room for around $49 a night. And do join the casino's players' club—they tend to offer free rooms with more or less minimal play. Perfect if you are coming to Vegas with no plans to spend time in your room except to sleep (if even that). Of course, the place just sold, so who knows what's in store for it?

That isn't to say there aren't other elements to like in place already, including the aforementioned casino, a midway area with kiddie-oriented rides, a pool with a view, and some of the friendliest, most accommodating staff in town. You can still ride the following incredible thrill rides (provided the wind isn't blowing too hard that day) on top of the tower: the **Big Shot,** a fabulous free-fall ride that thrusts passengers up and down the tower at speeds of up to 45 mph; **X-Scream,** a giant teeter-totter device that gives you the sensation of falling off the side of the building; and **Insanity: the Ride,** a whirly-gig contraption that spins you around more than 900 feet above terra firma, and another yet-to-be-announced ride to replace the closed roller coaster. (See p. 183 for a review of the three remaining adrenaline pumpers.) Indoor and outdoor observation decks offer the most stunning city views you will ever see, especially at night. For the price, this might be the right place for you. Just remember that you need a rental car or a lot of cash for cabs to get to the true thrills down the Strip.

In addition to the casino, the hotel sports two production shows: ***American Superstars*** (an impression-filled show, reviewed on p. 242) and ***BITE.***

2000 Las Vegas Blvd. S. (btw. St. Louis and Baltimore aves.), Las Vegas, NV 89104. ✆ **800/998-6937** or 702/380-7777. Fax 702/383-5334. www.stratospherehotel.com. 2,444 units. $49 and up double; $109 and up suite. Extra person $20. Children 12 and under stay free in parent's room. AE, DC, DISC, MC, V. Free self- and valet parking. **Amenities:** 9 restaurants; several fast-food outlets; casino; showrooms; wedding chapel; large pool area w/great views of the Strip; children's rides and games; concierge; tour desk; car-rental desk; shopping arcade; 24-hr. room service; laundry service; executive-level rooms. *In room:* A/C, TV w/pay movies, dataport, Wi-Fi (for a fee), hair dryer, iron/ironing board, safe.

INEXPENSIVE

Circus Circus Hotel & Casino ★ *Kids* This is the last bastion of family-friendly Las Vegas—indeed, for years, the only hotel with such an open mind. Which is also not to say that you should confuse this with a theme-park hotel. All the circus fun is still built around a busy casino. The midway level features dozens of carnival games, a large arcade (more than 300 video and pinball games), trick mirrors, and ongoing circus acts under the big top from 11am to midnight daily. The world's largest permanent circus, it features renowned trapeze artists, stunt cyclists, jugglers, magicians, acrobats, and high-wire daredevils. Spectators can view the action from much of the midway or get up close and comfy on benches in the performance arena. There's a "be-a-clown" booth where kids can be made up with clown makeup (easily washed off!) and red foam-rubber noses. They can grab a bite to eat in McDonald's (also on this level), and since the mezzanine overlooks the casino action, they can also look down and wave to Mom and Dad—or, more to the point, Mom and Dad can look up and wave to the kids without having to stray too far from the blackjack table. Circus clowns wander the midway, creating balloon animals and cutting up in various ways.

The thousands of rooms here occupy sufficient acreage to warrant a free Disney World–style aerial shuttle (another kid pleaser) and minibuses connecting its many components. Tower rooms have newish, just slightly better-than-average furnishings. The Manor section comprises five white, three-story buildings out back, fronted by rows of cypresses. Manor guests can park at their doors, and a gate to the complex that can be opened only with a room key ensures security. These rooms are usually among the least expensive in town, but we've said it before and we'll say it again: You get what you pay for. A renovation of these rooms added a coat of paint and some new photos on the wall but not much else. All sections of this vast property have their own swimming pools, additional casinos serve the main tower and sky-rise buildings, and both towers provide covered parking garages.

Adjacent to the hotel is **Circusland RV Park,** and is KOA-run, with 399 full-utility spaces and up to 50-amp hookups. It has its own 24-hour convenience store, swimming pools, saunas, whirlpools, kiddie playground, fenced pet runs, video-game arcade, community room, and Wi-Fi. The rate is $45 and up, with peak rates around $90. The very reasonably priced **Pink Pony** is Circus Circus's cheerful bubble-gum-pink-and-bright-red 24-hour eatery, with big paintings of clowns on the walls and pink pony carpeting. It offers a wide array of coffee-shop fare, including a number of specially marked "heart-smart" (low-fat, low-cholesterol) items. For gorging, there's always the **Circus Circus Buffet** (p. 168).

In addition to the ongoing circus acts, there's also the upgraded **Adventuredome** (p. 191) indoor theme park out back. There are three full-size casinos, all crowded and noisy, where you can gamble while trapeze acts take place overhead.

2880 Las Vegas Blvd. S. (btw. Circus Circus and Convention Center drives), Las Vegas, NV 89109. © 877/434-9175 or 702/734-0410. Fax 702/734-5897. www.circuscircus.com. 3,774 units. $59 and up double. Extra person $12. Children 16 and under stay free in parent's room. AE, DC, DISC, MC, V. Free self- and valet parking. **Amenities:** 7 restaurants; several fast-food outlets; casino; circus acts; midway-style carnival games; wedding chapel; 2 outdoor pools; video-game arcade; tour desk; car-rental desk; shopping arcade; 24-hr. room service; laundry service; dry cleaning; executive-level rooms. *In room:* A/C, TV w/pay movies, Wi-Fi (for a fee), hair dryer, iron/ironing board, safe.

6 East of the Strip

In this section, we cover hotels near the Convention Center, along with those farther south on Paradise Road, Flamingo Road, and Tropicana Avenue. Note that in the area around Paradise, there are more than a dozen chain-style hotels—various Marriotts (Courtyard, Residence Inn), a Budget Suites, and many others—any one of which is going to provide comfortable, reliable, utterly undistinguished lodging, and all of which often go for more money than they ought to. We've singled out a few here, but they are really quite interchangeable. Do some searching around online, and don't hesitate to try to play them off each other in an attempt to get a deal.

VERY EXPENSIVE

Hard Rock Hotel & Casino 🐸🐸 At press time, the hotel's new owners had announced plans for $750 million worth of new hotel towers, including one that is all suites for VIPs. The parking lot in front will become meeting and convention space plus a new, larger version of The Joint, while the old Joint is being removed and turned into additional casino area. All existing rooms and public spaces will get makeovers, so some of what you read below may have changed.

As soon as you check out the Hard Rock clientele, you'll know you are in a Vegas hotel that's like no other. The body-fat percentage (and median age) plummets; the percentage of black clothing skyrockets. Yep, the hip—including Hollywood and the music industry, among others—still flock to the Hard Rock, drawn by the cool 'n' rockin' ambience and the goodies offered by a boutique hotel (only in Vegas could 657 rooms be considered a "boutique hotel"). Our problem is that we are not famous pop stars and we do not look enough like Pamela Anderson to warrant the kind of attention that the staff seems to reserve for those types.

Arizona Charlie's Boulder **15**
Best Western
 Mardi Gras Inn **5**
Boulder Station **15**
Clarion Hotel & Suites—
 Emerald Springs **9**
Courtyard by Marriott **4**
Desert Rose Resort **13**
Fairfield Inn by Marriott **6**
Fiesta Henderson **14**

Green Valley Ranch
 Resort **14**
Hard Rock Hotel
 & Casino **11**
La Quinta Inn
 and Suites **7**
Las Vegas Hilton **1**
Marriott Suites **2**
Motel 6 **12**

Residence Inn
 by Marriott **3**
The Ritz-Carlton,
 Lake Las Vegas **14**
Sam's Town Hotel
 & Gambling Hall **15**
Terrible's **8**
Tuscany Suites
 & Casino **10**

It's that Boomer-meets-Gen-X sensibility that finds tacky-chic so very hip. Luckily, the "no-tell motel" look of the older rooms has been updated to more closely match the decor of the rooms in the newer addition. We still aren't crazy about the decor scheme in any of them—even the newer section is too '60s-futuristic hip to come off as posh, and all of it is showing more wear than it ought to. Bathrooms are a big step forward—bigger, brighter, and shinier, though in the older section, they can be cramped, spacewise, in suites. On a high note, the beds have feather pillows, and mattresses are surprisingly comfortable.

The lobby borders the casino (you can see how that immediately plunges you into the action, like it or not), which takes the center position in the round public area you immediately enter when arriving. On the perimeter is a collection of rock memorabilia, ranging from sad (a Kurt Cobain tribute) to cool (various guitars and outfits) to useless (various other guitars and outfits). The Hard Rock now has a permanent, if unwelcome, bit of rock trivia for its collection: John Entwistle, bassist for the Who, died in one of its rooms on the eve of the start of a tour with the band.

There are several fine restaurants, including AJ's Steakhouse, a tribute to original owner Peter Morton's dad, who brought us the legendary Morton's. You'll also find Nobu, a branch of highly famed Chef Nobu Matsuhisa's wildly popular Japanese restaurant, and AGO, a restaurant co-owned by Robert DeNiro. Kicky and funky Mexican food can be had at lunch and dinner in the folk-art-filled **Pink Taco** (p. 154), and **Mr. Lucky's 24/7** (p. 129) is the hotel's 'round-the-clock coffee shop, displaying rock memorabilia and old Las Vegas hotel signs. The **Hard Rock Cafe** (p. 127) is adjacent to the hotel. **The Joint** (p. 255) is a major showroom that often hosts big-name rock musicians.

If you've ever dreamed of being in a beach-party movie, or on the set of one of those MTV summer beach-house shows, the pool at the Hard Rock is for you. Multiple pools are joined by a lazy river and fringed in spots by actual sand beaches. You won't get much swimming done—the water is largely so shallow that it won't hit your knees—but there is swim-up blackjack (they give you little plastic pouches to hold your money), and a stage that features live music in the summer and is fronted by a sandy area, so you can make like Frankie, Annette, and Erik Von Zipper and do the Watusi. Or just pose in a thong bikini and new breasts. Whichever. On warm days and nights, this is *the* hangout scene.

The spa is smaller than its Strip counterparts but is soothing in its posh Space-Age-Zen way, and the health club is plenty large and well equipped, offering a full complement of Cybex equipment, stair machines, treadmills, massage, and steam rooms. There's a $20-per-day fee to use the health-club facilities.

4455 Paradise Rd. (at Harmon Ave.), Las Vegas, NV 89109. ✆ **800/473-ROCK** (473-7625) or 702/693-5000. Fax 702/693-5588. www.hardrockhotel.com. 657 units. $109 and up double; $250 and up suite. Extra person $50. Children 11 and under stay free in parent's room. AE, DC, MC, V. Free self- and valet parking. **Amenities:** 6 restaurants; casino; showroom; 2 outdoor pools w/lazy river and sandy-beach bottom; small health club; spa; concierge; tour desk; salon; 24-hr. room service; laundry service; dry cleaning; executive-level rooms. *In room:* A/C, TV w/pay movies, Wi-Fi (for a fee), hair dryer, iron/ironing board.

EXPENSIVE

Courtyard by Marriott ⭐   A complex of three-story buildings in an attractively landscaped setting of trees, shrubbery, and flower beds, the Courtyard is a welcome link in the Marriott chain. Although the services are limited, don't picture a no-frills establishment. This is a good-looking hotel (in a chain-establishment kind of way), with a pleasant, plant-filled lobby and very nice rooms indeed. Public areas and rooms still look brand-spanking new. Most rooms have king-size beds, and all have balconies or patios. It's also right across the street from a monorail station. Still, it's probably not worth the price given location and in comparison to what you can get at a comparably priced Strip hotel.

3275 Paradise Rd. (btw. Convention Center Dr. and Desert Inn Rd.), Las Vegas, NV 89109. ℂ **800/321-2211** or 702/791-3600. Fax 702/796-7981. www.courtyard.com. 149 units. $149 and up double (up to 4 people); $189 and up suite (up to 4 people). No charge for extra person. AE, DC, DISC, MC, V. Free parking at your room door. **Amenities:** Restaurant; outdoor pool; small exercise room; Jacuzzi; business center; limited room service; coin-op laundry; laundry service; dry cleaning; executive-level rooms; free computer and Wi-Fi in lobby. *In room:* A/C, TV w/pay movies, dataport, free high speed Internet access, coffeemaker, hair dryer, iron/ironing board.

La Quinta Inn and Suites ⍟   This is a tranquil and visually appealing alternative (within the limited range of chains) to the Strip's hubbub, featuring courtyards, rustic benches, attractive pools, barbecue grills, and picnic tables. The staff is terrific—friendly and incredibly helpful. The rooms are immaculate and attractive. Spend the extra money for an executive room, which features a queen-size bed, a small fridge, a wet bar, and a microwave oven. Double queens are larger but have no kitchen facilities. And two-bedroom suites are not just spacious, they are really full apartments, with large living rooms (some with sofa beds), dining areas, and full kitchens. Ground-floor accommodations have patios, and all accommodations feature bathrooms with oversized whirlpool tubs.

The hotel only recently became a La Quinta, and the property is undergoing a million-dollar renovation, which is expected to be complete by October 2008. It's unclear if the renovation will be noisy or otherwise bothersome, so you might want to ask when booking a room. Rooms and public areas have new paint, carpet, wallpaper, new flooring, and beds with pillow-top mattresses.

3970 Paradise Rd. (btw. Twain Ave. and Flamingo Rd.), Las Vegas, NV 89109. ℂ **800/531-5900** or 702/796-9000. Fax 702/796-3537. www.laquinta.com. 251 units. $89 and up double; $99 and up executive queen; $119 and up suite. Rates include continental breakfast. Up to 2 pets, free with security deposit. AE, DC, DISC, MC, V. Free self-parking. **Amenities:** Outdoor pool; Jacuzzi; tour desk; car-rental desk; free airport/Strip shuttle; coin-op laundry. *In room:* A/C, TV w/pay movies, dataport, Wi-Fi (free), kitchen in executive rooms and suites, coffeemaker, hair dryer, iron/ironing board.

Marriott Suites ⍟   Oh, sure, you don't lack for Marriotts in Las Vegas, but it is a reliable chain (if a tad overpriced), and you can't fault the location of this one. It's just 3 blocks off the Strip (and not much farther from the Convention Center)—a 10-minute walk at most, though in 100°F (38°C) heat, that may be too far. This is a solid choice for business travelers, but families might also like the lack of casino and accompanying mayhem, not to mention the extra-large, quite comfortable rooms. Each suite has a sitting area separated from the bedroom by French doors. And there are gorgeous prints on the walls—far, far better than you would expect in a hotel, much less in one of the chain variety.

325 Convention Center Dr., Las Vegas, NV 89109. ℂ **800/228-9290** or 702/650-2000. Fax 702/650-9466. www. marriott.com. 278 units. $159 and up suite (up to 4 people). AE, DC, DISC, MC, V. Free outdoor parking. **Amenities:** Restaurant; outdoor pool; small exercise room; Jacuzzi; tour desk; business center (w/free Wi-Fi); limited room service; laundry service; dry cleaning; coin-op laundry (at Residence Inn next door); executive-level rooms. *In room:* A/C, TV w/pay movies, dataport, Wi-Fi (for a fee), fridge, coffeemaker, hair dryer, iron/ironing board, safe.

Residence Inn by Marriott ⍟   Staying here is like having your own apartment in Las Vegas. The property occupies 7 acres of perfectly manicured lawns with tropical foliage, neat flower beds, and a big pool area. It's a great choice for families and business travelers.

Accommodations, most with working fireplaces, are housed in condolike, two-story wood-and-stucco buildings fronted by little gardens. Studios have adjoining sitting rooms with sofas and armchairs, dressing areas, and fully equipped eat-in kitchens complete with dishwashers. Every guest receives a welcome basket of microwave popcorn and coffee. All rooms have balconies or patios. Duplex penthouses, some with cathedral ceilings, add an upstairs bedroom (with its own bathroom, phone, TV, and radio) and a full dining room. A monorail station is just across the street.

3225 Paradise Rd. (btw. Desert Inn Rd. and Convention Center Dr.), Las Vegas, NV 89109. © **800/331-3131** or 702/796-9300. www.marriott.com. 192 units. $159 and up studio; $179 and up penthouse. Rates include breakfast buffet. AE, DC, DISC, MC, V. Free self-parking. Pets accepted with $100 non-refundable fee. **Amenities:** Outdoor pool; guest access to small exercise room next door at the Courtyard by Marriott; Jacuzzi; coin-op laundry; free Wi-Fi in public areas. *In room:* A/C, TV w/pay movies, dataport, free high-speed Internet access, kitchenette, coffeemaker, hair dryer, iron/ironing board.

MODERATE

Best Western Mardi Gras Inn *Value*   This well-run little casino hotel has a lot to offer and is apparently popular with budget-minded Europeans (which can sometimes result in some risqué Continental-style sunbathing around the pool). A block from the Convention Center and close to major properties, its three-story building sits on nicely landscaped grounds. There's a gazebo out back where guests can enjoy a picnic lunch.

Accommodations are all spacious: queen-size-bedded minisuites with sofa-bedded living-room areas and eat-in kitchens, the latter equipped with wet bars, refrigerators, and coffeemakers. All are what you'd expect from a midlevel motel, but the furnishings are well tended, if not exactly luxurious. Staying here is like having your own little Las Vegas apartment. A pleasant restaurant/bar off the lobby, open from 6:30am to 11pm daily, serves typical coffee-shop fare.

3500 Paradise Rd. (btw. Sands Ave. and Desert Inn Rd.), Las Vegas, NV 89109. © **800/634-6501** or 702/731-2020. Fax 702/731-4005. www.mardigrasinn.com. 314 units. $59 and up double. 4 people per room maximum. AE, DC, DISC, MC, V. Free parking at your room door. **Amenities:** Restaurant; small casino; outdoor pool; Jacuzzi; guest services desk; tour desk; car-rental desk; free airport shuttle; business center; salon; limited room service; coin-op laundry; dry cleaning. *In room:* A/C, TV w/pay movies, dataport, free Wi-Fi, kitchenette, fridge, coffeemaker, hair dryer, iron/ironing board, safe.

Clarion Hotel & Suites—Emerald Springs *Value*   Housed in three peach-stucco buildings, the Emerald Springs offers a friendly, low-key alternative to the usual glitz and glitter of Vegas accommodations. You'll enter via a charming marble-floored lobby with a waterfall fountain and lush, faux tropical plantings under a domed skylight. There's a small lounge area with a television and comfortable couches off the main lobby. Although your surroundings here are serene, you're only 3 blocks from the heart of the Strip.

Public areas and rooms here are notably clean and spiffy. Pristine hallways are hung with nice abstract paintings and have small seating areas on every level, and rooms are nicely decorated with bleached-oak furnishings. Even the smallest accommodations (studios) offer small sofas, desks, and armchairs with hassocks.

325 E. Flamingo Rd. (btw. Koval Lane and Paradise Rd.), Las Vegas, NV 89109. © **800/732-7889** or 702/732-9100. Fax 702/731-9784. www.clarionlasvegas.com. 150 units. $99 and up studio; $119 and up whirlpool suite; $159 and up hospitality suite. Extra person $20. Children 17 and under stay free in parent's room. AE, DC, DISC, MC, V. Free self-parking. **Amenities:** Restaurant; outdoor pool; small exercise room; Jacuzzi; concierge; tour desk; car-rental desk;

courtesy limo to airport/Strip; executive-level rooms. *In room:* A/C, TV w/pay movies and Nintendo, dataport, free Wi-Fi, kitchenette or minibar w/fridge, coffeemaker, hair dryer, iron/ironing board.

Desert Rose Resort ⟨⟨

This all-suite hotel has plenty of extras, making it stand out from its brethren and extremely appealing to families. Sure, the suites themselves are bland, but they have full kitchens (perfect for families seeking to save some money) and actual balconies, a huge relief in stuffy Vegas where the windows usually don't open. There is a free, continental breakfast, and an evening happy hour (Mon–Thurs) with snacks and free beer, wine, and soda. The pool is large, and there is table tennis and barbecue grills. All this just a block from the corner of the Strip and the Trop! This is really a lifesaver for families looking for a nice place not too far off the beaten path; think of the savings with the free breakfast, the snacks, and that full kitchen for other meals.

5051 Duke Ellington Way, Las Vegas, NV 89119. ☎ 800/811-2450 or 702/739-7000. Fax 702/739-9350. www.desertroseresort.com. 278 units. $99 and up 1-bedroom suite (up to 4 people); $169 and up 2-bedroom suite (up to 6 people). Rates include continental breakfast and weekday snacks. AE, DC, DISC, MC, V. Free outdoor parking. **Amenities:** Outdoor pool; Jacuzzi; small exercise room; coin-op laundry; laundry service; dry cleaning. *In room:* A/C, TV w/pay movies, dataport, Wi-Fi (for a fee), full kitchen, hair dryer, iron/ironing board.

Fairfield Inn by Marriott ⟨*Value*⟩

This pristine property is a pleasant place to stay. It has a comfortable lobby with sofas and armchairs, where coffee, tea, and hot chocolate are provided free all day. Rooms are cheerful. Units with king-size beds have convertible sofas, and all accommodations offer well-lit work areas with desks; TVs have free movie channels as well as pay-movie options. Local calls and high-speed Internet access are free. Breakfast pastries, fresh fruit, juice, and yogurt are served free in the lobby each morning, and many restaurants are within easy walking distance.

3850 Paradise Rd. (btw. Twain Ave. and Flamingo Rd.), Las Vegas, NV 89109. ☎ 800/228-2800 or 702/791-0899. Fax 702/791-2705. www.fairfieldinn.com. 129 units. $62 and up (up to 5 people). Rates include continental breakfast. AE, DC, DISC, MC, V. Free self-parking. **Amenities:** Outdoor pool; small exercise room; Jacuzzi; tour desk; car-rental desk; free airport shuttle; dry cleaning; free Wi-Fi in lobby and breakfast areas. *In room:* A/C, TV w/pay movies, dataport, free high-speed Internet access, hair dryer, iron/ironing board.

Las Vegas Hilton ⟨⟨

It's easy for us to overlook this dinosaur—look, we even called it a dinosaur. Totally unfair. It's one of the last of the dying breed of old Vegas hotels, but unlike many of its peers, it's still offering fine accommodations and even a bit more than that. A good place for adults—we mean that in a good way—looking for Vegas fun, all the better with yet another room renovation. The overall vibe is still old-school Vegas—we mean that in a good way—with an old-fashioned glitzy casino that is small enough to navigate without a GPS device. Consider it even if you aren't an old-timer, and don't be put off by the distance from the Strip; the monorail stops here, making access easier than ever. When you consider that on nights when you can't touch a room on the Strip for less than $175, the Hilton will put you in a nice room with plenty of marble and clean, well-maintained furnishings for a decent price, it seems silly to not make the Hilton a top choice more often. The clientele is a mix of savvy business travelers who know a good hotel deal when they see it. There are quite a few solidly good restaurants, too. Those very same facilities, however, mean that even a small convention can sometimes drive the prices up at odd times—then again, since conventions are often booked for weekdays, an atypical drop in price can occur on weekends. Just call or look at the website. The recently renovated, generously sized rooms do look fresh and include very good pillow-top mattresses and excellent amenities. Baths are smallish but do have nifty oval tubs. Upgrading to club level gets some complementary food and beverages served in a grown-up lounge.

The Hilton has a strong showing of restaurants, including TJ's Steakhouse, a Benihana, and a **buffet** (p. 169). The **Shimmer Cabaret,** a first-rate casino lounge/nightclub, has live entertainment and ongoing shows nightly. It's a great place to hang out in the evening, when it features regular sets by local cover bands. One of Elvis's sequined jumpsuits is enshrined in a glass case in the front, near the entrance to the lobby/casino (he played 837 sold-out shows here and Colonel Tom Parker's memorial service was held here in the hotel). There's also a major **showroom** (see chapter 9), featuring resident headliner Barry Manilow and other guest performers.

The third-floor roof comprises a well-landscaped 8-acre recreation deck with a large swimming pool, a 24-seat whirlpool spa, six Har-Tru tennis courts lit for night play, and more. Also on this level is a luxurious 17,000-square-foot state-of-the-art health club offering Nautilus equipment, Lifecycles, treadmills, rowing machines, three whirlpool spas, steam, sauna, massage, and tanning beds. There's a $20-per-day fee to use the facilities, but guests are totally pampered: All toiletries are provided; there are comfortable TV lounges; complimentary bottled waters and juices are served in the canteen; and treatments include facials and oxygen pep-ups. Discounts on health club fees are available for multiple-day use.

3000 Paradise Rd. (at Riviera Blvd.), Las Vegas, NV 89109. (C) **888/732-7117** or 702/732-5111. Fax 702/732-5805. www.lvhilton.com. 3,174 units. $49 and up double. Extra person $35. Children 17 and under stay free in parent's room. AE, DC, DISC, MC, V. Free self- and valet parking. **Amenities:** 8 restaurants; food courts; casino; showrooms; outdoor pool; 6 night-lit tennis courts; health club; spa; video-game arcade; car-rental desk; business center; shopping arcade; salon; 24-hr. room service; laundry service; dry cleaning; executive-level rooms. *In room:* A/C, TV w/pay movies, dataport, Wi-Fi (for a fee), hair dryer, iron/ironing board.

Sam's Town Hotel & Gambling Hall ✪

Just 5 miles from the Strip (which means it's not precisely near anything, but if you have a car, it's also not far), Western-themed Sam's Town is immensely popular with locals and tourists alike. This unexpectedly pleasing resort is well worth considering for the price. Off the beaten track though it may be, regular (if not exactly frequent), free shuttles to the Strip and Downtown may help you with any feelings of isolation. The addition of a new entertainment complex (including an 18-screen movie theater, a 56-lane bowling alley, and a child-care center) makes it an even more positive option, particularly for families.

Sam's Town's main draw is its centerpiece atrium, a high-rising edifice that is part park, part Western vista. With living trees and splashing fountains, plus silly animatronic animals, it's kind of goofy, but also a nice, albeit artificial (as if that's unusual for Vegas) place to wander through and sit (which is a rare thing for this town). And if it's a bit noisy, well, we'll take the splashing sounds of the water over the ka-ching-ing of slots any day. The other public areas, including the casino, have gotten a face-lift. If it isn't up to the impossible standards set by the new Strip hotels, everything is certainly less dated and dark.

Rooms are adequately sized, if a tad dim, thanks to the Western/Native American–themed decor, but they are clean and fine, especially for the price. All have either mountain views (higher up is much better) or inside-atrium views, which are great fun.

And bless it, the hotel continues to find ways to improve through almost nonstop remodeling or expansion. And while we love it when a place does not rest on its laurels but constantly seeks the improvements of change, that also means that every time we come here, some wall is up indicating that construction is going on, and every place within the hotel is subject to the whims of fortune and decor. The point being, don't totally count on anything we've mentioned above being here forever—after all, they took out a diner with the best burger in town and a large country-and-western dance hall of considerable tradition.

Sam's Town Firelight Buffet is described on p. 169. There are a variety of other dining options, including a cart in the atrium that serves homemade ice cream.

Roxy's Saloon, one of a dozen bars on the premises, offers live entertainment (country and western) for dancing, daily from noon to the wee hours. There's also a deli in the race-and-sports-book area, a bowling alley snack bar, a food court, an ice-cream parlor, and the aforementioned 18-screen movie theater and entertainment complex, complete with child-care facility.

The Sunset Stampede is a laser-and-water show that takes place four times daily (at 2, 6, 8, and 10pm) in the Mystic Falls Park. It begins with a howl from an animatronic wolf atop the waterfall, and then water spurts in sync with orchestral themes, as lasers fire pretty colors around the room. A 10-minute show, it's not long enough or special enough to be worth the drive from the Strip (though there are free buses to transport you—call for details), but if you happen to be around, grab a seat at the bar early. This is particularly important for kids, as it gets pretty crowded, and it's tough to see the show unless you are up close.

The enormous three-floor casino has a friendly, casual atmosphere.

5111 Boulder Hwy. (at Flamingo Rd.), Las Vegas, NV 89122. ℂ **800/634-6371** or 702/456-7777. Fax 702/454-8014. www.samstownlv.com. 648 units. $50 and up double; $140 and up suite. AE, DC, DISC, MC, V. Free self- and valet parking. **Amenities:** 7 restaurants; 12 bars; food court; casino; showrooms; 18-screen movie theater; 56-lane bowling center; outdoor pool; video-game arcades; tour desk; car-rental desk; shuttle to Strip/Downtown; laundry service; coin-op laundry machines in adjoining RV park. *In room:* A/C, TV w/pay movies, dataport, Wi-Fi (for a fee), coffeemaker.

Tuscany Suites & Casino ℱ   This may be the right kind of hybrid between chain hotel and fancier resort—not as lush as the latter but not anywhere near as expensive, either, with far more personal detail and indulgent touches than you can find at chains. It's another all-suite hotel, and another where "suite" really means "very big room." The rooms aren't memorable, just like the chain rooms, but they are smart enough that you won't get depressed like you might when you see some of the rooms in similarly priced hotels. The large complex (27 acres, complete with a winding pool) isn't so much Italian as it is vaguely evocative of the idea of Italian architecture, but it, too, is more stylish than most of the chains in town. And, unlike those other chains, this one comes with a large casino, roped off in such a way that this is still an appropriate place for families who want the best of all worlds (price, looks, family-friendly atmosphere, and gambling), especially as each room has a separate dining area, a kitchenette, and large TVs, plus convertible couches, on request. While the kids play, there is a large soaking tub for their folks to relax in. There's a good Italian restaurant on the premises, plus a lounge.

255 E. Flamingo Rd., Las Vegas, NV 89169. ℂ **877/887-2261** or 702/893-8933. Fax 702/947-5994. www.tuscany lasvegas.com. 700 units. $79 and up suite. AE, DISC, MC, V. **Amenities:** Restaurant; lounge; casino; outdoor pool; fitness center; concierge; car-rental access; business center; room service; laundry service; dry cleaning. *In room:* A/C, TV, Nintendo, dataport, Wi-Fi (for a fee), fridge, coffeemaker, hair dryer, iron/ironing board, safe.

INEXPENSIVE

Motel 6 ⓥ*alue*   Fronted by a big neon sign, this Motel 6 is the largest in the country, and it happens to be a great budget choice. Most Motel 6 properties are a little out of the way, but this one is quite close to major Strip casino hotels (the MGM is nearby).

Tips **Inexpensive Hotel Alternatives**

If you're determined to come to Vegas during a particularly busy season and you find yourself shut out of the prominent hotels, here's a list of moderate to very inexpensive alternatives.

On or Near the Strip
    Budget Suites of America, 4205 W. Tropicana Ave.; ✆ **702/889-1700**
    Budget Suites of America, 3655 W. Tropicana Ave.; ✆ **702/739-1000**
    Travelodge, 3735 Las Vegas Blvd. S.; ✆ **800/578-7878**

Paradise Road & Vicinity
    AmeriSuites, 4250 Paradise Rd.; ✆ **800/833-1516**
    Candlewood Suites, 4034 Paradise Rd; ✆ **877/226-3539**

Downtown & Vicinity
    Econo Lodge, 1150 Las Vegas Blvd. S.; ✆ **877/424-6423**

East Las Vegas & Vicinity
    Motel 6 Boulder Highway, 4125 Boulder Hwy.; ✆ **800/466-8356**
    Super 8 Motel, 5288 Boulder Hwy.; ✆ **800/800-8000**

West Las Vegas & Vicinity
    Motel 6, 5085 Dean Martin Dr.; ✆ **800/466-8356**

It has a big, pleasant lobby, and the rooms, in two-story, cream-stucco buildings, are clean and attractively decorated. Some rooms have showers only; others have tub/shower combo bathrooms. Local calls are free. And their Wi-Fi fee is the lowest town!

195 E. Tropicana Ave. (at Koval Lane), Las Vegas, NV 89109. ✆ 800/466-8356 or 702/798-0728. Fax 702/798-5657. www.motel6.com. 607 units. $45 and up single. Extra person $6. Children 16 and under stay free in parent's room. AE, DC, DISC, MC, V. Free parking at your room door. Small pets accepted. **Amenities:** 2 outdoor pools; tour desk; coin-op laundry; mini-mart. *In room:* A/C, TV w/pay movies, dataport (in some), Wi-Fi (for a fee).

Terrible's ✯ *Finds*   First of all, this place isn't terrible at all. (The owner is Ed "Terrible" Herbst, who operates a chain of convenience stores and gas stations.) Second, it isn't a bit like the hotel it took over, the rattrap known as the Continental. The Continental is gone, and good riddance. In its place is an unexpected bargain, a hotel frequently offering ridiculously low prices. Try this on for size: $39 a night! Near the Strip! Near a bunch of really good restaurants! Hot diggity! So what do you get?

Well, don't expect much in the way of memorable rooms; they are as basic as can be (despite some sweet attempts with artwork depicting European idylls), and some have views of a wall (though even those get plenty of natural light). Some, however, are considerably larger than others, so ask. The new hotel tower has both suites and standard rooms with new furnishings and flatscreen TVs, plus high-speed Internet. The pool area is a surprise; it looks like what you might find in a nice apartment complex (which, actually, is what Terrible's resembles on the outside), with plenty of palms and other foliage. There's a small but thoroughly stocked casino (not to mention penny slots, continuing the budget theme), plus a very good 24-hour coffee shop. How could you want for anything more? Did we mention the price and location? Plus a free airport shuttle? Okay, so we wish they had used a bit more imagination with the rooms.

4100 Paradise Rd. (at Flamingo Rd.), Las Vegas, NV 89109 © **800/640-9777** or 702/733-7000. Fax 702/765-5109. www.terribleherbst.com. 325 units. $39 and up double. Extra person $10. Children 12 and under stay free in parent's room. AE, DC, DISC, MC, V. Free self- and valet parking. **Amenities:** 2 restaurants; outdoor pool; 24-hr. room service. *In room:* A/C, TV w/pay movies, Nintendo (for a fee), dataport, high-speed Internet (for a fee, in some), coffeemaker, hair dryer.

7 Downtown

EXPENSIVE

Golden Nugget 🎔🎔 Always the standout hotel in the Downtown area, a recent face-lift has made it more appealing than ever, so while it's not the cheapest accommodations, it is by far the nicest. A massive face-lift has made the place look terrific; a new color scheme has given it a rich, deep look that is most posh and fresh. Everything feels brighter, lighter, and more spacious. The re-do is a good complement of the best of old and new Vegas; new enough not to be dated, but still user friendly.

The Golden Nugget opened in 1946 as the first building in Las Vegas constructed specifically for casino gambling. Steve Wynn, who is basically responsible for the "new" Vegas hotel look, took over the Golden Nugget as his first major project in Vegas in 1973. He gradually transformed the Old West/Victorian interiors (typical for Downtown) into something more high-rent and genuinely luxurious, especially for downtown Vegas. The sunny interior spaces are a welcome change from the Las Vegas tradition of dim artificial lighting. Don't forget their mascot (well, it ought to be): the world's largest gold nugget. The *Hand of Faith* nugget weighs in at 61 pounds, 11 ounces, and is on display for all to see.

Deluxe rooms are done in pretty floral schemes, and are attractive and comfortable enough that you don't need to splash out on the more contemporary gold-club rooms. In the North Tower, the rooms are slightly larger than in the South (smaller than the newer Strip places but not at all "small"). You don't have to walk through the casino to get to your room, but you do have to walk a distance to get to the newly redone pool, a chic and snazzy highlight, complete with a water slide that goes right through a glass tunnel in the shark tank. And check out that underwater restaurant! The presence of the pool, and general overall quality, makes this the best hotel Downtown for families; the other Downtowners seem geared toward the much older set and/or the single-minded gambler set.

The **Golden Nugget Buffet,** which is home to a fine Sunday brunch, is described in chapter 5. Oh, and yes, there is a casino. Don't think they'd forget that!

The Nugget's top-rated health club ($20 per day) offers a full line of Universal equipment, Lifecycles, stair machines, treadmills, rowing machines, free weights, steam sauna, and massage. Salon treatments include everything from leg waxing to seaweed-mask facials. Free Sebastian products are available for sprucing up afterward. The spa's opulent Palladian-mirrored foyer is modeled after a room in New York's Frick Museum.

129 E. Fremont St. (at Casino Center Blvd.), Las Vegas, NV 89101. © **800/846-5336** or 702/385-7111. Fax 702/386-8362. www.goldennugget.com. 1,907 units. $69 and up double; $275 and up suite. Extra person $20. No discount for children. AE, DC, DISC, MC, V. Free self- and valet parking. **Amenities:** 5 restaurants; casino; showroom; outdoor pool; health club; spa; tour desk; car-rental desk; salon; 24-hr. room service; laundry service; dry cleaning; executive-level rooms. *In room:* A/C, TV w/pay movies, dataport, Wi-Fi (for a fee), hair dryer, iron/ironing board, safe, robe/slippers.

MODERATE

Fitzgeralds Casino & Hotel 🎔 A few years ago, Fitzgeralds got a new owner, the first African-American man to own a Vegas casino, an interesting bit of history. Positive changes have come in his wake with total overhauls of the public areas and rooms. Largely gone is the luck-o'-the-Irish theme, which makes us sad when we think about Mr. O'Lucky, the hotel's longtime mascot, but not so much when it comes to all the rest of the leprechauns and shamrocks and other bits of Blarney nonsense. The casino has been brightened up, so it's now one of the nicer places to gamble Downtown; the hallways and check-in area have been redone, and a new outdoor pool—a rare amenity for Downtown in general, and open until the unheard-of (in Vegas) hour of 9pm—opened. Right now, you can expect a sort of Irish country-village walkway, complete with giant fake trees, leading to the room elevators. Fitzgeralds has the only balcony in Downtown from which you can watch the Fremont Street Experience. You can also sit in its McDonald's and gawk at the light show through the atrium windows.

The rooms are clean and comfortable, featuring standard hotel-room decor you will forget the moment you walk into the hallway. Because this is the tallest building Downtown (34 stories), you get excellent views: snowcapped mountains, Downtown lights, or the Strip. Whirlpool-tub rooms are slightly larger, offering wraparound windows.

301 Fremont St. (at 3rd St.), Las Vegas, NV 89101. *C* 800/274-LUCK (274-5825) or 702/388-2400. Fax 702/388-2181. www.fitzgeralds.com. 638 units. $59 and up double. Extra person $20. Children 11 and under stay free in parent's room. AE, DC, DISC, MC, V. Free self- and valet parking. **Amenities:** 5 restaurants; lounge; casino; unheated outdoor pool; concierge; car-rental desk; business center w/high-speed Internet (for a fee); 24-hr. room service; laundry service; dry cleaning. *In room:* A/C, TV w/pay movies, dataport, iron/ironing board, safe.

Four Queens *&* Opened in 1966 with a mere 120 rooms, the Four Queens (named for the owner's four daughters) has evolved over the decades into a major Downtown property occupying an entire city block. One of the last bastions of original Vegas glamour that still exists, and if this isn't the luxurious place it once was—and certainly it pales to the point of vanishing when compared with, say, The Palazzo—there is still plenty to like here, including sometimes very low rates. As the staff says, this is the place to stay if you just want to gamble—or if you want a genuine retro experience. A remodel has given the place a bit of a lift. Newly redone rooms come in a bright color palate, which is jarring given the monochromes that otherwise rule local decor. They can be rather wee, but the ones in the South Tower are a shade larger than the others, though we wouldn't hold any multi-person slumber parties in either. In most cases, rooms in the North Tower offer views of the Fremont Street Experience. The restaurant, **Hugo's Cellar** (p. 160), has a cozy lounge with a working fireplace, and two bars serve the casino.

202 Fremont St. (at Casino Center Blvd.), Las Vegas, NV 89101. *C* 800/634-6045 or 702/385-4011. Fax 702/387-5122. www.fourqueens.com. 690 units. $49 and up double; $119 and up suite. Extra person $15. AE, DC, DISC, MC, V. Free self- and valet parking. **Amenities:** 3 restaurants; 2 bars; casino; room service. *In room:* A/C, TV w/pay movies, Wi-Fi (for a fee), coffeemaker, hair dryer, iron/ironing board, safe.

INEXPENSIVE
California Hotel & Casino This is a hotel with a unique personality. California-themed, it markets itself mostly in Hawaii, and since 85% of its guests are from the Aloha State, it offers Hawaiian entrees in several of its restaurants and even has an on-premises store specializing in Hawaiian foodstuffs. You'll also notice that dealers are wearing colorful Hawaiian shirts. The rooms, however, reflect neither California nor Hawaii; they have mahogany furnishings and attractive marble bathrooms.

12 Ogden Ave. (at 1st St.), Las Vegas, NV 89101. *C* 800/634-6255 or 702/385-1222. Fax 702/388-2660. www.thecal.com. 781 units. $40 and up double. AE, DC, DISC, MC, V. Free self- and valet parking. **Amenities:** 4 restaurants; casino; small rooftop pool; video-game arcade; tour desk; laundry service; dry cleaning. *In room:* A/C, TV w/pay movies, coffeemaker, dataport, hair dryer, iron/ironing board, safe.

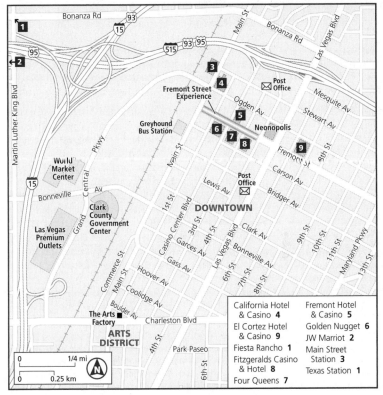

California Hotel & Casino **4**
El Cortez Hotel & Casino **9**
Fiesta Rancho **1**
Fitzgeralds Casino & Hotel **8**
Four Queens **7**
Fremont Hotel & Casino **5**
Golden Nugget **6**
JW Marriot **2**
Main Street Station **3**
Texas Station **1**

El Cortez Hotel & Casino 🏚🏚 Finally, a much-needed (as opposed to just done because everyone else is doing it) and well-conceived renovation has given an old-timer an unexpected new shot of life. The public areas are totally refreshed: Check out those cherrywood and oxidized metal panel sheets on the walls—you just don't see something that contemporary and design-intensive all that often in Downtown. By daringly removing half the slot machines, the casino floor has been opened up and aired out. The new entrance exterior with its stonework, planters, hitching posts, and stone drive-way feels like an entirely new hotel. Even more exciting, there are plans to take out a parking lot and turn it into a proper plaza with trees, fountains, and the like, which seems totally alien to the concept of Vegas. Additional plans include a South Beach–themed upscale annex in an adjacent, currently shabby property. Rooms (some quite large) have gotten new traditional furnishings; admittedly, nothing stands out, but with amenities like flatscreen TVs, nice new (if small) bathrooms, armoires with actual minifridges, and Wi-Fi (for a fee), they are right behind Main Street Station for recommendable affordable downtown lodgings. There is a new, popular Chinese buffet, and the steakhouse Roberta's is solidly good. Many of the employees have been here well over a dozen years, which says a lot. Local legend Jackie Gaughan still lives in the penthouse and wanders through the property. Overall, it's now a cool old Vegas place of the variety that doesn't exist any more. Forget the manufactured versions. This is the real thing, updated but without losing its identity, and for probably half the price (or even a third).

600 Fremont St. (btw. 6th and 7th sts.), Las Vegas, NV 89101. © **800/634-6703** or 702/385-5200. Fax 702/474-3626. www.elcortezhotelcasino.com. 428 units. $35 and up double; $60 minisuite. Extra person $8. AE, DISC, MC, V. Free self- and valet parking. **Amenities:** 3 restaurants; casino; salon; barber shop; small food court. *In room:* A/C, TV, Wi-Fi (for a fee).

Fremont Hotel & Casino   When it opened in 1956, the Fremont was the first high-rise in Downtown Las Vegas. Wayne Newton got his start here, singing in the now-defunct Carousel Showroom. Step just outside the front door, and there you are, in the **Fremont Street Experience** (p. 174). Rooms are larger (the bathrooms, however, are the opposite of "large"), more comfortable, and more peaceful than you might expect. (Though up until midnight you can hear, sometimes all too well, music and noise from the Fremont St. Experience show. But then again, if you are in bed before midnight in Vegas, it's your own fault.) The staff is shockingly friendly, partly because you actually can have personal service with hotels this size (another advantage of staying Downtown), partly because they just are. The hotel encourages environmental awareness by changing linens only every other day; upon request, it can be more often, but why not help out Earth a bit? For that matter, why not help out your wallet a bit and stay here?

The Fremont boasts an Art Deco restaurant called the **Second Street Grill** (p. 162), along with the **Paradise Buffet** (p. 170). Guests can use the swimming pool at the nearby California Hotel, another Sam Boyd enterprise.

200 E. Fremont St. (btw. Casino Center Blvd. and 3rd St.), Las Vegas, NV 89101. © **800/634-6182** or 702/385-3232. Fax 702/385-6229. www.fremontcasino.com. 447 units. $40 and up double. AE, DC, DISC, MC, V. Free valet parking; no self-parking. **Amenities:** 5 restaurants; casino; access to outdoor pool at nearby California Hotel; tour desk; car-rental desk; free shuttle to Sam's Town; laundry service; dry cleaning. *In room:* A/C, TV w/pay movies, DVD players (upon request), fridge, coffeemaker, hair dryer, iron/ironing board.

Main Street Station ✰✰ *Finds*   Though not actually on Fremont Street, the Main Street Station is just 2 short blocks away, barely a 3-minute walk. Considering how terrific it is, this is hardly an inconvenience. Having taken over an abandoned hotel space, the Main Street Station remains, in our opinion, one of the nicest hotels in Downtown and one of the best bargains in the city.

The overall look here, typical of Downtown, is early-20th-century San Francisco. However, unlike everywhere else, the details here are outstanding, resulting in a beautiful hotel by any measure. Outside, gas lamps flicker on wrought-iron railings and stained-glass windows. Inside, you'll find hammered-tin ceilings, ornate antique-style chandeliers, and lazy ceiling fans. The small lobby is filled with wood panels, long wooden benches, and a front desk straight out of the Old West, with an old-time key cabinet with beveled-glass windows. Check out the painting of a Victorian gambling scene to the left of the front desk. Even the cashier cages look like antique brass bank tellers' cages. They are proud of their special antiques, such as stained glass from the Lillian Russell mansion and doors from the Pullman mansion. It's all very appealing and just plain pretty. An enclosed bridge connects the hotel with the California Hotel across the street, where you will find shopping and a kids' arcade.

The long and narrow rooms are possibly the largest in Downtown, though the ornate decorating downstairs does not extend up here, but the rooms are plenty nice enough. The bathrooms are small but well appointed. Rooms on the north side overlook the freeway, and the railroad track is nearby. The soundproofing seems quite strong—we couldn't hear anything when inside, but then again, we're from L.A. A few people have complained about noise in these rooms, but the majority of guests haven't had any problems. If you're concerned, request a room on the south side.

The Pullman Grille is the steak-and-seafood place and is much more reasonably priced than similar (and considerably less pretty) places in town. The stylish **Triple 7 Brew Pub** is described in detail in chapter 9. The excellent buffet, **Main Street Station Garden Court,** is described in chapter 5. And the casino, thanks to some high ceilings, is one of the most smoke-free around.

200 N. Main St. (btw. Fremont St. and I-95), Las Vegas, NV 89101. ℂ 800/465-0711 or 702/387-1896. Fax 702/386-4466. www.mainstreetcasino.com. 406 units. $59 and up double. AE, DC, DISC, MC, V. Free self- and valet parking. **Amenities:** 3 restaurants; casino; access to outdoor pool at nearby California Hotel; car-rental desk; gift shop; dry cleaning; free Wi-Fi in lobby; free shuttle to Strip and sister properties. *In room:* A/C, TV w/pay movies and games, coffeemaker, safe.

8 Henderson

VERY EXPENSIVE

The Ritz-Carlton, Lake Las Vegas ✪✪✪ *(Kids)*   Vegas prides itself, these days, on offering all sorts of "luxury resorts." Vegas exaggerates—in some cases, by a lot. Truth be told, this is the *only* luxury resort (Four Seasons Las Vegas is a luxury hotel more than anything else because of its setup), and it's not even in Las Vegas. It's on the outskirts of next-door suburb Henderson, on the shores of Lake Las Vegas, meaning a 30-minute or so drive from the Strip.

Why on Earth are we recommending it? Because to come here is to come to a gob-smackingly beautiful resort—between the sparkling water and the crisp mountains, all the better in the early evening with a warm breeze blowing, this is the serene oasis everyone dreams of when he or she comes to the desert. Plus, it has all the pampering bells and whistles you could want. Here's the thing you have to remember: Those Strip "resorts" aren't in the hotel business; they are in the casino business, and the hotel is just a sideline. Ritz-Carlton is a proper hotelier, and you are the beneficiary. Certainly, the price is not cheap (though watch the website for some *great* deals), but once you realize what's included—all manner of treats that Strip "resorts" will charge you for as extras, plus impeccable service and a setting that's a dream—it's not a bad deal. Come here for a true getaway, and treat Vegas as a nearby attraction, an additional perk for your vacation.

Set right on the shores of the man-made (but so's Lake Mead, and we've gotten over it) Lake Las Vegas, and styled like an Italian lakeside resort, this property couldn't be more handsome, from the lobby to the cool-palette rooms, with plump beds, comforters, and Frette linens. All bathrooms are large and fully marbled (not tile, but real marble), with deep and long soaking tubs and amenities for miles. Most rooms have water views (make sure you get one of those) either of the serpentine lake (our favorite) or of the little bay that abuts the property. Some have balconies, and all have windows that open. Keep an eye on the lake for sightings of the big fish that occasionally cruise just below the surface.

The health club is the sort where all machines have flatscreen TVs, and the spa offers hot and cold plunge pools, plus a 360-degree Vichy shower and Prada skin treatments and products. There is one basic pool (with nice gazebos for shade) and one little "sandy beach" dipping area. And the overall service? We felt like if we sneezed, three people would have rushed at us with tissues, and four would have called doctors, just to make sure we were okay. It's also quiet, a great change from the hurly-burly found at most Strip hotels. And yet, it's not at all stuffy; no one minds if you run around in a bathing suit and bare feet.

The activities are the best around, from a large array of desert and mountain hikes, both on your own and guided (including a restful one that includes a round of Tai Chi in the evening), to stargazing (you are far enough from city lights, so the looking is good) to boating on the lake to honest-to-gosh fly-fishing. Daily yoga sessions and other physical fitness classes are also offered. And the hotel has access to two high-level golf courses.

Parents, in particular, should note that the club-level rooms offer, for an extra $100 a night, access to a lounge (complete with its own concierge and even more fabulous service), with nearly 'round-the-clock free "snacks," generous (and most of the time, rather fancy) enough to cover all your meal needs—that, plus free drinks, alcoholic and otherwise, makes this option a bargain. Think how much you spend on meals and drinks, and tell us that it doesn't routinely go over an extra $100 a day. Right next door is a charming faux-Italian village with nearly 40 shops and restaurants (so you need not rely on the hotel's restaurant, though it is excellent), plus a large, if borderline dull, casino, if you want that kind of action but don't want to drive to the Strip. There are regular shuttles to the Strip for a $35 fee, though why anyone would leave here is beyond us.

1610 Lake Las Vegas Pkwy., Henderson, NV 89011. ⓒ **800/686-2759** or 702/567-4700. Fax 702/567-4777. www.ritzcarlton.com. 349 units. $179 and up double (additional charge for rollaway bed). AE, DC, DISC, MC, V. Free self-parking. Pets accepted. **Amenities:** Restaurant; bar; casino; 2 pools; health club w/some free exercise classes; spa; summer children's program; concierge; tour desk; business center; shuttle to Strip; salon; 24-hr. room service; in-room massage; laundry service; dry cleaning; executive-level rooms. *In room:* A/C, TV w/pay movies, Nintendo, data-port, high-speed Internet access (for a fee), Wi-Fi (included in resort fee), minibar, hair dryer, iron/ironing board, safe.

EXPENSIVE

Green Valley Ranch Resort, Spa and Casino ⓖⓖ
Now, for all our heartfelt rhapsodizing above about the Ritz, do not think that we love Green Valley any less. It's not fair to this flat-out fabulous resort to compare the two—they can't quite compete on the same playing field because Green Valley doesn't have the same pedigree as the Ritz, nor does it have the knockout physical positioning on the lake. But it makes up for that with earnest efforts and slightly lower prices (plus it's about half the distance to the Strip, which is visible from the pool area), and if you can't stay at the one, you won't be unhappy staying at the other. Two different experiences, but each will make you feel like a resort should. Anyway, it seems that Green Valley's designers took careful notes on places like the Ritz-Carlton when coming up with their design—the interiors, rooms and public spaces both, feel completely influenced by the same, while the exterior pool area borrowed much from hip hotel concepts such as the Standard and the W. This sounds like a potentially risky combination, but it works smashingly. You can stay here with your parents or your kids, and every age group should be happy.

Inside, all is posh and stately—a dignified, classy lobby, large rooms with the most comfortable beds in town (high-thread-count linens, feather beds, plump down comforters), and luxe marble bathrooms. A recent expansion by the pool added more rooms, some of which have grand views.

Outside is the hippest pool area this side of the Hard Rock: part lagoon, part geometric, with shallow places for reading and canoodling, and your choice of poolside lounging equipment, ranging from teak lounge chairs to thick mattresses strewn with pillows, plus drinks served from the trendy Whiskey Beach. There is also a secluded topless bathing area for daring adults. The tiny health club is free, and the spa is also modern and hip.

At night, you can hang out at the ultratrendy **Whiskey Bar** (p. 262), where more mattresses and pillows get strewn about, all the better to attract the most beautiful bodies in town (desperate souls try to get past the velvet rope—you can pass with ease because you are staying here), or **Drop Bar** (p. 258); or you can head over to the entirely separate (as in, an adjoining building) casino area, which offers a disappointingly old school–looking gambling area, plus a variety of restaurants and a multiscreen movie theater. A shopping area, the District, conveniently located next door, features a simulated street scene, where you'll find your usual mall and catalog favorites (Williams-Sonoma, Pottery Barn), plus still more restaurants. This addition does help alleviate the resort's somewhat isolated nature.

2300 Paseo Verde Pkwy. (at I-215), Henderson, NV 89052. © **866/782-9487** or 702/617-7777. Fax 702/617-7778. www.greenvalleyranchresort.com. 490 units. $129 and up double. Extra person $35. Children 17 and under stay free in parent's room. AE, DC, DISC, MC, V. Free self- and valet parking. **Amenities:** 10 restaurants; food court; lounge; casino; movie theater; beautiful outdoor pool; health club; spa; concierge; business center; shopping arcade; free shuttle service to the Strip and the airport; 24-hr. room service; in-room massage; laundry service; dry cleaning; executive-level rooms. *In room:* A/C, TV w/pay movies, dataport, Wi-Fi (for a fee), coffeemaker, hair dryer, iron/ironing board, safe.

9 Summerlin

VERY EXPENSIVE

Red Rock Resort 🌟🌟🌟   The same people who brought you the fantastic Green Valley Ranch Resort trumped themselves by opening the swank Red Rock Resort in 2006, a hotel and casino complex that pretty much outdoes every other non-Strip hotel and most of the Strip hotels, also.

Built at a cost of nearly a billion dollars (an outrageous sum for a 400-room hotel not located on Las Vegas Blvd.), the hotel is named for its perch right on the edge of the **Red Rock Canyon National Conservation Area** (see chapter 10), a stunning natural wonderland of red-hued rock formations and desert landscape. It's a toss-up, really, which view you should choose—to the west, you get the beautiful natural vistas, and to the east, you get an unimpeded view of the Strip and Downtown Las Vegas, about 11 miles away.

Yes, it is a bit of a trek out here, but people seeking a luxury resort experience with the added bonus of a casino, restaurants, and more will find it worth the drive. Start with that casino, an 80,000-square-foot monster that is one of the most appealing in town, meandering through the building wrapped in natural woods, stonework, glass sculptures, and stunning amber-hued chandeliers. Eight restaurants serve up a wide variety of food selections, including a buffet and a branch of the famed Salt Lick BBQ out of Austin, Texas. Even the food court knocks it up a notch with a Capriotti's outlet offering some of the best submarine sandwiches we've ever tasted. Throw in a 16-screen movie theater, a day-care center, nightclubs and bars (including two from Rande Gerber, of Whiskey Sky renown), a sumptuous spa and health club, and a 3-acre circular "backyard" area with a sandy beach, swimming and wading pools (eagle-eyed sunbathers caught a pre-second-pregnancy-announcement Britney Spears wandering around here after a spousal tiff, so you know this is an instant celeb hot spot and getaway), Jacuzzis, private cabanas, and a stage where big-name entertainers perform, and you've got a terrific recipe for success.

The rooms are impressive, modern wonders with high-end furnishings and linens, 42-inch Hi-Def plasma TVs, iPod sound systems, giant bathrooms, and more, all wrapped up in clean, sleek lines and vibrant earth tones. Once ensconced in one, we were hard-pressed to leave.

One negative feature is a mandatory $20-per-night "amenities" charge that is tacked on to the room rate. This fee covers unlimited entry to the merely average health club and spa (services extra), nightly turndown service, and an airport shuttle, among other miscellanea. While it's a good deal if you plan to actually use any of that stuff, most people probably won't, so it's just another thing to jack up the room rates. Turndown, after all, should be automatically included. Then again, you can get rooms as low as $95 if you book on-line.

We're hoping that once the initial, well-deserved hype wears off, rates and fees will come down. Even if they don't, you may well find it worth the prices they charge to stay here.

11011 W. Charleston Rd., Las Vegas, NV 89135. ✆ **866/767-7773** or 702/797-7777. Fax 702/797-7053. www.redrocklasvegas.com. 816 units. $160 and up (up to 4 people). AE, DC, DISC, MC, V. **Amenities:** 10 restaurants; food court; bars, lounges, and nightclub; casino; 16-screen movie theater; outdoor pools and beach area; health club; spa; day-care center; concierge; business center; 24-hr. room service; in-room massage; laundry service; dry cleaning. *In room:* A/C, TV w/pay movies, dataport, Wi-Fi (for a fee), minibar, hair dryer, iron/ironing board, robe/slippers, safe.

5

Where to Dine

Among the images that come to mind when people think of Las Vegas are food bargains so good the food is practically free. They think of the buffets—all a small country can eat—for only $3.99!

While minor hotels still seek to attract guests with meal deals, frankly, eating in Las Vegas is no longer something you don't have to worry about budgeting for. The buffets are certainly there—no good hotel would be without one—as are the cheap meal deals, but you get what you pay for. Some of the cheaper buffets, and even some of the more moderately priced ones, are mediocre at best, ghastly and inedible at worst. And we don't even want to *think* about those 69¢ beef stew specials.

Meanwhile, the Vegas food scene has seen an enormous change. Virtually overnight, there was an explosion of new restaurants, most the creations of the so-called "celebrity chef" phenomenon. For this, we can thank those luxury-resort hotels, whose management realized that food today is a major indulgence and obsession and thus a significant part of the vacation experience. All of a sudden, Vegas can hold its head up alongside other big cities as a legitimate foodie destination.

Look at this partial list: Celebrity chefs Wolfgang Puck and Emeril Lagasse have ten restaurants in town between them; multi-Michelin-starred chef Joël Robuchon opened two restaurants in the MGM Grand; master Italian chef Mario Batali has two; deservedly famed chef Julian Serrano reigns at Bellagio's **Picasso;** Thomas Keller, the brains behind Napa Valley's French Laundry—considered by many to be the best restaurant in the United States—has a branch of his **Bouchon** bistro; legendary chef Alain Ducasse is behind **Mix** at THEhotel; and branches of L.A., New York, San Francisco, and Boston high-profile names such as **Pinot Brasserie, Le Cirque, Aureole, Olives, Border Grill, Nobu,** and others have all rolled into town. Not only are there more, but the 2006 James Beard Awards featured several Vegas nominees, while Robuchon's **L'Atelier** won Best New Restaurant in 2007. Unthinkable less than a decade ago.

Unfortunately, this boom has affected only the very highest end of the price category. In other words, boy, can you eat well, as long as you have a trust fund. Even as dedicated foodies, we can't, in good conscience, tell you to eat only at places that will require taking out a small bank loan—except we just don't really have any other options. For the moment, with a few exceptions, it's hard to eat extremely well or memorably in Vegas (especially on the Strip) for a down-to-earth price. The buffets remain, certainly, but they're not the bargains they once were; the midpriced food is, by and large, pretty forgettable; and the really low-end food found in the hotels—well, we try not to think of it as anything but fuel. That is, if you can still find it. Of course, this may not bother you as much as it bothers us.

If you get off the Strip, however, you can find some cheaper, more interesting alternatives, which we have listed below.

If you're staying on the Strip and you don't have the mobility of a car, your food options will be severely limited. Getting outside those enormous hotel resorts is a major proposition (and don't think that's not on purpose), which is why visitors often settle for what the hotel has to offer—long lines and diminished quality. Walking to another hotel—on the Strip, yet another major investment of time—means probably encountering much of the same thing. But not always: Once, when faced with dismal breakfast choices, we went from The Mirage over to Caesars, landing in their Forum Shops, where the Stage Deli stood, largely empty and with considerably better munchie options.

OUR BEST LAS VEGAS RESTAURANT ADVICE

GETTING IN   There are tricks to surviving dining in Vegas. If you can, make reservations in advance, particularly for the better restaurants. (You might get to town, planning to check out some of the better spots, only to find that they are totally booked throughout your stay.) Eat during off-hours when you can. Know that noon to, say, 1:30 or 2pm is going to be prime time for lunch, and 5:30 to 8:30pm (and just after the early shows get out) for dinner. Speaking of time, give yourself plenty of it, particularly if you have to catch a show. We once tried to grab a quick bite in the Riviera before running up to *La Cage.* The only choice was the food court, where long lines in front of all the stands (fast-food chains only) left us with about 5 minutes to gobble something decidedly unhealthy.

STAYING HEALTHY   "Unhealthy" is the watchword here; if you don't care about your heart or your waistline, you will do just fine in Vegas. (And really, what says "vacation" more than cream sauce?) But there are healthy choices on many menus. You just have to look for them. And we certainly don't mean to take away any enjoyment of those extravagant buffets; heck, that's a major part of the fun of Vegas! "Excess" is the other watchword here, and what better symbol is there than mounds of shrimp and unlimited prime rib?

SAVING MONEY   So you want to sample the creations of a celebrity chef, but you took a beating at the craps table? Check our listings to see which of the high-profile restaurants are open for lunch. Sure, sometimes the more interesting and exotic items are found at dinner, but the midday meal is usually no slouch and can be as much as two-thirds cheaper.

Or skip that highfalutin' stuff altogether. The late-night specials—a complete steak meal for just a few dollars—are also an important part of a good, decadent Vegas experience (and a huge boon for insomniacs). And having complained about how prices are going up, we'll also tell you that you can still eat cheaply and decently (particularly if you are looking upon food only as fuel) all over town. The locals repeatedly say that they almost never cook because in Vegas it is always cheaper to eat out. To locate budget fare, check local newspapers (especially Fri editions) and free magazines (such as *What's On in Las Vegas*), which are given away at hotel reception desks. Sometimes these sources also yield money-saving coupons.

ABOUT PRICE CATEGORIES   The restaurants in this chapter are arranged first by location, then by the following price categories (based on the average cost of a dinner entree): **Very Expensive,** more than $35; **Expensive,** $25 to $35; **Moderate,** $15 to $25; **Inexpensive,** under $15 (sometimes well under). In expensive and very expensive restaurants, expect to spend no less than twice the price of the average entree for your entire meal, with a tip; you can usually get by on a bit less in moderate and inexpensive restaurants. Buffets and Sunday brunches are gathered in a separate section at the end of this chapter.

A FINAL WORD   As welcome as the influx of designer chefs is—and, good lord, is it welcome—you can't help but notice that the majority are simply re-creating their best work (and sometimes not even that) from elsewhere rather than producing something new. So the Vegas food scene remains, like its architecture, a copy of something from somewhere else. And as happy as we are to encourage you to throw money at these guys, please don't forget the mom-and-pop places, which struggle not to disappear into the maw of the big hotel machines and which produce what comes the closest to true local quality. If you can, get in a car and check out some of the options listed below that are a bit off the beaten track. Show Vegas you aren't content—you want a meal you can brag about and afford, now!

1 Restaurants by Cuisine

AMERICAN
Carson Street Cafe (Downtown, $, p. 162)
Dick's Last Resort ★★ (South Strip, $$, p. 128)
ESPN (South Strip, $$, p. 126)
Fix ★★ (Mid-Strip, $$$$, p. 133)
Hard Rock Cafe ★ (East of the Strip, $$, p. 127)
Harley-Davidson Cafe ★ (South Strip, $$, p. 127)
Ice House Lounge ★ (Downtown, $, p. 162)
Jillian's ★ (Downtown, $, p. 163)
Margaritaville (Mid-Strip, $$, p. 127)
Rainforest Cafe ★ (South Strip, $$, p. 127)
Table 10 ★★★ (Mid-Strip, $$, p. 142)
Top of the World (North Strip, $$$$, p. 136)

ASIAN
Dragon Noodle Co. ★★ (South Strip, $, p. 128)
Grand Wok ★★ (South Strip, $$, p. 128)
Red 8 ★★ (North Strip, $$, p. 147)
Spago ★ (Mid-Strip, $$$$, p. 136)

BAGELS
Einstein Bros. Bagels ★ (East of the Strip, $, p. 152)

BARBECUE
Memphis Championship Barbecue ★★ (East of the Strip, $$, p. 151)
RUB ★ (Mid-Strip, $$, p. 142)
Salt Lick ★★ (West of the Strip, $$, p. 157)

BISTRO
Bouchon ★★★ (Mid-Strip, $$$, p. 137)
Daniel Boulud Brasserie ★ (North Strip, $$$$, p. 145)
Mon Ami Gabi ★★ (Mid-Strip, $$, p. 141)
Payard Patisserie & Bistro ★★★ (Mid-Strip, $$, p. 141)
Pinot Brasserie ★★ (Mid-Strip, $$$, p. 139)

BUFFETS/BRUNCHES
Bally's Sterling Sunday Brunch ★★ (Mid-Strip, $$$$, p. 165)
Bellagio Buffet ★★ (Mid-Strip, $$$$, p. 166)
The Buffet at the Las Vegas Hilton ★ (East of the Strip, $$, p. 169)

Key to Abbreviations: $$$$ = Very Expensive $$$ = Expensive $$ = Moderate $ = Inexpensive

The Buffet at TI ⭐⭐ (Mid-Strip, $$, p. 167)

Circus Circus Buffet (North Strip, $, p. 168)

Excalibur's Roundtable Buffet ⭐ (South Strip, $$, p. 164)

Flamingo Paradise Garden Buffet ⭐ (Mid-Strip, $$, p. 167)

Flavors at Harrah's ⭐ (Mid-Strip, $$, p. 168)

Fremont Paradise Buffet ⭐ (Downtown, $, p. 170)

Gold Coast Ports O' Call ⭐ (West of the Strip, $, p. 169)

Golden Nugget Buffet ⭐⭐ (Downtown, $$, p. 169)

Le Village Buffet ⭐⭐⭐ (Mid-Strip, $$$, p. 166)

Main Street Station Garden Court ⭐⭐⭐ (Downtown, $, p. 170)

Mandalay Bay's Bayside Buffet ⭐ (South Strip, $$$, p. 164)

MGM Grand Buffet (South Strip, $$$, p. 164)

Mirage Cravings Buffet ⭐⭐ (Mid-Strip, $$$, p. 166)

Monte Carlo Buffet ⭐ (South Strip, $$, p. 165)

MORE, The Buffet at Luxor ⭐⭐ (South Strip, $$, p. 165)

Rio's Carnival World Buffet ⭐⭐ (Mid-Strip, $$$, p. 167)

Sam's Town Firelight Buffet ⭐ (East of the Strip, $, p. 169)

Spice Market Buffet ⭐⭐ (South Strip, $$, p. 165)

Wynn Las Vegas Buffet ⭐⭐⭐ (North Strip, $$$$, p. 168)

CALIFORNIA

Gordon-Biersch Brewing Company ⭐ (East of the Strip, $$, p. 151)

Spago ⭐ (Mid-Strip, $$$$, p. 136)

Wolfgang Puck Bar & Grill ⭐⭐ (South Strip, $$, p. 125)

CHINESE

Cathay House (West of the Strip, $$, p. 154)

Fin ⭐ (Mid-Strip, $$$$, p. 132)

Harbor Palace ⭐ (West of the Strip, $$, p. 157)

CONTINENTAL

Alex ⭐⭐⭐ (North Strip, $$$$, p. 143)

Red Square ⭐⭐ (South Strip, $$$$, p. 124)

Top of the World (North Strip, $$$$, p. 136)

CREOLE

Delmonico Steakhouse ⭐⭐ (Mid-Strip, $$$$, p. 132)

Emeril's New Orleans Fish House ⭐ (South Strip, $$$$, p. 122)

CUBAN

Rincon Criollo (North Strip, $, p. 148)

DELI

Canter's Deli ⭐⭐ (Mid-Strip, $, p. 143)

Capriotti's ⭐⭐⭐ (North Strip, $, p. 147)

Carnegie Deli ⭐⭐ (Mid-Strip, $, p. 143)

Jason's Deli ⭐ (East of the Strip, $, p. 152)

Jody Maroni's Sausage Kingdom ⭐⭐⭐ (South Strip, $, p. 129)

DINER

Bougainvillea ⭐⭐ (East of the Strip, $, p. 152)

Burger Bar ⭐ (South Strip, $$, p. 126)

Sherwood Forest Café (South Strip, $, p. 140)

Tiffany's ⭐⭐ (North Strip, $, p. 148)

ECLECTIC

Cafe Ba Ba Reeba ⭐ (North Strip, $$, p. 146)

Sensi ⭐⭐ (Mid-Strip, $$$, p. 139)

FOOD COURT

Cypress Street Marketplace 𝕲𝕲 (Mid-Strip, $, p. 142)

FRENCH

Alizé 𝕲𝕲𝕲 (Mid-Strip, $$$$, p. 130)
Andre's 𝕲𝕲 (Downtown, $$$$, p. 160)
Eiffel Tower Restaurant (Mid-Strip, $$$$, p. 136)
Fleur de Lys 𝕲𝕲𝕲 (South Strip, $$$$, p. 122)
Joël Robuchon at the Mansion 𝕲𝕲𝕲 (South Strip, $$$$, p. 123)
L'Atelier de Joël Robuchon 𝕲𝕲𝕲 (South Strip, $$$$, p. 123)
Le Cirque 𝕲 (Mid-Strip, $$$$, p. 133)
Pamplemousse 𝕲 (East of the Strip, $$$$, p. 150)
Picasso 𝕲𝕲𝕲 (Mid-Strip, $$$$, p. 135)

GERMAN

Cafe Heidelberg German Deli & Restaurant 𝕲 (North Strip, $$, p. 146)

INTERNATIONAL

Hugo's Cellar 𝕲 (Downtown, $$$$, p. 160)
Second Street Grill 𝕲 (Downtown, $$$, p. 162)

IRISH

Nine Fine Irishmen 𝕲 (South Strip, $$, p. 128)

ITALIAN

B&B Ristorante 𝕲𝕲 (Mid-Strip, $$$$, p. 132)
Bartolotta Ristorante di Mare 𝕲𝕲𝕲 (North Strip, $$$$, p. 144)
Canaletto 𝕲𝕲 (Mid-Strip, $$$, p. 138)
Carluccio's Tivoli Gardens 𝕲𝕲 (East of the Strip, $$, p. 151)
Circo 𝕲𝕲 (Mid-Strip, $$$, p. 138)
Fellini's 𝕲 (North Strip, $$, p. 147)
Olives 𝕲𝕲 (Mid-Strip, $$$, p. 138)

Rao's 𝕲 (Mid-Strip, $$$, p. 139)
Valentino 𝕲 (Mid-Strip, $$$$, p. 137)

JAPANESE

Hyakumi 𝕲 (Mid-Strip, $$$$, p. 133)

MEDITERRANEAN

Olives 𝕲𝕲 (Mid-Strip, $$$, p. 138)
Paymon's Mediterranean Cafe & Lounge 𝕲 (East of the Strip, $, p. 153)

MEXICAN

Border Grill 𝕲𝕲𝕲 (South Strip, $$$, p. 125)
Dona Maria Tamales 𝕲𝕲 (North Strip, $, p. 147)
El Sombrero Cafe 𝕲𝕲 (Downtown, $, p. 162)
Isla 𝕲𝕲 (Mid-Strip, $$, p. 141)
Pink Taco 𝕲 (East of the Strip, $, p. 154)
Toto's 𝕲𝕲 (East of the Strip, $, p. 154)
Viva Mercado's 𝕲𝕲 (West of the Strip, $$, p. 157)

NOUVELLE AMERICAN

Aureole 𝕲𝕲𝕲 (South Strip, $$$$, p. 120)
Mix 𝕲𝕲 (South Strip, $$$$, p. 124)
Rosemary's Restaurant 𝕲𝕲𝕲 (West of the Strip, $$$, p. 156)

PACIFIC RIM

Second Street Grill 𝕲 (Downtown, $$$, p. 162)

PUB FARE

Gordon-Biersch Brewing Company 𝕲 (East of the Strip, $$, p. 151)
Monte Carlo Pub & Brewery 𝕲𝕲𝕲 (South Strip, $, p. 129)
Nine Fine Irishmen 𝕲 (South Strip, $$, p. 128)

RUSSIAN

Red Square 𝕲𝕲 (South Strip, $$$$, p. 124)

SANDWICHES

Earl of Sandwich ★★★ (Mid- Strip, $, p. 143)

SEAFOOD

Austins Steakhouse ★★ (West of the Strip, $$$, p. 154)

Bartolotta Ristorante di Mare ★★★ (North Strip, $$$$, p. 144)

Fin ★ (Mid-Strip, $$$$, p. 132)

Lawry's The Prime Rib ★★★ (East of the Strip, $$$$, p. 148)

Michael Mina ★ (Mid-Strip, $$$$, p. 134)

Morton's Steakhouse ★ (East of the Strip, $$$$, p. 150)

The Palm ★★ (Mid-Strip, $$$$, p. 135)

SOUL FOOD

M&M Soul Food ★★ (Downtown, $, p. 163)

SOUTHERN

House of Blues ★★ (South Strip, $$$, p. 126)

SOUTHWESTERN

Mesa Grill ★★ (Mid-Strip, $$$$, p. 134)

STEAK

Austins Steakhouse ★★ (West of the Strip, $$$, p. 154)

Charlie Palmer Steak ★★ (South Strip, $$$$, p. 121)

Delmonico Steakhouse ★★ (Mid-Strip, $$$$, p. 132)

Lawry's The Prime Rib ★★★ (East of the Strip, $$$$, p. 148)

Morton's Steakhouse ★ (East of the Strip, $$$$, p. 150)

The Palm ★★ (Mid-Strip, $$$$, p. 135)

The Range Steakhouse ★★ (Mid-Strip, $$$$, p. 135)

SUSHI

Dragon Sushi (West of the Strip, $, p. 150)

Hyakumi ★ (Mid-Strip, $$$$, p. 133)

THAI

Komol (East of the Strip, $, p. 152)

Lotus of Siam ★★★ (East of the Strip, $, p. 153)

Thai Spice (West of the Strip, $, p. 160)

2 South Strip

In addition to the restaurants listed in this section, the Monte Carlo has a branch of **Andre's,** a restaurant that has long been a favorite in Downtown (p. 160). The South Strip branch is just as highly recommended for fabulous food and attentive service.

VERY EXPENSIVE

Aureole ★★★ NOUVELLE AMERICAN   This branch of a New York City fave (it's pronounced are-ree-*all*) run by Charlie Palmer is noted for its glass wine tower. It's four stories of probably the finest wine collection in Vegas, made even more sensational thanks to catsuit-clad lovelies who are hoisted on wires to reach bottles requested from the uppermost heights. Amid this Vegas-show glitz is one of the better of the fine-dining experiences around. The menu is a three-course prix-fixe, though if you are winsome enough, they might send out luxurious extras such as pâté on brioche topped with shaved truffles or an espresso cup of cold yellow-pepper soup with crab. Otherwise, expect such marvels as a tender roasted lamb loin and braised shoulder, or a rack of venison accompanied by sweet-potato purée and chestnut crisp. Everything demonstrates the hand of a true chef in the kitchen, someone paying close attention to his work and to his customers. Service is solicitous; on a recent visit, with one diner not feeling up to an actual meal, the concerned server presented special clear

RESTAURANTS
Andre's **3**
Aureole **8**
Border Grill **8**
Burger Bar **8**
Charlie Palmer Steak **9**
Chocolate Swan **8**
Dick's Last Resort **6**
Dragon Noodle Co. **3**
Earl of Sandwich **1**
Emeril's New Orleans
Fish House **5**
ESPN **4**
Fleur de Lys **8**
Grand Wok **5**
Harley-Davidson Cafe **2**
House of Blues **8**
Jody Maroni's
Sausage Kingdom **4**
Joël Robuchon at
the Mansion **5**
L'Atelier de Joël
Robuchon **5**
Mix **8**
Monte Carlo Brew Pub
& Brewery **3**
Monte Carlo
food court **3**
New York–New York
food court **4**
Nine Fine Irishmen **4**
Rainforest Cafe **5**
Red Square **8**
Wolfgang Puck
Bar & Grill **5**

BUFFETS
Excalibur's Roundtable Buffet **6**
Mandalay Bay's Bayside Buffet **8**
MGM Grand Buffet **5**
Monte Carlo Buffet **3**
MORE, The Buffet at Luxor **7**
Spice Market Buffet **1**

consommé and mild sorbets. Desserts are playful, including a bittersweet chocolate soufflé with blood-orange sorbet and a Bartlett pear crisp with toasted cinnamon brioche and lemon grass foam. There is also an excellent cheese plate. Oh, and that wine tower? You can navigate it from your table with the innovative and highly engrossing handheld computer that not only helps you through the vast depths of the list but also makes suggestions for you, based on your meal choices.

In Mandalay Bay, 3950 Las Vegas Blvd. S. ✆ **877/632-1766.** www.aureolelv.com. Reservations required. Prix-fixe dinner $75; tasting menu $95. AE, DISC, MC, V. Sun–Thurs 6–10:30pm; Fri–Sat 5:30–10:30pm.

Charlie Palmer Steak ★★ STEAK   There are many, many steakhouses in Vegas, as if there were some natural law stating that any hotel without one will suffer from entropy and eventually collapse into a black hole. Discerning palates know there can be a significant difference between steakhouses; discerning wallets might not care. If you find yourself among the former, do try Charlie Palmer's, probably the best of the costlier shrines to beef. Those with the latter can be reassured that with entrees weighing in at around 22 to 45 ounces *each,* diners can legitimately—and in the name of decency ought to—share portions, which makes this a much more affordable experience than it might appear at first glance. And why not? Those enormous slabs o' meat are as tender as anything because with the big bucks, you do get the best cuts. We prefer the flavorful rib-eye to the other favorite, the Kansas City. Be sure to try the spinach salad topped with truffled fried egg and warm bacon vinaigrette as a starter (it gets a plus for presentation), and split sides like citrus-braised asparagus or a truffled potato purée (we are such suckers for what we call "gourmet baby food"). Desserts are stylish creations, and the entire thing is set in a generic fancy Vegas restaurant space that can be a bit noisy and crowded, so if romance is on the agenda, ask for one of the two-person tables in the back. Charlie Palmer, by the way, is the chef mind behind Aureole on the other side of Mandalay Bay; this makes two-for-two for this one celeb chef.

In Four Seasons Hotel, 3960 Las Vegas Blvd. S. ⓒ **702/632-5120.** www.charliepalmersteaklv.com. Reservations recommended. Main courses $30–$42. AE, DC, DISC, MC, V. Daily 5–10:30pm.

Emeril's New Orleans Fish House ⭐ CREOLE   As with Wolfgang Puck, the ubiquitous Emeril Lagasse has probably spread himself too thin. Although we thoroughly enjoy his shows on the Food Network and can attest that his flagship restaurant in New Orleans remains as good as ever, this Vegas outpost seems to have slipped. Part of that may be our prejudice about seafood restaurants in the desert—yes, we know about airplanes and refrigeration, but we rarely have good fish in Vegas, so there you go.

For that matter, at our last meal here, the most successful dish was the Creole-spiced aged rib-eye, drizzled with a horseradish Worcestershire sauce (with Emeril's famous kick that is neatly tempered by the mashed potatoes). A salad of duck comfit left us feeling the duck would be better on its own, but the sweet toasted-pecan vinaigrette was so good, it reconciled one diner toward eating previously loathed spinach. A signature dish remains the foie gras–topped ahi tuna, a combination that makes no more sense to us now than it did when we first tried it (because it tasted just fine with the side of spaghetti sauce). But the portions of foie gras can be generous, so you could just deconstruct it into a two-part appetizer. Still, you should try Emeril's famous lobster cheesecake appetizer, a savory delight like nothing you've tried before. The garlic-and-herb butter sauce that comes with the barbecued shrimp will have you mopping your plate with bread and asking for more of the petite rosemary biscuits that accompany it. And a slice of the banana-cream pie with banana crust and caramel drizzle is simple in its decadence.

In MGM Grand, 3799 Las Vegas Blvd. S. ⓒ **702/891-7374.** www.emerils.com. Reservations required. Main courses $17–$30 at lunch, $28–$45 at dinner (more for lobster). AE, DC, DISC, MC, V. Daily 11:30am–2:30pm and 5:30–10:30pm.

Fleur de Lys ⭐⭐⭐ FRENCH   One of the most sophisticated restaurants in Las Vegas, this is an offshoot of a highly regarded San Francisco establishment run by Chef Hubert Keller. Continuing the tradition of visually show-stopping restaurant spaces in Mandalay Bay, most tables are set in the semicircular two-story interior consisting half of '70s-style stone brick walls, half of billowing drapes, behind which are concealed a few dining booths. The tasting table is in the "wine loft" above the action, allowing fortunate diners a candle-framed view of the action below, surely the choicest table at what we consider one of the choicest restaurants in town. The entire thing is just sexy, right down to the playful, fanciful composition of the food. It's one of the few places in Vegas where you ought to dress up to dine, but in a good way.

Although the bustling servers do seem to know the difference between prompt care and unctuous crowding, it does feel a bit rushed—this is food you want to linger over. At this writing, one orders from a three-, four-, or five-course tasting menu (including a well-thought-out vegetarian option), featuring seasonal choices such as delicate seared ahi tuna with a gelée of chili and garlic, a silly appearing but hearty ocean "baeckeoffe" (a collection of seafood options, such as a sort of seafood burger–style crab cake on a brioche), pan-seared diver scallops with parsnip fries served in a cunning mini flower pot, perfect roasted Maine lobster with an artichoke purée soup, and roasted guinea hen breast and leg confit topped with crispy basil. Our descriptions won't do these playful, sexy dishes justice. Despite the presence of a perfect white and dark chocolate mousse on the "Chocolate Feast" sampler plate, you owe it to yourself to try the fresh fruit minestrone—basic sorbet, raspberries, and poppy seed *langue de chat,* all strong fresh fruit flavors that harmonize beautifully. There's no fat, and you won't care.

In Mandalay Place, 3930 Las Vegas Blvd. S. ☎ 702/632-7200. Reservations recommended. Jacket recommended. 3- to 5-course menu $79–$99. AE, DC, DISC, MC, V. Daily 5:30–10:30pm.

Joël Robuchon at the Mansion 👍👍👍 FRENCH   This is listed under "very expensive" only because there is no category for "unbelievably, heart stoppingly, stratospherically expensive." But it's here because legendary chef Joël Robuchon—the first (and youngest) chef to win three consecutive Michelin stars—who closed his restaurants in France (where he was proclaimed "chef of the century") at the height of his fame, has proven that all the hype is justified. The *Los Angeles Times* gave Robuchon four stars (their highest rating)—only the second time they've done so—while the *New York Times* reviewer proclaimed this "some of the very best French food I've eaten on this continent." These are no pushovers. All exclaim over the perfect combination of gastronomic feats and culinary artistry. This is not food as fuel, food to bolt down greedily (even though you may want to), but to slowly savor. Pay attention as you chew, and notice how many layers of interest are revealed. Great care was taken in choosing and combining ingredients, to create not fuss but both surprise and a sense of rightness. Exquisite, superb—name your superlative, and it's been levied toward this remarkable restaurant.

Chef Robuchon is not personally in the kitchen that often, but he has entrusted this kitchen to some of his former top employees, and if they stay (no implied criticism, merely a reality of the restaurant world), so should the quality. The menu changes very frequently, with many key ingredients flown in daily from France. And the service reminds one that Michelin ratings take that into account, too. None of this comes cheap. Could it possibly be worth it? When restaurant critics claim they would spend their own money to dine here, quite very possibly, yes. Look at it this way: You can easily lose the cost of a meal here in 15 forgettable minutes at a blackjack table (not that we did just that, ahem) or you can spend 3 hours slowly enjoying a meal, storing up much more pleasurable (presumably) memories. And then there is always the somewhat less expensive—that's relative, of course—neighbor **L'Atelier de Joël Robuchon,** where the focus is on counter seating, an intimate interactive experience between diner, server, and chef.

In MGM Grand, 3799 Las Vegas Blvd. S. ☎ 702/891-7925. Reservations strongly recommended. Jacket required. 6-course tasting menu $250, 16-course tasting menu $385. AE, DC, DISC, MC, V. Sun–Thurs 5:30–10pm; Fri–Sat 5:30–10:30pm.

L'Atelier de Joël Robuchon 👍👍👍 FRENCH   Despite the four-star L.A. and N.Y. *Times* reviews for the main establishment reviewed above, trustworthy foodies tipped this place as actually superior. Then it won the James Beard Award for best new restaurant in 2007, which only adds to the debate. You won't go wrong either way. Certainly, it's relatively cheaper here, but the casual, almost entirely counter seating (it's like an extremely high-style diner) might dismay those looking for a different sort of atmospheric experience. But food is supposed to be fun, and interacting with the charming (and often handsome and French) staff on the other side only adds to the great good pleasure.

Portions are small but exquisitely conceived and constructed. The tasting menu, which will likely change seasonally, is probably your best way to go, but consider coming just to treat yourself to a couple of dishes, such as the wee, perfect burgers topped with foie gras, or the Maine lobster with curry scent and fennel foam, a dish that sent us into a fit of uncontrollable giggles of delight. *La Pied de Cochon* is pâté made of pigs' feet, a robust and yet unctuous pork topped with shaved truffle and parmesan on toast. An *amuse-bouche* of foie gras parfait with port wine and parmesan foam comes layered in a teeny parfait glass with all three flavors clear and distinct and yet harmonizing into a powerful whole. The artistry only continues with dessert. A marvelous culinary experience.

In MGM Grand, 3799 Las Vegas Blvd. S. ℭ 702/891-7925. Reservations strongly recommended. Eight-course discovery menu $135; small plates $16–$32; main courses $38–$70. AE, DC, DISC, MC, V. Sun–Thurs 5:30–10:30pm; Fri–Sat 5–11pm.

Mix ⭑⭑ NOUVELLE AMERICAN   This is highly revered French chef Alain Ducasse's first Vegas venture, and such a Big Deal needs a Big Deal setting, in this case, on the 64th (by their counting) floor of THEhotel at Mandalay Bay. It's yet another spectacular restaurant space in a hotel full of them, this one white on white on silver, a futuristic fantasy including a set design sort of like a giant beaded curtain made of blown-glass balls, which envelopes a curving stairway plopped down in the middle. Some tables are set in silver "pods" that remind one of Woody Allen's *Sleeper.* It looks like where the Jetsons might eat. It also has drama outside, thanks to top-of-the-tall-hotel Strip views.

The playful yet hip attitude is reflected in the food, which is a little self-conscious. Still, it's hard to resist a place that starts with bread flavors such as ketchup or bacon, with a side of homemade peanut butter. But it's the sort of meal that grows progressively less "wow" as the evening wears on; early courses of melting amberjack sashimi topped with osetra caviar and a little lemon and salt are superb, as are the lovely foie gras terrines with nifty accompaniments. The signature Ducasse pressed chicken with foie gras in black truffle sauce probably would be just that much better if Chef himself were making it. Fish dishes are solidly good but not transcendent, and by the time the meal gets to, say, the rack of lamb, you may be thinking "Well, this is excellent, certainly, but not mind blowingly so." Which sounds like terrible nitpicking, but given the remarkable things going on in some other kitchens around town, and given the prices here, it's a fine line worth delineating. Still, the setting may make up for it.

In THEhotel, 3950 Las Vegas Blvd. S. ℭ 702/632-9500. www.chinagrillmgt.com/mixlv. Main courses $39–$60. AE, DISC, DC, MC, V. Daily 6–10:30pm.

Red Square ⭑⭑ CONTINENTAL/RUSSIAN   The beheaded and pigeon-dropping-adorned statue of Lenin outside Red Square only hints at the near-profane delights on the interior. Inside you will find decayed posters that once glorified the Worker, cheek by jowl with a patchwork mix of remnants of Czarist trappings, as pillaged from toppled Bolsheviks and Stalinists. It is disconcerting to see the hammer and sickle so blithely and irreverently displayed, but then again, what better way to drain it of its power than to exploit it in a palace of capitalistic decadence? And then there's the ice-covered bar—all the better to keep your drinks nicely chilled. After all, they have 150 different kinds of vodka, perhaps the largest collection in the world. It's all just one big post-Communist party (sorry, we had to say it).

Anyway, if you can tear your eyes away from the theme-run-amok, you might notice that the menu is quite good, one of our favorites around. Blow your expense account on some caviar (we found we liked nutty osetra better than stronger beluga), properly chilled in ice, served with the correct pearl spoon. Or, more affordably, nosh on Siberian nachos—smoked salmon, citron caviar, and crème fraîche. The chef's special is a Roquefort-crusted tender filet mignon, with some soft caramelized garlic and a fine reduction sauce; it's a grand piece of meat, one of the best in town and more cheaply priced than similarly ranked places. We also very much liked the pan-seared halibut with a roasted beet vinaigrette and basil oil on a mushroom risotto. Try a silly themed drink, such as the Cuban Missile Crisis, which is Rain vodka, dark rum, sugar-cane syrup, and lime juice, or better still, take advantage of that vodka menu and try a tasting flight of four kinds, joined by theme (in our case, the "Ultimate Flight" paired Polish, Russian, Scottish, and Estonian vodkas). Desserts are not so clever but are worth saving room for, especially the warm chocolate cake with a liquid center and the strawberries Romanoff.

In Mandalay Bay, 3950 Las Vegas Blvd. S. ℂ **702/632-7407.** Reservations recommended. Main courses $22–$46. AE, DC, MC, V. Daily 4–10:30pm.

EXPENSIVE

Border Grill 🎿🎿🎿 MEXICAN   For our money, here's the best Mexican food in town. This big, cheerful space (like a Romper Room for adults) houses a branch of the much-lauded L.A. restaurant, conceived and run by the Food Network's "Two Hot Tamales," Mary Sue Milliken and Susan Feniger. This is truly authentic Mexican home cooking—the Tamales learned their craft from the real McCoy south of the border—but with a *nuevo* twist. So don't expect precisely the same dishes you'd encounter in your favorite corner joint, but do expect fresh and fabulous food, sitting as brightly on the plates as the decor on the walls. Stay away from the occasionally bland fish and head right toward rich and cheesy dishes such as *chiles rellenos* (with perfect black beans) and chicken *chilaquiles* (a sister to the taco), or try new items such as mushroom empanadas. Don't miss the dense but fluffy Mexican chocolate-cream pie (with a meringue crust).

In Mandalay Bay, 3950 Las Vegas Blvd. S. ℂ **702/632-7403.** www.bordergrill.com. Reservations recommended. Main courses lunch $15–$24, dinner $21–34. AE, DC, DISC, MC, V. Mon–Fri 11:30am–11pm; Sat–Sun 11:30am–10pm.

Wolfgang Puck Bar & Grill 🎿🎿 CALIFORNIA   This transformed Puck Café is still a desirable, if slightly less affordable, option in the MGM Grand. There is nothing surprising on the menu if you've eaten in any modern cafe in the post-Puck era; it's not his fault his influence has extended so far. Frankly, it's still a relief in Vegas, and there is enough variety that all in your party should find something to please them, from crab cakes with basil aioli to a prime rib sandwich to homemade veal ravioli to Puck's pizzas, plus a good wine cellar. The fresh salads (we love the seasonal roasted beet) are better constructed than those at comparable eateries in town while Puck's hand is still on someone's helm; witness the silly potato chips drizzled with truffle oil and melted bleu cheese. It's all set in an almost entirely open space, a minimalist art take on a country kitchen, and a bit noisy thanks to proximity to the casino floor and

You Gotta Have a Theme

It shouldn't be too surprising to learn that a town devoted to gimmicks has just about every gimmick restaurant there is. Almost all have prominent celebrity co-owners and tons of "memorabilia" on the walls, which in virtually every case means throwaway items from blockbuster movies, or some article of clothing a celeb wore once (if that) on stage or on the playing field. Almost all have virtually identical menus and have gift shops full of logo items.

This sounds cynical, and it is—but not without reason. Theme restaurants are for the most part noisy, cluttered, overpriced places that are strictly tourist traps, and, though some have their devotees, if you eat at one of these places, you've eaten at them all. We don't want to be total killjoys. Fans should have a good time checking out the stuff on the walls of the appropriate restaurant. And while the food won't be the most memorable ever, it probably won't be bad (and will be moderately priced). But that's not really what you go for.

The **House of Blues** ★★, in Mandalay Bay, 3950 Las Vegas Blvd. S. (✆ **702/632-7607;** www.hob.com; Sun–Thurs 7:30am–midnight, Fri–Sat 7:30am–1am), is, for our money, food- and theme-wise, the best of the theme restaurants. The food is really pretty good (if a little more costly than it ought to be in a theme restaurant), and the mock Delta/New Orleans look works well, even if it is unavoidably commercial. You can dine here without committing to seeing whatever band is playing, as the dining room is separate from the club (note, though, that HOB gets very good bookings from nationally known acts). The gospel brunch might also be worth checking out (the food is good, though there's too much of it), but be warned: It's served inside the actual club, which can be unbelievably loud, so bring earplugs (we left with splitting headaches).

Presumably filling the hole left by the demise of the All Star Café, so that you sports fans won't feel left out in the theme restaurant race, **ESPN,** in New

cheers from the nearby sports book. Expect it to be crowded right before and after *KÀ*, but quiet during.

In MGM Grand, 3799 Las Vegas Blvd. S. ✆ **702/891-3019.** www.wolfgangpuck.com. Reservations accepted for dinner. Lunch $12–$35; dinner $18–$38 (most under $28). AE, DISC, DC, MC, V. Sun–Thurs 11:30am–10pm; Fri–Sat 10:30am–11pm.

MODERATE

Burger Bar ★ DINER See how Vegas is? They know you might be watching your budget or just wanting something simple but not boring, so they give you a place that specializes in hamburgers "your way," as the ads go. We love this concept, but we can't help but wince when we see how loading up a basic burger into a personalized creation turns a humble patty into a check for $15, and that's before we order fries and shakes. But we will eat at Burger Bar again because they start with Ridgefield Farm (most recommended) and Black Angus beef, and all the toppings (the usuals, such as

York–New York, 3790 Las Vegas Blvd. S. (© 702/933-3776; www.espnzone.com; Sun–Thurs 11am–11pm, Fri–Sat 11am–midnight), is a gigantic facility featuring rather wacky and entertaining sports memorabilia (such as Evel Knievel set up as the old "Operation" game, displaying his many broken bones), plus additions such as a rock-climbing wall/machine. It's pretty fun, actually, and the food, in a couch-potato-junk-food-junkie way, is not bad either, especially when you're sitting in one of the La-Z-Boy recliners, ordering delights such as three Krispy Kreme doughnuts topped with ice cream, whipped cream, and syrup, and watching sports.

There are those who rave about the warm Tollhouse-cookie pie at the **Harley-Davidson Cafe** 🍴, 3725 Las Vegas Blvd. S., at Harmon Avenue (© 702/740-4555; www.harley-davidsoncafe.com; Sun–Fri 11am–11pm, Sat 11am–midnight).

The **Hard Rock Cafe** 🍴, 4475 Paradise Rd., at Harmon Avenue (© 702/733-8400; www.hardrockcafe.com; Sun–Thurs 11am–11pm, Fri–Sat 11am–midnight, bar stays open an hour later than restaurant), has decent burgers. The serious hipster quotient at the adjacent hotel means that the people-watching opportunities are best here.

Visually, the **Rainforest Cafe** 🍴 *Kids*, in MGM Grand, 3799 Las Vegas Blvd. S. (© 702/891-8580; www.rainforestcafe.com; Sun–Thurs 8am–11pm, Fri–Sat 8am–midnight), with its jungle interior, complete with sound effects and animatronic animals, is the best of the bunch.

Parrot Heads like to party it up at **Margaritaville,** singer Jimmy Buffet's tropical-themed cafe/bar/club, at The Flamingo ("Parrot Heads" is how his fans refer to themselves). The menu runs a range from Mexican to something sort of Caribbean-themed to basic American, and it's not all that bad, considering. Partaking in lots of fruity tropical drinks doesn't hurt, either. In The Flamingo, 3555 Las Vegas Blvd. S. (© 702/733-3302; www.margaritaville lasvegas.com; Mon–Thurs 7am–2am, Fri–Sun 7am–3am).

bacon and avocado, but also six kinds of cheese, prosciutto, chopped scallions, and even anchovies and lobster, for Pete's sake), plus a choice of bun. It adds up to a hilarious and, if you have a deft touch, delicious experience (though we have not yet gotten them to prepare the doneness of the burgers to our proper specifications, so we advise you to be very clear about your pink-to-gray meat ratio preference).

Shakes are creamy, fries aren't bad (we like the skinny ones better than the fat ones), though if you haven't before, try the sweet-potato fries. One of the most clever desserts in town lurks on this menu, a "sweet burger"—a slab of really fine chocolate pâté "burger," on a warm donut "bun," topped with cunningly crafted strawberry "tomato" slices, mint "lettuce" and translucent passion-fruit "cheese." Note the weekend late hours. And skip the highfalutin' burger options—Kobe beef is too soft to use as burger meat, while foie gras is just wasted in this context. In other words, don't show off, but do have fun.

In Mandalay Place, 3930 Las Vegas Blvd. S. ☎ 702/632-9364. Main courses $8–$24 (burgers start at $8, depending on kind of beef; toppings start at 65¢ and go way up). AE, DISC, MC, V. Sun–Thurs 10:30am–11pm; Fri–Sat 10:30am–2am.

Dick's Last Resort ☆☆ AMERICAN Boy food for the boisterous. This is not the place to go for a relaxing or dainty meal. The gimmick is customer abuse—yes, you pay for the privilege of having a waitstaff hurl napkins and cheerful invective at you. But they mean it with love. Sounds a bit strange, but it works, in a party-hearty way. Speaking of, the food itself is hearty indeed, with house specialties (BBQ ribs, honey-glazed chicken) arriving in buckets. Entrees are substantial, both in quantity and construction—look for chicken-fried steak, fried chicken, meats or pastas covered in cream sauces. The most successful item could well be their burger, a juicy mammoth. Probably best for rowdy teenagers or stag parties, but both attitude and grub might be a relief after all those houses of reverent culinary worship.

In Excalibur, 3850 Las Vegas Blvd. S. ☎ 702/597-7991. Main courses $13–$24. AE, MC, V. Daily 11am–"late."

Grand Wok ☆☆ *Value* ASIAN No longer thoroughly pan-Asian but still a solid choice for sushi and, more importantly, budget fare in the form of the combo soup full of noodles and different kinds of meat. It's particularly nice and more affordable than the usual hotel restaurant—and the primarily Asian clientele clearly agrees. Note that soup portions are most generous; four people could easily split one order and have a nice and very inexpensive lunch, an unexpected bargain option for the Strip.

In MGM Grand, 3799 Las Vegas Blvd. S. ☎ 702/891-7777. Reservations not accepted. Main courses $15–$38; sushi rolls and pieces $7–$30. AE, DC, DISC, MC, V. Restaurant Sun–Thurs 11am–10pm, Fri–Sat 11am–1am; sushi bar Mon–Thurs 5–10pm, Fri–Sat 11am–1am, Sun 11am–10pm.

Nine Fine Irishmen ☆ IRISH/PUB FARE Travelin' foodies swear the once-maligned food in Ireland has improved enormously, so perhaps it's justified to have an Irish restaurant in the pantheon of new Vegas foodie destinations, though given our not-so-secret love of insta-decor, the interior of this one, mocked up to look like a rambling old Irish manor house, is enough for us. (Though once we start thinking about the complicated relationship the Irish have to New York City and vice versa, and the meta-implications of a faux-Irish restaurant set in a fantasy Irish house in the middle of a Vegas casino homage to NYC, our heads begin to hurt.) We will say that the caramelized apricot and pork sausage on a bed of potatoes was sweet and tangy and the Irish stew a right honest interpretation, complete with soda bread. Protestants and monarchists might want to try the beer-battered fish and chips, served as God and Queen intended, in a newspaper cone. You'll find bacon rashers at breakfast and a large selection of Irish beer most of the time. Desserts are more silliness, including items such as the Dunbrody Kiss, fluffy chocolate mousse on a crunchy caramel base.

In New York–New York, 3790 Las Vegas Blvd. S. ☎ 702/740-6969. www.ninefineirishmen.com. Reservations suggested. Dinner main courses: sandwiches $9–$12, entrees $18–$30. AE, MC, V. Daily 11am–11pm; bar daily 11am–3am.

INEXPENSIVE

Dragon Noodle Co. ☆☆ ASIAN A strong choice for a reasonably priced meal, Dragon Noodle is one of the better Chinese restaurants in town. We were glad to see that in addition to the usual suspects, there are some other interesting (if not radically less commonplace) choices on the menu. Note also the many Asian clients (part of our

┌───┐
│ (Value **Great Meal Deals**   │

Value Great Meal Deals

We've already alluded to the rock-bottom budget meals and graveyard specials available at casino hotel restaurants. Quality not assured and Pepto-Bismol not provided. As prices and deals can change without notice, we don't want to list examples, but finding a full prime-rib dinner for around $5 is not rare (pun definitely intended).

Your best bet is to keep your eyes open as you travel through town, as hotels tend to advertise their specials on their marquees. Or you can go to **www.vegas.com** and click **"Dining"** and then **"Dining Bargains,"** though the tips and prices may be similarly somewhat out-of-date. Following are three examples of current options for late-night munchies: **Ellis Island** offers a $4.95 10-ounce steak (plus potato and other sides), and $7.99 gets you a Porterhouse steak at **Arizona Charlie's Boulder. Mr. Lucky's 24/7** at the Hard Rock Hotel is a particularly good diner, with particularly good people-watching. And then ask your server about the $7.77 steak, three barbequed shrimp, and sides; it's not on the menu, so you have to know about it. And while it's not a "meal" it is certainly a "deal": **Onda** at The Mirage has a comp wine tasting, complete with nibbles, from 5 to 7pm on Fridays.

criteria for the authenticity of a place) and that the restaurant can handle large groups. Food is served family style and prepared in an open kitchen, so you know it's fresh. Be sure to try the very smooth house green tea. You might let your waiter choose your meal for you, but try the crispy Peking pork, the sweet pungent shrimp, the pot stickers, and perhaps the generous seafood soup. We were a little disappointed by the popular sizzling black-pepper chicken, but you may not be, so don't let us stop you. And they now have a sushi bar!

In Monte Carlo Resort & Casino, 3770 Las Vegas Blvd. S. (C) 702/730-7965. www.dragonnoodleco.com. Main courses $5.50–$17 (many under $10). AE, DC, DISC, MC, V. Sun–Thurs 11am–11pm; Fri–Sat 11am–midnight.

Jody Maroni's Sausage Kingdom ✸✸✸ DELI   There are several worthy fast-food stands in the New York–New York food court, but this one deserves an individual mention. What began as a humble stand on the Venice boardwalk in Los Angeles has expanded into a sausage empire, and we are glad. You will be, too, especially if you take a chance on their menu and don't just stick with the basic hot dog (though they do offer three tempting varieties) and instead try something a little more adventurous, like the tequila chicken sausage made with jalapeños, corn, and lime. (We wish that they offered samples and an even larger menu, as the original stand still does.) Or just vary your basic sweet Italian sausage with a hotter variety. Either way, you can top it with raw or grilled onions and peppers as it gets stuffed into a sesame-seed soft roll. Maybe some chili fries, too. This is our first choice for fast food in the immediate area.

In New York–New York, 3790 Las Vegas Blvd. S. (C) 702/740-6969. www.jodymaroni.com. Main courses $6–$11. AE, DC, MC, V. Daily 11am–6pm.

Monte Carlo Pub & Brewery ✸✸✸ Finds Kids PUB FARE   Lest you think we are big, fat foodie snobs who can't appreciate a meal unless it comes drenched in truffles and caviar, we hasten to direct you to this lively, working microbrewery (with a sort

Value Quick Bites

Food courts are a dime a dozen in Vegas, but the one in **New York–New York,** 3790 Las Vegas Blvd. S. (© **702/740-6969**), deserves a mention for two reasons: It's the nicest setting for this sort of thing on the Strip, sitting in the Greenwich Village section of New York–New York, which means scaled replica tenement buildings, steam rising from the manhole covers, and more than a little (faux, naturally) greenery, a nice change from unrelentingly shrill and plastic mall decor. The selections are the usual, with one exception listed below **(Jody Maroni's Sausage Kingdom),** but it's a better-than-average food court, with Chinese food and pizza (as befitting an ode to NYC), and excellent if expensive (for this situation) double-decker burgers, plus **Schraft's** ice cream.

The **Monte Carlo,** 3770 Las Vegas Blvd. S., between Flamingo Road and Tropicana Avenue (© **702/730-7777**), has some surprisingly good options, too. There's the always-reliable **McDonald's,** and for sweets there is **Häagen-Dazs. Sbarro** offers enticing pizza slices. If you want a good, cheap meal on the Strip and want to avoid some of those dubious night-owl specials, come here. It's open daily from 6am to 3am.

And if you head farther down the Strip, to the **Grande Canal Shoppes** at The Venetian, 3355 Las Vegas Blvd. S. (© **702/414-1000**), you can find another decent food court, with a **Panda Express,** a good pizza place (despite the confusing name of **LA Italian Kitchen**), a burrito stand, and a juice joint. Plus, it's right by the canals of this faux Venice, one of our favorite places in Vegas.

of rustic factory appearance) and its hearty, not-so-highfalutin' food. No fancy French frills and, best of all, no inflated prices. Combine the general high quality with generous portions—a nachos appetizer could probably feed eight (though it was not the best nachos appetizer ever)—and this may be a better deal than most buffets. It's not, however, the place for a quiet rendezvous, with about 40 TVs spread throughout (a sports fan's dream) and music blaring.

Earning recent raves were the short ribs in a fine barbecue sauce, cooked just right; the excellent appetizer of chicken fingers and shrimp fried in beer; the garlic pizza with mounds of our favorite aromatic herb; the pizza topped with lamb, grilled eggplant, and goat cheese (well, maybe that has more frills than we promised); and the avocado-and-shrimp salad. We also highly enjoyed the double-chocolate-fudge suicide brownie, though, really, what's not to love about something like that?

In Monte Carlo Resort & Casino, 3770 Las Vegas Blvd. S. © **702/730-7777**. Reservations not accepted. Main courses $6–$15. AE, DC, DISC, MC, V. Wed–Sun 11am–11pm; Fri–Sat 11am–1am.

3 Mid-Strip

VERY EXPENSIVE

Alizé 👍👍👍 FRENCH   Just a perfect restaurant, thanks to a combination of the most divine dining room and view in Vegas, not to mention one of the best chefs in Vegas. Situated at the top of the Palms Hotel, three sides of full-length windows allow

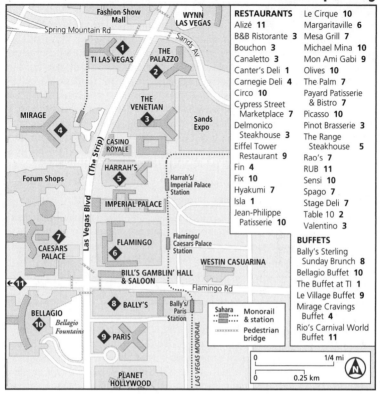

RESTAURANTS

Alizé **11**	Le Cirque **10**
B&B Ristorante **3**	Margaritaville **6**
Bouchon **3**	Mesa Grill **7**
Canaletto **3**	Michael Mina **10**
Canter's Deli **1**	Mon Ami Gabi **9**
Carnegie Deli **4**	Olives **10**
Circo **10**	The Palm **7**
Cypress Street	Payard Patisserie
Marketplace **7**	& Bistro **7**
Delmonico	Picasso **10**
Steakhouse **3**	Pinot Brasserie **3**
Eiffel Tower	The Range
Restaurant **9**	Steakhouse **5**
Fin **4**	Rao's **7**
Fix **10**	RUB **11**
Hyakumi **7**	Sensi **10**
Isla **1**	Spago **7**
Jean-Philippe	Stage Deli **7**
Patisserie **10**	Table 10 **2**
	Valentino **3**

BUFFETS

Bally's Sterling
  Sunday Brunch **8**
Bellagio Buffet **10**
The Buffet at TI **1**
Le Village Buffet **9**
Mirage Cravings
  Buffet **4**
Rio's Carnival World
  Buffet **11**

a panoramic view of the night lights of Vegas; obviously, window-side tables are best, but even seats in the center of the room have a good view (though seats on the right are now bedeviled by the recent Palms tower addition). Many great chefs have restaurants locally but are rarely in their kitchens (Emeril and Wolfgang, we love them, but they can't be in 25 different places at once). This operation is carefully overseen by Andre, he of the eponymous (and excellent) restaurants Downtown and in the Monte Carlo. The menu changes seasonally, but anything you order will be heavenly.

We've rarely been disappointed in either the appetizer or main course department. For the former, look for a shrimp and artichoke timbale trimmed with avocado and cucumber relish, or a tissue-thin Kobe beef carpaccio with dark pesto topping and tomato comfit. The foie gras can come in a pink-grapefruit-and-citrus-honey reduction, a tangy combination. Fish can be a little dry here, so we suggest either the stunning New York steak with summer truffle jus and potato herb pancakes, or the meltingly tender lamb chops with some shredded lamb shank wrapped in a crispy fried crepe. Desserts are similarly outstanding and often of great frivolity, such as sorbet in a case of browned marshmallow, floating in raspberry soup. Yeah, we're going over the top on this one, but we bet you won't think we're wrong.

In Palms Casino Resort, 4321 W. Flamingo Rd. ℭ **702/951-7000**. Fax 702/951-7002. www.alizelv.com. Reservations strongly recommended. Entrees $34–$67; 5-course tasting menu $95; 7-course tasting menu $125. AE, DC, DISC, MC, V. Sun–Thurs 5:30–10pm; Fri–Sat 5:30–11pm, last reservation at 10:30.

B&B Ristorante ☆☆ ITALIAN   Long-time Food Network staple Mario Batalli has a couple of Vegas outposts, and this is perhaps the most notable. It looks like an uber-Italian trattoria, full of dark wood, quite inviting and unfortunately very loud. Naturally, the desirable room is in the wine cellar. The menu options are a little too casual for the price, and might be intimidating for those uninitiated in Batalli, but there's probably no one in Vegas doing such interesting Italian food. To that end, you might be best served sticking with the *primi* (pasta selections), which are cheaper and arguably more interesting than the *secondi,* though portions are not hearty. Don't miss the beef-cheek ravioli with duck liver, but other notables are the mint love letters with lamb sausage and the stinging nettle *pappardelle* with wild boar ragu. Or just do the rather reasonable $75 pasta tasting menu. Meanwhile, if you are lucky, Chef himself might be roaming the place in his famous clogs.

In The Venetian, 3355 Las Vegas Blvd. S. ℂ 702/266-9977. Main courses $21–$49. AE, DISC, MC, V. Daily 5–11pm.

Delmonico Steakhouse ☆☆ CREOLE/STEAK   You might well feel that Emeril Lagasse is omnipresent. This incarnation is a steakhouse version of his hard-core classic Creole restaurant; this ever-so-slight twist is just enough to make it a superior choice over the more disappointing New Orleans locale. It's set in two dining rooms; the left one is '70s den ugly—choose instead the Neutra/Schindler–influenced right side.

You can try Emeril's concoctions, plus fabulous cuts of red meat. You can't go wrong with most appetizers, especially the superbly rich smoked mushrooms with homemade tasso ham over pasta—it's enough for a meal in and of itself. The same advice holds for any of the specials, or the gumbo, particularly if it's the hearty, near-homemade country selection. If you want to experiment, definitely do it with the appetizers; you're better off steering clear of complex entrees, no matter how intriguing they sound (such as a 1-night special of foie gras–stuffed ahi tuna). The tableside-made Caesar was dubbed "transcendental" by one astute diner. We've found the entree specials to be generally disappointing; the deceptively simple choices are more successful. The bone-in rib-eye steak is rightly recommended (skip the gummy béarnaise sauce in favor of the fabulous homemade Worcestershire or A.O.K. sauce). Sides are hit-or-miss—the creamed spinach was too salty, but a sweet-potato purée (a special, but maybe they'll serve you a side if you ask sweetly) is most definitely a winner. Too full for dessert? No, you aren't. Have a bananas-Foster cream pie, butterscotch crème brûlée, or the lemon icebox pie, a chunk of curd that blasts tart lemon through your mouth.

In The Venetian, 3355 Las Vegas Blvd. S. ℂ 702/414-3737. www.emerils.com. Reservations strongly recommended for dinner. Main courses $40–$50. AE, DC, DISC, MC, V. Daily 11:30am–2pm; Sun–Thurs 5–10pm; Fri–Sat 5–10:30pm.

Fin ☆ SEAFOOD/CHINESE   Elegant and decorous, perhaps a little higher on style (love the glass ball curtains, evocative of bubbles rising in water) than on substance, though that may just be our reaction to the prices, especially when you see how cheap dim sum is in other (admittedly, much less convenient) parts of town. Still, the quiet flourish of ritual that accompanies course presentation makes for a peaceful break from casino madness. Highlights include the rice cooked in chicken fat; the crispy shitake mushrooms in a sweet-and-sour sauce that ought to convert even a non-mushroom fan; and the deeply spicy seared black-pepper beef tenderloin.

In The Mirage, 3400 Las Vegas Blvd. S. ℂ 866/339-4566 or 702/791-7353. Reservations recommended. Main courses lunch $11–$27, dinner $19–$48. AE, DC, DISC, MC, V. Daily 11am–3pm and 5–11pm.

Fix 🇷🇷 AMERICAN   A just-right synthesis of gourmet dining, fun dining, and accessible dining, created by the people behind Bellagio's The Bank nightclub. Looking, as one visitor described it, like a "giant clam opening up toward the casino," the menu continues this playful vibe. Look for the silly presentation called "Forks," appetizers of smoked salmon and caviar skewed on forks and served tines in the air. Or desserts like "Shake and Cake" (espresso shake and a brownie), a peanut butter and jelly crème brûlée (misconceived? Or an idea whose time has come? You decide!), and delightful banana sugared-doughnuts with chocolate-and-peanut butter dipping sauce.

But before those clever conclusions come particularly good (in a town not known for same) fish selections, including scallops stacked with a crust of potatoes on applewood-smoked bacon, and "The Ultimate Shell," a selection of seafood (from clams to lobster) that comes in an XL size of dreamy decadence. Best of all are the steaks, which are grilled over cherrywood, giving the meat a smoky yet fruity flavor, reminding you that meat is supposed to have dimensions to its taste. From the trendy "small plates" to hamburgers, this is one complete menu, all right. All in all, a good compromise fancy location for a special occasion or just a treat of a meal: not so froufrou that basic eaters will be dismayed, not so simplistic that foodies will feel cheated, and not in the least bit stodgy or intimidating. Given the late hours and the origins, though, expect a lively and young crowd, especially as the night wears on.

In Bellagio, 3600 Las Vegas Blvd. S. ✆ **702/693-8400.** Reservations recommended. Main courses $29–$75. AE, MC, V. Sun–Thurs 5pm–midnight; Fri–Sat 5pm–2am.

Hyakumi 🇷 JAPANESE/SUSHI   Hyakumi (Yah-*koo*-me) is a quaint little oasis in the midst of a bustling casino. Tastefully decorated with hardwood floors in a tea-garden atmosphere, it is a relaxing respite from the madness of Vegas, as kimono-clad waitresses cater to your every need with a never-ending cup of particularly good green tea, plus hot towels, to put you in a Zen-like state.

But the setting, as serene and beautiful as it is, is not the reason for a visit to Hyakumi; it's the sushi. Supervised by Executive Chef Hiroji Obayashi, famed for his award-winning Hirozen Gourmet Restaurant in Los Angeles, Hyakumi offers some of the best sushi in town. It's not the cheapest, but it is well worth the extra cost. From the *toro* to the salmon roll, every bite melts in your mouth. The fish is shipped in daily and is prepared by friendly sushi chefs who obviously love what they do. If sushi isn't your thing, there is also a restaurant serving up traditional (but very expensive) Japanese fare in a lovely garden setting.

In Caesars Palace, 3570 Las Vegas Blvd. S. ✆ **877/346-4642.** Reservations recommended. Sushi $6–$10 per roll or piece; main courses $25–$60. AE, DC, DISC, MC, V. Daily lunch 11am–3pm, dinner 5–11pm.

Le Cirque 🇷 FRENCH   The influx of haute-cuisine, high-profile restaurants in Vegas means there are ever so many places now where you may feel like you have to take out a bank loan in order to eat—and you may wonder why you ought to. Though generally we always feel free to spend your money for you, we actually are going to suggest that you hold on to it in the case of Le Cirque, unless someone else is doing the buying. It's not that the food is bad—quite the contrary—but it's not the very best in town, and it is among the most expensive. And remember what we said about most of Vegas being quite casual? Here, forget it. If you didn't bring your nicest black, you are going to feel very uncomfortable.

The surprisingly small dining room (you may be virtually rubbing elbows with your neighbor, so keep inflammatory secrets out of the conversation) is decorated with murals of quaint bygone circus themes and a ceiling draped with gay fabric meant to evoke the Big Top. The busy decor adds to the cramped feeling. The menu changes seasonally, but you can expect genuine French cuisine—heavy, with lots of butter, though a recent visit brought a duo of cold cucumber and heirloom tomato soups that were so refreshing, every restaurant in this desert town ought to serve them. The lobster salad is sweet and tender, with a perfect black-truffle dressing; risotto is French style, almost soupy, perfect with fresh morels (in season) and Parmesan. The filet mignon is, oddly, not as good a cut as served elsewhere, but it does come with a generous portion of foie gras. For dessert, we loved the white chocolate cream (solid but not overwhelming), layered with banana and wrapped in phyllo, along with a milk chocolate dome with crème brûlée espresso.

In Bellagio, 3600 Las Vegas Blvd. S. ℂ **877/234-6358**. Reservations required. Jacket preferred; no jeans, shorts, t-shirts, or sneakers. Prix-fixe dinner $105 or $145. AE, DC, DISC, MC, V. Daily seating 5:30–10pm.

Mesa Grill ⭐⭐ SOUTHWESTERN   Food Network darling Bobby Flay has his fans and his detractors, and we aren't going to mediate that argument here, especially since the man isn't cooking in the kitchen any more often than most celebrity chefs in this town. More significantly, regardless of where you fall in the debate, this is a worthy restaurant, if, like so much in Vegas, a bit overpriced. Just about every well-spiced entree is over $30, and sometimes well over.

Still, there is so much that is fun here; blue-corn pancakes with barbeque duck, even the chicken quesadilla (made in a special dedicated oven) comes with garlic crème fraîche. Presentation is over the top—yes, yes, this is playful food, we get it, now stop it—but those who are a bit on the wimpy side when it comes to spices will appreciate how each entree comes with its own cooling element (the aforementioned crème fraîche, for example). Desserts are equally frivolous, though not particularly theme-intensive (unless you consider an exceptional raspberry and white-chocolate cheesecake "Southwestern"). Those wishing to try it without breaking the bank should either come at lunch or consider splitting appetizers as a light meal.

In Caesars Palace, 3570 Las Vegas Blvd. S. ℂ **702/731-7731**. Main courses $12–$24 for brunch and lunch, $23–$45 for dinner. Mon–Fri 11am–3pm and 5–10:30pm; Sat–Sun 10:30am–3pm and 5–10:30pm.

Michael Mina ⭐ SEAFOOD   What is it about Vegas and fish? Even this premier San Francisco piscine palace let us down. The signature lobster potpie is good, a splashy presentation that includes the wheeling of the pie to the table and the careful excising of the contents, including the broth and crusty top, which then fails to stay crusty thanks to the broth contact. Oh, well. But then again, at these prices, one cannot simply brush it off with "Oh, well." The miso-glazed sea bass in mushroom consommé tasted like nothing more than seafood sukiyaki. Really good sukiyaki, but even so. Starters of langoustine and crab ravioli are mealy and dull, while the "tasting" of foie gras, instead of multiple presentations of same, was just one serving of seared liver, with a nice parsnip tarte tatin. Desserts, including an actual root-beer float and a (this time, genuine) chocolate tasting, are much more successful. Service is a bit too rushed, with bread and water delivered in the heedless manner of a coffee shop.

In Bellagio, 3600 Las Vegas Blvd. S. ℂ **702/693-7223**. www.michaelmina.net. Reservations recommended. Main courses $36–$72 (lobster and whole foie gras higher). AE, DC, DISC, MC, V. Daily 5:30–10pm.

The Palm 🎭🎭 STEAK/SEAFOOD   A branch of the venerable New York eatery, which has been branching ever farther afield recently, this place attracts a star-studded clientele fond of the reliable and hearty, if not terribly exciting, bill of fare. (The famous may also be hoping to find their faces among the many caricatures that cover the walls.) This is plain but filling food—at manly prices. Red-meat lovers will be happy with the high-quality steaks found here, though those on a budget will shudder in horror. The tendency is to give the meat a good charring, so if you don't like yours blackened, start with it less well done and send it back for more if necessary. If you've hit a jackpot, your money will be well spent on one of The Palm's Buick-size lobsters. They're utterly succulent and outrageously priced, but given their size—they start at 3 pounds—they can easily be shared. If you're worried that all this won't be enough, add one of the delicious appetizers (plump but high-priced shrimp cocktails or a perfect prosciutto with melon) or toss in a side of crispy deep-fried onions. Desserts are heavy and unspectacular.

In Caesars Palace Forum Shops, 3570 Las Vegas Blvd. S. © 702/732-7256. www.thepalm.com. Reservations recommended. Main courses $13–$22 at lunch, $27–$83 at dinner. AE, DC, MC, V. Daily 11:30am–11pm.

Picasso 🎭🎭🎭 FRENCH   A Spanish chef who cooks French cuisine in an Italian-themed hotel in Vegas? Trust us, it works. This is one of the best restaurants in Vegas, and given the sudden serious competition for such a title, that says a lot. Steve Wynn spent months trying to talk Madrid-born chef Julian Serrano (whose Masa was considered the finest French restaurant in San Francisco) into coming to Bellagio. His bulldog tenacity paid off, and we should all thank him. This is an extraordinary dining experience, including the thrill of having $30 million worth of Picassos gaze down over your shoulders while you eat. It's not like dining in a stuffy museum, however—the water fountains going off outside every 15 minutes (with staid diners rushing to the windows to check it out) pretty much take care of that. Many of the furnishings were designed by one of Picasso's sons, and even the paintings themselves are challenged for beauty by the exceptional floral arrangements.

Serrano's cooking is a work of art that can proudly stand next to the masterpieces. The menu changes nightly and always offers a choice between a four- or five-course prix-fixe dinner or a tasting menu. The night we ate there, we were bowled over by roasted Maine lobster with a trio of corn—kernels, sauce, and a corn flan—that was like slightly solid sunshine. Hudson Valley foie gras was crusted in truffles and went down most smoothly. A filet of roasted sea bass came with a light saffron sauce and dots of cauliflower purée. And finally, pray that they're serving the lamb rôti—it was an outstanding piece of lamb, perfectly done, tender, and crusted with truffles. Portions are dainty but so rich that you'll have plenty to eat without groaning and feeling heavy when you leave. Desserts are powerful yet prettily constructed. A molten chocolate cake leaves any other you may have tried in the dust and comes with ice cream made with imported European chocolate. A crisp banana tart with coconut ice cream is a fine nonchocolate (foolish you) choice, while a passion-fruit flan in a citrus-soup sauce is perfect if you don't have much room left. Everything is delivered by attentive staff who make you feel quite pampered. Can we go back soon and try it all again?

In Bellagio, 3600 Las Vegas Blvd. S. © 877/234-6358. Reservations recommended. Prix-fixe 4-course dinner $113; 5-course degustation $123. AE, DC, DISC, MC, V. Wed–Mon 6–9:30pm.

The Range Steakhouse 🎭🎭 STEAK   This place is worth visiting if only for the spectacular view of the Strip (few Strip restaurants take advantage of this view, oddly

---

Moments A Dining Room, or Two, with a View

As we keep noting, the Strip at night is a dazzling sight, which is why hotel rooms with Strip views come at such a premium. Regardless of whether you were able to get the proverbial room with a view, consider dining at the chic **Eiffel Tower Restaurant,** in Paris Las Vegas, 3655 Las Vegas Blvd. S. (© **702/948-6937;** www.eiffeltowerrestaurant.com; daily 11:30am–2:30pm and Sun–Thurs 5–10:30pm, Fri–Sat 5–11pm), located on the 11th floor of said Mid-Strip hotel. Or choose the Stratosphere's **Top of the World,** in Stratosphere Hotel & Casino, 2000 Las Vegas Blvd. S. (© **702/380-7711;** www.topoftheworldlv.com; daily 11am–2:45pm and Sun–Thurs 5:30–10:30pm, Fri–Sat 5:30–11pm), which is almost at the top of the North Strip's Stratosphere Tower, the tallest structure west of the Mississippi. Both offer fantastic views. The latter even revolves 360 degrees, while the former also looks down on the Bellagio fountains. Both, however, also match sky-high views with sky-high prices, and, unfortunately, neither has food worth the price. Go for a special night out, or see if you can get away with just ordering appetizers and dessert (which are both superior to the entrees, anyway). You can also just have a drink at their respective bars, though each is set back far enough from the windows that drinkers have less-optimal views than diners.

---

enough) from 40-foot-high wraparound windows. Muted copper and wood tones make for a formal but not intimidating environment and a fine-looking room. The small menu features the usual steakhouse offerings—various cuts of beef and some chicken dishes, plus a few salads—but at a high-medium price. That said, the quality is better than we've found at the usual Vegas steakhouse suspects. We particularly liked the filet mignon on a Gorgonzola-onion croustade. All entrees come with family-style side dishes (they change nightly but can include such items as marinated mushrooms or horseradish mashed potatoes). Appetizers are also worth noting. The five-onion soup is thick, heavy, creamy, and served in a giant hollowed-out onion. It's delicious, as was a smoked chicken quesadilla. Don't miss the bread, which comes with a sweet-and-savory apricot-basil butter.

In Harrah's, 3475 Las Vegas Blvd. S. © 702/369-5084. Reservations strongly recommended. Main courses $20–$59. AE, DC, DISC, MC, V. Daily 5:30–10:30pm.

Spago (*R* _Overrated_ ASIAN/CALIFORNIA   At this point in the game, Spago represents both the best and the worst of the celebrity chef phenomenon. If you eat at the Beverly Hills location, you might well have the very best meal of your life, and almost certainly something that demonstrates the reason why such a fuss is made about creative cooking. The problem is that Wolfgang Puck, the man who virtually invented the Chef-as-Household-Name concept, and certainly had as much to do as anyone with California cuisine becoming a viable food genre, has stretched himself too thin—seven restaurants in Vegas alone. No one can keep a personal watch on that many locations, and the result is that this one, the first sign that Vegas was becoming a viable restaurant destination, is now simply not our first, nor even second, choice for you to spend your hard-won jackpot money.

The inside menu changes seasonally, but the signature—and reliable—dish is a Chinese-style duck, moist but with a perfectly crispy skin. It's about as good as duck gets, served with a doughy, steamed bun and Chinese vegetables. Our other suggestion is to come here for lunch, and that's still not the worst plan. Salads, sandwiches, and pastas are all pretty and generously portioned, and the signature Puck pizzas, like prosciutto and goat cheese and pear, are still quite good (ask for the off-the-menu and legendary "Jewish pizza," with salmon and crème fraîche). Nothing is all that innovative, however (braised leek and ham quiche with apple-smoked bacon—good, but you've seen it before), and nothing stands out. Desserts can actually be so poor—such as a dry chocolate cake—we won't even bother finishing them.

In Caesars Palace, 3570 Las Vegas Blvd. S. (C) 702/369-6300. www.wolfgangpuck.com. Reservations recommended for the dining room, not accepted at the cafe. Dining room main courses $28–$68; cafe main courses $15–$33. AE, DC, DISC, MC, V. Dining room daily 5:30–10pm; cafe Sun–Thurs 11am–11pm, Fri–Sat 11am–midnight.

Valentino ⋒ ITALIAN   Valentino was long considered the best Italian restaurant in L.A., and even the best in America (per *Bon Appetit*, and we suppose they oughta know). But this branch (with generic nice restaurant decor) isn't quite as successful as its Southern California counterpart, with complicated offerings that too often just miss the mark. Quail stuffed with snails and served with white-and-yellow polenta, for example, or house-smoked shrimp with crispy veggies and an apple-balsamic sauce—they're all interesting, but the combinations don't quite work. Working entirely well, however, are the four-cheese ravioli with truffle-cream sauce and fresh truffle shavings—we shamelessly mopped our plate with our bread—and the wild-rabbit loin in rhubarb-encrusted prosciutto. Their wine list is superb.

In The Venetian, 3355 Las Vegas Blvd. S. (C) 702/414-3000; www.pieroselvaggio.com. Reservations strongly recommended. Main courses $20–$49; tasting menus $70–$95, with wine pairing, $110–$145. AE, DC, DISC, MC, V. Valentino daily 5:30–11pm; The Grill daily 11:30am–11pm.

EXPENSIVE

Bouchon ⋒⋒⋒ BISTRO   Thomas Keller made his name with his Napa Valley restaurant French Laundry, considered by many to be the best restaurant in the United States. Bouchon is a version of his Napa Valley bistro. We had mixed expectations. On the one hand, he's a certifiably genius chef. On the other hand, he's not going to be in the kitchen, which will be producing bistro (which is to say, not innovative) food and, what's more, based on the rather lackluster Napa Bouchon.

Our negative expectations were confounded by the right, left, and center of the menu—yeah, we've tried nearly all of it and can report that humble though these dishes sound, in nearly every case they are gold-standard versions of classics. Someone is certainly keeping a close eye on this kitchen, and that someone has learned the lessons well. Ever wondered why people get worked up over raw oysters? The sweet and supremely fresh (kept in water until the moment they are served to you) Snow Creek oysters will enlighten you as they seem to melt on contact with your tongue. Fifty dollars seems like a lot for pâté, but here a complex multiday preparation produces a buttery whip that is so rich, it's an appropriate—and highly recommended—appetizer for four. Don't miss the bacon and poached-egg frisée salad, or the cleanly seared salmon over poached leeks, prepared to such perfection it doesn't need the accompanying sauce. Gnocchi is earthy and assertive, a peasant version of an Italian favorite, while beef bourguignon is exactly as you expect it to be, in the divine perfection sense. Leg of lamb has all chewy bits excised before cooking, leaving it a garlic-permeated bit of

tenderness. This is a superlative Vegas restaurant, and while it may be hard to recon-
cile the prices with the apparent simplicity of the food, recall that it takes serious skill
to make even the most humble of dishes correctly, as your palate will reassure you.

In The Venetian, 3355 Las Vegas Blvd. S. ✆ 702/414-6200; www.bouchonbistro.com. Reservations strongly recommended. Main courses $10–$20 at breakfast, $22–$45 at dinner; Sat–Sun brunch $21–$25. AE, DC, DISC, MC, V. Daily
7–10:30am and 5–11pm; Sat–Sun brunch 8am–2pm; oyster bar daily 3–11pm.

Canaletto ✶✶ ITALIAN   Come here for solid, true Italian fare—and that means
less sauce-intensive than the red-checked-tablecloth establishments of our American
youths. Here, the emphasis is on the pasta, not the accompaniments. This place is all
the more enjoyable for being perched on the faux St. Mark's Square; in theory, you can
pretend you are sitting on the edge of the real thing, a fantasy we don't mind admitting we briefly indulged in. A risotto of porcini, sausage, and white-truffle oil was full
of strong flavors, while the wood-fired roast chicken was perfectly moist. You know, a
properly roasted chicken should be a much-celebrated thing, and that alone may be a
reason to come here.

In The Venetian Grand Canal Shoppes, 3377 Las Vegas Blvd. S. ✆ 702/733-0070. Reservations recommended for
dinner. Main courses $14–$36. AE, DC, MC, V. Sun–Thurs 11:30am–11pm; Fri–Sat 11:30am–midnight.

Circo ✶✶ ITALIAN   Yes, this is the less expensive offering from the same family
that brings you Le Cirque, but going to one does not excuse you from going to the
other. (By the way, "less expensive" is a relative term.)

Le Cirque's gourmet French haute cuisine does not prepare you for what to expect
from Circo, or, for that matter, vice versa. Ignore the bright primary-color scheme,
meant to evoke the circus but instead sadly recalling outdated hotel buffets (albeit
with expensive wood grain), in favor of watching the dancing fountains outside. And
then order the *mista di Campo,* a lovely little salad, both visually and in terms of taste;
it's a creative construction of vegetables bound with cucumber and topped with a fab
balsamic vinaigrette. Follow that with a perfect tagliatelle with rock shrimp—it comes
loaded with various crustacean bits in a light sauce. Note that appetizer portions of
pastas are plenty filling and cheaper than full-size servings. Entrees usually include
more elaborate dishes, such as breast of Muscovy duck with dried organic fruit in port-
wine sauce. Save room for desserts such as *panna cotta* (Italian cream–filled doughnuts) or *tutto cioccolato,* consisting of chocolate mousse, ice cream, and crumb cake.

In Bellagio, 3600 Las Vegas Blvd. S. ✆ 702/693-8150. Reservations recommended. Main courses $16–$59. AE, DC,
DISC, MC, V. Daily 5–10:30pm, last seating at 10pm.

Olives ✶✶ ITALIAN/MEDITERRANEAN   If there were an Olives in our neighborhood, we would eat there regularly. A branch of Todd English's original Boston-
based restaurant, Olives is a strong choice for a light lunch that need not be as
expensive as you might think. Here's how to enjoy a moderately priced meal here:
Munch on the focaccia bread, olives, and excellent tapenade they give you at the start,
have a lovely salad (maybe of Bibb lettuce, Maytag bleu cheese, and walnut dressing),
and then split a flatbread—think pizza with an ultrathin crust (like a slightly limp
cracker), topped with delicious combinations such as the highly recommended
Moroccan-spiced lamb, eggplant purée, and feta cheese, or our other favorite, fig, prosciutto, and Gorgonzola. They are rich and wonderful—split one between two people, and you have an affordable and terrific lunch. Or try a pasta; we were steered
toward the simple but marvelous spaghettini with roasted tomatoes, garlic, and
Parmesan, and were happy with it. The constructed, but not too fussy, food gets more

complicated and costly at night, adding an array of meats and chickens, plus pastas such as butternut squash with brown butter and sage.

In Bellagio, 3600 Las Vegas Blvd. S. ✆ **702/693-7223**. www.toddenglish.com. Reservations recommended. Main courses $17–$25 at lunch, flatbreads $15; $24–$52 at dinner, flatbreads $17. AE, DC, DISC, MC, V. Daily 11am–10:30pm.

Pinot Brasserie ☆☆ BISTRO   This is one incarnation of a series of well-regarded Los Angeles restaurants whose mother ship, Patina, regularly tops "Best of" lists among City of Angels foodies. While the more innovative cooking is going on back in L.A., Pinot reliably delivers French and American favorites that are thoughtfully conceived and generally delicious. It's an excellent choice if you want a special meal that is neither stratospherically expensive nor too complex. And the space is highly attractive, with various props culled from French auctions and flea markets forming the archetypal, clubby bistro feel. We particularly like the small room off the bar to the right—just perfect for a tête-à-tête.

Salads are possibly fresher and more generous than other similar starters in town (thank that California influence), and they can come paired with various toppings for *crostini* (toasted slices of French bread) such as herbed goat cheese. Word is that they might add Patina's delightful butternut-squash soup to the menu here, and if so, you should try it. The signature dish, beloved by many, is a roasted chicken accompanied by heaping mounds of garlic fries; but if you wish to get a little more elaborate (and yet rather light), thin slices of smoked salmon with celery remoulade could be a way to go. Desserts are lovely, and the ice cream is homemade—the chocolate alone should make you wish you'd never eaten at 31 Flavors because it was wasted calories compared to this.

In The Venetian, 3355 Las Vegas Blvd. S. ✆ **702/414-8888**. www.patinagroup.com. Reservations recommended for dinner. Main courses $10–$19 at breakfast; $12–$25 at lunch; $21–$36 at dinner. AE, DISC, MC, V. Mon–Fri 8–10am, 11:30am–3pm, and 5:30–10pm; Sat–Sun 8am–3pm and 5:30–10:30pm.

Rao's ☆ ITALIAN   This is a meticulous recreation of the famous 110-year-old East Harlem restaurant, which is notorious in equal measure for "Uncle Vincent's lemon chicken" and the near-impossibility of getting a seat (there are only 10 tables, which are reserved a year in advance!). It was thoughtful of Vegas to replicate it at more than three times the size, allowing common folks to check it out (though keep an eye out for famous homesick New Yorkers holding court). On the other hand, since this isn't revelatory Italian cooking, you may justly wonder what all the fuss is about, especially since the "family portions" are smaller than that phrase implies. Expect comfort food—sweet Italian sausage, ravioli with ricotta and brown-butter sage sauce. A safe and budget way to go is to try that lemon chicken, which really does live up to the hype, and split one of their "sides" of enormous meatballs (toss in some of the complimentary bread and you've got a meatball sandwich), along with expectation-fulfilling *pot au crème* and gelato. That is, assuming you can get in. Reservations here are at a premium, too!

In Caesars Palace, 3570 Las Vegas Blvd. S. ✆ **877/346-4642**. Main courses $18–$40. AE, DC, DISC, MC, V. Daily 6am–3pm and 5–11pm.

Sensi ☆☆ ECLECTIC   It's usually a truism, as far as restaurants go, "jack of all trades, master of none." Sensi seems to be an exception, given that its menu is made up of Italian (fancy pizzas and pastas), wood-grilled American options (burgers, fish, chicken), and Asian-influenced dishes (and they mean "pan-Asian," thus tandoori and

(Kids) Family-Friendly Restaurants

Buffets Cheap meals for the whole family. The kids can choose what they like, and there are sometimes make-your-own sundae machines. Section 8 of this chapter reviews all the buffets and notes which ones have reduced prices for kids.

Cypress Street Marketplace (p. 142) Caesars Palace's food court (stylish enough to offer real plates and cloth napkins) offers a range of food (from very good hot dogs to wrap sandwiches to Vietnamese noodles) wide enough to ensure that bottomless-pit teenagers, picky grade-schoolers, and health-conscious parents will all find something that appeals, at affordable prices.

Fellini's (p. 147) With a menu that admittedly veers toward Italian-American rather than authentic food from the motherland, this is all the more appropriate for families, who probably want a good red-sauce pasta dish and some solid pizza rather than anything more elaborate.

Monte Carlo Pub & Brewery (p. 129) Despite the "pub" part of the name, this noisy place in the Monte Carlo hotel has many TVs to distract short-attention kids and brooding teenagers, all of whom will like the barbecue, pizza, and chicken fingers. Parents will be pleased with the low prices.

Pink Pony This bubble-gum-pink, circus-motif 24-hour coffee shop at Circus Circus will appeal to kids. Mom and Dad can linger while the kids race upstairs to watch circus acts and play carnival games.

Rainforest Cafe (p. 127) This is like eating in the Jungle Book ride at Disneyland. Animals howl, thunder wails, everywhere there is something to marvel at. There is a decent kids' menu, and they might even learn a little bit about ecology and the environment.

Sherwood Forest Café Kids love to climb on the lavender dragons fronting this 24-hour coffee shop at Excalibur, while finicky eaters can get burgers at breakfast and pancakes for dinner.

Toto's (p. 154) This Mexican restaurant that features enormous portions served family style is a casual place favored by locals.

---

sushi both). And yet, it does it all very well indeed. You are probably best off here at lunchtime, sampling pizza al prosciutto or wok-fried shrimp, for more moderate prices than found at dinner. Best of all is the "Sensi 41," a healthy take on the bento box, featuring such things as miso-glazed Chilean sea bass, some tender sashimi, piquant rice, and, disconcertingly, mozzarella salad. They finish it up with two small, cunning servings of fancy ice cream in wee cones. And do try that homemade ginger ale. A fun menu in a fun-looking space, laid out to surround one very busy and versatile kitchen.

In Bellagio, 3600 Las Vegas Blvd. S. © 877/234-6358. Main courses $14–$22 at lunch, $22–$44 at dinner. AE, DC, DISC, MC, V. Daily 11am–2:30pm and 5–10:30pm.

MODERATE

See also the listing for **Spago** (p. 136), an expensive restaurant fronted by a more moderately priced cafe.

Isla 👩‍🍳👩‍🍳 MEXICAN   We tend to get a little snobby about Mexican restaurants, particular those in casinos, because so often they seem careless. But unless you absolutely do not consider Mexican food anything other than a specific form of Southern California burrito, you really should try this establishment specializing in "modern Mexican cuisine." This means dishes both traditional and with potentially dangerous twists, but since the place starts with handmade tortillas and heads right to guacamole made on demand, it's all trustworthy, even if some of that guac contains lobster and passion fruit (it's a sweet and curious take on tradition). Roast pork pipian with tamarind marinade and pumpkin-seed sauce is a lovely dish, as are the needlessly fried (though pleasantly crunchy) beef empanadas with dried cherries and chipotle tomato sauce—a mix of sweet and spiced. For the more timid, there is a nice assortment of particularly good tacos and burritos. They also have a charming dessert menu, with Mexican themes both culinary and visually, such as a chocolate cactus stuck into a fudge hill, to complement the caramel cupcakes. The collection of 118 brands of tequila and a slightly modern nightclub interior remind you that dining in Vegas is still a gimmick.

In TI–Treasure Island, 3300 Las Vegas Blvd. S. ✆ **866/286-3809** or 702/894-7223. Main courses $10–$30. AE, DC, DISC, MC, V. Sun, Mon, Thurs 4–10:45pm; Wed, Fri–Sat 4–11:45pm; Tues 4–10:30pm. Limited bar menu served 24 hrs.

Mon Ami Gabi 👩‍🍳👩‍🍳 BISTRO   This charming bistro is one of our favorite local restaurants. It has it all: a delightful setting, better-than-average food, and affordable prices. Sure, it goes overboard in trying to replicate a classic Parisian bistro, but the results are less cheesy than most Vegas attempts at atmosphere, and the patio seating on the Strip (no reservations taken there—first-come, first-served, but a recent addition of 70 more seats probably helps matters) actually makes you feel like you're in a real, not a pre-fab, city. You can be budget-conscious and order just the very fine onion soup, or you can eat like a real French person and order classic steak (the filet mignon is probably the best cut, if not the cheapest) and *pommes frites* (french fries). There are plenty of less expensive options (which is why we listed this place in the "moderate" category, by the way). Yes, they have snails, and we loved 'em. Desserts, by the way, are massive and should be shared (another way to save). The baseball-size profiteroles (three or four to an order) filled with fine vanilla ice cream and the football-size bananas-Foster crepe are particularly recommended.

In Paris Las Vegas, 3655 Las Vegas Blvd. S. ✆ **702/944-4224**. www.monamigabi.com. Reservations recommended. Main courses $18–$40. AE, DC, DISC, MC, V. Mon–Fri 11:30am–11pm; Sat–Sun 11am–midnight.

Payard Patisserie & Bistro 👩‍🍳👩‍🍳👩‍🍳 BISTRO   Breakfast here offers one of the few real remaining bargains in Vegas, given quality-to-price ratio. Surely it can't last, considering the state of things in modern-day Vegas. But with some luck, this is what you have to look forward to—a continental breakfast like no other. $16 gets you cereals, fruits, yogurt, lox and bagel and, most significantly, all the breakfast pastries you can eat. Since the chef has his roots in Paris, these buttery bits of brioche and croissant perfection are as good as any you could consume by the Seine. One can easily spend that much on a breakfast buffet or a lunch entree elsewhere in town, but there is no comparison for quality. Lunch is light and of the French variety, while evening brings dessert tastings of delicate, inspired flights of sugary whimsy. Both are of particularly high quality and worth investigating, but it's the breakfast that has already earned it a strong reputation, and justly so.

In Caesars Palace, 3570 Las Vegas Blvd. S. ✆ 702/731-7110. Breakfast $16, lunch entrees $16–$26, evening desserts $15, prix-fixe dinner $45. AE, MC, V. Daily 6:30–11:30am, noon–7:30pm, 9–11:30pm.

RUB ✿ BARBEQUE   Goodness, we do love a good barbeque. While this won't have you renouncing your favorite back-roads juke joint, it still is quite credible for a hotel BBQ spot, and a good change of pace from either high-end dining spots or generic eateries. The name stands for Righteous Urban Barbeque, which either tells you everything or nothing at all. The owner is a championship smoker and they do take their work seriously—and playfully—as meats are smoked for 12 hours and offered with a choice of 4 different regional BBQ sauces. Look for sausages, ribs, pulled pork, brisket—really, anything meaty you can smoke. Burnt ends are available for those fetishists. Don't overlook the Frito pie, and especially the appetizer of thick barbequed bacon chunks.

In the Rio, 3700 W. Flamingo Rd. ✆ 702/227-0779. www.rubbbq.net. Main courses $9.95–$25. AE, MC, V. Mon–Tues 4–11pm, Wed–Sun 11am–2am.

Table 10 ✿✿✿ AMERICAN   The natural conclusion to draw about celebrity chefs with multiple restaurants is that they are spreading themselves too thin. That may or may not be true as a whole, but this latest venture by New Orleans-based and TV-ubiquitous Emeril belies conventional wisdom. Not a copy of another holding in the Emeril empire (as are the excellent Delmonico and the hit-and-miss Emeril's Seafood) but a new endeavor with its own personality—albeit one that clearly benefits from its Emeril origins. Named after a special seating spot in Emeril's flagship New Orleans restaurant, the food at this locale hits a high note on a level with that standout eatery. Further, at this writing, while not cheap, meals here come off as a bargain in comparison to comparable fine-dining options in town. (As is often the case, you may want to consider dropping by for an even more affordable lunch.) The menu will likely change regularly, but look for appetizers such as oyster fritters with Rockefeller sauce and Bibb salad with housemade bacon, and entrees such as tender roasted lamb with black truffle reduction, and sides including a sumptuous lobster macaroni and cheese. Desserts are clever, while standout is the *malassadas,* deep-fried dough balls filled with white chocolate.

In The Palazzo, 3328 Las Vegas Blvd. S. ✆ 702/607-6363. www.emerils.com. Reservations recommended. Main courses lunch $11–$29, dinner $25–$38. AE, MC, V. Sun–Thurs 11am–11pm; Fri–Sat 11am–midnight.

INEXPENSIVE

Cypress Street Marketplace ✿✿ (Kids) FOOD COURT   Often when we go to a Vegas buffet (and we are not alone in this), we sigh over all the choices, all those different kinds of pretty good, if not better, cuisines there for the taking, but, of course, we can't possibly try everything. And yet, in some of the higher-priced venues, we are charged as if we can. Here, in this modern version of the classic food court, it's sort of like being at a well-stocked buffet: There's darn fine barbecue (including North Carolina–influenced pulled pork), wrap sandwiches (grilled shrimp, for one example), Asian (including pot stickers and Vietnamese noodles), decent NY pizza, plump Chicago hot dogs, peel-and-eat shrimp and lobster chowder, a bargain-priced salad bar, plus pastries and even wine. And with the range of food, an entire family with very different tastes will all find something satisfactory.

In Caesars Palace, 3570 Las Vegas Blvd. S. ✆ 702/731-7110. Most items under $15. AE, MC, V. Daily 11am–11pm.

DELI DELIGHTS

It's East Coast vs. West Coast in the battle of the famous delis, here in sister properties The Mirage and TI–Treasure Island. The former has brought in New York's beloved **Carnegie Deli** ✰✰ ((℮ **702/791-7310**; daily 7am–1:30am), home of the towering sandwich, so large that no mere mortal can clamp his or her jaws around it. It's hardly the same joint you New Yorkers are used to, given that this sleek and modern interpretation is crammed into a small corner of a casino. Bad puns still run amok on the menu ("Tongues for the Memory," "Nova on a Sunday," and "The Egg and Oy!"). We aren't happy that the famously huge sandwiches come with huge prices to match, along with a miserly $3 sharing fee. TI–Treasure Island is home to the first offshoot of Los Angeles's **Canter's Deli** ✰✰ ((℮ **702/894-7111**; daily11am–midnight), where many a musician has whiled away many an hour, staring moodily into a bowl of matzo-ball soup. Whole families have been rend apart by stating preferences for one style over the other, so we will just say this: As much as we admit that NYC is right to claim it has superior bagels—there, we said it—and the Carnegie definitely has better hours, the Canter's smells just like the one we spent much pleasurable time in during our formative years. Ah, just go do some pastrami taste-testing yourselves, youse.

Earl of Sandwich ✰✰✰ SANDWICHES   It seems credulity-straining, but the sandwich was something that had to be invented, and thus someone got their simple yet ingenious idea named after them. At least, so the story goes, so sufficiently accepted as historical lore that it carries enough weight for the intrepid inventor's descendent, the 11th Earl of Sandwich, to lend their name to a chain of sandwich shops. It's a gimmick, but a good one, and so is the food. The eponymous, and largely excellent, sandwiches are served warm (wraps are cold) on bread made for the shop, and include combos such as grilled Swiss; bleu and brie with applewood-smoked bacon; and roast beef with horseradish cream and cheddar cheese. There are also complex if unoriginal salads, smoothies, and breakfast sandwiches. Portions aren't huge, but it's not a problem if you are devoted to Vegas-sized meals; the low prices make it possible to order two of everything if appetites demand.

In Planet Hollywood, 3667 Las Vegas Blvd. S. (℮ **702/463-0259**. www.earlofsandwichusa.com. Everything under $6. AE, MC, V. Daily 6am–midnight.

4 North Strip

VERY EXPENSIVE

Alex ✰✰✰ CONTINENTAL   Alex Strada (possibly familiar to you from his stint on the American "Iron Chef") followed his once and present boss Steve Wynn from The Mirage, closing his Renoir venue to open this eponymous one instead. A dramatic room, all swooping drapes and inlaid wood, it's about two fussy steps away from true elegance but still a place where grown-ups come to dine, while appreciating the venture as "occasion." Strada comes from a cosmopolitan and international background; add to that both some years working under Alain Ducasse and a general sense of food as pleasure and art, and you have one of the most special dining experiences in Vegas. The menu changes regularly—Chef Alex is as exacting as a chef should be, and so the readiness of seasonal ingredients dictates any particular evening's selection. If in a European restaurant, the result would almost certainly earn a Michelin star.

Diners have their choice of two set tasting menus or a three-course prix-fixe choice of appetizer, main course, and dessert. Expect starters such as carpaccio of Santa Barbara prawn topped with osetra caviar, or roasted scallop with basil purée, and don't neglect to ponder touches such as tiny vegetables ever so lightly cooked so crunch and flavor come through, the whole topped by translucent fried zucchini flower. Porcini gnocchi dissolves in the mouth, a terrine of foie gras is paired with the chef's interpretation of Waldorf salad, a main course of squab and sautéed foie gras, rhubarb, and spiced pineapple is deep, rich, and bold. Even the palate cleansers are serious, such as apricot gelée topped with coconut granita ringed by passion fruit, or strawberry gelée with lemon-grass crème fraîche. As for wine, Master Sommelier Paolo Barbieri's thoughtful list includes over 1,000 labels, many of them French, with some 200 burgundies alone. Those on a budget should fear not, as the list includes innovative treats like a "splash" of Chateau d'Yquem, which is plenty to accompany a foie gras starter and quite affordable. Desserts are of such gorgeous complexity that we cannot describe them adequately, but know that the construction is not served to the sacrifice of taste. You are in a master chef's hands; enjoy it.

In Wynn Las Vegas, 3131 Las Vegas Blvd. S. © **888/352-3463** or 702/248-3463. Reservations strongly recommended. Jacket recommended. 3-course prix-fixe menu $145; 7-course tasting menu $195. AE, DC, DISC, MC, V. Thurs–Mon 6–10pm.

Bartolotta Ristorante di Mare ✪✪✪ ITALIAN/SEAFOOD   James Beard Foundation Award–winning chef Paul Bartolotta trained in Italy under master chefs before opening his highly acclaimed Spiaggia in Chicago. Now he's here, in this eponymous (and Best New Restaurant 2006 Beard finalist) kitchen, yet more proof that celebrity chefs are all very well and good, but it's not the same as having them on the premises. In this case, the result is as authentic Italian food as one can find outside Italy. Determined to produce just that, Bartolotta went to his boss, Steve Wynn, and insisted that his fish not just be ultrafresh but also be flown daily straight from the Mediterranean to his Vegas kitchen, saying "I can't make authentic Italian food with American fish." Wynn's response? "Give the man his fish." (And you will be introduced to the results after you sit down!)

Bartolotta is nonchalant about what goes on here; all you have to do, he claims, is know what you are doing, and then do it with the best ingredients—best olive oil, best tomatoes, and best fish. He's right. It works, and so well that this is the restaurant we are currently most likely to tout in Vegas; as in, go here, do. You can choose your whole cooked fish right from that day's batch (you can get them big enough so one can be split among several people), which may include new-to-you (they were to us) possibilities like orata and purple snapper, each topped with a chunky "sauce" of sweet pachino tomatoes, arugula, garlic, and red onion. Pastas are perfect, as well, especially the delicate sheep's milk ricotta handkerchief-style ravioli, made both sweet and savory with a veal Marsala wine-reduction glaze. *Spaghetti allo Scoglio* comes with large chunks of lobster, langoustines are grilled to charred smoky rightness, seared scallops with porcini mushrooms in browned butter are what scallops should be—and all because this Italian staff learned their lessons well, and they are passing that knowledge on to you.

Meanwhile, Sommelier Claudio Vilani, who honed his skills in his native Italy, created and oversees the (almost) all-Italian list. Those in the know will leave themselves in his capable hands, as he pairs a regionally appropriate wine with the seafood cuisine.

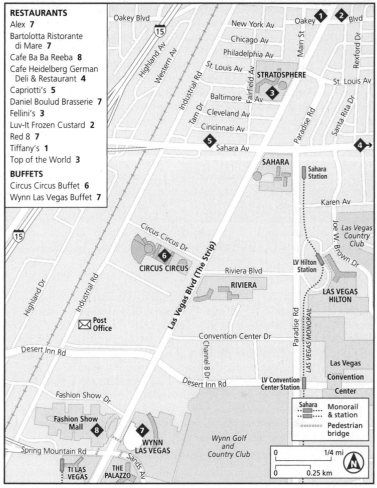

RESTAURANTS
Alex **7**
Bartolotta Ristorante di Mare **7**
Cafe Ba Ba Reeba **8**
Cafe Heidelberg German Deli & Restaurant **4**
Capriotti's **5**
Daniel Boulud Brasserie **7**
Fellini's **3**
Luv-It Frozen Custard **2**
Red 8 **7**
Tiffany's **1**
Top of the World **3**
BUFFETS
Circus Circus Buffet **6**
Wynn Las Vegas Buffet **7**

The space itself is perhaps the nicest in the hotel, which has done well by all its restaurants, a multilevel construction that gives a cafe feeling on the top level, a more elegant dining area down below (accessed by a dramatic curving, sweeping stairway), and, best of all, outdoor cabana seating by a small pond filled with reflecting balls, so fine for a long (as the Italians like to do it), sultry evening meal. A jewel box of a place for cooking that is a treasure.

In Wynn Las Vegas, 3131 Las Vegas Blvd. S. (C) **888/352-3463** or 702/248-3463. Reservations recommended. Main courses dinner $20–$58; family-style tasting $135 per person; Grand Seafood Feast served family style $155 per person. AE, DC, DISC, MC, V. Daily 5:30–10:30pm.

Daniel Boulud Brasserie ✿ BISTRO   Best known as the man who gave New York City the $29 hamburger (because it was filled with foie gras, short rib meat, and truffles), which is a mistake you should not make—not the hamburger itself, which is on this menu, and is fine, if extremely silly and now much imitated—but because there is more to his cuisine than burgers. This is classic French bistro food, and while Boulud himself is not in the house, he does have a superb French chef (at this writing) running the show, and very well. Still, you can always tell when someone is cooking off another master chef's menu, as opposed to working their own magic (especially when compared to, say, Alex or Bartolotta, here at Wynn itself).

But the cuisine here is still lovely; look at the beautifully composed salads, as roasted beets are laid out in precise order with endive and bleu cheese, or the stunning *tartin du tomato,* a whole reconstructed roasted tomato layered on goat cheese and puff pastry. The *foie gras chaud* is two fat lobes of liver on grilled pineapple, topped with a nearly see-through thin pineapple chip. Lean toward the slow-cooked dishes, such as braised short ribs Bourguignon with *pomme mousseline* and spring ramps—earthy and hearty. Save some room for a cheese plate and go through the evening's artisanal selections with your server. This restaurant is one of only two that allows viewing of the Lake of Dreams show at night. A way to get around some of the high-end cost is to work with the appetizers—cheese and charcuterie (try the duck confit terrine) are filling—because the entree is a little too small to split satisfyingly.

In Wynn Las Vegas, 3131 Las Vegas Blvd. S. ✆ **888/352-3463** or 702/248-3463. Reservations recommended. Main courses $26–$44. AE, DC, DISC, MC, V. Daily 5:30–10:30pm.

MODERATE

Cafe Ba Ba Reeba ⚑ ECLECTIC   One of the rare dining places in Vegas with an outdoor patio and easily accessed from The Mirage, TI, and The Venetian, Cafe Ba Ba Reeba bills itself as "tapas" but it's really "small plates." And they mean small: Order, say, a beef skewer with creamy horseradish sauce, and that's what you get—one skewer. And that skewer will cost you $9. Then again, the portions are actually what a real portion ought to be, not these behemoth, gut-busting and waistline-enlarging servings. Your dessert cake might be but five bites and not the size of a softball, but again, it's properly proportioned. It's our expectations that are outsized. So it's a little pricey, but the large menu means you can have a moderately priced, reasonably sized meal. Other possibilities include the bleu cheese–topped tenderloin, roasted bacon-wrapped dates, and some hearty mushroom soup.

In Fashion Show Mall, 3200 Las Vegas Blvd. S. ✆ **702/258-1211.** Tapas $6–$30. AE, DC, DISC, MC, V. Sun–Thurs 11:30am–11pm; Fri–Sat 11:30am–midnight.

Cafe Heidelberg German Deli & Restaurant ⚑ GERMAN   Configured to look like a beer garden, this German cafe brings in locals and homesick Bavarians alike. It's a small, not typically Vegas place, and because it's close enough to the Strip, it's a good place for refuge, though it could be crowded when you go. The food is better than fine, though certainly not "lite" fare, by any means. Recommended is the sausage sampler platter, so you can finally learn the difference between knockwurst and bratwurst, with sides such as potato pancakes, dumplings, excellent potato salad (choice of German or American style) and the like. Lunch brings sandwiches such as perfect schnitzel, with the pork loin twice the size of the roll. Wash it down with an imported beer. There is live entertainment on the weekends in the early evening. This is also a full-service deli and German market, so it's a good place to pick up a picnic for sightseeing outside the city. Sundays dinner is served all day.

604 E. Sahara Ave. (at 6th St.). ✆ **702/731-5310.** Reservations strongly recommended Fri–Sat nights. Main courses mostly under $13 at lunch, $20–$26 at dinner. AE, DC, DISC, MC, V. Mon–Tues 11am–3pm; Wed–Sun 11am–8pm; the deli opens daily at 10am.

Fellini's 👶 *Kids* ITALIAN   A Vegas institution (in its original West Las Vegas location), much beloved by in-the-know locals, Fellini's is a classic Italian restaurant—you
know, red gloopy sauce, garlicky cheesy bread—which isn't meant to be an insult at
all. It might not be ambitious, but it is reliable and more than satisfying. They do a
strong version of pasta (rigatoni, in this case) Amatriciana, and they are generous with
the pancetta, and while some Italian food purists would shudder at the gnocchi with
tenderloin tips topped with Gorgonzola and shallot cream sauce, they are just missing
out, that's all. The well-proportioned menu offers a variety of options from osso buco
to basic pizza, and, given the prices, that makes it a good option for families with a
similar range of tastes and needs.

In Stratosphere Hotel & Casino, 2000 Las Vegas Blvd S. ② 702/383-4859. www.fellinislv.com. Main courses
$11–$27. AE, DISC, MC, V. Mon–Thurs 5–11pm; Fri–Sat 5pm–midnight.

Red 8 👶👶 ASIAN   Such a relief, in the otherwise pricey Wynn, to find a dining spot
that is both good and affordable. This visual standout is a small cafe—as you wander
by, you think "Cool! Some of the tables overlook the casino!" Then you realize those
are *all* of the tables—with a decor that screams the place's colorful name. It's probably
going to be popular, given the location, size, and pricing—not to mention the quality of the food. Covering a sort of pan-Asiatic (Southeast Asia, anyway) terrain, look
for noodle dishes both wet (soup) and dry (pan-fried), rice (including porridge), dim
sum, Korean barbeque, Mongolian beef, vegetarian options, and more. There are
some "market price" specials that can quadruple a bill pretty fast, but otherwise, this
is a pretty budget-friendly option.

In Wynn Las Vegas, 3131 Las Vegas Blvd. S. ② 702/770-3380. No reservations required. Main courses $12–$28. AE,
DISC, MC, V. Sun–Thurs 11:30am–11pm; Fri–Sat 11:30am–1am.

INEXPENSIVE

Capriotti's 👶👶👶 *Finds* DELI   It looks like a dump, but Capriotti's is one of the
great deals in town, for quality and price. They roast their own beef and turkey on the
premises and stuff them (or Italian cold cuts, or whatever) into sandwiches mislabeled
"small," "medium," and "large"—the last clocks in at 20 inches, easily feeding two for
under $10 total. And deliciously so. The "Bobby" (turkey, dressing, and cranberry
sauce, like Thanksgiving dinner in sandwich form) would be our favorite sandwich in
the world had we not tried the "Slaw B Joe": roast beef, coleslaw, and Russian dressing. But other combos, such as the aforementioned Italian cold cuts, have their fans,
too, and Capriotti's even has veggie varieties. There are outlets throughout the city, but
this one is not only right off the Strip but also right by the freeway. We never leave
town without a stop here, and you shouldn't either.

322 W. Sahara Ave. (at Las Vegas Blvd. S.). ② 702/474-0229. www.capriottis.com. Most sandwiches under $10. AE,
MC, V. Mon–Fri 10am–5pm; Sat 11am–5pm.

Dona Maria Tamales 👶👶 MEXICAN   Decorated with Tijuana-style quilt work
and calendars, this quintessential Mexican diner is convenient to both the north end
of the Strip and Downtown. The cooks use lots of lard, lots of cheese, and lots of
sauce. As a result, the food is really good—and really fattening. Yep, the folks who did
those health reports showing how bad Mexican food can be for your heart probably
did some research here. The fat just makes it all the better, in our opinion. Locals
apparently agree; even at lunchtime, the place is crowded.

You will start off with homemade chips and a spicy salsa served in a mortar. Meals
are so large that it shouldn't be a problem getting full just ordering off the sides, which

can make this even more of a budget option. Naturally, the specialty is the fantastic tamales, which come in red, green, cheese, or sweet. They also serve up excellent enchiladas, *chiles rellenos,* burritos, and fajitas. All dinners include rice, beans, tortillas, and soup or salad. Sauces are heavy but oh-so-good. For dessert, they have flan, fried ice cream, and Mexican-style pumpkin pie.

910 Las Vegas Blvd. S. (at Charleston Blvd.). ℭ 702/382-6538. www.donamariatamales.com. Main courses $8–$12 breakfast; $8–$12 lunch; $12–$15 dinner. AE, MC, V. Sun–Thurs 8am–10pm; Fri–Sat 8am–11pm.

Rincon Criollo CUBAN   Located beyond the wedding chapels on Las Vegas Boulevard, Rincon Criollo has all the right details for a good, cheap ethnic joint: It's full of locals and empty of frills. It's not the best Cuban food ever, but it gets the job done. The main courses (featuring Cuban pork and chicken specialties) are hit-or-miss; try the marinated pork leg or, better still, ask your server for a recommendation. Paella is offered, but only for parties of at least five people (and starts at $25). The side-course *chorizo* (a spicy sausage) is excellent, and the Cuban sandwich (roast pork, ham, and cheese on bread, which is then pressed and flattened out) is huge and tasty. For only $3.50, the latter makes a fine change-of-pace meal.

1145 Las Vegas Blvd. S. ℭ 702/388-1906. Reservations not accepted. Main courses $7.50–$13; paella (for 5) $25. AE, DISC, MC, V. Tues–Sun 11am–9:30pm.

Tiffany's 🎖🎖 *Value* DINER   Why bother with theme restaurants that pretend to be cheap diners when the real thing is just past the end of the Strip? This decidedly unflashy soda fountain/lunch counter was Las Vegas's first 24-hour restaurant, and it has been going strong for 60 years. Plunk down at the counter and watch the cooks go nuts trying to keep up with the orders. The menu is basic comfort food: standard items (meatloaf, ground round steak, chops, and so on), fluffy cream pies, and classic breakfasts served anytime—try the biscuits and cream gravy at 3am. But the best bet is a ⅓-pound burger and "thick, creamy shake," both about as good as they get. At around $6, this is half what you would pay for a comparable meal at the Hard Rock Cafe. Places like this are a vanishing species—it's worth the short walk from the Stratosphere. Note, however, that the neighborhood remains stubbornly rough in appearance, and that can be a turnoff. Stay alert if you come here at night.

1700 Las Vegas Blvd. S. (at East Oakey Blvd.). ℭ 702/444-4459. Reservations not accepted. Most items under $8. No credit cards. Daily 24 hr.

5 East of the Strip

In this section, we cover restaurants close to the Convention Center, along with those farther south on Paradise Road, Flamingo Road, and Tropicana Avenue.

VERY EXPENSIVE

Lawry's The Prime Rib 🎖🎖🎖 STEAK/SEAFOOD   If you love prime rib, come here. If you could take or leave prime rib, Lawry's will turn you into a believer. Lawry's does one thing, and it does it better than anyone else. Lawry's first opened in Los Angeles in 1938 and remains a popular tradition. Over the years, they have added three branches; the most recent landed in Las Vegas at the beginning of 1997. Yes, you can get prime rib all over town for about $5. But, to mix a food metaphor, that's a tuna sandwich when you can have caviar at Lawry's.

Eating at Lawry's is a ceremony, with all the parts played the same way for the past 60 years. Waitresses in brown-and-white English-maid uniforms, complete with starched

RESTAURANTS
Bougainville **11**
Carluccio's Tivoli Gardens **17**
Einstein Bros. Bagels **15**
Freed's Bakery **20**
Gordon-Biersch Brewing
  Company **8**
Hard Rock Cafe **12**
Jason's Deli **6**
Komol **2**
Lawry's The Prime Rib **9**
Lotus of Siam **2**
Memphis Championship
  Barbecue **18**

Mr. Lucky's 24/7 **12**
Morton's Steakhouse **10**
Pamplemousse **1**
Paymon's Mediterranean
  Cafe & Lounge **7**
Pink Taco **12**
Toto's **19**

BUFFETS
The Buffet at the
  Las Vegas Hilton **3**
Sam's Town
  Firelight Buffet **5**

NIGHTLIFE
The Buffalo **14**
Champagne's Cafe **4**
Dispensary Lounge **20**
Double Down Saloon **14**
The Eagle **20**
Gipsy **13**
Good Times **16**

white cap, take your order—for side dishes, that is. The real decision, what cut of rib you are going to have, comes later. Actually, that's the only part of the tradition that has changed. Originally, all Lawry's offered was prime rib, which they did perfectly and with tremendous style. Now they have added fresh fish (halibut, salmon, or swordfish, depending on the evening) to the menu. Anyway, you tell the waitress what side dishes you might want (sublime creamed spinach, baked potato, and so on) for an extra price. Later, she returns with a spinning salad bowl. (Think of salad preparation as a Busby Berkeley musical number.) The bowl, resting on crushed ice, spins as she pours Lawry's special dressing in a stream from high over her head. Tomatoes garnish. Applause follows. Eventually, giant metal carving carts come to your table, bearing the meat. You name your cut (the regular Lawry's, the extra-large Diamond Jim Brady for serious carnivores, and the wimpy, thin English cut) and specify how you'd like it cooked. It comes with terrific Yorkshire pudding, nicely browned and not soggy, and some creamed horseradish that is combined with fluffy whipped cream, simultaneously sweet and tart.

Flavorful, tender, perfectly cooked, and lightly seasoned, this will be the best prime rib you will ever have. Okay, maybe that's going too far, but the rest is accurate, honest. It just has to be tasted to be believed. You can finish off with a rich dessert (English trifle is highly recommended), but it almost seems pointless. Incidentally, the other Lawry's are decorated English-manor style, but the Vegas branch has instead tried to re-create a 1930s restaurant, with Art Deco touches all around and big-band music on the sound system.

4043 Howard Hughes Pkwy. (at Flamingo Rd., btw. Paradise Rd. and Koval Lane). ⓒ 702/893-2223. www.lawrysonline. com. Reservations recommended. Main courses $32–$49. AE, DC, DISC, MC, V. Sun–Thurs 5–10pm; Fri–Sat 5–11pm.

Morton's Steakhouse ⓖ STEAK/SEAFOOD   A venerable steakhouse with branches throughout the U.S.—in fact, Mr. Morton is the proud papa of Peter Morton, formerly of the Hard Rock Hotel over yonder. Like **The Palm** (p. 135), this place serves "boy food"—steaks, really good steaks—and we are not prepared to say which (The Palm or Morton's) has the better hunk o' red meat because, frankly, after a while, these subtle distinctions elude us. Anyway, this approximates an old-time Vegas hangout (most actual old-time Vegas hangouts have closed), even in its off-Strip location. In addition to your cut of beef, suggested sides include flavorfully fresh al dente asparagus served with hollandaise, or hash browns. And it's a good place to hang around post-dinner, drink Scotch, and smoke.

400 E. Flamingo Rd. (at Paradise Rd.). ⓒ 702/893-0703. www.mortons.com. Reservations recommended. Main courses $28–$52. AE, DC, MC, V. Mon–Sat 5–11pm; Sun 5–10pm.

Pamplemousse ⓖ FRENCH   A little bit off the beaten path, Pamplemousse is a long-established Vegas restaurant that shouldn't be overlooked in the crush of new high-profile eateries. Evoking a cozy French-countryside inn (at least, on the interior), it's a catacomb of low-ceilinged rooms and intimate dining nooks with rough-hewn beams. It's all very charming and un-Vegasy. There's additional seating in a small garden sheltered by a striped tent. The restaurant's name, which means "grapefruit" in French, was suggested by the late singer Bobby Darin, one of the many celebrity pals of owner Georges La Forge.

Your waiter recites the menu, which changes nightly. The meal always begins with a large complimentary basket of crudités (about 10 different crisp, fresh vegetables), a big bowl of olives, and, in a nice country touch, a basket of hard-boiled eggs. Recent menu offerings have included out-of-this-world soups (French onion and cream of asparagus, to name a couple) and appetizers such as shrimp in cognac cream sauce and Maryland crab cakes with macadamia nut crust. Recommended entrees include a sterling veal with mushrooms and Dijon sauce and an even-better rack of lamb with pistachio nut crust and rosemary cream sauce (all sauces, by the way, are made with whatever the chef has on hand that evening in the kitchen). Leave room for the fabulous desserts, such as homemade ice cream in a hard chocolate shell.

400 E. Sahara Ave. (btw. Santa Paula and Santa Rita drives, just east of Paradise Rd.). ✆ **702/733-2066**. www. pamplemousserestaurant.com. Reservations required. Main courses lunch $12–$21, dinner $27–$58. AE, DC, DISC, MC, V. Lunch Mon–Sat 11:30am–2:30pm; dinner daily 5:30–10:30pm.

MODERATE

Carluccio's Tivoli Gardens ★★ *Finds* ITALIAN   A bit of a drive, but well worth it for those seeking an authentic (read: dining in a restaurant that's been around more than 10 years) Vegas experience. This joint used to be owned by none other than the Rhinestone King himself, Liberace. See, it was formerly Liberace's Tivoli Gardens, and he designed the interior himself, so you can guess what that looks like (it was reopened a few years after his death, and they kept the decor pretty much intact). This kind of history is more and more rare in this town with no memory, plus it's right next door to the Liberace Museum, no coincidence, so go pay your giggling respects in the late afternoon and then stop here for dinner. Expect traditional Italian food (pasta, pasta, pasta, and scampi), but done very, very well.

1775 E. Tropicana Blvd. (at Spencer St.). ✆ **702/795-3236**. Main courses $10–$18. AE, DC, DISC, MC, V. Tues–Sun 4:30–10pm.

Gordon-Biersch Brewing Company ★ CALIFORNIA/PUB FARE   This is a traditional brewpub (exposed piping and ducts, but still comfortable and casual), but it's worth going to for a meal as well. The menu is pub fare meets California cuisine (kids will probably find the food too complicated), and naturally, there are a lot of beers (German-style lagers) to choose from. Appetizers include satays (marinated meat on skewers served with spicy peanut sauce), pot stickers, calamari, baby back ribs, delicious beer-battered onion rings, and amazing garlic-encrusted fries. A wood-burning pizza oven turns out pies with California-type toppings: eggplant, shrimp, and so forth. For lunch, there are various pastas, stir-fries, sandwiches, and salads. The dinner menu eliminates the sandwiches and adds rosemary chicken, steaks, fish items, and, just in case you forgot it was a brewpub-type joint, beer everything: beer-glazed ham, beer meatloaf, and beer-barbecued glazed ribs. Doesn't that make you want to order a glass of milk?

3987 Paradise Rd. (just north of Flamingo Rd.). ✆ **702/312-5247**. www.gordonbiersch.com. Main courses $18–$23; sandwiches and pizzas $10–$13. AE, DISC, MC, V. Sun–Thurs 11am–midnight; Fri–Sat 11am–1am; bar daily until midnight or later.

Memphis Championship Barbecue ★★ BARBECUE   Okay, we refuse, simply refuse, to get into the debate about Texas vs. Kansas City vs. Mississippi barbecue (and if you've got another place with the best dang barbecue, we really don't want to hear about it). But we can say that if you aren't physically in those places, you gotta take what you can get—and luckily for Vegas visitors, eating at Memphis Championship Barbecue is hardly settling. Its vinegar-based sauce is sweet but has a kick. Food is cooked over mesquite applewood, and the meat falls off the bone just the way you want it to. They have hot links, baked beans, everything you would want and hope for. Standouts include a pulled-barbecue-chicken sandwich, onion straws, and delicious mac and cheese. *Note this special:* A $70 feast includes a rack of St. Louis ribs, ½ pound of pork, ½ pound of beef brisket, ½ pound of hot links, a whole chicken, baked beans, coleslaw, rolls, cream corn, and fries. It feeds four; we think even if two of those four are teenage boys, you might have leftovers.

2250 E. Warm Springs Rd. (near 215 Fwy.). ℂ 702/260-6909. www.memphis-bbq.com. Entrees $10–$20; special barbecue dinner for 4 people $70. AE, MC, V. Sun–Thurs 11am–10pm; Fri–Sat 11am–10:30pm.

INEXPENSIVE

Bougainvillea ★★ *Value* DINER   Oh, how we love a Vegas coffee shop. You've got your all-day breakfasts, your graveyard-shift specials, your prime rib, and, of course, your full Chinese menu. And it's all hearty and well priced; we're talkin' build your own three-egg, three-ingredient omelet for around $5. You can get a full dinner entree or a nice light lunch of a large half-sandwich and soup, also for around $5. And 24-hour specials—a slab of meat, potato or rice, veggies, soup or salad, and a 12-ounce draft beer—are an astounding $10. Yep. That's the ticket.

In Terrible's, 4100 Paradise Rd. ℂ 702/733-7000. Entrees $5–$13. AE, MC, V. Daily 24 hr.

Einstein Bros. Bagels ★ BAGELS   You may not like digging into an enormous buffet first thing in the morning, and the continental breakfast in most hotels is a rip-off. A welcome alternative is a fresh-baked bagel, of which there are 15 varieties here—everything from onion to wild blueberry. Cream cheeses also come in many flavors, anything from sun-dried tomato to vegetable and jalapeño. Einstein's is a pleasant place for a morning meal, with both indoor seating and outdoor tables cooled by misters. Service is friendly, and four special-blend coffees are available each day.

Note: Bagel buffs might also want to check out the nearby **Bagelmania** at 855 E. Twain Ave. (ℂ 702/369-3322). The bagels are sometimes chilled for freshness, which is heresy, but you can avoid this problem by catching them early in the morning, when their extensive selection is hot and fresh.

In the University Gardens Shopping Center, 4626 S. Maryland Pkwy. (btw. Harmon and Tropicana). ℂ 702/795-7800. www.einsteinbros.com. All items under $6. MC, V. Mon–Fri 5:30am–6pm; Sat–Sun 6am–4pm.

Jason's Deli ★ DELI   A chain popular with locals, there are four Jason's in the area, but this one is convenient to those staying east of the Strip. It's a busy, bustling deli where all items are advertised as free of artificial trans fat, plus a section of "slimwiches," so as multipurpose diner/delis go, this may be a fairly healthy option. They also do a brisk take-out business, again useful for those staying in nearby chain hotels without much in the way of room service. There is the usual deli fare—at least a dozen soups, sandwiches, wraps, and junior meals. The wraps tip you off that this is not a Brooklyn-style pastrami deli but fancy California-cuisine influenced froofy versions of sandwiches. A wild card is the New Orleans–inspired muffalettas. The sandwiches are piled with meat, and the chicken potpie is huge. Naturally, the salad bar contains pudding and vanilla wafers—wouldn't want to carry "healthy" too far.

3910 S. Maryland Pkwy. ℂ 702/893-9799. www.jasonsdeli.com. All items under $10. AE, DISC, MC, V. Daily 8am–9pm.

Komol THAI   This is a hole-in-the-wall dive, like most good ethnic places. The menu is pretty large, divided into different sections for poultry, beef, and pork, plus a separate section for vegetarian dishes, plus many rice and noodle selections. They'll spice the food to your specifications. Unless you know your spicy Asian food, it might be best to play it on the safe side. Although we don't want things bland, too much heat can overwhelm all other flavors. The mild to medium packs enough of a kick for most people.

Among the items tried during a recent visit were a vegetarian green curry and the *pud-kee-mao* (flat rice noodles stir-fried with ground chicken, mint, garlic, and hot peppers). *Nam sod* is ground pork with a hot-and-sour sauce, ginger, and peanuts, all of which you wrap up in lettuce leaves—sort of an Asian burrito. Sort of. The Thai iced tea was particularly good—just the right amount of sweetness and tea taste for a drink that is often served overly sweet.

Worth noting: The Commercial Center also has a number of other ethnic (mostly Asian) restaurants, including Korean barbecue.

In the Commercial Center, 953 E. Sahara Ave. (℃) **702/731-6542**. www.komolrestaurant.com. Main courses $8–$13. AE, DISC, MC, V. Mon–Sat 11am–10pm; Sun noon–10pm.

Lotus of Siam ★★★ (Finds) THAI   So we drag you out to a strip mall in the east end

of nowhere and you wonder why? Because here is what critic Jonathan Gold of *Gourmet* magazine called no less than the best Thai restaurant in North America.

What makes this place so darn special? First of all, in addition to all the usual beloved Thai favorites, they have a separate menu featuring lesser-known dishes from northern Thailand—they don't routinely hand this one out (since most of the customers are there for the more pedestrian, if still excellent, $9 lunch buffet). Second, the owner drives at least twice a week back to Los Angeles to pick up the freshest herbs and other ingredients needed for his dishes' authenticity. That's dedication that should be rewarded with superlatives.

You might be best off letting them know you are interested in Northern food (with dried chiles and more pork; it's not un-Cajunlike, says the owner) and letting them guide you through, though you must assure them that you aren't of faint heart or palate (some customers complain the heat isn't enough, even with "well spiced" dishes, though others find even medium spice sufficient). Standouts include the Issan sausage (a grilled sour pork number), the *nam kao tod* (that same sausage, ground up with lime, green onion, fresh chile, and ginger, served with crispy rice), *nam sod* (ground pork mixed with ginger, green onion, and lime juice, served with sticky rice), jackfruit *larb* (spicy ground meat), and *sua rong hai* ("weeping tiger"), a dish of soft, sliced, and grilled marinated beef. If you insist on more conventional Thai, that's okay, in that it's unlikely you are going to have better *mee krob* noodles or *tom kah kai* (that beloved soup can also be served northern style, if asked, which is without the coconut milk). If in season, finish with mango with sticky rice, or if not, coconut ice cream with sticky rice, something you would find at many a street stall in Thailand.

In the Commercial Center, 953 E. Sahara Ave. (℃) **702/735-3033**. www.saipinchutima.com. Reservations strongly recommended for dinner; call at least a day in advance. Lunch buffet $9; other dishes $9–$20. AE, MC, V. Mon–Thurs 11:30am–2:30pm and 5:30–9:30pm; Fri–Sun 5:30–10pm.

Paymon's Mediterranean Cafe & Lounge ★ MEDITERRANEAN   The empha-

sis on safe, mainstream food for the masses, to say nothing of the basic economy involved in running a Vegas restaurant (take your pick, either pay costly rent to a Strip hotel or get less tourist traffic with an off-Strip site), means that the kind of eateries other big cities take for granted—you know, cheap holes-in-the-wall, or charming little quirky joints, or the kind of ethnic places the chowhound folks brag about discovering—are rare indeed. And when you do find them, they are always, but always, in a strip mall. Paymon's Mediterranean Cafe is no exception, and its main dining room has no decor worth mentioning. But it gets extra points for having a courtyard seating area full of Middle Eastern touches and an honest-to-goodness hookah lounge—it's a good break from an otherwise often stifled, insulating time in Sin City.

Plus, it's just so darn nice to find ethnic food in this town. As the menu warns, kabobs take 25 minutes, so order an appetizer plate with various dips to while away the time. The hummus here is too reminiscent of its chickpea origins, but the *baba ghanouj* is properly smoky, and the falafel has the right crunch. Gyros may not be the most adventurous thing to order, but who cares about that when you've got a well-stuffed pocket pita, gloopy with yogurt sauce. *Fresenjan* is a dish of falling-apart chicken swimming in a tangy pomegranate sauce; ask them to ensure that the ratio of sauce to chicken is greater than 10:1.

4147 S. Maryland Pkwy. (at Flamingo Rd., in the Tiffany Sq. strip mall). ✆ 702/731-6030. www.paymons.com. Reservations not accepted. Main courses $10–$19; most sandwiches under $8. AE, DISC, MC, V. Restaurant Sun–Thurs 11am–1am, Fri–Sat 11am–3am; lounge Mon–Thurs 5pm–1am, Fri–Sat 5pm–3am.

Pink Taco 𝕲 MEXICAN   A mega-hip Mexican cantina, this folk-art–bedecked spot is a scene just waiting to happen, or rather, has already happened. There are no surprises in terms of the food; you know the drill—tacos, burritos, quesadillas—but it's all tasty and filling, and some of it comes with some surprising accompaniments, such as tapenade, along with the usual guacamole and sour cream. This is hip Mexican as opposed to a mom-and-pop joint, and it's a good place to eat on this side of town.

In the Hard Rock Hotel & Casino, 4455 Paradise Rd. ✆ 702/693-5525. www.pinktaco.com. Reservations not accepted except in cases of 10 or more. Main courses $7.50–$15. AE, DC, DISC, MC, V. Sun–Thurs 11am–10pm; Fri–Sun 11am–midnight (bar stays open later).

Toto's 𝕲𝕲 𝒱alue 𝒦ids MEXICAN   A family-style Mexican restaurant favored by locals, with enormous portions and quick service, this is good value for your money. With all that food, you could probably split portions and still be satisfied. There are no surprises on the menu, though there are quite a few seafood dishes. Everything is quite tasty, and they don't skimp on the cheese. The nongreasy chips come with fresh salsa, and the nachos are terrific. Chicken tamales got a thumbs-up, while the veggie burrito was happily received by non–meat eaters (although it's not especially healthful, all the ingredients were fresh, with huge slices of zucchini and roasted bell peppers). The operative word here is *huge;* the burritos are almost the size of your arm. The generous portions continue with dessert—a piece of flan was practically pie size. The Sunday margarita brunch is quite fun, and the drinks are large (naturally) and yummy.

2055 E. Tropicana Ave. ✆ 702/895-7923. Main courses $7–$15. AE, DISC, MC, V. Mon–Thurs 11am–10pm; Fri–Sat 11am–11pm; Sun 9:30am–10pm.

6 West of the Strip

EXPENSIVE

Austins Steakhouse 𝕲𝕲 𝐹inds STEAK/SEAFOOD   Now, understand that we don't send you out to nether regions such as Texas Station lightly. We do so here because, improbably, Austins Steakhouse has gained a reputation for the best steak in town. Really. Even the snooty critics at the *Las Vegas Review-Journal* agree with the hubbub about this place. And here's what has everyone, including us, raving: a 24-ounce rib-eye—yes, we know, just split it—aged and marinated, cooked over mesquite

Dining & Nightlife West of the Strip

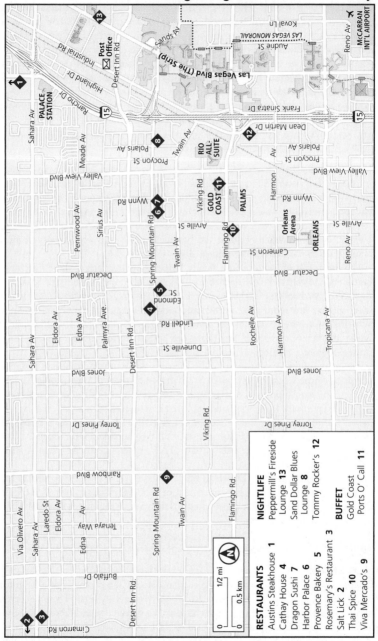

RESTAURANTS
Austins Steakhouse **1**
Cathay House **4**
Dragon Sushi **7**
Harbor Palace **6**
Provence Bakery **5**
Rosemary's Restaurant **3**
Salt Lick **2**
Thai Spice **10**
Viva Mercado's **9**

NIGHTLIFE
Peppermill's Fireside
   Lounge **13**
Sand Dollar Blues
   Lounge **8**
Tommy Rocker's **12**

BUFFET
Gold Coast
Ports O' Call **11**

applewood, then rubbed with peppercorns and pan-seared in garlic, butter, and cilantro. A massive chunk of meat with a smoky, garlicky flavor like no other steak we can think of. Most of the dishes have a Southern twist, like the fried green tomatoes with remoulade dipping sauce, and for those not watching their cholesterol, or at least only watching it go up, the shrimp sautéed in garlic-butter sauce, dipped in cheese, and wrapped in bacon. The Maui onion soup is also a standout, as is, over in the desserts, the chocolate decadence cake, which actually has a molten center, sort of a semi-soufflé. Note that a comparable meal on the Strip would cost $10 to $20 more per person—yet another reason to head out to the hinterlands.

In Texas Station, 2101 Texas Star Lane. © 702/631-1033. Reservations recommended. Main courses $15–$50. AE, DC, DISC, MC, V. Sun–Thurs 5–10pm; Fri–Sat 5–11pm.

Rosemary's Restaurant ★★★ *Finds* NOUVELLE AMERICAN　No visitor would be blamed for never leaving the Vegas Strip—it's the raison d'être of any Vegas tourist—but a true foodie should make a point of finding the nearest moving vehicle that can get them to Rosemary's Restaurant. A 15-minute (or so) drive down Sahara (hardly anything) is all it takes to eat what may well be the best food in Las Vegas. (Certainly, it is consistently voted the best food in the *Las Vegas Review-Journal's* annual poll, by food critics and readers alike.)

The brainchild of Michael and Wendy Jordan, both veterans of the New Orleans food scene (Michael actually opened Emeril's here in Vegas), Rosemary's Restaurant (named for Michael's mother) shows more than a few NOLA touches, from the food to the service, in a room that's warmer and more inviting than most others in Vegas. Note that you can get seats at the bar overlooking the open kitchen, great fun for foodie interaction and not a bad choice for singles, or for couples looking for an unusual romantic evening.

The cuisine covers most regions of the U.S., though Southern influences dominate. Fifty local farmers help supply products. Seared foie gras with peach coulis, candied walnuts, and vanilla bean–scented arugula is like a quilt, with distinct flavors that all hang together nicely. Interesting sides include ultrarich bleu-cheese slaw, slightly spicy crispy fried tortilla strips, and perfect cornmeal jalapeño hush puppies. A recent visit found the crispy striped bass fighting it out with the pan-seared honey-glazed salmon for "best fish dish we've ever had." Desserts are similarly Southern—lemon icebox pie!—and most pleasant.

There is a nice little wine list with a broad range, especially when it comes to half-price bottles. They also specialize, unusually, in beer suggestions to pair with courses, including some fruity Belgian numbers; this is such a rare treat, if you drink, you must try some of their suggestions.

8125 W. Sahara. © 702/869-2251. www.rosemarysrestaurant.com. Reservations strongly recommended. Lunch $14–$17; dinner $27–$42. AE, DISC, MC, V. Mon–Fri 11:30am–2:30pm and 5:30–10:30pm; Sat–Sun 5:30–10:30pm.

MODERATE

Cathay House CHINESE　Las Vegas actually has a Chinatown—a very large strip mall (naturally) on Spring Mountain Road near Wynn Las Vegas. There are several Asian restaurants there, but ask locals who look like they know, and they will send you instead farther up Spring Mountain Road to the Cathay House (on the opposite side of the street). This only looks far from the Strip on a map; it's really about a 7-minute drive from TI–Treasure Island.

Ordering dim sum, for those of you who haven't experienced it, is sort of like being at a Chinese sushi bar, in that you order many individual, tasty little dishes. Of course, dim sum itself is nothing like sushi. Rather, it's a range of pot stickers, pan-fried dumplings, *baos* (soft, doughy buns filled with such meat as barbecued pork), translucent rice noodles wrapped around shrimp, sticky rice in lotus leaves, chicken feet, and so forth. Some of it is steamed; some is fried—for that extra-good grease! You can make your own dipping sauce by combining soy sauce, vinegar, and hot-pepper oil. The waitstaff pushes steam carts filled with little dishes; point, and they'll attempt to tell you what each one is. Better, just blindly order a bunch and dig in. Each dish ranges from approximately $1 to $3; each server makes a note of what you just received, and the total is tallied at the end. (For some reason, it almost always works out to about $9 per person.) Dim sum is usually available only until mid-afternoon.

5300 W. Spring Mountain Rd. © **702/876-3838**. www.cathayhouse.com. Reservations recommended. Main courses $6.75–$19. AE, DC, DISC, MC, V. Daily 10:30am–10pm.

Harbor Palace ⌖ CHINESE   Located in a mega–strip mall with quite a few other Asian restaurants as competition, we point this out to you as another dim sum option. When you can get an order of commendable shrimp *hai gow* (little steamed rice noodle–wrapped balls of fresh shrimp) or pork *shiu mai* for $1.90, or pan-fried chive dumplings for $2.70, you might feel foolish eating dim sum on the Strip, where it will set you back five times as much. They also have a full menu of other Chinese dishes (as do their neighbors; you can pretty much head into whichever one looks the most popular and take a chance), and they do takeout. Given those late-night hours, this is a good spot for post-clubbing snacks, though the dim sum is usually not offered late.

4275 Spring Mountain Rd. © **702/253-1688**. Dim sum $1.90–$6.50; main courses $10–$20. AE, MC. V. Daily 10am–5am.

Salt Lick ⌖⌖ BARBEQUE   An outpost of the much-beloved Austin barbeque spot, this looks both not at all like the Driftwood original and yet related in a double-first-cousin kind of way, with the same heavy pine wood tables and more importantly, the same heavenly smell. Many believe Salt Lick serves the platonic ideal of barbeque. That's not the case here. The meat is smoky, and the dry rub has its kick, but the results aren't as tender or as memorably flavorful. The sausage and ribs are better than the brisket, which is sublime back in Texas. Still, the all-you-can-eat plate is a good deal, and you can do takeout either on your way to a picnic in Red Rock Canyon or to munch back in your hotel after a long day of hiking.

In Red Rock Resort, 10972 W. Charleston. © **702/797-7535**. Main courses $9–$17. AE, MC, V. Sun–Thurs 11am–10pm; Fri–Sat 11am–11pm.

Viva Mercado's ⌖⌖ MEXICAN   Ask any local about Mexican food in Vegas, and almost certainly they will point to Viva Mercado's as the best in town. That recommendation, plus the restaurant's health-conscious attitude, makes this worth the roughly 10-minute drive from the Strip.

Given all those warnings about Mexican food and its heart-attack-inducing properties, the approach at Viva Mercado's is nothing to be sniffed at. No dish is prepared with or cooked in any kind of animal fat. Nope, the lard so dear to Mexican cooking is not found here. The oil used is an artery-friendly canola. This makes the place particularly appealing to vegetarians, who will also be pleased by the regular veggie specials. Everything is quite fresh, and they do particularly amazing things with seafood.

Sweet Sensations

Plenty of opportunities exist in Vegas for satisfying your sweet tooth, but for the discriminating, here are six spots that you may have to make a detour for.

Jean-Philippe Patisserie (in Bellagio, 3600 Las Vegas Blvd. S.; © 702/693-8788) makes us swoon, not just because it has the world's largest chocolate fountain (20 ft. high! Though only 11 ft. are on view, and they won't let us drink from it. Darn.), but perhaps, more to the point, it's the home of World Pastry Champion Jean-Philippe Maury. (Yes, you can win gold medals for pastries.) Each visit causes us to spin around distractedly, trying to take in all the choices, both visually and gastronomically. From perfect gourmet chocolates to ice cream (diet-conscious folks will be relieved to learn the sorbets are excellent) to the eponymous pastries (each a little work of art), we hit greed overload. For us, this is true Vegas decadence—if only "what happens in Vegas, stays in Vegas" applied to calories. Our current favorites include a witty-looking version of lemon meringue pie that was proclaimed by one aficionado as her favorite ever, to a chocolate hazelnut bombe with so many layers of interest we couldn't quite keep track, to brioches filled with either *dulce de leche* or Nutella. They also serve some solidly good sandwiches, which often need heating, which can be a problem if the ingredients are better cold (prosciutto, for example), and some adequate savory crepes. Open daily from 7am to midnight.

The **Chocolate Swan** (Mandalay Place, 3930 Las Vegas Blvd. S.; © 702/632-9366; www.chocolateswan.com) is here because a Mandalay Bay executive fell in love with the owners' work back at their original Midwestern shop and convinced them to close and reopen in Vegas. Patronize them so they know their decision was a good one; you will know it is as soon as you try one of their entirely-from-scratch-and-fresh products: gorgeous, elaborate baked goods, carefully created candies, and too much more to list. Have a slice of cake and homemade hot chocolate, and take back a few pastries and other sweets for a late-night orgy in your room. Prices aren't cheap (particularly for slices of cake), but that seems to be the way of gourmet sweets shops. Open daily 8am to 10pm.

A local favorite is **Freed's Bakery**, 4780 S. Eastern Ave., at Tropicana Boulevard (© 702/456-7762; www.freedsbakery.com), open Monday through Saturday from 9am to 6:30pm and Sunday from 9am to 3pm. If you've got a serious sugar craving, this is worth the 15-minute drive from the Strip.

Try the *Maresco Vallarta*, which is orange roughy, shrimp, and scallops cooked in a coconut-tomato sauce, with capers and olives. They have all sorts of noteworthy shrimp dishes and 11 different salsas, ranked 1 to 10 for degree of spice. The staff is friendly (try to chat with owner Bobby Mercado) and the portions hearty. ***Note:*** At press time, the restaurant was planning to move to a new address at 3553 South Rainbow Rd. Call before you head out to confirm the correct location.

Despite the minimalist setting, it's like walking into Grandma's kitchen (provided you had an old-fashioned granny who felt pastries should not be fancy but should definitely be gooey, chocolaty, and buttery). The chocolate coffeecake is especially good. They also have fresh bread, napoleons, strawberry cheesecake, cream puffs, sweet rolls, Danishes, and doughnuts, many of which are made with surprisingly fresh ingredients. Some may find the goodies too heavy and rich, but for those of us with a powerful sweet tooth, this place hits the spot.

Those staying at the Green Valley Resort can rejoice over their proximity to **The Cupcakery,** 9680 S. Eastern, in Henderson (© **702/207-2253;** www. thecupcakery.com). Thus far, Vegas's only entry into the cupcake wars currently raging in major U.S. cities, the delectable cakes here aren't large, but they pack a wallop of moist cake and creamy frosting. Clever combinations include the Boston cream pie (filled with custardy cream), but even the basic chocolate-on-chocolate is a buttercream pleasure. They even have sugar-free cupcakes for those with such dietary needs. Since they offer sit-down seating as well as take-away, you can make this a stop if you are out visiting any Henderson sights. Open Monday to Friday 8am to 6pm, Saturday 10am to 6pm.

Hot Vegas days call for cool desserts, and frozen custard (softer than regular ice cream, but harder than soft serve) is a fine way to go. Head for **Luv-It Frozen Custard,** 505 E. Oakey (© **702/384-6452;** www.luvitfrozencustard. com), open Tuesday through Thursday from 1 to 10pm, Friday and Saturday from 1 to 11pm. Since it has less fat and sugar than premium ice cream, you can even fool yourself into thinking this is somewhat healthful (ha!). Made every few hours using fresh cream and eggs, Luv-It Frozen Custard has basic flavors available for cup or cone, but more exotic ones (maple walnut, apple spice, and more) in tubs.

Another Chinatown alternative for baked goods is the French/Asian **Provence Bakery** ⊛, 5115 Spring Mountain, no. 225 (© **702/341-0168**). Try custard buns, sweet bread, and all manner of cookies, but definitely grab one of their packages of little cream puffs, superior in many ways to the cream-puff chains popping up in other parts of the U.S. It all makes for good snack-grabbing to and from Red Rock or as a post-Chinese meal dessert in the complex. They also have shaved ice and smoothies. Open Monday through Saturday from 9:30am to 9pm, Sunday from 10am to 9pm.

6182 W. Flamingo Rd. (at Jones Blvd.). © **702/871-8826.** www.vivamercadoslv.com. Reservations accepted only for large parties. Main courses $10–$20. AE, DISC, MC, V. Sun–Thurs 11am–9:30pm; Fri–Sat 11am–10pm.

INEXPENSIVE

Dragon Sushi SUSHI   Those used to really extraordinary sushi need to remember that you are in the middle of the desert, and so there is no way the fish you are going to eat here were swimming the ocean all that recently. That said, they do pretty good sushi here, with rolls that pack a wallop, such as the Tuna Tuna Roll (spicy tuna with fresh tuna wrapped around it and, unless we miss our guess, some kind of chile oil for good measure). Don't say we didn't warn you about the Hell Roll. If the incongruously named sushi chef Bruce is working, let this talented man do his work for you. Better still, let him make all your choices.

4115 Spring Mountain Rd. (at Valley View Blvd.). ℭ **702/368-4336**. Sushi $4–$7 per portion, daily specials more; main courses all under $20. AE, MC, V. Mon–Sat 11am–10:30pm; Sun 4–10:30pm.

Thai Spice ✓*Value* THAI Just off the Strip and across from the Rio, this modern-looking, nonglitzy Thai restaurant offers decent food at reasonable prices. The sub-dued ambience, quick service, and good food make it a local favorite. The menu is extensive and offers an array of Thai dishes and even some Chinese fare. For appetiz-ers, the *tom kah kai* soup and pork or chicken satay (served on skewers with a spicy peanut sauce) are excellent. Skip the terrible *moo goo gai pan* in favor of terrific *pad Thai* and tasty lemon chicken. Lunch specials are $6.95 and include spring rolls, salad, soup, and steamed rice. Make sure you tell the waitress how spicy you want your food.

4433 W. Flamingo Rd. (at Arville St.). ℭ **702/362-5308**. Main courses $7 at lunch, $9–$15 at dinner. AE, DISC, MC, V. Sun–Thurs 11am–10pm, Fri–Sat 11am–10:30pm.

7 Downtown

VERY EXPENSIVE

Andre's ✶✶ FRENCH Andre's has long been the bastion of gourmet dining in Vegas, but with all the new big boys crowding the Strip, it runs the risk of getting over-looked. It shouldn't—Andre may not have a show on the Food Network, but he ought to be a household name. Besides, his first restaurant still dominates Downtown. This is also a celebrity haunt where you're likely to see Strip headliners. One night, Tom Hanks, Steven Spielberg, and James Spader were all spotted joining some pals for a bachelor party. The staff played it cool, though. In a small, converted 1930s house, you'll find an elegant French provincial atmosphere, overseen by owner-chef Andre, who brings over 40 years of experience to the table. Much of the waitstaff is also French, and they will happily lavish attention on you and guide you through the menu.

The food presentation is exquisite, and choices change seasonally. On a recent visit, an appetizer of Northwest smoked salmon *mille feuille* with cucumber salad and sevruga caviar was especially enjoyed, as was a main course of grilled veal *tournedos* with chive sauce accompanied by a mushroom and foie gras crepe. You get the idea. Desserts are similarly lovely, an exotic array of rich delights. An extensive wine list (more than 900 labels) is international in scope and includes many rare vintages; con-sult the sommelier.

Note: An additional branch of Andre's is in the **Monte Carlo Hotel & Casino,** 3775 Las Vegas Blvd. S. (ℭ **702/798-7151**), and is also highly recommended, as is their slightly different take, **Alizé** (p. 130), in the Palms.

401 S. 6th St. (at Lewis St., 3 blocks south of Fremont St.). ℭ **702/385-5016**. www.andrelv.com. Reservations required. Main courses $33–$68. AE, DC, MC, V. Tues–Sat 5:30–10:30pm.

Hugo's Cellar ✶ INTERNATIONAL Hugo's Cellar is indeed in a cellar, or at least below street level in the Four Queens hotel. No, they aren't ashamed of it—quite the opposite. This is their pride and joy, and it is highly regarded by the locals. This is Old School Vegas Classy Dining. Each female guest is given a red rose when she enters the restaurant—the first of a series of nice touches. The restaurant proper is dimly lit,

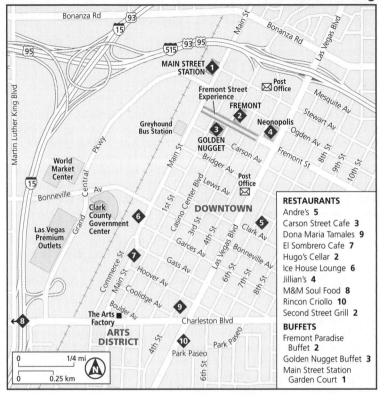

RESTAURANTS

Andre's **5**
Carson Street Cafe **3**
Dona Maria Tamales **9**
El Sombrero Cafe **7**
Hugo's Cellar **2**
Ice House Lounge **6**
Jillian's **4**
M&M Soul Food **8**
Rincon Criollo **10**
Second Street Grill **2**

BUFFETS

Fremont Paradise
   Buffet **2**
Golden Nugget Buffet **3**
Main Street Station
   Garden Court **1**

lined with dark wood and brick. It's fairly intimate, but if you really want to be cozy, ask for one of the curtained booths against the wall.

The meal is full of ceremony, perfectly delivered by a well-trained and cordial waitstaff. Salads, included in the price, are prepared at your table, from a cart full of choices. In Vegas style, though, most choices are on the calorie-intensive side, ranging from chopped egg and bleu cheese to pine nuts and bay shrimp. Still, with a honey-orange-walnut vinaigrette, it's good enough to consider paying the $14 a la carte fee and just sticking with it. Unfortunately, the main courses are not all that novel (various cuts of meat, seafood, and chicken prepared in different ways), but on a recent visit, not one of six diners was anything less than delighted. The filet of beef stuffed with crabmeat and wrapped with bacon is over the top for us, but others loved it, while the roast duckling rubbed with anise and flambéed at the table is a guilty pleasure, just the right effect for this Old School Vegas dining experience. The T-bone steak was tender enough to cut with a fork. Vegetables and excellent starchy sides are included, as is a finish of chocolate-dipped fruits with cream.

The service is impeccable, and it really makes you feel pampered. The fact that salad, the small dessert, and so forth are included makes an initially hefty-seeming price tag appear a bit more reasonable, especially compared to Strip establishments that aren't much better and can cost the same for just the entree. While it's not worth going out of your way for the food (though here we admit that well-prepared Old School is better than careless nouvelle any day), perhaps it is worth it for the entire package.

In the Four Queens, 202 Fremont St. ✆ **702/385-4011.** www.hugoscellar.com. Reservations required. Main courses $36–$52. AE, DC, DISC, MC, V. Daily 5:30–11pm.

EXPENSIVE

Second Street Grill ✪ *Finds* INTERNATIONAL/PACIFIC RIM   Our categorization notwithstanding, Second Street Grill calls itself "Continental American with Euro and Asian influences." And, yes, that translates to a bit of a muddle, culinary-wise, but the portions are extremely generous, and it's hard to resist a place that plants two long potato chips in a pile of mashed potatoes, thereby creating a bunny rabbit. You are probably best off with grill dishes (various steaks and other cuts of meat), though here might be your best ratio of quality to price for lobster tail. Play around with the Hunan pork and beef lettuce wrap appetizers, and the Peking duck and shrimp tacos—don't wince, the shell was a won ton wrapper. The waist-conscious will be very pleased with the bamboo-steamed snapper in a nice broth, while others may want to try the grilled salmon with goat cheese Parmesan crust. Desserts are disappointing, unfortunately. Overall, a nice place for a family event dinner Downtown, and certainly more affordable than fancy places on the Strip.

In Fremont Hotel & Casino, 200 E. Fremont St. ✆ **702/385-3232.** Reservations recommended. Main courses $17–$30. AE, DC, DISC, MC, V. Sun–Mon and Thurs 6–10pm; Fri–Sat 6–11pm.

INEXPENSIVE

Carson Street Cafe AMERICAN   Here's a slightly better-than-adequate hotel coffee shop, though it's a mixed bag in terms of quality of food. Sandwiches are better than ribs, burgers, and fries, all of which are merely just filling. On the other hand, the linguine with shrimp is surprisingly good, while desserts, especially pecan pie a la mode, more than earn their rep.

In the Golden Nugget, 129 E. Fremont St. ✆ **702/385-7111.** Reservations not accepted. Main courses $6–$18. AE, DC, DISC, MC, V. Daily 24 hr.

El Sombrero Cafe ✪✪ MEXICAN   This kind of hole-in-the-wall Mexican joint can be found all over California but not always so readily elsewhere. It's also the kind of family-run (since 1950) place increasingly forced out of Vegas by giant hotel conglomerates, making it even more worth your time (it's becoming harder and harder, particularly in Downtown, to find budget options that serve food that is more than just mere fuel). Mexican-food fans, in particular, should seek out this friendly place, though it's not in an attractive part of town. Portions are generous, better than average, and unexpectedly spicy. They also cater to special requests—changing the beef burrito to a chicken one (an option that comes highly recommended), for example, without batting an eyelash. The enchilada and taco combo also won raves.

807 S. Main St. (at Gass Ave.). ✆ **702/382-9234.** Lunch $8; dinner $13. MC, V. Mon–Thurs 11am–4pm; Fri–Sat 11am–8:30pm.

Ice House Lounge ✪ *Value* AMERICAN   This eatery, part nightclub/bar, part diner, believes a Downtown revitalization is still possible, which is why the owners set up shop in a particularly grungy industrial part of the city. Don't let the dismal surroundings put you off; inside is a lively, popular modern-appearing club, with a menu full of reliable (if not inspired) and well-priced menu options. The late-night hours also make this a good choice for those located near Downtown. Lunch, in particular, is a bargain, as vinyl-record-size plates are loaded with towering sandwiches or wide-reaching flatbread-style pizzas, mounds of coleslaw, or piles of crinkly fries. We like the plate of three miniburgers. None of it is thrillingly spiced or especially cleverly crafted, but it's all solidly good and, given the portions, eminently shareable. The bar borrows the "ice bar" concept from Red Square, while the walls feature historical photos of Vegas and of the actual icehouse that once stood on the site.

650 S. Main St. (at Bonneville). ✆ 702/315-2570. www.icehouselounge.com. Most items under $15. AE, DISC, MC, V. Mon–Fri 10am–2am; Sat 11am–3am.

Jillian's ✦ AMERICAN   This is a branch of a national chain, and while the fare is strictly coffee shop, it's a good representative of same. Since it's well located at the foot of Fremont Street, in the Neonopolis complex, and is open late, it should be considered for both hungry night owls and families on a budget (especially those with hungry and/or picky teens, since the large menu has something for just about everyone, except maybe those watching their diet). You will find the usual playful concept chain food starters—Buffalo wings, mozzarella sticks, plus a more clever spinach and artichoke dip with chips—and then everything from multiburger styles (the barbecue-bacon burger oozed cheese and was piled with bacon and onion rings) to steak and seafood combos, pizzas, and some unexpected New Orleans–influenced entrees such as jambalaya and even crawfish. Portions are enormous, so you can split items and save even more money, and everything is what you might expect in terms of quality—not transcendent, but solidly good. The atmosphere is lively, if not downright noisy.

In Neonopolis, 450 Fremont St. (at Las Vegas Blvd. S.). ✆ 702/759-0450. www.jillianslasvegas.com. Main courses all under $18. AE, MC, V. Sun–Thurs 11am–10pm; Fri–Sat 11am–12:30am.

M&M Soul Food ✦✦ (Finds SOUL FOOD   Though we've listed this in Downtown, it's really not too far from the Strip. At first glance, the neighborhood seems intimidating, but it's not actually threatening. Why come here? Because locals have voted this their favorite soul food place, and while the competition may not be all that high, the quality stands out regardless. Appropriately, it's a hole in the wall, with somewhat higher prices than one might expect, but the generous portions make up for it. Mini cornbread pancakes are served to every table. Smothered fried chicken is moist, slightly spicy, and topped with a robust gravy. The menu includes hot links, collard greens, and other typical options.

3923 W. Charleston. ✆ 702/453-7685. $6–$17. AE, DISC, MC, V. Daily 7am–8pm.

8 Buffets & Sunday Brunches

Lavish, low-priced buffets are a Las Vegas tradition, designed to lure you to the gaming tables and to make you feel that you got such a bargain for your meal that you can afford to drop more money. They're gimmicks, and we love them. Something about filling up on too much prime rib and shrimp just says "Vegas" to us.

Unfortunately, like so much else that was Vegas tradition, the buffets are evolving. The higher-end ones no longer put out heaping mounds o' stuff, which is probably for the best in terms of waste but is a departure from decadence that we are loath to see. And prices have been steadily creeping upward; the higher-end buffets are no longer a true bargain because it's unlikely you can (or should) eat enough to make you feel like you really got away with something. With the more expensive buffets, some of which have pretty good food, consider it this way: You would pay much more, per person, at one of the fancier restaurants in town, and you could order just one, potentially disappointing, item. Consider the higher-end recommended buffet as an alternative to a nice meal at a traditional restaurant. More variety per person means more options, less likelihood for disappointment. (Hate what you picked? Dump your plate and start all over.) Not nearly as atmospheric as a proper restaurant, but how else can you combine good barbecue with excellent Chinese and a cupcake or 10?

There is a lot of variety within the buffet genre. Some are just perfunctory steam-table displays and salad bars that are heavy on the iceberg lettuce, while others are unbelievably opulent spreads with caviar and free-flowing champagne. Some are quite beautifully presented as well. Some of the food is awful, some of it is decent, and some of it is memorable.

No trip to Las Vegas is complete without trying one or two buffets. Of the dozens, the most noteworthy are described below. Bear in mind that, appearance and layout aside, almost all buffets have some things in common. Unless otherwise noted, every one listed below will have a carving station, a salad bar (quality differs), and hot main courses and side dishes. We will try to point out only the more notable and original elements at the various buffets.

Note: Buffets are extremely popular, and reservations are usually not taken (we've indicated when they are, and in all those cases, they are highly recommended). Arrive early (before opening) or late to avoid a long line, especially on weekends.

SOUTH STRIP
EXPENSIVE
Mandalay Bay's Bayside Buffet ✦ BUFFET   This is a particularly pretty, not overly large buffet. Floor-to-ceiling windows overlooking the beach part of the elaborate pool area make it less stuffy and eliminate the closed-in feeling that so many of the other buffets in town have. The buffet itself is adequately arranged but features nothing particularly special, though there are some nice salads, hearty meats, and a larger and better-than-average dessert bar—they make their own desserts, and it shows.

In Mandalay Bay, 3950 Las Vegas Blvd. S. ℂ 702/632-7777. Breakfast $17; lunch $21; dinner $28; Sun brunch $25; Shark Reef Brunch package $36. Reduced prices for children ages 4–11; free for children 3 and under. AE, DC, DISC, MC, V. Mon–Fri 7am–2:30pm and 4:45–9:45pm; Sat–Sun 7am–10pm.

MGM Grand Buffet BUFFET   This rather average buffet does feature a fresh Belgian waffle station at breakfast. Dinner also has an all-you-can-eat shrimp and prime rib option. Also available: low-fat, sugar-free desserts! And at all meals, you get a full pot of coffee on your table. Still, those dinner prices do not justify a trip here.

In MGM Grand, 3799 Las Vegas Blvd. S. ℂ 702/891-7777. Breakfast $14; lunch $16; Sun–Thurs dinner $26, Fri–Sat dinner $28; Sat–Sun brunch $28. Reduced prices for children ages 4–11; free for children 3 and under. AE, DC, DISC, MC, V. Daily 7am–2:30pm; Sun–Thurs 4:30–10pm and Fri–Sat 4:30–10:30pm.

MODERATE
Excalibur's Roundtable Buffet ✦ BUFFET   This one strikes the perfect balance of moderate prices, forgettable decor, and adequate food. It's what you want in a cheap Vegas buffet—except it's just not that cheap anymore. Then again, none are anymore, so this still qualifies and, thus, usually has long lines.

In Excalibur, 3850 Las Vegas Blvd. S. ℂ 702/597-7777. Breakfast $13; lunch $14; dinner $17. Prices reduced for children ages 4–12. Free for children 3 and under. AE, DC, DISC, MC, V. Daily 6:30am–11pm.

Monte Carlo Buffet ⊛ BUFFET   A "courtyard" under a painted sky, the Monte Carlo's buffet room has a Moroccan market theme, with murals of Arab scenes, Moorish archways, Oriental carpets, and walls hung with photographs of and artifacts from Morocco. Dinner includes a rotisserie (for chicken and pork loin, or London broil), a Chinese food station, a taco/fajita bar, a baked potato bar, numerous salads, and more than a dozen desserts, plus frozen yogurt and ice-cream machines. Lunches are similar. At breakfast, the expected fare is supplemented by an omelet station, and choices include crepes, blintzes, and corned-beef hash. Fresh-baked bagels are a plus.

In Monte Carlo Resort & Casino, 3770 Las Vegas Blvd. S. ℂ 702/730-7777. Breakfast $13; lunch $15; dinner $20; Sun brunch $21. All meals include tax. Reduced prices for children ages 5–9; free for children 4 and under. AE, DC, DISC, MC, V. Daily 7am–10pm (closed btw. 3:30 and 4pm).

MORE, The Buffet at Luxor ⊛⊛ BUFFET   Once one of our favorite buffets not just for the excellent price-to-quality ratio, but also because it reflected the excellent theme in its Indiana Jones–invoking decor, the Luxor buffet has been redesigned and renamed as part of the ongoing de-Egypt-ing of the hotel. Dang. We are sick of neato modern-classy already and want our mummies back. That said, the food is the best in its price range, and it is one of the top buffets in town. There's a Mexican station with some genuinely spicy food, a Chinese stir-fry station, and different Italian pastas. Desserts were disappointing, though they do offer a pretty large selection of diabetic-friendly options. The quality-to-price ratio is no secret, and, as a result, the lines are always enormous.

In Luxor, 3900 Las Vegas Blvd. S. ℂ 702/262-4000. Breakfast $12; lunch $14; dinner $20; Sun brunch $18 until 3pm; $20 3–7pm. Reduced prices for children ages 4–10; free for children 3 and under. AE, DC, DISC, MC, V. Daily 7am–10pm.

Spice Market Buffet ⊛⊛   Despite the switch over from Aladdin to Planet Hollywood, there are no plans to reconfigure this excellent buffet. This comes as a relief, as this is one of the better choices in the city, thanks to unexpected, and pretty good, Middle Eastern specialties, including the occasional Moroccan entrees. Look for tandoori chicken, hummus, couscous, stuffed tomatoes with ground lamb, and at dinner, lamb skewers. The Mexican station is particularly good as well, even if it confuses the palate to go from guacamole to hummus. The dim sum also gets a vote of confidence. There is cotton candy at lunch and a crepe-making station at dinner. We still wish it were a bit cheaper; at these prices, it's edging toward the high end.

3667 Las Vegas Blvd. S. ℂ 702/785-5555. Breakfast $15; lunch $18; dinner $26. AE, DC, DISC, MC, V. Daily 7–10:30am, 11am–3pm, and 4–10pm.

MID-STRIP
VERY EXPENSIVE

Bally's Sterling Sunday Brunch ⊛⊛ BUFFET   Now, the admittedly high cost of this brunch seems antithetical to the original purpose of a buffet: a lot of food for minimal money. However, if you're a dedicated buffet fan, this is probably a better spree than one of the many new high-priced restaurants. It works out to less money in the long run, and you will get, for your purposes, more bang for your buck. It's a fancy deal—linen and silver-bedecked tables, waiters to assist you, if you choose—and while the variety of food isn't as massive as at regular buffets, the quality is much higher in terms of both content and execution. We're talking unlimited champagne, broiled lobster, caviar, sushi, and rotating dishes of the day (items such as monkfish with pomegranate essence, tenderloin wrapped in porcini mushroom mousse, and even ostrich). No French toast that's been sitting out for days here! Perfect for a wedding breakfast or just a big treat; stay a long time and eat as much as you can.

Inside Bally's Steakhouse, 3645 Las Vegas Blvd. S. ✆ **702/967-7999**. Reservations recommended. Brunch $75. AE, DC, MC, V. Sun 9:30am–2pm (last reservation at 1:30pm).

Bellagio Buffet 🐦🐦 BUFFET   Though one of the priciest of the buffets, the Bellagio still gets high marks from visitors. The array of food is fabulous, with one ethnic cuisine after another (Japanese, Chinese that includes unexpected buffet fare such as dim sum, build-it-yourself Mexican items, and so on). There are elaborate pastas and semitraditional Italian-style pizza from a wood-fired oven. The cold fish appetizers at each end of the line are not to be missed—scallops, smoked salmon, crab claws, shrimp, oysters, and assorted condiments. Other specialties include breast of duck and game hens. There is no carving station, but you can get the meat precarved. The salad bar is more ordinary, though prepared salads have some fine surprises, such as the eggplant-tofu salad and an exceptional Chinese chicken salad. Desserts, unfortunately, look better than they actually are.

In Bellagio, 3600 Las Vegas Blvd. S. ✆ **877/234-6358**. Mon–Fri breakfast $15; Sat–Sun brunch $24–$29; Mon–Fri lunch $20; Sun–Thurs dinner $28, Fri–Sat dinner $36. Children 2 and under eat free. AE, DC, DISC, MC, V. Daily 7am–10pm.

EXPENSIVE

Le Village Buffet 🐦🐦🐦 BUFFET   One of the more ambitious buffets, with a price to match—still, you do get, even at the higher-priced dinner, a fine assortment of food and more value for the dollar than you are likely to find anywhere else. Plus, the Paris buffet is housed in the most pleasing room of the buffet bunch. It's a Disneyland-esque two-thirds replica of your classic French village clichés; it's either a charming respite from Vegas lights or it's sickening, depending on your tolerance level for such things.

Buffet stations are grouped according to French regions, and though in theory entrees change daily, there do seem to be some constants: In Brittany, you'll find such things as made-to-order crepes, surprisingly good roasted duck with green peppercorn and peaches, and steamed mussels with butter and shallots. In Normandy, there's quiche and some dry bay scallops with honey cider. The carving station shows up in Burgundy but distinguishes itself by adding options of Chateaubriand sauce and cherry sauce Escoffier. Lamb stew is a possibility for Alsace, while Provence has pasta to order and a solidly good braised beef. The salad station isn't strong on flavors, but the veggies are fresh, and there is even some domestic (darn it) cheese. You can skip the dessert station in favor of heading back to Brittany for some made-to-order crepes, but you might want to try the bananas Foster.

In Paris Las Vegas, 3655 Las Vegas Blvd. S. ✆ **888/266-5687**. Breakfast $15; lunch $18; dinner $25; Sun brunch $25. Reduced price for children ages 4–10; free for children 3 and under. AE, DC, DISC, MC, V. Sun–Thurs 7am–10pm; Fri–Sat 7am–11pm.

Mirage Cravings Buffet 🐦🐦 BUFFET   Aesthetically, an incredible transformation from classic Vegas buffet (read: blah) style to a gleaming, streamlined look, all shining steel and up-to-the-minute high-design concept shades of green, blue, and red. Gone are the heaping mounds of shrimp and other symbols of Vegas excess and bargain. In its place are plenty of live-action stations, but minimal offerings, just a scant few in the (admittedly inclusive) categories. This probably helps with waste, but if you are used to matters the other way, it does feel mingy. Seniors won't like the poor signage; kids may get tired long before completing the lengthy circuit. No worries:

The line starts with excellent pizza. Look for pot stickers and Chinese barbecue pork, quite good barbecue, tangy Japanese cuke salad, slightly dry but flavorful Mexican slow-roasted pork. A trip to the made-to-order salad station is so pokey, you'll need to find the other salads that are hidden with the open-faced sandwiches (where you can also find the gefilte fish). The desserts are generally disappointing. Despite the drawbacks—we're probably just overthinking it anyway—this remains popular with buffet connoisseurs.

In The Mirage, 3400 Las Vegas Blvd. S. ✆ 702/791-7111. Breakfast $14; lunch $18; dinner $25; Sat–Sun brunch $23. Reduced prices for children ages 5–10; free for children 4 and under. AE, DC, DISC, MC, V. Daily 7am–10pm.

Rio's Carnival World Buffet ⭐⭐ BUFFET   This buffet has long been voted by locals as the best in Vegas. Quality-wise, it's probably as good as ever, and maybe even better. Decor-wise, it's better still, since an overhaul was devoted mostly to improving the dining areas. Overall, this is simply more mainstream, an upscale food court with "South American" cooked-to-order stir-fries, Mexican taco fixings and accompaniments, Chinese fare, a Japanese sushi bar and *teppanyaki* grill, a Brazilian mixed grill, Italian pasta and antipasto, and fish and chips. There's even a diner setup for hot dogs, burgers, fries, and milkshakes. All this is in addition to the usual offerings of most Las Vegas buffets. Best of all, a brand-new dessert station features at least 70 kinds of pies, cakes, and pastries from an award-winning pastry chef, plus a large selection of gelatos and sorbets.

In Rio All-Suite Hotel & Casino, 3700 W. Flamingo Rd. ✆ 702/252-7777. Breakfast $15; lunch $17; dinner $24; Sat–Sun champagne brunch $24. Reduced prices for children ages 4–7; free for children 3 and under. AE, DC, MC, V. Mon–Fri 7am–10pm; Sat–Sun 7:30am–10pm.

MODERATE

The Buffet at TI ⭐⭐ BUFFET   Another gorgeous buffet makeover, now easily the handsomest buffet space in town, sort of contemporary diner, all dark gleaming wood, mirrors, and geometric lines. We feel mixed on the food choices; this is a smaller buffet than one might expect for such a big hotel, and while there is a reasonable range of cuisines (Italian; Japanese, with sushi chefs who will make up fresh plates just for you; Southern, including unexpected spoon bread; deli), there isn't the overwhelming bounty we've come to consider our right when it comes to Vegas buffets. However, there are some well-considered and fine-tasting deli sandwiches (brie and honey, roast beef with goat cheese), plus better-than-decent barbecue ribs and Chinese options. Best of all, some of the most charming dessert choices, focusing on such childhood tastes as cupcakes, fresh cotton candy, quite good crème brûlée (yes, not exactly real kiddie fare, but, let's face, it's just exceptionally good vanilla custard!) and best of all, adorable minidoughnuts, fresh out of the fryer. We ate two dozen and we are not ashamed.

In TI–Treasure Island, 3300 Las Vegas Blvd. S. ✆ 702/894-7111. Breakfast $15; lunch $17; dinner Sun–Thurs $21, Fri–Sun $26; Sat–Sun champagne brunch $17–22. Reduced prices for children ages 4–11; free for children 3 and under. AE, DC, DISC, MC, V. Daily 7am–10:30pm.

Flamingo Paradise Garden Buffet ⭐ BUFFET   This buffet occupies a vast room, with floor-to-ceiling windows overlooking a verdant tropical landscape of cascading waterfalls and koi ponds. At dinner, there is an extensive international food station (which changes monthly), presenting French, Chinese, Mexican, German, or Italian specialties. A large salad bar, fresh fruits, pastas, vegetables, potato dishes, and a vast dessert display round out the offerings. Lunch is similar, featuring international cuisines as well as a stir-fry station and a soup/salad/pasta bar. At breakfast, you'll find all the expected fare, including a made-to-order omelet station and fresh-baked breads. The seafood is dry and tough, and desserts are uninspired. Drinks are unlimited but are served in small glasses, so expect to call your server for many refills.

In The Flamingo Las Vegas, 3555 Las Vegas Blvd. S. ℂ **702/733-3111.** Mon–Fri lunch $17; Sat–Sun champagne brunch $20; dinner $22. Reduced for children ages 4–8; free for children 3 and under. Prices may be higher on holidays. AE, DC, DISC, MC, V. Breakfast Mon–Fri 7:30–11:30am; lunch daily 11:30am–3pm; dinner daily 4–10pm, brunch Sat–Sun 7:30am–3pm.

Flavors at Harrah's ✿ BUFFET   Not as bold a makeover as other recently refurbished buffets, but the redone room is certainly an improvement. Oddly, here it's the carving station that stands out, with simultaneous servings of turkey, ham, prime rib, chicken, game hen, sausage, roast vegetables (talk about a wild card), and lamb. The other stations are typical—Mexican, Italian, seafood, Chinese. A particularly good dessert area is heavy on the cookies, cakes, and little pastries such as Oreo mousse tarts and mini crème brûlées. Best of all, there is a chocolate fountain with pound cake, fruit, brownies, and the like ready for dipping. It nearly overshadows the make-your-own root beer float station.

In Harrah's, 3475 Las Vegas Blvd. S. ℂ **702/369-5000.** Breakfast $15; lunch $17; dinner $24; brunch Sat–Sun $21. AE, MC, V. Daily 7am–10pm.

NORTH STRIP
VERY EXPENSIVE
Wynn Las Vegas Buffet ✿✿✿ BUFFET   Goodness, we do love a nice buffet, and this one is particularly nice (if notably super-expensive), more thoughtful and artful than the average, starting with the *Alice in Wonderland*–evoking atrium styled with towers of fruit flowers and foliage and even some natural light. Don't worry if you don't score one of the few tables set there; it's a bit far from the food lines, and you want to be close to the action, after all. And once there, you may get the impression that instead of the usual bunch of often gloppy dishes, someone's thinking about items not just with flavor but that can sit for periods of time better than the usual buffet suspects, or that translate better to large-quantity preparation. Don't just take our word for it; on a visit not many weeks after it opened, we chatted with one regular buffet diner who said he had already sworn off all other buffets in favor of loyal devotion to Wynn. Look for such items as jerk chicken, wood-fired pizza, honey-glazed pork, nice little salmon rolls, five kinds of ceviche, sweet Kansas City–style barbecue, and tandoori chicken among the stations, which include Mexican, Southern, seafood, and Italian. Best of all, desserts are superior to those at probably all the other buffets, in construction and in taste, giving the impression that a pastry chef is active on the premises. Don't miss the mini floating islands, the unusual tiramisu, the excellent chocolate mousse and ice creams, and even a plate full of madeleines.

In Wynn Las Vegas, 3131 Las Vegas Blvd. S. ℂ **702/770-3463.** Breakfast $18; lunch $22; dinner $34–38; Sat–Sun brunch $29–$35. AE, DC, DISC, MC, V. Sun–Thurs 8am–10pm; Fri–Sat 8am–10:30pm.

INEXPENSIVE
Circus Circus Buffet BUFFET   Here's a tradeoff: It's just about the cheapest buffet on the Strip but also what some consider the worst buffet food in town. Here you'll find 50 items of typical cafeteria fare, and none of them is all that good. If food is strictly fuel for you, you can't go wrong here. Otherwise, find another buffet.

2880 Las Vegas Blvd. S. ℂ **702/734-0410.** Breakfast $11; lunch $13; dinner $14. AE, DC, DISC, MC, V. Daily 7am–2pm and 4:30–10pm.

EAST OF THE STRIP
MODERATE
The Buffet at the Las Vegas Hilton ⋆ BUFFET   A surprisingly stylish-looking room, with the usual suspects (salad bar, bagel bar, desserts) and a good selection of Chinese food (including Peking duck). The fare is fresh and delicious, with special mention going to the prime rib, the outstanding cream puffs, and the superior rice pudding. (It's hard to find good desserts at Vegas buffets.) There's plenty to eat here, but the place feels small compared to the newer lavish spreads on the Strip.

In Las Vegas Hilton, 3000 Paradise Rd. ℂ 702/732-5111. Breakfast $13; lunch $14; dinner $18 (includes complimentary beer and wine); Sat–Sun brunch $18 (includes unlimited champagne). Half-price for children 12 and under. DC, DISC, MC, V. Mon–Fri 7am–2:30pm and 5–10pm; Sat–Sun 8am–2:30pm and 5–10pm.

INEXPENSIVE
Sam's Town Firelight Buffet ⋆ BUFFET   This buffet has a nice room with actual natural lighting and a big wall of flames—hence, firelight—plus lighting that changes throughout the day, according to mood requirements, and a view of the water and laser-light show in the atrium of the hotel (kind of alfresco dining, in a Vegas artificial way). The buffet has international stations (Chinese, Mexican), a bar, and a dessert station with hand-scooped ice cream. The food is fine—for a buffet, anyway.

In Sam's Town, 5111 Boulder Hwy. ℂ 702/456-7777. Breakfast $6; lunch $8; theme dinner nights (seafood, barbeque, and so forth) $11–$18; Sat–Sun brunch $10. Discount prices for children 4–10; free for children 3 and under. AE, DC, DISC, MC, V. Mon–Thurs 7am–3pm and 4–9pm; Fri 7am–2pm and 3–9pm; Sat–Sun 8am–3pm and 4–9pm.

WEST OF THE STRIP
INEXPENSIVE
Gold Coast Ports O' Call ⋆ BUFFET   As formerly bargain buffet prices skyrocket—and we aren't helping matters by highly recommending $30-and-up places such as the Wynn buffet—it's getting harder and harder to find anything budget-minded on the Strip. Well, anywhere worth eating, certainly. This isn't on the Strip, but it is nearby, and the prices are cheaper than at any buffet on the Strip. Plus, you are less likely to find tremendous lines here. Having said that, don't expect anything miraculous, though they get points for keeping the food at the correct temperature (many a buffet's hot food suffers from a cooling effect as it sits out). Options run the usual gamut: Asian (decent pot stickers), Mexican (fine beef fajitas), and a carving station (with full rotisserie chickens). They have an all-you-can-eat steak night and an all-you-can-eat seafood night.

In the Gold Coast, 4400 West Flamingo Rd. ℂ 702/367-7111. Breakfast $7; lunch $9; dinner $13–$17; brunch Sun $13 (for specialty nights). Reduced prices for children 4–9; free for children 3 and under. Mon–Sat 7–10am, 11am–3pm, and 4–10pm; Sun 8am–3pm and 4–10pm.

DOWNTOWN
MODERATE
Golden Nugget Buffet ⋆⋆ BUFFET   This buffet has often been voted number one in Las Vegas and while we wouldn't go that far, it certainly is top quality. Most of the seating is in plush booths. The buffet tables are laden with an extensive salad bar (about 50 items), fresh fruit, and marvelous desserts. Fresh seafood is featured every night. Most lavish is the all-day Sunday champagne brunch, which adds such dishes as eggs Benedict, blintzes, pancakes, creamed herring, and smoked fish with bagels and cream cheese.

In the Golden Nugget, 129 E. Fremont St. ℂ 702/385-7111. Breakfast $10; lunch $11; Mon–Thurs dinner $18, Fri dinner $30, Sat–Sun dinner $21; Sat–Sun brunch $18. Half-price for children 3–12; free for children 2 and younger. AE, DC, DISC, MC, V. Mon–Fri 7am–10pm; Sat–Sun 8am–10pm.

INEXPENSIVE

Fremont Paradise Buffet ✷ BUFFET   Another buffet that makes us cross about rising Vegas prices; this was (at dinnertime) one of the cheapest buffets we could recommend, but now? Not so much (seems like every night's a theme night). However, lunchtime still brings a price that is a bargain. The selection isn't extensive (though with some surprises in the form of a "Southwestern" station and some Chinese), but the space is adequately attractive. Expect long lines.

In the Fremont Hotel & Casino, 200 E. Fremont St. ℂ 702/385-3232. Breakfast $8; lunch $8; dinner $10; Sun brunch $10; various "theme" (steak or seafood) nights $13–$16. Free for children 3 and under. AE, DC, DISC, MC, V. Mon–Fri 7–10:30am, 11am–3pm, and 4–10pm; Sat–Sun 7am–3pm and 4–10pm.

Main Street Station Garden Court ✷✷✷ (Finds) BUFFET   Set in what is truly one of the prettiest buffet spaces in town (and certainly in Downtown), with very high ceilings and tall windows bringing in much-needed natural light, the Main Street Station Garden Court buffet is one of the best in town, let alone Downtown. It features nine live-action stations where you can watch your food being prepared, including a wood-fired, brick-oven pizza (delicious); many fresh salsas at the Mexican station; a barbecue rotisserie; fresh sausage at the carving station; Chinese, Hawaiian, and Southern specialties (soul food and the like); and so many more we lost count. On Friday night, it has all this and nearly infinite varieties of seafood, all the way up to lobster. We ate ourselves into a stupor and didn't regret it.

At Main Street Station, 200 N. Main St. ℂ 702/387-1896. Breakfast $7; lunch $8; dinner $11–$16; Sat–Sun champagne brunch $11. Free for children 3 and under. AE, DC, DISC, MC, V. Daily 7–10:30am, 11am–3pm, and 4–10pm.

6

What to See & Do in Las Vegas

You aren't going to lack for things to do in Las Vegas. More than likely, you've come here for the gambling, which should keep you pretty busy. (We say that with some understatement.) But you can't sit at a slot machine forever. (Or maybe you can.) In any event, it shouldn't be too hard to find ways to fill your time between poker hands.

Just walking on the Strip and gazing at the gaudy, garish, absurd wonder of it all can occupy quite a lot of time. This is the number-one activity we recommend in Vegas; at night, it is a mind-boggling sight. And, of course, there are shows and plenty of other nighttime entertainment. But if you need something else to do beyond resting up at your hotel's pool, or if you are trying to amuse yourself while the rest of your party gambles away, this chapter will guide you. Having said that, Vegas is firmly set in such an "adult" entertainment direction that many attractions, particularly those with kid appeal, have closed, and though new, equally expensive options may come along to take their place, the emphasis right now seems to be on mature fun—drinking, gambling, nightclubbing,

and the like—and spas to help you recover from the effects of same. Put it that way, and it doesn't sound all that bad.

Don't forget to check out the **free hotel attractions,** such as Bellagio's water-fountain ballet, The Mirage's volcano, the MGM lions, and the Mardi Gras show at the Rio. Oh, yeah, and the utter piece of hooey that masquerades as the pirate show at TI–Treasure Island. (The pirates now battle scantily clad women. Except it's even worse than that.) You can probably give that a miss.

You could also consider using a spa at a major hotel; they seem too pricey (as high as $30 a day) to fill in for your daily gym visit if you are just going to use a few machines, but spending a couple of hours working out, sweating out Vegas toxins in the steam room, and generally pampering yourself will leave you feeling relaxed, refreshed, and ready to go all night again.

There are also plenty of out-of-town sightseeing options, such as **Hoover Dam** (a major tourist destination), **Red Rock Canyon,** and excursions to the Grand Canyon. We've listed the best of these in chapter 10.

SUGGESTED LAS VEGAS ITINERARIES

The itineraries outlined here are for adults. If you're traveling with kids, incorporate some of the suggestions from "Especially for Kids," listed later in this chapter. The activities mentioned briefly here are described more fully later in this chapter.

IF YOU HAVE 1 DAY   Spend most of the day **casino-hopping.** These are buildings like no other (thank goodness). Each grandiose interior tops the last. You'll want to see Wynn Las Vegas, no longer the newest thing going thanks to The Venetian's Palazzo annex, but the latter is less of a destination in and of itself. But also be sure to see The Venetian, Bellagio, The Mirage, TI–Treasure Island, Paris Las Vegas, Caesars

Palace (including The Forum Shops and the talking statues), New York–New York, MGM Grand, and the exteriors of Excalibur and Luxor. Then at night, take a drive (if you can) down **the Strip.** As amazing as all this is during the day, you just can't believe it at night. Aside from just the Strip itself, there are Bellagio's **water fountains,** which "perform" to various musical numbers, the dreadful (and even though it's free, still not worth the money) sexy **sirens vs. pirate battle** at TI–Treasure Island, and the newly refurbished **volcano explosion** next door at The Mirage. Eat at a buffet (see chapter 5 for details and options) and have a drink at the top of the Stratosphere, goggling at the view from the tallest building west of the Mississippi. Oh, and maybe you should gamble a little, too.

IF YOU HAVE 2 DAYS   Do more of the above since you may not have covered it all. Then do something really Vegasy and visit the **Liberace Museum.** The **Dolphin Habitat** at The Mirage is also worth a look, in that it's unexpectedly not Las Vegas. At night, take in a show. We think *KÀ, O,* and *Mystère,* productions from the avant-garde **Cirque du Soleil,** are the finest in Vegas, but there are plenty to choose from, including a selection of Broadway babies, such as *Phantom of the Opera,* and divas galore, including Cher, Bette Midler, and Toni Braxton. Though buffets are still the most Vegas-appropriate food experience, genuine haute cuisine by celebrity chefs has invaded the town and you should take advantage of it. **Bartolotta, Fleur de Lys, Bouchon,** and **Picasso** are our top choices (not to mention **Joël Robuchon** and **L'Atelier de Joël Robuchon** at the MGM Grand, if you can afford the supreme pleasure), but you can't go wrong with **Alex, Alizé,** or **Aureole,** plus there are branches of **Olives, Pinot Brasserie,** and the **Border Grill.** Be sure to leave some time to go Downtown to check out the much more affordable casinos in the classic Glitter Gulch and to visit the **Fremont Street Experience** light show.

IF YOU HAVE 3 DAYS   By now you've spent 2 days gambling and gawking. So take a break and drive out to **Red Rock Canyon.** The panoramic 13-mile Scenic Loop Drive is best seen early in the morning, when there's little traffic. If you're so inclined, spend some time hiking here. If you want to spend the entire day out, bring lunch from nearby **Red Rock Resort,** and then do a stop at nearby **Bonnie Springs Ranch,** where you can enjoy a guided trail ride into the desert wilderness or enjoy the silliness at **Old Nevada** (see chapter 10 for details).

IF YOU HAVE 4 DAYS OR MORE   Plan a tour to **Hoover Dam.** Leave early in the morning, returning to Las Vegas after lunch via **Valley of Fire State Park,** stopping at the **Lost City Museum** in Overton en route (see chapter 10 for details). Alternatively, you can rest up by spending the day by the hotel pool or going to the hotel spa. At night, presumably refreshed and toxins purged, hit the casinos and/or catch another show. Even if you aren't a big fan of magic, **Lance Burton** is a wonderful show for a reasonable (by current Vegas standards) price, or there is the arty weirdness of the **Blue Man Group** at The Venetian, or *Jubilee!,* if your trip won't be complete without a topless revue. You can also feast at dinner since you certainly haven't tried all there is. There is some great work being done by restaurants not associated with brand-name chefs, such as Rosemary's, Alizé, and Andre's.

As you plan any additional days, consider excursions to other nearby attractions such as **Lake Mead** and the **Grand Canyon.** Inquire about interesting possibilities at your hotel's tour desk.

1 The Top Attractions

See also the listings for theme parks and other fun stuff in section 4, "Especially for Kids."

The Arts Factory ★★ *(Finds* Believe it or not, Las Vegas has a burgeoning art scene (what some would consider soul-crushing is what others consider inspirational), and this complex, located in the Gateway district, is the place to find proof. It features a few galleries and a number of work spaces for local artists. Several of the spaces are closed to the public. On the first Friday of each month, they have a party event (unimaginatively named "First Friday") showcasing local artists and arts-oriented businesses, with live music, street performances, and other entertainment and activities. Visit their website for further details.

101–109 E. Charleston Blvd. ⓒ **702/676-1111**. www.theartsfactory.com. Free admission. Hours vary by gallery.

The Atomic Testing Museum ★★★ *(Finds* From 1951 until 1992, the Nevada Test Site was this country's primary location for testing nuclear weapons. Aboveground blasts in the early days were visible to the tourists and residents of Las Vegas. This well-executed museum, library, and gallery space (a Smithsonian affiliate) offers visitors a fascinating glance at the test site from ancient days through modern times, with memorabilia, displays, official documents, videos, interactive displays, motion-simulator theaters (like sitting in a bunker, watching a blast), and emotional testimony from the people who worked there. It respectfully treads that tricky line between honoring the work done at the site and understanding its terrible implications. Not to be missed, even if it's only because of the Albert Einstein action figure in the gift shop. Visitors should plan on spending at least an hour.

755 E. Flamingo Rd. ⓒ **702/794-5151**. www.atomictestingmuseum.org. $12 adults; $9 seniors, military, students with ID, and Nevada residents; free for children 6 and under. Mon–Sat 9am–5pm; Sun 1–5pm.

Bellagio Gallery of Fine Art ★ Everyone (ourselves not nearly least among them) scoffed when then–Bellagio owner Steve Wynn opened an art gallery on his fabulous property. Sure, Wynn's been a serious and respected fine-arts collector for years, and consequently there was good stuff on display (though there are no masterpieces, there certainly are serious works by masters), but who would go see *art* in Las Vegas? Tons of tourists, as it happens, so many that they had to almost immediately relocate the gallery to a larger space.

When the MGM MIRAGE company bought Wynn's empire, the future of the gallery, which did rely on his collection (he took most of it with him), was in doubt. Surprise again, you scoffers (and that again includes us). The gallery is not only open again, but it's also getting written up by real art critics, thanks in part to such well-chosen shows as Warhol, Monet, Picasso ceramics, and Ansel Adams retrospectives, and an exhibit from the collection of none other than Steve Martin—yes, we mean the stand-up-comedian-turned-actor-turned-playwright/author. See, he's a longtime, well-respected collector, too, and, consequently, there were real-life reviewers, hushed with happy reverence, who took the entire show seriously indeed.

Now, will there be as interesting a show when you go? Beats us. (When we wrote this, it was a collection of American Modernism organized with Boston's Museum of Fine Arts.) Then there's that ticket price. Do let us point out that the Louvre—needless to say, quite a bit larger and with, one can safely say, some notable works—is about $5 cheaper than the entry fee to this museum.

Fun Fact **When Downtown Ruled**

Fremont Street was the hub of Las Vegas for almost 4 decades, before the first casino hotel, El Rancho, opened on the Strip in 1941.

In Bellagio, 3600 Las Vegas Blvd. S. ℂ 702/693-7871. ww.bellagio.com. Reservations suggested, but walk-ins taken every 15 min. Admission $17 adults, $14 seniors and Nevada residents, $14 teachers and students with ID. Sun–Thurs 10am–6pm; Fri–Sat 10am–9pm. Last admission half-hour prior to closing.

Bodies: The Exhibition 𝕽𝕽   A stunning and controversial exhibit featuring what can be perhaps best described as Real Live Dead Bodies. Utilizing a patented freeze-dry–sort of operation, full bodies (donated by their former inhabitants, though that's where the controversy comes in), artfully dissected body parts, and stripped cadavers are on display not for sensationalism—though it is pretty sensational in nearly all senses of the word—but for visitors to fully appreciate the wonder and mechanics that go into this too, too transient flesh. When a body is positioned in an athletic pose you can see how the muscles work, and when a cross section of a lung afflicted with cancer is right in front of you, you may well be glad Vegas is increasingly a nonsmoking town. It's educational and bizarre and not something you are likely to forget soon. Surprisingly not grotesque, but not for the ultra-squeamish.

In the Luxor, 3900 Las Vegas Blvd. S. Prices and hours still forthcoming at press time.

Eiffel Tower Experience *Overrated*   Whether this is worth the dough depends on how much you like views. An elevator operator (we refuse to call them guides) delivers a few facts about this Eiffel Tower (this is a half-size exact replica, down to the paint color of the original) during the minute or so ride to the uppermost platform, where you are welcome to stand around and look out for as long as you want, which probably isn't 2 hours, the length of the average movie, which costs about what this does. Nice view, though.

In Paris Las Vegas, 3655 Las Vegas Blvd. S. ℂ 702/946-7000. Admission $10 adults, $7 seniors over 65 and children 6–12, free for children 5 and under. Daily 9:30am–12:30am, weather permitting.

Fremont Street Experience 𝕽𝕽   Poor Downtown. For years now, it's been overlooked in favor of the Strip. And no wonder: It's so...small...by comparison. Even its once-dazzling collection of hotel marquee lights seems like candles next to the klieg-light voltage of the Strip. But things are cheaper down here, people; and speaking of people, if you get tired of feeling not pretty or rich enough for the Strip, you are not alone. Come join us in admiring the project that closed off the heart of "Glitter Gulch" and turned it into a much more user-friendly pedestrian mall.

The Fremont Street Experience is a 5-block open-air landscaped strip of outdoor snack shops, vendor carts, and colorful kiosks purveying food and merchandise. Overhead is a 90-foot-high steel-mesh "celestial vault"; at night, it is the most successfully revamped **Viva Vision,** a high-tech light-and-laser show (the canopy is equipped with more than 12.5 million lights) enhanced by a concert-hall-quality sound system that takes place five times nightly. There are a number of different shows, and there's music between the light performances as well. Not only does the canopy provide shade, but it also cools the area through a misting system in summer and warms you with radiant heaters in winter. It's really cool, in that Vegas over-the-top way that we love so

Las Vegas Attractions

The Adventuredome **10**
The Arts Factory **6**
The Atomic Testing
Museum **26**
Bellagio Conservatory **18**
Bellagio Fountains **18**
Bellagio Gallery of Fine Art **18**
Bodies: The Exhibition **22**
Eiffel Tower Experience **19**
The Forum Shops
Fountain Shows **17**
Fremont Street Experience **5**
GameWorks **20**
Kids Quest **16**
Las Vegas Mini Gran Prix **1**
Las Vegas Motor Speedway **2**
Las Vegas Natural History
Museum **4**
Liberace Museum **24**
Lied Discovery
Children's Museum **3**
Madame Tussauds
Las Vegas **14**
Marjorie Barrick Museum **25**
Masquerade Show
in the Sky **16**
MGM Grand Lion Habitat **21**
Mirage Volcano **15**
Secret Garden &
Dolphin Habitat **15**
Shark Reef at
Mandalay Bay **23**
Sirens of TI **13**
SPEED: The Ride/Las Vegas
Cyber Speedway **8**
Springs Preserve **11**
Star Trek: The Experience
& Borg Invasion 4-D **9**
Stratosphere Thrill Rides **7**
Titanic: The Exhibition **22**
Wynn Conservatory **12**
Wynn Lake of Dreams **12**

much. Go see for yourself; you will be pleased to see how a one-time ghost town of tacky, rapidly aging buildings, in an area with more undesirables than not, is now a bustling (at least at night), friendly, safe place (they have private security guards who hustle said undesirables away). It's a place where you can stroll, eat, or even dance to the music under the lights. The crowd it attracts is more upscale than in years past, and, of course, it's a lot less crowded than the hectic Strip. This helps give a second life to a deserving neighborhood. *Note:* A good place to view the Sky Parade light show is from the balcony at Fitzgerald's Casino & Hotel.

And in a further effort to retain as much of classic Las Vegas as possible, the **Neon Museum** is installing vintage hotel and casino signs along the promenade. The first installation was the horse and rider from the old Hacienda, which presently rides the sky over the intersection of Fremont Street and Las Vegas Boulevard, while the Lamp from the old Aladdin Hotel twinkles at the northwest corner. Eventually, the Neon Museum hopes to have a complex at their Neon Boneyard, using the old La Concha Motel, itself a piece of classic Vegas architecture thankfully saved from the wrecking ball, as a centerpiece. It's uncertain when the complex will open, but in the meantime, you can do a self-guided walking tour of sign installations in downtown. (Go to www. neonmuseum.org for information.)

Fremont St. (btw. Main St. and Las Vegas Blvd.), Downtown. www.vegasexperience.com. Free admission. Shows nightly.

GameWorks ☆☆ (Kids)   What do you get when Steven Spielberg and his Dream-Works team get in on the arcade video-game action? Grown-up, state-of-the-art fun. High-tech movie magic has taken over all sorts of traditional arcade games and turned them interactive, from a virtual-reality batting cage to a *Jurassic Park* game that lets you hunt dinosaurs. There are motion-simulator rides galore and even actual-motion activities such as rock climbing. But classic games, from Pac-Man to pool tables, are here, too, though sometimes with surprising twists, such as air hockey where multiple pucks occasionally shoot out at once.

All this doesn't exactly come cheap. Games are priced via a point system: $5 gets you $7 worth of play points, $10 gets you $16 in game play, $20 delivers $36, $25 brings $50. On Thursday nights from 9pm until the midnight closing you can purchase a card to play for the final three hours for $30. Purchased points go on a debit card that you then insert into the various machines to activate them. But you do get value for your money, which makes this a viable alternative to casinos, particularly if you have children (though it's clearly geared toward a high-school-age-and-older demographic). Children probably should be 10 years old and up—any younger and parents will need to stand over them rather than go off and have considerable fun on their own. *Note:* If you don't like crowds, come here earlier rather than later, when it can get packed. They also have a dress code (no excessively baggy clothes, no tattoos or clothing with profanity, no chains, and so on) that they enforce occasionally, and no one under 18 is allowed without parental supervision after 9pm.

In the Showcase Mall, 3785 Las Vegas Blvd. S. ⓒ **702/432-4263.** www.gameworks.com. See game prices listed above in the review. Sun–Thurs 10am–midnight; Fri–Sat 10am–1am. Hours may vary.

Las Vegas Mini Gran Prix ☆☆☆ (Kids)   Finally, after all our yammering about how Vegas isn't for families and how most of the remaining options are really overpriced tourist traps, we can wholeheartedly recommend an actual family-appropriate entertainment option. Part arcade, part go-kart racetrack, this is exactly what you want to help your kids (and maybe yourselves) work their ya-yas out. The arcade is well stocked, with a better quality of prizes than one often finds, but we suggest not spending too much time in there and instead hustling outside to the slide, the little roller coaster, and best of all, the four go-kart tracks. Each offers a different thrill, from the longest track in Vegas, full of twists and turns as you try to outrace other drivers (be a sport, let the little kids win occasionally), to a high-banked oval built just so you can try to make other drivers take spills onto the grass, to, best of all, a timed course. The last requires a driver's license, so it's for you rather than your kids (but the wee ones will find the fourth course is just for them), and here you can live out your Le Mans or police-chase fantasies as you blast through twisting runs one kart at a time, trying to beat your personal best. A good kind of adrenaline rush, believe us. The staff is utterly friendly, and the pizzas at the food court are triple the size and half the price of those found in your hotel. The one drawback: It's far away from main Strip action—here's where you'll need that rental car, for sure. *Note:* Kids have to be at least 36 inches tall to ride any of the attractions.

1401 N. Rainbow Rd., just off U.S. 95 N. © 702/259-7000. www.lvmgp.com. Ride tickets $6.50 each, $6 for 5 or more; tickets good on all rides and at any time. Sun–Thurs 10am–10pm; Fri–Sat 10am–11pm.

Las Vegas Motor Speedway ★★   This 176,000-seat facility was the first new super-speedway to be built in the Southwest in over 2 decades. A $200-million state-of-the-art motorsports entertainment complex, it includes a 1½-mile super-speedway, a 2½-mile FIA-approved road course, paved and dirt short-track ovals, and a 4,000-foot drag strip. Also on the property are facilities for go-kart, Legends Car, Sand Drag, and Motocross competition, as well as driving schools, attractions, and more. The place is so popular that they are even building condos overlooking the track for those who apparently don't want to sleep on race days. Some major hotels have shuttles to the speedway during big events, so check with the front desk or concierge.

7000 Las Vegas Blvd. N., directly across from Nellis Air Force base (take I-15 north to Speedway exit 54). © 702/644-4443 for ticket information. www.lvms.com. Tickets $10–$75 (higher prices for major events). Race days vary.

Liberace Museum ★★★ (Moments   Forget all that stuff we said before about the great museums of the world. You can keep your Louvres and Vaticans and Smithsonians: *This* is a museum. Housed in a strip mall, this is a shrine to the glory and excess that was the art project known as Liberace. You've got your costumes (bejeweled), your many cars (bejeweled), your many pianos (bejeweled), and many jewels (also bejeweled). Also, the entrance itself is a giant jewel. It just shows what can be bought with lots of money and no taste.

The thing is, Liberace was in on the joke. We think. The people who come here largely aren't. Many of these guests would not have liked him living next door to them if his name was, say, Bruce Smith, but they idolize the man, the myth. Not found here is any reference to AIDS or chauffeurs who had plastic surgery to look more like him. But you will find a Czar Nicholas uniform with 22-karat-gold braiding and a blue-velvet cape styled after the coronation robes of King George V and covered with $60,000 worth of rare chinchilla. Not to mention a 50½-pound rhinestone costing $50,000, the world's largest, presented to him by the grateful (we bet they were) Austrian firm that supplied all his costume stones.

The museum is now better than ever, thanks to a costly renovation that turned what was once a too-low-key exhibition, especially given the subject matter, into something much more gaudy and over-the-top—and, better still, properly enshrined. Expect a ridiculously outrageous entrance (three words: giant pink piano) into rooms with

⟨Value⟩ Free Vegas

Vegas used to be the land of freebies—or at least, stuff so cheap it seemed free. Those days are an increasingly dim memory, but some hotels still offer free attractions designed to lure you, the unsuspecting visitor, into their casinos, where you might well then drop far more than the cost of a day ticket to Disney World. Do not give them the satisfaction. Or do. Whatever. It's your money. Meanwhile, here's a handy list of the best of the free bait, er, sights:

Bellagio Conservatory (in Bellagio) ⭐⭐⭐ A totally preposterous idea, a larger-than-life greenhouse atrium, filled with seasonal living foliage in riotous colors and styles, changed with meticulous regularity. From Easter to Chinese New Year, events are celebrated with carefully designed splashes of flowers, plants, and remarkable decorations—it's an incredible amount of labor for absolutely no immediate financial payoff. No wonder it's one of the most popular sights in Vegas. Open 24 hours.

Bellagio Fountains (outside Bellagio) ⭐⭐⭐ Giant spouts of water shoot up and down and sideways, and dance their little aquatic hearts out, to pieces carefully choreographed to tunes ranging from show to Chopin. We tell people about this, they roll their eyes when they think we aren't looking, then they go see it for themselves... and end up staying for several numbers. Daily every half-hour, starting early afternoon, then every 15 minutes 8pm to midnight. Closed when it's windy.

The Forum Shops Fountain Shows (in The Forum Shops at Caesars) ⭐ The first-established of the free shows, and easily the stupidest. We love it, in theory at least, as giant "marble" Greco-Roman statues come to creaky animatronic life and deliver a largely unintelligible speech, mostly exhorting the crowds to eat, drink, and get so merry they will think nothing of dropping a bundle on the slots. Not quite so bad it's good, but one day they are going to wise up and make the thing more high-tech, and a little something special will be lost. Daily every hour, starting at 10am.

Masquerade Show in the Sky (in the Rio) ⭐ Like TI's pirates, this formerly wholesome, if a bit weird, show has undergone a revamp to make it more sexy and adult-oriented. It's still staged on floats that move above viewers' heads, but now those floats include "bedroom" and "spa" scenes peopled with what the company calls "high energy performers of seduction." This gives you an idea of the kind of action contained therein. Prepare to try to distract your kid's attention elsewhere, though if you want a better view, grab a spot on the second floor of the village. Performed several times in the evening Thursday through Sunday.

Mirage Volcano (outside The Mirage) ⭐ The first curbside free attraction, and one of the reasons Wynn designed it so you can't see his new mountain and lake show from the street (see "Wynn Lake of Dreams," below)—because that doesn't bring guests *into* the property. This had paled in comparison to such things as dancing fountains and pirates, but a multi-million-dollar overhaul seeks to make the volcano as much of a must-see attraction as the Bellagio fountains. Actual fireballs will be spat in synched time to a percussion soundtrack by Grateful Dead drummer Mickey Hart.

Sirens of TI (outside TI–Treasure Island) ⍟ We gave it the star because it has such high production values, but man, it hurt us to do even that. See, this used to be a fun, hokey stunt show, where pirates attacked a British sailing vessel. Lusty men swashed and buckled, cannons exploded, ships sank, the pirates always won. But Vegas is—repeat after us, please—*not for families anymore,* and to prove it, the British were removed (first India, now this) and now the pirates are lured by singing and dancing lingerie-clad lovelies more suited to the Victoria's Secret catalog than Homer. Stuff happens, but no one really cares; either you like the nekkid chicks, or you are so horrified by the whole spectacle because it's so appallingly bad that plot twists don't matter much. *Parents, be warned:* Between the gals and their undies, and the 24-foot stark-raving-naked female figurehead on the ship right by the Strip entrance to TI–Treasure Island, you may be in for an interesting conversation with your children. Daily at 7, 8:30, 10, and 11:30pm, weather permitting.

Wynn Conservatory (in Wynn Las Vegas) ⍟ Yes, remarkably like the one at Bellagio, only we have to admit this one is better placed, situated just inside the door, and laid out so that you can stroll through it on your way to other parts of the hotel, as opposed to the tucked-in-a-corner Bellagio version. The floral displays change regularly, though they may reflect the striking floral mosaics on the floor below. We do hope it won't get as wacky as its Bellagio counterpart and will stick to the merely festive. Open 24 hours.

Wynn Lake of Dreams (in Wynn Las Vegas) ⍟ This is the most peculiar of the "free" shows in several ways: It's not easily defined (not dancing fountains, not a parade in the sky), and it's not easily seen. The 150-foot-tall mountain, complete with mature trees saved from the old Desert Inn golf course, plus several waterfalls, cannot be seen in its entirety from anywhere other than hotel rooms facing west. The show itself can be watched only if you are dining in the Daniel Boulud Brasserie or SW Steakhouse, the Parasol or Chanel bars, or a small viewing platform set above those venues on the casino level. Nab a coveted spot there or else pay double (or more) digits to dine or drink while waiting for the shows. Should you bother? Maybe. Basically, twice an hour, the lake lights up with pretty colors, cued to tunes ranging from classical to Louis Armstrong for "interludes." At the top of the hour are bigger extravaganzas of weird hologram erotic-psychedelic images projected on the wall waterfall, while shapes and puppets pop out for even more weird action, with some rather adult imagery at times. Not worth an overpriced drink unless you can nurse it all night, but the restaurants are good enough to try, so the shows are a bonus. Note that if you can't get a table outside, you do have to go there to see the shows properly. Shows are every 20 minutes, from 7pm to midnight.

various exhibits that finally give detailed attention to facts and figures. Admission has been cranked up, probably to pay for the renovations, but we don't mind—this is a one-of-a-kind place, all the better thanks to a reconceived gift shop that finally understands what a lure Liberace branding is. (Think Elvis kitsch only bejeweled.) Unless you have a severely underdeveloped appreciation for camp or take your museum-going very seriously, you shouldn't miss it. The museum is 2½ miles east of the Strip, on your right.

1775 E. Tropicana Ave. (at Spencer St.). ℭ 702/798-5595. www.liberace.org. Admission $15 adults, $10 seniors over 64 and student with ID, free for children 10 and under. Tues–Sat 10am–5pm; Sun noon–4pm. Closed Mon, Thanksgiving, Dec 25, and Jan 1.

Madame Tussauds Las Vegas ℛℛ *Kids*

Madame Tussauds's waxworks exhibition has been the top London attraction for nearly 2 centuries, so even if you aren't a fan of wax museums, this, its sole branch west of the Mississippi, is probably worth a stop—if you can stomach the price. Figures here are state-of-the-art, painstakingly constructed to perfectly match the original person. Truth be told, though some are nearly identical to their living counterparts—Brad Pitt gave us a start—others look about as much like the celebrity in question as a department-store mannequin. All the waxworks are free-standing, allowing, and indeed encouraging, guests to get up close and personal—there's interactive fun! Go ahead, lay your cheek next to Elvis's or Sinatra's and have your photo taken. Or put on a wedding dress and get "married" to "George Clooney" (you know you want to). Or fondle J. Lo's butt (you know you want to). Live performers make the Haunted House section more stimulating than expected in a facility dedicated to statues. Exhibits change, but someone sheepishly enjoyable ought to be on display when you go through. There's also a behind-the-scenes look at the lengthy process involved in creating one of these figures.

In The Venetian, 3355 Las Vegas Blvd. S. ℭ 702/862-7800. www.mtvegas.com. Admission $24 adults, $18 seniors, $15 students, $14 children 7–12, free for children 6 and under. Daily 10am–10pm, but hours vary seasonally, and museum may close early for private events.

Marjorie Barrick Museum ℛ

Formerly known as the Natural History Museum (as opposed to the Las Vegas Natural History Museum, which still exists—and now you can see why they changed the name), this is a cool place to beat the heat and noise of Vegas while examining some attractive, if not overly imaginative, displays on Native American craftwork and Las Vegas history. Crafts include 19th-century Mexican religious folk art, a variety of colorful dance masks from Mexico, and Native American pottery. The first part of the hall is often the highlight, with impressive traveling art exhibits. Children won't find much that's entertaining, other than some glass cases containing examples of local, usually poisonous, reptiles (who, if you are lucky—or unlucky, depending on your view—will be dining on mice when you drop by). Outside is a pretty garden that demonstrates how attractive desert-appropriate plants (in other words, those requiring little water) can be. You just wish the local casinos, with their lush and wasteful lawns, would take notice.

On the UNLV campus, 4505 Maryland Pkwy. ℭ 702/895-3381. http://hrcweb.nevada.edu/museum. Free admission. Mon–Fri 8am–4:45pm; Sat 10am–2pm. Closed on state and federal holidays.

MGM Grand Lion Habitat ℛℛ *Kids*

Hit this attraction at the right time, and it's one of the best freebies in town. It's a large, multilevel glass enclosure in which various lions frolic during various times of day. In addition to regular viewing spots, you can walk through a glass tunnel and get a worm's-eye view of the underside of a lion (provided one is in position); note how very big Kitty's paws are. Multiple lions share show duties (about 6 hr. on and then 2 days off at a ranch for some free-range activity, so they're never cooped up here for long). You could see any combo, from one giant male to a pack of five females who have grown from cub to adult size during their MGM time. Each comes with a trainer or three, who are there to keep the lions busy with play so they don't act like the big cats they are and sleep the entire time. But obviously, photo ops are more likely to occur as the more frisky younger set tussles, so what you observe definitely depends on who is in residence when you drop by. And, of course, actually seeing anything depends on how many other people think this is a two-star attraction; hordes of tourists are often pressed against the glass, preventing you, not to mention your kids, from doing the same.

In MGM Grand, 3799 Las Vegas Blvd. S. ⓒ 702/891-7777. Free admission. Daily 11am–10pm.

Secret Garden & Dolphin Habitat ⭐⭐⭐ (Kids)
Siegfried & Roy's famous white tigers went from famous to infamous when one of them either did what tigers all do eventually and attacked his beloved owner/trainer, or—depending on whether you buy the following story—helped said beloved owner/trainer when the latter was having a medical emergency. Either way this saga is played, it explains why the **Secret Garden** attraction is still up; no matter what, the tiger is not to blame. We hope this attraction, a gorgeous area behind the dolphin exhibit, stays put for a long time. Here, white lions, Bengal tigers, an Asian elephant, a panther, and a snow leopard join the white tigers. (The culprit, Montecore, may sometimes be on exhibit.) It's really just a glorified zoo featuring only the big-ticket animals; however, it is a very pretty place, with plenty of foliage and some bits of Indian- and Asian-themed architecture. Zoo purists will be horrified at the smallish spaces the animals occupy, but all the animals are rotated between here and their more lavish digs at the illusionist team's home. What this does allow you to do is get safely very close up to a tiger, which is quite a thrill—those paws are massive indeed. Visitors are given little portable phonelike objects on which they can play a series of programs, listening to Roy and former Mirage owner Steve Wynn discuss conservation or the attributes of each animal, and deliver anecdotes.

The **Dolphin Habitat** is more satisfying than the Secret Garden. It was designed to provide a healthy and nurturing environment and to educate the public about marine mammals and their role in the ecosystem. Specialists worldwide were consulted in creating the habitat, which was designed to serve as a model of a quality, human-made environment. The pool is more than eight times larger than government regulations require, and its 2.5 million gallons of human-made seawater are cycled and cleaned once every 2 hours. It must be working because the adult dolphins here are breeding regularly. The Mirage displays only dolphins already in captivity—no dolphins are taken from the wild. You can watch the dolphins frolic both above and below ground through viewing windows, in three different pools. There is nothing quite like the kick you get from seeing a baby dolphin play. The knowledgeable staff, who surely have the best jobs in Vegas, will answer questions. If they aren't doing it already, ask them to play ball with the dolphins; they toss large beach balls into the pools, and the dolphins hit them out with their noses, leaping out of the water, cackling with dolphin glee. You catch the ball, getting nicely wet, and toss it back to them. If you have never played ball with a dolphin, shove that happy child next to you out of the way and go for it. There is also a video of a resident dolphin (Duchess) giving birth (to Squirt) underwater; her fourth calf (30 lb. and 3 ft. long) was born just before Mother's Day in 2003. You can stay as long as you like, which might just be hours.

In The Mirage, 3400 Las Vegas Blvd. S. © **702/791-7111.** www.mirage.com. Admission $15 adults, $10 children 4–10, free for children 3 and under if accompanied by an adult. Memorial Day–Labor Day daily 10am–7pm; Labor Day–Memorial Day Mon–Fri 11am–5:30pm, Sat–Sun 10am–5:30pm. Hours subject to change.

Shark Reef at Mandalay Bay 𝒜   Given that watching fish can lower your blood pressure, it's practically a public service for Mandalay Bay to provide this facility in a city where craps tables and other gaming areas can bring your excitement level to dangerous heights. Unfortunately, it's just a giant aquarium (though we admire the style—it's built to look like a sunken temple), which, hey, we like, but gee, not at these prices (though standing in the all-glass tunnel surrounded by sharks and finny friends was kinda cool). Note also that it is *waaay* off in a remote part of Mandalay Bay, which might be a hassle for those with mobility problems.

In Mandalay Bay, 3950 Las Vegas Blvd. S. © **702/632-4555.** www.mandalaybay.com. Admission $16 adults, $11 children 5–12, free for children 4 and under. Daily 10am–11pm. Last admission at 10pm.

SPEED: The Ride/Las Vegas Cyber Speedway 𝒜𝒜   Auto racing is the fastest-growing spectator sport in America, so it's no surprise that these two attractions at the Sahara are a popular stop. The first is an 8-minute virtual-reality ride, **Cyber Speedway,** featuring a three-quarter-size replica of a NASCAR race car. Hop aboard for an animated, simulated ride—either the Las Vegas Motor Speedway or a race around the streets of Las Vegas (start with the Strip, with all the hotels flashing by, and then through the Forum Shops—whoops! There goes Versace!—and so forth). Press the gas and you lean back and feel the rush of speed; hit a bump and you go flying. Should your car get in a crash, off you go to a pit stop. At the end, a computer-generated report tells you your average speed, how many laps you made, and how you did racing against the others next to you. It's a pretty remarkable experience.

Speed junkies and race-car buffs will be in heaven here, though those with tender stomachs should consider shopping at the well-stocked theme gift shop instead.

SPEED: The Ride is a roller coaster that blasts riders out through a hole in the wall by the NASCAR Cafe, then through a loop, under the sidewalk, through the hotel's marquee, and finally straight up a 250-foot tower. At the peak, you feel a moment of weightlessness, and then you do the entire thing backward! Not for the faint of heart.

In the Sahara, 2535 Las Vegas Blvd. S. © **702/737-2111.** www.nascarcafelasvegas.com. $20 for all-day pass on both rides. Cyber Speedway (simulator) $10; $6 per re-ride (you must be at least 54 in. tall to ride); SPEED: The Ride (roller coaster) $10 for single ride; $13 for all day pass on SPEED only. Sun–Thurs 11am–midnight; Fri–Sat 11am–1am. Hours may vary.

Springs Preserve 𝒜𝒜𝒜   By now, perhaps you've learned that "Las Vegas" is Spanish for "the meadows." This facility is set on the 180-acre site of the original springs that fed Las Vegas until it dried in the 1960s (told you that Hoover Dam comes in handy). These days, Las Vegas is an environmental nightmare, along with much of the rest of this planet, and this remarkable recreational attraction is here to educate us about the possibilities to reverse some of the damage.

Set amidst nature and hiking trails, plus man-made wetlands, which is an interesting concept, the focal point is a large interpretive center that gives the history of Las Vegas from a land- and water-use perspective. The displays are creative and interactive, including a room with a reproduction flash flood that uses 5,000 gallons of water and one with a simulation of the experience of working on Hoover Dam. The other buildings are all done according to standards that have the least environmental impact, using modern construction versions of adobe and other green concepts. There are only 30 such structures in the world and seven of them are here. Each building tackles an aspect of desert living and the environment, including one that instructs kids on the glories of recycling, complete with a compost tunnel to crawl through! Other displays focus on environmentally friendly kitchens and bathrooms while the gardens demonstrate environmentally friendly gardening, including a section instructing older people and those with disabilities how to garden despite their physical limitations.

The outdoor kids' play area is made from recycled materials and has big animals to climb on, in case the kiddies have grown tired about learning responsible stuff. The cafe menu is designed by Wolfgang Puck with further green emphasis. Finally, this will be the eventual location of the Nevada state historical museum. Given the care, knowledge, and urgency of the issues addressed, this is a extraordinary facility for any town but particularly for this one.

3333 S. Valley View Blvd. ℂ 702/822-8344. www.springspreserve.com. $19 adults, $17 seniors and students with ID, $11 children 5–17. Free admission to trails. Summer daily 10am–10pm summer; winter daily 10am–6pm.

Stratosphere Thrill Rides 🎟🎟 (Kids)   Atop the 1,149-foot Stratosphere Tower are three marvelous thrill rides. There used to be four, but they closed the roller coaster to make way for something even more stomach-churning. That's okay—it was the least thrilling of the thrills. The **Big Shot** is a breathtaking free-fall ride that thrusts you 160 feet in the air along a 228-foot spire at the top of the tower, and then plummets back down again. Sitting in an open car, you seem to be dangling in space over Las Vegas. We have one relative, a thrill-ride enthusiast, who said he never felt more scared than when he rode the Big Shot. After surviving, he promptly put his kids on it; they loved it. Amping up the terror factor is **X-Scream,** a giant teeter-totter style device that propels you in an open car off the side of the 100-story tower and lets you dangle there weightlessly before returning you to relative safety. And now they have the aptly named **Insanity,** a spinning whirly-gig of a contraption that straps you into a seat and twirls you around 1,000 feet or so above terra firma. Insanity is right. *Note:* The rides are shut down in inclement weather and high winds.

Atop Stratosphere Las Vegas, 2000 Las Vegas Blvd. S. ℂ 702/380-7777. www.stratospherehotel.com. Admission: $10 each for Big Shot, X-Scream, or Insanity, plus fee to ascend Tower: $12 adults; $8 locals, seniors, hotel guests, and children 4–12; free for children 3 and under and those dining in the buffet room or Top of the World. Multiride and all-day packages also available for varying costs. Sun–Thurs 10am–1am; Fri–Sat 10am–2am. Hours vary seasonally. Minimum height requirement for Big Shot is 48 inches, minimum height requirement for X-Scream and Insanity is 52 inches.

Titanic: The Exhibition 🎟   It's too easy to say "you've seen the movie, now see the exhibit." But that is sort of the case; if you were captivated by the Oscar-winning epic, you will definitely want to take in this exhibit on the unsinkable luxury liner that sank on its maiden voyage. While it's a can't-miss for buffs, it might still be of some interest for those with only marginal feelings about the massive 1912 disaster. It's a strangely somber subject for Vegas, but what can you do? It features displays explaining the ship's ill-fated maiden voyage; relics salvaged from the sunken liner; and even recreations of sample cabins from first, second, and third class, including atmospheric conditions, giving you a sense of how it felt to travel aboard what was an incredible vessel. There is even a large chunk of real ice standing in for the culprit berg. It's tastefully done, except for the proposed adjoining bar wherein patrons will be lifted into the establishments via lifeboat. Let's hope that one doesn't come to pass.

In the Luxor, 3900 Las Vegas Blvd. S. No prices or hours available at press time.

2 Getting Married

Getting hitched is one of the most popular things to do in Las Vegas. Just ask Britney. As she rather infamously revealed, it's very easy to get married here. Too easy. See that total stranger/childhood friend standing next to you? Grab him or her and head down to the **Clark County Marriage License Bureau,** 201 Clark Ave. (© **702/761-0600;** daily, including holidays, 8am–midnight), to get your license. Find a wedding chapel (not hard, as there are about 50 of them in town; they line the north end of the Strip, and most hotels have them) and tie the knot. Just like that. No blood test, no waiting period—heck, not even an awkward dating period. Though a potentially very awkward time explaining it afterward to your mother, your manager, and the press.

Even if you have actually known your intended for some time, Las Vegas is a great place to get married. The ease is the primary attraction, but there are a number of other appealing reasons. You can have any kind of wedding you want, from a big, traditional production number to a small, intimate affair; from a spur-of-the-moment "just-the-happy-couple-in-blue-jeans" kind of thing to an "Elvis-in-a-pink-Cadillac-at-a-drive-through-window" kind of thing. (Oh, yes. More on that later. See the box "An Elvis Impersonator's Top 10 Reasons to Get Married in Las Vegas," below.) The wedding chapels take care of everything; usually they'll even provide a limo to take you to the license bureau and back. Most offer all the accessories, from rings to flowers to a videotaped record of the event.

We personally know several very happy couples who opted for the Vegas route. Motivations differed, with the ease factor heading the list (though the Vegas-ness of the whole thing came in a close second), but one and all reported having great fun. Really, is there a more romantic way to start off your life together than in gales of laughter?

In any event, the more than 100,000 couples who yearly take advantage of all this can't be wrong. If you want to follow in the footsteps of Elvis and Priscilla (at the first incarnation of the Aladdin Hotel), Michael Jordan, Jon Bon Jovi, Richard Gere and Cindy Crawford, Pamela Anderson and ill-fated husband #3, Angelina Jolie and Billy Bob, and, of course, Britney and What's-His-Name, you'll want to peruse the following list of the most notable wedding chapels on or near the Strip. There are many more in town, and almost all the major hotels offer chapels as well; though the latter are cleaner and less tacky than some of the Strip chapels, they do tend to be without any personality at all. One exception might be the chapel at the Excalibur Hotel, where you can dress in medieval costumes, and the lovely chapel at Bellagio, which has personal wedding coordinators and a high level of customer service, holding only 8 to 10 weddings a day—seems like a lot, but it's nothing compared to the volume on the Strip.

With regard to decor, there isn't a radical difference between the major places—hence, no star ratings here—though some are decidedly spiffier and less sad than others. Attitude certainly makes a difference with several and varies radically, depending on who's working at any given time. Given how important your wedding is—or should be—we encourage you to give yourself time to comparison-shop and spurn anyone who doesn't seem eager enough for your business. ***Passing note:*** Standing outside a wedding chapel for a couple of hours makes for interesting people-watching, as you see brides in full white gowns accompanied by a whole retinue, pregnant brides in ordinary dresses, or happy couples wearing sweats, all ready to march down that aisle.

Fun Fact   An Elvis Impersonator's Top 10 Reasons to Get Married in Las Vegas

Jesse Garon has appeared in numerous Las Vegas productions as "Young Elvis." He arrives at any special event in a 1955 pink, neon-lit Cadillac, and does weddings, receptions, birthdays, conventions, grand openings, and so on. For all your Elvis impersonator needs, call © **702/588-8188,** or visit his website at **www.vegaselvis.com**.

1. It's the only place in the world where Elvis will marry you, at a drive-up window, in a pink Cadillac—24 hours a day.
2. Chances are, you'll never forget your anniversary.
3. Where else can you treat all your guests to a wedding buffet for only 99¢ a head?
4. Four words: One helluva bachelor party.
5. On your wedding night, show your spouse that new "watch me disappear" act you learned from Siegfried & Roy.
6. Show your parents who's boss—have your wedding your way.
7. Wedding bells ring for you everywhere you go. They just sound like slot machines.
8. You can throw dice instead of rice.
9. Easy to lie about age on the marriage certificate—just like Joan Collins did!
10. With all the money you save, it's dice clocks for everyone!

You can also call **Las Vegas Weddings** (© **800/488-MATE;** www.lasvegasweddings. com), which offers one-stop shopping for wedding services. They'll find a chapel or outdoor garden that suits your taste (not to mention such only-in-Vegas venues as the former mansions of Elvis Presley and Liberace); book you into a hotel for the honeymoon; arrange the ceremony; and provide flowers, a photographer (and/or videographer), a wedding cake, a limo, car rental, music, champagne, balloons, and a garter for the bride. Basically, they can arrange anything you like. Theme weddings are a specialty. They even have a New Age minister on call who can perform a Native American ceremony. And yes, you can get married by an Elvis impersonator. Las Vegas Weddings can also arrange your honeymoon stay, complete with sightseeing tours, show tickets, and meals.

Weddings can be very inexpensive in Vegas: A license is $55 and a basic service not much more. Even a full-blown shebang package—photos, music, some flowers, video, cake, and other doodads—will run only about $500 total. We haven't quoted any prices here because the ultimate cost depends entirely on how much you want to spend. Go cheap, and the whole thing will set you back maybe $100, including the license (maybe even somewhat less); go elaborate, and the price is still reasonable by today's wedding-price standards. Be sure to remember that there are often hidden charges, such as expected gratuities for the minister (about $25 should do; no real need to tip anyone else), and so forth. If you're penny-pinching, you'll want to keep those in mind.

Be aware that Valentine's Day is a very popular day to get married in Vegas. Some of the chapels perform as many as 80 services on February 14. On 7/7/07, 1,600 wedding licenses were issued—four times the regular number for a Friday—as couples, some of whom booked chapel time a year or more in advance, chose what seemed to be the luckiest day of the year to get hitched. But remember, you also don't have to plan ahead. Just show up, get your paperwork, close your eyes, and pick a chapel. And above all, have fun. Good luck and best wishes to you both.

Note: When we describe the following chapels and say "flowers," don't think fresh (unless it's part of a description of services provided); the permanent decorations are artificial, of varying levels of quality, though usually well dusted.

Chapel of the Bells   Sporting perhaps the largest and gaudiest wedding chapel sign on the Strip, this is also one of the longest-running chapels, operating since 1957. This combination of classic Vegas "style" and "tradition" is most of what this place has going for it. The chapel is pretty, garnished with swaths of white material, seating about 25, but nothing dazzling. It's not particularly distinctive, but Kelly Ripa got married here, so there is that. They prefer advance booking but can do same-day ceremonies.

2233 Las Vegas Blvd. S. (at Sahara Ave.). (C) **800/233-2391** or 702/735-6803. www.chapelofthebellslasvegas.com. Mon–Thurs 9am–10pm; Fri–Sat 9am–1am. Open as late as needed on holidays.

Cupid's Wedding Chapel ☞   "The little chapel with the big heart." Well, it just might be. The manager explains that, unlike other chapels on the Strip, this one schedules weddings an hour apart to provide time for the full production number. The folks at Cupid's pride themselves on offering "a traditional church wedding at a chapel price." This includes a bridal processional, dimmed lights as the minister introduces the happy couple, and then a tape of the couple's favorite song so they can have their first dance right there at the pulpit after their "first" kiss. They also offer family weddings for those couples blending preexisting families; the children become a part of the service, and as their parents exchange rings with each other, the kids are given their own small token, to let them know the parents are marrying them as well. The chapel is pleasantly low-frills and down-to-earth, with white walls and pews, and modern stained glass with doves and roses. (Kitsch-phobes will be pleased to know that the cupids are only in the lobby.) It seats 60 to 70. They added a classic banquet hall (and by that we mean New Jersey banquet hall) so you can have your reception and wedding all in one place. Look for Internet-savvy packages like a live webcast of your wedding and a DVD of the ceremony included in most packages.

827 Las Vegas Blvd. S. (btw. Gass and Hoover aves.). (C) **800/543-2933** or 702/598-4444. www.cupidswedding.com. Weddings by appointment only, hours vary.

Graceland Wedding Chapel ☞   Housed in a landmark building that's one of the oldest wedding chapels in Vegas, the Graceland bills itself as "the proverbial mom and pop outfit. We offer friendly, courteous service, and are willing to go that extra step." No, Elvis never slept here; one of the owners was friends with Elvis and asked his permission to use the name. This is a tiny New England church building with a small bridge and white picket fence out front. Inside is a 30-seat chapel; the walls are off-white, with a large, modern stained-glass window of doves and roses behind the pulpit. The pews are dark-blond wood. It's not the nicest of the chapels, but Jon Bon Jovi and Billy Ray Cyrus got married here, though not to each other. Elvis package available. Weddings available for viewing online 45 minutes after ceremony.

619 Las Vegas Blvd. S. (at E. Bonneville Ave.). ℭ 800/824-5732 or 702/382-0091. www.gracelandchapel.com. Daily 9am–midnight.

Little Chapel of the Flowers ℱ   This chapel's claim to fame is that Dennis Rodman and Carmen Electra exchanged their deathless vows here. Don't hold it against the place; this is the slickest operation on the Strip, a big complex that offers your best shot at a traditional wedding. The La Capella Chapel fits 50 and has a cutesy church feel, with wood pews and electric candle chandeliers. The Victorian chapel, which holds only 30, has white walls and dark-wood pews and doesn't look very Victorian at all—but as the plainest, it's also the nicest. The smallest is the Magnolia Chapel, full of artificial flowers and a freestanding archway. If you want an outdoor vow exchange, you might choose the gazebo by a running stream and waterfall that nearly drowns out Strip noise. There's also a medium-size reception room and live organ music upon request. It's a pretty, friendly place that seems to keep an eye on its bustling business. It does not allow rice or confetti throwing.

1717 Las Vegas Blvd. S. (at E. Oakey Blvd.). ℭ 800/843-2410 or 702/735-4331. www.littlechapel.com. Mon–Thurs 8am–8pm; Fri–Sat 8am–9pm; Sun noon–6pm (sometimes).

Little White Wedding Chapel   This is arguably the most famous of the chapels on the Strip, maybe because they have the big sign saying Michael Jordan and Joan Collins were married here (again, not to each other), maybe because they were the first to do the drive-up window, or maybe because this is where Britney and that guy who isn't the guy from *Seinfeld* began their 51 hours of wedded bliss (no, we will never, ever get tired of mocking that bit of bad decision-making). It is indeed little and white. However, it has a factory-line atmosphere, processing wedding after wedding after wedding, 24 hours a day. Move 'em in, and move 'em out. No wonder they put in that drive-up window! The staff, dressed in hot-pink smocks, is brusque, hasty, and has a bit of an attitude (though we know one couple who got married here and had no complaints). They do offer full wedding ceremonies, complete with candlelight service and traditional music. There are two chapels, the smaller of which has a large photo of a forest stream. There's also a gazebo for outdoor services, but since it's right on the Strip, it's not as nice as it sounds. If you want something special, there are probably better choices, but for a true Vegas wedding experience, this is Kitsch Wedding Central.

1301 Las Vegas Blvd. S. (btw. E. Oakey and Charleston boulevards). ℭ 800/545-8111 or 702/382-5943. www.alittle whitechapel.com. Daily 24 hr.

Mon Bel Ami Wedding Chapel ℱ   Formerly the Silver Bells chapel, this is a spanking new redo, a pretty little churchlike building complete with a big gold- and flower-bedecked chapel room (maybe the taller peaked ceiling gives that effect) fitted with surround-sound speakers, new wood fittings, carpet, and paint. The cupid bas-relief is a bit much. They do frilly and fancy wedding receptions, as well as events where white doves are released. Perhaps because of this, the establishment seems to attract fewer walk-ins than prebooked weddings, so you should call in advance, or you might be stuck in the Strip-side gazebo. Along with Elvis, they can provide Tom Jones, Marilyn Monroe, and Elvira (!) impersonators.

607 Las Vegas Blvd. S. (at E. Bonneville Ave.). ℭ 866/503-4400 or 702/388-4445. www.monbelami.com. Sun–Fri 10am–8pm; Sat 10am–10pm.

A Special Memory Wedding Chapel ℱ   This is a very nice wedding chapel, particularly compared to the rather tired facades of the classics on the Strip. This is absolutely the place to go if you want a traditional, big-production wedding; you won't feel it the least bit tacky. It's a New England church–style building, complete with steeple. The interior looks like a proper church (well, a plain one—don't think ornate Gothic cathedral) with a peaked roof, pews with padded red seats, modern stained-glass windows of doves and flowers, and lots of dark wood. It's all very clean and new, and seats about 87 comfortably. There is a short staircase leading to an actual bride's room; she can make an entrance coming down it or through the double doors at the back. The area outside the chapel is like a mini-mall of bridal paraphernalia stores. Should all this just be too darned nice and proper for you, they also offer a drive-up window (where they do about 300 weddings a month!). It'll cost you $25—just ring the buzzer for service. They have a photo studio on-site and will do receptions featuring a small cake, cold cuts, and champagne. There is a gazebo for outside weddings, and they sell T-shirts!

800 S. 4th St. (at Gass Ave.). ⓒ 800/962-7798 or 702/384-2211. www.aspecialmemory.com. Sun–Thurs 8am–10pm; Fri–Sat 8am–midnight.

Wee Kirk O' the Heather 🎀   This is the oldest wedding chapel in Las Vegas (it's been here since 1940; ah, Vegas, and its mixed-up view of age) and the one at the very end of the Strip, right before Downtown (and thus close to the license bureau). It would be declared a historic landmark except that some renovations in the past moved just enough of the interior walls to alter it sufficiently to keep it from being official. An even more recent face-lift invigorated it. The decor is entirely fresh, and while that means gold-satin-patterned wallpaper in the chapel, we still like it a great deal. Just the right balance between kitsch and classic, and that's what you want in a Vegas wedding chapel. After all, what else is the point?

231 Las Vegas Blvd. S. (btw. Bridger and Carson aves.). ⓒ 800/843-2566 or 702/382-9830. www.weekirk.com. Daily 10am–8pm.

3 Attractions in Nearby Henderson

About 6 miles from the Strip in the town of Henderson are a couple of attractions that seem small-time in comparison with the glitz offered elsewhere. But if you need a break from all the high-tech, multimedia energy that buffets you in the city, you won't be alone. It's surprising how many people wander over this way for a bit more staid, though engaging, older-fashioned amusement.

To get to Henderson, drive east on Tropicana Avenue, make a right on Mountain Vista, then go 2 miles to Sunset Way; turn left into Green Valley Business Park. You will soon see Ethel M Chocolates, a good place to begin. Use the map in this section to find your way to the other facility.

Clark County Heritage Museum 🎀🎀 *(Finds)* *(Kids)*   Someday, one of these casino moguls (yeah, we're lookin' at you, Trump) is going to take just some of those megamillions they are pouring into yet another Strip hotel and put it into the museum that this bizarre town, and its ridiculously rich 100-year history, deserves. Until then, this dear little place will have to do its best—and that best is actually pretty good. With everything from dioramas of dinosaurs to a small street filled with original buildings, including the 1932 Boulder City train depot, this is a throwback to ghost towns and other low-tech diversions. Sweet, informative, and you can't beat the price. Note that hot days will make the outdoor portions less than bearable.

Henderson

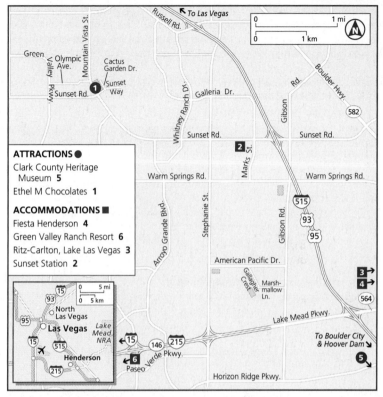

1830 S. Boulder Hwy., Henderson. ✆ 702/455-7955. Admission $1.50 adults, $1 seniors and children 3–15, free for children 2 and under. Daily 9am–4:30pm. Closed Thanksgiving, Dec 25, and Jan 1.

Ethel M Chocolates ⟨⟩ *(Kids)*   This tourist attraction draws about 2,000 visitors a day. Ethel Mars began making fine chocolates in a little candy kitchen in the early 20th century. Her small enterprise evolved to produce not only dozens of varieties of superb boxed chocolates, but also some of the world's most famous candies: M&Ms, Milky Way, 3 Musketeers, Snickers, and Mars bars.

Alas, the tour lasts only about 10 minutes and consists entirely of viewing stations with an audiotape explaining the chocolate-baking process. You learn very little. But the place does look like a bakery rather than a factory, which is nice, as no one wants to see their chocolates handled without love. Even more sadly, you get only one small chocolate as a sample—delicious, but hardly satisfying. Surely, this is by design; now overwhelmingly in the mood for sugar, you are more likely to buy some of their expensive chocolate. *Note:* Come before 2:30pm, which is when the workers start to pack up and go home.

What's really worth seeing is outside: a lovely and extensive **2½-acre garden** ⟨⟩ displaying 350 species of rare and exotic cacti with signs provided for self-guided tours. It's best appreciated in spring, when the cacti are in full bloom. There's a little gazebo

190 CHAPTER 6 · WHAT TO SEE & DO IN LAS VEGAS

in which to sit and enjoy the garden, which would be quite peaceful were it not for the busloads of tourists in the area. Behind the garden, also with a self-guided tour, is Ethel M's "Living Machine," a natural wastewater treatment and recycling plant that consists of aerated tanks, ecological fluid beds, constructed wetlands, reed beds, and a storage pond.

2 Cactus Garden Dr. (just off Mountain Vista and Sunset Way in the Green Valley Business Park). ✆ 888/627-0990 or 702/433-2500 for recorded information. www.ethelschocolate.com. Free admission. Daily 8:30am–7pm. Closed Dec 25.

4 Especially for Kids

Like much of the rest of the world, you may be under the impression that Las Vegas has evolved from an adults-only fantasyland into a vacation destination suitable for the entire family. The only explanation for this myth is that Las Vegas was referred to as "Disneyland for adults" by so many and for so long that the town became momentarily confused and decided it actually *was* Disneyland. Some of the gargantuan hotels then spent small fortunes on redecorating in an attempt to lure families, with vast quantities of junk food and a lot of hype. They now vehemently deny that any such notion ever crossed their collective minds, and, no, they don't know how that roller coaster got into the parking lot.

To put things simply, Las Vegas makes money—lots and lots of money—by promoting gambling, drinking, and sex. These are all fine pursuits if you happen to be an adult, but if you haven't reached the magical age of 21, you really don't count in this town. In any case, the casinos and even the Strip itself are simply too stimulating, noisy, and smoky for young kids.

Older progeny may have a tolerance for crowds and the incessant pinging of the slot machines, but they will be thoroughly annoyed with you when casino security chastises them if they so much as stop to tie their shoelaces anywhere near the gaming tables. Since you can't get from your hotel room to the parking lot without ambling through a casino, you can't reasonably expect a teenager to be in a good mood once you stagger outside. And those amusement parks and video halls that haven't yet been purged are very expensive places to park your kids for an afternoon or evening, assuming they are old enough to be left unsupervised.

Nevertheless, you may have a perfectly legitimate reason for bringing your children to Las Vegas (like Grandma was busy, or you were just stopping off on your way from somewhere else), so here are some places to take the children both on and off the Strip.

Circus Circus (p. 97) has ongoing circus acts throughout the day, a vast video-game-and-pinball arcade, and dozens of carnival games on its mezzanine level. Behind the hotel is the **Adventuredome,** detailed below.

Excalibur (p. 72) also offers video, carnival, and thrill cinemas.

At **Caesars Palace** (p. 78), animated talking statues in the **Forum Shops** are also a kick though smaller kids might be scared by them. Calm them down with a visit to the aquarium nearby in the Atlantis wing of the shops.

The erupting volcano might divert kids, as the **Secret Garden** and **Dolphin Habitat** at The Mirage (p. 181) surely will, and the **Shark Reef** at Mandalay Bay (p. 182) is worth a look.

Consider carefully the attractions at Luxor Las Vegas: **Bodies: the Exhibition** may be too intense for kids depending on their age, though others will be happily grossed out and might even learn a thing or two, while only those with interest in the high seas, disasters, the Titanic or the eponymous movie will want to browse through **Titantic: The Exhibition.**

Cyber Speedway and **Speed: The Ride** (p. 182) at the Sahara is the place for thrill ride kids to get their kicks.

Children 10 and up will love the many options for play (from high-tech to low-tech, from video wonders to actual physical activity) offered at **GameWorks** (p. 176), as will their parents.

Of moderate interest to youngsters is the **Ethel M Chocolates factory tour** in Henderson (see "Attractions in Nearby Henderson," above), not for the educational value but for the sweets at the end. More educational is the **Marjorie Barrick Museum** at UNLV (p. 180), but only the reptile exhibit will really interest kids. The **Clark County Heritage Museum** (p. 188) is also a dear little throwback, and uncynical kids may enjoy wandering through the old buildings and checking out some of the dioramas.

Appropriate shows for kids include *Tournament of Kings* at Excalibur, **Lance Burton** at the Monte Carlo, **Mac King** at Harrah's, and Cirque du Soleil's *Mystère* at TI–Treasure Island. As a general rule, early shows are less racy than late-night shows. All these productions are reviewed in detail in chapter 9, where you'll also find a few more suggestions for kid-friendly shows.

Beyond the city limits (see chapter 10 for details on all of these) is **Bonnie Springs Ranch/Old Nevada,** with trail and stagecoach rides, a petting zoo, old-fashioned melodramas, stunt shootouts, a Nevada-themed wax museum, crafts demonstrations, and more. **Lake Mead** has great recreational facilities for family vacations. Finally, organized tours (see the following section) to the Grand Canyon and other interesting sights in southern Nevada and neighboring states can be fun family activities. Check with your hotel sightseeing desk. Kids should also be entertained by the personalized tours offered by **Creative Adventures** (© **702/893-2051;** www.creative adventuresltd.net); see p. 193.

Specifically kid-pleasing attractions are described below.

The Adventuredome 🍭 *Kids*   This an okay place to spend a hot afternoon, especially now that it's about all that remains of the great Vegas-Is-For-Kids-Too experiment. Plus, unlike most theme parks, it's indoors! The glass dome that towers overhead lets in natural light. Even so, the place is looking a little ragged, like it knows it's now an afterthought rather than a centerpiece. A double-loop roller coaster careens around the simulated Grand Canyon, and there's the requisite water flume, a laser-tag area, some bouncy/twirly/stomach-churning rides, and a modest number of other tamer rides for kids of all ages. Video games and a carnival-style arcade are separate from the attractions, though it all still feels pretty hectic. The SpongeBob SquarePants 4-D ride is disappointing, since the technology is about 10 years behind the times and the story is hard to follow, thanks to bad acoustics. We suggest that you not leave kids here alone; they could easily get lost.

2880 Las Vegas Blvd. S. (behind Circus Circus). © 702/794-3939. www.adventuredome.com. Free admission; pay per ride $4–$7; daily pass $25 adults, $15 children 33–47 in. tall. AE, DC, DISC, MC, V. Park hours vary seasonally but are usually Mon–Thurs 10am–6pm; Fri–Sat 10am–midnight; Sun 10am–9pm.

Kids Quest 🍭 *Kids*   This is part of a well-regarded chain of activity and babysitting centers, oddly located in the otherwise very adult Palms and Red Rock resorts. Given the loss of the MGM Grand's child-care facility, it's a boon to parents who have business or want a little quality adult time, and frankly to kids who might not be enjoying the Vegas experience as much as older folks.

The Red Rock facility is quite large, including a gym with a basketball court and a salon for the girlie-minded. Kids can play dress-up, scoot around a doll's house, or try out air hockey and video games. The ratio of staff to kids is 1 to 10, and 1 to 4 for babies and toddlers. The employees are all cute and earnest, and have to pass certain qualifications to work here. It's certainly an option for parents who wish to have dinner or see a show.

In the Palms, 4321 W. Flamingo Rd.; © 866/942-7777. In Red Rock Resort, 11011 W. Charleston Blvd.; © 702/797-7646. www.kidsquest.com. $6.25–$7.25 per hr. Hours vary according to location; generally until 11pm on weekdays and 1am on weekends.

Las Vegas Natural History Museum 🌟 *Kids*

Conveniently located across the street from the Lied Discovery Children's Museum (described below), this humble temple of taxidermy harkens back to elementary-school field trips, circa 1965, when stuffed elk and brown bears forever protecting their kill were as close as most of us got to exotic animals. Worn around the edges but very sweet and relaxed, the museum is enlivened by a hands-on activity room and two life-size dinosaurs that roar at one another intermittently. A small boy was observed leaping toward his dad upon watching this display, so you might want to warn any sensitive little ones that the big tyrannosaurs aren't going anywhere. Surprisingly, the gift shop here is particularly well stocked with neat items you won't too terribly mind buying for the kids. When you are finished, you might as well scoot around the corner to the **Old Fort,** which isn't a strong enough attraction on its own but is a logical transition from this destination.

900 Las Vegas Blvd. N. (at Washington Ave.). © 702/384-3466. www.lvnhm.org. Admission $8 adults; $7 seniors, students, and military; $4 children 3–11; free for children 2 and under. Daily 9am–4pm.

Lied Discovery Children's Museum 🌟🌟 *Finds* *Kids*

A hands-on science museum designed for curious kids, the bright, airy, two-story Lied makes an ideal outing for toddlers and young children. With lots of interactive exhibits to examine, including a miniature grocery store, a tube for encasing oneself inside a soap bubble, a radio station where attendees can perform karaoke, and music and drawing areas, you'll soon forget your video/poker losses. Clever, thought-inducing exhibits are everywhere. Learn how it feels to be physically disabled by playing basketball from a wheelchair. Feed a wooden "sandwich" to a cutout of a snake and to a human cutout, and see how much nutrition each receives. See how much sunscreen their giant stuffed mascot needs to keep from burning. On Saturday afternoons from 1 to 3pm, free drop-in art classes are offered, giving adults a bit of time to ramble around the gift store or read the fine print on the exhibit placards. The Lied also shares space with a city library branch, so after the kids run around, you can calm them back down with a story or two.

833 Las Vegas Blvd. N. (half-block south of Washington, across from Cashman Field). © 702/382-3445. www.ldcm.org. Admission $8 adults; $7 seniors, military, and children 1–17. Tues–Fri 9am–4pm; Sat 10am–5pm; Sun noon–5pm. Closed Easter, Thanksgiving, Dec 24, Dec 25, and Jan 1.

5 Organized Tours

Just about every hotel in town has a tour desk offering a seemingly infinite number of sightseeing opportunities in and around Las Vegas. You're sure to find a tour company that will take you where you want to go.

Gray Line (© **800/634-6579;** www.grayline.com) offers a rather comprehensive roster, including the following:

- A pair of 5- to 6-hour **city tours** (1 day, 1 night), with various itineraries, including visits to Ethel M Chocolates, the Liberace Museum, and the Fremont Street Experience
- Half-day excursions to **Hoover Dam** and **Red Rock Canyon** (see chapter 10 for details)
- A half-day tour to **Lake Mead** and **Hoover Dam** (see chapter 10 for details)
- Several full-day **Grand Canyon excursions** (see chapter 10 for details)

Call for details or inquire at your hotel's tour desk, where you'll also find free magazines with coupons for discounts on these tours.

UNIQUE DESERT TOURS BY CREATIVE ADVENTURES 🏛🏛🏛

A totally different type of tour is offered by Char Cruze of **Creative Adventures** 🏛🏛🏛 (© 702/893-2051; www.creativeadventuresltd.net). Char, a charming fourth-generation Las Vegan (she was at the opening of The Flamingo), spent her childhood riding horseback through the mesquite and cottonwoods of the Mojave Desert, discovering magical places you'd never find on your own or on a commercial tour. Char is a lecturer and storyteller as well as a tour guide. She has extensively studied southern Nevada's geology and desert wildlife, its regional history, and its Native American cultures. Her personalized tours, enhanced by fascinating stories about everything from miners to mobsters, visit haunted mines, sacred Paiute grounds, ghost towns, canyons, and ancient petroglyphs. She also has many things to entertain and educate children, and she carries a tote bag full of visual aids, such as a board covered in labeled rocks to better illustrate a lecture on local geology. Char has certain structured tours, but she loves to do individual tours tailored to the group. This is absolutely worth the money—you are definitely going to get something different than you would on a conventional tour, while Char herself is most accommodating, thoughtful, knowledgeable, and prompt. Char rents transport according to the size of the group and can handle clients with physical disabilities; foreign language translators are also available.

Mayor Oscar B. Goodman's Top 10 Places to Recapture Old Las Vegas

1. The proposed "Mob" Museum in the old U.S. Courthouse and Post Office (300 E. Stewart Ave.)
2. The "Bugsy" Suite at The Flamingo Hotel & Casino
3. Bob Taylor's Ranch House at 6250 Rio Vista (where the old-timers went)
4. Fellini's Restaurant at 5555 W. Charleston (ambience of yore)
5. Piero's Italian Cuisine at 355 Convention Center Dr. (characters eating pasta)
6. Two hundred feet at the bottom of Lake Mead
7. Six feet in the desert near the state line
8. Howard Hughes's bungalow behind Channel 8
9. The WELCOME TO LAS VEGAS sign south of the Strip
10. The Huntridge Theater at 1208 E. Charleston

Oscar B. Goodman is the Mayor of Las Vegas through 2011.

Each tour is customized based on your interests so pricing varies dramatically, but figure at least $150 for the basics (which are much more than basic), with costs going up from there. It's a good idea to make arrangements with Char prior to leaving home.

6 Fore! Great Desert Golf

In addition to the listings below, there are dozens of local courses, including some very challenging ones that have hosted PGA tournaments. *Note:* Greens fees vary radically depending on time of day and year. Also, call for opening and closing times because these change frequently. Because of the heat, you will want to take advantage of the cart that in most cases is included in the greens fee.

Note also that the **Rio All-Suite Hotel** (p. 89) has an affiliated golf course. Also, **Wynn Las Vegas** (p. 93) has a state-of-the-art course, but we aren't including it for two reasons; at this writing, it is for guests only—and they mean it. If anyone in your party is not also staying at the hotel, they can't play. And the greens fees? A mere $500 a person. Call when you get to town to see whether they've come to their senses.

Angel Park Golf Club 𝕽𝕽   This 36-hole, par-70/71 public course is a local favorite. Arnold Palmer originally designed the Mountain and Palm courses (the Palm Course was redesigned several years later by Bob Cupp). Players call this a great escape from the casinos, claiming that no matter how many times they play it, they never get tired of it. The Palm Course has gently rolling fairways that offer golfers of all abilities a challenging yet forgiving layout. The Mountain Course has rolling natural terrain and gorgeous panoramic views. In addition to these two challenging 18-hole courses, Angel Park offers a night-lit Cloud 9 Course (12 holes for daylight play, 9 at night), where each hole is patterned after a famous par 3. You can reserve tee times up to 60 days in advance with a credit card guarantee.

Yardage: Palm Course 6,525 championship and 5,438 resort; Mountain Course 6,722 championship and 5,718 resort.

Facilities: Pro shop, night-lit driving range, 18-hole putting course, restaurant, snack bar, cocktail bar, and beverage cart.

100 S. Rampart Blvd. (btw. Summerlin Pkwy. and Alta St.; 20 min. NW of the Strip). ✆ **888/629-3929** or 702/254-0566. www.angelpark.com. Greens fees for 18 hole courses (includes cart rental, practice balls, and tax) $75–$155; short course fees $25, excluding optional cart rental. Discounted twilight rates available for 18-hole course.

Bali Hai Golf Club 𝕽𝕽𝕽   One of the newest and most exclusive golf addresses belongs to this multimillion-dollar course built in 2000 on the Strip just south of Mandalay Bay. Done in a wild South Seas theme, the par-72 course has over 7 acres of water features, including an island green, palm trees, and tropical foliage everywhere you look. Not impressed yet? How about the fact that all their golf carts are equipped with GPS (global positioning systems)? Or that celebrity chef Wolfgang Puck chose to open his newest Vegas eatery here? Okay, if that doesn't convince you of the upscale nature of the joint, check out the greens fees. Even at those prices, tee times are often booked 6 months in advance.

Yardage: 7,002 championship.

Facilities: Pro shop, putting green, gourmet restaurant, grill, and lounge.

5150 Las Vegas Blvd. S. ✆ **888/427-6678**. www.balihaigolfclub.com. Greens fees (includes cart, range balls, and tax) $99–$395.

Black Mountain Golf & Country Club 💰💰 Two new greens have recently been added to this 27-hole, par-72 semiprivate course, which requires reservations 4 days in advance. It's considered a great old course, with lots of wildlife, including roadrunners. However, unpredictable winds may affect your game.

Yardage: 6,550 championship, 6,223 regular, and 5,518 ladies.

Facilities: Pro shop, putting green, driving range, restaurant, snack bar, and cocktail lounge.

500 Greenway Rd., Henderson. ✆ 866/596-4833. www.golfblackmountain.com. Greens fees (includes cart rental) $75–$120. Call for twilight rates.

Craig Ranch Golf Club *Value* This is a flat 18-hole, par-70 public course with many trees and bunkers; both narrow and open fairways feature Bermuda turf. The greens fees are a bargain, and you can reserve tee times 7 days in advance.

Yardage: 6,001 regular and 5,221 ladies.

Facilities: Driving range, pro shop, PGA teaching pro, putting green, and snack bar.

628 W. Craig Rd. (btw. Losee Rd. and Martin Luther King Blvd.). ✆ 702/642-9700. Greens fees $19 walking, $30 in golf cart.

Desert Rose Golf Club 💰 *Value* This is an 18-hole, par-71 public course built in 1963 and designed by Dick Wilson and Joe Lee. Narrow fairways feature Bermuda turf. You can reserve tee times up to 7 days in advance.

Yardage: 6,511 championship, 6,135 regular, and 5,458 ladies.

Facilities: Driving range, putting and chipping greens, PGA teaching pro, pro shop, restaurant, and cocktail lounge.

5483 Clubhouse Dr. (3 blocks west of Nellis Blvd., off Sahara Ave.). ✆ 800/470-4622 or 702/566-7618. Greens fees (includes cart rental) $60–$80.

Las Vegas National Golf Club 💰 This is an 18-hole (about 8 with water on them), par-71 public course, and a classic layout (not the desert layout you'd expect). If you play from the back tees, it can really be a challenge. The 1996 Las Vegas Invitational, won by Tiger Woods, was held here. Discounted tee times are often available. Reservations are taken up to 60 days in advance.

Yardage: 6,815 championship, 6,418 regular, and 5,741 ladies.

Facilities: Pro shop, golf school, driving range, restaurant, and cocktail lounge.

1911 Desert Inn Rd. (btw. Maryland Pkwy. and Eastern Ave.). ✆ 702/734-1796. www.lasvegasnational.com. Greens fees (some include cart rental) $60–$179.

7 Staying Active

You need not be a slot-hypnotized slug when you come to Vegas. The city and surrounding areas offer plenty of opportunities for active sports. In addition to many highly rated golf courses (described above), just about every hotel has a large swimming pool and health club, and tennis courts abound. All types of watersports are offered at Lake Mead National Recreation Area; there's rafting on the Colorado, horseback riding at Mount Charleston and Bonnie Springs, great hiking in the canyons, and much, much more. Do plan to get out of those smoke-filled casinos and into the fresh air once in a while. It's good for your health and your finances.

For information on cycling, hiking, horseback riding, skiing, and snowboarding, see chapter 10.

Note: When choosing a hotel, check out its recreational facilities, all listed in chapter 4.

BOWLING   There are a number of serious bowling options listed in this section, but for those who take their strikes less soberly—more on that in a moment—there is **Lucky Strike at the Rio,** 3700 W. Flamingo Blvd. (© **702/777-7777**). It has only 10 lanes, but you don't come to this clublike spot to bowl. You come to eat items like fried mac 'n' cheese and other salty, tasty snacks. This then makes you thirsty for various goofy drinks, such as cotton candy–flavored martinis (the glass is lined with the vibrant spun sugar, and when the drink is poured into it, a curious colored effect appears) or the Mambo for Two, from which dry ice dramatically froths out. You then lounge on some couches and think "Bowling? Eh." Open daily from 2pm to 2am; no one under 21 admitted after 9pm.

More serious bowlers have some good options to choose from. **Gold Coast Hotel,** 4000 W. Flamingo Rd. (at Valley View; © **702/367-7111**), has a 72-lane bowling center open daily 24 hours. The **Orleans,** 4500 W. Tropicana Ave. (© **702/365-7111**), has 70 lanes, a pro shop, lockers, meeting rooms, and more; it's also open daily 24 hours.

Out on the east side of town, you'll find 56 lanes at **Sam's Town,** 5111 Boulder Hwy. (© **702/456-7777**), plus a snack shop, cocktail lounge, video arcade, day-care center, pro shop, and more. Open daily 24 hours.

In 2005, **Sunset Station,** 1301 W. Sunset Rd., in Henderson (© **702/547-7777**) added a high-tech 72-lane facility called Strike Zone. It's got all the latest automated scoring gizmos, giant video screens, a full bar, a snack shop, a pro shop, a video arcade, and more.

Up north at **Santa Fe Station,** 4949 N. Rancho Rd. (© **702/658-4900**), you'll find a remodeled 60-lane alley with the most modern scoring equipment, new furnishings, a fun and funky bar, a small cafe, and much more. Just down the road is sister hotel **Texas Station,** 2101 Texas Star Lane (© **702/631-8128**), with a 60-lane alley, video arcade, billiards, snack bar and lounge, and more. Open 24 hours.

Suncoast, 9090 Alta Dr., in Summerlin (© **702/636-7111**), offers 64 lanes divided by a unique center aisle. The high-tech center with touch-screen scoring has become a regular stop on the Pro Bowlers tours. Open daily 24 hours.

South Point, 9777 Las Vegas Blvd. (© **702/796-7400**), opened in 2006 and features a 64-lane facility with a similar divided layout to its sister at Suncoast. It has all the latest gee-whiz scoring and automation plus the usual facilities. Open 24 hours.

ROCK CLIMBING   **Red Rock Canyon** 𝕬𝕬𝕬, just 19 miles west of Las Vegas, is one of the world's most popular rock-climbing areas. In addition to awe-inspiring natural beauty, it offers everything from boulders to big walls. If you'd like to join the bighorn sheep, Red Rock has more than 1,000 routes to inaugurate beginners and challenge accomplished climbers. Experienced climbers can contact the **visitor center** (© **702/515-5350;** www.redrockcanyon.blm.gov) for information. See chapter 10 for details about Red Rock.

TENNIS   Tennis used to be a popular pastime in Vegas, but these days, buffs only have a couple of choices at hotels in town that have tennis courts.

Bally's 𝕬𝕬 (© **702/739-4111**) has eight night-lit hard courts. Fees per hour start at $15 for guests of Bally's or Paris Las Vegas, and $20 for nonguests, with rackets available for rental. Facilities include a pro shop. Hours vary seasonally. Reservations are advised.

Tips Desert Hiking Advice

Except in summer, when temperatures can reach 120°F (49°C) in the shade, the Las Vegas area is great for hiking. The best hiking season is November through March. Great locales include the incredibly scenic Red Rock Canyon and Valley of Fire State Park (see chapter 10 for details on both).

Hiking in the desert is exceptionally rewarding, but it can be dangerous. Here are some safety tips:

1. Don't hike alone.
2. Carry plenty of water and drink it often. Don't assume that spring water is safe to drink. A gallon of water per person per day is recommended for hikers.
3. Be alert for signs of heat exhaustion (headache, nausea, dizziness, fatigue, and cool, damp, pale, or red skin).
4. Gauge your fitness accurately. Desert hiking may involve rough or steep terrain. Don't take on more than you can handle.
5. Check weather forecasts before starting out. Thunderstorms can turn into raging flash floods, which are extremely hazardous to hikers.
6. Dress properly. Wear sturdy walking shoes for rock scrambling, long pants (to protect yourself from rocks and cacti), a hat, sunscreen, and sunglasses.
7. Carry a small first-aid kit.
8. Be careful when climbing on sandstone, which can be surprisingly soft and crumbly.
9. Don't feed or play with animals, such as the wild burros in Red Rock Canyon. (It's actually illegal to approach them.)
10. Be alert for snakes and insects. Though they're rarely encountered, you'll want to look into a crevice before putting your hand into it.
11. Visit park or other information offices before you start out, and acquaint yourself with rules and regulations and any possible hazards. It's also a good idea to tell the staff where you're going, when you'll return, how many are in your party, and so on. Some park offices offer hiker-registration programs.
12. Follow the hiker's creed: Take only photographs and leave only footprints.

The Flamingo Las Vegas ★★ (© 702/733-3444) has four outdoor hard courts (all lit for night play) and a pro shop. It's open to the public daily from 8am to 5pm. Rates are $15 per hour for guests of The Flamingo, $20 per hour for nonguests. Lessons are available. Reservations are required.

8 Spectator Sports

Las Vegas isn't known for its sports teams. Except for minor-league baseball and hockey, the only consistent spectator sports are those at UNLV. For the pros, if watching Triple A ball (in this case, a Los Angeles Dodgers farm team) in potentially triple-degree heat sounds like fun, the charmingly named and even-better merchandized **Las Vegas 51s** (as in Area 51, as in alien-themed gear!) is a hot ticket. The team's schedule and ticket info are available at **www.lv51.com**, or call ✆ **702/386-7200.** Ice hockey might be a better climate choice; get info for the **Las Vegas Wranglers** at **www.lasvegas wranglers.com** or ✆ **702/471-7825.**

The **Las Vegas Motor Speedway** (p. 177) is a main venue for car racing that draws major events to Las Vegas.

Because the city has several top-notch sporting arenas, important annual events take place in Las Vegas, details for which can be found in the "Las Vegas Calendar of Events" in chapter 2. The **LPGA Tour's Takefuji Classic** is held every April, and the **PGA Tour's Frys.com Open** takes place in Las Vegas every October. The **National Finals Rodeo** is held in UNLV's Thomas and Mack Center in December. From time to time, you'll find NBA exhibition games, professional ice-skating competitions, or gymnastics exhibitions. Then there are the only-in-Vegas spectaculars, such as Evel Knievel's ill-fated attempt to jump the fountains in front of Caesars.

Finally, Las Vegas is well known as a major location for **boxing matches.** These are held in several Strip hotels, most often at Caesars or the MGM Grand, but sometimes at The Mirage. Tickets are hard to come by and quite expensive.

Tickets to sporting events at hotels are available either through **Ticketmaster** (✆ **702/893-3000;** www.ticketmaster.com) or through the hotels themselves. (Why pay Ticketmaster's exorbitant service charges if you don't have to?)

MAJOR SPORTS VENUES IN HOTELS

Caesars Palace (✆ **800/634-6698** or 702/731-7110) has a long tradition of hosting sporting events, from Evel Knievel's attempted motorcycle jump over its fountains in 1967 to Gran Prix auto races. Mary Lou Retton has tumbled in gymnastic events at Caesars, and Olympians Brian Boitano and Katarina Witt have taken to the ice, as has Wayne Gretzky. And well over 100 world-championship boxing contests have taken place here since the hotel opened. In the spirit of ancient Rome, Caesars awards riches and honors to the "gladiators" who compete in its arenas.

The **MGM Grand's Garden Events Arena** (✆ **800/929-1111** or 702/891-7777) is a major venue for professional boxing matches, rodeos, tennis, ice-skating shows, World Figure Skating Championships, and more.

Mandalay Bay (✆ **877/632-7400**) has hosted a number of boxing matches in its 12,000-seat Events Center.

7

About Casino Gambling

What? You didn't come to Las Vegas for the Liberace Museum? We are shocked. *Shocked.*

Yes, there are gambling opportunities in Vegas. We've noticed this. You will, too. The tip-off will be the slot machines in the airport as soon as you step off the plane. Or the slot machines in the convenience stores as soon as you drive across the state line. Let's not kid ourselves: Gambling is what Vegas is about. The bright lights, the shows, the showgirls, the food—it's all there just to lure you in and make you open your wallet. The free drinks certainly help ease the latter as well.

You can disappoint them if you want, but what would be the point? *This is Las Vegas.* You don't have to be a high roller. You would not believe how much fun you can have with a nickel slot machine. You won't get rich, but neither will most of those guys playing the $5 slots, either.

Of course, that's not going to stop anyone from trying. Almost everyone plays in Vegas with the hopes of winning The Big One. That only a few ever do win doesn't stop them from trying again and again and again. That's how the casinos make their money, by the way.

It's not that the odds are stacked so incredibly high in their favor—though the odds *are* in their favor, and don't ever think otherwise. Rather, it's that if there is one constant in this world, it's human greed. Look around in any casino, and you'll see countless souls who, having doubled their winnings, are now trying to quadruple them, and are losing it all and then trying to recoup their initial bankroll and losing still more in the process.

We don't mean to dissuade you from gambling. Just be sure to look at it as recreation and entertainment, *not* as an investment or a moneymaking opportunity. Spend only as much as you can afford to lose. It doesn't matter if that's $10 or $100,000. You can have just as good a time with either. (Though if you can afford to lose $100,000, we would like to meet you.)

Remember also that there is no system that's sure to help you win. We all have our own systems and our own ideas. Reading books and listening to others at the tables will help you pick up some tips, but if there were a surefire way to win, the casinos would have taken care of it (and we will leave you to imagine just what that might entail). Try to have the courage to walk away when your bankroll is up, not down. Remember, your children's college fund is just that, and not a gambling-budget supplement.

Impressions
Stilled forever is the click of the roulette wheel, the rattle of dice, and the swish of cards.

—Shortsighted editorial in the *Nevada State Journal* after gambling was outlawed in 1910

The first part of this chapter is a contribution from James Randi, a master magician, who looks at the four major fallacies people bring with them to the gaming tables in Las Vegas; it's fascinating, and we thank him for this contribution.

The second part tells you the basics of betting. Knowing how to play the games not only improves your odds but also makes playing more enjoyable. In addition to the instructions here, you'll find dozens of books on how to gamble at all casino hotel gift shops, and many casinos offer free gaming lessons.

The third part of this chapter describes all the major casinos in town. Remember that gambling is supposed to be entertainment. Picking a gaming table where the other players are laughing, slapping each other on the back, and generally enjoying themselves tends to make for considerably more fun than a table where everyone is sitting around in stony silence, morosely staring at their cards. Unless you really need to concentrate, pick a table where all seem to be enjoying themselves, and you will, too, even if you don't win. Maybe.

1 The 4 Most Pervasive Myths about Gambling

by James Randi

Most of us know little, if anything, about statistics. It's a never-never land we can live without, something for those guys in white coats and thick glasses to mumble over. And because we don't bother to learn the basics of this rather interesting field of study, we sometimes find ourselves unable to deal with the realities that the gambling process produces.

I often present my audiences with a puzzle. Suppose that a mathematician, a gambler, and a magician are walking together on Broadway and come upon a small cluster of people who are observing a chap standing at a small table set up on the sidewalk. They are told that this fellow has just tossed a quarter into the air and allowed it to fall onto the table, nine times. And that has produced nine "tails" in a row. Now the crowd is being asked to bet on what the next toss of the coin will bring. The question: How will each of these three observers place their bets?

The mathematician will reason that each toss of the coin is independent of the last toss, so the chances are still exactly 50/50 for heads or tails. He'll say that either bet is okay and that it doesn't make any difference which decision is made.

The gambler will go one of two ways; either he'll reason that there's a "run" taking place here—and that a bet on another tail will be the better choice—or he'll opine that it's time for the head to come up, and he'll put his wager on that likelihood.

The magician? He has the best chance of winning because he knows that there is only 1 chance in 512 that a coin will come up tails nine times in a row—*unless there's something wrong with that coin!* He'll bet tails, and he'll win!

The reasoning of the mathematician is quite correct, that of the gambler is quite wrong (in either one of his scenarios), but just as long as that isn't a double-tailed coin. The point of view taken by the magician is highly specialized, but human nature being what it is, that view is probably the correct one.

In professional gambling centers such as Las Vegas, great care is taken to ensure that there are no two-tailed quarters or other purposeful anomalies that enable cheating to take place. The casinos make their percentages on the built-in mathematical advantage, which is clearly stated and available to any who ask, and though that is a very tiny "edge," it's enough to pay for the razzle-dazzle that lures in the customers. It's volume

The Amazing Randi

James Randi is a world-class magician (the Amazing Randi), now involved in examining supernatural, paranormal, and occult claims. He is the author of 11 books on these subjects and is the president of the James Randi Educational Foundation in Fort Lauderdale, Florida. The JREF offers a prize of $1 million to any person who can produce a demonstration of any paranormal activity. His website is **www.randi.org**, where details of the offer can be found.

that supports the business. The scrutiny that is applied to each and every procedure in Vegas is evident everywhere.

So, **Fallacy Number One:** Cheating of some sort is necessary for an operation to prosper. It isn't.

Fallacy Number Two: Some people just have "hunches" and "visions" that enable them to win at the slots and tables. Sorry folks, it just ain't so. The science of parapsychology, which has studied such claims for many decades now, has never come up with evidence that any form of clairvoyance (clear seeing, the supposed ability to know hidden data, such as the next card to come up in a deal or the next face on the dice) or telepathy (mind reading) actually exists. It's remarkably easy for us to imagine that we have a hot streak going, or that the cards are falling our way, but the inexorable laws of chance prevail and always will.

Fallacy Number Three: There are folks who can give us systems for winning. Now, judicious bet placing is possible, and there are mathematical methods of minimizing losses, it's true. But the investment and base capital needed to follow through with these methods makes them a rather poor investment. The return percentage can be earned much more easily by almost any other form of endeavor, at less risk and less expenditure of boring hours following complicated charts and equations. The best observation we can make on the "systems" is this: Why would the inventors of the "systems" sell something that they themselves could use to get rich, which is what they say you can do with it? Think about that!

Of course, the simplest of all the systems is bet doubling. It sounds great in theory, but an hour spent tossing coins in your hotel room, or at the gaming tables, will convince you that theory and practice are quite different matters. Bet doubling, as applied to heads or tails (on a fair coin!), consists of placing a unit bet on the first coin toss, then pocketing the proceeds if you win but doubling your bet on the next toss if you lose. If you get a lose, lose, win sequence, that means you will have lost three units (one plus two) and won four. You're up one unit. You start again. If you get a lose, lose, lose, win sequence, you've put out 15 units and brought in 16. Again, you're up only one unit. And no matter how long your sequences go, you'll always be up only one unit at the end of a sequence. It requires you to make that "unit" somewhat sizable if you want to have any significant winnings at all, and that may mean going bankrupt by simply running out of capital before a sequence ends—and if you hang on, you'll have been able to end up only one unit ahead, in any case. Not a good investment at all.

Fallacy Number Four: Studying the results of the roulette wheels will provide the bettor with useful data. We're peculiar animals, in that we constantly search for meaning in all sets of observations. That's how subjects of Rorschach tests find weird faces, figures, and creatures in inkblots that are actually random patterns with single symmetry. Similarly, any sets of roulette results are, essentially, random numbers; there are no patterns to be found there that can give indications of probable future spins of the wheels. Bearing in mind that those wheels are carefully monitored to detect any biases or defects, we should conclude that finding clues in past performances is futile.

I recall that when I worked in Wiesbaden, Germany, just after World War II, I stuck around late one night after closing at the *Spielbank* and watched as an elderly gentleman removed all the rotors of the 12 wheels they had in operation, wrote out the numbers 1 to 12 on separate scraps of paper, and reassembled the wheels according to the random order in which he drew each slip of paper from a bowl. He was ensuring that any inconsistencies in the wheels would be essentially nullified. Yet, as he told me, the front desk at the casino continued to sell booklets setting out the results of each of the wheels because patrons insisted on having them and persisted in believing that there just had to be a pattern there, if only it could be found.

We're only human. We can't escape certain defects in our thinking mechanism, but we can resist reacting to them. When we see Penn & Teller or Lance Burton doing their wonders, we smile smugly and assure ourselves that those miracles are only illusions. But if we haven't solved those illusions, and we haven't, how can we assume that we aren't being fooled by our own self-created delusions? Let's get a grip on reality and enjoy Las Vegas for what it really is: a grand illusion, a fairyland, a let's-pretend project, but not one in which the laws of nature are suspended or can be ignored.

Enjoy!

2 The Games

As you walk through the labyrinthine twists and turns of a casino floor, your attention will likely be dragged to the various games and, your interest piqued, your fingers may begin to twitch in anticipation of hitting it big. Before you put your money on the line, it's imperative to know the rules of the game you want to play. Most casinos offer free gambling lessons at scheduled times on weekdays. This provides a risk-free environment for you to learn the games that tickle your fancy. Some casinos follow their lessons with low-stakes game play, enabling you to put your newfound knowledge to the test at small risk. During those instructional sessions, and even when playing on your own, dealers in most casinos will be more than happy to answer any questions you might have. Remember, the casino doesn't need to trick you into losing your money . . . the odds are already in their favor across the board; that's why it's called *gambling*. Another rule of thumb: Take a few minutes to watch a game being played in order to familiarize yourself with the motions and lingo. Then go back and reread this section—things will make a lot more sense at that point. Good luck!

BACCARAT

The ancient game of baccarat, or *chemin de fer,* is played with eight decks of cards. Firm rules apply, and there is no skill involved other than deciding whether to bet on the bank or the player. No, really—that's all you have to do. The dealer does all the other work. You can essentially stop reading here. Oh, all right, carry on.

Any beginner can play, but check the betting minimum before you sit down, as baccarat tends to be a high-stakes game. The cards are shuffled by the croupier and then placed in a box called the "shoe." Players may wager on "bank" or "player" at any time. Two cards are dealt from the shoe and given to the player who has the largest wager against the bank, and two cards are dealt to the croupier, acting as banker. If the rules call for a third card, the player or banker, or both, must take the third card. In the event of a tie, the hand is dealt over. *Note:* The guidelines that determine whether a third card must be drawn (by the player or banker) are provided at the baccarat table upon request.

The object of the game is to come as close as possible to the number 9. To score the hands, the cards of each hand are totaled and the *last digit* is used. All cards have face value. For example: 10 plus 5 equals 15 (score is 5); 10 plus 4 plus 9 equals 23 (score is 3); 4 plus 3 plus 3 equals 10 (score is 0); and 4 plus 3 plus 2 equals 9 (score is 9). The closest hand to 9 wins.

Each player has a chance to deal the cards. The shoe passes to the player on the right each time the bank loses. If the player wishes, he or she may pass the shoe at any time.

Note: When you bet on the bank and the bank wins, you are charged a 5% commission. This must be paid at the start of a new game or when you leave the table.

BIG SIX

Big Six provides pleasant recreation and involves no study or effort. The wheel has 56 positions on it, 54 of them marked by bills from $1 to $20. The other two spots are jokers, and each pays 40 to 1 if the wheel stops in that position. All other stops pay at face value. Those marked with $20 bills pay 20 to 1, the $5 bills pay 5 to 1, and so forth. The idea behind the game is to predict (or just blindly guess) what spot the wheel will stop at and place a bet accordingly.

BLACKJACK

In this popular game, the dealer starts the game by dealing each player two cards. In some casinos, they're dealt to the player face up, in others face down, but the dealer always gets one card up and one card down. Everybody plays against the dealer. The object is to get a total that is higher than that of the dealer without exceeding 21. All face cards count as 10; all other number cards, except aces, are counted at their face value. An ace may be counted as 1 or 11, whichever you choose it to be.

Starting at his or her left, the dealer gives additional cards to the players who wish to draw (be "hit") or none to a player who wishes to "stand" or "hold." If your count is nearer to 21 than the dealer's, you win. If it's under the dealer's, you lose. Ties are a "push" (standoff) and nobody wins. After all the players are satisfied with their counts, the dealer exposes his or her face-down card. If his or her two cards total 16 or less, the dealer must hit until reaching 17 or over. If the dealer's total exceeds 21, he or she must pay all the players whose hands have not gone "bust." It is important to note here that the blackjack dealer has no choice as to whether he or she should stay or draw. A dealer's decisions are predetermined and known to all the players at the table.

If you're a novice or just rusty, do yourself a favor and buy one of the small laminated cards available in shops all over town that illustrate proper play for every possible hand in blackjack. Even longtime players have been known to pull them out every now and then, and they can save you from making costly errors.

HOW TO PLAY

Here are eight "rules" for blackjack:

1. Place the number of chips that you want to bet on the betting space on your table.
2. Look at the first two cards the dealer starts you with. If you wish to "stand," then wave your hand over your cards, palm down (watch your fellow players), indicating that you don't wish any additional cards. If you elect to draw an additional

Tips Look, but Don't Touch!

1. *Never* touch your cards (or anyone else's), unless it's specifically stated at the table that you may. While you'll receive only a verbal slap on the wrist if you violate this rule, you *really* don't want to get one.
2. Players must use hand signals to indicate their wishes to the dealer. All verbal directions by players will be politely ignored by the dealer, who will remind players to use hand signals. The reason for this is the "eye in the sky," the casino's security system, which focuses an "eye" on every table and must record players' decisions to avoid accusations of misconduct or collusion.

---

card, you tell the dealer to "hit" you by tapping the table with a finger. (Watch your fellow players.)

3. If your count goes over 21, you are "bust" and lose, even if the dealer also goes "bust" afterward.

4. If you make 21 in your first two cards (any picture card or 10 with an ace), you've got blackjack. You will be paid 1½ times your bet, provided that the dealer does not have blackjack, too, in which case it's a "push," and nobody wins.

5. If you find a "pair" in your first two cards (say, two 8s or two aces), you may "split" the pair into two hands and treat each card as the first card dealt in two separate hands. You will need to place an additional bet, equal to your original bet, on the table. The dealer will then deal you a new *second* card to the first split card and play commences as described above. This will be done for the second split card as well. *Note:* When you split aces, you will receive only one additional card per ace and must "stand."

6. After seeing your two starting cards, you have the option to "double down." You place an amount equal to your original bet on the table and you receive only one more card. Doubling down is a strategy to capitalize on a potentially strong hand against the dealer's weaker hand. *Tip:* You may double down for less than your original bet, but never for more.

7. Anytime the dealer deals himself or herself an ace for the "up" card, you may insure your hand against the possibility that the hole card is a 10 or face card, which would give him or her an automatic blackjack. To insure, you place an amount up to one-half of your bet on the "insurance" line. If the dealer does have a blackjack, you get paid 2 to 1 on the insurance money while losing your original bet: You break even. If the dealer does not have a blackjack, he or she takes your insurance money and play continues in the normal fashion.

8. *Remember:* The dealer must stand on 17 or more and must hit a hand of 16 or less.

PROFESSIONAL TIPS

Advice of the experts in playing blackjack is as follows:

1. *Do not* ask for an extra card if you have a count of 17 or higher, *ever.*
2. *Do not* ask for an extra card when you have a total of 12 or more if the dealer has a 2 through 6 showing in his or her "up" card.

3. *Ask* for an extra card or more when you have a count of 12 through 16 in your hand if the dealer's "up" card is a 7, 8, 9, 10, or ace.

There's a lot more to blackjack strategy than the above, of course. So consider this merely as the bare bones of the game. Blackjack is played with a single deck or with multiple decks; if you're looking for a single-deck game, your best bet is to head to a Downtown casino.

A final tip: Avoid insurance bets; they're sucker bait!

CRAPS

The most exciting casino action is usually found at the craps tables. Betting is frenetic, play fast-paced, and groups quickly bond while yelling and screaming in response to the action.

THE POSSIBLE BETS

The craps table is divided into marked areas (Pass, Come, Field, Big 6, Big 8, and so on), where you place your chips to bet. The following are a few simple directions.

PASS LINE   A "Pass Line" bet pays even money. If the first roll of the dice adds up to 7 or 11, you win your bet; if the first roll adds up to 2, 3, or 12, you lose your bet. If any other number comes up, it's your "point." If you roll your point again, you win, but if a 7 comes up again before your point is rolled, you lose.

DON'T PASS LINE   Betting on the "Don't Pass" is the opposite of betting on the "Pass Line." This time, you lose if a 7 or an 11 is thrown on the first roll, and you win if a 2 or a 3 is thrown on the first roll.

If the first roll is 12, however, it's a "push" (standoff), and nobody wins. If none of these numbers is thrown and you have a point instead, in order to win, a 7 will have to be thrown before the point comes up again. A "Don't Pass" bet also pays even money.

COME   Betting on "Come" is the same as betting on the Pass Line, but you must bet after the first roll or on any following roll. Again, you'll win on 7 or 11 and lose on 2, 3, or 12. Any other number is your point, and you win if your point comes up again before a 7.

DON'T COME   This is the opposite of a Come bet. Again, you wait until after the first roll to bet. A 7 or an 11 means you lose; a 2 or a 3 means you win; 12 is a push, and nobody wins. You win if 7 comes up before the point. (The point, you'll recall, was the first number rolled if it was none of the above.)

FIELD   This is a bet for one roll only. The "Field" consists of seven numbers: 2, 3, 4, 9, 10, 11, and 12. If any of these numbers is thrown on the next roll, you win even money, except on 2 and 12, which pay 2 to 1 (at some casinos 3 to 1).

BIG 6 AND 8   A "Big 6 and 8" bet pays even money. You win if either a 6 or an 8 is rolled before a 7. Mathematically, this is a sucker's bet.

ANY 7   An "Any 7" bet pays the winner 5 to 1. If a 7 is thrown on the first roll after you bet, you win.

"HARD WAY" BETS   In the middle of a craps table are pictures of several possible dice combinations together with the odds the casino will pay you if you bet and win on any of those combinations being thrown. For example, if double 3s or 4s are rolled and you had bet on them, you will be paid 7 to 1. If double 2s or 5s are rolled and you had bet on them, you will be paid 9 to 1. If either a 7 is rolled or the number you bet on was rolled any way other than the "Hard Way," then the bet is lost. In-the-know gamblers tend to avoid "Hard Way" bets as an easy way to lose their money.

ANY CRAPS   Here you're lucky if the dice "crap out"—if they show 2, 3, or 12 on the first roll after you bet. If this happens, the bank pays 7 to 1. Any other number is a loser.

PLACE BETS   You can make a "Place Bet" on any of the following numbers: 4, 5, 6, 8, 9, or 10. You're betting that the number you choose will be thrown before a 7 is thrown. If you win, the payoff is as follows: 4 or 10 pays at the rate of 9 to 5, 5 or 9 pays at the rate of 7 to 5, 6 or 8 pays at the rate of 7 to 6. "Place Bets" can be removed at any time before a roll.

SOME PROBABILITIES

The probability of a certain number being rolled at the craps table is not a mystery. Because there are only 36 possible outcomes when the dice are rolled, the probability for each number being rolled is easily ascertained. See the "Dice Probabilities" chart to help you, in case you decided it was fun to pass notes or sleep during math classes.

Dice Probabilities

Number	Possible Combinations	Actual Odds	Percentage Probability
2	1	35:1	2.8%
3	2	17:1	5.6%
4	3	11:1	8.3%
5	4	8:1	11.1%
6	5	6.2:1	13.9%
7	6	5:1	16.7%
8	5	6.2:1	13.9%
9	4	8:1	11.1%
10	3	11:1	8.3%
11	2	17:1	5.6%
12	1	35:1	2.8%

So 7 has an advantage over all other combinations, which, over the long run, is in favor of the casino. You can't beat the law of averages, but if you can't beat 'em, join 'em (that is, play the "Don't Pass" bet).

KENO

Originating in China, this is one of the oldest games of chance. Legend has it that funds acquired from the game were used to finance construction of the Great Wall of China.

Chinese railroad construction workers first introduced keno into the United States in the 1800s. Easy to play, and offering a chance to sit down and converse between bets, it is one of the most popular games in town—despite the fact that *the house percentage is greater than that of any other casino game!*

To play, you must first obtain a keno form, available at the counter in the keno lounge and in most Las Vegas coffee shops. In the latter, you'll usually find blank keno forms and thick black crayons on your table. Fill yours out, and a miniskirted keno runner will come and collect it. After the game is over, she'll return with your winning or losing ticket. If you've won, it's customary to offer a tip, depending on your winnings.

For those of you with state lotteries, this game will appear very familiar. You can select from 1 to 15 numbers (out of a total of 80), and if all of your numbers come up, you win. Depending on how many numbers you've selected, you can win smaller amounts if less than all of your numbers have come up. For example, if you bet a "3 spot" (selecting a total of three numbers) and two come up, you'll win something but not as much as if all three had shown up. A one-number mark is known as a 1-spot, a two-number selection is a 2-spot, and so on. After you have selected the number of spots you wish to play, write the amount you want to wager on the ticket, in the right-hand corner where indicated. The more you bet, the more you can win if your numbers come up. Before the game starts, you have to give the completed form to a keno runner, or hand it in at the keno lounge desk, and pay for your bet. You'll get back a duplicate form with the number of the game you're playing on it. Then the game begins. As numbers appear on the keno board, compare them to the numbers you've marked on your ticket. After 20 numbers have appeared on the board, the game is over, and if you've won, turn in your ticket to collect your winnings.

The more numbers on the board matching the numbers on your ticket, the more you win (in some cases, you get paid if *none* of your numbers come up). If you want to keep playing the same numbers over and over, you can replay a ticket by handing in your duplicate to the keno runner; you don't have to keep rewriting it.

In addition to the straight bets described above, you can split your ticket, betting various amounts on two or more groups of numbers. It does get a little complex, as combination-betting options are almost infinite. Helpful casino personnel in the keno lounge can assist you with combination betting.

POKER

Poker is the game of the Old West. There's at least one sequence in every Western where the hero faces off against the villain over a poker hand. In Las Vegas, poker is just about the biggest thing going, thanks to the prevalence and popularity of celebrity poker TV shows, poker tours, books, magazines, and who knows what all else. Just about every casino now has a poker room, and it's just a matter of time before the others catch up.

There are lots of variations on the basic game, but one of the most popular is **Hold 'Em.** Two cards are dealt, face down, to the players. After a betting round, five community cards (everyone can use them) are dealt face up on the table. Players make the best five-card hand, using their own cards and the "board" (the community cards), and the best hand wins. The house dealer takes care of the shuffling and the dealing, and moves a marker around the table to alternate the start of the deal. The house rakes 1% to 5% (depending on the casino) from each pot. Most casinos also provide tables for playing Seven-Card Stud, Omaha High, and Omaha Hi-Lo. A few even have Seven-Card Stud Hi-Lo split. To learn how these variations are played, either read a book or take lessons.

Warning: If you don't know how to play poker, don't attempt to learn at a table. Card sharks are not a rare species in Vegas; they will gladly feast on fresh meat (you!). Find a casino that provides free gaming lessons and learn, to quote Kenny Rogers, when to hold 'em, and when to fold 'em.

PAI GOW

Pai Gow is a variation on poker that has become popular. The game is played with a traditional deck plus one joker. The joker is a wildcard that can be used as an ace or to complete a straight, a flush, a straight flush, or a royal flush. Each player is dealt seven cards to arrange into two hands: a two-card hand and a five-card hand. As in standard poker, the highest two-card hand is two aces, and the highest five-card hand is a royal flush. The five-card hand *must* be higher than the two-card hand (if the two-card hand is a pair of sixes, for example, the five-card hand must be a pair of sevens or better). Any player's hand that is set incorrectly is an automatic loser. The object of the game is for both of the players' hands to rank higher than both of the banker's hands. Should one hand rank exactly the same as the banker's hand, this is a tie (called a "copy"), *and the banker wins all tie hands.* If the player wins one hand but loses the other, this is a "push," and no money changes hands. The house dealer or any player may be the banker. The bank is offered to each player, and each player may accept or pass. Winning hands are paid even money, less a 5% commission.

CARIBBEAN STUD

Caribbean Stud is yet another variation of poker that is gaining in popularity. Players put in a single ante bet and are dealt five cards, face down, from a single deck; they play solely against the dealer, who receives five cards, one of them face up. Players are then given the option of folding or calling, by making an additional bet that is double their original ante. After all player bets have been made, the dealer's cards are revealed. If the dealer doesn't qualify with *at least an ace/king combination,* players are paid even money on their ante, and their call bets are returned. If the dealer does qualify, each player's hand is compared to the dealer's. On winning hands, players receive even money on their ante bets, and call bets are paid out on a scale according to the value of their hands. The scale ranges from even money for a pair, to 100 to 1 on a royal flush, although there is usually a cap on the maximum payoff, which varies from casino to casino.

An additional feature of Caribbean Stud is the inclusion of a progressive jackpot. For an additional side bet of $1, a player may qualify for a payoff from a progressive jackpot. The jackpot bet pays off only on a flush or better, but you can win on this bet even if the dealer ends up with a better hand than you do. Dream all you want of getting that royal flush and taking home the jackpot, but the odds of it happening are astronomical, so don't be so quick to turn in your resignation letter. Most veteran gamblers will tell you this is a bad bet (from a strict mathematical standpoint, it is), but considering that Caribbean Stud already has a house advantage that is even larger than the one in roulette, if you're going to play, you might as well toss in the buck and pray.

LET IT RIDE

Let It Ride is another popular game that involves poker hands. You place three bets at the outset and are dealt three cards. The dealer is dealt two cards that act as community cards (you're not playing against the dealer). Once you've seen your cards, you can choose to pull the first of your three bets back or "let it ride." The object of this game is to get a pair of 10s or better by combining your cards with the community cards. If you're holding a pair of 10s or better in your first three cards (called a "no-brainer"), you want to let your bets ride the entire way through. Once you've decided whether or not to let your first bet ride, the dealer exposes one of his or her two cards. Once again, you must make a decision to take back your middle bet or keep on going. Then the dealer exposes the last of his or her cards; your third bet must stay. The dealer then turns over the hands of the players and determines whether you've won. Winning bets are paid on a scale, ranging from even money for a single pair up to 1,000 to 1 for a royal flush. These payouts are for each bet you have in play. Similarly to Caribbean Stud, Let It Ride has a bonus that you can win for high hands if you cough up an additional dollar per hand, but be advised that the house advantage on that $1 is obscene. But hey, that's why it's called gambling.

3-CARD POKER

Three-Card Poker is rapidly gaining popularity, and now you'll find at least one table in most major Vegas casinos. It's actually more difficult to explain than to play. For this reason, we recommend watching a table for a while. You should grasp it pretty quickly.

Basically, players are dealt three cards with no draw and have to make the best poker hand out of those three cards. Possible combinations include a straight flush (three sequential cards of the same suit), three of a kind (three queens, for example), a straight (three sequential cards of any suit), a flush (three cards of the same suit), and a pair (two queens, for example). Even if you don't have one of the favored combinations, you can still win if you have cards higher than the dealer's.

On the table are three betting areas—Ante, Play, and Pair Plus. There are actually two games in one on a 3-Card Poker table—"Pair Plus" and "Ante and Play." You can play only the Pair Plus or only the Ante or both. You place your chips in the areas you want to bet in.

In Pair Plus, you are betting only on your hand, not competing against anyone else at the table or the dealer. If you get a pair or better, depending on your hand, the payoff can be pretty fab—straight flush: 40 to 1; three of a kind: 30 to 1; straight: 6 to 1; flush: 3 to 1; pair: 1 to 1.

In Ante and Play, you are betting that your hand will be better than the dealer's but are not competing against anyone else at the table. You place an Ante bet, view your cards, and then, if you decide you like your hand, you place a bet in the Play area equal to your Ante bet. If you get lousy cards and don't want to go forward, you can fold, losing only your Ante bet and your Pair Plus bet, if you made one. Once all bets are made, the dealer's hand is revealed—he or she must have at least a single queen for the bet to count; if not, your Ante and Play bets are returned. If you beat the dealer's hand, you get a 1 to 1 payoff, but there is a bonus for a particularly good winning hand: straight flush, 5 to 1; three of a kind, 4 to 1; straight, 1 to 1.

Your three cards are dealt. If you play only Pair Plus, it doesn't matter what the dealer has—you get paid if you have a pair or better. If you don't, you lose your bet. If you play the Ante bet, you must then either fold and lose the Ante bet or match the Ante bet by placing the same amount on the Play area. The dealer's hand is revealed, and payouts happen accordingly. Each hand consists of one fresh 52-card deck.

Meanwhile, as if all this weren't enough, new variations on table games keep popping up. The latest is Crazy 4 Poker—similar to 3-Card Poker, only with five cards dealt, no draw, make your best 4-card poker hand out of it.

ROULETTE

Roulette is an extremely easy game to play, and it's really quite colorful and exciting to watch. The wheel spins, and the little ball bounces around, finally dropping into one of the slots, numbered 1 to 36, plus 0 and 00. You can place bets "Inside" the table and "Outside" the table. Inside bets are bets placed on a particular number or a set of numbers. Outside bets are those placed in the boxes surrounding the number table. If you bet on a specific number and it comes up, you are paid 35 to 1 on your bet. Bear in mind, however, that the odds of a particular number coming up are actually 38 to 1 (don't forget the 0 and 00!), so the house has an advantage the moment you place an inside bet. The methods of placing single-number bets, column bets, and others are fairly obvious. The dealer will be happy to show you how to make many interesting betting combinations, such as betting on six numbers at once. Each player is given different-colored chips so that it's easy to follow the numbers you've bet on.

SLOTS

You put the coin in the slot and pull the handle. What, you thought there was a trick to this?

Actually, there is a bit more to it. But first, some background. Old-timers will tell you slots were invented to give wives something to do while their husbands gambled. Slots used to be stuck at the edges of the casino and could be counted on one hand, maybe two. But now they *are* the casino. The casinos make more from slots than from craps, blackjack, and roulette combined. There are more than 140,000 slot machines (not including video poker) in the county. Some of these are at the airport, steps from you as you deplane. It's just a matter of time before the planes flying into Vegas feature slots that pop up as soon as you cross the state line.

But to keep up with the increasing competition, the plain old machine, where reels just spin, has become nearly obsolete. Now they are all computerized and have added buttons to push so you can avoid getting carpal tunnel syndrome from yanking the handle all night (though the handles are still there on some of them). Many don't even have reels anymore but are entirely video screens, which offer a number of little bonus extras that have nothing to do with actual play. The idea is still simple: Get three (sometimes four) cherries (clowns, sevens, dinosaurs, whatever) in a row, and you win something. Each machine has its own combination. Some will pay you something with just one symbol showing; on most, the more combinations there are, the more opportunities for loot. Some will even pay if you get three blanks. Study each machine to learn what it does. *Note:* The **payback** goes up considerably if you bet the limit (from 2 to as many as 45 coins).

Progressive slots are groups of linked machines (sometimes spread over several casinos) where the jackpot gets bigger every few moments (just as lottery jackpots build up). Bigger and better games keep showing up; for example, there's Anchor Gaming's much-imitated **Wheel of Gold,** wherein if you get the right symbol, you get to spin a roulette wheel, which guarantees you a win of a serious number of coins. **Totem Pole** is the Godzilla of slot machines, a behemoth that allows you to spin up to three reels at once (provided you put in the limit).

Other gimmick machines include the popular **Wheel of Fortune** machines, slots that have a gorilla attempting to climb the Empire State Building, heading up as you win, and machines with such themes as Elvis or the Three Stooges. And, of course, there are always those **giant slot machines,** gimmicky devices found in almost every casino. They may not win as often as regular slots (though there is no definite word on it one way or the other), but not only are they just plain fun to spin, they also often turn into audience-participation gambling, as watchers gather to cheer you on to victory.

Players' Clubs

If you play slots or video poker, or, indeed, just gamble quite a bit, or even just gamble, it definitely pays to join a players' club. These so-called clubs are designed to attract and keep customers in a given casino by providing incentives: meals, shows, discounts on rooms, gifts, tournament invitations, discounts at hotel shops, VIP treatment, and (more and more) cash rebates. Join a players' club (it doesn't cost a cent to sign up), and soon you, too, will be getting those great hotel-rate offers—$20-a-night rooms, affordable rooms at the luxury resorts, even free rooms. This is one way to beat the high hotel rates. Of course, your rewards are often greater if you play just in one casino, but your mobility is limited.

When you join a players' club (inquire at the casino desk), you're given something that looks like a credit card, which you must insert into an ATM-like device whenever you play. Yes, many casinos even have them for the tables as well as the machines. The device tracks your play and computes bonus points. Don't forget, as we sometimes do, to retrieve your card when you leave the machine—though that may work in your favor if someone comes along and plays the machine without removing it.

Which players' club should you join? Actually, you should join one at any casino where you play because even the act of joining usually entitles you to some benefits. It's convenient to concentrate play where you're staying; if you play a great deal, a casino-hotel's players' club benefits may be a factor in your accommodations choice. Consider, though, particularly if you aren't a high roller, the players' clubs Downtown. You get more bang for your buck because you don't have to spend as much to start raking in the goodies.

Another advantage is to join a players' club that covers many hotels under the same corporate umbrella. Caesars Entertainment operates the Total Rewards club, which is good at any of their casinos in Vegas (Harrah's, Rio, Caesars Palace, The Flamingo, Paris Las Vegas, and Bally's) or elsewhere around the world. The same goes for casinos in the MGM MIRAGE stable (The Mirage, Bellagio, MGM Grand, TI–Treasure Island, Mandalay Bay, Luxor, Circus Circus, and Excalibur; www.playersclub.com), the locals' favorite Station Casinos (Palace, Sunset, Texas, and more), and the other interlinked properties, which include Arizona Charlie's and the Stratosphere Casino Hotel & Tower.

Choosing the best club(s) for you can be a complex business. To get into it in depth, see **www.lasvegasadvisor.com**. Also visit the sites for the individual casinos, many of which allow you to join their clubs online. Try it, and you might find yourself receiving discounts and freebies before you even set foot in Vegas.

Nickel slots, which for a long time had been overlooked, relegated to a lonely spot somewhere by a back wall because they were not as profitable for the casinos as quarter and dollar slots, have made a comeback. Many machines now offer a 45-nickel maximum (meaning a larger bet on those machines than on the five-quarter-maximum slots), and gamblers have been flocking to them. As a result, more cash is pocketed by the casino (which keeps a higher percentage of cash off of nickel slots than it does off of quarter slots), which is happy to accommodate this trend by offering up more and more nickel slots. See how this all works? Are you paying attention? Ultratightwads will be pleased by the increased presence of the humble penny slot, but few, if any, allow for only a penny bet—in fact, the maximum bet is $3!

The most recent prominent move in Las Vegas, though, is the use of cashless machines. Now when gambling, players insert their money, they play, and when they cash out, they get—instead of the clanging sound of coins cascading out into the tray—a little paper ticket with their total winnings on it. Those of us who find the sound of the coins pouring out a comfort are only slightly pleased to learn that the same noise plays, as a computer-generated audio effect, when the ticket is disgorged. Hand in your ticket at a cashier's window (or use the omnipresent ATM-style redemption machines), and you get your winnings. It's not nearly as viscerally satisfying, but the future is now. The casinos are all but entirely cashless. Why take this cheap thrill from us? Because it saves gambling time (instead of waiting for the flow of coins to stop, you can grab your ticket and pop it into another machine) and maintenance time (keeping the machines stocked with coins), and the casinos no longer need worry about having enough quarters on hand. We are not pleased about this. *Note:* As a result of cashless machine trend, the casinos are much quieter, as many of the formerly chatty machines have been largely silenced, and that famous Vegas clang-clang is somewhat dimmed.

Are there surefire ways to win on a slot machine? No. But you can lose more slowly. The slot machines use minicomputers known as random number generators (RNGs) to determine the winning combinations on a machine; depending on how many numbers have been programmed into the RNG, some machines are "looser" than others. A bank of empty slots probably (but not certainly) means the machines are tight. Go find a line where lots of people are sitting around with trays full of money. (Of course, yours will be the one that doesn't hit.) A good rule of thumb is that if your slot doesn't hit something in four or five pulls, leave it and go find another. It's not as though you won't have some choice in the matter. Also, each casino has a bank of slots that they advertise as more loose or with a bigger payback. Try these. It's what they want you to do, but what the heck.

Note: Many slot machines no longer accept coins at all for bets. For these new machines, bets have to start with bills accepted into special slots. This makes all but extinct the famous change carts that used to roam the floors, helping people get rolls of quarters and the like.

SPORTS BOOKS

Most of the larger hotels in Las Vegas have sports-book operations, which look a lot like commodities-futures trading boards. In some, almost as large as theaters, you can sit comfortably, occasionally in recliners and sometimes with your own video screen, and watch ball games, fights, and, at some casinos, horse races on huge TV screens. To add to your enjoyment, there's usually a deli/bar nearby that serves sandwiches, hot dogs, soft drinks, and beer. As a matter of fact, some of the best sandwiches in Las

Vegas are served next to the sports books. Sports books take bets on virtually every sport (and not just who'll win, but what the final score will be, who'll be first to hit a home run, who'll be MVP, who'll wear red shoes, you name it). They are best during important playoff games or big horse races, when everyone in the place is watching the same event—shrieking, shouting, and moaning, sometimes in unison. Joining in with a cheap bet (so you feel like you, too, have a personal stake in the matter) makes for bargain entertainment.

VIDEO POKER

Rapidly gaining on slots in popularity, video poker works the same way as regular poker, except you play against the machine. You are dealt a hand, you pick which cards to keep and which to discard, and then you get your new hand. And, it is hoped, you collect your winnings. This is somewhat more of a challenge and more active than slots because you have some control (or at least the illusion of control) over your fate, and it's easier than playing actual poker with a table full of folks who probably take it very seriously.

There are a number of varieties of this machine, including **Jacks or Better, Deuces Wild,** and so forth. Be sure to study your machine before you sit down. (The best returns are offered on the **Bonus Poker** machines; the payback for a pair of jacks or better is two times your bet, and three times for three of a kind.) The Holy Grail of video-poker machines is the 9/6 (it pays nine coins for a full house, six coins for a flush), but you'll need to pray a lot before you find one in town. Some machines offer **double down:** After you have won, you get a chance to draw cards against the machine, with the higher card the winner. If you win, your money is doubled, and you are offered a chance to go again. Your money can increase nicely during this time, and you can also lose it all very quickly, which is most annoying.

Technology is catching up with video poker, too. Now they even have touch screens, which offer a variety of different poker games, blackjack, and video slots—just touch your screen and choose your poison.

3 The Casinos

Casino choice is a personal thing. Some like to find their lucky place and stick with it, while others love to take advantage of the nearly endless choices that Las Vegas offers. Everyone should casino-hop at least once to marvel (or get dizzy) at the decor/spectacle and the sheer excess of it all. But beyond decoration, there isn't too much difference between the different venues. You've got your slot machines, your gaming tables, and your big chandeliers.

Virtually all casinos make sure they have no clocks or windows—they do not want you to interrupt your losing streak by realizing how much time has passed. Of course, we've all heard the legend that Las Vegas casinos pump in fresh oxygen to keep the players from getting tired and wanting to pack it in. The veracity of this is hard to confirm, but we can only hope it's true, especially when we think of that time we looked up after a long stretch of gambling and discovered it was Thursday.

Don't be a snob, and don't be overly dazzled by the fancy casinos. Sometimes you can have a better time at one of the older places Downtown, where stakes are lower, pretensions are nonexistent, and the clientele is often friendlier. Frankly, real gamblers—and by that we don't necessarily mean high rollers, but those who play to win, regardless of the amount of said win—head straight for Downtown (and most often, straight for Binion's) for these precise reasons, caring not a whit about glitz and glamour. Even if you don't take your gambling as seriously as that, you may well want to follow their example. After all, it's getting harder and harder to find cheap tables (where you can play a hand of blackjack, for example, for less than $10) on the Strip—so take your hard-earned money to where you can lose it more slowly!

We would also call your attention to less glamorous, less readily accessible casinos, such as local favorites Sunset Station, Texas Station, the Cannery, Fiesta Rancho, Fiesta Henderson, and Fiesta Santa Fe, where payoffs are often higher than on the Strip, and the limits are lower.

You can expect to find in every casino the usual and expected assortment of games—slot machines, of course, video poker, blackjack, table poker (making a big comeback after years of decline), a race and sports book, a keno lounge, a poker room, baccarat, minibaccarat, Caribbean Stud, Let It Ride, craps, roulette, Pai Gow, and more, more, more. If you want a particular game, and it's not one of the most obvious, you might want to call before heading over to a particular casino, just to make sure.

What follows is a description of most of the major casinos in Vegas, including their level of claustrophobia, and a completely arbitrary assessment based on whether we won there.

SOUTH STRIP

Excalibur   As you might expect, the Excalibur casino is replete with suits of armor, stained-glass panels, knights, dragons, and velvet and satin heraldic banners, with gaming action taking place beneath vast iron-and-gold chandeliers fit for a medieval castle fortress. This all makes it fine for kitsch-seekers, but anyone who hates crowds or is sensitive to noise will hate it. The overall effect is less like a castle than like a dungeon. One of us won a lot of money here and refused to share it with the other, so our final judgment about the casino is, well, mixed. Excalibur is part of the MGM MIRAGE Players Club, which is also used at MGM Grand, The Mirage, TI–Treasure Island, Bellagio, Luxor, Mandalay Bay, Circus Circus, and others (www.playersclub.com). 3850 Las Vegas Blvd. S. ℂ **702/597-7777**. www.excalibur.com.

Luxor Las Vegas   The good news: more accessible than you might think, thanks to the air-conditioned people-mover from Excalibur and the monorail from Mandalay Bay. The bad news: Luxor has been systematically stripping away anything Egypt about the place. The result—a casino that looks like all the other casinos in town. Bring back the talking camels and Tut! The casino did get a remodel that removed the space-wasting central area that used to contain the bathrooms, cashiers, and casino offices. This additional space gives the casino a much more airy feel, which produces a low claustrophobia level—in parts of the place, you can see all the way up the inside of the pyramid. There is also a casino lounge called Aurora that is very nice. The MGM MIRAGE Players Club offers rewards of cash, merchandise, meals, and special

---

Impressions

Tip Number 3: Win a bunch of money. I can't recommend this too highly. If it hasn't occurred to you, win $1,200 and see for yourself. It's very energizing and really adds to your Vegas fun.

—Merrill Markoe, *Viva Las Wine Goddesses!*

services to slot and table players. Sports action unfolds on 17 large-screen TVs and 128 personalized monitors in Luxor's race and sports book. We felt inclined to like this casino, thanks to a good run at blackjack, but we are most cranky about the de-Egypt-ification process. 3900 Las Vegas Blvd. S. ℂ 702/262-4000. www.luxor.com.

Mandalay Bay You'll find "elegant" gaming in a pre-fab, deliberate way, with a very high ceiling that produces a very low claustrophobia factor. This is definitely the right place to gamble if you're looking for less hectic, less gimmick-filled play. The layout makes it look airy, and it's marginally less confusing and certainly less overwhelming than many other casinos. Because it is so far down the Strip, there are fewer walk-in players, but the presence of the House of Blues and the increasing popularity of the **rumjungle nightclub** can mean a late-night influx of customers. There's a big, ultracomfortable sports-book area (complete with armchairs that could well encourage a relaxed gambler to fall asleep), including a live daily sports-radio show. Players can sign up for the MGM MIRAGE Players Club (www.playersclub.com). 3950 Las Vegas Blvd. S. ℂ 702/632-7777. www.mandalaybay.com.

MGM Grand Las Vegas's largest casino (171,500 sq. ft.)—we've been to countries that were smaller!—is divided into four areas, in a futile attempt to make it seem smaller. Most of the *Wizard of Oz* decorations have been removed, but spend an hour in here, and you may feel like Dorothy after she was whisked away by the twister. You will get lost at least once. One section features a high-roller slot area with machines that operate on coins valued at $100 and $500! The sports casino houses a big poker room, a state-of-the-art race and sports book with private luxury sky boxes, and the Turf Club Lounge. Carousels of progressive slots unique to the MGM Grand include the very popular Majestic Lions high-frequency $1 slot machines, which pay out more than $1 million daily, and the Lion's Share $1 slots, which are capable of jackpots exceeding $1 million each at any time. This hotel takes part in the MGM MIRAGE Players Club. 3799 Las Vegas Blvd. S. ℂ 702/891-7777. www.mgmgrand.com.

Monte Carlo Resort & Casino This place is all huge ceilings and white-light interior: Obviously, they're trying to evoke gambling in Monaco. While the decor shows lots of attention, it perhaps had too much attention. Bulbs line the ceiling, and everywhere you look is some detail or other. It's busy on both your eyes and your ears. So despite the effort put in, it's not a pleasant place to gamble. However, there is a large and comfortable race and sports-book area, with its own cocktail lounge. This casino takes part in the MGM MIRAGE Players Club system. 3770 Las Vegas Blvd. S. ℂ 702/730-7777. www.montecarlo.com.

New York–New York Another theme-run-wild place: tuxes on the backs of gaming chairs and so forth, all set in a miniature New York City. It's all fabulous fun, but despite a low claustrophobia level (thanks to an unusually high ceiling), it is a major case of sensory overload. This may prove distracting. On the other hand, we won repeatedly here, so we love it. And in places, it is, if one can say this about anything in Vegas with a straight face, quite beautiful—or at least dazzling. Serious gamblers understandably may sniff at it all and prefer to take their business to a more seemly casino, but everyone else should have about the most Vegasy time they can. New York–New York participates in the MGM MIRAGE Players Club. 3790 Las Vegas Blvd. S. ℂ 702/740-6969. www.nynyhotelcasino.com.

Orleans This is not a particularly special gambling space, though it does have a low claustrophobia level. Another plus is that they sometimes play Cajun and zydeco

Memories of a Longtime Dealer

Lou has been a part of the gaming industry for over 40 years, the first 20 of which he spent as a dealer in Las Vegas.

"My favorite places were The Flamingo, the Sands, and the Desert Inn. That's when the corporations weren't there. That's when the other folks were in. The mob guys—I never knew it, but that's what they were. I was just a kid. Bugsy had just gotten killed when I went to work at The Flamingo. The Sands was my very first favorite. That was the hotel of all hotels. They had the very best management team. They took care of their help. Their benefits were better than any union. It was the place.

"Years ago, you had great entertainment. You could go to a lounge and catch better acts than in the showroom. Major stars were in the lounges, or they would come in and sit in with the acts after the showroom closed. Don Rickles: Sinatra would get up with him once in a while. Sinatra gave me my first $100 tip. He was playing blackjack. Then he said, 'Do you want to play it or keep it?' I wanted to be polite, so I said, 'Bet it.' And he lost. In those days when the stars would appear on stage, between shows they would come out into the casinos. Sinatra and Sammy would deal. They would blow money, but the casinos didn't care. It was a fun, fun place.

"The casinos were run the way they were supposed to be run—for the customer, not so corporate-minded. In those days, you could go to Vegas, get your room very reasonable, your food was practically free, your shows were practically free, you would spend $500 in the casino, but you would come back and be happy because gaming was a form of entertainment. When they ran the casinos, you would have a ball, come home, and be happy. They were very happy if the restaurants and shows lost money—you still lost that $500. Now it would cost you $100 to stay at a hotel, and food

music over the sound system, so you can two-step while you gamble, which can make losing somewhat less painful. It has all the needed tables—blackjack, craps, and so forth—plus plenty of slots, including the popular Wheel of Fortune machine, which works like those other roulette-wheel slots, but in this case, actually plays the theme song from the TV show. It even applauds for you if you win. Since Orleans is popular with locals, there are lots of video-poker options. And because it's not on the Strip, you'll find better odds for craps and cheaper table minimums. Their players' club card (www.clubcoast.com) gains you points at all Coast Casinos, such as Gold Coast, Suncoast, and others, and may be linked in the future to new corporate owner Boyd Casinos at places such as the Main Street Station. 4500 W. Tropicana Ave. ℂ **702/365-7111.** www.orleanscasino.com.

Tropicana   It's not quite as good-looking as it once was, but it's highly tropical, with gaming tables situated beneath a massive stained-glass archway and Art Nouveau lighting fixtures. In summer, it offers something totally unique: swim-up blackjack tables located in the hotel's 5-acre tropical garden and pool area. Slot and table-game players can earn bonus points toward rooms, shows, and meals by obtaining a Tropicana is much more expensive, and to get a ticket to one of these shows is ridiculous. Now you gamble only $150 and you aren't as happy when you come home because you don't feel like you've been treated to anything. It all goes into the same pocket—what difference does it make? It gives the customer the same hours and more fun. They don't understand that. It's not the same industry as when they ran it. And it shows."

LOU THE DEALER'S GAMING TIPS

If you are a **craps** shooter, just look around at the tables where they have the most chips. Find the guy with the most chips, and do what he does. Follow him along.

For **blackjack,** everybody will tell you in all your books to try to play single and double decks. I don't agree with that, and I never will. The average player goes in to enjoy himself and to win a few dollars. So he is not a professional card counter. Play a shoe. If that shoe is going bad and you catch a run, you will make a lot more money than with a single deck.

Look at gaming as a form of entertainment. Look at that $100 that you might have spent on dinner or a club, where we laughed and had a few drinks and had a good time. Think of it that way.

If you double your money, quit. Not quit gambling, but quit that table. Go have a sandwich or watch a show. And *then* come back. The odds aren't that tremendously in favor of the casinos. How they make their money is through greed; gamblers doubling their money then trying to quadruple it and losing it all, and more.

Try to survive. Don't try to win the hotel. Just try to win a few dollars. Then stop and enjoy it.

Winners Club card in the casino. A luxurious high-end slot area has machines that take up to $100 on a single pull. Numerous tournaments take place here, and free gaming lessons are offered weekdays. *Note:* Because of the plans to completely renovate the Trop, the casino may be altered or under construction during your stay. 3801 Las Vegas Blvd. S. (C) 702/739-2222. www.tropicanalv.com.

MID-STRIP

Bally's Las Vegas   Bally's casino is large (the size of a football field), with lots of colorful signage. The big ceiling makes for a low claustrophobia level. The casino hosts frequent slot tournaments and offers free gaming lessons. Their Total Rewards players' club is valid at sister properties such as Harrah's, Caesars, Paris Las Vegas, and others, offering members cash rebates, room discounts, free meals and show tickets, and invitations to special events, among other perks. 3645 Las Vegas Blvd. S. (C) 702/739-4111. www.ballys.com.

Bellagio   The slot machines here are mostly encased in marble and fine woods. How's that for upping the ante on classy? Bellagio comes the closest to re-creating the feel of gambling in Monte Carlo (the country, not the next-door casino), but its relentless good taste means that this is one pretty forgettable casino. After all, we are suckers for a wacky theme that screams "Vegas," and European class just doesn't cut it. Then again, we brought a pal of more refined sensibility, and she adored it, finding it the perfect antidote to New York–New York. Sure, there are good touches—we always like a high ceiling to reduce the claustrophobia index, and the place is laid out in an easy-to-navigate grid with ultrawide aisles, so walking through doesn't seem like such a crowded collision-course maze. (*Tip:* The main casino path is identified with black carpets.) And we won big here, so there's that. Anyway, the cozy sports book has individual TVs and entirely denlike leather chairs—quite, quite comfortable. Bellagio is part of the MGM MIRAGE Players Club. 3600 Las Vegas Blvd. S. © 888/987-6667. www.bellagio.com.

Bill's Gamblin' Hall & Saloon   Bill's Gamblin' Hall & Saloon is an 1890s-style casino ornately decorated with $2 million worth of gorgeous stained-glass skylights and signs, as well as immense crystal-dangling globe chandeliers over the gaming tables. It's kind of small, dark, and cluttered, but it's also Old Las Vegas (and we mean "old" loosely), and small is rare on the Strip. The casino is now part of Harrah's and is tied into their players' club. 3595 Las Vegas Blvd. S. © 702/737-7111. www.billslasvegas.com.

Caesars Palace   The Caesars casino is simultaneously the ultimate in gambling luxury and the ultimate in Vegas kitsch. Cocktail waitresses in very short togas parade about as you gamble under the watchful gaze of faux-marble Roman statues. The very high ceiling in certain newer areas of the casino makes for a very low claustrophobia level. Unfortunately, some spots in the casino are still dark and entirely too claustrophobic. Although we love it, the casino has become somewhat confusing and unmanageable because of its size and meandering layout, like Caesars itself. The new Pussycat Dolls section (Tues and Fri–Sun 9pm–5am) features hot-pink and black leather tables, nubile dealers dressed in the Dolls' signature scanties, and dancers in cages above, all the better to help you concentrate on your game. Given that table limits start at $50, this could really be an issue.

A notable facility is the state-of-the-art race and sports book, with huge electronic display boards and giant video screens. Caesars pioneered computer-generated wagering data that can be communicated in less than half a second, and it has sophisticated satellite equipment that can pick up the broadcast of virtually any sporting event in the world. It's quite comfortable, but is located right by the line of foot traffic. The domed VIP slot arena of the Forum Casino (minimum bet is $5, but you can wager up to $1,500 on a single pull!) is a plush, crystal-chandeliered precinct with seating in roomy, adjustable chairs. They also have the largest poker room in the city. Gamblers can accumulate bonus points toward cash back, gifts, gratis show tickets, meals, and rooms by joining the Total Rewards players' club. Club membership also lets you in on grand-prize drawings, tournaments, and parties. The most upscale of the Caesars gaming rooms is the intimate, European-style casino adjoining the Palace Court restaurant. It's a gorgeous and elegant place to gamble, but we've never won there, so we hate it. 3570 Las Vegas Blvd. S. © 702/731-7110. www.harrahs.com.

Flamingo Las Vegas   If you've seen the movie *Bugsy,* you won't recognize this as Mr. Siegel's baby. We can't say for sure what the seemingly years-long casino renovation actually did. It all looks pretty much the same as it used to, but it might be marginally less confusing and tortuous a layout (trust us, anything is an improvement), with better, and most welcome, access to the street (before, you needed a trail of bread crumbs and a lot of stamina to find your way out). Still, the claustrophobia factor is moderately high, thanks to a still-low ceiling with electric bulbs and pink neon everywhere. It's old school and retro in the unintentional (that is to say, authentic) way, which means it looks tired compared to the fancy high-class operations across the street. But while it's uncoordinated and gaudy, it's also not threateningly chic or chilly or overrun with Paris Hilton wannabes. So there's something to be said for old school. We have to say that of all the casinos that qualify as older, this is the most pleasant one in which to play. Unfortunately, the gambler seems to be paying for it—no more daytime $3 blackjack. The Flamingo takes part in the Total Rewards players' club. 3555 Las Vegas Blvd. S. ✆ 702/733-3111. www.flamingolasvegas.com.

Gold Coast   Adjacent to the Rio, this casino is not only well lit but also totally unique in Vegas: It has windows! It's a little thing, but it made us really excited. They also have a higher ratio of video-poker machines to slot machines, rather than the other way around. A remodeling made it much bigger, with high ceilings, and it's very bright overall. Nice job. The casino and the players' club (www.clubcoast.com) are tied to other Coast properties, such as Orleans and Barbary Coast, and may eventually be linked to new corporate owner Boyd Casinos at such places as Stardust and Main Street Station. 4000 W. Flamingo Rd. ✆ 702/367-7111. www.goldcoastcasino.com.

Harrah's   This is a mixed bag of a casino, one that is both dated (low ceilings, old lighting, stuffy) and fun (parts have high-enough ceilings, and there are special attractions). It's also super crowded, noisy, flashy, and claustrophobic. At night, the popular party pit (allegedly fun dealers, rowdy music) packs them in, but the entire place gets crowded by the end of the day. Slot and table-game players can earn bonus points toward complimentary rooms, meals, and show tickets by joining Harrah's Total Rewards players' club in the casino. Free gaming lessons are offered on weekdays. 3475 Las Vegas Blvd. S. ✆ 702/369-5000. www.harrahs.com.

The Mirage   The Mirage is more inviting than in its chaotic past, thanks to a design switch from heavy tropics to more soothing Asian wood accents. But it's still twisting and meandering, and the relatively low ceiling is still a medium claustrophobia issue. This remains one of our favorite places to gamble. Facilities include a plush European-style *salon privé* for high rollers at baccarat, blackjack, and roulette; an elegant dining room serves catered meals to gamblers there. Slot and table players can join the MGM MIRAGE Players Club and work toward bonus points for cash rebates, special room rates, complimentary meals and/or show tickets, and other benefits. The elaborate race and sports book offers theater stereo sound and a movie theater–size screen. It's one of the most pleasant and popular casinos in town, so it's crowded more often than not. 3400 Las Vegas Blvd. S. ✆ 702/791-7111. www.mirage.com.

The Palazzo   This brand new casino is so lacking in distinguishing features that when it came time to write it up, we couldn't remember if The Palazzo even *had* a casino. See the review below for the one at the adjoining Venetian and just lather, rinse, and repeat. Sure it's big and grand, but it's also beige and bland. Signage is just as confusing as over at The Venetian. Slots are almost all multi-payline video screen rather than the traditional single-payline model, which is disappointing. The sports book is located on a different level, and unlike others does not have seats—instead you go into the adjoining club/bar, 40/40 (owned in part by Jay Z), where there are any number of couches and the like for sprawling, and flatscreens for following the action. At night this area becomes a hip-hop club. If you want a traditional sports book, you are better off going elsewhere. 3335 Las Vegas Blvd St. ✆ 866/263-3001. www.palazzolasvegas.com.

Palms Resort & Casino   Here's where this desperately-seeking-the-hip hotel has a bit of an identity crisis, because it also wants to be a place where locals feel comfortable gambling. You know, like Palace and Texas Station. Huh? That's right, the Palms wants to mirror those hotels off the Strip that offer loose slots and other incentives to make the locals feel at home. This rarely makes for a chic playing area (because locals don't want to have to get glammed up to go out and play some slots). On the other hand, the area is—especially on weekend nights—ringed with the beautiful and slender and aloof, desperate to get into ghostbar and Rain. If they aren't inside, they are surly about it. Let's hope everyone just keeps getting along. It's actually a pretty fun place to play, so something works. The gaming area covers most of the ground floor and is replete with Miami tropical–inspired details. 4321 W. Flamingo Rd. ⓒ 702/942-7777. www.palms.com.

Paris Las Vegas Casino   Surrounded by a rather Disney-esque one-third-scale replica of the streets of Paris, this 83,000-square-foot casino is a very pleasant place to gamble, in that Vegas-gimmick kind of way. It's one of those kitschy places that "real" gamblers are appalled by. To heck with them, we say. A tall ceiling gives the illusion that you are trying to bust the bank while strolling outside and results in an airy effect. The place doesn't feel all that large, thanks to its layout. It has more than 2,000 slot machines and more than 100 table games. A state-of-the-art race and sports book features live satellite feeds of sporting events from around the world. The Paris is part of Harrah's Total Rewards players' club. 3655 Las Vegas Blvd. S. ⓒ 702/946-7000. www.harrahs.com.

Planet Hollywood   A top-to-bottom remodel of the former Aladdin has newly classed this place up with nary a hint of its former identity. The interior is impressive, classic Hollywood glamour, with plenty of curving lines and dramatic folderol on columns and the like. In sharp contrast to the chaotic entrance, the interior is actually much calmer than it used to be. Check out the imaginative slot toppers, which usually proclaim "Double Diamond." All the usual casino suspects are still around, including thousands of slots, video-poker machines, plenty of table games, a high-limit salon, a poker room, and more. The sports book serves food by Pink's, the famous L.A. hot dog stand, and you need not gamble there in order to nosh. 3667 Las Vegas Blvd. S. ⓒ 702/736-0111. www.aladdincasino.com.

Rio All-Suite Hotel & Casino   This Brazilian-themed resort's 85,000-square-foot casino is, despite the presence of plenty of glitter and neon, very dark. It has about the highest claustrophobia rating of the major casinos and seems very dated these days. Its sports book feels a little grimy. The waitresses wear scanty costumes (particularly in the back), probably in an effort to distract you and throw your game off (all the more so now that they are adding "Bev-entertainment"—those poor waitresses are required to burst into song and/or dance while delivering beer). Do not let them. The part of the casino in the Masquerade Village is considerably more pleasant (the very high ceilings help), though still crowded, and the loud live show here adds even more noise. In the high-end slot area ($5–$100 a pull), guests enjoy a private lounge and gratis champagne. There are nonsmoking slot and gaming table areas. The Rio participates in the Harrah's Total Rewards players' club. 3700 W. Flamingo Rd. ⓒ 702/252-7777. www.harrahs.com.

TI–Treasure Island   We really loved it when this place was a casino set in Disneyland's Pirates of the Caribbean—or so it seemed. It doesn't seem like a big deal, the loss of those pirate chests dripping gold, jewels, and skulls with eye patches, but with the removal of the theme, this is now just a very nice casino. But it is that, so you should come here. There are nonsmoking gaming tables in each pit. A race and sports book boasts state-of-the-art electronic information boards and TV monitors at every seat, as well as numerous large-screen monitors. MGM MIRAGE Players Club members can earn points toward meals, services, show tickets, and cash rebates. 3300 Las Vegas Blvd. S. ℂ 702/894-7111. www.treasureisland.com.

The Venetian "Tasteful" is the watchword in these days of classy Vegas gaming, and consequently, with the exception of more hand-painted Venetian art re-creations on parts of the ceiling, The Venetian's casino is interchangeable with those found at Mandalay Bay, the Monte Carlo, and, to a certain extent, Bellagio. All that gleaming marble, columns, and such is very nice, but after a while, it's also a bit ho-hum. Besides, this is Vegas, and we want our tacky theme elements, by gosh. The lack thereof, combined with poor signage, may be why this casino is so hard to get around—every part looks exactly the same as every other part. It's not exactly claustrophobic, but it can be confusing. On the other hand, we made a killing at blackjack, and one of our editors struck it rich at the slots, so we have to love the place for those reasons. Another (less personal) plus is that you can access the casino directly from the St. Mark's Square re-creation out front. The smoke-sensitive report that the ventilation system here is tops. 3355 Las Vegas Blvd. S. ℂ 702/414-1000. www.venetian.com.

NORTH STRIP

Circus Circus This vast property has three full-size casinos that, combined, comprise one of the largest gaming operations in Nevada (more than 100,000 sq. ft.). More important, they have an entire circus midway set up throughout, so you are literally gambling with trapeze stunts going on over your head. The other great gimmick is the slot machine carousel—yep, it turns while you spin the reels. The Circus Bucks progressive slot machines here build from a jackpot base of $500,000, which players can win on a $2 pull. Gaming facilities include a 10,000-square-foot race and sports book with 30 video monitors ranging from 13 to 52 inches, and 40-seat and 89-seat keno lounges. Circus Circus participates in the MGM MIRAGE Players Club. Unfortunately, the casino is crowded and noisy, and there are lots of children passing through (making it more crowded and noisy). That, plus some low ceilings (not in the Big Top, obviously), makes for a very high claustrophobia rating, though the current commedia dell'arte clown motif (as opposed to the old garish circus motif) has upgraded the decor. 2880 Las Vegas Blvd. S. ℂ 702/734-0410. www.circuscircus.com.

The Riviera The Riviera's 100,000-square-foot casino, once one of the largest in the world, offers plenty of opportunities to get lost and cranky. Especially if you, as one of us recently did, lose all your recent blackjack winnings at a table here. (What? Like you have fond memories of places where you've dropped a bundle?) A wall of windows lets daylight stream in (most unusual), but as the hotel gets shabbier, every inch of the casino smells like smoke and age. The casino's players' clubs allow slot players to earn bonus points toward free meals, rooms, and show tickets. Nickeltown is just that—nothin' but nickel slots and video poker. The race and sports book here offers individual monitors at each of its 250 seats. 2901 Las Vegas Blvd. S. ℂ 702/734-5110. www.rivierahotel.com.

Sahara This is one place where there seem to be more tables than slots and video-poker machines. On a recent visit, the high ceilings and the unexpected *Arabian Nights* touches over the tables were nicer than we remembered from previous visits (maybe it all got dusted), and we made a killing at blackjack, so now we love this place again. (What? We told you it was entirely arbitrary!) Still, plans to morph the Sahara into something more like the Palms can only be a good move. The Sahara runs frequent slot tournaments and other events, and its slot club, Club Sahara, offers cash rebates and other perks. 2535 Las Vegas Blvd. S. ⓒ 702/737-2111. www.saharavegas.com.

Stratosphere Casino Hotel & Tower   Originally set up to evoke a world's fair but ending up more like a circus, Stratosphere redid its entire casino area to make it more appealing to the many adults who were staying away in droves. This should lure many of you because it is a nicer, and less crowded, place to play. They heavily advertise their good odds: single deck blackjack, single-zero roulette, and 10-times odds on craps. We can't say we noticed a difference, but other people around us were winning like crazy. The Ultimate Rewards players' club sponsors frequent tournaments, and its members can earn points toward gifts, VIP perks, discounted room rates, meals, and cash rebates—just a bit of play here, and you may be getting more free-room offers than you know what to do with. 2000 Las Vegas Blvd. S. ⓒ 702/380-7777. www.stratospherehotel.com.

Wynn Las Vegas   Sprawling off the registration and conservatory/atrium/garden walkway, this looks like every other casino in a good-taste Vegas hotel (but most notably like Bellagio's, down to the little shade canopies over the tables, though without the marble on the side of the slot machines. Pity. We like that fancy touch.), and thus is instantly forgettable. Excessive geometric detailing on the ceiling gives it the illusion of lower height and so delivers a medium-high claustrophobia rating. It's also perhaps the quietest of the major casinos, which is kind of a good thing. Since this is a Grown-Up Place, playfulness is mostly missing, though we did overhear at least one slap-happy craps dealer exhorting his customers in a party-hearty way. All the games you could want, plus a poker room and the rest, are here, though good luck finding a blackjack table under $15 a hand. And we aren't just saying that because we remain bitter about that losing streak at blackjack. 3131 Las Vegas Blvd. S. ⓒ 702/770-7700. www.wynnlasvegas.com.

EAST OF THE STRIP

Casino MonteLāgo   We are including this casino in case you find yourself staying in Lake Las Vegas (it's the only casino near the Ritz) or simply in the neighborhood, admiring the lake, or eating at the Ritz (all excellent uses of your time). It's only half the size of Strip casinos, but with exposed wood beams and stonework (in keeping with the location's Italian village theme, it's meant to evoke a 17th-century Tuscan winery; PR stuff like that makes us laugh), it has its own style. The very high ceiling gives this an especially low claustrophobia rating, and overall, the absence of neon-light madness continues to support the belief that this general area is for grown-ups. Also, we won a truckload of money here twice, so you know we might be a tad biased. There are all the latest slots and video poker, plus the usual mainstay tables, staffed by a sometimes friendly, sometimes surly staff. 8 Strada di Villaggio, Henderson. ⓒ 702/939-8888. www.casinomontelago.com.

Green Valley Ranch Resort   It's probably too far for the average traveler to drive—after all, when there is a casino just steps (or floors) away from your hotel room (and between you and anywhere in the world apart from your hotel room), to say nothing of several dozen more within a few blocks of your hotel room, you may be disinclined to drive out to one that is isolated from many other decent casinos. But given that this is a swank resort (or at least, trying to be); that it's smallish and elegant; that it's got a happening, decadent bar with girls prancing in go-go boots right in the center; and that more bars attracting the young and beautiful and well-heeled are opening here, you might want to make a visit, just to see the scene. And they have penny slots. 2300 Paseo Verde Dr. (at I-215), Henderson. ⓒ 702/617-7777. www.greenvalleyranch resort.com.

Hard Rock Hotel & Casino   The Hard Rock certainly took casino decor to an entirely new level. The attention to detail and the resulting playfulness is admirable, if not incredible. Gaming tables have piano keyboards at one end, some slots have Fender guitar fret boards as arms, gaming chips have band names and/or pictures on them, slot machines are similarly rock-themed (check out the Jimi Hendrix machine!), and so it goes. The entire thing is set in the middle of a circular room, around the outskirts of which is rock memorabilia in glass cases. Rock blares over the sound system, allowing boomers to boogie while they gamble. Plans to greatly expand the casino (by taking over the space formerly occupied by The Joint) are way overdue, given the relatively small space.

A Back Stage Pass allows patrons to rack up discounts on meals, lodging, and gift-shop items while playing slots and table games. The race and sports book here provides comfortable seating in leather-upholstered reclining armchairs. All this is genuinely amazing, but the noise level is above even that of a normal casino, and we just hated it. We are in the minority, though; most people love it, so assume you will be one of them. 4455 Paradise Rd. © 702/693-5000. www.hardrockhotel.com.

Las Vegas Hilton   In an area designed to look like a spaceport, you find space-themed slot machines, many of which have no handles—just pass your hand through a light beam to activate. You'll find other gimmicks throughout the casino (though already some have been dropped since the opening), including urinals that give you an instant "urinalysis"—usually suggesting this is your lucky day to gamble. We do like a well-designed space in which to lose our money.

Over in the original casino section, a makeover has given the place a much more modern and polished feel, although you'll be happy to note they kept the trademark Austrian-crystal chandeliers, which still add a strong touch of class. The casino is actually medium-size, but it does have an enormous sports book—at 30,500 square feet, it's the world's largest race and sports book facility. It, too, is a luxurious precinct equipped with the most advanced audio, video, and computer technology available, including 60 TV monitors, some as large as 15 feet across. In fact, its video wall is second in size only to NASA's. The casino is adjacent to the lobby but is neither especially loud nor frantic. Especially plush is the vast 6,900-square-foot baccarat room—with gorgeous crystal chandeliers, silk-covered walls, and velvet-upholstered furnishings—and the VIP slot area where personnel are attired in tuxedos. Both areas offer gracious service to players. 3000 Paradise Rd. © 702/732-7111. www.lvhilton.com.

Sam's Town   On its two immense floors of gaming action (over 153,000 sq. ft., second only to the MGM Grand in size), Sam's Town maintains the friendly, just-folks ambience that characterizes the entire property. The casino is adorned with Old West paraphernalia (horseshoes, Winchester rifles, holsters, and saddlebags) and is looking a bit less dated, thanks to some recent sprucing up (it's subtle, but believe us, it's better). Sam's Town claims its friendliness extends to looser slots. Join the Sam's Town Prime Rewards players' club to earn points toward rooms, meals, and cash rebates. Free gaming lessons are offered weekdays from 11am to 4pm, with poker lessons at other times. 5111 Boulder Hwy. (at Nellis Blvd.). © 702/456-7777. www.samstownlv.com.

WEST OF THE STRIP

Red Rock Resort   A bit of a distance to travel just for gambling but perhaps worth it because for sheer design, this is the best-looking casino in town. It utilizes natural woods, glass ornaments, and stone. As with the rest of the resort, it's a stunner. It's also a convivial place to play, but our good wins at blackjack probably had very little to do with that.

Not only does Red Rock have traditional gaming tables, slots (from penny slots to high-roller $100 pulls!), a race and sports book, and a 24-hour Poker Room, it also has Bingo. Jumbo Bingo! Part of Station Casinos players' club, Red Rock participates in JUMBO games, including the aforementioned Jumbo Bingo, Jumbo Keno, Jumbo Race, Jumbo Hold 'em, Jumbo Pennies, and Jumbo Jackpot. 10973 W. Charleston Blvd. ✆ 702/797-7625. www.redrockstation.com.

DOWNTOWN

Binion's *(Finds* Binion's has had quite the ride lately. Here's the back story: Professionals in the know say that "for the serious player, the Binions are this town." Benny Binion could neither read nor write, but, boy, did he know how to run a casino. His venerable establishment has been eclipsed over the years, but it claims the highest betting limits in Las Vegas on all games (probably in the entire world, according to a spokesperson). Unfortunately, its last couple of years read like a Vegas soap opera—you know, in-family fighting, murder of one scion at the (alleged) hands of his stripper girlfriend, another taking out many of the elements that made Binion's famous, and the whole thing getting shuttered in early 2004, thanks to nonpayment of bills. To everyone's relief, after 3 months, the casino reopened, thanks to the then dual owners, one of which was Harrah's, which managed it for a year before running off with the Horseshoe name (and rumors are running wild over what that might one day mean, including speculation that they will build a new "Harrah's Horseshoe" on the spot currently occupied by Bally's) and the rights to Binion's famous World Series of Poker, which was moved to the Rio in 2005. Binion's has since changed hands twice more; the current owners were behind the very nice makeover for the Four Queens, so they clearly get classic Vegas. Let's hope they bring the old man back to great glory.

Until that happens, here's what to expect: Binion's has about 400 fewer slot machines than it used to, in an effort to improve flow, and some parts got painted, so it looks less dingy (but still like an Old West bordello), but it remains otherwise essentially the same. That includes the relatively high claustrophobia level. It offers single-deck blackjack and low minimums, 10-times odds on craps, and high progressive jackpots. Real gamblers still won't consider going anywhere else. 128 E. Fremont St. (btw. Casino Center Blvd. and 1st St.). ✆ 702/382-1600. www.binions.com.

California Hotel & Casino   The California is a festive place filled with Hawaiian shirts and balloons. This friendly facility actually provides sofas and armchairs in the casino area—an unheard-of luxury in this town. Players can join the Players Gold club (which is also good at Main Street Station and the Fremont Hotel & Casino) and amass points toward gifts and cash prizes, or participate in daily slot tournaments. 12 Ogden Ave. (at 1st St.). ✆ 702/385-1222. www.thecal.com.

El Cortez   One of the last shreds of pre-1980s Las Vegas, this old gal just got a fantastic new face-lift, with an appeal based less on kitsch and more natural. By removing half the slot machines, the casino has been opened up and aired out. Plus, they gave it more contemporary decor. And local legend Jackie Gaughin (who lives in the penthouse) wanders through at least once a day. It features frequent big-prize drawings and special events designed to bring the locals in. It's also popular for low limits (10¢ roulette and 25¢ craps). 600 Fremont St. (btw. 6th and 7th sts.). ✆ 702/385-5200. www. elcortezhotelcasino.com.

The World Series, Las Vegas Style

Binion's was internationally known as the home of the **World Series of Poker.** "Nick the Greek" Dondolos first approached Benny Binion in 1949 with the idea for a high-stakes poker marathon between top players. Binion agreed, with the stipulation that the game be open to public viewing. The competition, between Dondolos and the legendary Johnny Moss, lasted 5 months, with breaks only for sleep. Moss ultimately won about $2 million. As Dondolos lost his last pot, he rose from his chair, bowed politely, and said, "Mr. Moss, I have to let you go."

In 1970, Binion decided to re-create the battle of poker giants, which evolved into the annual World Series of Poker. Johnny Moss won the first year and went on to snag the championship again in 1971 and 1974. Thomas "Amarillo Slim" Preston won the event in 1972 and popularized it on the talk-show circuit. In 2002, there were more than 7,595 entrants from over 22 countries, each ponying up the $10,000 entrance fee, and total winnings were in excess of $19 million (the tournament was also televised on ESPN). During one memorable year, the participants included actors Matt Damon and Edward Norton, fresh from *Rounders,* a movie in which they played a couple of card sharks. They decided to try out their newly acquired moves against the pros, who were unhappy that these kids were barging in on their action and so, rumor has it, offered a separate, large bounty to whatever player took them out. Both actors got knocked out on the first day but took it with good grace and apparently had a blast. Matt's buddy Ben Affleck, an experienced player, tried in 2003—the line on him to win (he didn't) was 400:1. *Note:* In 2005, the World Series of Poker moved to the Rio under the auspices of Harrah's Entertainment, which bought the rights to the event in 2004. The 2008 purse is $8.25 million.

Fitzgeralds This casino is done up in greens and golds, and the overall effect is not quite as tacky as you might expect, though the now near-total absence of any overt Irish theme means it's rather forgettable. In fact, it's rather friendly and with a medium-to-low claustrophobia level, thanks in part to some windows to the outside Fremont Street. The casino actually has two levels: From the upstairs part, you can access a balcony from which you get an up-close view of the Fremont Street Experience.

Blackjack, craps, and keno tournaments are frequent events here. The Club Fitz card offers slots, video poker, and video keno players gifts, meals, and other perks for accumulated points. Several slot machines have cars as prizes, fun books provide two-for-one gaming coupons, and if you're lucky, you might find a blackjack table with something less than a $5 per-hand minimum. 301 Fremont St. (at 3rd St.). ✆ **702/388-2400.** www.fitzgeraldslasvegas.com.

Four Queens The Four Queens is New Orleans–themed, with late-19th-century–style globe chandeliers, which make for good lighting and a low claustrophobia level. It's small, but the dealers are helpful, which is one of the pluses of gambling in the more manageably sized casinos. Slots tournaments are frequent events, and there are major poker tournaments throughout the year. The casino also offers exciting multiple-action blackjack (it's like playing three hands at once, with separate wagers on each). The Royal Players Club offers players bonus points toward cash rebates. 202 Fremont St. (at Casino Center Blvd.). ℂ **702/385-4011.** www.fourqueens.com.

Fremont Hotel & Casino   This 32,000-square-foot casino—it's much bigger than it initially looks—offers a relaxed atmosphere. In some ways, it's more comfortable gambling here than on the Strip, possibly in part because the beautiful people don't bother with places like this. But lots of other people do, and so it can be more crowded than other Downtown casinos, even during the day. Low gambling limits ($2 blackjack, 25¢ roulette, though not as many tables with these as we would like) help. It's also surprisingly open and bright for a Downtown casino. Just 50¢ could win you a Cadillac or Ford Mustang here, plus a progressive cash jackpot. Casino guests can accumulate bonus points redeemable for cash by joining the Players Gold club (which is also good at Main Street Station and the California Hotel & Casino). Guests can also take part in frequent slot and keno tournaments. No giant slot machine, though. 200 E. Fremont St. (btw. Casino Center Blvd. and 3rd St.). ℂ **702/385-3232.** www.fremontcasino.com.

The Golden Gate   This is one of the oldest casinos in Downtown, and though its age is showing, it's still fun to go there. As you might expect from the name, old San Francisco artifacts and decor abound (think earthquake time). At one end of the narrow casino is the bar, where a piano player performs ragtime jazz, which is better than the homogenized pop offered in most casino lounges. Unfortunately, the low ceiling, dark period wallpaper, and small dimensions give this a high claustrophobia level. 1 Fremont St. ℂ **702/382-3510.** www.goldengatecasino.net.

Golden Nugget   While this is not the standout among casino properties developed by Steve Wynn (now owned by Landry's Restaurants), it's still one of the nicest places to gamble, looks-wise, in Downtown. We prefer Main Street Station, but you might prefer the more obvious attempts at class that this place exudes. The new owners gave it a gorgeous makeover, all rich tones with splashes of color, and it's now even nicer than ever. Some tables are only $5 minimum, at least during the day. And compared to most other Downtown properties, this is the most like the Strip. Look for more improvements from the new owners. Of course, it has a players' club. 129 E. Fremont St. (at Casino Center Blvd.). ℂ **702/385-7111.** www.goldennugget.com.

Main Street Station *Finds*   This is the best of the Downtown casinos, at least in terms of comfort and a pleasant environment. Even the Golden Nugget, nice as it is, has more noise and distractions. The decor here is, again, classic Vegas/old-timey (Victorian-era) San Francisco, but with extra touches (check out the old-fashioned fans above the truly beautiful bar) that make it work much better than other attempts at the same decor. Strangely, it seems just about smoke-free, perhaps thanks in part to a very high ceiling. The claustrophobia level is zero. Players can join the Players Gold club, which is also good at Fremont Hotel & Casino and the California Hotel & Casino. 200 N. Main St. (btw. Fremont St. and I-95). ℂ **702/387-1896.** www.mainstreetcasino.com.

Plaza Hotel & Casino   This is Old Vegas, with an attempt at '60s glamour (think women in white go-go boots). It had gotten worn, and every time the owners try to spruce it up, it seems to get worn again quickly. Cautious bettors will appreciate the $1 blackjack tables and penny slots here. The Plaza Play Club lets members earn points toward room offers and other promotions. 1 Main St. (at Fremont St.). ℂ **702/386-2110.** www.plazahotelcasino.com.

8

Shopping

Shopping in Vegas—Nirvana or an endless Sisyphean repetition of every mall you've ever been to? Depends on your viewpoint. If you are looking for quaint, clever, unique stores, this isn't the town for you (with a few notable exceptions, most of which will require you to drive some blocks off the Strip). But if you are looking for general shop-till-you-drop fun, this is your kind of town. In addition to some extensive (and recently revamped) malls, many hotels have comprehensive, and sometimes highly themed, shopping arcades. The most notable of the arcades are in Caesars Palace, Planet Hollywood, and The Venetian (details below). Thankfully catering to the weird schedules kept by many Vegas visitors, most shops in the major hotel malls stay open until 11pm or midnight, so your spending isn't curtailed by limited retail hours. However, given the unstable Vegas landscape, to save you a potential inconvenience, if you are interested in a particular shop listed at a specific mall, shopping arcade, or especially an outlet, you probably should call first to ensure that the establishment in question is still there.

In addition to exploring the malls, outlets, and shops listed below, you might consider driving **Maryland Parkway,** which runs parallel to the Strip on the east and has just about one of everything: Target, Toys "R" Us, several major department stores, major drugstores (in case you forgot your shampoo and don't want to spend $8 on a new bottle in your hotel's sundry shop), some alternative-culture stores (tattoo parlors and hip clothing stores), and so forth. It goes on for blocks.

1 The Malls

The Boulevard ⟨★⟩   The Boulevard is the second largest mall in Las Vegas—Fashion Show on the Strip has it beat. Its 150-plus stores and restaurants are arranged in arcade fashion on a single floor occupying 1.2 million square feet. Geared to the average consumer, it has anchors such as Sears, JCPenney, Macy's, Dillard's, and Marshalls. There's a wide variety of shops offering all sorts of items—moderately priced shoes and clothing for the entire family, books and gifts, jewelry, and home furnishings. There are also more than a dozen fast-food eateries. In short, you can find just about anything you need here. And there's free valet parking. The mall is open Monday through Saturday from 10am to 9pm and Sunday from 11am to 6pm. 3528 S. Maryland Pkwy. (btw. Twain Ave. and Desert Inn Rd.). ⟨C⟩ **702/732-8949.** www.blvdmall.com.

Fashion Show ⟨★★⟩   What was a nondescript, if large, mall has now been revamped with a *yowsa* exterior much more fitting Las Vegas. It's capped by a giant . . . well . . . they call it a cloud, but we call it "that weird thingy that looks like a spaceport for UFOs. What in the heck were they thinking?" Inside, it's still, more or less, a basic mall, including the city's first Nordstrom, a Bloomingdale's, Saks Fifth Avenue, a Neiman Marcus, and other high-end retailers. The mall hosts more than 250 shops, restaurants, and services. And the cloud/alien spaceport thingy has giant LED screens, music, and other distractions—again, much more fitting for Vegas, where even the malls have to light up. Valet parking is available, and you can even arrange to have your car hand-washed while you shop. The Fashion Show is open Monday through Saturday from 10am to 9pm and Sunday from 11am to 7pm. 3200 Las Vegas Blvd. S. (at the corner of Spring Mountain Rd.). ✆ 702/784-7000. www.thefashionshow.com.

The Galleria at Sunset ✿   This is the farthest-away mall of the bunch (9 miles southeast of Downtown Las Vegas, in Henderson) but the most aesthetically pleasing, a 1-million-square-foot Southwestern-themed shopping center, with topiary animals adding a sweet touch to the food court. Anchored by Dillard's, JCPenney, Mervyn's California, and Macy's, the Galleria's 140 emporia include branches of Gap/Gap Kids/Baby Gap, The Limited Too, Ann Taylor, bebe, Caché, Lane Bryant, Victoria's Secret, The Body Shop, B. Dalton, and Sam Goody. In addition to shoes and clothing for the entire family, you'll find electronics, eyewear, gifts, books, home furnishings, jewelry, and luggage here. Dining facilities include an extensive food court and two restaurants. Open Monday through Saturday from 10am to 9pm and Sunday from 11am to 7pm. 1300 W. Sunset Rd. (at Stephanie St., just off I-15), Henderson. ✆ 702/434-0202. www.galleriaatsunset.com.

Meadows Mall ✿   Another immense mall, this one has more than 144 shops, services, and eateries, anchored by four department stores: Macy's, Dillard's, Sears, and JCPenney. In addition, there are more than a dozen shoe stores, a full array of apparel for the entire family (including maternity wear, petites, and large sizes), an extensive food court, and shops purveying toys, books, music, luggage, gifts, jewelry, home furnishings (The Bombay Company, among others), accessories, and so on. Fountains and trees enhance Meadows Mall's ultramodern, high-ceilinged interior, and there are a few comfortable seating areas for resting your feet a moment. The Meadows Mall is open Monday through Saturday from 10am to 9pm and Sunday from 10am to 6pm. 4300 Meadows Lane (at the intersection of Valley View and U.S. 95). ✆ 702/878-3331. www.meadows mall.com.

Showcase Mall ✿   Less a traditional mall than an entertainment center, it has plenty of shopping and fun—we rarely miss a chance to drop by M&M's World. Other occupants include GameWorks, the World of Coca-Cola store, Grand Canyon Experience, and the United Artists theaters—the only regular movie theater complex on the Strip. Hours vary by store. 3785 S. Las Vegas Blvd. (right next to the MGM Grand). ✆ 702/597-3122.

2 Factory Outlets

Las Vegas has a big factory-outlet center just a few miles past the southern end of the Strip (see below). If you don't have a car, you can take a no. 301 CAT bus from anywhere on the Strip and change at Vacation Village to a no. 303. You can see from the review below that it doesn't do much for us, which is why we usually head to Primm to drop more money than we do at the tables (Williams-Sonoma outlet, how we love you).

Fashion Outlets Las Vegas ✿✿✿   Dedicated bargain hunters (we stop here every time we drive by) may want to make the roughly 40-minute drive along I-15 to this big outlet complex, right on the border of California and Nevada. There's also a shuttle from the MGM Grand or the mall at Planet Hollywood. Round-trip fare is $15 and includes a savings book for discounts at the outlets. Also, check the website for a shuttle discount coupon. On your left is a large factory outlet with some designer names prominent enough to make the trip worthwhile—Kenneth Cole, Versace, Coach, Gap, Banana Republic, Old Navy, even a rare Williams-Sonoma, among several others. Why so far out of town? Our guess is because some of these companies have full-price boutiques in various hotels and malls, and they don't want you ignoring those in favor of discounted items. Open daily from 10am to 8pm. 32100 Las Vegas Blvd. S. © **888/424-6898** or 702/874-1400. www.fashionoutletlasvegas.com.

Las Vegas Outlet Center ⚑ This massive complex houses 130 air-conditioned outlets, including a few dozen clothing stores and shoe stores. It offers a range of merchandise, but even with our understanding of the hit-and-miss nature of outlets, we never buy anything here and feel nothing but apathy for the center. Among other stores (which you will perhaps find less disappointing than we have), you'll find Liz Claiborne, Perry Ellis, Ashworth-Callaway Golf, Levi's, Nike, Oshkosh B'Gosh, Gymboree, Reebok, Jockey, Springmaid, Danskin, Van Heusen, Tommy Hilfiger, Burlington, Royal Doulton, Waterford (crystal), Black & Decker (tools), and Calvin Klein. There are also a carousel and a food court. Hours vary by store. 7400 Las Vegas Blvd. S. (at Warm Springs Rd.). © **702/896-5599.** www.premiumoutlets.com.

Las Vegas Premium Outlets We had such high hopes for this, the most conveniently located, and largest (ever more so thanks to a recently completed major expansion), outlet mall in Las Vegas. We can say that it looks nice, in that pretty outdoor mall kind of way. But the key here is "outdoor." It's fine on a regular day, but on a hot Vegas day—and there are plenty of those—this is an open oven of misery. They should put a roof over the thing or at least install a whole bunch of misters. You'll roast away while shopping among disappointingly dull stores, some of which are "outlets" only because they aren't in regular malls. (The Bath & Body Works shop, for example, consists mostly of regular products at regular prices.) Maybe we are just feeling bitter about that pair of Bass shoes that were half a size too small. Or that we can't quite fit into the Dolce & Gabbana sample sizes. Still, bring a lot of water if you go during the summer. *Warning:* Parking here is often a nightmare. Consider taking a cab. Stores include Armani, Bernini, Brooks Brothers, Calvin Klein, Coach, Crabtree & Evelyn, Dolce & Gabbana, Kenneth Cole, Lacoste, Nike, Perry Ellis, Ralph Lauren, Quicksilver, Samsonite, Timberland, Tommy Hilfiger, Wilson's Leather, and Zales. Open Monday through Saturday from 10am to 9pm, Sunday from 10am to 8pm. 875 S. Grand Central Pkwy. (at I-15). © **702/474-7500.** www.premiumoutlets.com.

3 Hotel Shopping Arcades

Just about every Las Vegas hotel offers some shopping opportunities. The following have the most extensive arcades. The physical spaces of these shopping arcades are always open, but individual stores keep unpredictable hours. For addresses and telephone numbers, see the hotels' listings in chapter 4.

Note: The Forum Shops at Caesars, the Grand Canal Shoppes at The Venetian, and the Miracle Mile Shops at Planet Hollywood—as much sightseeing attractions as shopping arcades—are in the must-see category.

BALLY'S Bally's **Avenue Shoppes** consist of around 20 emporia offering, you know, stuff (kitschy card-shop knickknacks and the like). In addition, there are several gift shops, art galleries, and a pool-wear shop. There are blackjack and slot tournaments right in the mall, as well as a race and sports book. You can dispatch the kids to a video arcade here while you shop (or gamble). A recent addition of a walkway to neighbor Paris Las Vegas features more stores and restaurants.

BELLAGIO 🏵🏵   The **Via Bellagio** collection of stores isn't as big as some of the other megahotel shopping arcades, but here it's definitely quality over quantity. It's a veritable roll call of glossy magazine ads: Armani, Prada, Chanel, Tiffany, Hermès, Fred Leighton, Gucci, Dior, and Yves Saint Laurent. That's about it. You need anything else? Well, yes—money. If you can afford this stuff, good for you, you lucky dog. (Actually, we've discovered affordable, good-taste items in every store here, from Tiffany's $30 silver key chains to $100 Prada business-card holders.) A nice touch is a parking lot by the far entrance to Via Bellagio, so you need not navigate the great distance from Bellagio's main parking structure; instead, you can simply pop in and pick up a little something.

CAESARS PALACE 🏵🏵🏵   Since 1978, Caesars has had an impressive arcade of shops called the **Appian Way,** highlighted by an immense white Carrara-marble replica of Michelangelo's *David* standing more than 18 feet high. All in all, a respectable grouping of hotel shops. But in the hotel's tradition of constantly surpassing itself, in 1992 Caesars inaugurated the fabulous **Forum Shops,** an independently operated 375,000-square-foot Rodeo-Drive-meets-the-Roman-Empire affair complete with a 48-foot triumphal arch entranceway, a painted Mediterranean sky that changes as the day progresses from rosy-tinted dawn to twinkling evening stars, acres of marble, lofty Corinthian columns with gold capitals, and a welcoming goddess of fortune under a central dome. The architecture and sculpture span a period from 300 B.C. to A.D. 1700, so you've got all your ancient Italian cityscape clichés. Then there is the Festival Fountain, where some seemingly immovable "marble" animatronic statues of Bacchus (slightly in his cups), a lyre-playing Apollo, Plutus, and Venus come to life for a 7-minute revel with dancing waters and high-tech laser-light effects. The shows take place every hour on the hour. The entire thing is pretty incredible, but also very Vegas—particularly the Bacchus show, which is truly frightening and bizarre. Even if you don't like shopping, it's worth the stroll just to giggle.

In 1998 the Forum Shops added an extension. The centerpiece is a giant **Roman Hall,** featuring a 50,000-gallon circular aquarium and another fountain that also comes to life with a show involving fire (don't stand too close—it gets really hot), dancing waters, and animatronic figures, as the mythical continent of Atlantis rises and falls every hour. The production values are much higher than those of the Bacchus extravaganza, but this "performance" takes itself more seriously, so the giggle factor remains. A 2004 expansion upped an already high ante. The three-story addition tacked on a new Strip entryway complete with a deliriously audacious circular escalator and another 175,000 square feet of retail space. The multistoried extension tries to permanently move past kitsch and into "classy rich person's shopping experience"—though any sort of movement, literal or metaphoric, is tricky, what with all the giant marbled pillars, statues, and fountains, plus an atrium that actually admits sunlight.

So with all the gawking opportunities, it may be easy to forget that there are actually stores here where you can shop and buy things (so much so that Caesars claims this is the most profitable mall in America). Tenants are mostly of the exclusive variety, although there are a few more Average Joe kind of stores (yes, of course there's a Gap). Some examples: Louis Vuitton, Bernini, Christian Dior, Christian Lacroix (sweetie darling), A/X Armani Exchange, Nanette Lapore (drop-dead cute clothing with only a handful of stores worldwide), Gucci, Gianni Versace, Harry Winston jewelers, Brooks Brothers, Juicy Couture, Taryn Rose, a branch of the famed barbershop to the Royal Family Truefitt and Hill, a Playboy store, Kiehl's cosmetics (worth a trip just for that), M.A.C., FAO Schwartz (complete with two-story horse towering over the entrance), and especially Vosages Haut Chocolate—makeup and sweets, that sounds like shopping heaven to us!

The majority of the Caesars Palace shops are open Sunday through Thursday from 10am to 11pm, Friday and Saturday from 10am to midnight.

CIRCUS CIRCUS There are about a dozen shops between the casino and the Adventuredome (p. 191), offering a selection of gifts and sundries, logo items, toys and games, jewelry, liquor, resort apparel for the entire family, T-shirts, homemade fudge/candy/soft ice cream, and, fittingly, clown dolls and puppets. Adjacent to the Adventuredome, there's a shopping arcade (with the usual souvenir stores and such) themed as a European village, with cobblestone walkways, fake woods, and so forth, decorated with replicas of vintage circus posters.

EXCALIBUR For the most part, the shops of the **Realm** reflect the hotel's medieval theme. Dragon's Lair, for example, features items ranging from pewter swords and shields to full suits of armor, plus crystal balls and the like. Other shops carry more conventional wares—gifts, candy, jewelry, women's clothing, and Excalibur logo items. And most importantly, they have a branch of that medieval staple—Krispy Kreme Doughnuts!

THE FLAMINGO LAS VEGAS The **Crystal Court** shopping promenade here accommodates men's and women's clothing/accessories stores, gift shops, and a variety of other emporia selling jewelry, beachwear, Southwestern crafts, fresh-baked goods, logo items, children's gifts, toys, and games.

HARRAH'S ⚓ Carnaval Court is a small outdoor shopping promenade, a concept unique to the Strip. It consists mostly of little stalls selling bits and bobs, like hippie-inspired floaty dresses and tops, saucy underwear with catchy phrases on it, jewelry, and knock-off purses. A store highlight is a Ghirardelli chocolate shop, a branch of the famous San Francisco–based chocolate company. It's remarkably like a smaller version of the one in San Francisco (alas, without the vats of liquid chocolate being mixed up), and in addition to candy, you can get a variety of delicious sundaes and other ice-cream treats.

LUXOR A 20,000-square-foot shopping arcade with eight full shops. Most of the stores emphasize clothing. Adjacent is the Cairo Bazaar, a trinket shop, though with the de-emphasis on anything Egypt, it may well have taken a different shape by the time you read this.

MANDALAY PLACE ⚓ In appearance, more like an actual indoor mall than a hotel shopping arcade, but in content it is neither the rarified atmosphere of Via Bellagio or the Wynn Promenade, nor does it have the collection of the Forum Shops. But there is a men's shop called the Art of Shaving, a great wine store, a shop for way-too-pampered pets (Lush Puppy), and a superior chocolatier.

MGM GRAND The hotel's **Star Lane Shops** include more than a dozen mostly pedestrian emporia lining the corridors en route from the monorail entrance. **Studio Walk** is another shopping area adjacent to the main casino, featuring some upscale boutiques and several restaurants.

MIRACLE MILE SHOPS AT PLANET HOLLYWOOD ✿✿ To our dismay, our favorite hotel-related shopping area is currently undergoing a $50-million total redo. The one-time Desert Passage, all Middle Eastern *souk*–themed, is getting made over with some vague "Miracle Mile" theme meant to invoke every high-end shopping district in any major metropolis. (Note to designers: L.A.'s own Miracle Mile lost its luster years ago—way to be on top of the trends.) Though not without some eye-catching details, the result isn't even all that glamorous: It's pretty much a new-Vegas, whiz-bang version of every nice upper-end mall in America, a generic letdown all the worse because the original version was so charming. The one bright spot may be the "rainstorm" (pouring water from the ceiling, and thunder and lightning effects) that takes place in Merchant's Harbor, though other free entertainment offers are being considered.

At least the shops somewhat stand out, including several listed separately below, plus a Showcase Slots (where you can bring home your own one-armed bandit), Frederick's of Hollywood, Crocs, Two Lips Shoes (affordable stylish and comfortable shoes), Steve Madden, Ann Taylor, Urban Outfitters, bebe, BCBG, Sephora, and a branch of the insanely popular H&M clothing store. You can also get your Tiki on at a branch of L.A.'s late, lamented Trader Vic's restaurant, not to mention all kinds of loud big-screens and other electronic gizmos because that's the way Vegas is these days. Interior changes have continued throughout 2008. For information, see **www.miraclemile shopslv.com**.

The shops are open Sunday through Thursday from 10am to 11pm, Friday and Saturday from 10am to midnight.

MONTE CARLO A cobblestone arcade of retail shops, the **Street of Dreams,** includes several upscale clothing, timepiece, eyewear, and gift boutiques, plus a Lance Burton magic shop.

THE PALAZZO ✿✿ The new addition to The Venetian couldn't hold its resort head up without its own luxury shopping area. As with the super high-end experience at Bellagio and Wynn, this brings all kinds of names to town, names sure to thrill the souls—and diminish the wallets—of dedicated fashionistas. A branch of Barney's New York is the star of the retail show, but Christian Louboutin, Bottega Veneta, Chloe, Diane von Fusternberg, Michael Kors, and Van Cleef & Arpels are hardly second string. It's like the pages of Vogue come to life!

RIO The **Masquerade Village** is an adequately executed shopping arcade at Rio. It's done as a European village, and is two stories tall, featuring a few shops, mostly selling clothes, jewelry, and gifts. One notable outlet is Nawlins, which includes "authentic" voodoo items, Mardi Gras masks, and so forth.

THE RIVIERA Though nothing like the higher-end shopping galleries, the Riviera has a fairly extensive shopping arcade comprising art galleries, jewelers, shops specializing in women's shoes and handbags, clothing for the entire family, furs, gifts, logo items, toys, phones and electronic gadgets, and chocolates.

STRATOSPHERE The internationally themed (though in a high-school production kind of way, compared to what's over at Planet Hollywood and The Venetian) second-floor **Tower Shops** promenade, housing more than 40 stores, is entered via an escalator from the casino. Some shops are in "Paris," along the Rue Lafayette and Avenue de l'Opéra (there are replicas of the Eiffel Tower and Arc de Triomphe in this section). Others occupy Hong Kong and New York City streetscapes.

TI–TREASURE ISLAND   TI's shopping promenade is nowhere near as interesting since they took out all the pirate-themed bits. Emporia here include the TI Store (your basic hotel gift/sundry shop, also offering much pirate-themed merchandise) plus the *Sirens of TI*–themed lingerie shop. Cirque du Soleil and *Mystère* logo wares are also sold in a shop near the ticket office in the hotel.

THE VENETIAN ⚘⚘   After you've shopped Ancient Rome at Caesars, come to **The Grand Canal Shoppes** and see if shopping in Renaissance- (more or less) era Venice is any different. Certainly the production values stay high: This is a re-created Italian village, complete with a painted, cloud-studded blue sky overhead, and a canal right down the center on which gondoliers float and sing. Pay them ($15), and you can take a lazy float down and back, serenaded by your boatman (actors hired especially for this purpose and with accents perfect enough to fool Roberto Benigni). As you pass by, under, and over bridges, flower girls will serenade you and courtesans will flirt with you, and you may have an encounter with a famous Venetian or two, as Marco Polo discusses his travels and Casanova exerts his famous charm. The stroll (or float) ends at a miniature (though not by all that much) version of St. Mark's Square, the central landmark of Venice. Here, you'll find opera singers, strolling musicians, glass blowers, and other bustling marketplace activity. It's all most ambitious and beats the heck out of animatronic statues.

The Shoppes are accessible directly from outside (so you don't have to navigate miles of casino and other clutter), via a grand staircase whose ceiling features more of those impressive hand-painted art re-creations. It's quite smashing. The Venetian's Palazzo hotel addition, due to open in late 2007, will eventually adjoin the Shoppes at the far end of St. Mark's Square (and include a branch of Barneys New York).

Oh, the shops themselves? The usual high- and medium-end brand names: Jimmy Choo, Mikimoto, Movado, Davidoff, Kenneth Cole, Ann Taylor, BCBG, bebe, Banana Republic, Rockport, and more, plus Venetian glass and paper shops. Madame Tussaud's Celebrity Encounter (p. 180) is also located here, and so is the Canyon Ranch Spa Club. The shops are open Sunday through Thursday from 10am to 11pm, Friday and Saturday from 10am to midnight.

WYNN LAS VEGAS ⚘⚘   The **Esplanade** is along the same rarified lines of the Bellagio shopping area, in that it's a Euro-style-esque (love those Vegas qualifiers!) shopping street lined with pricey places with famous names—Chanel, Cartier, Dior, Judith Leiber, Jean Paul Gaultier, Manolo Blahnik, Oscar de la Renta (his only store outside of NYC), La Flirt (a sort of mini-Sephora), Chocolat (excellent pastries and gourmet chocolates), and Jo Malone. We prefer it some to the one at Bellagio because it seems like it has just enough shops (like La Flirt) that nearly reach an average person's budget.

4 Fashion & Beauty

There are any number of clothing shops in Vegas, though most are of the name brand chain variety, from high to low end. Here are a couple of more interesting standouts. In addition to those listed below, Miracle Mile has an **H&M,** where the clothes are cheap and fashionable and the lines to try them on are very long. Go as soon they open to avoid the crowds.

Agent Provocateur ⚘⚘⚘   Vegas doesn't lack for lingerie stores (including Frederick's of Hollywood and Playboy), but if you can only make time for one, it has to be this British import. The designs are clever and witty, in addition to drop-dead sexy and ultracool. Kate Moss has long been the face and body of the line, and even starred in a short movie ad for the line directed by Mike Figgis. Seduction should start someplace special. Open Sunday through Thursday from 10am to 11pm, Friday and Saturday from 10am to midnight. In the Forum Shops at Caesars Palace, 3500 Las Vegas Blvd. S. ⓒ 702/696-7174.

Ben Sherman ⍟ British designer Ben Sherman started during the mod era, but now his clean-lined clothes seem more Sloane Ranger–conservative than cutting-edge London irony. Given that there are only seven outposts in the world, Anglo fashionphiles will still need to make a pilgrimage. Open Sunday through Thursday from 10am to 11pm, Friday and Saturday from 10am to midnight. In Miracle Mile, 3663 Las Vegas Blvd. S. ⓒ 702/688-4227.

Bettie Page Boutique ⍟⍟ It's the old story. Needing a job, curvaceous gal poses for naughty photos, and her cheery good humor in all kinds of bondage photos, not to mention a gleaming black pageboy hairdo, makes her an icon. The next thing you know, there's a store dedicated to all things Bettie. Dress like a pin-up thanks to a line of Page-inspired '50s-style dresses, corsets, hosiery, and more. You can't have a venture like this without a wink, and so the shop, all done up in leopard, is a hoot. There is also plenty of Bettie artwork by renowned pin-up artist Olivia de Berardinis for sale. Open Sunday through Thursday from 10am to 11pm, Friday and Saturday from 10am to midnight. In Miracle Mile, 3663 Las Vegas Blvd. S. ⓒ 702/636-1100. www.bettiepage clothing.com.

5 Vintage Clothing

The Attic ⍟ The Attic, former star of a Visa commercial, is the sort of place where they make poodle skirts in all sizes, in addition to the usual vintage and vintage-influenced wares stuffed on the crowded racks. Not so much of a scenester hangout as it used to be, but still worth a browse. Open Monday through Thursday from 10am to 5pm, Friday from 10am to 6pm, and Saturday from 11am to 6pm. 1018 S. Main St. ⓒ 702/388-4088. www.theatticlasvegas.com.

Buffalo Exchange ⍟ This is actually a branch of a chain of stores spread out across the United States. If the chain part worries you, don't let it—this merchandise doesn't feel processed. Staffed by plenty of incredibly hip alt-culture kids (ask them what's happening in town during your visit), it is stuffed with dresses, shirts, pants, and so forth. You can easily go in one day and come out with 12 fabulous new outfits, but you can just as easily go in and come up dry. But it's still probably the most reliable of the local vintage shops. The store is open Monday through Saturday from 10am to 8pm, Sunday from 11am to 7pm. 4110 S. Maryland Pkwy. (at Flamingo Rd.). ⓒ 702/791-3960. www.buffaloexchange.com.

6 Souvenirs

The **Arts Factory Complex** ⍟⍟⍟, 103 E. Charleston Blvd. (ⓒ 702/382-3886), is full of galleries of local artists working in a variety of different mediums, and one of their works would make for an original souvenir.

If you prefer your souvenirs to be a little less class and a little more kitsch, head over to the **Bonanza Gift and Souvenir Shop** ⍟⍟, 2460 Las Vegas Blvd. S. (ⓒ 702/ 384-0005). It's the self-proclaimed "World's Largest Gift Shop," and it certainly is big. T-shirts, Native American "handicrafts," all kinds of playing cards, both new and used (casinos have to change decks frequently, so this is where used packs go), dice, things covered in rhinestones, snowglobes—in short, something for everyone, provided "everyone" has a certain sensibility. We looked, and we felt the tackiest item available was the pair of earrings made out of poker chips. The coolest? Some inexpensive, old-fashioned-style dice.

For reverent camp, encrusted with sequins, take a peek at the **Liberace Museum gift store** 𝒦𝒦, 1775 E. Tropicana Ave. (② **702/798-5595**). Now better than ever thanks to a new team that really understands the value of branding and has greatly expanded the glittery, Liberace–adorned merch. For mixed emotions, little can beat items emblazoned with vintage images of bomb tests and other glories to the good old days of atomic blasts, at the **Atomic Testing Museum gift store** 𝒦𝒦, 755 E. Flamingo Rd. (② **702/794-5161**).

7 Reading Material & Music

USED BOOKS

Dead Poet Bookstore 𝒦𝒦 *Finds* The dead poet in question was the man from whose estate the owners bought their start-up stock. He had such good taste in books that they "fell in love with him" and wanted to name the store in his memory. Just one problem—they never did get his name. So they just called him "the dead poet." His legacy continues at this book-lover's haven. Open Monday through Saturday from 10am to 6pm. 937 S. Rainbow Blvd. ② **702/227-4070**.

LAS VEGAS SPECIALTY BOOKSTORES

Gambler's Book Shop 𝒦 Here you can buy a book on any system ever devised to beat casino odds. Owner Edna Luckman carries more than 4,000 gambling-related titles, including many out-of-print books, computer software, and videotapes. She describes her store as a place where "gamblers, writers, researchers, statisticians, and computer specialists can meet and exchange information." On request, knowledgeable clerks provide on-the-spot expert advice on handicapping the ponies and other aspects of sports betting. The store's motto is "knowledge is protection." Open Monday through Saturday from 9am to 5pm. 630 S. 11th St. (just off Charleston Blvd.). ② **800/522-1777** or 702/382-7555. www.gamblersbook.com.

Gamblers General Store 𝒦 This is a gambler's paradise stocked with a massive book collection, antique and current slot machines, gaming tables (blackjack, craps, and so on), roulette wheels, collectible chips, casino dice, classic Vegas photos, and a ton of gaming-related souvenirs. Open daily from 9am to 6pm. 800 S. Main St. (Downtown). ② **800/322-2447** or 702/382-9903. www.gamblersgeneralstore.com.

COMIC BOOKS

Alternate Reality Comics 𝒦 This is the best place in Vegas for all your comic-book needs. They have a nearly comprehensive selection, with a heavy emphasis on underground comics. But don't worry—the superheroes are here, too. Open Sunday through Tuesday from noon to 6pm, and Wednesday through Saturday from 11am to 7pm. 4800 S. Maryland Pkwy., Ste. D. ② **702/736-3673**. www.alternaterealitycomics.net.

MUSIC

Zia Record Exchange 𝒦𝒦 A sign that individual Vegas culture might not be dead after all, this fairly large shop mixes new and used records. The emphasis is on CDs but they do have a big vinyl section, and both show a varied selection of music styles (rock, punk, jazz, soundtracks, and so on). Cleverly, they spotlight bands coming to Vegas, both large and small, with special displays, plus always have bins of music from local acts. On Fridays and Saturdays, live local acts play in the shop. Please note the signs cautioning against slam dancing! Open daily from 10am to midnight. 4225 S. Eastern Ave., no. 17. © 702/735-4942. www.ziarecords.com.

8 Candy & Food

The Chocolate Swan and Jean Phillipe Patisserie, which also sell chocolates in addition to pastries and more, are listed in chapter 5.

British Foods, Inc. ☆☆   Here's a wild card even for this city: an import shop dedicated to all things U.K. Mostly edibles, though there are some Union Jack and other national imagery–inspired trinkets, and not just from Blighty—they also import from Australia and other parts of the Commonwealth. Come here for your Cadbury fix; there's a wide range of that favorite candy line, including items not regularly found on these shores. Stock up on teas, biscuits, bangers, jams, Ambrosia custards and puddings, British bacon, pasties, and even haggis. No lager, though. Sorry. Open daily from 10am to 6pm. 3375 S. Decatur Blvd., no. 11. © 702/579-7777. www.britishgrocer.com.

Ethel's Chocolate Lounge ☆   A creation of local confectioner Ethel M that is part cafe, part lounge. "You love chocolate. We are here to help." is their motto. This location isn't as large or as immediately fun as others around the country, but it's still a fun blood-sugar pick-me-up. Choose fancy chocolates from the carefully designed ones on display, such as pomegranate, champagne cocktail, and even margarita flavor, or savor a fondue or other appropriate nosh. Because they keep mall hours—Monday through Saturday from 10am to 9pm, Sunday from 11am to 7pm—they are more of a mid-afternoon snack spot than a post-dinner wind-down option. In Fashion Show Mall, 3200 Las Vegas Blvd. S. © 702/796-6662.

M&M's World ☆☆ (Kids)   What can one do when faced with a wall of M&Ms in colors never before seen by man or woman (purple! teal! lime green!)? Overpriced? Yeah! Who cares? There are doodads galore, replete with the M&M's logo, and a surprisingly enjoyable short film and comedy routine, ostensibly about the "history" of the candy but really just a cute little adventure with a decent budget behind it. Open Sunday through Thursday from 9am until 11pm, Friday and Saturday from 9am until midnight. In the Showcase Mall, 3785 Las Vegas Blvd. S. (just north of the MGM Grand Hotel). © 702/736-7611.

9 Antiques

Antiques in Vegas? You mean really old slot machines, or the people playing the really old slot machines?

Actually, Vegas has quite a few antiques stores—nearly two dozen—of consistent quality and price, nearly all located within a few blocks of each other. We have one friend, someone who takes interior design very seriously, who comes straight to Vegas for most of her best finds. You should see her antique chandelier collection!

To get to this antiquing mecca, start in the middle of the **1600 block of East Charleston Boulevard** and keep driving east. The little stores, nearly all in old houses dating from the '30s, line each side of the street. Or you can stop in at **Silver Horse Antiques,** 1651 E. Charleston Blvd. (© **702/385-2700**), and pick up a map to almost all of the locations, with phone numbers and hours of operation.

Antiques at the Market ☞ This is an antiques mini-mall (for lack of a better phrase) with a number of individuals operating stalls under one roof. Open Monday through Saturday from 10am to 6pm, Sunday from noon to 5pm. 6665 S. Eastern Ave. (btw. Sunset and Warm Springs rds.). ☏ 702/307-3960.

Antique Square ☞ It's a cruddy-looking collection of stores in several remodeled houses arranged in a square, but every good antiques shopper knows that these kinds of crammed junk stores are the places to find real treasures and to do real antiques hunting (because once they've been really picked through and prettily displayed by pros, you can kiss bargains and real finds goodbye). Individual store hours vary, but most are closed on Sunday and Monday. 2014–2034 E. Charleston Blvd. (at Eastern Ave.). ☏ 702/471-6500.

Red Rooster Antique Mall ☞ The Red Rooster is a mini-mall of sorts, only with "antiques" instead of a 7-Eleven and a nail salon. The place is older and battered, but features individual stalls selling all categories of stuff, from junk to treasures. Individual store hours vary, but most are open Monday through Saturday 10am to 6pm, Sunday from 11am to 5pm. 1109 Western Ave. (at Charleston and I-15). ☏ 702/382-5253.

10 Wigs

Serge's Showgirl Wigs ☞ Oh, you probably thought all those showgirls just naturally had bountiful thick manes. Sorry to burst your bubble. If you have a desire to look like a showgirl yourself (and why not?), come to Serge's, which for over 2 decades has been supplying Vegas's wiggy needs, with more than 2,000 wigs to choose from. This, by the way, is not just for showgirls or the similarly delusional. Not only can wigs be fun for everyone (we treasure our own turquoise number), but at least one sassy gal we know with thinning hair issues recently bought two natural-looking models and reports that the sales staff was as nice and helpful as could be. Wigs range in price from $130 to over $1,500, depending on quality and realness, and you can pick from Dolly Parton's wig line or get something custom-made. They also make hairpieces and toupees and carry hair-care products. Open Monday through Saturday from 10am to 5:30pm.

If the prices at Serge's are too rich to bring your fantasy alive, right across the way is **Serge's Showgirl Wigs outlet,** with prices running from a more reasonable $60 to $70. 953 E. Sahara Ave., no. A-2. ☏ 800/947-9447 or 702/732-1015. www.showgirlwigs.com.

9

Las Vegas After Dark

You will not lack for things to do at night in Vegas. This is a town that truly comes alive only after dark. Don't believe us? Just look at the difference between the Strip during the day, when it's kind of dingy and nothing special, and at night, when the lights hit and the place glows in all its glory. Night is when it's happening in this 24-hour town. In fact, most bars and clubs don't even get going until close to midnight. That's because it's only around then that all the restaurant workers and people connected with the shows get off the clock and can go out and play themselves. It's extraordinary. Just sit down in a bar at 11pm; it's empty. You might well conclude it's dead. Return in 2 hours, and you'll find it completely full and jumping.

But you also won't lack for things to do before 11pm. There are shows all over town, though traditional variety and magic shows have largely given way to Cirque du Soleil. The showgirls remain, topless and otherwise, but the current trend is toward Big Name Headliners and Big Broadway Productions. Every hotel has at least one lounge, usually offering live music. But the days of fabulous Vegas lounge entertainment, when the lounge acts were sometimes of better quality than the headliners (and headliners like Sinatra would join the lounge acts on stage between their own sets), are gone. Most of what remains is homogeneous and bland, and serves best as a brief respite or background noise. On the other hand, finding the most awful lounge act in town can be a rewarding

pursuit of its own. Many lounges and bars have replaced live music with DJs and go-go dancers.

Vegas still attracts some dazzling headliner entertainment in its showrooms and arenas. Madonna's 2006 shows commanded the top prices on her tour; Bruce Springsteen played his first Vegas show ever in 2000; U2 started their PopMart tour at UNLV's stadium; the Rolling Stones played both the MGM Grand and the Hard Rock Hotel's The Joint; Pavarotti inaugurated Mandalay Bay's Arena, and Bob Dylan did the same for the House of Blues; Cher opened up The Venetian, and Sting got a reported $1 million to open Red Rock Resort with a 60-minute set. The Red Hot Chili Peppers gave a free concert to celebrate the city's centennial. It is still a badge of honor for comedians to play Vegas, and there is almost always someone of marquee value playing one showroom or the other.

Admission to shows runs the gamut, from about $25 for Mac King (comedy magic show at Harrah's) to $250 and more for top headliners. Prices occasionally include two drinks.

To find out who's performing during your stay and for up-to-date listings of shows (prices change, shows close), you can call the various hotels, using their toll-free numbers. Or call the **Las Vegas Convention and Visitors Authority** (© **877/VISIT-LV** or 702/892-0711) and ask them to send you a free copy of *Showguide* or *What's On in Las Vegas* (one or both of which will probably be in your hotel room). You can also check out

Moments   Lounge Lizard Supreme

All those faux-hipster artists doing woeful lounge-act characters in Hollywood and New York only wish they could be **Mr. Cook E. Jarr,** whose sincerity and obvious drive to entertain puts mere performance artists to shame. With George Hamilton's tan, Cher's first shag haircut (it's certainly not his factory-original coif), and a bottomless, borderless catalog of rock, pop, soul, swing, and standard favorites, he's more Vegas than Wayne Newton.

Cook has a cult following of blue-collar casino denizens and the youthful cocktail set, who listen enraptured as he plays human jukebox, complete with karaoke-style backing recordings, terrible jokes, an array of disco-era lights, and (his favorite) a smoke machine. He's actually a solid, throaty singer, with a gift for vocal mimicry as he moves from Ben E. King to Bee Gees to Tony Bennett turf. And his tribute the night Sinatra died—a version of "My Way" in which he voiced, alternately, Sammy, Dino, and Elvis welcoming Ol' Blue Eyes to Heaven—was priceless.

He moves around a lot, but you can often catch him on Friday and Saturday nights, late, at **Harrah's Carnaval Court Lounge,** at 3475 Las Vegas Blvd. S. (© **702/369-5222;** www.cookejarr.com). Don't miss him! (And if he has left there by the time you read this, try to track him down.)

what's playing at **www.visitlasvegas.com.** It's best to plan well ahead if you have your heart set on seeing one of the most popular shows or catching a major headliner.

The hotel entertainment options described in this chapter include information on ticket prices, what's included in that price (drinks, dinner, taxes, and/or gratuities), showroom policies (whether it's preassigned or maitre d' seating, and smoking policies), and how to make reservations. Whenever possible, reserve in advance, especially on weekends and holidays. If the showroom has **maitre d' seating** (as opposed to preassigned seats), you may want to tip him to upgrade your seat. A tip of $15 to $20 per couple will usually do the trick at a major show, less at a small showroom. An alternative to tipping the maitre d' is to wait until the captain shows you to your seat. Perhaps it will be adequate, in which case you've saved some money. If not, you can offer the captain a tip for a better seat. If you do plan to tip,

have the money ready; maitres d' and captains tend to get annoyed if you fumble around for it, since they have other people to seat. You can also tip with casino chips (from the hotel casino where the show is taking place only) in lieu of cash. Whatever you tip, the proper etiquette is to do it rather subtly—a kind of palm-to-palm action. There's really no reason for this, since everyone knows what's going on, but being blatant is in poor taste. Arrive early at maitre d' shows to get the best choice of seats.

If you buy tickets for an assigned-seat show in person, you can look over a seating chart. Avoid sitting right up by the stage, if possible, especially for big-production shows. Dance numbers are better viewed from the middle of the theater. With headliners, you might like to sit up close.

Note: All these caveats and instructions aside, most casino-hotel showrooms offer good visibility from just about every seat in the house.

If you prefer alternative or real rock music, your choices used to be limited, but that's all changed. Most touring rock bands make at least once stop in the city, so that means you can actually see such folks as Marilyn Manson and Beck in Vegas. But otherwise, the alternative club scene in town is no great shakes. If you want to know what's playing during your stay, consult the local free alternative papers: the *Las Vegas Weekly* (biweekly, with great club and bar descriptions in their listings; on the web at www.lasvegas weekly.com), and *City Life* (weekly, with no descriptions but comprehensive listings of what's playing where all over town; www.lasvegascitylife.com). Both can be picked up at restaurants, bars, record and music stores, and hip retail stores. If you're looking for good alt-culture tips, try asking the cool staff at **Zia Records** (*©* **702/ 735-4942**); not only do they have bins dedicated to local artists but also local acts play live in stores on the weekend.

In addition to the listings in this chapter, consider the **Fremont Street Experience,** described on p. 174.

Be aware that there is a curfew law in Vegas: Anyone under 18 is forbidden from being on the Strip without a parent after 9pm on weekends and holidays. In the rest of the county, minors cannot be out without parents after 10pm on school nights, and midnight on weekends.

1 What's Playing Where

It used to be that a show was an essential part of the Vegas experience. Back in those days, a show was pretty simple: A bunch of scantily (and we mean scantily) clad show-girls paraded around while a comedian engaged in some raunchy patter. The showgirls are still here and still scantily clad (though not as often topless; guess cable TV has taken some of that thrill away), but the productions around them have gotten impossibly elaborate. And they have to be because they have to compete with a free dancing water fountains show held several times nightly right on the Strip. Not to mention a volcano, a Mardi Gras parade in the sky, lounge acts galore, and the occasional imploding building—all free.

The big resort hotels, in keeping with their general over-the-top tendencies, are pouring mountains of money into high-spectacle extravaganzas, luring big-name acts into decades-long residencies and surrounding them with special effects that would put some Hollywood movies to shame. Which is not to say the results are Broadway quality—they're big, cheesy fun. Still, with the exception of the astonishing work done by the Cirque du Soleil productions, most of what passes for a "show" in Vegas is just a flashier revue, with a predictable lineup of production number/magic act/production number/acrobatics/production number.

Unfortunately, along with big budgets and big goals come big-ticket prices. Sure, you can still take the entire family of four to a show for under $100, but you're not going to get the same production values that you'd get by splurging on a Cirque du Soleil show. Which is not to say you always get what you pay for: There are some reasonably priced shows that are considerably better values than their more expensive counterparts.

Note: Although every effort has been made to keep up with the volatile Las Vegas show scene, keep in mind that the following reviews may not be indicative of the actual show you'll see, but the basic concept and idea will be the same. What's more, the show itself may have closed, so it's a good idea to always call the venue and check.

The following section describes the major production shows currently playing in Las Vegas, arranged alphabetically by the title of the production. But first, here's a handy list arranged by hotel:

> ## ⓘ Tips Our Favorites
>
> Our vote for **best show?** It's a toss-up between *KÀ* at the MGM Grand, *O* at Bellagio, and *Mystère* at TI–Treasure Island, all by Cirque du Soleil. Each has to be seen to be believed—and even then you may not believe it, but you won't be forgetting the experience anytime soon. The **most intelligent show** is put on by Penn & Teller, and we are grateful. The **best magic show** is Lance Burton at Monte Carlo. The **best classic Vegas topless revue** is *Jubilee!* at Bally's. The **best we aren't sure what the heck to call it, but you should really try to see it** is Blue Man Group, at The Venetian.

- **Bally's:** *Jubilee!* (Las Vegas–style revue), *The Price is Right*
- **Bellagio:** Cirque du Soleil's *O* (unique circus-meets-performance-art theatrical experience)
- **Caesars Palace:** Bette Midler (music and variety), Elton John: *The Red Piano* (music), and Cher (music and variety)
- **Excalibur:** Tournament of Kings (medieval-themed revue)
- **The Flamingo Las Vegas:** *The Second City* (improvisational comedy)
- **Harrah's:** Mac King (comedy and magic) and Rita Rudner (comedy)
- **The Las Vegas Hilton:** Barry Manilow: *Music & Passion* (he writes the songs)
- **Luxor:** *Believe* (Illusionist Criss Angel and Cirque de Soliel collaborate)
- **The Mirage:** Cirque du Soleil's *Love* (featuring the music of The Beatles)
- **MGM Grand:** Cirque du Soleil's *KÀ* (astounding martial arts and acrobatics); *Crazy Horse Paris* (adults-only topless dancing)
- **Monte Carlo:** Lance Burton: *Master Magician* (magic show and revue)
- **New York–New York:** Cirque du Soleil's *Zumanity* (adults-only provocative revue)
- **Rio All-Suite Hotel & Casino:** Penn & Teller (illusions), *Tony & Tina's Wedding*, Chippendales
- **The Riviera:** *La Cage* (female impersonators), *Crazy Girls* (sexy Las Vegas–style revue), and *ICE*
- **Stratosphere Hotel & Casino:** *American Superstars* (an impression-filled production show) and *Viva Las Vegas* (Vegas-style variety show)
- **TI–Treasure Island:** Cirque du Soleil's *Mystère* (unique circus performance)
- **Tropicana:** *Folies Bergere* (Las Vegas–style revue) and Dirk Arthur (magic)
- **The Venetian:** Blue Man Group (hilarious performance art) and *Phantom of the Opera* (Andrew Lloyd Webber's most popular musical), Jersey Boys (award winning Broadway musical)
- **Wynn Las Vegas:** *Le Rêve* (water-themed production show), *Danny Gans* (impressions)

2 The Major Production Shows

This category covers all the major Las Vegas production shows and a few of the minor ones as well. In addition to the following, we recommend **Donny and Marie**'s wholesome nostalgia at Harrah's and **Louie Anderson's** comic stylings at Excalibur, but we urge you to stay away from the musical family the **Scintas** at the Las Vegas Hilton—a fossilized Vegas act full of near-parody-level lounge singing and jokes at the expense of every ethnicity, handicap, and sexual orientation out there.

⟨Value⟩ HOT TIP!

Tickets2Nite (© 702/939-2222) is a service that puts any unsold seats for that evening on sale, starting at 2pm, for—get this!—*half price*. Hot diggity! Of course, there are some drawbacks. It's downright unlikely that really ultra super-duper shows are ever going to have unsold seats (because the hotel will just sell them to the always-waiting-and-happy-to-pay-full-price standby line), but you'd be shocked at the range otherwise, from basic crap to stuff that we would recommend even at full price (they aren't allowed to say on the record which shows' tickets often come up for sale). Alas, the very nature of the service means you can't plan; you have to stand in line and take your chances starting at about noon (we advise getting in line even earlier than that). So if you have your heart set on ambiguously gendered contortionists, don't rely on Tickets2Nite, but, if like a good gambler, you like taking chances, head for 3785 Las Vegas Blvd. S. (in the giant Coke bottle at the Showcase Mall). Another possibility is **Tix4Tonight,** which offers the same service but has more locations. © 877/849-4868; www.tix4tonight.com.

There is also a new trend of major headliners doing semipermanent but irregular stints in the big showrooms. If you are in town when **Elton John** is performing *The Red Piano* on Bette Midler and Cher's off days at Caesars Palace, you owe it to yourself to see it (even if the top $275 ticket prices are way on the ridiculous side—it's such a good show that it's worth saving up for). **Stevie Nicks** also does a couple of stints at Caesars throughout the year. Similarly, **Reba McEntire** was doing a bunch of shows at the Las Vegas Hilton when Barry Manilow wasn't there.

Note: Shows can close without warning, even ones that have been running just shy of forever, so please call first. You might also want to double check on days and times of performances; schedules can change without notice. Note also that some ticket prices may not include tax or drinks, so you might also check for those potential hidden costs.

American Superstars ⟨⟩ ⟨Kids⟩   One of a number of celebrity-impersonator shows (well, it's cheaper than getting the real headliners), *American Superstars* is one of the few shows where the impersonators actually sing live. Five performers do their thing; the celebs impersonated vary depending on the evening.

A typical Friday night featured Christina Aguilera, Britney Spears, Tim McGraw, Michael Jackson, and Elvis. The performers won't be putting the originals out of work any time soon, but they aren't bad. Actually, they were closer in voice than in looks to the celebs in question (half the black performers were played by white actors), which is an unusual switch for Vegas impersonators. The "Charlie Daniels" actually proved to be a fine fiddler in his own right and was the hands-down crowd favorite. The live band actually had a look-alike of their own: Kato Kaelin on drums (it's good that he's getting work). The youngish crowd (by Vegas standards) included a healthy smattering of children and seemed to find no faults with the production. The action is also shown on two large, and completely unnecessary, video screens flanking the stage, so you don't have to miss a moment. Sunday through Tuesday 7pm; Wednesday, Friday, and Saturday 6:30 and 8:30pm. In the Stratosphere Casino Hotel & Tower, 2000 Las Vegas Blvd. S. © 800/99-TOWER or 702/380-7711. www.stratospherehotel.com. Tickets $43 adults, $33 children 5–12; show and buffet package $52 (package includes taxes and fees, 2 drinks, and tower admission).

Bette Midler ⚜⚜⚜   At the beginning of 2008, the Divine Miss M brought her delicious self to a 2-year-plus residency in Caesars, taking over Céline Dion's remarkable run. The Coliseum venue was built just for Céline, but the diva has left the building. Midler's bawdy jokes and belting vocals belie her 60-something age, as she delivers a classic *show*. You know, singing, dancing, joke telling, charisma, not to mention mermaid costumes and Sophie Tucker homages. Ticket prices are high for the good seats, to be sure, but the dame delivers; her voice and her stage presence are as strong as ever. This is Vegas entertainment as it was—a great performer doing what she does best, no gimmicks, night after night. There will be 100 shows throughout the year, usually in 4-week blocks, Tuesday, Wednesday, and Friday through Sunday at 8pm. In Caesars Palace, 3570 Las Vegas Blvd. S. ✆ 877/7BETTEM, or through www.ticketmaster.com. Tickets $95–$250 (plus booking fee).

Blue Man Group ⚜⚜⚜   Are they blue? Indeed they are—three hairless, nonspeaking men dipped in azure paint (you may have seen them on a commercial or two and wondered what in the heck they were all about), doing decidedly odd stunts with marshmallows, art supplies, audience members, tons of paper, and an amazing array of percussion instruments fashioned fancifully from PVC piping. If that doesn't sound very Vegas, well, it's not. It's a franchise of a New York–born performance-art troupe that seems to have slipped into town through a side door opened by Cirque du Soleil's groundbreaking successes. Don't get the wrong idea: This is no Cirque clone. There are no acrobatics or flowing choreography, no attempt to create an alternate universe—just a series of surreal, unconnected bits. But even if the whole is no greater than the sum of the parts, the parts are pretty great themselves. It's funny in the weirdest and most unexpected ways, and the crowd is usually roaring by the end. Fans of typical Vegas shows may leave scratching their heads, but we are glad there is another color in the Vegas entertainment spectrum. The Blue Man Group theater at The Venetian is not quite as comfy as its former home at Luxor, but most folks are so amused by the onstage antics that they forget about elbow room. Nightly at 7:30pm, with an additional 10:30pm show on Saturdays. At The Venetian, 3355 Las Vegas Blvd. S. ✆ 866/641-7469 or 702/414-7469. www.venetian.com. Tickets $85–$140 (includes tax and service fees).

Cher ⚜⚜⚜   Cherilyn Sarkisian has had a nice little career—the kind that gets you a headliner slot at Ceasars Palace in rotation with Elton John and Bette Midler. And the kind that gets you the ultimate status symbol of stardom, having the whole world know you on a first-name basis. That's Cher, who though at times has been dismissed as a mere "I Got You Babe" pawn of ex-hubby Sonny, a disco-era cartoon, high-profile serial romancer and anachronistic relic, has time and again proven herself one of the most resilient figures in pop culture, almost on the force of her sheer will (and good sportsmanship) alone. Let's face it, she's not a great singer, can't really dance, isn't known as a songwriter or musician. Yet she's just plain likable—and knows how to make the most of her personality, sense of (often self-effacing) humor, and talents. Having her name on dozens of hits, one of the '70s top TV variety shows, and a 1988 best actress Academy Award for her "Moonstruck" role, are not things to sneeze at. Oh, and no one wears Bob Mackie gowns like she does! So can she excel with her own Vegas show? Just say the title of one of her signature comeback hits. No, not "Half Breed"! We mean "Believe." Tuesday, Wednesday, Saturday, and Sunday at 7:30pm. In Caesars Palace. 3570 Las Vegas Blvd. S. ✆ 866/510-2437. Tickets $95–$250 (plus tax).

Cirque du Soleil's KÀ ⚜⚜⚜ *Kids*   Our initial reaction to the opening of this was, "Does Vegas really need *another* Cirque show?" And, for that matter, "Is there anything

Vegas on the Upswing

Vegas: Everything old is new again, and again. Whereas once it was the thing to do—to have a regular Vegas act, back in the Frankie and the Rat Pack days, and then again in the Elvis days—so it went that such acts became cornball and cheese. Then you couldn't get a performer with any critical or commercial legitimacy to touch the place with a 10-foot roll of quarters. And now? Céline Dion has made it safe again, and here comes **Elton John**, filling Bette Midler's spot on some of her off nights with his *The Red Piano* ✸✸ show. It's a gorgeously mounted production, featuring Elton and his lacquered piano, plus artistic video installations and other touches that have earned the show critical raves. Too bad he does it only a few weeks a year. Oh, and the prices make even Midler's look cheap. Call ✆ **888/4ELTONJ** (435-8665) for tickets, which run $110 to $275 plus a Ticketmaster surcharge (no charge for box office walk-ups).

Less technical pizzazz, but no less showmanship (not to mention more frequent dates and lower ticket prices) comes from **Barry Manilow: *Music & Passion*** ✸✸, who, bless him, knows just who he is and how to use it. He's at the Las Vegas Hilton, 3000 Paradise Rd. (✆ **800/222-5361**); tickets are $95 to $225, and shows are Wednesday through Saturday at 8pm. We really wish these artists, in making Vegas safe again for legit performers, also made it safe again for those on budgets. Meanwhile, Wayne Newton is currently MIA. Bring back Mr. Las Vegas!

else Cirque can possibly *do?*" The answer to the latter is "Apparently, yes" and to the former "Certainly, as long as it's this one."

To begin with, *KÀ* subverts expectations by largely eschewing the usual Cirque format—wide-eyed innocent is taken on surreal adventure, beautiful but aimless, complete with acrobats and clowns and lots of weird floaty things—in favor of an actual plot, as a brother and sister from some mythical Asian kingdom are separated by enemy raiders and have to endure various trials and tribulations before being reunited. Gleefully borrowing imagery from magical realist martial arts movies such as *Hero* and *Crouching Tiger, Hidden Dragon,* the production makes use of a technically extraordinary set that shifts the stage not just horizontally but vertically, as the action moves from under the sea to the side of a steep cliff and beyond. The circus elements—acrobats, clowns—are for once incorporated into the show in a way that makes some loose narrative sense, though this does mean that the physical stunts are mostly pretty much that rather than feats of derring-do, and between the stage's antics and the clever lighting effects, the show is more about hydraulics than humans.

Except not; there really is a story, and it is by turns funny, tragic, and whimsical. There are at least two moments that are nothing but simple stagecraft and yet are exquisite, among the most memorable of any current Vegas show. The theater is cavernous, but extensive catwalks and other staging tricks mean that those in the back won't feel cheated or that far from the action. It might be a little long and intense for younger children, but older ones will be enthralled—and so will you. Don't sit here reading this any longer; go see it. Friday through Tuesday at 7:30 and 10:30pm. In the

MGM Grand, 3799 Las Vegas Blvd. S. ℂ 866/774-7117 or 702/531-2000. www.cirquedusoleil.com. Tickets $69–$150 (plus tax).

Cirque du Soleil's LOVE 🔥 *Kids*   A collaboration between the Beatles (by way of Sir George Martin's son, who remixed and reconfigured the music with a free hand that may distress purists) and Cirque du Soleil, this is the usual Cirque triumph of imaginative design, but it also feels surprisingly hollow. In one sense, it's an inspired pairing, in that the Beatles' music provides an apt vehicle for Cirque's trademark exuberant, joyous spectacle. But while Cirque shows have never been big on plot, the particular aimlessness of this production means that the show too quickly dissolves into simply the introduction of one creative, novel staging element after another. In other words, its visual fabulousness ends up repetitious rather than thrilling. There is a missed opportunity here for a fractured retelling of the Beatles' personal history, a saga that contains much the same myth, wonder, and melancholy as expressed in other Cirque shows. Beatles fans—though who, at this stage in the game, is not, really?—will still have a good time, but others may wish to spend their Cirque money on one of the other options. Daily 7:30 and 10:30pm. At The Mirage, 3400 Las Vegas Blvd. S. ℂ 800/963-9637 or 702/792-7777. www.beatles.com. Tickets $94–$150 (plus tax).

Cirque du Soleil's *Mystère* 🔥🔥🔥 *Kids*   The in-house ads for *Mystère* (Miss-*tair*) say "Words don't do it justice," and for once, that's not just hype. The show is so visual that trying to describe it is a losing proposition. And simply calling it a circus is like calling the Hope Diamond a gem or the Taj Mahal a building. It's accurate but, as the ad says, doesn't begin to do it justice.

Cirque du Soleil began in Montréal as a unique circus experience, not only shunning traditional animal acts in favor of gorgeous feats of human strength and agility, but also adding elements of the surreal and the absurd. The result seems like collaboration between Salvador Dalí and Luis Buñuel, with a few touches by Magritte and choreography by Twyla Tharp. MGM MIRAGE has built the troupe its own theater, an incredible space with an enormous dome and superhydraulics that allow for the Cirque performers to fly in space. Or so it seems.

While part of the fun of the early Cirque was seeing what amazing stuff they could do on a shoestring, seeing what they can do with virtually unlimited funds is spectacular. Cirque took full advantage of MGM MIRAGE's largesse, and their art only rose with their budget. The show features one simply unbelievable act after another (seemingly boneless contortionists and acrobats, breathtakingly beautiful aerial maneuvers), interspersed with Dadaist/commedia dell'arte clowns, and everyone clad in costumes like nothing you've ever seen before. All this and a giant snail!

The show is dreamlike, suspenseful, funny, erotic, mesmerizing, and just lovely. At times, you might even find yourself moved to tears. For some children, however, it might be a bit too sophisticated and arty. Even if you've seen Cirque before, it's worth coming to check out, thanks to the large production values. It's a world-class show, no matter where it's playing. That this arty and intellectual show is playing in Vegas is astonishing. Catch it Wednesday through Saturday 7:30 and 10:30pm, Sunday 4:30 and 7:30pm. In TI–Treasure Island, 3300 Las Vegas Blvd. S. ℂ 800/963-9634 or 702/796-9999. www.cirquedusoleil.com. Tickets $60–$95 (plus tax and service fee).

Cirque du Soleil's O 🔥🔥🔥   How to describe the seemingly indescribable wonder and artistry of Cirque du Soleil's still utterly dazzling display? An Esther Williams–Busby Berkeley spectacular on peyote? A Salvador Dalí painting come to life? A stage show by Fellini? The French troupe has topped itself with this

---

Kids   Family-Friendly Shows

Appropriate shows for kids, all described in this chapter, include the following:

- *American Superstars* at the Stratosphere (p. 242)
- Cirque du Soleil's *KÀ* at the MGM Grand (p. 243)
- Cirque du Soleil's *LOVE* at The Mirage (p. 245)
- Cirque du Soleil's *Mystère* at TI–Treasure Island (p. 245)
- *Lance Burton: Master Magician* at the Monte Carlo (p. 249)
- *Mac King* at Harrah's (p. 250)
- *Stomp Out Loud* at Planet Hollywood (p. 252)
- *Tournament of Kings* at Excalibur (p. 254)

---

production—and not simply because it's situated its breathtaking acrobatics in, on, around, and above a 1.5-million-gallon pool (*eau*—pronounced *O*—is French for "water"). Even without those impossible feats, this might be worth the price just to see the presentation, a constantly shifting dreamscape tableau that's a marvel of imagination and staging. If you've seen *Mystère* at TI–Treasure Island or other Cirque productions, you'll be amazed that they've once again raised the bar to new heights without losing any of the humor or stylistic trademarks, including the sensuous music. If you've never seen a Cirque show, prepare to have your brain turned inside out.

We know—those ticket prices, especially when we keep pointing you in the direction of other Cirque shows—*ouch*. We want to say that we can guarantee it's worth it, but that's a decision only you can make. (Though no one we've personally sent has come back regretting having went.) But we can say this: Watch this show, and you know where a good chunk of the money is going (in other words, they spend a bundle nightly to mount this thing). Note that no tank tops, shorts, or sneakers are allowed. Wednesday through Sunday 7:30 and 10:30pm. In Bellagio, 3600 Las Vegas Blvd. S. ✆ **888/488-7111** or 702/693-7722. www.cirquedusoleil.com. Tickets $94–$150 (plus tax).

Cirque du Soleil's *Zumanity (Overrated)*   If we really need to tell you one more time, Las Vegas is not for kids. And here is the final proof: Cirque du Soleil, long considered the smartest family entertainment around, now produces this, an adult show dedicated to celebrating human sexuality. (Or celebrating how they can shamelessly empty your pockets, but hold on—more cynicism to come.) Staunch warnings tell audience members this is 18-and-over, and you know it as ushers dressed—and we feel terrible for them—in comic T-shirts designed to make them look naked escort you to seats while the usual pre-show Cirque business gets under way, this time in the form of a self-loving, well-muscled male egoist who oozes and seduces gullible patrons. And thus begins the least subtle show on the Strip (appropriately for the least subtle hotel on the Strip), an erotic cabaret of the sort that stopped being shocking in fin-de-siècle Paris, not that that stops the crowd from eating it up.

A rhinestone-bedecked transvestite hostess introduces a bevy of acts that are all meant to be lewd or alluring or both. But if you pay attention, they are mostly just basic Cirque acts (and worse, just basic striptease acts, which you can see anywhere in town for a great deal less money), though instead of giving the illusion of near-nakedness, they give the illusion of total nakedness (an illusion that works better the farther you sit from the stage). As they contort and writhe and feign pleasure or apathy, we feel sympathy for all the parents who spent money on gymnastics and ballet lessons over the years, only to have their poor kids end up in this. See, Cirque is naturally sexy and erotic, so all this is gilding the lily until it chokes from lack of oxygen and dies. But if you were feeling sexy despite this stuff, the comic antics of the clowns, as they beat each other with blow-up dolls and faux phalli, should quench your ardor, while a triple-jointed contortionist should put you off sex—and your lunch—for good.

There are some visually stunning moments (two women splashing about in a large glass, a woman performing with a dozen hula hoops), and at least one sketch (involving a woman and a muscled little person) that actually says something about love, romance, and tenderness. But overall, this is an endeavor of such cynicism that it makes our own look faint-hearted. Save your money for MGM Grand's *Crazy Horse Paris* across the street, or just go to Sapphire and tip the best dancer there. Friday through Tuesday at 7:30 and 10:30pm. In New York–New York, 3790 Las Vegas Blvd. S. ☎ **866/ 606-7111** or 702/740-6815. www.zumanity.com. Ages 18 and over only. Tickets $85–$99 (theater seats), $69 (cabaret stools and balcony with partially obstructed views), $79 (upper orchestra), $129 per person (duo sofas, sold in pairs), plus tax and service fee.

Crazy Girls   *Crazy Girls*, presented in an intimate theater, is probably the raciest revue on the Strip. It features sexy showgirls with perfect bodies in erotic song-and-dance numbers enhanced by innovative lighting effects. Think of *Penthouse* poses coming to life. Perhaps it was best summed up by one older man from Kentucky: "It's okay if you like boobs and butt. But most of the girls can't even dance." Wednesday through Monday 9:30pm. In the Riviera Hotel & Casino, 2901 Las Vegas Blvd. S. ☎ **877/892-7469** or 702/794-9433. www.rivierahotel.com. Ages 18 and over only. Tickets $55–$75 (plus tax).

Criss Angel: *Believe with Cirque de Soliel*   Flashy set pieces with magicians aren't unfamiliar territory to Vegas, though the city hasn't seen anything along the huge budget lines since the abrupt departure of Seigfried & Roy. That's all set to change with the arrival (in fall 2008) of this collaboration between charismatic Angel and the always eye-catching Cirque. While "plot" may be too strong a word to associate with a Cirque production, this does promise a narrative of sorts, probably paying dream-like homage to Angel's love of Houdini (as does the title). Given Angel's penchant for hypnotic fantastical illusions and escapist scenarios and the Cirque's own surreal human-generated special effects, this could well be a thrilling show, an organic mélange of artistic visions, not to mention an updated version of Vegas razzle-dazzle. Friday through Tuesday 7 and 10pm. In the Luxor, 3900 Las Vegas Blvd. S. ☎ **800/288-1000.** Tickets $59–$150.

Danny Gans: *The Man of Many Voices* ✷✷   In a town where the consistent sell-outs are costly, elaborate extravaganzas, it's a tribute to Danny Gans's charisma and appeal that his one-man variety act can draw the same crowds with nothing more than a backup band and a few props. Gans is "the man of many voices"—more than 400 of them—and his show features impressions of 80 different celebrities, usually a different mix each night, depending on audience demographics.

The emphasis is on musical impressions (everyone from Sinatra to Springsteen), with some movie scenes (Hepburn and Fonda from *On Golden Pond,* Tom Hanks in *Forrest Gump*) thrown in. A standout (though he doesn't always do it) is "The Twelve Months of Christmas" sung by 12 different celebrities (Paul Lynde, Clint Eastwood, Woody Allen, and so on). Gans's vocal flexibility is impressive, though his impersonations are hit-or-miss (his Springsteen needs work). That said, when we last saw him, he did a dead-on impression of comedian Jeff Foxworthy that had the crowd rolling, a hilarious bit involving George Burns imitating MC Hammer, and a somewhat freaky but totally on-target impression of Macy Gray. Truth be told, he's better than his current material (particularly if the mood strikes and he improvises), which is padded with obvious jokes and mawkish sentimentality. Still, he's a consistent crowd-pleaser, and the lack of bombast can be a refreshing change of pace. Wednesday and Friday through Saturday at 8pm. In The Mirage, 3400 Las Vegas Blvd. S. © **800/963-9634** or 702/792-7777. www.mirage.com. Tickets $100 (plus tax). *Note:* This show will play to the end of November 2008 in The Mirage before moving to the Wynn Encore sometime early in 2009.

An Evening at La Cage   No, it wasn't inspired by the French movie or the American remake, or even the Broadway musical. Actually, it's more like the stage show derived from the movie *Priscilla, Queen of the Desert*. Female impersonators dress up as various entertainers (with varying degrees of success) to lip-sync to those celebrity entertainers' greatest hits (with varying degrees of success). The celebs lampooned can include Céline Dion (one of the funniest moments, as they accurately parody her show down the Strip), Cher, Bette Midler, Judy Garland, Britney Spears, and, intriguingly, Michael Jackson. A Joan Rivers impersonator, looking not unlike the original but sounding not at all like her, is the hostess, delivering scatological phrases and jokes both current and that have been in the show for years. It's really close to being good without quite getting there. But it's been running forever, so for some folks, they are doing something right. Wednesday through Monday at 7:30pm. In the Riviera Hotel & Casino, 2901 Las Vegas Blvd. S. © **877/892-7469** or 702/794-9433. www.rivierahotel.com. Ages 12 and over only. Tickets $75 (plus tax).

Folies Bergere ☆☆   The longest-running production show in town has recently undergone a "sexier than ever" face-lift, but the result is far from that. It's more like tamed-down burlesque, as done by a college drama department. Bare breasts pop up (sorry) at odd moments (late shows only): not during the cancan line, but rather during a fashion show and an *en pointe* ballet sequence. The effect is neither erotic nor titillating, suggesting only that absent-minded dancers simply forgot to put their shirts on. The dance sequences (more acrobatics than true dance) range from the aforementioned ballet and cancan to jazz and hoedown, and are only occasionally well costumed. A coyly cute '50s striptease number on a *Hollywood Squares*–type set is more successful, as is a clever and funny juggling act (don't miss his finale with the vest and hat). Monday, Wednesday, Thursday (covered) at 7:30 and Saturday (topless) at 7:30 and 10pm; Tuesday and Friday (topless) at 8:30pm. In Tropicana Resort & Casino, 3801 Las Vegas Blvd. S. © **800/829-9034** or 702/739-2411. www.tropicanalv.com. Tickets $69–$76 (plus tax).

Jersey Boys Vegas ☆☆   Between 1962 and 1975, Frankie Valli and the Four Seasons racked up an astonishingly long string of catchy, well-crafted pop hits that are as well-known—and well-loved—as any in pop music. These time-tested songs are the central draw of the massively popular, Tony-winning (for Best Musical) "Jersey Boys." But this is far more than a rote musical revue, or just another re-creation of a popular oldies act. It's a real musical play, with a compelling street-to-suite storyline, a fair share of drama, and enough humor and uplift to satisfy both the theater veteran and the vacationing family (with a mild warning for some salty, Jersey-esque language). A dazzlingly visual production that crackles with energy and shines with precision stage-craft, "Jersey Boys" has already had an enthusiastic post-Broadway. With its visual wow factor and an excitingly faithful re-creation of the Four Seasons' music, it just may be the perfect vehicle to break the theatrical Vegas jinx (which has seen other

Tony winners such as "Hairspray," "The Producers," "Spamalot" and "Avenue Q" slink off in defeat) and settle in for a long, flashy run. Monday, Thursday, and Friday at 7pm, Tuesday and Saturday at 7 and 10pm. The Palazzo, 3325 Las Vegas Blvd. © 866/641-SHOW. $65–$135.

Jubilee! ⭒⭒⭒   A classic Vegas spectacular, crammed with singing, dancing, magic, acrobats, elaborate costumes and sets, and, of course, bare breasts. It's a basic revue, with production numbers featuring homogenized versions of standards (Gershwin, Cole Porter, some Fred Astaire numbers) sometimes sung live, sometimes lip-synced, and always accompanied by lavishly costumed and frequently topless showgirls. Humorous set pieces about Samson and Delilah, and the sinking of the *Titanic* (!) show off some pretty awesome sets. They were doing the *Titanic* long before a certain movie, and recent attendees claimed the ship-sinking effect on stage here was better than the one in the movie. The finale features aerodynamically impossible feathered and bejeweled costumes and headpieces designed by Bob Mackie. So what if the dancers are occasionally out of step, and the action sometimes veers into the dubious (a Vegas-style revue about a disaster that took more than 1,000 lives?) or even the inexplicable (a finale praising beautiful and bare-breasted girls suddenly stops for three lines of "Somewhere Over the Rainbow"?). Note that *Jubilee!* offers a marvelous backstage walking tour Mondays, Wednesdays, and Saturdays at 11am. Saturday through Thursday at 7:30 and 10:30pm. In Bally's Las Vegas, 3645 Las Vegas Blvd. S. © 800/237-7469 or 702/946-4567. www.ballys.com. Ages 18 and over only. Tickets $68–$110 (plus tax).

Lance Burton: *Master Magician* ⭒⭒⭒ *Kids*   Magic acts are a dime a dozen in Vegas of late. Along with impersonator acts, they seem to have largely replaced the topless showgirls of yore. Most magic shows seem more than a little influenced by the immeasurable success of Siegfried & Roy. So when someone pops up who is original—not to mention charming and, yes, actually good at his job—it comes as a relief. Handsome and folksy (he hails from Lexington, KY), Burton is talented and engaging, for the most part shunning the big-ticket special effects that seem to have swamped most other shows in town. Instead, he offers an extremely appealing production that starts small, with "close-up" magic. These lovely, precise tricks, he tells us, are what won him a number of prestigious magic competitions. They are truly extraordinary, we are told by other professional magicians. We swear that he tossed a bird up in the air, and the darn thing turned into confetti in front of our eyes. Really.

Burton doesn't have patter, per se, but his dry, laconic, low-key delivery is plenty amusing and contrasts nicely with other performers in town, who seem as if they have been spending way too much time at Starbucks. He does eventually move to bigger illusions, but his manner follows him—he knows the stuff is good, but he also knows the entire thing is a bit silly, so why not have fun with it? His longtime support act is comedian/juggler Michael Goudeau, who is not only perhaps the only genuinely funny and talented support act on the Strip, but who also can juggle a beanbag chair, a chainsaw, and a peanut M&M all at once. His presence is just further proof of how right Burton's show is overall. All this and extremely comfortable movie theater–style plush seats with cup holders. Tuesday and Saturday at 7 and 10pm, Wednesday through Friday at 7pm. In the Monte Carlo Resort & Casino, 3770 Las Vegas Blvd. S. © 877/386-8224 or 702/730-7160. www.montecarlo.com. Tickets $61–$73 (plus tax).

Le Rêve ⭒   Challenged from the get-go, thanks to a decision to base this Cirque-like around a stage of water, thus prompting inevitable comparisons with *O* down the street, this production is receiving an ongoing major revamp, both in staging and choreography, to address some of the issues. By and large, the choices—particularly to get revered avant-garde choreographer and Momix genius Moses Pendleton to take over the choreography (thus increasing the presence of dance)—have been good ones. But the show still comes off as a copy rather than an original.

Le Rêve, named for the most significant of the paintings owned by Steve Wynn, is an extravaganza featuring all the usual elements: gorgeously sculpted athletic performers who twist, contort, and mostly pose in filmy tattered outfits before and after diving in and splashing out of a giant pool. Intermittently funny clowns do their thing. Magritte figures float by. Fountains rise out of the stage. The result is pure spectacle, with a slight narrative suggesting the proceedings are the dreams of a woman dealing with a turbulent romantic issue. It's like the biggest, most impressive Esther Williams production you can imagine. Speaking of which, you may wish to avoid sitting in the front rows, unless you don't mind spending 90 minutes huddling under the provided towels—not only does the in-the-round staging mean the performers routinely splash water, but also that long, filmy costumes, when hauled out of said water and lifted high in the air, drip most impressively and most wetly on the first couple of rows. Since no seat is that far from the stage, and since the farther back, the more of the complex imagery you can take in, there really isn't a bad seat, so stay back and stay dry.

Speaking of, one advantage this production has over *O* are the top-end seats: placed in the back row, in cushy armchairs, equipped with video screens that show the off-stage action (so when a performer plunges into the pool, patrons can see where they go when they disappear from regular view), plus a bottle of champagne and some chocolate-dipped strawberries. A nice gimmick. Monday, Thursday, and Sunday at 7 and 9:30pm; Friday at 8:30pm; and Saturday at 8 and 10:30pm. In Wynn Las Vegas, 3131 Las Vegas Blvd. S. (✆ **888/320-7110**. www.wynnlasvegas.com. Ages 13 and over. Tickets $99–$179.

Mac King ✮✮✮ (Value) (Kids)   One of the best entertainment values in Vegas, this is an afternoon comedy-magic show—and note the order of precedence in that introduction. King does magic, thankfully, as far as we are concerned, emphasizing the only kind that's really mind-blowing these days—those close-up tricks that defy your eyes and mind. But he surrounds his tricks with whimsy and wit, and sometimes gut-busting guffaws, which makes you wonder how someone else can still perform stunts with a straight face. Check out how he takes a $100 bill and—wait, we don't want to give it away, but suffice it to say it involves an old shoe, a Fig Newton, and several other unexpected props. Perfect for the kids, perfect for the budget, perfect timing if you need something in the afternoon before an evening of gambling, dining, and cavorting. Then again, we are rather surprised he's still just an afternoon gig. One day, someone is going to wise up and move him to the big time, and his ticket prices will move up, too. So catch him while he's still a bargain. Tuesday through Saturday at 1 and 3pm. In Harrah's, 3475 Las Vegas Blvd. S. (✆ **800/427-7247**. www.harrahs.com. Tickets $25 (plus tax and service fees).

MGM Grand's *Crazy Horse Paris* ✮✮   Further proof that Vegas is trying to distance itself from the "Vegas Is for Families" image, "Classy Adult Entertainment" are the new watchwords in several hotels, with *Crazy Horse Paris* leading the pack. Allegedly the same show that has been running for years in a famous racy French nightclub, this show is just a bunch of pretty girls taking their clothes off. Except that the girls are smashingly pretty, with the kind of bodies just not found on real live human beings, and they take their clothes off in curious and, yes, artistic ways, gyrating *en pointe* while holding on to ropes or hoops, falling over sofas while lip-syncing to French torch songs—in short, it's what striptease ought to be, and by gosh, if strip clubs were this well staged, we'd go to them all the time. But $60 a ticket is a great deal to pay for arty nudie fun, especially when the routines, no matter how clever or how naked (the girls get down to a postage-stamp-size triangle soul patch covering the naughtiest of their bits, so they aren't "nude," but talk about a technicality), start to seem alike after a while. At press time, noted burlesque artist (and former Mrs. Marilyn Manson) Dita Von Teese was doing a stint in the production. Wednesday through Monday at 8 and 10:30pm. In the MGM Grand, 3799 Las Vegas Blvd. S. (C) 877/880-0880 or 702/891-7777. www.mgmgrand.com. Ages 18 and over. Tickets $59 (plus tax).

Penn & Teller ★★★ *(Moments)*   The most intelligent show in Vegas, as these two—magicians? illusionists? truth-tellers? BS artists? geniuses?—put on 90 minutes of, yes, magic and juggling, but also acerbic comedy, mean stunts, and great quiet beauty. Looking like two characters out of Dr. Seuss, big, loud Penn and smaller, silent Teller (to reduce them to their basic characteristics) perform magic, reveal the secrets behind a few major magic tricks, discuss why magic is nothing but a bunch of lies, and then turn around and show why magic is as lovely an art form as any other. We won't tell

---

Penn & Teller's Top 10 Things One Should *Never* Do in a Vegas Magic Show

Penn & Teller have been exercising their acerbic wit and magical talents in numerous forums together for more than 25 years, and their show at the Rio is one of Vegas's best and most intelligent. We must confess that we couldn't get the quieter half of the duo, Teller, to cough up a few words, but the more verbose Penn Jillette was happy to share.

1. Costume yourself in gray business suits totally lacking in rhinestones, animal patterns, Mylar, capes, bell-bottoms, shoulder pads, and top hats.
2. Wear your hair in any style that could *not* be described as "feathered" or "spiked."
3. Use really good live jazz music instead of canned sound-alike cheesy rip-off fake pop "music."
4. Cruelly (but truthfully) make fun of your siblings in the magic brotherhood.
5. Do the dangerous tricks on each other instead of anonymous show women with aftermarket breasts and/or endangered species.
6. Toss a cute little magic bunny into a cute little chipper-shredder.
7. Open your show by explaining *and* demonstrating how other magicians on the Strip do their most amazing tricks, and then do that venerable classic of magic "The Cups and Balls," with transparent plastic cups.
8. Treat the audience as if they had a brain in their collective head.
9. Allow audience members to sign real bullets, load them into real guns, and fire those bullets into your face.
10. Bleed.

(You will find **all** 10 of these "don'ts" in the *Penn & Teller* show at the Rio All-Suite Hotel and Casino.)

you much about the various tricks and acts for fear of ruining punch lines, but watching Teller fish money out of an empty glass aquarium or play with shadows is to belie Penn's earlier caveats about learning how tricks are done—it doesn't ruin the wonder of it, not at all, nor the serenity that settles in your Vegas-sensory-overloaded brain. Saturday through Thursday at 9pm. In the Rio Hotel, 3700 W. Flamingo. ✆ **888/746-7784.** www.riolasvegas.com. Ages 5 and over only. Tickets $75–$85 (plus tax).

Phantom of the Opera This is a 90-minute, intermission-free, heavy-on-the-special-effects, costly staging of Andrew Lloyd Webber's ubiquitous musical *The Phantom of the Opera.* The show's fans (and they are legion) will doubtless yowl, but they survived the movie adaptation, while the rest of us might be a little happier with some of the fat trimmed away, though somewhat befuddled by the plot. The lowdown: There's a guy in a mask, and he loves a girl who sings, and she loves him, but she also loves another boy, and there are caverns and canals and romance and tragedy and mystery and murder and light opera. Staged on the former site of the failed Guggenheim Museum (transformed into a $40-million theater), the musical is even more high-tech than the original Broadway staging, with increased special effects and whatnot (like anything can top that chandelier crash). *Phantom* is over the top, but then, so is Vegas, and this seems like a good fit. Monday through Saturday at 7pm; Monday and Saturday at 9:30pm; and Thursday at 10pm. At The Venetian, 3355 Las Vegas Blvd. S. ✆ **866/641-7469** or 702/414-7469. www.venetian.com. Tickets $80–$175 (plus tax).

Rita Rudner ✹✹ She stands in front of an audience for about an hour and tells the truth. It's that simple. It's also funny as heck, and oddly endearing, as Rudner's successful shtick is to present herself as Every Woman, not to mention the audience's Best Friend Forever. She wryly and dryly tosses out one-liners about gender relationships in an attempt to explain that age-old problem—What Do Women Want? And Why Don't Men Understand It's Shoes? At Harrah's, 3475 Las Vegas Blvd. S. ✆ **702/369-5222.** Tickets $54–$105.

The Second City ✹✹ *Value* Second City is the Chicago-based comedy group that spawned not only *SCTV* but also some of the best modern-day comics (such as the late Gilda Radner and John Belushi, Martin Short, and Mike Myers). This is an improv comedy show, with cast members performing stunts similar to those you might have seen on *Whose Line Is It Anyway?*—you know, taking suggestions from the audience and creating bizarre little skits and such out of them, all of it done at lightning speed with wit and a wink. Some of it can turn R-rated, so be careful about bringing the kids, but do not hesitate to see it yourself. And join in—any improv group is only as good as the material fed it. (So remember, there's only so much a group can do with jokes about sex and vomiting, especially if every single audience member thinks that would be funny material with which to work.) One of the best values and highest-quality shows in Vegas. Monday, Tuesday, and Friday at 8pm; and Thursday, Saturday, and Sunday at 8 and 10:30pm. In The Flamingo Las Vegas, 3555 Las Vegas Blvd. S. ✆ **800/221-7299** or 702/733-3333. www.secondcity.com. Tickets $45 (plus tax and fees).

Stomp Out Loud ✹✹ *Kids* A happy-go-lucky bunch of young people come on stage and make some noise. Lots of noise. They clap, they bang on trashcans, they—yes—stomp. A peculiar theatrical phenomena that finally gives drummers respect, the *Stomp* troupes are percussion whizzes. There is nothing they can't make a beat out of or even turn into primitive music. Why is this "out loud"? Apparently because the cast is bigger, with 16 people, which makes it louder. Or something. Performers start with

Afternoon Delight?

By now, it will not have escaped your attention that most of the nighttime shows in Vegas, at least the ones of any quality, cost a lot. Except for the ones that cost a whole heck of a lot. And that we tend to prefer the latter. "Isn't there *any* cheap entertainment in this town?" you may have begun to wonder, and trust us, even if we are awfully liberal with the contents of your wallets, we feel your pain.

So, barring the possibility that you might be the kind of gambler we wish to be—the sort who gets comped free tickets to expensive shows (that you could probably afford anyway, in typical Vegas irony)—there are some alternatives. Several Vegas hotels offer afternoon shows, at much more reasonable prices—that, of course, being a relative term. Here are a couple of the better offerings: (**Note:** Mac King, because he's quite a bit better, gets his own full review above.) **Ronn Lucas** ⍟⍟ (Excalibur, 3850 Las Vegas Blvd. S.; ✆ 800/933-1334; Tues–Sun 1pm; $30–$40 plus tax, includes drink and program) seems like a throwback to corny vaudeville days—after all, he's a ventriloquist. But his puppets are maladjusted (why not?), with bite and wit, and he is fearless in the manner of Penn & Teller; he gleefully deconstructs his art form, confident that after he shows you how it all works, he can still bamboozle you. Watch if you don't suddenly start thinking of those puppets as real characters, even though you know exactly how it all works. He's clever, funny, and weird.

Dirk Arthur ⍟ (Tropicana Las Vegas, 3801 Las Vegas Blvd. S.; ✆ 800/829-9034; www.tropicanalv.com; Sat–Thurs 2 and 4pm; $22–$28 per person) is an entertaining magician, though one wonders why he merits his own afternoon show but not his own nighttime show, or a part of one of the big nighttime production revues (as he once did).

Viva Las Vegas (Stratosphere Casino Hotel & Tower, 2000 Las Vegas Blvd. S.; ✆ 800/99-TOWER or 702/380-7777; www.stratospherehotel.com; Mon–Sat 2 and 4pm; $17, including tax), an everything-but-the-kitchen-sink Vegas variety show, is good only if you really need an hour's respite from the slots in the afternoon.

Note: Discount coupons for the afternoon shows are often found in those free magazines in hotel rooms. Sometimes the discount gets you in free, with just the price of a drink.

a set of push brooms and move to the aforementioned trashcans, plus water jugs, boxes, key rings, lighters (which makes for a great affect in a dark theater), even newspapers and garbage bags. The onstage joy is infectious, plus it's refreshing to see a racially and physically mixed cast, as opposed to the usual line-up of generic impossibly pretty people. Hardly mentally challenging, perhaps just a bit repetitious, and certainly not for those who would consider it all just noise (and for any parents who have to endure their kid's post-show imitative pounding, we apologize), but it is as fun and funny as it is clever. Monday 6 and 9pm; Tuesday, Thursday, Friday, and Sunday 7pm;

and Saturday 7 and 10pm. In Planet Hollywood, 3663 Las Vegas Blvd. S. ℂ **877/333-0474**. Tickets $60–$100 (plus tax).

Tournament of Kings ☀ (Kids)   If you've seen the Jim Carrey movie *The Cable Guy*, you probably laughed at the scene in which the two protagonists go to a medieval dinner and tournament. Perhaps you thought it was satire, created just for the movie. You would be wrong. It's actually part of a chain, and something very like it can be found right here in Vegas, though in a new and improved version. Those of us who shuddered at the former incarnation find this new one to be, at worst, highly tolerable, and at times downright entertaining.

For a fixed price, you get a dinner that's better than you might expect (Cornish game hen, very fine baked potato, and more), which you eat with your hands (in keeping with the theme), while Merlin (or someone like him) spends too much time trying to work the crowd up with a singalong. This gives way to a competition among the kings of various medieval countries, competing for titles in knightly contests (jousting, horse races, and such) that are every bit as unrehearsed and spontaneous as a professional wrestling match. Eventually, good triumphs over evil and all that.

Each section of the arena is given a king to be the subject of and to root for, and the audience is encouraged to hoot, holler, and pound on the tables, which kids love but teens will be too jaded for (though we know some from whom a spontaneous "way cool" slipped out, unchecked, a few times). Many adults might find it tiresome, particularly when they insist you shout "huzzah!" and other period slang. Acrobatics are terrific, and certain buff performers make for a different sort of enjoyment. Daily at 6 and 8:30pm. In Excalibur, 3850 Las Vegas Blvd. S. ℂ **800/933-1334** or 702/597-7600. www.excalibur.com. Tickets $55 (plus tax).

3 Headliner Showrooms

Vegas entertainment made its name with its showrooms, though its glory days are somewhat behind it, gone with the Rat Pack themselves. For a long time, Vegas headliners were something of a joke; only those on the downhill side of fame were thought to play here. But with all the new performance spaces—and high fees—offered by the new hotels, Vegas suddenly has respect again, especially, on (of all things) the rock scene. Both the Hard Rock Hotel's The Joint (currently undergoing a massive reconstruction) and the House of Blues attract very current and very popular acts who find it hip, rather than humiliating, to play Sin City. However, the classic Vegas showroom itself does seem headed the way of the dinosaurs; many of the hotels have shuttered theirs. As for the remainder, one is pretty much like the other, with the exception of the Hard Rock and HOB (hence their detailed descriptions), and in any case, audiences go based on the performer rather than the space itself. Check with your hotel, or those free magazines in your room, to see who is in town when you are.

Major headliner showrooms in Vegas include the following:

- **Center for the Performing Arts**   In the Planet Hollywood Hotel & Casino, 3667 Las Vegas Blvd. S. (ℂ **877/333-9474** or 702/785-5555)
- **Las Vegas Hilton Showroom**   In the Las Vegas Hilton, 3000 Paradise Rd. (ℂ **800/222-5361** or 702/732-5755)
- **Mandalay Bay Events Center**   In Mandalay Bay, 3950 Las Vegas Blvd. S. (ℂ **877/632-7400** or 702/632-7580)

- **MGM Grand Garden Events Arena** In the MGM Grand Hotel & Casino, 3799 Las Vegas Blvd. S. (© **800/929-1111** or 702/891-7777)
- **MGM Grand Hollywood Theatre** In the MGM Grand Hotel & Casino, 3799 Las Vegas Blvd. S. (© **800/929-1111** or 702/891-7777)
- **Orleans Showroom** In the Orleans, 4500 W. Tropicana Ave. (© **800/ ORLEANS**)

Hard Rock Hotel's The Joint 🎸 Formerly just about the only game in town in terms of good rock bookings, The Joint, with its 1,400-seat capacity, faces some stiff competition from the House of Blues. For example, when Alanis Morrisette came to town, she played the Hard Rock, but her opening act, Garbage, played the House of Blues. On the other hand, it was here the Rolling Stones chose to do a show during their arena tour—this was the smallest venue the band had played in years, and, as you can imagine, it was one hot ticket. When the Hard Rock Hotel opened in 1995, the Eagles were the first act to appear. Since then the facility has presented Bob Dylan, Ziggy Marley, Marilyn Manson, Green Day, the Black Crowes, David Bowie, Donna Summer, Stephen Stills, Jimmy Cliff, Tears for Fears, Lyle Lovett, and James Brown. The venue is not a preferred one, however; it's worth going only if a favorite performer is playing or if it's an opportunity to see a big artist play a smaller-than-usual room.

At press time, The Joint was closed for an entire reconception; the club is changing locations, which will allow for a much larger space when it reopens in late 2008. Expect a bigger rival to the House of Blues, which outstripped its rival some time ago.

Showroom Policies: Smoking is permitted for some shows; seating is either preassigned or general, depending on the performer. **Price:** $20 to $250, depending on the performer (tax and drinks extra). **Showtimes:** Times and nights of performance vary. **Reservations:** You can reserve up to 30 days in advance. In the Hard Rock Hotel & Casino, 4455 Paradise Rd. © **800/693-7625** or 702/693-5000. www.hardrockhotel.com.

House of Blues 🎸🎸 The House of Blues goes head to head with The Joint at the Hard Rock Hotel, and it does seem as though acts looking to do spontaneous shows pick HOB over The Joint. On its own merits, the House of Blues is a good, intimate room with a cozy floor surrounded by a bar area, and an upstairs balcony area that has actual theater seating. (The balcony might be a better place to see a show since the sightlines are unobscured, unlike down below, where posts and such can get in the way.) It's probably the most comfortable and user-friendly place to see a rock show in Vegas.

Headliner Stadiums

Two arenas are worth a mention. **Sam Boyd Stadium,** the outdoor stadium at the University of Nevada, Las Vegas (UNLV), has been host to such major acts as Paul McCartney, the Eagles, and Metallica. Still, both it and the **Thomas and Mack Center,** the university's indoor arena, have been losing headliners to the MGM Grand Garden and the Mandalay Bay Center. (These two, for example, recently saw acts such as the Police reunion, Gwen Stefani, Christina Aguilera, U2, and Justin Timberlake.) Both are more likely to have sporting events these days. Both are located on the **UNLV campus** at Boulder Highway and Russell Road (© **702/895-3900**). Ticketmaster (© **702/474-4000;** www.ticketmaster.com) handles ticketing for both arenas.

Fun Fact   **Wayne Newton's Top 10 Favorite Lounge Songs**

Wayne Newton is the consummate entertainer. He has performed more than 25,000 concerts in Las Vegas alone, and in front of more than 25 million people worldwide. Wayne has received more standing ovations than any other entertainer in history. Along with his singing credits, his acting credits are soaring—one of his most fun credits is *Vegas Vacation*. Make sure you catch him. No trip to Vegas is complete without seeing the "King of Las Vegas."

1. "You're Nobody, 'Til Somebody Loves You" (You don't have a body unless somebody loves you!)
2. "Up a Lazy River" (or "Up Your Lazy River!")
3. "Don't Go Changing (Just the Way You Are)" (The clothes will last another week!)
4. "Having My Baby" (Oh, God!)
5. "The Windmills of My Mind" (A mind is a terrible thing to waste!)
6. "The Wind Beneath My Wings" (Soft and Dry usually helps!)
7. "Copacabana"
8. "When the Saints Go Marching In"
9. "I Am, I Said" (Huh?!)
10. "The Theme from *The Love Boat*" (or "Would a Dinghy Do?")

The heavy theme decor (a constant evocation of the Delta region and New Orleans) is a bit too Disneyland-meets-Hearst-Castle, with corrugated-tin this and weathered-wood that, plus walls covered in outsider/primitive/folk art from various Southern artists. But it annoys us less in Vegas than it does in New Orleans; here it's sort of a welcome touch of the genuine amid the artificial, while in the actual Big Easy, it comes off as prefab.

The House of Blues has rock and blues shows just about every night, and, as mentioned, nationally recognized acts flock to the place, starting with Bob Dylan on opening night and continuing with shows by Seal, X, Garbage, Taylor Dane, Al Green, James Brown, the Go-Go's, the Neville Brothers, Chris Isaak, and even spoken word by Henry Rollins. During the summer, Mandalay Bay hosts outdoor concerts on its poolside beach. Acts have included the Go-Go's and B-52's.

Showroom Policies: Smoking is permitted; seating is either preassigned or general, depending on the performer. (Some shows are all general admission, with everyone standing on the floor.) **Price:** $18 to $250, depending on the performer. **Showtimes:** Vary, but usually 8pm. **Reservations:** You can buy tickets as soon as shows are announced; lead time varies with each artist. In Mandalay Bay, 3950 Las Vegas Blvd. S. © 877/632-7400 or 702/632-7600. www.hob.com.

4 Comedy Clubs

Comedy Club   The Riviera's comedy club, on the second floor of the Mardi Gras Plaza, showcases several comedians nightly. They are usually nobody you've ever heard of, and the place tends to draw a breed of comic that goes for the gross-out, insult-every-minority brand of "humor" instead of actual humor. Daily 8:30 and 10:30pm.

In the Riviera Hotel & Casino, 2901 Las Vegas Blvd. S. © **800/634-6753** or 702/794-9433. Tickets $25 (plus tax and fees).

Comedy Stop   Similar to the other comedy clubs in town, the Comedy Stop features several of what they call "nationally known comedy headliners" nightly, although let's just say you shouldn't expect to see Jerry Seinfeld performing here anytime soon. Daily 8 and 10:30pm. In Tropicana Resort & Casino, 3801 Las Vegas Blvd. S. © **800/829-9034** or 702/739-2411. Tickets $22 (includes tax, tip, and 1 drink).

The Improv 𝒞𝒞   This offshoot of Budd Friedman's famed comedy club (the first one opened in 1963 in New York City) presents about four comedians per show in a 400-seat showroom. These are talented performers—the top comics on the circuit, ones you're likely to see on Leno and Letterman. You can be sure of an entertaining evening. Tuesday through Sunday 8:30 and 10:30pm. In Harrah's Las Vegas, 3475 Las Vegas Blvd. S. © **800/392-9002** or 702/369-5111. Tickets $40 (includes taxes and fees).

5 Bars

In addition to the venues listed below, consider hanging out, as the locals quickly began doing, at **Aureole** 𝒞𝒞, **Red Square** 𝒞𝒞, and the **House of Blues** 𝒞𝒞, all in Mandalay Bay. There's a separate bar at Aureole (p. 120), facing the wine tower, where your wish for wine sends comely lasses flying up four stories, courtesy of *Peter Pan*–style harnesses, to fetch your desired bottle. At Red Square (p. 124), keep your drink nicely chilled all night long on the ice bar, created by water that's freshly poured and frozen daily. Or hang out and feel the blues at the small bottle-cap-bedecked bar in the corner of the House of Blues restaurant (see the "You Gotta Have a Theme" feature on p. 126), which gets quite lively with off-duty locals after midnight.

You might also check out the incredible nighttime view at the bar atop the **Stratosphere Casino Hotel & Tower** (p. 96)—nothing beats it.

There's also the **Viva Las Vegas Lounge** at the Hard Rock Hotel (p. 98), which every rock-connected person in Vegas will eventually pass through.

Caramel 𝒞𝒞   It's small, but worlds away from the Bellagio-business-as-usual just outside its doors. How happy the 20-somethings are that there is this hip-hop spinning, nonthreatening (and non-Euro-stodgy), scene-intensive hangout with caramel-and-chocolate-coated drink glasses and glowing bar in the middle of Bellagio. How much does this prove Bellagio is trying to lure the ghost-bar crowd away from the Palms? Not that this will do it, but if you are here and young, it's where you should be. Open daily 5pm to 5am. In Bellagio, 3600 Las Vegas Blvd. S. © **702/693-7111.**

Champagnes Cafe 𝒞𝒞   Wonder where Old Vegas went? It ossified right here. Red- and gold-flocked wallpaper and other such trappings of "glamour" never die— in fact, with this ultralow lighting, they will never even fade. It's a seedy old bar with seedy old scary men leering away. They even serve ice-cream shakes spiked with booze—two indulgences wrapped into one frothy package, and quite a double addiction delight. Some might run screaming from the place, while others will think they've died and gone to heaven. It's the kind of place that refuses to serve food any more because that would mean they would have to ban smoking. So cool it's going to keep going from passé to hot and back again in the course of an evening. Karaoke Friday through Saturday 10pm to 2am. Open daily 24 hours. 3557 S. Maryland Pkwy. (btw. Twain Ave. and Desert Inn Rd.). © **702/737-1699.**

Coyote Ugly ⊛   You've seen the movie, now go have some of that prepackaged fun for yourself. Oh, come on—you don't think those bartender girls really dance on the bar and hose down the crowd just because they are so full of spontaneous rowdy high spirits, now do you? Not when the original locale built a reputation (and inspired a bad movie) on just such behavior, creating a success strong enough to start an entire chain of such frat-boy fun places? By the way, sarcastic and cynical as we are, can we say it's a totally fun place? Open daily from 6pm to 4am. In New York–New York, 3790 Las Vegas Blvd. S. (at Tropicana Ave.). ℂ 702/740-6969. www.coyoteuglysaloon.com. Cover varies, usually $10 and up after 8pm.

Dispensary Lounge ⊛   Stuck in a '70s time warp (the water wheel and the ferns are the tip-off, though the Muzak songs confirm it), this is a fine place for a nice, long drink. One that lasts decades, perhaps. It's very quiet, low-key, and often on the empty side. Things pick up on weekends, but it still isn't the sort of place that attracts raucous drunks. (Of course, if it were on the Strip instead of being tucked away, it probably would.) "We leave you alone if you don't want to be bothered," says the proprietor. (We still worry about what happens if you sit here long enough.) If you are a hep cat, but one on the mild side, you'll love it. Open daily 24 hours. 2451 E. Tropicana Ave. (at Eastern Ave.). ℂ 702/458-6343.

Double Down Saloon ⊛⊛⊛ *(Finds*   "House rule: You puke, you clean." Okay, that about sums up the Double Down. Well, no, it doesn't really do the place justice. This is a big local hangout, with management quoting an old *Scope* magazine description of its clientele: "Hipsters, blue collars, the well-heeled lunatic fringe." Rumored to have been spotted here: director Tim Burton and the late Dr. Timothy Leary. Need to know more? Okay, trippy hallucinogenic graffiti covers the walls, the ceiling, the tables, and possibly you if you sit there long enough. Decor includes Abbey Rents–type chairs, thrift-store battered armchairs and sofa, a couple of pool tables, and a jukebox that holds everything from the Germs and Frank Zappa to Link Wray, Dick Dale, and Reverend Horton Heat. Oddly, they swear they invented the bacon martini here. On Wednesday night, they have a live blues band, while other nights might find local alternative, punk, or ska groups performing. On the last Sunday of every month, the Blue Man Group plays, but under another name, as a percussion band. Call about that, for sure. There's no cover unless they have some out-of-town band that actually has a label deal. Open daily 24 hours. 4640 Paradise Rd. (at Naples Dr.). ℂ 702/791-5775. www.doubledownsaloon.com.

Downtown Cocktail Lounge ⊛⊛   One of three (and counting) friendly and individualistic bars just a couple blocks from the Fremont Street Experience, these are the places to go for true modern Vegas cool, as opposed to the prefab (not to mention costly) Strip-side hotel bars. Once you find the door (it's hidden behind an industrial metal sheet on the left) you enter an Asian *moderne* space, complete with lounges that invite posing. It feels a little more young-executive friendly than its neighbor, the gothic Griffin. The cocktail menu is as substantial as it ought to be. Daily 5pm until close (usually till about 2am, but it can vary). 111 Las Vegas Blvd. ℂ 702/880-3696.

Drop Bar ⊛   Smack in the middle of the Green Valley Ranch Resort, with '60s-inspired go-go girls dancing away. Open daily 24 hours. In Green Valley Ranch Resort, 2300 Paseo Verde Pkwy., Henderson. ℂ 702/221-6560. No cover.

Eiffel Tower Bar ⊛   From this chic and elegant room, in the restaurant on the 11th floor of the Eiffel Tower, you can look down on everyone (in Vegas)—just like a real

Parisian! (Just kidding, Francophiles.) But really, this is a date-impressing bar, and, since there's no cover or minimum, it's a cost-effective alternative to the overly inflated food prices at the restaurant. Drop by for a drink, but try to look sophisticated. And then you can cop an attitude and dismiss everything as *gauche*—or *droit,* depending on which way you are seated. A business-attire dress code is enforced after 4:30pm. Open daily 11am to 11pm. In Paris Las Vegas, 3655 Las Vegas Blvd. S. ✆ 702/948-6937.

ghostbar ✿✿   Probably the most interesting aspect of this desperate-to-get-into-the-gossip-pages-as-the-trendy-bar-of-the-moment place (decorated with a '60s mod/futuristic silver-gleam look) is that though much is made of the fact that it's on the 55th floor, it's really on the 42nd. Something about the number 4 being bad luck in Asian cultures. Whatever. The view still is fabulous, which is the main reason to come here, that and to peer at those tousled-hair beauties copping an attitude on the couches and see if any of them have the kind of names that will make tomorrow's gossip pages. This may be the hot bar of the moment by the time you get here (dress up), or everyone may have moved on. Who knows? Open daily 8pm until dawn. In the Palms Resort & Casino, 4321 W. Flamingo Rd. (just west of the Strip). ✆ 702/938-2666. Cover varies, usually $10 and up.

Griffin ✿✿   Part of a promising trend to revitalize the Fremont East District (just a couple of blocks from the Fremont Street Experience), the fun starts with the old stone facade and eponymous sign and continues inside with the stone pillars, arched cave ceiling and two fire pits. Just what you want in a stylish bar that revels in its history but at the same time doesn't try too hard. Given its proximity to other top-notch downtown hangouts such as Beauty Bar and Downtown Cocktail Lounge, this is a must-stop on the anti-Strip and hotel bar tour. There are DJs on the weekends. Open Monday through Saturday 5pm until close, Sunday 9pm until close (closing time can vary, but 2am is a safe bet). 511 E. Fremont St. ✆ 702/382-0577.

Gordon-Biersch Brewing Company ✿   This is part of a chain, and while it does feel like it, it's better than the average lounge chain. The interior is both contemporary and rustic, and warmer than its semi-industrial look suggests it would be. It's roomy, so you don't feel stacked up on top of other customers. The house lager (they specialize in German brews) was tasty and the noise level acceptable. A good place to go hoist a few. Open Sunday through Thursday 11am to midnight, Friday and Saturdays 11am to 1am. 3987 Paradise Rd. (just north of Flamingo Rd.). ✆ 702/312-5247. www.gordon biersch.com.

Hogs & Heifers Saloon ✿   While there is a chain of Coyote Ugly nightclubs (including one here in Vegas), the movie of the same name was actually based on the high jinks that happened at the New York version of this rowdy roadhouse saloon. In Sin City since 2005, the hogs here are of the motorcycle variety, and the place definitely draws a crowd that can look intimidating but is usually a friendly (and boisterous) bunch. Saucy, heckling bar maidens and outdoor barbecues on select weekends make this one of the few good options for nightlife in the Downtown area. Open daily, usually 10am to 6am (call to check on hrs., as they vary by month). 201 N. 3rd St. (btw. Ogden and Stewart aves., 1 block from the Fremont Street Experience). ✆ 702/676-1457.

Ivan Kane's Forty Deuce ✿✿   The brainchild of Los Angeles club impresario Ivan Kane, this is a supremely hot combo bar/nightclub/burlesque revue, a modern take on the classic girlie shows, featuring va-va-voom clever dancers (with shows every 90 min. for at least 15 min.—longer if there are more dancers) who strip down to little pasties, short-shorts, and g-strings. Drinks are obscenely expensive, and tables are entirely bottle service, and naturally, the view of the show is better from those seats. DJs spin between sets, and you can't fit a piece of paper inside on the weekends. The beautiful people love it, and we kind of do, too. Open Thursday through Monday from 10:30pm until dawn. Shows at 12:30am and 3am. In Mandalay Bay, 2950 Las Vegas Blvd. S. ℭ 702/632-7000. www.fortydeuce.com. Cover varies.

Peppermill's Fireside Lounge ⍟ *(Finds)* Walk through the classic Peppermill's coffee shop (not a bad place to eat, by the way) on the Strip, and you land in its fabulously dated view of hip bars. It has low, circular banquette seats, fake floral foliage, a whole bunch of pink neon, and electric candles. But best of all is the water and fire pit as the room's centerpiece—a piece of kitsch thought to be long vanished from Earth, and attracting nostalgia buffs like moths to a flame. The neon (a recent edition, just adding to the wrongness of the decor) detracts somewhat from the fire-pit centerpiece, but it's still wonderfully retro for unwinding a bit after some time spent on the hectic Strip. You might well be joined by all kinds of entertainers and others winding down after a late night. The enormous, exotic froufrou tropical drinks (including the signature bathtub-size margaritas) will ensure that you sink into a level of comfortable stupor. Open daily 24 hours. 2985 Las Vegas Blvd. S. ℭ 702/735-4177.

Petrossian ⍟⍟⍟ Those despairing of a grown-up place to drink, a place for people who want a real cocktail made by people who know that martinis really do require vermouth (none of this "just wave the bottle in the general direction of the glass" nonsense) and that "shaken not stirred" is a silly debate, rejoice and come here. Located just off the Bellagio lobby, this is one of the prettiest places to imbibe in the city as the glorious Dale Chihuly glass flowers "bloom" near your head. The bartenders are required to attend ongoing cocktail education, so they really know their stuff. Said stuff is made with the finest ingredients, which means none of the drinks come cheap. But the extra is worth it if you want it done right. They also have a good selection of high-end snacks. A little Beluga with your booze? In Bellagio, 3600 Las Vegas Blvd. S. ℭ 702/693-7111.

Playboy Club ⍟ A generation mourned when the last of the Playboy Clubs closed. Once the *sine non qua* of naughty, sexy, mature fun, somehow it lost its mojo. This new incarnation doesn't capture the vibe of exclusive adult cool, but its presence is still a happy thing for swingers, ironically retro and deadly serious alike. Positioned so that attendees can move between it and the Moon nightclub, there's expensive gambling and vintage magazine covers rotating on video screens. Although it's not nearly the bastion of cool that it once was, it's still kind of swell to see the Bunnies again—Gloria Steinem's lessons notwithstanding—even if they do make lousy dealers. Open daily at 8pm. In the Palms, 4321 W. Flamingo Rd. ℭ 702/942-777. Cover varies, includes admission to Moon nightclub.

Pussycat Dolls Lounge ⍟⍟ A Los Angeles novelty club act turned ubiquitous international stars, major brand, and reality TV show. Don't expect to see the recording stars perform in this lounge just off the PURE nightclub. (As if the difference between one pretty, vacuous face and plastic surgery–enhanced body and another is detectable anyway.) Still, the local gals strut their stuff (a couple of times an hour) well enough that you probably won't mind. Open daily at 5pm. In Caesars Palace, part of PURE. 3570 Las Vegas Blvd. S. ℭ 702/731-7873. Cover varies.

(Tips) Coolest House in Town?

Ice House Lounge, 650 S Main St. (© **702/315-2570**), a $5-million, two-story, 12,800-square-foot restaurant, bar, and gaming facility, is another effort to get Downtown on an upswing. The Art Deco–inspired building evokes images of South Beach rather than a Downtown dive, with an interior accented by retrospective photos of Old Vegas and '60s-style furniture. Both of the Ice House's two lounges sport frozen bar tops made of solid ice to keep drinks cold. Down a drink, grab a bite, and then play video poker or watch sports. (See p. 162 for a review of the restaurant.)

Revolution (ℛ This place is tied to the Beatles-themed Cirque *LOVE* show, so think White Album, not Chairman Mao. While we dig the Ginger Spice, Union Jack miniskirt–clad go-go dancer greeters, we wish the somewhat sterile interior was a bit more Peter Max, over-the-top shagadelic. Apart from some random Beatles-esque—rather, *LOVE*-esque—elements, the furnishings are pretty much beanbag chairs, silver mirrors, and a whiff of Austin Powers. Plus, the music relates not at all to the '60s. Having said that, lots of oddballs show up to spin records; in one week, Tommy Lee and Kevin Federline both headlined. The Abbey Road Bar, which fronts the place, is a good hangout, especially if you can kick out a go-go dancer and nab one of the seats in the REVOLUTION letters. Bar open noon to 4am, club open 6pm to 4am. In The Mirage, 3400 Las Vegas Blvd. S. © 702/791-1111.

Sand Dollar Blues Lounge   Reopened after a brief sprucing up, in part to get rid of a "bad element" (think too many bikers), this is the kind of funky, no-decor (think posters and beer signs), atmosphere-intensive, slightly grimy, friendly bar you either wish your town had or wish it had something other than. Just up the road from TI–Treasure Island, this is a great antidote to artificial Vegas. Attracting a solid mix of locals and tourists (employees claim the former includes everything from bikers to chamber of commerce members), the Sand Dollar features live blues (both electric and acoustic, with a little Cajun and zydeco thrown in) every night. We wondered how Vegas had enough blues bands to fill out an entire weekly bill. The answer? All the musicians play in multiple bands in different configurations. The dance floor is tiny and often full. The minimal cover always goes to the band. Drinks are happily affordable ($3 for a beer!). Depending on your desires, it's either refreshingly not Las Vegas or just the kind of place you came to Vegas to escape. Go before someone has the idea to build a theme hotel based on it. Open daily 24 hours. 3355 Spring Mountain Rd. (at Polaris Ave.). © 702/871-6651. www.sanddollarblues.com. No cover Sunday through Tuesday; Wednesday through Saturday $5–$7.

Triple 7 Brew Pub (ℛ *(Finds*   Yet another of the many things the Main Street Station hotel has done right. Stepping into its microbrew pub feels like stepping out of Vegas. Well, except for the dueling-piano entertainment. The place has a partially modern warehouse look (exposed pipes, microbrew fixtures visible through exposed glass at the back, and a very high ceiling), but a hammered-tin ceiling continues the hotel's Victorian decor; the overall effect seems straight out of San Francisco's North Beach. It's a bit on the yuppified side but escapes being pretentious. And frankly, it's a much-needed modern space for the Downtown area. This place has its own brew master and

> ### *Tips* Bathroom Break
>
> When you gotta go, you gotta go, particularly if you've tried drinking at every bar listed here, and so when you do, do try to do so in the unisex, free-standing Space Age pods at **Mandalay Bay's China Grill.**

a number of microbrews ready to try, and if you want a quick bite, there's also an oyster-and-sushi bar, plus fancy burgers and pizzas. It can get noisy during the aforementioned piano-duel act, but otherwise casino noise stays out. Since all of Downtown is too heavy on the Old Las Vegas side (which is fine, but not *all* the time), this is good for a suitable breather. Open daily from 11am to 7am. In Main Street Station, 200 N. Main St. ℂ **702/387-1896.**

Whiskey Bar ⊛⊛   Probably your best bet for a trendy place that might actually have either beautiful locals or out-of-town celebs looking for a cool time but wanting a lower profile. This cool, low-key vibe is due to the bar's off-the-Strip location and also its creator, hip-bar-master Rande Gerber (Cindy Crawford's hubby). Think beds instead of couches, and you've got a sense of the gestalt. Open Thursday and Sunday 6pm to 2am and Friday and Saturday 6pm to 4am. In the Green Valley Ranch Resort, 2300 Paseo Verde Pkwy., Henderson. ℂ **702/617-7560.** Cover varies, usually $10 and up.

Zuri ⊛   This is the best of the casino-hotel free bars (free as in no admission price), probably because of its construction, a semicurtained enclave just off the elevators (as opposed to a space just plunked down right off or right in the middle of a casino). With swooping wood and red-velvet couches, the drinks are expensive, but at least you can hear your partner's whispered sweet nothings (a rare thing in a Vegas hotel). Open 24 hours. In the MGM Grand, 3799 Las Vegas Blvd. S. ℂ **702/891-7777.**

6 Piano Bars

The Bar at Times Square ⊛   If you're looking for a quiet piano bar, this is not the place for you. It's smack in the middle of the Central Park part of the New York–New York casino. Two pianos are going strong every night, and the young hipster, cigar-smoking crowd overflows out the doors. It always seems to be packed with a singing, swaying, drinking throng full of camaraderie and good cheer—or at least, full of booze. Hugely fun, provided you can get a foot in the door. Shows daily from 8pm to 2:15am. In New York–New York, 3790 Las Vegas Blvd. S. ℂ **702/740-6969.** Cover $10 after 7pm.

Napoleon's ⊛⊛   A formerly nice but rather sedate space near the back of the Paris Las Vegas shopping gallery has been transformed into a rollicking good-time venue with the addition of dueling piano performances. The bar is a mixture of French old-world charm and Las Vegas showmanship, done all in reds and dark browns with lots of comfy seating scattered about. The pianists play daily 9pm to 1am. In Paris Las Vegas, 3570 Las Vegas Blvd. S. ℂ **702/946-7000.**

PJ McRae's ⊛   This low-key, sophisticated piano bar—its walls lined with oil paintings of icons such as Elvis, Bogart, James Dean, and Marilyn Monroe (not to mention Rodney Dangerfield, finally getting respect)—is a romantic setting for cocktails and classic piano-bar entertainment every night except Sunday and Monday. There's a small dance floor. On Friday and Saturday a talented vocalist is on hand as well. Far from a meat market, but it's a relaxed atmosphere in which to meet people, with an over-30 crowd. A menu offers salads, burgers, steak sandwiches, pastas, and gourmet appetizers such as oysters Rockefeller and escargot-stuffed mushrooms. Open daily 24 hours. 1487 E. Flamingo Rd. (btw. Maryland Pkwy. and Tamarus St.; on your right as you come from the Strip). ⓒ **702/737-6212.**

7 Gay Bars

Hip and happening Vegas locals know that some of the best scenes and dance action can be found in the city's gay bars. And no, they don't ask for sexuality ID at the door. All are welcome at any of the following establishments—as long as you don't have a problem with the people inside, they aren't going to have a problem with you. For women, this can be a fun way to dance and not get hassled by overeager Lotharios. (Lesbians, by the way, are just as welcome at any of the gay bars.)

If you want to know what's going on in gay Las Vegas during your visit, pick up a copy of *Q Vegas,* which is also available at any of the places described below. You can also call ⓒ **702/650-0636** or check out the online edition at **www.qvegas.com**. Gay nightlife listings can also be found on the Web at **www.gaylasvegas.com** or **www.gay vegas.com**.

The Buffalo 𝄐 Close to Gipsy and several other gay bars and establishments, this is a leather/Levi's bar popular with motorcycle clubs. It features beer busts (all the beer you can drink for a small cover) and other drink specials throughout the week. There are pool tables and darts, and music videos play in this not-striking environment. It's very cheap, with longnecks going for a few bucks, and it gets very, very busy, very late (3 or 4am). Open daily 24 hours. 4640 Paradise Rd. (at Naples Dr.) ⓒ **702/733-8355.**

The Eagle Off the beaten track in just about every sense of the phrase, the Eagle is the place to go if well-lit bars make you nervous. It's dark and slightly seedy, but in that great '70s gay bar kind of way. All in all, it's a refreshing change from the over-processed slickness that is Las Vegas. The crowd, tending toward middle age, is mostly male and of the Levi's/leather group. There is a small dance area (calling it a dance floor would be generous), a pool table, video poker, and a nice-size bar. Drinks are inexpensive, and special events make them even more so. For instance, the Eagle is rapidly becoming famous for its twice-weekly underwear parties (if you check your pants, you receive draft beer and drinks for free—that's right, free). The 20-minute drive from the Strip makes it a questionable option, but try it out if you've got a sense of adventure. Open daily 24 hours. 3430 E. Tropicana Ave. (at Pecos Rd.). ⓒ **702/458-8662.**

Gipsy 𝄐𝄐 For years, Gipsy reigned supreme as the best gay dance place in the city, and for good reason: great location (Paradise Rd. near the Hard Rock), excellent lay-out (sunken dance floor and two bars), and very little competition. A few years ago, some fierce competition stole some of its spotlight, along with a good portion of the clientele, and so the Gipsy fought back with a $750,000 renovation that seemed to recapture past glories. The drink specials, along with special events, shows, male dancers, and theme nights, make this place a good party bar. Open daily from 10pm to dawn. 4605 Paradise Rd. (at Naples Dr.). ⓒ **702/731-1919.** www.gipsylasvegas.com. Cover varies but is usually $5 and up on weekends, less or even free on weekdays.

Good Times 𝄐 This quiet neighborhood bar is located (for those of you with a taste for subtle irony) in the same complex as the Liberace Museum, a few miles due east of the MGM Grand. There's a small dance floor, but on a recent Friday night, nobody was using it, the crowd preferring instead to take advantage of the cozy bar area. A small conversation pit is a perfect spot for an intimate chat. Of course, there's the omnipresent pool and video poker if you're not interested in witty repartee. We remember this place as being a lot more crowded than it was during our most recent visit (but perhaps we were there on an off night). It makes a nice respite after the Liberace Museum (after which you may very well need a stiff drink). Open daily 24 hours. In the Liberace Plaza, 1775 E. Tropicana Ave. (at Spencer St.). ✆ 702/736-9494. www. goodtimeslv.com.

Krave ✪✪ Most notably the first gay club on the Strip, not that anyone's admitting it's a gay club anymore, using "alternative" as the winking buzzword. The result is a more mixed crowd than you might get at other, openly gay clubs. The interior is a well-crafted Gothic explosion, with a dance floor and some go-go platforms that can feature dancers of either gender. Overall, a toss-up; clearly, more money is going into the place, and the Strip access is important since most other local gay bars take some doing to get to. On the other hand, it has limited hours and a possibly even more competitive crowd. Note that if you don't pay the club valet, you have to park in the regular hotel parking, and that calls for a long jog through the evening-deserted Desert Passage shopping mall, which might be uncomfortable in club togs—limited access may well explain why there have already been two failed nightclubs in this space. Open daily except Monday from 8pm until late (after hours until dawn Fri and Sat). At Planet Hollywood Hotel & Casino, 3667 Las Vegas Blvd. S. (entrance on Harmon). ✆ 702/836-0830. www.kravelasvegas.com. Cover varies.

8 Dance Clubs

In addition to the options listed below, country-music fans might want to wander on in to **Toby Keith's I Love This Bar & Grill,** Harrah's, 3475 Las Vegas Blvd. S. (✆ 702/ 369-5084), not for the grill part—the food is definitely on the overpriced and unex-ceptional side—but for the bar portion of the program, with live entertainment Wednesday through Sunday from 9pm to 2am. The eponymous owner has been known to drop in and play from time to time.

Note about entrance fees: Many of the following have absurdly high door charges, prices that go up—way, way, way up—if you either encounter one of those doormen who will accept discrete (and significant) tips to let you bypass the inevitable line, or if you reserve one of the obnoxious "bottle service tables." Many of the clubs reserve all tables (and thus, chairs) for "bottle service," which require the purchase of a bottle or two of booze, usually running triple digits and way up. By the time you factor in the inflated cost of the bottle (which is often smaller than usual), taxes and other fees, not to mention the original door charge, your evening out has hit mid-three figures or more. Unless your wallets are heavy, skip this racket and resign yourself to maneu-vering for a place to stand on the floor.

One bright note—women are often charged less for admission than men (some-times even allowed in free), and any guest can get a comped ticket to even the hottest clubs, if you play it right. If there is a sign advertising the club (or even just the hotel) as you walk around the ground floor, and there is a person from the hotel standing by it (who will be in a suit with a nametag), go talk to them. Odds are good they will offer you comps to the club for that night. If you are gambling for any length of time, ask the pit boss for comps.

Note: As far as a dress code is concerned, you are going to go farther with more obviously expensive clothes, but you may not have the budget or fashion sense for that (and who travels with really good clothes, anyway?). When in doubt, all black should do it, and showing skin helps. Otherwise, just dress as nicely as you can and hope they don't notice your sneakers. But do avoid sports team–affiliated jerseys and baseball hats, baggy pants, and other things that might fall under the heading "gangsta-wear" because that's one sure way of not getting past the velvet rope.

The Bank 🍒🍒 Because Vegas can never sit still, the otherwise alluring Light night-club had to be demolished while it was still new-ish to make room for yet another hot spot. The entrance, lined with 500 bottles of Crystal, with crystal hanging from the ceiling, and the bar lined with gold crocodile skin, puts a guest on notice: This is high-end clubbing. Look for hefty cover charges (though ladies are often free), and as a result, it attracts the deep-pocket crowd. Top-of-the-line everything nearly justifies prices; the lights respond to the music, ten snow machines pump snow effects over the hot crowd, the staff are in couture suits. They may or may not let you in if you aren't dressed to the nines. Open Thursday through Sunday, 10:30pm to 4am. In Bellagio, 3600 Las Vegas Blvd. S. ✆ 702/693-8300.

Body English 🍒🍒 To our way of thinking, this is exactly what a Las Vegas club should be—because all the other hot nightclubs in town look exactly like a hot night-club in any old town, and so we always want Vegas places to be *Vegas*—over the top and just a little bit wrong. So this clash of Anne Rice and Cher Gothic–themed wacky decadence, with fabrics on top of wood on top of mirrors, not to mention the sort of layout that allows for intimate corners and voyeuristic balcony viewing of the dance floor, is just the sort of overly rich dessert of a place we crave. So do many others; it's one of the hottest spots in town, and the wait in line is so long you might well polish off a Rice novel while standing in it. Well, you gotta pass the time somehow. Expect a hefty cover charge, too. Open Friday through Sunday 10pm to 4:30am. In the Hard Rock Hotel, 4455 Paradise Rd. ✆ 702/693-5000. www.bodyenglish.com. Cover varies, but can be as high as $30.

Cherry 🍒 All of Vegas is style over substance, and given how similar the city's night-clubs can look after awhile, this fantastically designed space—thank Rande Gerber again—is enough of said style to make it instantly fabulous. It echoes the red of the Red Rock Canyon and the titular fruit. The enveloping tunnel entrance just starts the experience. A circular bar and raised circular dance floor dominate the inside, while outside the decadent action takes in the pool area, including fire pit and rotating beds. Don't miss the bathrooms—we don't want to give anything away but there are several surprises waiting. In Red Rock Resort, 11011 W. Charleston Rd. ✆ 702/423-3112. www.redrock lasvegas.com.Cover varies.

Cleopatra's Barge 🍒 This is a small, unique nightclub set in part on a floating barge—you can feel it rocking. The bandstand, a small dance floor, and a few (usually reserved) tables are here, while others are set around the boat on "land." It's a gimmick (in fact, it was the first themed nightclub in America) but one that makes this far more fun than other, more pedestrian, hotel bars. Plenty of dark makes for romance, but blaring volume levels mean you will have to scream those sweet nothings. It's still a landmark; trying to meet someone in the increasingly massive Caesars? Arrange to meet at the barge. Open nightly from 10:30pm to 3am. In Caesars Palace, 3570 Las Vegas Blvd. S. ✆ 702/731-7110. 2-drink minimum.

Drai's After Hours ⍟ Young Hollywood film execs and record-company types are likely to be found here, schmoozing and dancing it up to house, techno, and tribal music. Open Wednesday through Sunday from 1am until dawn. In Bill's Gambling Hall (formerly Barbary Coast), 3595 Las Vegas Blvd. S. ⓒ **702/737-0555.** Cover varies, usually $20.

Jet ⍟⍟ Done by the same folks who did the now defunct Light, this 2006 addition to The Mirage takes everything they did right at Bellagio and throws more money, more space, and more everything at it. The club is stunning, with three dance floors, each with its own vibe and musical style, and four bars on multiple levels to keep you entertained and give you something to look at. Wildly successful if you are of a certain age, but the combination of higher-than-average cover charges and the "club of the moment" vibe can be a bit exhausting for anyone looking for a slightly less competitive experience. Open Friday, Saturday, and Monday from 10:30pm until 4am. In The Mirage, 3400 Las Vegas Blvd. S. ⓒ **702/792-7900.** Cover varies, usually $30.

Monte Carlo Pub & Brewery ⍟ *(Finds* After 9pm nightly, this immense warehouselike pub and working microbrewery (details on p. 129) turns from a casual restaurant into something of a dance club. Rock videos blare forth from a large screen and 40 TV monitors around the room, while on stage, dueling pianos provide music and audience-participation entertainment. The pub is cigar-friendly and maintains a humidor. There's a full bar, and, of course, the house microbrews are featured. You can also order pizza. Open Wednesday, Thursday, and Sunday until 1am, Friday and Saturday until 2am. In the Monte Carlo Resort & Casino, 3770 Las Vegas Blvd. S. ⓒ **702/730-7777.**

Moon ⍟ Here is exactly the point we were alluding to above in the review of Cherry. This is another basic trendy nightclub—dance floor, smoke machines, house music—not nearly as inviting as Jet or Rain, its closest competitors, and certainly not a design stunner like Cherry or Tao. You go one night, and it's raging, you go another night and the DJ has misread the crowd and the dance floor is empty. The beat pounds and either so will your pulse or your head, and out you will go in search of something more interesting. You can quickly take it in after a brief tour of the Playboy Club just above it, as one (pricey) admission gets you into both. Opens daily at 8pm. In the Palms Resort & Casino, 4321 W. Flamingo Rd. ⓒ **702/492-3960.** Cover varies.

Polly Esther's Nightclub ⍟ This late-night club features four different rooms each themed to a different decade—'70s, '80s, '90s, and '00s—which just means big black boxes with decade-appropriate images projected on the walls and the music of the era blasting from the DJ. In the '70s room you can pose in the Brady Bunch square. The "This Decade" (What did we decide to call it? The Aughties?) room is more like an ultralounge. It's an appealing concept, less threatening and, frankly, more generic than the bigger names down the Strip. Plus, it seems the demographic is more spread out, thanks to theme and music, which makes it an alternative if you want to go out and dance, and don't want to deal with—or compete with, whatever—the 21-year-olds. Open Wednesday through Saturday from 11:30pm to 4am. In the Stratosphere, 2000 Las Vegas Blvd. S. ⓒ **702/380-7777.** Cover varies.

Privé and the Living Room ⍟⍟⍟ For once, a user-friendly club that's hot but not intimidating. While as dazzling as any of the other high-end joints on the Strip, this one is surprisingly egalitarian. There is no dress code (though dress up anyway, because it's more fun), which means all manner of patrons are mingling together. And mingle they do; with the exception of one row of bottle tables, all seating and other areas of the club are open to all patrons—no VIP ropes or other barriers, just move about the spacious, amphitheatre-inspired setup as you will. No matter where you stand, there is a good view. For that matter, if the spirit moves you, jump on the tables and couches and dance; they encourage that. Smashing visuals include a stage (they claim spontaneous performances bust out occasionally), two-story fireplace, projection screens showing Godzilla movies and the like, plus actual dance coordinators for the table-top-dancing waitresses. Because of the eclectic mix of clientele, the energy is great. Plus, one cover gets you two clubs: The Living Room is a much smaller space, evoking its name with a fireplace, leather couches, chandeliers, and a booming, deafening sound system. Open Monday, Friday, Saturday 10pm to 4am. In Planet Hollywood, 3667 Las Vegas Blvd. S. ✆ 702/492-3960. Cover $20 for women, $30 for men.

PURE 🞷🞷 The biggest club on the Strip, PURE is everything a big, loud nightclub ought to be. People line up hours before opening for the chance to share in the mayhem. (This is the place where Britney passed out on New Year's instead of completing her hostess duties, while Christina Aguilera held an after-show party here.) The theme is reflected in the decor—or lack of it, since just about everything is as white as Ivory Soap (get the name?)—which is either minimalist brilliant or reflects the fact that even Vegas designers get tired. In any event, the noise and lack of cushy corners means this is a definite get-your-booty-in-motion kind of place, though there is ample space (seriously, there are airline hangars that are smaller) for just standing around watching other booties in motion. There is also a rooftop club, itself bigger than most regular Vegas clubs, with views of the Strip, for those who need a little fresh air. Open Friday through Sunday and Tuesday 10pm to 4am. In Caesars Palace, 3570 Las Vegas Blvd. S. ✆ 702/731-7110. Cover varies.

Rain Nightclub 🞷🞷 Despite considerable competition, still one of the hottest nightclubs in Vegas. Which means you (and we—don't think we aren't standing there with you, shoulder-to-shoulder in solidarity) probably will spend most of your time trying to convince someone, anyone, to let you in—you and a couple thousand size-2 Juicy Couture jeans–clad 20-somethings who feel they will simply cease to exist if they don't get inside. We smirk and snicker at their desperation because it makes us feel superior. But we also have to be honest; if you can brave the wait, the crowds, and the attitude, you will be inside a club that has done everything right, from the multi-level layout that allows them to pack the crowds in and allows those crowds to peer up and down at their brethren, to DJs who play the right house and techno cuts (at a pulse-thumping tempo, so don't expect your good pickup lines to be heard), to the scaffolding that holds pyrotechnics and other mood-revvers, to the ubiquitous-of-late go-go girls dressed like strippers. If this is your choice, then note that they start lining up way before the opening time. Open Friday and Saturday from 11pm until 5am. 4321 W. Flamingo Rd. ✆ 702/940-7246. Cover usually $25.

rumjungle 🞷 Now, normally our delicate sensibilities wince at such overkill, and we tend to write off such efforts as just trying a bit too hard. But surprisingly, rumjungle really delivers the great fun it promises. The fire-wall entrance gives way to a wall of water; the two-story bar is full of the largest collection of rum varieties anywhere, each bottle illuminated with a laser beam of light; go-go girls dance and prance between bottles of wine to dueling congas; and the food all comes skewered on swords. It's all a bit much, but it works, it really does. A great deal of thought went into the various clever designs and schemes, and it's paid off. Almost instantly, rumjungle became and stayed one of the hottest clubs in Vegas, with lines of partiers out the door every night, ready to dance to live world-beat music. Get there early (before 10pm) to avoid lines/guest lists/the cover charge, and consider having dinner (served till 11pm); it's costly, but it's a multicourse, all-you-can-eat feast of flame pit–cooked Brazilian food. For the amount of food and the waiving of the cover charge, dinner is a good deal. Then dance it off all night long! Open Sunday to Wednesday 'til 2am, Thursday through Saturday'til 4am. In Mandalay Bay, 3950 Las Vegas Blvd. S. ℂ **702/632-7408.** Cover Fri–Sat $20–$25, ladies always free.

Seamless After Hours ⚘⚘ Proving that the line between the latest hot nightclub and the latest hot strip club is getting blurred to the point of invisibility, by day, and much of the night, this is a strip club. But around 4am the girls leave the stage and morph into slightly more-clad go-go dancers, while the tables and chairs are cleared for a dance floor that is the site of the most intense after-hours action in Vegas. It's ingenious, because with some exceptions, most of even the hottest clubs are closing around the same time, and not everyone wants to go to a strip bar to continue the party. Said party goes on until everyone gives up, which can be as late as noon the next day, whereupon the girls reappear and their clothes again disappear. 4740 S. Arville St. ℂ **702/227-5200.** Cover $20 if you come in a cab, free if you drive yourself (because drivers get a cut of the door).

Studio 54 *Overrated* The legendary Studio 54 has been resurrected here in Las Vegas, but with all the bad elements and none of the good ones. Forget Truman, Halston, and Liza doing illegal (or at least immoral) things in the bathroom stalls; that part of Studio 54 remains but a fond memory. The snooty, exclusive door attitude has been retained, however. Hooray. Red-rope policies are all well and good if you're trying to build mystique in a regular club, but for a tourist attraction, where guests are likely to be one-time-only (or, at best, once a year), it's obnoxious. Oddly, this doesn't lead to a high-class clientele; of all the new clubs, this is the trashiest (though apparently the hot night for locals is Tuesday, so if you do go, go then). The large dance floor has a balcony overlooking it, the decor is industrial (exposed piping and the like), the music is hip-hop and electronic, and there is nothing to do other than dance. If the real Studio 54 were this boring, no one would remember it today. Open Tuesday through Saturday 10pm until dawn. In the MGM Grand, 3799 Las Vegas Blvd. S. ℂ **702/891-1111.** www. studio54lv.com. Cover varies, but usually $10–$20.

Tabú ⚘ A little by-the-numbers for a nightclub, but still, despite the name, less stripper-saucy than the other new "ultralounges" (which here means "noisy, high-priced bar") and consequently is more grown up, and just as loud. With an interior of late '90s high-tech/industrial meets cheesy '80s bachelor's den, it's nothing aesthetically special, though there are some nice spots for canoodling. But do find a wall or the circular couch if you want to hear yourself think. Open Wednesday through Sunday 10pm to early morning. At MGM Grand, 3799 Las Vegas Blvd. S. ℂ **702/891-7183.** www. tabulv.com. Cover varies, but expect it to be about $10–$20; ladies free.

Tao Nightclub ⚘ As of this writing, one of the hottest of the Vegas hotspots. Yes, that has been mentioned in other reviews here, and yes, it changes on an almost daily basis, but welcome to the Las Vegas club scene. Done as a Buddhist temple run amok, this multilevel club is drawing the party faithful and the celebrity entourages in droves, so expect long lines and high cover charges. Some may find the wall-to-wall crowds, flashing lights, pounding music, and general chaos overwhelming, but Tao is obviously doing something right. Open Tuesday through Saturday 10pm until dawn. At The Venetian, 3355 Las Vegas Blvd. S. ℂ **702/388-8588.** Cover varies.

Tryst 🎐   Wynn's first stab at a nightclub, La Bête, tanked, and mere months after it opened with the hotel in April 2005, they shut it down, brought in new management, revamped the place, and tried again. The result is much more subtle than the beast-themed original, but this is the Vegas nightclub scene, so it's definitely a sliding scale. After all, the dance floor opens up onto a 90-foot waterfall, so it's all relative. Expect a slightly more refined crowd than you usually find at such places, which may be a good or bad thing, depending on your viewpoint. Then again, during their brief BFF phase, this was Britney and Paris's Vegas nightspot of choice, so "refined" is definitely open to interpretation. Open Thursday through Sunday 10pm to 4am. At Wynn Las Vegas, 3131 Las Vegas Blvd. S. ✆ 702/770-3375. Cover varies.

VooDoo Lounge 🎐   Occupying, along with the VooDoo Cafe, two floors in the newer addition to the Rio, the Lounge almost successfully combines Haitian voodoo and New Orleans Creole in its decor and theme. There are two main rooms: one with a large dance floor and stage for live music, and a disco room, which is filled with large video screens and serious light action. Big club chairs in groups form conversation pits, where you might actually be able to have a conversation. The big seller? The bartenders put on a show, a la Tom Cruise in *Cocktail.* They shake, jiggle, and light stuff on fire. Supposedly, the live music includes Cajun acts, but when it comes down to it, rock seems to rule the day. And if you don't suffer from paralyzing vertigo (who, us?), be sure to check out the dramatic outdoor, multilevel patio, which offers some amazing views of the Strip. The mid- to late-20s crowd is more heavily local than you might expect; the dress code calls for no sneakers, flip-flops, torn jeans, or t-shirts. It's open nightly 5pm to 3am. In the Rio All-Suite Hotel & Casino, 3700 Las Vegas Blvd. S. ✆ 702/252-7777. Cover $10 and up.

9 Strip Clubs

No, we don't mean entertainment establishments on Las Vegas Boulevard South. We mean the other kind of "strip." Yes, people come to town for the gambling and the wedding chapels, but the lure of Vegas doesn't stop there. Though prostitution is not legal within the city, the sex industry is an active and obvious force in town. Every other cab carries a placard for a strip club, and a walk down the Strip at night will have dozens of men thrusting fliers at you for clubs, escort services, phone-sex lines, and more. And some of you are going to want to check it out.

And why not? An essential part of the Vegas allure is decadence, and naked flesh would certainly qualify, as does the thrill of trying something new and daring. Of course, by and large, the nicer bars aren't particularly daring, and if you go to more than one in an evening, the thrill wears off, and the breasts don't look quite so bare.

In the finest of Vegas traditions, the "something for everyone" mentality extends to strip clubs. Here is a guide to the most prominent and heavily advertised; there are plenty more, of increasing seediness, out there. You don't have to look too hard. The most crowded and zoolike times are after midnight, especially on Friday and Saturday nights. Should you want a "meaningful" experience, you might wish to avoid the rush and choose an off-hour for a visit.

In addition to the listings below, keep an eye out for a new addition to the scene: In a "If you can't beat 'em, join 'em" move, longtime bar owner and local musician Tommy Rocker decided to revamp his frat-boy fave, at 4275 Dean Martin Dr. (✆ 702/ 261-6688; www.tommyrocker.com), and turn it into a strip club, gleefully saying his new place's motto will be "Fun for the whole family, except for your wife and kids." Tommy still plays on Saturday nights.

Cheetah's ⚘ This is the strip club used as the set in the movie *Showgirls,* but thanks to the magic of Hollywood and later renovations by the club, only the main stage will look vaguely familiar to those few looking for Nomi Malone. There's also a smaller stage, plus three tiny "tip stages" so that you can really get close to (and give much money to) the woman of your choice. Eight TVs line the walls; the club does a brisk business during major sporting events. The management believes "If you treat people right, they will keep coming back," so the atmosphere is friendlier than at other clubs. They "encourage couples—people who want to party—to come here. We get a 21- to 40-aged party kind of crowd," the manager told us. Indeed, there is a sporty, frat-bar feel to the place (though on a crowded Saturday night, some unescorted women were turned away, despite policy). Lap dances are $20. Open daily 24 hours. 2112 Western Ave. ☎ 702/384-0074. Topless. Cover $30 8pm until 5am.

Club Paradise ⚘ Until the new behemoths moved into town, this was the nicest of the strip clubs. Which isn't to say it isn't still nice; it's just got competition. The outside looks a lot like the Golden Nugget; the interior and atmosphere are rather like that of a hot nightclub where most of the women happen to be topless. The glitzy stage looks like something from a miniature showroom: The lights flash and the dance music pounds, there are two big video screens (one featuring soft porn, the other showing sports!), the chairs are plush and comfortable, the place is relatively bright by strip-club standards, and they offer champagne and cigars. Not too surprisingly, they get a very white-collar crowd here. The result is not terribly sleazy, which may please some and turn others off.

The women ("actual centerfolds") are heavy (and we do mean heavy) on the silicone. They don't so much dance as pose and prance, after which they don skimpy evening dresses and come down to solicit lap dances, which eventually fills the place up with writhing females in thongs. The club says it is "women-friendly," and indeed there were a few couples, including one woman who was receiving a lap dance herself—and didn't seem too uncomfortable. Occasionally, the action stops for a minirevue, which ends up being more like seminaked cheerleading than a show. Lap dances are $20. Open Monday through Friday 5pm to 8am, Saturday and Sunday 6pm to 8am. 4416 Paradise Rd. ☎ 702/734-7990. Unescorted women allowed. Topless. Cover $30.

Déjà Vu Showgirls ⚘⚘ This place both deeply perturbs us and amuses the heck out of us. The latter because it's one of the rare strip clubs where the women actually perform numbers. Instead of just coming out and taking off an article or two of clothing and then parading around in a desultory manner before collecting a few tips and running off to solicit lap dances, each stripper comes out and does an actual routine—well, okay, maybe not so much, but she does remove her clothes to personally chosen music, shedding an outfit tailored to her music selection (like *Flashdance*—except naked-er). And so it happened that we have now seen a punk-rock chick strip to "Anarchy in the UK" and a Ramones tune. But it also distresses us because it's the kind of place where guys bring their buds the night before their wedding to make sure they get photographed with a naked girl (yes, the girls get totally naked here) performing something raunchy with a sex toy—that's the kind of fun that leaves a bad taste in the mouth. "Shower" and "couch" dances are $20, "theme" dances $30. Open Monday through Saturday 11am to 6am, Sunday 6pm to 4am. 3247 Industrial Rd. ☎ 702/894-4167. Unescorted women allowed. Totally nude. Cover charge $15. 18 and over. No alcohol.

Eden ⭐⭐ Formerly Strip Tease Cabaret, this club has been redone to eliminate the rather disturbing "fantasy rooms" (where lap dances could occur in private), replacing them with a generic "classy" gentlemen's-club look, all shiny runways and stages (three total, plus the "shower" stage, where periodically two girls will soap each other up). One of the bouncers was in the film *Ocean's Eleven* as a thug menacing George Clooney. With live DJs and girls far more interested in working the lap-dance angle than dancing, it's a fine, safe first-time strip-bar experience, but not one to make you see what all the fuss is about. Lap dances are $20 and up. Open daily 1pm to 5am. 3750 S. Valley View Blvd. ✆ 702/253-1555. Unescorted women allowed, couples encouraged. Topless. Cover $30.

Glitter Gulch ⭐ Right there in the middle of the Fremont Street Experience, Glitter Gulch is either an eyesore or the last bastion of Old Las Vegas, depending on your point of view. One of the most venerable strip clubs in town, it has undergone a $3.5-million renovation, which just shows you what kind of money there is in nearly nekkid girls. Gone are the old burlesque gaudy trappings and fixtures, and in their place is an interior that rivals some of the mid-level Strip ultralounges. It's still a little cramped and naturally dark. The location is the most convenient all of the strip clubs—right on Fremont Street—but it's also the most conspicuous—given that you have to exit right on Fremont Street. Good for the curious lookie-loo, not so good for the bashful or discrete. Still, it means customers include groups of women and even a 90-year-old couple. Given its convenient location, this is the perfect place for the merely curious—you can easily pop in, check things out, goggle and ogle, and then hit the road. Table dances are $35. Open daily 1pm to 4am. 20 Fremont St. ✆ 702/385-4774. Topless. 2-drink minimum (drinks $7 and up) before 8pm; after 8pm cover is $20 (includes 1 drink).

Olympic Gardens Topless Cabaret ⭐ Once the largest of the strip clubs, this almost feels like a family operation, thanks to the middle-age women often handling the door—maybe they're the reason for the equal-opportunity male strippers on special nights. It also has a boutique that sells lingerie and naughty outfits. (They get a lot of couples coming in, so perhaps this is in case someone gets inspired and wants to try out what they learned here at home.) There are two rooms: one with large padded tables for the women to dance on, the other featuring a more classic strip runway. The girls all seemed really cute—perhaps the best-looking of the major clubs. The crowd is a mix of 20s to 30s geeks and blue-collar guys. As the place fills up and the chairs are crammed in next to each other, it's hard to see how enjoyable, or intimate, a lap dance can be when the guy next to you is getting one as well. That didn't seem to stop all the guys there, who seemed appropriately blissed out. Oh, and by the way, they also have male strippers most nights of the week, so you ladies won't feel left out. Lap dances are $20, more in the VIP room. Open daily 24 hours. 1531 Las Vegas Blvd. S. ✆ 702/385-8987. Unescorted women allowed. Topless. Cover $30 after 6pm.

The Palomino ⭐ This one-time classically elegant nudie bar—you know, red flocked wallpaper and the like—became pretty seedy over the years, as places like that generally do. Even the offer of total nudity was not quite enough to lure visitors to this seedy part of town. The owners then came up with an ingenious makeover. In addition to updating the downstairs (gone, sadly, is the aforementioned vintage look in favor of a flashy runway, neon, flatscreen TVs, and other modern gizmos; it's new, but it's also generic), they had the inspiration to introduce male stripping—yes, still totally nude—upstairs on the weekends. This something-for-everyone equality approach results in a bustling crowd, packed with women, with an atmosphere that can be a little intense rather than bachelorette ribald. Expect a largely urban crowd and a lot of couples. And in case you wondered, the guys do lap dances too. Topless lap dances are $20, totally nude dances are $40. Open daily 4pm to 5am. 1848 Las Vegas Blvd. N. ℂ 702/642-2984. Totally nude. Cover $20.

Sapphire Gentleman's Club ★★★ Ladies and gentlemen (particularly the latter), Las Vegas, home of the largest everything else, now brings you—drum roll—the largest strip club *in the world!* That's right, 71,000 square feet of nakedity. Of course, you have to see it—and, of course, that's what they are counting on. But let's say this: While really it's nothing you haven't seen before strip-club-wise, if you haven't seen a strip club, this is the place to start (though the size and looks are atypical, to say the least; it's all downhill from here) because it's modern and clean, and, frankly, it's not all that different, looks-wise, from Rain, the super-hot nightclub over at the Rio, except that here you can actually hear yourself think, and the girls sometimes wear more clothes than at Rain. It's also more friendly and less attitudinal.

Expect three stages in a bridge shape (including one where gawkers who paid for the privilege can watch the action from below, thanks to a glass floor), and a fourth in a separate—and still large—room, with several poles and strippers all working it at the same time. Giant video screens occasionally act as a JumboTron for the action on the other side of the cavernous room. Upstairs are incredibly posh and incredibly expensive rooms for wealthy sports and movie figures to utilize. Oh, and ladies are not only allowed to visit, but they'll also have their very own male strippers to leer at. Lap dances start at $20. Open daily 24 hours. 3025 S. Industrial. ℂ 702/796-6000. Unescorted women allowed. Topless. Cover $30 6pm–6am.

Seamless ★★★ Between the big-screen TVs, the mirrors, the pounding beat of house music at eardrum-bursting volumes, the smoke machines, and the party atmosphere, it's hard to tell the difference between this high-end strip club and an equally high-end Vegas nightclub. Sure, the girls have on less clothing here, and visitors tend to sit in armchairs designed for interaction with the entertainers as opposed to tearing it up on the dance floor, but that's about it. To prove the point, at 4am, the girls morph into go-go dancers, the chairs vanish, and the entire thing turns into a hot after-hours club. It is kind of one-stop nightlife shopping in that regard. Lap dances start at $30. 4740 S. Arville St. ℂ 702/227-5200. Cover $20.

Spearmint Rhino ★ Did you know that even strip bars come in chains? They do, and this is a familiar brand to those in the know, or who read billboards close to airports. The runway (where some of the dancers get a little personal with each other) is actually in a separate back area, so it is possible to have a drink at the front (where there are many TVs and other manly accoutrements) and never see a naked girl (save for the smaller stage and pole nearby). On a busy night, it's crammed with grown-up frat boys enjoying a clubby space. There can be a veritable factory assembly line of lap dances during these busy periods, which frankly, seems the opposite of a turn-on to us. Unescorted women should also note that while normally they are permitted, lately it seems that they might also be taken for hookers and turned away from the door (lest they come inside and lure customers away). Lap dances are $20. Open daily 24 hours. 3444 Highland Dr. ℂ 702/796-3600. Unescorted women allowed. Topless. Cover $30.

Treasures ★★★ Right now, along with Sapphire, this is our favorite of the strip clubs, for several reasons. From the outside, this looks like one of the new fancy casino-hotels (if considerably smaller), but inside it's straight out of a Victorian sporting house (that's a brothel, by the way), down to replicas of 19th-century girlie pictures on the walls. On stage, the performers actually perform; anyone who has witnessed the desultory swaying of the hips and vacant stare of a bored, can't-be-bothered stripper will appreciate not just the bump-and-grind (some of which gets on the raunchy side) dance routines but also the special effects, from hair-blowing fans to smoke machines to a neon pole, that makes it all the more memorable. We are suckers for this combination of period-inspired style and contemporary approach to the business at hand. However, and we don't mean this in an off-putting way, "suckers" is a word to bear in mind; this is a place of commerce, and any adult-industry professional knows it. Try not to forget that, especially couples and first-timers, for whom this is still an excellent and comfortable venue. *Note:* The entrance to the parking lot can be hard to spot after dark. Go down Highland and keep your eyes peeled. Lap dances $30 and up. Open Sunday through Thursday 4pm to 6am, Friday and Saturday 4pm to 9am. 2801 Westwood Dr. ⓒ 702/257-3030. No unescorted women. Topless. Cover $20.

10

Side Trips from Las Vegas

Though Vegas is designed to make you forget that there is an outside world, it might do you and your pocketbook some good to reacquaint yourself with the non-Vegas realm. Actually, if you're spending more than 3 days in Vegas, this may become a necessity; 2 days with kids, and it absolutely will.

Plus, there is such a startling contrast between the artificial wonders of Sin City and the natural wonders that, in some cases, lie just a few miles away. Few places are as developed and modern as Vegas; few places are as untouched as some of the canyons, desert, and mountains that surround it. The electrical and design marvel that is the Strip couldn't exist without the extraordinary structural feat that is Hoover Dam. Need some fresh air? There are plenty of opportunities for outdoor recreation, all in a landscape all the more jarring for the contrast it has with the city.

The excursions covered in this chapter will take you from 20 to 60 miles out of town. Every one of them offers a memorable travel experience.

GRAND CANYON TOURS

Generally, tourists visiting Las Vegas don't drive 300 miles to Arizona to see the Grand Canyon, but dozens of sightseeing tours depart from the city daily. In addition to the Gray Line tours described in chapter 6, a major operator, **Scenic Airlines** (© **800/634-6801** or 702/638-3300; www.scenic.com), runs several tours, including its most popular: a deluxe, full-day guided air-ground tour for $279 per person ($249 for children 2–11); the price includes a bus excursion through the national park, a flight over the canyon, and lunch. All scenic tours include flightseeing. The company also offers both full-day and overnight tours with hiking.

Scenic Airlines also offers tours to other points of interest and national parks, including Bryce Canyon and Monument Valley. Ask for details when you call.

1 Hoover Dam ✦✦✦ & Lake Mead ✦✦

30 miles SE of Las Vegas

This is one of the most popular excursions from Las Vegas. Hoover Dam is visited by 2,000 to 3,000 people daily. Why should you join them? Because Hoover Dam is an engineering and architectural marvel, and it changed the Southwest forever. Without it, you wouldn't even be going to Vegas. Kids may be bored, unless they like machinery or just plain big things, but expose them to it anyway, for their own good. Buy them ice cream and a Hoover Dam snow globe as a bribe. Obviously, if you are staying at Lake Mead, it's a must.

The tour itself is a bit cursory, but you do get up close and personal with the dam. Wear comfortable shoes; the tour involves a bit of walking. Try to take the tour in the morning to beat the desert heat and the really big crowds. You can have lunch out in

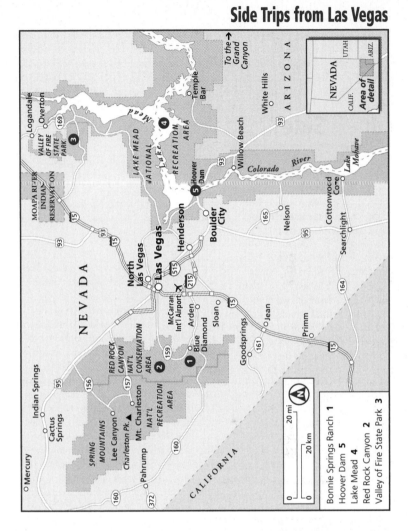

Boulder City, and then perhaps drive back through the **Valley of Fire State Park** (a landscape of wind- and water-hewn formations of red sandstone; described later in this chapter), which is about 60 magnificently scenic miles from Lake Mead (purchase gas before you start!). Or you can spend the afternoon on Lake Mead–centered pursuits such as hiking, boating, even scuba diving in season, or perhaps a rafting trip down the Colorado River.

GETTING THERE

Drive east on Flamingo Road or Tropicana Avenue to U.S. 515 South, which automatically turns into I-93 South and takes you right to the dam. This will involve a rather dramatic drive as you go through Boulder City and come over a rise, and Lake Mead suddenly appears spread out before you. It's a beautiful sight. At about this point, the road narrows to two lanes, and traffic can slow considerably. On normal busy tourist days, this drive would take about an hour. But between construction, security measures that call for most trucks and many other vehicles to be stopped and searched during peak hours (particularly Sun, and Mon of holiday weekends, when visitors are returning through Arizona), the drive is taking longer than ever. Plan accordingly.

Go past the turnoff to Lake Mead. As you near the dam, you'll see a five-story parking structure tucked into the canyon wall on your left. Park here ($5 charge) and take the elevators or stairs to the walkway leading to the new visitor center.

If you would rather go on an **organized tour,** check out **Gray Line** (✆ 800/ 634-6579; www.grayline.com), which offers a Hoover Dam package that includes a buffet lunch and a side trip to the Ethel M Chocolate factory. When you're in Las Vegas, look for discount coupons in the numerous free publications available at hotels. The 7½-hour **Deluxe Hoover Dam Tour** departs daily at 7:30am; the price is $53, and admission to the dam's Discovery Tour is an additional $11.

THE HOOVER DAM ✹✹✹

There would be no Las Vegas as we know it without the Hoover Dam. Certainly, the neon and glitz that we know and love would not exist. In fact, the growth of the entire Southwest can be tied directly to the electricity created by the dam.

Until the Hoover Dam was built, much of the southwestern United States was plagued by two natural problems: parched, sandy terrain that lacked irrigation for most of the year, and extensive flooding in spring and early summer, when the mighty Colorado River, fed by melting snow from its source in the Rocky Mountains, overflowed its banks and destroyed crops, lives, and property. On the positive side, raging unchecked over eons, the river's turbulent, rushing waters carved the Grand Canyon.

In 1928, prodded by the seven states through which the river runs during the course of its 1,400-mile journey to the Gulf of California, Congress authorized construction of a dam at Boulder Canyon (later moved to Black Canyon). The Senate's declaration of intention stated, "A mighty river, now a source of destruction, is to be curbed and put to work in the interests of society." Construction began in 1931. Because of its vast scope and the unprecedented problems posed in its realization, the project generated significant advances in many areas of machinery production, engineering, and construction. An army of more than 5,200 laborers was assembled, and work proceeded 24 hours a day. Completed in 1936, 2 years ahead of schedule and $15 million under budget (it is, no doubt, a Wonder of the Modern Fiscal World), the dam stopped the annual floods and conserved water for irrigation, industry, and domestic uses. Equally important, it became one of the world's major electrical-generating plants, providing low-cost, pollution-free hydroelectric power to a score of surrounding communities. Hoover Dam's $165-million cost has been repaid with interest by the sale of inexpensive power to a number of California cities and the states of Arizona and Nevada. The dam is a government project that paid for itself—a feat almost as awe-inspiring as its engineering.

The dam itself is a massive curved wall, 660 feet thick at the bottom, tapering to 45 feet where the road crosses it at the top. It towers 726 feet above bedrock (about the height of a 60-story skyscraper) and acts as a plug between the canyon walls to hold back up to 9.2 trillion gallons of water in Lake Mead, the reservoir created by its construction. Four concrete intake towers on the lake side drop the water down about

600 feet to drive turbines and create power, after which the water spills out into the river and continues south.

All the architecture is on a grand scale, and the design has beautiful Art Deco elements, unusual in an engineering project. Note, for instance, the monumental 30-foot bronze sculpture, *Winged Figures of the Republic,* flanking a 142-foot flagpole at the Nevada entrance. According to its creator, Oskar Hansen, the sculpture symbolizes "the immutable calm of intellectual resolution, and the enormous power of trained physical strength, equally enthroned in placid triumph of scientific achievement."

The dam has become a major sightseeing attraction, along with Lake Mead, America's largest artificial reservoir and a major Nevada recreation area.

Seven miles northwest of the dam on U.S. 93, you'll pass through **Boulder City,** which was built to house managerial and construction workers. Sweltering summer heat (many days it is 125°F/52°C) ruled out a campsite by the dam. The higher elevation of Boulder City offered lower temperatures. The city emerged within a single year, turning a desert wasteland into a community of 6,000. By 1934, it was Nevada's third-largest town.

TOURING THE DAM

The very nice **Hoover Dam Visitor Center,** a vast three-level circular concrete structure with a rooftop overlook, opened in 1995. You'll enter the Reception Lobby (bags were not allowed inside after the Sept 11 terrorist attacks, but ask about current security measures, as they may have changed), where you can buy tickets; peruse informational exhibits, photographs, and memorabilia; and view three 12-minute video presentations about the importance of water to life, the events leading up to the construction of Hoover Dam, and the construction itself, as well as the many benefits it confers. Exhibits on the Plaza Level include interactive displays on the environment, habitation, and development of the Southwest, the people who built the dam, and related topics.

Yet another floor up, galleries on the Overlook Level demonstrate, via sculpted bronze panels, the benefits of Hoover Dam and Lake Mead to the states of Arizona, Nevada, and California. The Overlook Level additionally provides an unobstructed view of Lake Mead, the dam, the power plant, the Colorado River, and Black Canyon. There are multiple photo opportunities throughout this trip.

You can visit an exhibit center across the street where a 10-minute presentation in a small theater focuses on a topographical map of the 1,400-mile Colorado River. It also has a cafeteria. Notice, by the way, how the restrooms in the exhibition center have only electric dryers and no paper towels? A tribute?

The center closes at 6pm, and 5:15pm is the last admission time, though hours vary seasonally. There are two tours available, the Power Plant Tour and the Hoover Dam Tour. Admission to the former is $11 for adults; $9 for seniors, military personnel and their dependents, and all children 4 to 16; and free for military in uniform and children under 4. The more extensive Hoover Dam Tour is $30 per person, no children under 8 allowed. Parking is $7 no matter which tour you take, and the lot takes cash only. There is no need to call ahead to reserve a place, but for more information, call © **866/730-9097** or 702/494-2517.

At this writing, because of post–September 11 security measures, tours of the dam are somewhat restricted. It's no longer the quite nifty, and lengthy, experience it once was because access is so limited. On the Power Plant tour visitors go to the center, see a movie, and walk on top of the dam. While both tours include a 530-foot descent via elevator into the dam to view the massive generators, the Power Plant tour is a self-guided tour aided by the occasional information kiosk or guide/docent stationed at intervals along the way; the pricier tour offers the same attractions and viewing opportunities, but it is guided, lasts an hour and a half, and is limited to 20 people. If you plan on taking that tour, be aware that it covers over a mile and a half of walking on concrete and gravel, with no handicapped access. The Hoover Dam tour is offered every half-hour, with the last tour at 3:30, while the final Power Plant admission is at 5:15.

Some fun facts you might hear along the way: It took 6½ years to fill the lake. Though 96 workers were killed during the construction, contrary to popular myth, none were accidentally buried as the concrete was poured (it was poured only at a level of 8 in. at a time). Look for a monument outside dedicated to the workers who were killed—"they died to make the desert bloom"—along with a tombstone for their doggy mascot who was also killed, albeit after the dam was completed. Compare their wages of 50¢ an hour to those of their Depression-era peers, who made 5¢ to 30¢.

For more information on the dam, and sometimes discount coupons, visit **www. usbr.gov/lc/hooverdam**.

LAKE MEAD NATIONAL RECREATION AREA 🐂🐂

Under the auspices of the National Park Service, 1.5-million-acre Lake Mead National Recreation Area was created in 1936 around Lake Mead (the reservoir lake that is the result of the construction of Hoover Dam) and later Lake Mohave to the south (formed by the construction of Davis Dam). Before the lakes emerged, this desert region was brutally hot, dry, and rugged—unfit for human habitation. Today, it's one of the nation's most popular playgrounds, attracting about 9 million visitors annually. The two lakes comprise 291 square miles. At an elevation of 1,221 feet, Lake Mead itself extends some 110 miles upstream toward the Grand Canyon. Its 550-mile shoreline, backed by spectacular cliff and canyon scenery, forms a perfect setting for a wide variety of watersports and desert hiking.

Having said all that, Lake Mead is in the beginning stages of a crisis so large that unchecked would spell the end for Vegas entirely. The nation's largest reservoir has experienced a severe drop-off in levels since 2000, a combination of drought, global warming, and increased use. Whole portions of the lake's edges are now dry, in the process exposing the remains of some of the small towns that were flooded to build the thing in the first place. These have become tourist spots themselves. There is a 50% chance the lake will go dry by 2021 and since it supplies water to Las Vegas (not to mention hydroelectric power), that has grave implications for that city. Let's encourage those fancy new hotels to put in drought-tolerant plants instead of more grass. And don't ask for your towels to be changed every day.

Keep in mind that if the lake water shortage continues, many of the following activities will probably be affected in one way or another, if they aren't already.

The **Alan Bible Visitor Center,** 4 miles northeast of Boulder City on U.S. 93 at NV 166 (© **702/293-8990**), can provide information on all area activities and services. You can pick up trail maps and brochures here, view informative films, and find out about scenic drives, accommodations, ranger-guided hikes, naturalist programs and lectures, bird-watching, canoeing, camping, lakeside RV parks, and picnic facilities. The center has some sweet exhibits about the area and is staffed by friendly folks full of local pride. It's open daily from 8:30am to 4:30pm except Thanksgiving, Christmas, and New Year's Day.

Lake Mead & Vicinity

For information on accommodations, boat rentals, and fishing, call **Seven Crown Resorts** (© 800/752-9669 or 702/293-3484; www.sevencrown.com). You can also find Lake Mead info on the Web at **www.nps.gov/lame**.

The **entry fee** for the area is $5 per vehicle, which covers all passengers, or $3 per person if you're walking, motorcycling, or biking in.

OUTDOOR ACTIVITIES

This is a lovely area for scenic drives amid the dramatic desert landscape. One popular route follows the Lakeshore and Northshore Scenic drives along the edge of Lake Mead. From these roads there are panoramic views of the blue lake, set against a backdrop of the browns, blacks, reds, and grays that make up the desert mountains. Northshore Scenic Drive also leads through areas of brilliant red boulders and rock formations, and you'll find a picnic area along the way.

BOATING & FISHING   A store at **Lake Mead Resort and Marina,** under the auspices of **Seven Crown Resorts** (© 800/752-9669 or 702/293-3484; www.seven crown.com), rents fishing boats, ski boats, personal watercraft, and patio boats. It also carries groceries, clothing, marine supplies, sporting goods, water-skiing gear, fishing equipment, and bait and tackle. Nonresidents can get a fishing license here ($69 for a year or $18 for 1-day plus $7 for each additional day; discounts for children under 15 are available; additional fees apply for special fishing classifications, including trout, which require a $10 stamp for taking or possessing that fish). The staff is knowledgeable and can apprise you of good fishing spots. Largemouth bass, striped bass, channel catfish, crappie, and bluegill are found in Lake Mead; rainbow trout, largemouth bass, and striped bass in Lake Mohave. You can also arrange here to rent a fully equipped houseboat at **Echo Bay,** 40 miles north.

Other convenient Lake Mead marinas offering similar rentals and equipment are **Las Vegas Boat Harbor** (© 702/293-1191; www.lasvegasbaymarina.com), which is even closer to Las Vegas, and **Callville Bay Resort & Marina** (© 800/255-5561 or 702/565-8958; www.callvillebay.com), which is the least crowded of the five on the Nevada Shore.

CAMPING   Lake Mead's shoreline is dotted with campsites, all of them equipped with running water, picnic tables, and grills. Available on a first-come, first-served basis, they are administered by the **National Park Service** (© 702/293-8990; www.nps.gov/lame). There's a charge of $10 per night at each campsite.

CANOEING   The **Alan Bible Visitor Center** (see above) can provide a list of outfitters that rent canoes for trips on the Colorado River. There's one catch, however: A canoeing permit ($10 per person) is required in advance for certain areas near the dam and is available from the **Bureau of Reclamation** (Attn.: Canoe Launch Permits), Box 60400, Boulder City, NV 89006-0400 (© 702/293-8204; www.usbr.gov/lc). You can apply for and receive the permit on the same day that you plan to canoe.

HIKING   The best season for hiking is November through March (it's too hot the rest of the year). Some ranger-guided hikes are offered via the **Alan Bible Visitor Center** (see above), which also stocks detailed trail maps. Three trails, ranging in length from .75 mile to 6 miles, originate at the visitor center. The 6-mile trail goes past remains of the railroad built for the dam project. Be sure to take all necessary desert-hiking precautions. (See "Desert Hiking Advice" on p. 197.)

LAKE CRUISES   A delightful way to enjoy Lake Mead is on a cruise aboard the **Lake Mead Cruises** boat *Desert Princess* (© 702/293-6180; www.lakemead-cruises.com), a Mississippi-style paddle-wheeler. Cruises depart year-round from a terminal near **Lake Mead Resort** (p. 281). It's a relaxing, scenic trip (enjoyed from an open promenade deck or one of two fully enclosed, climate-controlled decks) through Black Canyon and past colorful rock formations known as the "Arizona Paint Pots" en route to Hoover Dam, which is lit at night. Options include narrated midday cruises ($22 adults, $10 children), pizza party cruises ($26 adults, $15 children), dinner cruises ($46 adults, $25 children), and sunset dinner/dance cruises with live music ($58 adults, children not permitted). Dinner is served in a pleasant, windowed, air-conditioned dining room. There's a full onboard bar. Call for departure times.

SCUBA DIVING   October through April, there's good visibility, lessened in summer months when algae flourishes. A list of good dive locations, authorized instructors, and nearby dive shops is available at the **Alan Bible Visitor Center** (see above). There's a designated underwater-diving area near Lake Mead Marina.

BOULDER CITY

You might want to consider poking around Boulder City on your way back to Vegas. Literally the company town for those building Hoover Dam, it was created by the wives who came with their husbands and turned a temporary site into a real community, since aided by the recreational attractions and attendant businesses of Lake Mead. It doesn't look like much as you first approach it, but once you are in the heart, you'll discover that it's quite charming, an old-fashioned town all the more preserved and quiet due to its status as the only city in Nevada where gambling is illegal. It's worth getting out and taking a little stroll. There are some antiques and curio shops, and a number of family-style restaurants and burger and Mexican joints, including **Toto's,** a reasonably priced Mexican restaurant at 806 Buchanan Blvd. (© **702/293-1744**); it's in the Von's shopping center. Or you could try the **Coffee Cup Diner,** 512 Nevada Hwy. (© **702/294-0517**), which is right on the road to and from the dam. A '50s diner in looks and menu, it has the usual burgers, shakes, and fries, plus complete breakfasts, and is inexpensive, friendly, and a good place to take the kids.

WHERE TO STAY

In addition to the hotel below (the only place to stay right on Lake Mead itself, aside from campsites), there are a number of little hotels in Boulder City.

Lake Mead Resort *(Value*   If camping isn't your bag, spend your night or nights at this rustic and comfortable bungalow-style lodge. It's an easy drive from Hoover Dam and is right on the lake but also right on the desert, so don't picture it as a wooded resort. The rooms are pleasant, with wood-paneled ceilings and walls of white-painted brick or rough-hewn pine. Each has a full private bathroom. Two suites have three rooms and a small kitchen, which might be good for families staying a few days. The pool is rudimentary, but you might want to relax with a good book in one of the gazebos on the property. About a half-mile down the road is the marina, where you can while away a few hours over cocktails on a lakeside patio. The marina (the Lake Mead Resort and Marina) is the headquarters for boating, fishing, and watersports; it also houses a large shop (see marina details above, under "Boating & Fishing").

There's a nautically themed restaurant (© **702/293-2074**) at the marina, its rough-hewn pine interior embellished with various seafaring iconography. It's open Sunday through Thursday 7am to 8pm, and Friday and Saturday until 9pm (it closes an hour later during the summer). The restaurant serves hearty breakfasts; sandwiches, salads, and burgers at lunch; and steak-and-seafood dinners. And Boulder Beach, also an easy walk from the lodge, has waterfront picnic tables and barbecue grills.

322 Lakeshore Rd., Boulder City, NV 89005. © **800/752-9669** or 702/293-2074. www.sevencrown.com. 42 units. Apr–Oct $95 and up double; rest of the year $80 and up double. Extra person $15. Children 5 and under stay free in parent's room. DISC, MC, V. Pets accepted, $50 refundable deposit and $10 per pet per night. **Amenities:** Restaurant; outdoor pool; watersports equipment/rentals; picnic area w/barbecue pit. *In room:* A/C, TV w/basic cable.

2 Valley of Fire State Park ★★

60 miles NE of Las Vegas

Most people visualize the desert as a vast expanse of undulating sands punctuated by the occasional cactus or palm-fringed oasis. But the desert of America's Southwest bears little relation to this Lawrence of Arabia image. Stretching for hundreds of miles around Las Vegas in every direction is a seemingly lifeless tundra of vivid reddish earth, shaped by time, climate, and subterranean upheavals into majestic canyons, cliffs, and ridges.

The 36,000-acre Valley of Fire State Park typifies the mountainous, red Mojave Desert. It derives its name from the brilliant sandstone formations that were created 150 million years ago by a great shifting of sand and that continue to be shaped by the geologic processes of wind and water erosion. These are rock formations like you'll never see anywhere else. There is nothing green, just fiery red rocks, swirling unrelieved as far as the eye can see. No wonder various sci-fi movies have used this place as a stand-in for another planet—it has a most otherworldly look. The entire place is very mysterious, loaded with petroglyphs, and totally inhospitable. It's not hard to believe that for the Indians it was a sacred place, where men came as a test of their manhood. It is a natural wonder that must be seen to be appreciated.

Although it's hard to imagine in the sweltering Nevada heat, for billions of years, these rocks were under hundreds of feet of ocean. This ocean floor began to rise some 200 million years ago, and the waters became more and more shallow. Eventually, the sea made a complete retreat, leaving a muddy terrain traversed by ever-diminishing streams. A great sandy desert covered much of the southwestern part of the American continent until about 140 million years ago. Over eons, winds, massive fault action, and water erosion sculpted fantastic formations of sand and limestone. Oxidation of iron in the sands and mud—and the effect of groundwater leaching the oxidized iron—turned the rocks the many hues of red, pink, russet, lavender, and white that can be seen today. Logs of ancient forests washed down from faraway highlands and became petrified fossils, which can be seen along two interpretive trails.

Human beings occupied the region, a wetter and cooler one, as far back as 4,000 years ago. They didn't live in the Valley of Fire, but during the Gypsum period (2000 B.C.–300 B.C.), men hunted bighorn sheep (a source of food, clothing, blankets, and hut coverings) here with notched sticks called *atlatls* that are depicted in the park's petroglyphs. Women and children caught rabbits, tortoises, and other small game. In the next phase, from 300 B.C. to A.D. 700, the climate became warmer and drier. Bows and arrows replaced *atlatls,* and the hunters and gatherers discovered farming. The ancestral Puebloan people began cultivating corn, squash, and beans, and communities began replacing small nomadic family groups. These ancient people wove watertight baskets, mats, hunting nets, and clothing. Around A.D. 300, they learned how to make sun-dried ceramic pottery. Other tribes, notably the Paiute, migrated to the area. By A.D. 1150, they had become the dominant group. Unlike the ancestral Puebloans, they were still nomadic and used the Valley of Fire region seasonally. These were the inhabitants whom white settlers found when they entered the area in the early to mid-1800s. The newcomers diverted river and spring waters to irrigate their farmlands, destroying the nature-based Paiute way of life. About 300 descendants of those Paiute tribespeople still live on the Moapa Indian Reservation (about 20 miles northwest) that was established along the Muddy River in 1872.

GETTING THERE

From Las Vegas, take I-15 north to exit 75 (Valley of Fire turnoff). However, the more scenic route is to take I-15 north, and then travel Lake Mead Boulevard east to Northshore Road (NV 167) and proceed north to the Valley of Fire exit. The first route takes about an hour, the second 1½ hours.

There is a $5-per-vehicle admission charge to the park, regardless of how many people you cram inside.

Plan on spending a minimum of an hour in the park, though you can spend a great deal more time. It can get very hot in there (there is nothing to relieve the sun beating down on and reflecting off of all that red), and there is no water, so be certain to bring a liter, maybe two, per person in the summer. Without a guide, you must stay on paved roads, but don't worry if they end; you can always turn around and come back to the main road again. You can see a great deal from the car, and there are also hiking trails.

Numerous **sightseeing tours** go to the Valley of Fire. **Gray Line** (© 800/634-6579; www.grayline.com) offers tours, although at press time none to Valley of Fire, but that could change by the time you read this. Inquire at your hotel tour desk. Char Cruze of **Creative Adventures** (p. 193) also offers a fantastic tour.

The Valley of Fire can also be visited in conjunction with Lake Mead. From **Lake Mead Lodge,** take NV 166 (Lakeshore Rd.) north, make a right turn on NV 167 (Northshore Rd.), turn left on NV 169 (Moapa Valley Blvd.) West—a spectacularly scenic drive—and follow the signs. Valley of Fire is about 65 miles from Hoover Dam.

WHAT TO SEE & DO

There are no food concessions or gas stations in the park; however, you can obtain meals or gas on NV 167 or in nearby **Overton** (15 miles northwest on NV 169). Overton is a fertile valley town replete with trees, agricultural crops, horses, and herds of cattle—quite a change in scenery. On your way in or out of the teeming metropolis, do stop off at **Inside Scoop** (⍟, 395 S. Moapa Valley Blvd. (© 702/397-2055), open Monday through Saturday from 10am to 8pm and Sunday from 11am to 7pm. It's a sweet, old-fashioned ice-cream parlor run by extremely friendly people, with a proper menu that, in addition to classic sandwiches and the like, features some surprising options—a vegetarian sandwich and a fish salad with crab and shrimp, for example. Everything is quite tasty and fresh. They also do box lunches, perfect for picnicking inside the park. We strongly recommend coming by here on your way in for a box lunch, and then coming by afterward for a much-needed cooling ice cream.

At the southern edge of town is the **Lost City Museum** (⍟, 721 S. Moapa Valley Blvd. (© 702/397-2193), a sweet little museum, very nicely done, commemorating an ancient ancestral Puebloan village that was discovered in the region in 1924. Artifacts dating back 12,000 years are on display, as are clay jars, dried corn and beans, arrowheads, seashell necklaces, and willow baskets from the ancient Pueblo culture that inhabited this region between A.D. 300 and 1150. Other exhibits document the Mormon farmers who settled the valley in the 1860s. A large collection of local rocks—petrified wood, fern fossils, iron pyrite, green copper, and red iron oxide, along with manganese blown bottles turned purple by the ultraviolet rays of the sun—are also displayed here. The museum is surrounded by reconstructed wattle-and-daub pueblos. Admission is $3 for adults, $2 for seniors over 65, free for children under 18. It's open daily from 8:30am to 4:30pm, but closed Thanksgiving, Christmas, and New Year's Day.

Information headquarters for Valley of Fire is the **Visitor Center** on NV 169, 6 miles west of Northshore Road (© 702/397-2088). It's open daily 8:30am to 4:30pm and is worth a quick stop for information and a bit of history before entering the park. Exhibits on the premises explain the origin and geologic history of the park's colorful sandstone formations, describe the ancient peoples who carved their rock art on canyon walls, and identify the plants and wildlife you're likely to see. Postcards, books, slides, and films are for sale here, and you can pick up hiking maps and brochures. Rangers can answer your park-related questions. For online information about the park, see **http://parks.nv.gov/vf.htm.**

There are **hiking trails, shaded picnic sites,** and **two campgrounds** in the park. Most sites are equipped with tables, grills, water, and restrooms. A $12-per-vehicle, per-night camping fee is charged for use of the campground; if you're not camping, it costs $5 per vehicle to enter the park.

Some of the notable formations in the park have been named for the shapes they vaguely resemble—a duck, an elephant, seven sisters, domes, beehives, and so on. Mouse's Tank is a natural basin that collects rainwater, so named for a fugitive Paiute called Mouse who hid there in the late 1890s. And Native American petroglyphs etched into the rock walls and boulders—some dating from as long as 3,000 years ago—can be observed on self-guided trails. **Petroglyphs** at Atlatl Rock and Petroglyph Canyon are both easily accessible. In summer, when temperatures are usually over 100°F (38°C), you may have to settle for driving through the park in an air-conditioned car.

3 Red Rock Canyon ★★★

19 miles W of Las Vegas

If you need a break from the casinos of Vegas, with their windowless, claustrophobic, noisy interiors, Red Rock Canyon is balm for your overstimulated soul. Less than 20 miles away—but a world apart—this is a magnificent unspoiled vista that should cleanse and refresh you (and if you must, a morning visit should leave you enough time for an afternoon's gambling). You can drive the panoramic 13-mile **Scenic Drive** (daily 7am–dusk) or explore more in depth on foot, making it perfect for both athletes and armchair types. There are many interesting sights and trail heads along the drive itself. The **National Conservation Area** (www.nv.blm.gov/redrockcanyon) offers hiking trails and internationally acclaimed rock-climbing opportunities. Especially notable is 7,068-foot Mount Wilson, the highest sandstone peak among the bluffs; for information on climbing, contact the **Red Rock Canyon Visitor Center** at ✆ 702/515-5350. There are picnic areas along the drive and in nearby **Spring Mountain Ranch State Park** (www.parks.nv.gov/smr.htm), 5 miles south, which also offers plays in an outdoor theater during the summer. Since Bonnie Springs Ranch (see the next section) is just a few miles away, it makes a great base for exploring Red Rock Canyon.

GETTING THERE

Just drive west on Charleston Boulevard, which becomes NV 159. As soon as you leave the city, the red rocks will begin to loom around you. The visitor center will appear on your right, though the sign is not the best, so keep a sharp eye out.

You can also go on an **organized tour. Gray Line** (✆ 800/634-6579; www.grayline.com), among other companies, runs bus tours to Red Rock Canyon. Inquire at your hotel tour desk.

Finally, you can go **by bike.** Not very far out of town (at Rainbow Blvd.), Charleston Boulevard is flanked by a bike path that continues for about 11 miles to the visitor center/scenic drive. The path is hilly but not difficult if you're in reasonable shape. However, exploring Red Rock Canyon by bike should be attempted only by exceptionally fit and experienced bikers.

Just off NV 159, you'll see the turnoff for the **Red Rock Canyon Visitor Center** (✆ 702/515-5350; www.nv.blm.gov/redrockcanyon), which marks the actual entrance to the park. There, you can pick up information on trails and view history exhibits about the canyon. The center is open daily from 8am to 4:30pm. A visit to Red Rock Canyon can be combined with a visit to Bonnie Springs Ranch.

ABOUT RED ROCK CANYON

The geological history of these ancient stones goes back some 600 million years. Over eons, the forces of nature have formed Red Rock's sandstone monoliths into arches, natural bridges, and massive sculptures painted in a stunning palette of gray-white limestone and dolomite, black mineral deposits, and oxidized minerals in earth-toned sienna hues ranging from pink to crimson and burgundy. Orange and green lichens add further contrast, as do spring-fed areas of lush foliage. And formations such as **Calico Hill** are brilliantly white where groundwater has leached out oxidized iron. Cliffs cut by deep canyons tower 2,000 feet above the valley floor.

During most of its history, Red Rock Canyon was below a warm, shallow sea. Massive fault action and volcanic eruptions caused this seabed to begin rising some 225 million years ago. As the waters receded, sea creatures died, and the calcium in their bodies combined with sea minerals to form limestone cliffs studded with ancient fossils. Some 45 million years later, the region was buried beneath thousands of feet of windblown sand. The landscape was as arid as the Sahara. As time progressed, iron oxide and calcium carbonate infiltrated the sand, consolidating it into cross-bedded rock.

Shallow streams began carving the Red Rock landscape, and logs that washed down from ancient highland forests fossilized, their molecules gradually replaced by quartz and other minerals. These petrified stone logs, which the Paiute Indians believed were weapons of the wolf god Shinarav, can be viewed in the **Chinle Formation** at the base of the Red Rock Cliffs. About 100 million years ago, massive fault action began dramatically shifting the rock landscape here, forming spectacular limestone and sandstone cliffs and rugged canyons punctuated by waterfalls, shallow streams, and serene oasis pools. Especially notable is the **Keystone Thrust Fault,** dating back about 65 million years, when two of the Earth's crustal plates collided, forcing older limestone and dolomite plates from the ancient seas over younger red and white sandstones. Over the years, water and wind have been ever-creative sculptors, continuing to redefine this strikingly beautiful landscape.

Red Rock's valley is home to more than 45 species of mammals, about 100 species of birds, 30 reptiles and amphibians, and an abundance of plant life. Ascending the slopes from the valley, you'll see cactus and creosote bushes, aromatic purple sage, yellow-flowering blackbrush, yucca and Joshua trees, and, at higher elevations, clusters of forest-green pinyon, juniper, and ponderosa pines. In spring, the desert blooms with extraordinary wildflowers.

Archaeological studies of Red Rock have turned up pottery fragments, stone tools, pictographs (rock drawings), and petroglyphs (rock etchings), along with other ancient artifacts. They show that humans have been in this region since about 3000 B.C. (some experts say as early as 10,000 B.C.). You can still see remains of early inhabitants on hiking expeditions in the park. (As for habitation of Red Rock, the same ancient Puebloan-to-Paiute-to-white-settlers progression related in the Valley of Fire section above occurred here.)

In the latter part of the 19th century, Red Rock was a mining site and later a sandstone quarry that provided materials for many buildings in Los Angeles, San Francisco, and early Las Vegas. By the end of World War II, as Las Vegas developed, many people became aware of the importance of preserving the canyon. In 1967, the secretary of the interior designated 62,000 acres as Red Rock Canyon Recreation Lands under the auspices of the Bureau of Land Management, and later legislation banned all development except hiking trails and limited recreational facilities. In 1990, Red Rock Canyon became a National Conservation Area, further elevating its protected status. Its current acreage is 197,000.

WHAT TO SEE & DO

Begin with a stop at the **Visitor Center;** while there is a $5 per-vehicle fee, you also can pick up a variety of helpful literature: history, guides, hiking trail maps, and lists of local flora and fauna. You can also view exhibits that tell the history of the canyon and depict its plant and animal life. You'll see a fascinating video here about Nevada's thousands of wild horses and burros, protected by an act of Congress since 1971. Furthermore, you can obtain permits for hiking and backpacking. Call ahead to find out about ranger-guided tours as well as informative guided hikes offered by such groups as the Sierra Club and the Audubon Society. And if you're traveling with children, ask about the free *Junior Ranger Discovery Book* filled with fun family activities. Books and videotapes are for sale here, including a guidebook identifying more than 100 top-rated climbing sites.

The easiest thing to do is to **drive the 13-mile scenic loop** ✹✹✹. It really is a loop, and it only goes one way, so once you start, you are committed to driving the entire thing. You can stop the car to admire a number of fabulous views and sights along the way, or have a picnic, or take a walk or hike. As you drive, observe how dramatically the milky-white limestone alternates with iron-rich red rocks. Farther along, the mountains become solid limestone, with canyons running between them, which lead to an evergreen forest—a surprising sight in the desert.

If you're up to it, however, we can't stress enough that the way to really see the canyon is by **hiking.** Every trail is incredible—glance over your options and decide what you might be looking for. You can begin from the visitor center or drive into the loop, park your car, and start from points therein. Hiking trails range from a .7-mile-loop stroll to a waterfall (its flow varying seasonally) at Lost Creek to much longer and more strenuous treks. Actually, all the hikes involve a certain amount of effort, as you have to scramble over rocks on even the shortest hikes. Unfit or undexterous people should beware. Be sure to wear good shoes, as the rocks can be slippery. You must have a map; you won't get lost forever (there usually are other hikers around to help you out, eventually), but you can still get lost. It is often tough to find a landmark, and once deep into the rocks, everything looks the same, even with the map. Consequently, give yourself extra time for each hike (at least an additional hour), regardless of its billed length, to allow for the lack of paths, getting disoriented, and simply to slow down and admire the scenery.

A popular 2-mile round-trip hike leads to **Pine Creek Canyon** and the creekside ruins of a historic home site surrounded by ponderosa pine trees. Our hiking trail of choice is the **Calico Basin,** which is accessed along the loop. After an hour walk up the rocks (which is not that well marked), you end up at an oasis surrounded by sheer walls of limestone (which makes the oasis itself inaccessible, alas). In the summer, flowers and deciduous trees grow out of the walls.

As you hike, keep your eyes peeled for lizards, the occasional desert tortoise, herds of bighorn sheep, birds, and other critters. But the rocks themselves are the most fun, with many minicaves to explore and rock formations to climb on. (Relive childhood with a politically incorrect game of Cowboys and Indians!) On trails along Calico Hills and the escarpment, look for "Indian marbles," a local name for small, rounded sandstone rocks that have eroded off larger sandstone formations. Petroglyphs are also tucked away in various locales.

Biking is another option; riding a bicycle is a tremendous way to travel the loop. There are also terrific off-road mountain-biking trails, with levels from amateur to expert.

After you tour the canyon, drive over to Bonnie Springs Ranch (details in the next section) for some old-fashioned, hokey fun. See chapter 6 for further details on biking and climbing.

The opening of the gleaming new luxury **Red Rock Resort,** 10973 W. Charleston Rd. (② **866/767-7773;** www.redrocklasvegas.com), gives day-trippers a new, highly desirable refueling point on a trip to the canyon. It's a gorgeous new facility, already a place for celeb-spotting. There's a casino, if you are getting the jitters, and a set of movie theaters if you realize it's really, really hot and you don't want to take a hike after all but are too ashamed to come back without having done *something*. Best of all, the food court contains a **Capriotti's,** the economical submarine sandwich shop we have already suggested as a source for picnic munchies, and among the restaurants is a branch of the highly lauded **Salt Lick BBQ.** It doesn't quite measure up to the platonic perfection of the original in Austin, Texas, but it's here, and so are you. Both are ideal for takeout for picnics in the park (buy a cheap Styrofoam ice chest at a convenience store) or for in-room dining as you rest up in your hotel post-hike.

4 Bonnie Springs Ranch/Old Nevada ✶✶

About 24 miles W of Las Vegas, 5 miles past Red Rock Canyon

Bonnie Springs Ranch/Old Nevada is a kind of Wild West theme park with accommodations and a restaurant. If you're traveling with kids, a day trip to Bonnie Springs is recommended, but it is surprisingly appealing for adults, too. It could even be a romantic getaway, as it offers horseback riding, gorgeous mountain vistas, proximity to Red Rock Canyon, and temperatures 5° to 10° cooler than on the Strip.

For additional information, you can call **Bonnie Springs Ranch/Old Nevada** at ② **702/875-4191,** or visit them on the Web at **www.bonniesprings.com**.

If you're **driving,** a trip to Bonnie Springs Ranch can be combined easily with a day trip to Red Rock Canyon; it is about 5 miles farther. But you can also stay overnight.

Jeep tours to and from Las Vegas are available through **Action Tours.** Call ② **888/ 288-5200** or 702/566-7400 (www.actiontours.com) for details.

WHAT TO SEE & DO IN OLD NEVADA

Old Nevada ✶✶ (② **702/875-4191;** www.bonniesprings.com) is a re-creation of an 1880s frontier town, built on the site of a very old ranch. As tourist sights go, this is a classic one, if a bit worn around the edges; it's a bit cheesy, but knowingly, perhaps even deliberately, so. It's terrific for kids up to about the age of 12 or so (before teenage cynicism kicks in) but not all that bad for adults fondly remembering similar places from their own childhoods. Many go expecting a tourist trap, only to come away saying that it really was rather cute and charming. Still others find it old in the bad way. It's certainly low tech and low key.

Certainly, Old Nevada looks authentic, with rustic buildings made entirely of weathered wood. And the setting, right in front of beautiful mountains with layered red rock, couldn't be more perfect for a Western. You can wander the town (it's only about a block long), taking peeps into places of business, such as a blacksmith shop, a working mill, a saloon, and an old-fashioned general store (cum gift shop) and museum that has a potpourri of items from the Old West and Old Las Vegas: antique gaming tables and slot machines, typewriters, and a great display of old shoes, including lace-up boots. There is also a rather lame wax museum; the less said about it, the better.

Country music is played in the saloon during the day, except when **stage melodramas** take place (at frequent intervals btw. 11:30am and 5pm). These are entirely tongue-in-cheek—the actors are goofy and know it, and the plot is hokey and fully intended to be that way. Somehow, it just heightens the fun factor. It's interactive with the audience, which, in response to cue cards held up by the players, boos and hisses the mustache-twirling villain, sobs in sympathy with the distressed heroine, and laughs, cheers, and applauds. It's hugely silly and hugely fun, provided you all play along. Kids love it, though younger ones might be scared by the occasional gunshot.

Following each melodrama, a **Western drama** is presented outside the saloon, involving a bank robbery, a shootout, and the trial of the bad guy. A judge, a prosecuting attorney, and a defense attorney are chosen from the audience, the remainder of whom act as the jury. The action always culminates in a hanging. None of this is a particularly polished act, but the dialogue is quite funny, and the entire thing is performed with enthusiasm and affection.

Throughout the area, cowboys continually interact with visiting kids, who, on the weekends, are given badges so that they can join a posse hunting for bad guys. There are also ongoing **stunt shootouts** (maybe not at the level found at, say, Universal Studios) in this wild frontier town, and some rather unsavory characters occasionally languish in the town jail.

In the **Old Nevada Photograph Shoppe** you can have a tintype picture taken in 1890s Wild West costume (they have a fairly large selection) with a 120-year-old camera. There are replicas of a turn-of-the-20th-century church and stamp mill; the latter, which has original 1902 machinery, was used for crushing rocks to separate gold and silver from the earth. You can tour the remains of the **old Comstock lode silver mine,** though there isn't much to see there. There is also a nicely maintained **chapel** that would be a hoot to get married in. You can also shop for a variety of "Western" souvenirs (though to us, that's when the tourist-trap part kicks in). Eateries in Old Nevada are discussed below. There's plenty of parking; on weekends and holidays a free shuttle train takes visitors from the parking lot to the entrance.

Admission to Old Nevada is charged by vehicle—$20 per car, for up to six people in the car (the fee includes a $10 coupon to the restaurant). The park is open daily from 10:30am to 5pm November through April, and until 6pm the rest of the year.

WHAT TO SEE & DO AT BONNIE SPRINGS RANCH

There are several things to do here free of charge, and it's right next door to Old Nevada. It's quite a pretty place, in a funky, ramshackle kind of way, and in season, there are tons of flowers everywhere, including honeysuckle and roses. The main attraction is the small **zoo** ✪ on the premises. Now, when we say "zoo," unfortunately we mean that in addition to a petting zoo with the usual suspects (deer, sheep, goats, and rabbits) and some unusual animals (potbelly pigs and snooty, beautiful llamas) to caress and feed, there is also a mazelike enclosure of a series of wire-mesh pens that contain a variety of livestock, some of which should not be penned up (though they are well taken care of), including wolves and bobcats. Still, it's more than diverting for kids.

Less politically and ecologically distressing is the aviary, which houses peacocks, Polish chickens, peachface and blackmask lovebirds, finches, parakeets, ravens, ducks, pheasants, and geese. Keep your eyes peeled for the peacocks roaming free; with luck, they will spread their tails for a photo op. With greater luck, some of the angelic, rare white peacocks will do the same. It may be worth dropping by just in the hopes of spotting one in full fan-tailed glory.

Riding stables offer guided hour-long trail rides into the mountain area on a continuous basis throughout the day (spring–fall 9am–3:45pm, summer until 5:40pm). Children must be at least 6 years old to participate. Cost is $50 per person. There are also breakfast, lunch, and dinner rides, which are $134, $144, and $164 per person, respectively. For more information, call ✆ **702/875-4191.**

WHERE TO STAY & DINE

In Old Nevada, the **Miner's Restaurant** is a snack bar located in quite a large room that looks great thanks to Western-motif accessories. Inexpensive fare is served (sandwiches, decent burgers, pizza, and hot dogs), along with fresh-baked desserts. There are tables out on the porch. In summer you can also get beer and soft drinks in a similarly old-fashioned **Beer Parlor.**

Bonnie Springs Motel ✿   This is really a hoot: a funky, friendly little place in the middle of nowhere—except that nowhere is a gorgeous setting. The motel is in two double-story buildings and offers regular rooms, "Western" rooms, "specialty theme" rooms, and kitchen suites.

Where to begin? Here, the theme is expressed mostly through the use of fabrics, personally decorated by the owner, who did a pretty nice job. The "gay 1890s" room is done in black and pink, with a lace canopy over the bed, an old-fashioned commode, and liberal use of velvet. The American Indian room uses skins and feathers, and has a bearskin-covered burl-wood chair. You get the idea. The "Western" rooms have more burl-wood furniture and electric-log fireplaces that blow heat into the rooms.

All special theme rooms (also known as fantasy suites) have mirrors over the beds and big whirlpool tubs in the middle of the rooms (not in the bathrooms), and come with bottles of champagne (the empties of which you can see littering the road on your way out). All the rooms are quite large, though long and narrow, and have private balconies or patios, and mountain views. There are also large family suites with fully equipped kitchens, bedrooms, living rooms (with convertible sofas), and dressing areas; these are equipped with two phones and two TVs, and are available for long-term rentals (many of the people who work at Old Nevada actually rent these as apartments). Videotapes and players are available for rental, and there is even a tiny train that takes you around the grounds and on a short tour of the desert.

The **Bonnie Springs Ranch Restaurant** has a lot of character and is a perfect family place. It's heavily rustic (stone floors, log beams, raw wooden chairs made from tree branches, lanterns, a roaring fire in winter, and plenty of dead animals adorning the walls). It's a bit touristy, but small-town touristy. The food is basic—steak, ribs, chicken, burgers, and potato skins; pancakes and eggs for breakfast; it's all greasy but good. There is a cozy bar attached to the restaurant, its walls covered with thousands of dollar bills with messages on them—a classic neighborhood bar, if it were actually in a neighborhood.

1 Gunfighter Lane, Old Nevada, NV 89004. ✆ **702/875-4400.** Fax 702/875-4424. www.bonniesprings.com/ motel.html. 50 units. Sun–Thurs $65–$75 double, $105 family suite, $130 fantasy suite; Fri–Sat $80–$90 double, $120 family suite, $145 fantasy suite; weekly rates available. (Family suite rates based on 4 people; extra person $5.) AE, MC, V. **Amenities:** Restaurant; outdoor pool; nonsmoking rooms. *In room:* A/C, TV, coffeemaker, dial-up Internet.

5 A Close Encounter with Area 51 ⓧ

150 miles N of Las Vegas

Want to feel like an extra on the *X-Files?* Just want to get an idea of the kind of spots the government picks when it needs a place in which to do secret things? Take the drive from Vegas out to the **"E. T. Highway,"** where folks were spotting aliens years before it became fashionable. This is about a 150-mile trip one-way, so it's probably not something to do on a whim, but even for non–alien buffs, it can be a long, strange—and oddly illuminating—trip indeed.

WHAT TO SEE & DO

Area 51 is a secret military facility, containing a large air base that the government will not discuss. The site was selected in the mid-1950s for the testing of the U2 spy plane and is supposedly the current testing ground for "black budget" aircraft before their public acknowledgment. (Oh, heck, who are they trying to kid? *Of course* that's where they are testing high-tech gadgets.) But its real fame comes with the stories of aliens, whose bodies and ships were supposedly taken there when they "crashed" at Roswell.

Mind you, the only thing alien you are guaranteed to see is the landscape. Only fans of desert topography will find the scenery attractive. It's a desolate area, but that's part of the inexplicable charm. There is absolutely a weird vibe in the air; something is going on out here. And one thing's for sure: If you need a place for covert, or at least private, activities, you couldn't find a better location for it. Alien bodies? Shoot, you could hide an entire alien fleet.

But don't come looking for monuments, historical markers, or good shopping—with a few exceptions, there's a whole lot of nothing out there. You'd think the tourist possibilities would have led to more development, but even in Vegas, despite the presence of plenty of alien merchandise in the gift shops and an entire Area 51–themed shopping area at the airport expansion, there is not as much awareness as you might think. One waitress, when asked if she'd been there, responded, "Not since they remodeled."

All we know for sure is that you turn down one of the most well-maintained dirt roads you will ever encounter, drive a few miles, and come upon a fence with a sign that warns you against going any farther in the strictest of terms (though the language has been toned down from "use of deadly force authorized" to threats of fines and jail time). Along the way down that road, notice how there is absolutely no wildlife other than grasshoppers, that the Joshua trees suddenly turn to an enormous size and monstrous shape, and that the few cattle grazing around don't seem like any cattle you've seen before. Then notice those blasted-out craters in the earth, with the core sample holes in the center. When you realize you are looking at nuclear test sites, the desolation and mutations suddenly make sense. Wave hi at the guys in the military vehicles who are making damn sure you don't go through that gate, and hightail it out of there.

The other hot spot is the "town" of **Rachel** (www.rachel-nevada.com), really just a collection of trailer homes. Here's where you'll find the **Little A'Le'Inn** (ⓒ **866/ET-HWY51** or 775/729-2515; www.littlealeinn.com) diner and gift shop ("Earthlings Welcome")—where a very funny *X-Files* episode was filmed—and, in theory, chat with fellow E. T. spotters, who often gather at night to search the skies. The owners don't play along as much as one would like, though they do feel they were "called there for a special purpose," but their gift shop makes up for it with fine humorous souvenirs. (We liked the alien-head-shaped guitar pick.) Plus, they serve up satisfying diner food.

You can also drop in at the **Area 51 Research Center** (just look for the big yellow trailer), which was opened after its founder (Glenn Campbell, who is largely responsible for Area 51's recent cultural icon status, and who wrote the definitive book *Area 51 Viewer's Guide*) got kicked out of the Little A'Le'Inn. Their headquarters is now in Las Vegas, and their store may be opening only during spring and summer, so call before you visit. It stocks all manner of Area 51 logo items and a number of related books.

There is no place to stay out here, so unless you want to camp (which could be fun; aliens usually show up at night), plan this as a lengthy day trip. Be sure to fill your tank before you head out, as there are few opportunities to do so once you leave Vegas. The gas station in Rachel itself is closed as of press time, with the nearest fuel-up point 60 miles south in Ash Springs. If you'll be doing this drive in the heat of the summer, bring water for your car and for yourself. Along the way, keep your eyes peeled for little green men (or weather balloons, jackrabbits, tumbleweeds, broken-down cars), and should you spot one, don't forget to write us all about it.

By the way, word is starting to spread of a *really* mysterious secret base even farther out in the desert. Just mention Area 58, and watch people go nuts.

ESSENTIALS
GETTING THERE
Take I-15 north to U.S. 93 North (paying close attention—it's an easy exit to miss; if you do, you can take NV 168 at Moapa west back to U.S. 93), and get off at the E. T. Highway, a 98-mile stretch of NV 375. The town of Rachel is approximately 43 miles away; the "black mailbox" (it's now white) road, which leads you to Area 51, actually comes first, about 17 miles down the highway. (We strongly suggest going to Rachel first, to get your bearings, chat with knowledgeable locals and other alien-spotters, and pick up some literature, including a good local map.) Turn left and keep driving; any of the dirt roads that lead off of it will get you to the Area 51 fence and gates. Veer right at the fork in the road (not the ranch turnoff, which you come to first) if you want to go to the most commonly talked about entrance, the one at Groom Lake (though you can't see the lake from where you are forced to stop).

FOR MORE INFORMATION
For more information, call the **Nevada Commission on Tourism** (© **800/638-2328;** www.travelnevada.com) and ask them to send you their *Pioneer Territory* brochure and a list of E. T. Highway services (gas stations, chambers of commerce, restaurants, and more). On the Internet, check out **www.ufomind.com/area51** (this is a huge site maintained by the Area 51 Research folks that contains countless links and all sorts of information) and **www.ufo-hyway.com**.

Appendix: Fast Facts, Toll-Free Numbers & Websites

1 Fast Facts

AMERICAN EXPRESS There is an AmEx Travel office located at the **Fashion Show Mall,** 3200 Las Vegas Blvd. S., Las Vegas, NV 89109 (© **702/739-8474**).

AREA CODES The local area code is 702.

AUTOMOBILE ORGANIZATIONS Motor clubs will supply maps, suggested routes, guidebooks, accident and bail-bond insurance, and emergency road service. The **American Automobile Association (AAA)** is the major auto club in the United States. If you belong to a motor club in your home country, inquire about AAA reciprocity before you leave. You may be able to join AAA even if you're not a member of a reciprocal club; to inquire, call AAA (© **800/222-4357;** www.aaa.com). AAA is actually an organization of regional motor clubs, so look under "AAA Automobile Club" in the White Pages of the telephone directory. AAA has a nationwide emergency road service telephone number (© **800/AAA-HELP**).

BUSINESS HOURS Casinos and most bars are open 24 hours a day, nightclubs are usually open only late at night into the early morning hours, and restaurant and attraction hours vary.

CAR RENTALS See "Toll-Free Numbers & Websites," p. 298.

DRINKING LAWS The legal age for purchase and consumption of alcoholic beverages is 21; proof of age is required and often requested at bars, nightclubs, and restaurants, so it's always a good idea to bring ID when you go out. Beer, wine, and liquor are sold in all kinds of stores pretty much around the clock; trust us, you won't have a hard time finding a drink in this town.

Do not carry open containers of alcohol in your car or any public area that isn't zoned for alcohol consumption, which includes the Strip and the Fremont Street Experience downtown. The police can fine you on the spot. And nothing will ruin your trip faster than getting a citation for DUI ("driving under the influence"), so don't even think about driving while intoxicated.

ELECTRICITY Like Canada, the United States uses 110 to 120 volts AC (60 cycles), compared to 220 to 240 volts AC (50 cycles) in most of Europe, Australia, and New Zealand. Downward converters that change 220–240 volts to 110–120 volts are difficult to find in the United States, so bring one with you. Wherever you go, bring a **connection kit** of the right power and phone adapters, a spare phone cord, and a spare Ethernet network cable—or find out whether your hotel supplies them to guests.

EMBASSIES & CONSULATES All embassies are located in the nation's capital, Washington, D.C. Some consulates are located in major U.S. cities, and most nations have a mission to the United Nations in New York City. If your country isn't listed below, call for directory information in Washington, D.C. (© **202/555-1212**) or check **www.embassy.org/embassies**.

The embassy of **Australia** is at 1601 Massachusetts Ave. NW, Washington, DC 20036 (© **202/797-3000**; www.usa.embassy.gov.au). There are consulates in New York, Honolulu, Houston, Los Angeles, and San Francisco.

The embassy of **Canada** is at 501 Pennsylvania Ave. NW, Washington, DC 20001 (© **202/682-1740**; www.canadianembassy.org). Canadian consulates are in Buffalo (New York), Detroit, Los Angeles, New York, and Seattle.

The embassy of **Ireland** is at 2234 Massachusetts Ave. NW, Washington, DC 20008 (© **202/462-3939**; www.irelandemb.org). Irish consulates are in Boston, Chicago, New York, San Francisco, and other cities. See website for complete listing.

The embassy of **New Zealand** is at 37 Observatory Circle NW, Washington, DC 20008 (© **202/328-4800**; www.nzemb.com). New Zealand consulates are in Los Angeles, Salt Lake City, San Francisco, and Seattle.

The embassy of the **United Kingdom** is at 3100 Massachusetts Ave. NW, Washington, DC 20008 (© **202/588-7800**; www.britainusa.com). Other British consulates are in Atlanta, Boston, Chicago, Cleveland, Houston, Los Angeles, New York, San Francisco, and Seattle.

EMERGENCIES Dial © **911** to contact the police or fire department or to call an ambulance.

GASOLINE (PETROL) At press time, in the U.S., the cost of gasoline (also known as gas, but never petrol), is ridiculously high and climbing. Taxes are already included in the printed price. One U.S. gallon equals 3.8 liters or .85 imperial gallons. Fill-up locations are known as gas or service stations. Las Vegas prices typically fall near the nationwide average (higher than some areas but lower than others). You can also check **www.vegasgasprices.com** for recent costs.

HOLIDAYS Banks, government offices, post offices, and many stores, restaurants, and museums are closed on the following legal national holidays: January 1 (New Year's Day), the third Monday in January (Martin Luther King, Jr., Day), the third Monday in February (Presidents' Day), the last Monday in May (Memorial Day), July 4 (Independence Day), the first Monday in September (Labor Day), the second Monday in October (Columbus Day), November 11 (Veterans' Day/Armistice Day), the fourth Thursday in November (Thanksgiving Day), and December 25 (Christmas). The Tuesday after the first Monday in November is Election Day, a federal government holiday in presidential-election years (held every 4 years, and next in 2008).

HOSPITALS & PHYSICIANS Emergency services are available 24 hours a day at **University Medical Center,** 1800 W. Charleston Blvd., at Shadow Lane (© **702/383-2000**; www.umc-cares.org); the emergency-room entrance is on the corner of Hastings and Rose streets. **Sunrise Hospital and Medical Center,** 3186 Maryland Pkwy., between Desert Inn Road and Sahara Avenue (© **702/731-8080**; www.sunrisehospital.com), also has a 24-hour emergency room.

For more minor problems, try the **Harmon Medical Urgent Care Center,** the closest to the Strip, with doctors and X-ray machines; it's located at 105 E. Harmon at Koval, near the MGM Grand (© **702/796-1116**; www.harmonmedicalcenter.com). It's open 24 hours, and there is a pharmacy on-site.

Hotels usually have lists of doctors, should you need one. In addition, they are listed in the Yellow Pages. For physician referrals, call the **Desert Springs Hospital** (© **702/388-4888**; www.desertspringshospital.net). Hours are

Monday to Friday from 8am to 8pm and Saturday from 9am to 3pm.

HOTLINES Emergency hotlines include the **Rape Crisis Center** (✆ 702/366-1640), **Suicide Prevention** (✆ 702/731-2990), and **Poison Emergencies** (✆ 800/446-6179).

INSURANCE Medical Insurance Although it's not required of travelers, health insurance is highly recommended. Most health insurance policies cover you if you get sick away from home—but check your coverage before you leave.

International visitors to the U.S. should note that unlike many European countries, the United States does not usually offer free or low-cost medical care to its citizens or visitors. Doctors and hospitals are expensive, and in most cases will require advance payment or proof of coverage before they render their services. Good policies will cover the costs of an accident, repatriation, or death. Packages such as **Europ Assistance's "Worldwide Healthcare Plan"** are sold by European automobile clubs and travel agencies at attractive rates. **Worldwide Assistance Services, Inc.** (✆ 800/777-8710; www.worldwideassistance.com) is the agent for Europ Assistance in the United States.

Though lack of health insurance may prevent you from being admitted to a hospital in nonemergencies, don't worry about being left on a street corner to die: The American way is to fix you now and bill the daylights out of you later.

If you're ever hospitalized more than 150 miles from home, **MedjetAssist** (✆ 800/527-7478; www.medjetassistance.com) will pick you up and fly you to the hospital of your choice in a medically equipped and staffed aircraft 24 hours day, 7 days a week. Annual memberships are $225 individual, $350 family; you can also purchase short-term memberships.

Canadians should check with their provincial health plan offices or call **Health Canada** (✆ 866/225-0709; www.hc-sc.gc.ca) to find out the extent of their coverage and what documentation and receipts they must take home in case they are treated in the United States.

Travelers from the U.K. should carry their European Health Insurance Card (EHIC), which replaced the E111 form as proof of entitlement to free/reduced cost medical treatment abroad (✆ 0845/606-2030; www.ehic.ie). Note, however, that the EHIC only covers "necessary medical treatment," and for repatriation costs, lost money, baggage, or cancellation, travel insurance from a reputable company should always be sought. For other options visit **www.travelinsuranceweb.com**.

Travel Insurance The cost of travel insurance varies widely, depending on the destination, the cost and length of your trip, your age and health, and the type of trip you're taking, but expect to pay between 5% and 8% of the vacation itself. You can get estimates from various providers through **InsureMyTrip.com**. Enter your trip cost and dates, your age, and other information, for prices from more than a dozen companies.

U.K. citizens and their families who make more than one trip abroad per year may find an annual travel insurance policy works out cheaper. Check **www.moneysupermarket.com**, which compares prices across a wide range of providers for single- and multi-trip policies.

Most big travel agents offer their own insurance and will probably try to sell you their package when you book a holiday. Think before you sign. **Britain's Consumers' Association** recommends that you insist on seeing the policy and reading the fine print before buying travel insurance. **The Association of British Insurers** (✆ 020/7600-3333; www.abi.org.uk) gives advice by phone and publishes *Holiday Insurance,* a free guide to policy provisions and prices. You might also shop around for better deals: Try

Columbus Direct (© 0870/033- 9988; www.columbusdirect.net).

Trip Cancellation Insurance Trip-cancellation insurance will help retrieve your money if you have to back out of a trip or depart early, or if your travel supplier goes bankrupt. Trip cancellation traditionally covers such events as sickness, natural disasters, and State Department advisories. The latest news in trip-cancellation insurance is the availability of **expanded hurricane coverage** and the **"any-reason"** cancellation coverage—which costs more but covers cancellations made for any reason. You won't get back 100% of your prepaid trip cost, but you'll be refunded a substantial portion. **Travel-Safe** (© 888/885-7233; www.travelsafe. com) offers both types of coverage. Expedia also offers any-reason cancellation coverage for its air-hotel packages. For details, contact one of the following recommended insurers: **Access America** (© 866/807-3982; www.accessamerica. com); **Travel Guard International** (© 800/826-4919; www.travelguard.com); **Travel Insured International** (© 800/ 243-3174; www.travelinsured.com); and **Travelex Insurance Services** (© 888/ 457-4602; www.travelex-insurance.com).

INTERNET ACCESS **FedEx Kinkos,** 830 S. 4th St. (downtown) © 702/383-7022.

FedEx Kinkos, 395 Hughes Center Dr. (East Strip) © 702/951-2400.

Jitters East Trop, 2457 East Tropicana Ave. © 702/898-0056.

To find a **cybercafe** in Las Vegas, try www.cybercafe.com or www.jiwire.com.

LAUNDROMATS Most hotels provide laundry services.

LEGAL AID If you are "pulled over" for a minor infraction (such as speeding), never attempt to pay the fine directly to a police officer; this could be construed as attempted bribery, a much more serious crime. Pay fines by mail, or directly into the hands of the clerk of the court. If accused of a more serious offense, say and do nothing before consulting a lawyer. Here the burden is on the state to prove a person's guilt beyond a reasonable doubt, and everyone has the right to remain silent, whether he or she is suspected of a crime or actually arrested. Once arrested, a person can make one telephone call to a party of his or her choice. International visitors should call their embassy or consulate.

LOST & FOUND Be sure to tell all of your credit card companies the minute you discover your wallet has been lost or stolen and file a report at the nearest police precinct. Your credit card company or insurer may require a police report number or record of the loss. Most credit card companies have an emergency toll-free number to call if your card is lost or stolen; they may be able to wire you a cash advance immediately or deliver an emergency credit card in a day or two. Visa's U.S. emergency number is © **800/ 847-2911** or 410/581-9994. American Express cardholders and traveler's check holders should call © **800/221-7282.** MasterCard holders should call © **800/ 307-7309** or 636/722-7111. For other credit cards, call the toll-free number directory at © **800/555-1212.**

If you need emergency cash over the weekend when all banks and American Express offices are closed, you can have money wired to you via **Western Union** (© **800/325-6000;** www.westernunion. com).

MAIL At press time, domestic postage rates were 27¢ for a postcard and 42¢ for a letter. For international mail, a first-class letter of up to 1 ounce costs $1.40 (72¢ to Canada and Mexico); a first-class postcard costs the same as a letter. For more information go to **www.usps.com** and click on "Calculate Postage."

If you aren't sure what your address will be in the United States, mail can be sent to you, in your name, c/o General Delivery at the main post office of the city or region where you expect to be. (Call © 800/275-8777 for information on the nearest post office.) The addressee must pick up mail in person and must produce proof of identity (driver's license, passport, and so on). Most post offices will hold your mail for up to 1 month, and are open Monday to Friday from 8am to 6pm, and Saturday from 9am to 3pm.

Always include zip codes when mailing items in the U.S. If you don't know your zip code, visit **www.usps.com/zip4**.

The most convenient post office is immediately behind Circus Circus at 3100 S. Industrial Rd., between Sahara and Spring Mountain Road (© **800/ 275-8777**). It's open Monday through Friday from 8:30am to 5pm. You can also mail letters and packages at your hotel, and there's a drop-off box in the Forum Shops at Caesars Palace.

MAPS The **Las Vegas Convention and Visitors Authority,** 3150 Paradise Rd., Las Vegas, NV 89109 (© **877/ VISIT-LV** or 702/892-0711; www.visit lasvegas.com) can send you a comprehensive packet containing maps and much more. Motor clubs will also supply maps, suggested routes, and guidebooks. See "Automobile Associations," above.

MEASUREMENTS See the chart on the inside back cover of this book for details on converting metric measurements to nonmetric equivalents.

NEWSPAPERS & MAGAZINES There are two Las Vegas dailies: the *Las Vegas Review Journal* and the *Las Vegas Sun*. The *Review Journal's* Friday edition has a helpful "Weekend" section with a comprehensive guide to shows and buffets. There are two free alternative papers, with club listings and many unbiased restaurant and bar reviews. Both *City Life* and *Las*

Vegas Weekly are published weekly. All can be viewed online at their respective websites. Moreover, at every hotel desk, you'll find dozens of free local magazines, such as *Vegas Visitor, What's On in Las Vegas,* and *Where to Go in Las Vegas,* that are chock-full of helpful information—although probably of the sort that comes from paid advertising.

PASSPORTS The websites listed provide downloadable passport applications as well as the current fees for processing applications. For an up-to-date, country-by-country listing of passport requirements around the world, go to the "International Travel" tab of the U.S. State Department at **http://travel.state. gov.** International visitors to the U.S. can obtain a visa application at the same website. Even children are required to present a passport when entering the United States at airports; more information on obtaining a passport for a minor can be found at http://travel.state.gov. Allow plenty of time before your trip to apply for a passport; processing normally takes 4 to 6 weeks (3 weeks for expedited service) but can take longer during busy periods (especially spring). And keep in mind that if you need a passport in a hurry, you'll pay a higher processing fee.

For Residents of Australia You can pick up an application from your local post office or any branch of Passports Australia, but you must schedule an interview at the passport office to present your application materials. Call the **Australian Passport Information Service** at © **131-232,** or visit the government website at www.passports.gov.au.

For Residents of Canada Passport applications are available at travel agencies throughout Canada or from the central **Passport Office,** Department of Foreign Affairs and International Trade, Ottawa, ON K1A 0G3 (© **800/567-6868;** www.ppt.gc.ca). Canadian children who travel must have their own passport. However, if you hold a valid Canadian passport issued before December 11, 2001, that bears the name of your child, the passport remains valid for you and your child until it expires.

For Residents of Ireland You can apply for a 10-year passport at the **Passport Office,** Setanta Centre, Molesworth Street, Dublin 2 (© **01/671-1633;** www.irlgov.ie/iveagh). Those under age 18 and over 65 must apply for a 3-year passport. You can also apply at 1A South Mall, Cork (© **21/494-4700**) or at most main post offices.

For Residents of New Zealand You can pick up a passport application at any New Zealand Passports Office or download it from their website. Contact the **Passports Office** at © **0800/225-050** in New Zealand or 04/474-8100, or log on to www.passports.govt.nz.

For Residents of the United Kingdom To pick up an application for a standard 10-year passport (5-yr. passport for children under 16), visit your nearest passport office, major post office, or travel agency or contact the **United Kingdom Passport Service** at © **0870/521-0410** or search its website at www.ukpa.gov.uk.

POLICE For non-emergencies, call © **702/795-3111.** For emergencies, call © **911.**

SMOKING Increasingly strict smoking laws prohibit puffing virtually everywhere indoors except in designated hotel rooms, bars that don't serve food, and on the casino floor itself. Since it's frequently hard to tell where a casino ends and basic public area begins, don't fret too much about stepping across some invisible line. But Vegas is decidedly no longer a smoker's haven. Hotels still dedicate floors for smokers and nonsmokers. There is a significant charge, approximately $300, for smoking anything in a nonsmoking room.

TAXES The United States has no value-added tax (VAT) or other indirect tax at the national level. The sales tax in Las Vegas is 7.75% and will be added to food and drink bills. Taxes are also added to show tickets.

TELEPHONES For information about making local, long-distance, and international calls, please turn to "Staying Connected," p. 38.

TELEGRAPH, TELEX & FAX Telegraph and telex services are provided primarily by **Western Union** (© **800/325-6000;** www.westernunion.com). You can telegraph (wire) money, or have it telegraphed to you, very quickly over the Western Union system, but this service can cost as much as 15 to 20 percent of the amount sent.

Most hotels have **fax machines** available for guest use. (Be sure to ask about the charge to use them.) Many hotel rooms are wired for guests' fax machines. A less expensive way to send and receive faxes may be at stores such as the **UPS Store** or **FedEx Kinkos.**

TIME Las Vegas is in the Pacific Time zone, GMT+8, three hours behind the East Coast and two behind the Midwest. The continental United States is divided into **four time zones:** Eastern Standard Time (EST), Central Standard Time (CST), Mountain Standard Time (MST), and Pacific Standard Time (PST). Alaska and Hawaii have their own zones. For example, when it's 9am in Los Angeles (PST), it's 7am in Honolulu (HST), 10am in Denver (MST), 11am in Chicago (CST), noon in New York City (EST), 5pm in London (GMT), and 2am the next day in Sydney.

Daylight saving time is in effect from 1am on the second Sunday in March to 1am on the first Sunday in November, except in Arizona, Hawaii, the U.S. Virgin Islands, and Puerto Rico. Daylight saving time moves the clock 1 hour ahead of standard time.

TIPPING   Tips are a very important part of certain workers' income, and gratuities are the standard way of showing appreciation for services provided. (Tipping is certainly not compulsory if the service is poor!) In hotels, tip **bellhops** at least $1 per bag ($2–$3 if you have a lot of luggage) and tip the **chamber staff** $1 to $2 per day (more if you've left a disaster area for him or her to clean up). Tip the **doorman** or **concierge** only if he or she has provided you with some specific service (for example, calling a cab for you or obtaining difficult-to-get theater tickets). Tip the **valet-parking attendant** $1 to $2 every time you get your car.

In restaurants, bars, and nightclubs, tip **service staff** 15% to 20% of the check, tip **bartenders** 10% to 15%, tip **checkroom attendants** $1 per garment, and tip **valet-parking attendants** $1 per vehicle.

As for other service personnel, tip **cab drivers** 15% of the fare; tip **skycaps** at airports at least $1 per bag ($2–$3 if you have a lot of luggage); and tip **hairdressers** and **barbers** 15% to 20%.

TOILETS   The one thing Vegas does absolutely right is bathrooms. Each hotel-casino has numerous public restrooms, usually sparking clean, frequently large, and often quite fancy or stylish. They are usually well marked with signs, but any casino worker can point you toward the closest one. You won't find public toilets or "restrooms" on the streets in most U.S. cities but they can be found in hotel lobbies, bars, restaurants, museums, department stores, railway and bus stations, and service stations.

USEFUL PHONE NUMBERS U.S. Dept. of State Travel Advisory ℂ 202/647-5225 (manned 24 hr.).

U.S. Passport Agency ℂ 202/647-0518.

U.S. Centers for Disease Control International Traveler's Hotline ℂ 404/332-4559.

VISAS   For information about U.S. Visas go to **http://travel.state.gov** and click on "Visas." Or go to one of the following websites:

Australian citizens can obtain up-to-date visa information from the **U.S. Embassy Canberra,** Moonah Place, Yarralumla, ACT 2600 (ℂ **02/6214-5600**) or by checking the U.S. Diplomatic Mission's website at **http://us embassy-australia.state.gov/consular**.

British subjects can obtain up-to-date visa information by calling the **U.S. Embassy Visa Information Line** (ℂ **0891/200-290**) or by visiting the "Visas to the U.S." section of the American Embassy London's website at **www. usembassy.org.uk**.

Irish citizens can obtain up-to-date visa information through the **Embassy of the USA Dublin,** 42 Elgin Rd., Dublin 4, Ireland (ℂ **353/1-668-8777;** or by checking the "Consular Services" section of the website at **http://dublin.us embassy.gov**.

Citizens of **New Zealand** can obtain up-to-date visa information by contacting the **U.S. Embassy New Zealand,** 29 Fitzherbert Terrace, Thorndon, Wellington (ℂ **644/472-2068**), or get the information directly from the website at **http://wellington.usembassy.gov**.

2 Toll-Free Numbers & Websites

MAJOR U.S. AIRLINES

(*flies internationally as well)

Alaska Airlines/Horizon Air
ℂ 800/252/7522
www.alaskaair.com

American Airlines*/American Eagle
ℂ 800/433-7300 (in U.S. or Canada)
ℂ 020/7365-0777 (in U.K.)
www.aa.com

Continental Airlines*
℡ 800/523-3273 (in U.S. or Canada)
℡ 084/5607-6760 (in U.K.)
www.continental.com

Delta Air Lines*/Skywest
℡ 800/221-1212 (in U.S. or Canada)
℡ 084/5600-0950 (in U.K.)
www.delta.com

Frontier Airlines
℡ 800/432-1359
www.frontierairlines.com

Hawaiian Airlines*
℡ 800/367-5320 (in U.S. and Canada)
www.hawaiianair.com

JetBlue Airways
℡ 800/538-2583 (in U.S.)
℡ 080/1365-2525 (in U.K. or Canada)
www.jetblue.com

Midwest Airlines
℡ 800/452-2022
www.midwestairlines.com

Northwest Airlines
℡ 800/225-2525 (in U.S.)
℡ 870/0507-4074 (in U.K.)
www.flynaa.com

United Airlines*
℡ 800/864-8331 (in U.S. and Canada)
℡ 084/5844-4777 in U.K.
www.united.com

US Airways*
℡ 800/428-4322 (in U.S. and Canada)
℡ 084/5600-3300 (in U.K.)
www.usairways.com

Virgin America*
℡ 877/359-8474
www.virginamerica.com

MAJOR INTERNATIONAL AIRLINES

Aeroméxico
℡ 800/237-6639 (in U.S.)
℡ 020/7801-6234 (in U.K., information only)
www.aeromexico.com

Air Canada
℡ 800/776-3000
www.aircanada.ca

American Airlines
℡ 800/433-7300 (in U.S. and Canada)
℡ 020/7365-0777 (in U.K.)
www.aa.com

Continental Airlines
℡ 800/523-3273 (in U.S. or Canada)
℡ 084/5607-6760 (in U.K.)
www.continental.com

Delta Air Lines
℡ 800/221-1212 (in U.S. or Canada)
℡ 084/5600-0950 (in U.K.)
www.delta.com

Hawaiian Airlines
℡ 800/367-5320 (in U.S. and Canada)
www.hawaiianair.com

Japan Airlines
℡ 012/025-5931 (international)
www.jal.com

Philippine Airlines
℡ 800/435-9725 (in U.S. and Canada)
℡ 632/855-8888 (in Philippines)
www.philippineairlines.com

United Airlines*
℡ 800/864-8331 (in U.S. and Canada)
℡ 084/5844-4777 (in U.K.)
www.united.com

US Airways*
℡ 800/428-4322 (in U.S. and Canada)
℡ 084/5600-3300 (in U.K.)
www.usairways.com

Virgin Atlantic Airways
℡ 800/821-5438 (in U.S. and Canada)
℡ 087/0574-7747 (in U.K.)
www.virgin-atlantic.com

BUDGET AIRLINES

Frontier Airlines
© 800/432-1359
www.frontierairlines.com

Southwest Airlines
© 800/435-9792 (in U.S., U.K. and Canada)
www.southwest.com

CAR RENTAL AGENCIES

Advantage
© 800/777-5500 (in U.S.)
© 021/0344-4712 (outside of U.S.)
www.advantagerentacar.com

Alamo
© 800/462-5266
www.alamo.com

Avis
© 800/331-1212 (in U.S. and Canada)
© 084/4581-8181 (in U.K.)
www.avis.com

Budget
© 800/527-0700 (in U.S.)
© 087/0156-5656 (in U.K.)
© 800/268-8900 (in Canada)
www.budget.com

Dollar
© 800/800-4000 (in U.S.)
© 800/848-8268 (in Canada)
© 080/8234-7524 (in U.K.)
www.dollar.com

Enterprise
© 800/261-7331 (in U.S.)
© 514/355-4028 (in Canada)
© 012/9360-9090 (in U.K.)
www.enterprise.com

Hertz
© 800/645-3131
© 800/654-3001 (international)
www.hertz.com

National
© 800/227-7368
www.nationalcar.com

Payless
© 800/729-5377
www.paylesscarrental.com

Thrifty
© 800/367-2277
© 918/669-2168 (international)
www.thrifty.com

Index

See also Accommodations and Restaurant indexes, below.

RESTAURANTS

FROMMER'S® COMPLETE TRAVEL GUIDES

FROMMER'S® DAY BY DAY GUIDES

PAULINE FROMMER'S GUIDES: SEE MORE. SPEND LESS.

FROMMER'S® PORTABLE GUIDES

Acapulco, Ixtapa & Zihuatanejo
Amsterdam
Aruba, Bonaire & Curacao
Australia's Great Barrier Reef
Bahamas
Big Island of Hawaii
Boston
California Wine Country
Cancún
Cayman Islands
Charleston
Chicago
Dominican Republic

Florence
Las Vegas
Las Vegas for Non-Gamblers
London
Maui
Nantucket & Martha's Vineyard
New Orleans
New York City
Paris
Portland
Puerto Rico
Puerto Vallarta, Manzanillo &
    Guadalajara

Rio de Janeiro
San Diego
San Francisco
Savannah
St. Martin, Sint Maarten, Anguila &
    St. Bart's
Turks & Caicos
Vancouver
Venice
Virgin Islands
Washington, D.C.
Whistler

FROMMER'S® CRUISE GUIDES

Alaska Cruises & Ports of Call

Cruises & Ports of Call

European Cruises & Ports of Call

FROMMER'S® NATIONAL PARK GUIDES

Algonquin Provincial Park
Banff & Jasper
Grand Canyon

National Parks of the American West
Rocky Mountain
Yellowstone & Grand Teton

Yosemite and Sequoia & Kings
    Canyon
Zion & Bryce Canyon

FROMMER'S® WITH KIDS GUIDES

Chicago
Hawaii
Las Vegas
London

National Parks
New York City
San Francisco

Toronto
Walt Disney World® & Orlando
Washington, D.C.

FROMMER'S® PHRASEFINDER DICTIONARY GUIDES

Chinese
French

German
Italian

Japanese
Spanish

SUZY GERSHMAN'S BORN TO SHOP GUIDES

France
Hong Kong, Shanghai & Beijing
Italy

London
New York
Paris

San Francisco
Where to Buy the Best of Everything.

FROMMER'S® BEST-LOVED DRIVING TOURS

Britain
California
France
Germany

Ireland
Italy
New England
Northern Italy

Scotland
Spain
Tuscany & Umbria

THE UNOFFICIAL GUIDES®

Adventure Travel in Alaska
Beyond Disney
California with Kids
Central Italy
Chicago
Cruises
Disneyland®
England
Hawaii

Ireland
Las Vegas
London
Maui
Mexico's Best Beach Resorts
Mini Mickey
New Orleans
New York City
Paris

San Francisco
South Florida including Miami &
    the Keys
Walt Disney World®
Walt Disney World® for
    Grown-ups
Walt Disney World® with Kids
Washington, D.C.

SPECIAL-INTEREST TITLES

Athens Past & Present
Best Places to Raise Your Family
Cities Ranked & Rated
500 Places to Take Your Kids Before They Grow Up
Frommer's Best Day Trips from London
Frommer's Best RV & Tent Campgrounds in the U.S.A.

Frommer's Exploring America by RV
Frommer's NYC Free & Dirt Cheap
Frommer's Road Atlas Europe
Frommer's Road Atlas Ireland
Retirement Places Rated